Data Structures
and
Program Design
in C++

Data Structures
and
Program Design
in C++

Robert L. Kruse

Alexander J. Ryba

Prentice Hall
Upper Saddle River, New Jersey 07458

Library of Congress Cataloging–in–Publication Data

KRUSE, ROBERT L.
    Data structures and program design in C++ / Robert L. Kruse,
    Alexander J. Ryba.
        p.   cm.
    Includes bibliographical references and index.
    ISBN 0-13-768995-0
    1. C++ (Computer program language) 2. Data Structures
    (Computer Science)   I. Ryba, Alexander J. II. Title.
QA76.73.C153K79 1998   98–35979
005.13'3—dc21   CIP

Publisher: *Alan Apt*
Editor in Chief: *Marcia Horton*
Acquisitions Editor: *Laura Steele*
Production Editor: *Rose Kernan*
Managing Editor: *Eileen Clark*
Art Director: *Heather Scott*
Assistant to Art Director: *John Christiana*
Copy Editor: *Patricia Daly*

Cover Designer: *Heather Scott*
Manufacturing Buyer: *Pat Brown*
Assistant Vice President of Production and
      Manufacturing: *David W. Riccardi*
Editorial Assistant: *Kate Kaibni*
Interior Design: *Robert L. Kruse*
Page Layout: *Ginnie Masterson (PréTEX, Inc.)*
Art Production: *Blake MacLean (PréTEX, Inc.)*

Cover art: *Orange*, 1923, by Wassily Kandinsky (1866-1944), Lithograph in Colors.   Source: Christie's Images

 © 1999 by Prentice-Hall, Inc.
Simon & Schuster/A Viacom Company
Upper Saddle River, New Jersey 07458

The typesetting for this book was done with PreTEX, a preprocessor and macro package for the TEX typesetting system and the POSTSCRIPT page-description language. PreTEX is a trademark of PreTEX, Inc.; TEX is a trademark of the American Mathematical Society; POSTSCRIPT is a registered trademarks of Adobe Systems, Inc.

The authors and publisher of this book have used their best efforts in preparing this book. These efforts include the research, development, and testing of the theory and programs in the book to determine their effectiveness. The authors and publisher make no warranty of any kind, expressed or implied, with regard to these programs or the documentation contained in this book. The authors and publisher shall not be liable in any event for incidental or consequential damages in connection with, or arising out of, the furnishing, performance, or use of these programs.

Printed in the United States of America

10 9 8 7 6 5 4 3

ISBN 0-13-768995-0

Prentice-Hall International (U.K.) Limited, *London*
Prentice-Hall of Australia Pty. Limited, *Sydney*
Prentice-Hall Canada Inc., *Toronto*
Prentice-Hall Hispanoamericana, S.A., *Mexico*
Prentice-Hall of India Private Limited, *New Delhi*
Prentice-Hall of Japan, Inc., *Tokyo*
Simon & Schuster Asia Pte. Ltd., *Singapore*
Editora Prentice-Hall do Brasil, Ltda., *Rio de Janeiro*

Contents

v

9 **Tables and Information Retrieval _ 379**

10 **Binary Trees _____ 429**

Preface

THE APPRENTICE CARPENTER may want only a hammer and a saw, but a master builder employs many precision tools. Computer programming likewise requires sophisticated tools to cope with the complexity of real applications, and only practice with these tools will build skill in their use. This book treats structured problem solving, object-oriented programming, data abstraction, and the comparative analysis of algorithms as fundamental tools of program design. Several case studies of substantial size are worked out in detail, to show how all the tools are used together to build complete programs.

Many of the algorithms and data structures we study possess an intrinsic elegance, a simplicity that cloaks the range and power of their applicability. Before long the student discovers that vast improvements can be made over the naïve methods usually used in introductory courses. Yet this elegance of method is tempered with uncertainty. The student soon finds that it can be far from obvious which of several approaches will prove best in particular applications. Hence comes an early opportunity to introduce truly difficult problems of both intrinsic interest and practical importance and to exhibit the applicability of mathematical methods to algorithm verification and analysis.

Many students find difficulty in translating abstract ideas into practice. This book, therefore, takes special care in the formulation of ideas into algorithms and in the refinement of algorithms into concrete programs that can be applied to practical problems. The process of data specification and abstraction, similarly, comes before the selection of data structures and their implementations.

We believe in progressing from the concrete to the abstract, in the careful development of motivating examples, followed by the presentation of ideas in a more general form. At an early stage of their careers most students need reinforcement from seeing the immediate application of the ideas that they study, and they require the practice of writing and running programs to illustrate each important concept that they learn. This book therefore contains many sample programs, both short functions and complete programs of substantial length. The exercises and programming projects, moreover, constitute an indispensable part of the book. Many of these are immediate applications of the topic under study, often requesting that programs be written and run, so that algorithms may be tested and compared. Some are larger projects, and a few are suitable for use by a small group of students working together.

Our programs are written in the popular object-oriented language C++. We take the view that many object-oriented techniques provide natural implementations for basic principles of data-structure design. In this way, C++ allows us to construct safe, efficient, and simple implementations of data-structures. We recognize that C++ is sufficiently complex that students will need to use the experience of a data structures courses to develop and refine their understanding of the language. We strive to support this development by carefully introducing and explaining various object-oriented features of C++ as we progress through the book. Thus, we begin Chapter 1 assuming that the reader is comfortable with the elementary parts of C++ (essentially, with the C subset), and gradually we add in such object-oriented elements of C++ as classes, methods, constructors, inheritance, dynamic memory management, destructors, copy constructors, overloaded functions and operations, templates, virtual functions, and the STL. Of course, our primary focus is on the data structures themselves, and therefore students with relatively little familiarity with C++ will need to supplement this text with a C++ programming text.

SYNOPSIS

Programming Principles

By working through the first large project (Conway's game of Life), Chapter 1 expounds principles of object-oriented program design, top-down refinement, review, and testing, principles that the student will see demonstrated and is expected to follow throughout the sequel. At the same time, this project provides an opportunity for the student to review the syntax of elementary features of C++, the programming language used throughout the book.

Introduction to Stacks

Chapter 2 introduces the first data structure we study, the stack. The chapter applies stacks to the development of programs for reversing input, for modelling a desk calculator, and for checking the nesting of brackets. We begin by utilizing the STL stack implementation, and later develop and use our own stack implementation. A major goal of Chapter 2 is to bring the student to appreciate the ideas behind information hiding, encapsulation and data abstraction and to apply methods of top-down design to data as well as to algorithms. The chapter closes with an introduction to abstract data types.

Queues

Queues are the central topic of Chapter 3. The chapter expounds several different implementations of the abstract data type and develops a large application program showing the relative advantages of different implementations. In this chapter we introduce the important object-oriented technique of inheritance.

Linked Stacks and Queues

Chapter 4 presents linked implementations of stacks and queues. The chapter begins with a thorough introduction to pointers and dynamic memory management in C++. After exhibiting a simple linked stack implementation, we discuss destructors, copy constructors, and overloaded assignment operators, all of which are needed in the safe C++ implementation of linked structures.

Recursion Chapter 5 continues to elucidate stacks by studying their relationship to problem solving and programming with recursion. These ideas are reinforced by exploring several substantial applications of recursion, including backtracking and tree-structured programs. This chapter can, if desired, be studied earlier in a course than its placement in the book, at any time after the completion of Chapter 2.

Lists and Strings More general lists with their linked and contiguous implementations provide the theme for Chapter 6. The chapter also includes an encapsulated string implementation, an introduction to C++ templates, and an introduction to algorithm analysis in a very informal way.

Searching Chapter 7, Chapter 8, and Chapter 9 present algorithms for searching, sorting, and table access (including hashing), respectively. These chapters illustrate the *Sorting* interplay between algorithms and the associated abstract data types, data structures, and implementations. The text introduces the "big-O" and related notations for elementary algorithm analysis and highlights the crucial choices to be made *Tables and* regarding best use of space, time, and programming effort. These choices require *Information Retrieval* that we find analytical methods to assess algorithms, and producing such analyses is a battle for which combinatorial mathematics must provide the arsenal. At an elementary level we can expect students neither to be well armed nor to possess the mathematical maturity needed to hone their skills to perfection. Our goal, therefore, is to help students recognize the importance of such skills in anticipation of later chances to study mathematics.

Binary Trees Binary trees are surely among the most elegant and useful of data structures. Their study, which occupies Chapter 10, ties together concepts from lists, searching, and sorting. As recursively defined data structures, binary trees afford an excellent opportunity for the student to become comfortable with recursion applied both to data structures and algorithms. The chapter begins with elementary topics and progresses as far as such advanced topics as splay trees and amortized algorithm analysis.

Multiway Trees Chapter 11 continues the study of more sophisticated data structures, including tries, B-trees, and red-black trees.

Graphs Chapter 12 introduces graphs as more general structures useful for problem solving, and introduces some of the classical algorithms for shortest paths and minimal spanning trees in graphs.

Case Study: The case study in Chapter 13 examines the Polish notation in considerable *The Polish Notation* detail, exploring the interplay of recursion, trees, and stacks as vehicles for problem solving and algorithm development. Some of the questions addressed can serve as an informal introduction to compiler design. As usual, the algorithms are fully developed within a functioning C++ program. This program accepts as input an expression in ordinary (infix) form, translates the expression into postfix form, and evaluates the expression for specified values of the variable(s). Chapter 13 may be studied anytime after the completion of Section 10.1.

The appendices discuss several topics that are not properly part of the book's subject but that are often missing from the student's preparation.

Mathematical Appendix A presents several topics from discrete mathematics. Its final two *Methods* sections, Fibonacci numbers amd Catalan numbers, are more advanced and not needed for any vital purpose in the text, but are included to encourage combinatorial interest in the more mathematically inclined.

Random Numbers   Appendix B discusses pseudorandom numbers, generators, and applications, a topic that many students find interesting, but which often does not fit anywhere in the curriculum.

Packages and Utility Functions   Appendix C catalogues the various utility and data-structure packages that are developed and used many times throughout this book. Appendix C discusses declaration and definition files, translation units, the utility package used throughout the book, and a package for calculating CPU times.

Programming Precepts, Pointers, and Pitfalls   Appendix D, finally, collects all the Programming Precepts and all the Pointers and Pitfalls scattered through the book and organizes them by subject for convenience of reference.

COURSE STRUCTURE

prerequisite   The prerequisite for this book is a first course in programming, with experience using the elementary features of C++. However, since we are careful to introduce sophisticated C++ techniques only gradually, we believe that, used in conjunction with a supplementary C++ textbook and extra instruction and emphasis on C++ language issues, this text provides a data structures course in C++ that remains suitable even for students whose programming background is in another language such as C, Pascal, or Java.

A good knowledge of high school mathematics will suffice for almost all the algorithm analyses, but further (perhaps concurrent) preparation in discrete mathematics will prove valuable. Appendix A reviews all required mathematics.

content   This book is intended for courses such as the ACM Course CS2 (*Program Design and Implementation*), ACM Course CS7 (*Data Structures and Algorithm Analysis*), or a course combining these. Thorough coverage is given to most of the ACM/IEEE knowledge units[1] on data structures and algorithms. These include:

AL1 Basic data structures, such as arrays, tables, stacks, queues, trees, and graphs;

AL2 Abstract data types;

AL3 Recursion and recursive algorithms;

AL4 Complexity analysis using the big Oh notation;

AL6 Sorting and searching; and

AL8 Practical problem-solving strategies, with large case studies.

The three most advanced knowledge units, AL5 (complexity classes, NP-complete problems), AL7 (computability and undecidability), and AL9 (parallel and distributed algorithms) are not treated in this book.

---

[1] See *Computing Curricula 1991: Report of the ACM/IEEE-CS Joint Curriculum Task Force*, ACM Press, New York, 1990.

Most chapters of this book are structured so that the core topics are presented first, followed by examples, applications, and larger case studies. Hence, if time allows only a brief study of a topic, it is possible, with no loss of continuity, to move rapidly from chapter to chapter covering only the core topics. When time permits, however, both students and instructor will enjoy the occasional excursion into the supplementary topics and worked-out projects.

two-term course   A two-term course can cover nearly the entire book, thereby attaining a satisfying integration of many topics from the areas of problem solving, data structures, program development, and algorithm analysis. Students need time and practice to understand general methods. By combining the studies of data abstraction, data structures, and algorithms with their implementations in projects of realistic size, an integrated course can build a solid foundation on which, later, more theoretical courses can be built. Even if it is not covered in its entirety, this book will provide enough depth to enable interested students to continue using it as a reference in later work. It is important in any case to assign major programming projects and to allow adequate time for their completion.

SUPPLEMENTARY MATERIALS

A CD-ROM version of this book is anticipated that, in addition to the entire contents of the book, will include:

➡ All packages, programs, and other C++ code segments from the text, in a form ready to incorporate as needed into other programs;

➡ Executable versions (for DOS or Windows) of several demonstration programs and nearly all programming projects from the text;

➡ Brief outlines or summaries of each section of the text, suitable for use as a study guide.

These materials will also be available from the publisher's internet site. To reach these files with `ftp`, log in as user `anonymous` to the site `ftp.prenhall.com` and change to the directory

```
pub/esm/computer_science.s-041/kruse/cpp
```

Instructors teaching from this book may obtain, at no charge, an instructor's version on CD-ROM which, in addition to all the foregoing materials, includes:

➡ Brief teaching notes on each chapter;

➡ Full solutions to nearly all exercises in the textbook;

➡ Full source code to nearly all programming projects in the textbook;

➡ Transparency masters.

BOOK PRODUCTION

This book and its supplements were written and produced with software called PreTEX, a preprocessor and macro package for the TEX typesetting system.[2] PreTEX, by exploiting context dependency, automatically supplies much of the typesetting markup required by TEX. PreTEX also supplies several tools that greatly simplify some aspects of an author's work. These tools include a powerful cross-reference system, simplified typesetting of mathematics and computer-program listings, and automatic generation of the index and table of contents, while allowing the processing of the book in conveniently small files at every stage. Solutions, placed with exercises and projects, are automatically removed from the text and placed in a separate document.

For a book such as this, PreTEX's treatment of computer programs is its most important feature. Computer programs are not included with the main body of the text; instead, they are placed in separate, secondary files, along with any desired explanatory text, and with any desired typesetting markup in place. By placing tags at appropriate places in the secondary files, PreTEX can extract arbitrary parts of a secondary file, in any desired order, for typesetting with the text. Another utility removes all the tags, text, and markup, producing as its output a program ready to be compiled. The same input file thus automatically produces both typeset program listings and compiled program code. In this way, the reader gains increased confidence in the accuracy of the computer program listings appearing in the text. In fact, with just two exceptions, all of the programs developed in this book have been compiled and succesfully tested under the g++ and Borland C++ compilers (versions 2.7.2.1 and 5.0, respectively). The two exceptions are the first program in Chapter 2 (which requires a compiler with a full ANSI C++ standard library) and the last program of Chapter 13 (which requires a compiler with certain Borland graphics routines).

ACKNOWLEDGMENTS

Over the years, the Pascal and C antecedents of this book have benefitted greatly from the contributions of many people: family, friends, colleagues, and students, some of whom are noted in the previous books. Many other people, while studying these books or their translations into various languages, have kindly forwarded their comments and suggestions, all of which have helped to make this a better book.

We are happy to acknowledge the suggestions of the following reviewers, who have helped in many ways to improve the presentation in this book: KEITH VANDER LINDEN (Calvin College), JENS GREGOR (University of Tennessee), VICTOR BERRY (Boston University), JEFFERY LEON (University of Illinois at Chicago), SUSAN

---

[2] TEX was developed by DONALD E. KNUTH, who has also made many important research contributions to data structures and algorithms. (See the entries under his name in the index.)

HUTT (University of Missouri–Columbia), FRED HARRIS (University of Nevada), ZHI-LI ZHANG (University of Minnesota), and ANDREW SUNG (New Mexico Institute of Technology).

ALEX RYBA especially acknowledges the helpful suggestions and encouraging advice he has received over the years from WIM RUITENBURG and JOHN SIMMS of Marquette University, as well as comments from former students RICK VOGEL and JUN WANG.

It is a special pleasure for ROBERT KRUSE to acknowledge the continuing advice and help of PAUL MAILHOT of PreTeX, Inc., who was from the first an outstanding student, then worked as a dependable research assistant, and who has now become a valued colleague making substantial contributions in software development for book production, in project management, in problem solving for the publisher, the printer, and the authors, and in providing advice and encouragement in all aspects of this work. The CD-ROM versions of this book, with all their hypertext features (such as extensive cross-reference links and execution of demonstration programs from the text), are entirely his accomplishment.

Without the continuing enthusiastic support, faithful encouragement, and patience of the editorial staff of Prentice Hall, especially ALAN APT, Publisher, LAURA STEELE, Acquisitions Editor, and MARCIA HORTON, Editor in Chief, this project would never have been started and certainly could never have been brought to completion. Their help, as well as that of the production staff named on the copyright page, has been invaluable.

ROBERT L. KRUSE

ALEXANDER J. RYBA

Programming Principles

1

THIS CHAPTER summarizes important principles of good programming, especially as applied to large projects, and introduces methods such as object-oriented design and top-down design for discovering effective algorithms. In the process we raise questions in program design and data-storage methods that we shall address in later chapters, and we also review some of the elementary features of the language C++ by using them to write programs.

The greatest difficulties of writing large computer programs are not in deciding what the goals of the program should be, nor even in finding methods that can be used to reach these goals. The president of a business might say, "Let's get a computer to keep track of all our inventory information, accounting records, and personnel files, and let it tell us when inventories need to be reordered and budget lines are overspent, and let it handle the payroll." With enough time and effort, a staff of systems analysts and programmers might be able to determine how various staff members are now doing these tasks and write programs to do the work in the same way.

problems of large programs

This approach, however, is almost certain to be a disastrous failure. While interviewing employees, the systems analysts will find some tasks that can be put on the computer easily and will proceed to do so. Then, as they move other work to the computer, they will find that it depends on the first tasks. The output from these, unfortunately, will not be quite in the proper form. Hence they need more programming to convert the data from the form given for one task to the form needed for another. The programming project begins to resemble a patchwork quilt. Some of the pieces are stronger, some weaker. Some of the pieces are carefully sewn onto the adjacent ones, some are barely tacked together. If the programmers are lucky, their creation may hold together well enough to do most of the routine work most of the time. But if any change must be made, it will have unpredictable consequences throughout the system. Later, a new request will come along, or an unexpected problem, perhaps even an emergency, and the programmers' efforts will prove as effective as using a patchwork quilt as a safety net for people jumping from a tall building.

 OBJECTIVES

The main purpose of this book is to describe programming methods and tools that will prove effective for projects of realistic size, programs much larger than those ordinarily used to illustrate features of elementary programming. Since a piecemeal approach to large problems is doomed to fail, we must first of all adopt a consistent, unified, and logical approach, and we must also be careful to observe important principles of program design, principles that are sometimes ignored in writing small programs, but whose neglect will prove disastrous for large projects.

problem specification

The first major hurdle in attacking a large problem is deciding exactly what the problem is. It is necessary to translate vague goals, contradictory requests, and perhaps unstated desires into a precisely formulated project that can be programmed. And the methods or divisions of work that people have previously used are not necessarily the best for use in a machine. Hence our approach must be to determine overall goals, but precise ones, and then slowly divide the work into smaller problems until they become of manageable size.

program design

The maxim that many programmers observe, "First make your program work, then make it pretty," may be effective for small programs, but not for large ones. Each part of a large program must be well organized, clearly written, and thoroughly understood, or else its structure will have been forgotten, and it can no longer be tied to the other parts of the project at some much later time, perhaps by another programmer. Hence we do not separate style from other parts of program design, but from the beginning we must be careful to form good habits.

Even with very large projects, difficulties usually arise not from the inability to find a solution but, rather, from the fact that there can be so many different methods and algorithms that might work that it can be hard to decide which is best, which may lead to programming difficulties, or which may be hopelessly inefficient. The greatest room for variability in algorithm design is generally in the way in which the data of the program are stored:

choice of data structures

➡ How they are arranged in relation to each other.

➡ Which data are kept in memory.

➡ Which are calculated when needed.

➡ Which are kept in files, and how the files are arranged.

A second goal of this book, therefore, is to present several elegant, yet fundamentally simple ideas for the organization and manipulation of data. Lists, stacks, and queues are the first three such organizations that we study. Later, we shall develop several powerful algorithms for important tasks within data processing, such as sorting and searching.

When there are several different ways to organize data and devise algorithms, it becomes important to develop criteria to recommend a choice. Hence we devote attention to analyzing the behavior of algorithms under various conditions.

analysis of algorithms

The difficulty of debugging a program increases much faster than its size. That is, if one program is twice the size of another, then it will likely not take twice as long to debug, but perhaps four times as long. Many very large programs (such as operating systems) are put into use still containing errors that the programmers have despaired of finding, because the difficulties seem insurmountable. Sometimes projects that have consumed years of effort must be discarded because it is impossible to discover why they will not work. If we do not wish such a fate for our own projects, then we must use methods that will

testing and verification

program correctness

➡ Reduce the number of errors, making it easier to spot those that remain.

➡ Enable us to verify in advance that our algorithms are correct.

➡ Provide us with ways to test our programs so that we can be reasonably confident that they will not misbehave.

Development of such methods is another of our goals, but one that cannot yet be fully within our grasp.

maintenance

Even after a program is completed, fully debugged, and put into service, a great deal of work may be required to maintain the usefulness of the program. In time there will be new demands on the program, its operating environment will change, new requests must be accommodated. For this reason, it is essential that a large project be written to make it as easy to understand and modify as possible.

C++

The programming language C++ is a particularly convenient choice to express the algorithms we shall encounter. The language was developed in the early 1980s, by Bjarne Stroustrup, as an extension of the popular C language. Most of the new features that Stroustrup incorporated into C++ facilitate the understanding and implementation of data structures. Among the most important features of C++ for our study of data structures are:

Highlights

➡ C++ allows *data abstraction*: This means that programmers can create new types to represent whatever collections of data are convenient for their applications.

➡ C++ supports *object-oriented design*, in which the programmer-defined types play a central role in the implementation of algorithms.

➡ Importantly, as well as allowing for object-oriented approaches, C++ allows for the use of the *top-down approach*, which is familiar to C programmers.

➡ C++ facilitates *code reuse*, and the construction of general purpose libraries. The language includes an extensive, efficient, and convenient standard library.

➡ C++ improves on several of the inconvenient and dangerous aspects of C.

➡ C++ maintains the efficiency that is the hallmark of the C language.

It is the combination of flexibility, generality and efficiency that has made C++ one of the most popular choices for programmers at the present time.

We shall discover that the general principles that underlie the design of all data structures are naturally implemented by the data abstraction and the object-oriented features of C++. Therefore, we shall carefully explain how these aspects of C++ are used and briefly summarize their syntax (grammar) wherever they first arise in our book. In this way, we shall illustrate and describe many of the features of C++ that do not belong to its small overlap with C. For the precise details of C++ syntax, consult a textbook on C++ programming—we recommend several such books in the references at the end of this chapter.

1.2 THE GAME OF LIFE

If we may take the liberty to abuse an old proverb,

> *One concrete problem is worth a thousand unapplied abstractions.*

Study *CASE*

Throughout this chapter we shall concentrate on one case study that, while not large by realistic standards, illustrates both the principles of program design and the pitfalls that we should learn to avoid. Sometimes the example motivates general principles; sometimes the general discussion comes first; always it is with the view of discovering general principles that will prove their value in a range of practical applications. In later chapters we shall employ similar methods for larger projects.

The example we shall use is the game called *Life*, which was introduced by the British mathematician J. H. Conway in 1970.

1.2.1 Rules for the Game of Life

Life is really a simulation, not a game with players. It takes place on an unbounded rectangular grid in which each cell can either be occupied by an organism or not.

definitions Occupied cells are called *alive*; unoccupied cells are called *dead*. Which cells are alive changes from generation to generation according to the number of neighboring cells that are alive, as follows:

transition rules   1. The neighbors of a given cell are the eight cells that touch it vertically, horizontally, or diagonally.

2. If a cell is alive but either has no neighboring cells alive or only one alive, then in the next generation the cell dies of loneliness.

3. If a cell is alive and has four or more neighboring cells also alive, then in the next generation the cell dies of overcrowding.

4. A living cell with either two or three living neighbors remains alive in the next generation.

5. If a cell is dead, then in the next generation it will become alive if it has exactly three neighboring cells, no more or fewer, that are already alive. All other dead cells remain dead in the next generation.

6. All births and deaths take place at exactly the same time, so that dying cells can help to give birth to another, but cannot prevent the death of others by reducing overcrowding; nor can cells being born either preserve or kill cells living in the previous generation.

configuration   A particular arrangement of living and dead cells in a grid is called a ***configuration***. The preceding rules explain how one configuration changes to another at each generation.

1.2.2 Examples

As a first example, consider the configuration

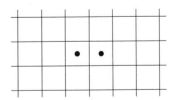

The counts of living neighbors for the cells are as follows:

0	0	0	0	0	0
0	1	2	2	1	0
0	1	•1	•1	1	0
0	1	2	2	1	0
0	0	0	0	0	0

moribund example   By rule 2 both the living cells will die in the coming generation, and rule 5 shows that no cells will become alive, so the configuration dies out.

On the other hand, the configuration

0	0	0	0	0	0
0	1	2	2	1	0
0	2	•3	•3	2	0
0	2	•3	•3	2	0
0	1	2	2	1	0
0	0	0	0	0	0

stability   has the neighbor counts as shown. Each of the living cells has a neighbor count of three, and hence remains alive, but the dead cells all have neighbor counts of two or less, and hence none of them becomes alive.

The two configurations

0	0	0	0	0
1	2	3	2	1
1	•1	•2	•1	1
1	2	3	2	1
0	0	0	0	0

and

0	1	1	1	0
0	2	•1	2	0
0	3	•2	3	0
0	2	•1	.2	0
0	1	1	1	0

alternation   continue to alternate from generation to generation, as indicated by the neighbor counts shown.

It is a surprising fact that, from very simple initial configurations, quite complicated progressions of Life configurations can develop, lasting many generations, and it is usually not obvious what changes will happen as generations progress. *variety*   Some very small initial configurations will grow into large configurations; others will slowly die out; many will reach a state where they do not change, or where they go through a repeating pattern every few generations.

popularity   Not long after its invention, MARTIN GARDNER discussed the Life game in his column in *Scientific American*, and, from that time on, it has fascinated many people, so that for several years there was even a quarterly newsletter devoted to related topics. It makes an ideal display for home microcomputers.

Our first goal, of course, is to write a program that will show how an initial configuration will change from generation to generation.

1.2.3 The Solution: Classes, Objects, and Methods

In outline, a program to run the Life game takes the form:

algorithm   Set up a Life configuration as an initial arrangement of living and dead cells.

Print the Life configuration.

While the user wants to see further generations:
Update the configuration by applying the rules of the Life game.
Print the current configuration.

class   The important thing for us to study in this algorithm is the Life configuration. In C++, we use a ***class*** to collect data and the methods used to access or change the *object*   data. Such a collection of data and methods is called an ***object*** belonging to the given class. For the Life game, we shall call the class Life, so that configuration becomes a Life *object*. We shall then use three methods for this object: initialize() will set up the initial configuration of living and dead cells; print() will print out the current configuration; and update() will make all the changes that occur in moving from one generation to the next.

C++ classes   Every C++ class, in fact, consists of ***members*** that represent either variables or functions. The members that represent variables are called the ***data members***; these are used to store data values. The members that represent functions belonging to *methods*   a class are called the ***methods*** or ***member functions***. The methods of a class are normally used to access or alter the data members.

clients   ***Clients***, that is, user programs with access to a particular class, can declare and manipulate objects of that class. Thus, in the Life game, we shall declare a Life object by:

Life configuration;

We can now apply methods to work with configuration, using the C++ operator *member selection*   . (the member selection operator). For example, we can print out the data in *operator*   configuration by writing:

configuration.print();

It is important to realize that, while writing a client program, we can use a *specifications*   C++ class so long as we know the ***specifications*** of each of its methods, that is, statements of precisely what each method does. We do not need to know how the data are actually stored or how the methods are actually programmed. For example, to use a Life object, we do not need to know exactly how the object is *information hiding*   stored, or how the methods of the class Life are doing their work. This is our first example of an important programming strategy known as ***information hiding***.

When the time comes to implement the class Life, we shall find that more goes on behind the scenes: We shall need to decide how to store the data, and *private and public*   we shall need variables and functions to manipulate this data. All these variables and functions, however, are *private* to the class; the client program does not need to know what they are, how they are programmed, or have any access to them. Instead, the client program only needs the *public* methods that are specified and declared for the class.

In this book, we shall always distinguish between methods and functions as follows, even though their actual syntax (programming grammar) is the same:

Convention

Methods of a class are public.
Functions in a class are private.

1.2.4 Life: The Main Program

The preceding outline of an algorithm for the game of Life translates into the following C++ program.

```
#include "utility.h"
#include "life.h"

int main()                        //    Program to play Conway's game of Life.
/* Pre:  The user supplies an initial configuration of living cells.
   Post: The program prints a sequence of pictures showing the changes in the
         configuration of living cells according to the rules for the game of Life.
   Uses: The class Life and its methods initialize(), print(), and update().
         The functions  instructions(), user_says_yes(). */
{
   Life configuration;
   instructions();
   configuration.initialize();
   configuration.print();
   cout << "Continue viewing new generations? " << endl;
   while (user_says_yes()) {
      configuration.update();
      configuration.print();
      cout << "Continue viewing new generations? " << endl;
   }
}
```

utility package   The program begins by including files that allow it to use the class **Life** and the standard C++ input and output libraries. The utility function **user_says_yes()** is declared in `utility.h`, which we shall discuss presently. For our Life program, the only other information that we need about the file `utility.h` is that it begins with the instructions

```
#include <iostream>
using namespace std;
```

which allow us to use standard C++ input and output streams such as **cin** and **cout**. (On older compilers an alternative directive #include <iostream.h> has the same effect.)

program specifications

The documentation for our Life program begins with its ***specifications***; that is, precise statements of the conditions required to hold when the program begins and the conditions that will hold after it finishes. These are called, respectively, the ***preconditions*** and ***postconditions*** for the program. Including precise preconditions and postconditions for each function not only explains clearly the purpose of the function but helps us avoid errors in the interface between functions. Including specifications is so helpful that we single it out as our first programming precept:

Programming Precept

*Include precise preconditions and postconditions
with every program, function, and method that you write.*

---

functions

A third part of the specifications for our program is a list of the classes and functions that it uses. A similar list should be included with every program, function, or method.

action of the program

The action of our main program is entirely straightforward. First, we read in the initial situation to establish the first configuration of occupied cells. Then we commence a loop that makes one pass for each generation. Within this loop we simply update the Life configuration, print the configuration, and ask the user whether we should continue. Note that the Life methods, initialize, update, and print are simply called with the member selection operator.

Plain Simple

In the Life program we still must write code to implement:

➡ The **class** Life.

➡ The method initialize( ) to initialize a Life configuration.

➡ The method print( ) to output a Life configuration.

➡ The method update( ) to change a Life object so that it stores the configuration at the next generation.

➡ The function user_says_yes( ) to ask the user whether or not to go on to the next generation.

➡ The function instructions( ) to print instructions for using the program.

The implementation of the class Life is contained in the two files `life.h` and `life.c`. There are a number of good reasons for us to use a pair of files for the implementation of any class or data structure: According to the principle of information hiding, we should separate the definition of a class from the coding of its methods. The user of the class only needs to look at the specification part and its list of methods. In our example, the file `life.h` will give the specification of the **class** Life.

Moreover, by dividing a class implementation between two files, we can adhere to the standard practice of leaving function and variable definitions out of files with a suffix `.h`. This practice allows us to compile the files, or compilation units, that make up a program separately and then link them together.

Each compilation unit ought to be able to include any particular .h file (for example to use the associated data structure), but unless we omit function and variable definitions from the .h file, this will not be legal. In our project, the second file life.c must therefore contain the implementations of the methods of the **class** Life and the function instructions().[1]

Another code file, utility.c, contains the definition of the function

user_says_yes( ).

utility package   We shall, in fact, soon develop several more functions, declarations, definitions, and other instructions that will be useful in various applications. We shall put all of these together as a ***package***. This package can be incorporated into any program with the directive:

#include "utility.h"

whenever it is needed.

Just as we divided the Life class implementation between two files, we should divide the utility package between the files utility.h and utility.c to allow for its use in the various translation units of a large program. In particular, we should place function and variable definitions into the file utility.c, and we place other sorts of utility instructions, such as the inclusion of standard C++ library files, into utility.h. As we develop programs in future chapters, we shall add to the utility package. Appendix C lists all the code for the whole utility package.

Exercises 1.2

Determine by hand calculation what will happen to each of the configurations shown in Figure 1.1 over the course of five generations. [*Suggestion*: Set up the Life configuration on a checkerboard. Use one color of checkers for living cells in the current generation and a second color to mark those that will be born or die in the next generation.]

1.3 PROGRAMMING STYLE

Before we turn to implementing classes and functions for the Life game, let us pause to consider several principles that we should be careful to employ in programming.

1.3.1 Names

In the story of creation (Genesis 2:19), the LORD brought all the animals to ADAM to see what names he would give them. According to an old Jewish tradition, it was only when ADAM had named an animal that it sprang to life. This story brings

---

[1] On some compilers the file suffix .c has to be replaced by an alternative such as .C, .cpp, .cxx, or .cc.

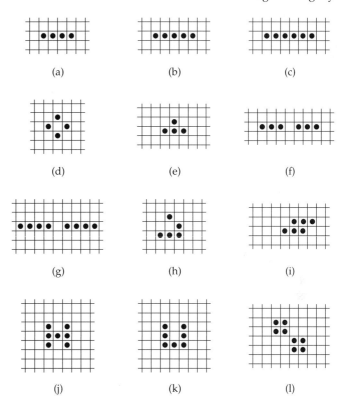

Figure 1.1. Simple Life configurations

an important moral to computer programming: Even if data and algorithms exist before, it is only when they are given meaningful names that their places in the program can be properly recognized and appreciated, that they first acquire a life of their own.

purpose of careful naming

For a program to work properly it is of the utmost importance to know exactly what each class and variable represents and to know exactly what each function does. Documentation explaining the classes, variables, and functions should therefore always be included. The names of classes, variables, and functions should be chosen with care so as to identify their meanings clearly and succinctly. Finding good names is not always an easy task, but is important enough to be singled out as our second programming precept:

Programming Precept

*Always name your classes, variables and functions
with the greatest care, and explain them thoroughly.*

C++ goes some distance toward enforcing this precept by requiring the declaration of variables and allows us almost unlimited freedom in the choice of identifying names. Constants used in different places should be given names, and so should different data types, so that the compiler can catch errors that might otherwise be difficult to spot.

We shall see that types and classes play a fundamental role in C++ programs, and it is particularly important that they should stand out to a reader of our programs. We shall therefore adopt a capitalization convention, which we have already used in the Life program: We use an initial capital letter in the identifier of any class or programmer defined type. In contrast, we shall use only lowercase letters for the identifiers of functions, variables, and constants.

The careful choice of names can go a long way in clarifying a program and in helping to avoid misprints and common errors. Some guidelines are

guidelines

1. Give special care to the choice of names for classes, functions, constants, and all global variables used in different parts of the program. These names should be meaningful and should suggest clearly the purpose of the class, function, variable, and the like.

2. Keep the names simple for variables used only briefly and locally. Mathematicians usually use a single letter to stand for a variable, and sometimes, when writing mathematical programs, it may be permissible to use a single-letter name for a mathematical variable. However, even for the variable controlling a **for** loop, it is often possible to find a short but meaningful word that better describes the use of the variable.

3. Use common prefixes or suffixes to associate names of the same general category. The files used in a program, for example, might be called

    input_file   transaction_file   total_file   out_file   reject_file

4. Avoid deliberate misspellings and meaningless suffixes to obtain different names. Of all the names

    index   indx   ndex   indexx   index2   index3

    only one (the first) should normally be used. When you are tempted to introduce multiple names of this sort, take it as a sign that you should think harder and devise names that better describe the intended use.

5. Avoid choosing cute names whose meaning has little or nothing to do with the problem. The statements

```
do {
    study();
} while (TV.in_hock());
if (!sleepy) play();
else nap();
```

may be funny but they are bad programming!

6. Avoid choosing names that are close to each other in spelling or otherwise easy to confuse.

7. Be careful in the use of the letter "I" (small ell), "O" (capital oh), and "0" (zero). Within words or numbers these usually can be recognized from the context and cause no problem, but "I" and "O" should never be used alone as names. Consider the examples

$$ \mathsf{I = 1;} \qquad \mathsf{x = 1;} \qquad \mathsf{x = I;} \qquad \mathsf{x = O;} \qquad \mathsf{O = 0} $$

1.3.2 Documentation and Format

the purpose of documentation

Most students initially regard documentation as a chore that must be endured after a program is finished, to ensure that the marker and instructor can read it, so that no credit will be lost for obscurity. The author of a small program indeed can keep all the details in mind, and so needs documentation only to explain the program to someone else. With large programs (and with small ones after some months have elapsed), it becomes impossible to remember how every detail relates to every other, and therefore to write large programs, it is essential that appropriate documentation be prepared along with each small part of the program. A good habit is to prepare documentation as the program is being written, and an even better one, as we shall see later, is to prepare part of the documentation before starting to write the program.

Not all documentation is appropriate. Almost as common as programs with little documentation or only cryptic comments are programs with verbose documentation that adds little to understanding the program. Hence our third programming precept:

Programming Precept

Keep your documentation concise but descriptive.

The style of documentation, as with all writing styles, is highly personal, and many different styles can prove effective. There are, nonetheless, some commonly accepted guidelines that should be respected:

guidelines

1. Place a prologue at the beginning of each function including
   (a) Identification (programmer's name, date, version number).[2]
   (b) Statement of the purpose of the function and algorithm used.
   (c) The changes the function makes and what data it uses.
   (d) Reference to further documentation external to the program.

2. When each variable, constant, or class is declared, explain what it is and how it is used. Better still, make this information evident from the name.

---

[2] To save space, programs printed in this book do not include identification lines or some other parts of the prologue, since the surrounding text gives the necessary information.

3. Introduce each significant section (paragraph or function) of the program with a comment stating briefly its purpose or action.

4. Indicate the end of each significant section if it is not otherwise obvious.

5. Avoid comments that parrot what the code does, such as

count++;   //   *Increase counter by* 1.

or that are meaningless jargon, such as

//   *Horse string length into correctitude.*

(This example was taken directly from a systems program.)

6. Explain any statement that employs a trick or whose meaning is unclear. Better still, avoid such statements.

7. The code itself should explain *how* the program works. The documentation should explain *why* it works and *what* it does.

8. Whenever a program is modified, be sure that the documentation is correspondingly modified.

format   Spaces, blank lines, and indentation in a program are an important form of documentation. They make the program easy to read, allow you to tell at a glance which parts of the program relate to each other, where the major breaks occur, and precisely which statements are contained in each loop or each alternative of a conditional statement. There are many systems (some automated) for indentation and spacing, all with the goal of making it easier to determine the structure of the program.

prettyprinting   A *prettyprinter* is a system utility that reads a C++ program, moving the text between lines and adjusting the indentation so as to improve the appearance of the program and make its structure more obvious. If a prettyprinter is available on your system, you might experiment with it to see if it helps the appearance of your programs.

consistency   Because of the importance of good format for programs, you should settle on some reasonable rules for spacing and indentation and use your rules consistently in all the programs you write. Consistency is essential if the system is to be useful in reading programs. Many professional programming groups decide on a uniform system and insist that all the programs they write conform. Some classes or student programming teams do likewise. In this way, it becomes much easier for one programmer to read and understand the work of another.

Programming Precept

The reading time for programs is much more than the writing time.
Make reading easy to do.

1.3.3 Refinement and Modularity

problem solving　Computers do not solve problems; people do. Usually the most important part of the process is dividing the problem into smaller problems that can be understood in more detail. If these are still too difficult, then they are subdivided again, and so on. In any large organization the top management cannot worry about every detail of every activity; the top managers must concentrate on general goals and problems and delegate specific responsibilities to their subordinates. Again, middle-level managers cannot do everything: They must subdivide the work and send it to
subdivision　other people. So it is with computer programming. Even when a project is small enough that one person can take it from start to finish, it is most important to divide the work, starting with an overall understanding of the problem, dividing it into subproblems, and attacking each of these in turn without worrying about the others.

Let us restate this principle with a classic proverb:

Programming Precept

Don't lose sight of the forest for its trees.

---

top-down refinement　This principle, called **top-down refinement**, is the real key to writing large programs that work. The principle implies the postponement of detailed consideration, but not the postponement of precision and rigor. It does not mean that the main pro-

gram becomes some vague entity whose task can hardly be described. On the contrary, the main program will send almost all the work out to various classes, data structures and functions, and as we write the main program (which we should
specifications　do first), we decide *exactly* how the work will be divided among them. Then, as we later work on a particular class or function, we shall know before starting exactly what it is expected to do.

It is often difficult to decide exactly how to divide the work into classes and functions, and sometimes a decision once made must later be modified. Even so, some guidelines can help in deciding how to divide the work:

Programming Precept

Use classes to model the fundamental concepts of the program.

For example, our Life program must certainly deal with the Life game and we therefore create a class **Life** to model the game. We can often pick out the important classes for an application by describing our task in words and assigning classes for the different nouns that are used. The verbs that we use will often signify the important functions.

Programming Precept

Each function should do only one task, but do it well.

That is, we should be able to describe the purpose of a function succinctly. If you find yourself writing a long paragraph to specify the preconditions or postconditions for a function, then either you are giving too much detail (that is, you are writing the function before it is time to do so) or you should rethink the division of work. The function itself will undoubtedly contain many details, but they should not appear until the next stage of refinement.

Programming Precept

Each class or function should hide something.

Middle-level managers in a large company do not pass on everything they receive from their departments to their superior; they summarize, collate, and weed out the information, handle many requests themselves, and send on only what is needed at the upper levels. Similarly, managers do not transmit everything they learn from higher management to their subordinates. They transmit to their employees only what they need to do their jobs. The classes and functions we write should do likewise. In other words, we should practice *information hiding*.

One of the most important parts of the refinement process is deciding exactly what the task of each function is, specifying precisely what its preconditions and postconditions will be; that is, what its input will be and what result it will produce. Errors in these specifications are among the most frequent program bugs and are among the hardest to find. First, the parameters used in the function must be precisely specified. These data are of three basic kinds:

parameters

➥ *Input parameters* are used by the function but are not changed by the function. In C++, input parameters are often passed by value. (Exception: Large objects should be passed by reference.[3] This avoids the time and space needed to make a local copy. However, when we pass an input parameter by reference, we shall prefix its declaration with the keyword **const**. This use of the type modifier **const** is important, because it allows a reader to see that we are using an input parameter, it allows the compiler to detect accidental changes to the parameter, and occasionally it allows the compiler to optimize our code.)

➥ *Output parameters* contain the results of the calculations from the function. In this book, we shall use reference variables for output parameters. In contrast, C programmers need to simulate reference variables by passing addresses of variables to utilize output parameters. Of course, the C approach is still available to us in C++, but we shall avoid using it.

➥ *Inout parameters* are used for both input and output; the initial value of the parameter is used and then modified by the function. We shall pass inout parameters by reference.

---

3   Consult a C++ textbook for discussion of call by reference and reference variables.

In addition to its parameters, a function uses other data objects that generally fall into one of the following categories.

variables   ➡ *Local variables* are defined in the function and exist only while the function is being executed. They are not initialized before the function begins and are discarded when the function ends.

➡ *Global variables* are used in the function but not defined in the function. It can be quite dangerous to use global variables in a function, since after the function is written its author may forget exactly what global variables were used and how. If the main program is later changed, then the function may mysteriously begin to misbehave. If a function alters the value of a global variable, it is said

side effects   to cause a *side effect*. Side effects are even more dangerous than using global variables as input to the function because side effects may alter the performance of other functions, thereby misdirecting the programmer's debugging efforts to a part of the program that is already correct.

Programming Precept

Keep your connections simple. Avoid global variables whenever possible.

Programming Precept

Never cause side effects if you can avoid it.
If you must use global variables as input, document them thoroughly.

While these principles of top-down design may seem almost self-evident, the only way to learn them thoroughly is by practice. Hence throughout this book we shall be careful to apply them to the large programs that we write, and in a moment it will be appropriate to return to our first example project.

Exercises 1.3   **E1.** What classes would you define in implementing the following projects? What methods would your classes possess?

(a) A program to store telephone numbers.
(b) A program to play Monopoly.
(c) A program to play tic-tac-toe.
(d) A program to model the build up of queues of cars waiting at a busy intersection with a traffic light.

E2. Rewrite the following class definition, which is supposed to model a deck of playing cards, so that it conforms to our principles of style.

```
    class a {            //   a deck of cards
int X; thing Y1[52];   /* X is the location of the top card in the deck. Y1 lists
the cards. */ public: a();
void Shuffle();        //   Shuffle randomly arranges the cards.
thing d();             //   deals the top card off the deck
}
        ;
```

E3. Given the declarations

$$\text{int a[n][n], i, j;}$$

where n is a constant, determine what the following statement does, and rewrite the statement to accomplish the same effect in a less tricky way.

```
for (i = 0; i < n; i++)
    for (j = 0; j < n; j++)
        a[i][j] = ((i + 1)/(j + 1)) * ((j + 1)/(i + 1));
```

E4. Rewrite the following function so that it accomplishes the same result in a less tricky way.

```
void does_something(int &first, int &second)
{
    first = second - first;
    second = second - first;
    first = second + first;
}
```

E5. Determine what each of the following functions does. Rewrite each function with meaningful variable names, with better format, and without unnecessary variables and statements.

(a)
```
int calculate(int apple, int orange)
{ int peach, lemon;
peach = 0; lemon = 0; if (apple < orange)
peach = orange; else if (orange <= apple)
peach = apple; else { peach = 17;
lemon = 19; }
return(peach);
}
```

(b) For this part assume the declaration **typedef float** vector[max];

```
float figure (vector vector1)
{ int loop1, loop4; float loop2, loop3;
loop1 = 0; loop2 = vector1[loop1]; loop3 = 0.0;
loop4 = loop1; for (loop4 = 0;
loop4 < max; loop4++) { loop1 = loop1 + 1;
loop2 = vector1[loop1 - 1];
loop3 = loop2 + loop3; } loop1 = loop1 - 1;
loop2 = loop1;
return(loop2 = loop3/loop2); }
```

(c)
```
int question(int &a17, int &stuff)
{ int another, yetanother, stillonemore;
another = yetanother; stillonemore = a17;
yetanother = stuff; another = stillonemore;
a17 = yetanother; stillonemore = yetanother;
stuff = another; another = yetanother;
yetanother = stuff; }
```

(d) **int** mystery(**int** apple, **int** orange, **int** peach)
  { **if** (apple > orange) **if** (apple > peach) **if**
  (peach > orange) **return**(peach); **else if** (apple < orange)
  return(apple); **else return**(orange); **else return**(apple); **else**
  if (peach > apple) **if** (peach > orange) **return**(orange); **else**
  return(peach); **else return**(apple); }

E6. The following statement is designed to check the relative sizes of three integers, which you may assume to be different from each other:

    if (x < z) **if** (x < y) **if** (y < z) c = 1; **else** c = 2; **else**
      if (y < z) c = 3; **else** c = 4; **else if** (x < y)
      if (x < z) c = 5; **else** c = 6; **else if** (y < z) c = 7; **else**
      if (z < x) **if** (z < y) c = 8; **else** c = 9; **else** c = 10;

(a) Rewrite this statement in a form that is easier to read.
(b) Since there are only six possible orderings for the three integers, only six of the ten cases can actually occur. Find those that can never occur, and eliminate the redundant checks.
(c) Write a simpler, shorter statement that accomplishes the same result.

E7. The following C++ function calculates the cube root of a floating-point number (by the Newton approximation), using the fact that, if y is one approximation to the cube root of x, then

$$z = \frac{2y + x/y^2}{3}$$

cube roots   is a closer approximation.

float function fcn(**float** stuff)
{ **float** april, tim, tiny, shadow, tom, tam, square; **int** flag;
tim = stuff; tam = stuff; tiny = 0.00001;
if (stuff != 0) **do** {shadow = tim + tim; square = tim * tim;
tom = (shadow + stuff/square); april = tom/3.0;
if (april*april * april − tam > −tiny) **if** (april*april*april − tam
    < tiny) flag = 1; **else** flag = 0; **else** flag = 0;
if (flag == 0) tim = april; **else** tim = tam; } **while** (flag != 1);
if (stuff == 0) **return**(stuff); **else return**(april); }

(a) Rewrite this function with meaningful variable names, without the extra variables that contribute nothing to the understanding, with a better layout, and without the redundant and useless statements.
(b) Write a function for calculating the cube root of x directly from the mathematical formula, by starting with the assignment y = x and then repeating

$$y = (2 * y + (x/(y * y)))/3$$

until abs(y * y * y − x) < 0.00001.
(c) Which of these tasks is easier?

E8. The *mean* of a sequence of numbers is their sum divided by the count of numbers in the sequence. The (population) *variance* of the sequence is the mean of the squares of all numbers in the sequence, minus the square of the mean of the numbers in the sequence. The **standard deviation** is the square root of the variance. Write a well-structured C++ function to calculate the standard deviation of a sequence of n floating-point numbers, where n is a constant and the numbers are in an array indexed from 0 to $n - 1$, which is a parameter to the function. Use, then write, subsidiary functions to calculate the mean and variance.

statistics

E9. Design a program that will plot a given set of points on a graph. The input to the program will be a text file, each line of which contains two numbers that are the x and y coordinates of a point to be plotted. The program will use a function to plot one such pair of coordinates. The details of the function involve the specific method of plotting and cannot be written since they depend on the requirements of the plotting equipment, which we do not know. Before plotting the points the program needs to know the maximum and minimum values of x and y that appear in its input file. The program should therefore use another function **bounds** that will read the whole file and determine these four maxima and minima. Afterward, another function is used to draw and label the axes; then the file can be reset and the individual points plotted.

plotting

(a) Write the main program, not including the functions.
(b) Write the function **bounds**.
(c) Write the preconditions and postconditions for the remaining functions together with appropriate documentation showing their purposes and their requirements.

1.4 CODING, TESTING, AND FURTHER REFINEMENT

The three processes in the section title go hand-in-hand and must be done together. Yet it is important to keep them separate in our thinking, since each requires its own approach and method. *Coding*, of course, is the process of writing an algorithm in the correct syntax (grammar) of a computer language like C++, and *testing* is the process of running the program on sample data chosen to find errors if they are present. For further refinement, we turn to the functions not yet written and repeat these steps.

1.4.1 Stubs

After coding the main program, most programmers will wish to complete the writing and coding of the required classes and functions as soon as possible, to see if the whole project will work. For a project as small as the Life game, this approach may work, but for larger projects, the writing and coding will be such a large job that, by the time it is complete, many of the details of the main program and the classes and functions that were written early will have been forgotten. In fact, different people may be writing different functions, and some of those who

early debugging and testing

started the project may have left it before all functions are written. It is much easier to understand and debug a program when it is fresh in your mind. Hence, for larger projects, it is much more efficient to debug and test each class and function as soon as it is written than it is to wait until the project has been completely coded.

Even for smaller projects, there are good reasons for debugging classes and functions one at a time. We might, for example, be unsure of some point of C++ syntax that will appear in several places through the program. If we can compile each function separately, then we shall quickly learn to avoid errors in syntax in later functions. As a second example, suppose that we have decided that the major steps of the program should be done in a certain order. If we test the main program as soon as it is written, then we may find that sometimes the major steps are done in the wrong order, and we can quickly correct the problem, doing so more easily than if we waited until the major steps were perhaps obscured by the many details contained in each of them.

stubs To compile the main program correctly, there must be something in the place of each function that is used, and hence we must put in short, dummy functions, called **stubs**. The simplest stubs are those that do little or nothing at all:

```
void instructions() { }
bool user_says_yes() { return(true); }
```

Note that in writing the stub functions we must at least pin down their associated parameters and return types. For example, in designing a stub for user_says_yes(), we make the decision that it should return a natural answer of **true** or **false**. This means that we should give the function a return type **bool**. The type **bool** has only recently been added to C++ and some older compilers do not recognize it, but we can always simulate it with the following statements—which can conveniently be placed in the utility package, if they are needed:

```
typedef int bool;
const bool false = 0;
const bool true = 1;
```

In addition to the stub functions, our program also needs a stub definition for the **class** Life. For example, in the file life.h, we could define this class without data members as follows:

```
class Life {
public:
    void initialize();
    void print();
    void update();
};
```

We must also supply the following stubs for its methods in life.c:

```
void Life :: initialize() {}
void Life :: print() {}
void Life :: update() {}
```

Note that these method definitions have to use the C++ scope resolution operator :: [4] to indicate that they belong to the scope of the class **Life**.

Even with these minimal stubs we can at least compile the program and make
sure that the definitions of types and variables are syntactically correct. Normally,
however, each stub function should print a message stating that the function was
invoked. When we execute the program, we find that it runs into an infinite loop,
because the function **user_says_yes()** always returns a value of **true**. However,
the main program compiles and runs, so we can go on to refine our stubs. For a
small project like the Life game, we can simply write each class or function in turn,
substitute it for its stub, and observe the effect on program execution.

1.4.2 Definition of the Class Life

1: living cell
0: dead cell

Each **Life** object needs to include a rectangular array,[5] which we shall call **grid**, to
store a Life configuration. We use an integer entry of 1 in the array **grid** to denote a
living cell, and 0 to denote a dead cell. Thus to count the number of neighbors of a
particular cell, we just add the values of the neighboring cells. In fact, in updating
a Life configuration, we shall repeatedly need to count the number of living neighbors of individual cells in the configuration. Hence, the class **Life** should include a
member function **neighbor_count** that does this task. Moreover, since the member
neighbor_count is not needed by client code, we shall give it **private** visibility. In
contrast, the earlier **Life** methods all need to have **public** visibility. Finally, we must
settle on dimensions for the rectangular array carried in a **Life** configuration. We
code these dimensions as global constants, so that a single simple change is all that
we need to reset grid sizes in our program. Note that constant definitions can be
safely placed in **.h** files.

```
const int maxrow = 20, maxcol = 60;   //   grid dimensions

class Life {
public:
   void initialize();
   void print();
   void update();
private:
   int grid[maxrow + 2] [maxcol + 2];
                              //   allows for two extra rows and columns
   int neighbor_count(int row, int col);
};
```

We can test the definition, without writing the member functions, by using our
earlier stub methods together with a similar stub for the private function **neigh-
bor_count**.

---

[4]   Consult a C++ textbook for discussion of the scope resolution operator and the syntax for class
methods.

[5]   An array with two indices is called *rectangular*. The first index determines the *row* in the array
and the second the *column*.

1.4.3 Counting Neighbors

function
neighbor_count

hedge

Let us now refine our program further. The function that counts neighbors of the cell with coordinates **row, col** requires that we look in the eight adjoining cells. We shall use a pair of **for** loops to do this, one running from **row** − 1 to **row** + 1 and the other from **col** − 1 to **col** + 1. We need only be careful, when **row, col** is on a boundary of the grid, that we look only at legitimate cells in the grid. Rather than using several **if** statements to make sure that we do not go outside the grid, we introduce a *hedge* around the grid: We shall enlarge the grid by adding two extra rows, one before the first real row of the grid and one after the last, and two extra columns, one before the first column and one after the last. In our definition of the **class** Life, we anticipated the hedge by defining the member **grid** as an array with **maxrow** + 2 rows and **maxcol** + 2 columns. The cells in the hedge rows and columns will always be dead, so they will not affect the counts of living neighbors at all. Their presence, however, means that the **for** loops counting neighbors need make no distinction between rows or columns on the boundary of the grid and any other rows or columns. See the examples in Figure 1.2.

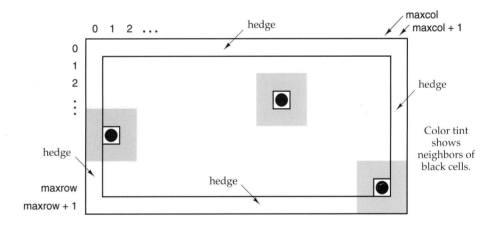

Figure 1.2. Life grid with a hedge

sentinel

Another term often used instead of hedge is **sentinel**: A sentinel is an extra entry put into a data structure so that boundary conditions need not be treated as a special case.

int Life :: neighbor_count(**int** row, **int** col)
/* **Pre:**   *The* Life *object contains a configuration, and the coordinates* row *and* col
          define a cell inside its hedge.
   Post: *The number of living neighbors of the specified cell is returned.* */

```
{
  int i, j;
  int count = 0;
  for (i = row − 1; i <= row + 1; i++)
    for (j = col − 1; j <= col + 1; j++)
      count += grid[i][j];   //   Increase the count if neighbor is alive.
  count −= grid[row][col];
                             //   Reduce count, since cell is not its own neighbor.
  return count;
}
```

1.4.4 Updating the Grid

method update

The action of the method to update a **Life** configuration is straightforward. We first use the data stored in the configuration to calculate entries of a rectangular array called **new_grid** that records the updated configuration. We then copy **new_grid**, entry by entry, back to the **grid** member of our **Life** object.

To set up **new_grid** we use a nested pair of loops on **row** and **col** that run over all non-hedge entries in the rectangular array **grid**. The body of these nested loops consists of the multiway selection statement **switch**. The function **neighbor_count(row, col)** returns one of the values $0, 1, \ldots, 8$, and for each of these cases we can take a separate action, or, as in our application, some of the cases may lead to the same action. You should check that the action prescribed in each case corresponds correctly to the rules 2, 3, 4, and 5 of Section 1.2.1.

```
void Life :: update()
/* Pre:   The Life object contains a configuration.
   Post:  The Life object contains the next generation of configuration. */
{
  int row, col;
  int new_grid[maxrow + 2][maxcol + 2];
  for (row = 1; row <= maxrow; row++)
    for (col = 1; col <= maxcol; col++)
      switch (neighbor_count(row, col)) {
      case 2:
        new_grid[row][col] = grid[row][col];   //   Status stays the same.
        break;
      case 3:
        new_grid[row][col] = 1;   //   Cell is now alive.
        break;
      default:
        new_grid[row][col] = 0;   //   Cell is now dead.
      }
  for (row = 1; row <= maxrow; row++)
    for (col = 1; col <= maxcol; col++)
      grid[row][col] = new_grid[row][col];
}
```

1.4.5 Input and Output

careful input and output

It now remains only to write the Life methods initialize() and print(), with the functions user_says_yes() and instructions() that do the input and output for our program. In computer programs designed to be used by many people, the functions performing input and output are often the longest. Input to the program must be fully checked to be certain that it is valid and consistent, and errors in input must be processed in ways to avoid catastrophic failure or production of ridiculous results. The output must be carefully organized and formatted, with considerable thought to what should or should not be printed, and with provision of various alternatives to suit differing circumstances.

Programming Precept

Keep your input and output as separate functions,
so they can be changed easily
and can be custom tailored to your computing system.

---

1. Instructions

stream output operators

The instructions() function is a simple exercise in use of the *put to* operator ≪ and the standard output stream called cout. Observe that we use the manipulator endl to end a line and flush the output buffer. The manipulator flush can be used instead in situations where we just wish to flush the output buffer, without ending a line. For the precise details of stream input and output in C++, consult a textbook on C++.

```
void instructions( )
/* Pre:   None.
   Post:  Instructions for using the Life program have been printed. */
{
   cout ≪ "Welcome to Conway's game of Life." ≪ endl;
   cout ≪ "This game uses a grid of size "
        ≪ maxrow ≪ " by " ≪ maxcol ≪ " in which" ≪ endl;
   cout ≪ "each cell can either be occupied by an organism or not." ≪ endl;
   cout ≪ "The occupied cells change from generation to generation" ≪ endl;
   cout ≪ "according to the number of neighboring cells which are alive."
        ≪ endl;
}
```

2. Initialization

input method

The task that the Life method initialize() must accomplish is to set up an initial configuration. To initialize a Life object, we could consider each possible coordinate pair separately and request the user to indicate whether the cell is to be occupied or not. This method would require the user to type in

$$maxrow * maxrow = 20 * 60 = 1200$$

entries, which is prohibitive. Hence, instead, we input only those coordinate pairs corresponding to initially occupied cells.

```
void Life :: initialize( )
/* Pre:   None.
   Post:  The Life object contains a configuration specified by the user. */
{
   int row, col;
   for (row = 0;  row <= maxrow + 1;  row++)
     for (col = 0;  col <= maxcol + 1;  col++)
        grid [row] [col] = 0;
   cout << "List the coordinates for living cells." << endl;
   cout << "Terminate the list with the the special pair −1 −1" << endl;
   cin >> row >> col;
   while (row != −1 || col != −1) {
     if (row >= 1 && row <= maxrow)
       if (col >= 1 && col <= maxcol)
          grid [row] [col] = 1;
       else
          cout << "Column " << col << " is out of range." << endl;
     else
       cout << "Row " << row << " is out of range." << endl;
     cin >> row >> col;
   }
}
```

output   For the output method **print( )** we adopt the simple method of writing out the entire rectangular array at each generation, with occupied cells denoted by * and empty cells by blanks.

```
void Life :: print( )
/* Pre:   The Life object contains a configuration.
   Post:  The configuration is written for the user. */
{
   int row, col;
   cout << "\nThe current Life configuration is:" << endl;
   for (row = 1;  row <= maxrow;  row++) {
     for (col = 1;  col <= maxcol;  col++)
       if (grid [row] [col] ==  1) cout << '*';
       else cout << ' ';
     cout << endl;
   }
   cout << endl;
}
```

response from user   Finally comes the function **user_says_yes()**, which determines whether the user wishes to go on to calculate the next generation. The task of **user_says_yes()** is to ask the user to respond yes or no. To make the program more tolerant of mistakes in input, this request is placed in a loop that repeats until the user's response is acceptable. In our function, we use the standard input function **get()** to process input characters one at a time. In C++, the function **get()** is actually just a method of the **class istream**: In our application, we apply the method, **cin.get()**, that belongs to the **istream** object **cin**.

```
bool user_says_yes()
{
   int c;
   bool initial_response = true;
   do {                              //    Loop until an appropriate input is received.
      if (initial_response)
         cout << " (y,n)? " << flush;
      else
         cout << "Respond with either y or n: " << flush;
      do {                           //    Ignore white space.
         c = cin.get();
      } while (c == '\n' || c == ' ' || c == '\t');
      initial_response = false;
   } while (c != 'y' && c != 'Y' && c != 'n' && c != 'N');
   return (c == 'y' || c == 'Y');
}
```

At this point, we have all the functions for the Life simulation. It is time to pause and check that it works.

1.4.6 Drivers

separate debugging   For small projects, each function is usually inserted in its proper place as soon as it is written, and the resulting program can then be debugged and tested as far as possible. For large projects, however, compilation of the entire project can overwhelm that of a new function being debugged, and it can be difficult to tell, looking only at the way the whole program runs, whether a particular function is working correctly or not. Even in small projects the output of one function may be used by another in ways that do not immediately reveal whether the information transmitted is correct.

One way to debug and test a single function is to write a short auxiliary program whose purpose is to provide the necessary input for the function, call it, and *driver program*   evaluate the result. Such an auxiliary program is called a *driver* for the function. By using drivers, each function can be isolated and studied by itself, and thereby errors can often be spotted quickly.

As an example, let us write drivers for the functions of the Life project. First, we consider the method **neighbor_count()**. In our program, its output is used but has not been directly displayed for our inspection, so we should have little confidence that it is correct. To test **neighbor_count()** we shall supply a **Life** object **configuration**, call **neighbor_count** for every cell of **configuration**, and write out the results.

The resulting driver uses **configuration.initialize()** to set up the object and bears some resemblance to the original main program. In order to call **neighbor_count()**, from the driver, we need to adjust its visibility temporarily to become **public** in the **class** Life.

```
int main ()                        //   driver for neighbor_count()
/* Pre:   None.
   Post:  Verifies that the method neighbor_count() returns the correct values.
   Uses:  The class Life and its method initialize(). */
{
  Life configuration;
  configuration.initialize();
  for (row = 1;  row <= maxrow;  row++){
    for (col = 1;  col <= maxrow;  col++)
      cout << configuration.neighbor_count(row, col) << " ";
    cout << endl;
  }
}
```

Sometimes two functions can be used to check each other. The easiest way, for example, to check the Life methods initialize() and print() is to use a driver whose action part is

```
configuration.initialize();
configuration.print();
```

Both methods can be tested by running this driver and making sure that the configuration printed is the same as that given as input.

1.4.7 Program Tracing

group discussion

After the functions have been assembled into a complete program, it is time to check out the completed whole. One of the most effective ways to uncover hidden defects is called a ***structured walkthrough***. In this the programmer shows the completed program to another programmer or a small group of programmers and explains exactly what happens, beginning with an explanation of the main program followed by the functions, one by one. Structured walkthroughs are helpful for three reasons. First, programmers who are not familiar with the actual code can often spot bugs or conceptual errors that the original programmer overlooked. Second, the questions that other people ask can help you to clarify your own thinking and discover your own mistakes. Third, the structured walkthrough often suggests tests that prove useful in later stages of software production.

print statements for debugging

It is unusual for a large program to run correctly the first time it is executed as a whole, and if it does not, it may not be easy to determine exactly where the errors are. On many systems sophisticated ***trace tools*** are available to keep track of function calls, changes of variables, and so on. A simple and effective debugging tool, however, is to take ***snapshots*** of program execution by inserting printing statements at key points in the main program; this strategy is often available as an option in a debugger when one is available. A message can be printed each time a function is called, and the values of important variables can be printed before and after each function is called. Such snapshots can help the programmer converge quickly on the particular location where an error is occurring.

temporary scaffolding

Scaffolding is another term frequently used to describe code inserted into a program to help with debugging. Never hesitate to put scaffolding into your programs as you write them; it will be easy to delete once it is no longer needed, and it may save you much grief during debugging.

When your program has a mysterious error that you cannot localize at all, then it is very useful to put scaffolding into the main program to print the values of important variables. This scaffolding should be put at one or two of the major dividing points in the main program. (If you have written a program of any significant size that does not subdivide its work into several major sections, then you have already made serious errors in the design and structure of your program that you should correct.) With printouts at the major dividing points, you should be able to determine which section of the program is misbehaving, and then you can concentrate on that section, introducing scaffolding into its subdivisions.

defensive programming

Another important method for detecting errors is to practice **defensive** programming. Put **if** statements at the beginning of functions to check that the preconditions do in fact hold. If not, print an error message. In this way, you will be alerted as soon as a supposedly impossible situation arises, and if it does not arise, the error checking will be completely invisible to the user. It is, of course, particularly important to check that the preconditions hold when the input to a function comes from the user, or from a file, or from some other source outside the program itself. It is, however, surprising how often checking preconditions will reveal errors even in places where you are sure everything is correct.

static analyzer

For very large programs yet another tool is sometimes used. This is a **static analyzer**, a program that examines the source program (as written in C++, for example) looking for uninitialized or unused variables, sections of the code that can never be reached, and other occurrences that are probably incorrect.

1.4.8 Principles of Program Testing

choosing test data

So far we have said nothing about the choice of data to be used to test programs and functions. This choice, of course, depends intimately on the project under development, so we can make only some general remarks. First we should note the following:

Programming Precept

The quality of test data is more important than its quantity.

Many sample runs that do the same calculations in the same cases provide no more effective a test than one run.

Programming Precept

Program testing can be used to show the presence of bugs,
but never their absence.

It is possible that other cases remain that have never been tested even after many sample runs. For any program of substantial complexity, it is impossible to perform exhaustive tests, yet the careful choice of test data can provide substantial confidence in the program. Everyone, for example, has great confidence that the typical computer can add two floating-point numbers correctly, but this confidence is certainly not based on testing the computer by having it add all possible floating-point numbers and checking the results. If a double-precision floating-point number takes 64 bits, then there are 2^{128} distinct pairs of numbers that could be added. This number is astronomically large: All computers manufactured to date have performed altogether but a tiny fraction of this number of additions. Our confidence that computers add correctly is based on tests of each component separately; that is, by checking that each of the 64 digits is added correctly and that carrying from one place to another is done correctly.

testing methods   There are at least three general philosophies that are used in the choice of test data.

1. The Black-Box Method

Most users of a large program are not interested in the details of its functioning; they only wish to obtain answers. That is, they wish to treat the program as a black box; hence the name of this method. Similarly, test data should be chosen according to the specifications of the problem, without regard to the internal details of the program, to check that the program operates correctly. At a minimum the test data should be selected in the following ways:

data selection

1. *Easy values.* The program should be debugged with data that are easy to check. More than one student who tried a program only for complicated data, and thought it worked properly, has been embarrassed when the instructor tried a trivial example.

2. *Typical, realistic values.* Always try a program on data chosen to represent how the program will be used. These data should be sufficiently simple so that the results can be checked by hand.

3. *Extreme values.* Many programs err at the limits of their range of applications. It is very easy for counters or array bounds to be off by one.

4. *Illegal values.* "Garbage in, garbage out" is an old saying in computer circles that should not be respected. When a good program has garbage coming in, then its output should at least be a sensible error message. Indeed, the program should provide some indication of the likely errors in input and perform any calculations that remain possible after disregarding the erroneous input.

2. The Glass-Box Method

The second approach to choosing test data begins with the observation that a program can hardly be regarded as thoroughly tested if there are some parts of its code that, in fact, have never been executed. In the *glass-box* method of testing, the logical structure of the program is examined, and for each alternative that may
path testing   occur, test data are devised that will lead to that alternative. Thus care is taken to choose data to check each possibility in every **switch** statement, each clause of

every **if** statement, and the termination condition of each loop. If the program has several selection or iteration statements, then it will require different combinations of test data to check all the paths that are possible. Figure 1.3 shows a short program segment with its possible execution paths.

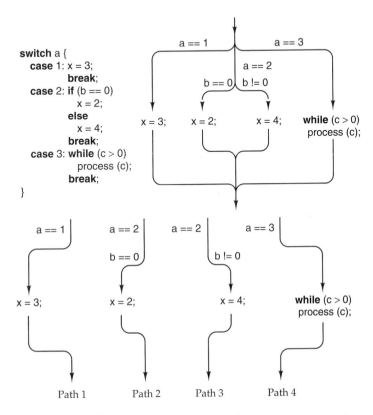

Figure 1.3. The execution paths through a program segment

For a large program the glass-box approach is clearly not practicable, but for a single small module, it is an excellent debugging and testing method. In a well-designed program, each module will involve few loops and alternatives. Hence only a few well-chosen test cases will suffice to test each module on its own.

modular testing   In glass-box testing, the advantages of modular program design become evident. Let us consider a typical example of a project involving 50 functions, each of which can involve 5 different cases or alternatives. If we were to test the whole program as one, we would need 5^{50} test cases to be sure that each alternative was tested. Each module separately requires only 5 (easier) test cases, for a total of $5 \times 50 = 250$. Hence a problem of impossible size has been reduced to one that, for a large program, is of quite modest size.

comparison   Before you conclude that glass-box testing is always the preferable method, we should comment that, in practice, black-box testing is usually more effective in uncovering errors. Perhaps one reason is that the most subtle programming

interface errors   errors often occur not within a function but in the interface between functions, in misunderstanding of the exact conditions and standards of information interchange between functions. It would therefore appear that a reasonable testing philosophy for a large project would be to apply glass-box methods to each small module as it is written and use black-box test data to test larger sections of the program when they are complete.

3. The Ticking-Box Method

To conclude this section, let us mention one further philosophy of program testing, a philosophy that is, unfortunately, quite widely used. This might be called the *ticking-box* method. It consists of doing no testing at all after the project is fairly well debugged, but instead turning it over to the customer for trial and acceptance. The result, of course, is a time bomb.

ÒUCH!

Exercises 1.4

E1. If you suspected that the Life program contained errors, where would be a good place to insert scaffolding into the main program? What information should be printed out?

E2. Take your solution to Section 1.3, Exercise E9 (designing a program to plot a set of points), and indicate good places to insert scaffolding if needed.

E3. Find suitable black-box test data for each of the following:

   (a) A function that returns the largest of its three parameters, which are floating-point numbers.

   (b) A function that returns the square root of a floating-point number.

   (c) A function that returns the least common multiple of its two parameters, which must be positive integers. (The *least common multiple* is the smallest integer that is a multiple of both parameters. Examples: The least common multiple of 4 and 6 is 12, of 3 and 9 is 9, and of 5 and 7 is 35.)

   (d) A function that sorts three integers, given as its parameters, into ascending order.

   (e) A function that sorts an array a of integers indexed from 0 to a variable n into ascending order, where a and n are both parameters.

E4. Find suitable glass-box test data for each of the following:

   (a) The statement

   ```
   if (a < b) if (c > d) x = 1;  else if (c ==  d) x = 2;
   else x = 3;  else if (a ==  b) x = 4;  else if (c ==  d) x = 5;
   else x = 6;
   ```

   (b) The Life method neighbor_count(row, col).

Programming Projects 1.4

P1. Enter the Life program of this chapter on your computer and make sure that it works correctly.

P2. Test the Life program with the examples shown in Figure 1.1.

P3. Run the Life program with the initial configurations shown in Figure 1.4. Several of these go through many changes before reaching a configuration that remains the same or has predictable behavior.

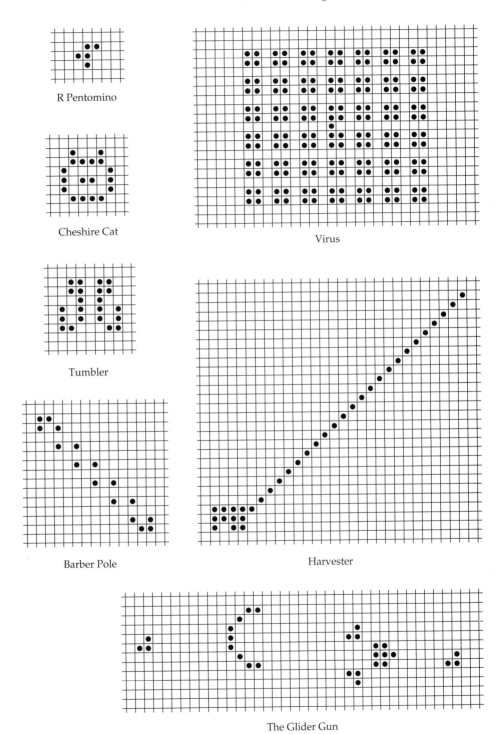

R Pentomino

Cheshire Cat

Virus

Tumbler

Barber Pole

Harvester

The Glider Gun

Figure 1.4. Life configurations

1.5 PROGRAM MAINTENANCE

Small programs written as exercises or demonstrations are usually run a few times and then discarded, but the disposition of large practical programs is quite different. A program of practical value will be run many times, usually by many different people, and its writing and debugging mark only the beginning of its use. They also mark only the beginning of the work required to make and keep the program useful. It is necessary to *review* and *analyze* the program to ensure that it meets the requirements specified for it, *adapt* it to changing environments, and *modify* it to make it better meet the needs of its users.

Maintenance of a computer program encompasses all this work done to a program after it has been fully debugged, tested, and put into use. With time and experience, the expectations for a computer program will generally change. The operating and hardware environment will change; the needs and expectations of users will change; the interface with other parts of the software system will change. Hence, if a program is to have continued usefulness, continuing attention must be given to keep it up to date. In fact, surveys show the following:

> **Programming Precept**
> *For a large and important program, more than half the work*
> *comes in the maintenance phase,*
> *after it has been completely debugged, tested, and put into use.*

1.5.1 Program Evaluation

The first step of program maintenance is to begin the continuing process of review, analysis, and evaluation. There are several useful questions we may ask about any program. The first group of questions concerns the use and output of the program (thus continuing what is started with black-box testing).

1. Does the program solve the problem that is requested, following the problem specifications exactly?

2. Does the program work correctly under all conditions?

3. Does the program have a good user interface? Can it receive input in forms convenient and easy for the user? Is its output clear, useful, and attractively presented? Does the program provide alternatives and optional features to facilitate its use? Does it include clear and sufficient instructions and other information for the user?

The remaining questions concern the structure of the program (continuing the process begun in glass-box testing).

4. Is the program logically and clearly written, with convenient classes and short functions as appropriate to do logical tasks? Are the data structured into classes that accurately reflect the needs of the program?

5. Is the program well documented? Do the names accurately reflect the use and meaning of variables, functions, types, and methods? Are precise pre- and postconditions given as appropriate? Are explanations given for major sections of code or for any unusual or difficult code?

6. Does the program make efficient use of time and of space? By changing the underlying algorithm, could the program's performance be improved?

Some of these criteria will be closely studied for the programs we write. Others will not be mentioned explicitly, but not because of any lack of importance. These criteria, rather, can be met automatically if sufficient thought and effort are invested in every stage of program design. We hope that the examples we study will reveal such care.

1.5.2 Review of the Life Program

Let us illustrate these program-evaluation criteria by reconsidering the program for the Life game. Doing so, in one sense, is really overkill, since a toy project like the Life game is not, in itself, worth the effort. In the process, however, we shall consider programming methods important for many other applications. Let us consider each of the preceding questions in turn.

1. Problem Specification

problem: the boundary

OUCH!

If we go back to review the rules for the Life game in Section 1.2.1, we will find that we have not, in fact, been solving the Life game as it was originally described. The rules make no mention of the boundaries of the grid containing the cells. In our program, when a moving colony gets sufficiently close to a boundary, then room for neighbors disappears, and the colony will be distorted by the very presence of the boundary. That is not supposed to be. Hence our program violates the rules.

It is of course true that in any computer simulation there are absolute bounds on the values that may appear, but certainly the use of a 20 by 60 grid in our program is highly restrictive and arbitrary. It is possible to write a Life program without restricting the size of the grid, but before we can do so, we must develop several sophisticated data structures. Only after we have done so can we, in Section 9.9, write a general Life program without restrictions on the size of the grid.

On a first try, however, it is quite reasonable to restrict the problem being solved, and hence, for now, let us continue studying Life on a grid of limited size. It is, nevertheless, very important to say exactly what we are doing:

Programming Precept

Be sure you understand your problem completely.
If you must change its terms, explain exactly what you have done.

---

2. Program Correctness

Since program testing can show the presence of errors but not their absence, we need other methods to *prove* beyond doubt that a program is correct. Constructing formal proofs that a program is correct is often difficult but sometimes it can be done, as we shall do for some of the sophisticated algorithms developed in later chapters. For the Life game, let us be content with more informal reasons why our program is correct.

First, we ask which parts of the program need verification. The Life configuration is changed only by the method update, and only update and neighbor_count involve any calculation that might turn out to be wrong. Hence we should concentrate on the correctness of these two methods.

correctness of
neighbor_count

The method neighbor_count looks only at the cell given as its parameters and at the neighbors of that cell. There are only a limited number of possibilities for the status of the cell and its neighbors, so glass-box testing of these possibilities is feasible, using a driver program for neighbor_count. Such testing would quickly convince us of the correctness of neighbor_count.

correctness of update

For update, we should first examine the cases in the **switch** statement to make sure that their actions correspond exactly to the rules in Section 1.2.1. Next, we can note that the action for each cell depends only on the status of the cell and it neighbor count. Hence, as for neighbor_count, we can construct a limited set of glass-box test data that verify that update performs the correct action in each possible case.

3. User Interface

problem: input

In running the Life program, you will have likely found that the poor method for input of the initial configuration is a major inconvenience. It is unnatural for a person to calculate and type in the numerical coordinates of each living cell. The form of input should instead reflect the same visual imagery that we use to print a configuration. At a minimum, the program should allow the user to type each row of the configuration as a line of blanks (for dead cells) and non-blank characters (for living cells).

file input and output

Life configurations can be quite complicated. For easier input, the program should be able to read its initial configuration from a file. To allow stopping the program to be resumed later, the program should also be able to store the final configuration in a file that can be read again later.

editing

Another option would be to allow the user to edit a configuration at any generation.

output improvements

The output from the program can also be improved. Rather than rewriting the entire configuration at each generation, direct cursor addressing should be used to change only the cells whose status has changed. Color or other features can be used to make the output both much more attractive and more useful. For example, cells that have newly become alive might be one color and those continuing alive other colors depending on how long they have been alive.

help screen

To make the program more self-contained, it would also be useful to have an optional display of a short description of the Life game and its rules, perhaps as a pop-up screen.

In general, designing a program to have an attractive appearance and feel to the user is very important, and in large programs a great deal of importance is given to the user interface, often more than to all other parts of the program combined.

Programming Precept

Design the user interface with the greatest care possible.
A program's success depends greatly on its attractiveness and ease of use.

---

4. Modularity and Structure

We have already addressed these issues in the original design. The decisions already made will continue to serve us well.

5. Documentation

Again, we have previously addressed issues of documentation, which need not be repeated here.

6. Efficiency

Where does the Life program spend most of its time? Surely it is not in the input phase, since that is done only once. The output too is generally quite efficient. The bulk of the calculation is in method update and in neighbor_count, which it invokes.

At every generation, update recalculates the neighbor counts of every possible cell. In a typical configuration, perhaps only five percent of the cells are living, often localized in one area of the grid. Hence update spends a great deal of time laboriously establishing that many dead cells, with no living neighbors, indeed have neighbor counts of 0 and will remain dead in the next generation. If 95 percent of the cells are dead, this constitutes a substantial inefficiency in the use of computer time.

But is this inefficiency of any importance? Generally, it is not, since the calculations are done so quickly that, to the user, each generation seems to appear instantaneously. On the other hand, if you run the Life program on a very slow machine or on a busy time-sharing system, you may find the program's speed *poor speed* somewhat disappointing, with a noticeable pause between printing one generation and starting to print the next. In this case, it might be worthwhile to try saving computer time, but, generally speaking, optimization of the Life program is not needed even though it is very inefficient.

Programming Precept

Do not optimize your code unless it is necessary to do so.
Do not start to optimize code until it is complete and correct.

Most programs spend 90 percent of their time
doing 10 percent of their instructions.
Find this 10 percent, and concentrate your efforts for efficiency there.

Another reason to think carefully before commencing optimization of a program is that optimizations often produce more complicated code. This code will then be harder to debug and to modify when necessary.

Programming Precept

Keep your algorithms as simple as you can.
When in doubt, choose the simple way.

1.5.3 Program Revision and Redevelopment

As we continue to evaluate a program, asking whether it meets its objectives and the needs of its users, we are likely to continue discovering both deficiencies in its current design and new features that could make it more useful. Hence program review leads naturally to program revision and redevelopment.

As we review the Life program, for example, we find that it meets some of the criteria quite well, but it has several deficiencies in regard to other criteria. The most serious of these is that, by limiting the grid size, it fails to satisfy its specifications. Its user interface leaves much to be desired. Finally, its computations are inefficient, but this is probably not important.

With some thought, we can easily improve the user interface for the Life program, and several of the projects propose such improvements. To revise the program to remove the limits on grid size, however, will require that we use data structures and algorithms that we have not yet developed, and hence we shall revisit the Life program in Section 9.9. At that time, we shall find that the algorithm we develop also addresses the question of efficiency. Hence the new program will both meet more general requirements and be more efficient in its calculations.

Programming Precept

Sometimes postponing problems simplifies their solution.

Exercises 1.5

E1. Sometimes the user might wish to run the Life game on a grid smaller than 20×60. Determine how it is possible to make **maxrow** and **maxcol** into variables that the user can set when the program is run. Try to make as few changes in the program as possible.

E2. One idea for speeding up the function Life :: neighbor_count(row, col) is to delete the hedge (the extra rows and columns that are always dead) from the arrays **grid** and **new_grid**. Then, when a cell is on the boundary, **neighbor_count** will look at fewer than the eight neighboring cells, since some of these are outside the bounds of the grid. To do this, the function will need to determine whether or not the cell (row, col) is on the boundary, but this can be done outside the nested loops, by determining, before the loops commence, the lower and upper bounds for the loops. If, for example, row is as small as allowed, then the lower bound for the row loop is row; otherwise, it is row − 1. Determine, in terms of the size of the grid, approximately how many statements are executed by the original version of neighbor_count and by the new version. Are the changes proposed in this exercise worth making?

Programming Projects 1.5

P1. Modify the Life function initialize so that it sets up the initial Life :: grid configuration by accepting occupied positions as a sequence of blanks and x's in appropriate rows, rather than requiring the occupied positions to be entered as numerical coordinate pairs.

P2. Add a feature to the function initialize so that it can, at the user's option, either read its initial configuration from the keyboard or from a file. The first line of the file will be a comment giving the name of the configuration. Each remaining line of the file will correspond to a row of the configuration. Each line will contain x in each living position and a blank in each dead position.

P3. Add a feature to the Life program so that, at termination, it can write the final configuration to a file in a format that can be edited by the user and that can be read in to restart the program (using the feature of Exercise E2).

P4. Add a feature to the Life program so, at any generation, the user can edit the current configuration by inserting new living cells or by deleting living cells.

P5. Add a feature to the Life program so, if the user wishes at any generation, it will display a help screen giving the rules for the Life game and explaining how to use the program.

P6. Add a step mode to the Life program, so it will explain every change it makes while going from one generation to the next.

P7. Use direct cursor addressing (a system-dependent feature) to make the Life method print update the configuration instead of completely rewriting it at each generation.

P8. Use different colors in the Life output to show which cells have changed in the current generation and which have not.

1.6 CONCLUSIONS AND PREVIEW

This chapter has surveyed a great deal of ground, but mainly from a bird's-eye view. Some themes we shall treat in much greater depth in later chapters; others must be postponed to more advanced courses; still others are best learned by practice.

This section recapitulates and expands some of the principles we have been studying.

1.6.1 Software Engineering

Software engineering is the study and practice of methods helpful for the construction and maintenance of large software systems. Although small by realistic standards, the program we have studied in this chapter illustrates many aspects of software engineering.

Software engineering begins with the realization that it is a very long process to obtain good software. It begins before any programs are coded and continues as maintenance for years after the programs are put into use. This continuing process is known as the *life cycle* of software. This life cycle can be divided into phases as follows:

phases of life cycle

1. *Analyze* the problem precisely and completely. Be sure to *specify* all necessary user interface with care.
2. *Build* a prototype and *experiment* with it until all specifications can be finalized.
3. *Design* the algorithm, using the tools of data structures and of other algorithms whose function is already known.
4. *Verify* that the algorithm is correct, or make it so simple that its correctness is self-evident.
5. *Analyze* the algorithm to determine its requirements and make sure that it meets the specifications.
6. *Code* the algorithm into the appropriate programming language.
7. *Test* and *evaluate* the program on carefully chosen test data.
8. *Refine* and *repeat* the foregoing steps as needed for additional classes and functions until the software is complete and fully functional.
9. *Optimize* the code to improve performance, but only if necessary.
10. *Maintain* the program so that it will meet the changing needs of its users.

Most of these topics have been discussed and illustrated in various sections of this and the preceding chapter, but a few further remarks on the first phase, problem analysis and specification, are in order.

1.6.2 Problem Analysis

Analysis of the problem is often the most difficult phase of the software life cycle. This is not because practical problems are conceptually more difficult than are computing science exercises—the reverse is often the case—but because users and programmers tend to speak different languages. Here are some questions on which the analyst and user must reach an understanding:

specifications

1. What form will the input and output data take? How much data will there be?
2. Are there any special requirements for the processing? What special occurrences will require separate treatment?
3. Will these requirements change? How? How fast will the demands on the system grow?
4. What parts of the system are the most important? Which must run most efficiently?
5. How should erroneous data be treated? What other error processing is needed?
6. What kinds of people will use the software? What kind of training will they have? What kind of user interface will be best?

7. How portable must the software be, so that it can move to new kinds of equipment? With what other software and hardware systems must the project be compatible?

8. What extensions or other maintenance are anticipated? What is the history of previous changes to software and hardware?

1.6.3 Requirements Specification

For a large project, the phase of problem analysis and experimentation should eventually lead to a formal statement of the requirements for the project. This statement becomes the primary way in which the user and the software engineer attempt to understand each other and establishes the standard by which the final project will be judged. Among the contents of this specification will be the following:

1. *Functional requirements* for the system: what it will do and what commands will be available to the user.

2. *Assumptions* and *limitations* on the system: what hardware will be used for the system, what form must the input take, what is the maximum size of input, what is the largest number of users, and so on.

3. *Maintenance requirements*: anticipated extensions of the system, changes in hardware, changes in user interface.

4. *Documentation requirements*: what kind of explanatory material is required for what kinds of users.

The requirements specifications state *what* the software will do, not *how* it will be done. These specifications should be understandable both to the user and to the programmer. If carefully prepared, they will form the basis for the subsequent phases of design, coding, testing, and maintenance.

1.6.4 Coding

specifications complete

In a large software project it is necessary to do the coding at the right time, not too soon and not too late. Most programmers err by starting to code too soon. If coding is begun before the specifications are made precise, then unwarranted assumptions about the specifications will inevitably be made while coding, and these assumptions may render different classes and functions incompatible with each other or make the programming task much more difficult than it need be.

Programming Precept

Never code until the specifications are precise and complete.

Programming Precept

Act in haste and repent at leisure.
Program in haste and debug forever.

---

top-down coding   It is possible but unlikely, on the other hand, to delay coding too long. Just as we design from the top down, we should code from the top down. Once the specifications at the top levels are complete and precise, we should code the classes and functions at these levels and test them by including appropriate stubs. If we then find that our design is flawed, we can modify it without paying an exorbitant price in low-level functions that have been rendered useless.

The same thought can be expressed somewhat more positively:

Programming Precept

Starting afresh is often easier than patching an old program.

A good rule of thumb is that, if more than ten percent of a program must be modified, then it is time to rewrite the program completely. With repeated patches to a large program, the number of bugs tends to remain constant. That is, the patches become so complicated that each new patch tends to introduce as many new errors as it corrects.

An excellent way to avoid having to rewrite a large project from scratch is to plan from the beginning to write two versions. Before a program is running, it is often impossible to know what parts of the design will cause difficulty or what features need to be changed to meet the needs of the users. Engineers have known for many years that it is not possible to build a large project directly from the drawing board. For large projects engineers always build *prototypes*; that is, scaled-down models that can be studied, tested, and sometimes even used for limited purposes. Models of bridges are built and tested in wind tunnels; pilot plants are constructed before attempting to use new technology on the assembly line.

software prototypes   Prototyping is especially helpful for computer software, since it can ease the communication between users and designers early in a project, thereby reducing misunderstandings and helping to settle the design to everyone's satisfaction. In building a software prototype the designer can use programs that are already written for input-output, for sorting, or for other common requirements. The building blocks can be assembled with as little new programming as possible to make a working model that can do some of the intended tasks. Even though the prototype may not function efficiently or do everything that the final system will, it provides an excellent laboratory for the user and designer to experiment with alternative ideas for the final design.

Programming Precept

Always plan to build a prototype and throw it away.
You'll do so whether you plan to or not.

Programming Projects 1.6

P1. A *magic square* is a square array of integers such that the sum of every row, the sum of every column, and sum of each of the two diagonals are all equal. Two magic squares are shown in Figure 1.5.[6]

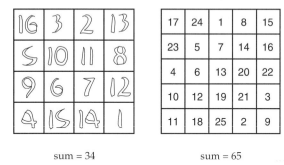

sum = 34   sum = 65

Figure 1.5. Two magic squares

(a) Write a program that reads a square array of integers and determines whether or not it is a magic square.

(b) Write a program that generates a magic square by the following method. This method works only when the size of the square is an odd number. Start by placing 1 in the middle of the top row. Write down successive integers 2, 3, . . . along a diagonal going upward and to the right. When you reach the top row (as you do immediately since 1 is in the top row), continue to the bottom row as though the bottom row were immediately above the top row. When you reach the rightmost column, continue to the leftmost column as though it were immediately to the right of the rightmost one. When you reach a position that is already occupied, instead drop straight down one position from the previous number to insert the new one. The 5×5 magic square constructed by this method is shown in Figure 1.5.

P2. *One-Dimensional Life* takes place on a straight line instead of a rectangular grid. Each cell has four neighboring positions: those at distance one or two from it on each side. The rules are similar to those of two-dimensional Life except (1) a dead cell with either two or three living neighbors will become alive in the next generation, and (2) a living cell dies if it has zero, one, or three living neighbors. (Hence a dead cell with zero, one, or four living neighbors stays dead; a living cell with two or four living neighbors stays alive.) The progress of sample communities is shown in Figure 1.6. Design, write, and test a program for one-dimensional Life.

---

[6] The magic square on the left appears as shown here in the etching *Melancolia* by ALBRECHT DÜRER. Note the inclusion of the date of the etching, 1514.

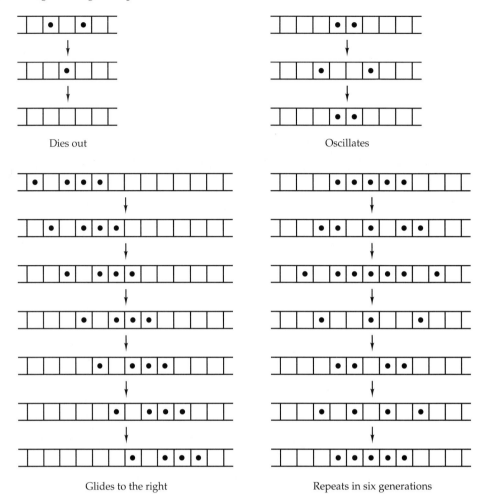

Figure 1.6. One-dimensional Life configurations

P3. (a) Write a program that will print the calendar of the current year.

(b) Modify the program so that it will read a year number and print the calendar for that year. A year is a leap year (that is, February has 29 instead of 28 days) if it is a multiple of 4, except that century years (multiples of 100) are leap years only when the year is divisible by 400. Hence the year 1900 is not a leap year, but the year 2000 is a leap year.

(c) Modify the program so that it will accept any date (day, month, year) and print the day of the week for that date.

(d) Modify the program so that it will read two dates and print the number of days from one to the other.

(e) Using the rules on leap years, show that the sequence of calendars repeats exactly every 400 years.

(f) What is the probability (over a 400-year period) that the 13th of a month is a Friday? Why is the 13th of the month more likely to be a Friday than any other day of the week? Write a program to calculate how many Friday the 13ths occur in this century.

POINTERS AND PITFALLS

1. To improve your program, review the logic. Don't optimize code based on a poor algorithm.

2. Never optimize a program until it is correct and working.

3. Don't optimize code unless it is absolutely necessary.

4. Keep your functions short; rarely should any function be more than a page long.

5. Be sure your algorithm is correct before starting to code.

6. Verify the intricate parts of your algorithm.

7. Keep your logic simple.

8. Be sure you understand your problem before you decide how to solve it.

9. Be sure you understand the algorithmic method before you start to program.

10. In case of difficulty, divide a problem into pieces and think of each part separately.

11. The nouns that arise in describing a problem suggest useful classes for its solution; the verbs suggest useful functions.

12. Include careful documentation (as presented in Section 1.3.2) with each function as you write it.

13. Be careful to write down precise preconditions and postconditions for every function.

14. Include error checking at the beginning of functions to check that the preconditions actually hold.

15. Every time a function is used, ask yourself why you know that its preconditions will be satisfied.

16. Use stubs and drivers, black-box and glass-box testing to simplify debugging.

17. Use plenty of scaffolding to help localize errors.

18. In programming with arrays, be wary of index values that are off by 1. Always use extreme-value testing to check programs that use arrays.

19. Keep your programs well formatted as you write them—it will make debugging much easier.

20. Keep your documentation consistent with your code, and when reading a program make sure that you debug the code and not just the comments.

21. Explain your program to somebody else: Doing so will help you understand it better yourself.

REVIEW QUESTIONS

Most chapters of this book conclude with a set of questions designed to help you review the main ideas of the chapter. These questions can all be answered directly from the discussion in the book; if you are unsure of any answer, refer to the appropriate section.

1.3
1. When is it appropriate to use one-letter variable names?

2. Name four kinds of information that should be included in program documentation.

3. What is the difference between *external* and *internal* documentation?

4. What are pre- and postconditions?

5. Name three kinds of parameters. How are they processed in C++?

6. Why should side effects of functions be avoided?

1.4
7. What is a program stub?

8. What is the difference between stubs and drivers, and when should each be used?

9. What is a structured walkthrough?

10. What is *scaffolding* in a program, and when is it used?

11. Name a way to practice *defensive* programming.

12. Give two methods for testing a program, and discuss when each should be used.

13. If you cannot immediately picture all details needed for solving a problem, what should you do with the problem?

14. What are preconditions and postconditions of a subprogram?

15. When should allocation of tasks among functions be made?

1.6
16. How long should coding be delayed?

17. What is *program maintenance*?

18. What is a *prototype*?

19. Name at least six phases of the software life cycle and state what each is.

20. Define software engineering.

21. What are requirements specifications for a program?

REFERENCES FOR FURTHER STUDY

C++

The programming language C++ was devised by BJARNE STROUSTRUP, who first published its description in 1984. The standard reference manual is

B. STROUSTRUP, *The C++ Programming Language*, third edition, Addison-Wesley, Reading, Mass., 1997.

Many good textbooks provide a more leisurely description of C++, too many books to list here. These textbooks also provide many examples and applications.

For programmers who already know the language, an interesting book about how to use C++ effectively is

SCOTT MEYERS, *Effective C++*, second edition, Addison-Wesley, Reading, Mass., 1997.

Programming Principles

Two books that contain many helpful hints on programming style and correctness, as well as examples of good and bad practices, are

BRIAN KERNIGHAN and P. J. PLAUGER, *The Elements of Programming Style*, second edition, McGraw-Hill, New York, 1978, 168 pages.

DENNIE VAN TASSEL, *Program Style, Design, Efficiency, Debugging, and Testing*, second edition, Prentice Hall, Englewood Cliffs, N.J., 1978, 323 pages.

EDSGER W. DIJKSTRA pioneered the movement known as structured programming, which insists on taking a carefully organized top-down approach to the design and writing of programs, when in March 1968 he caused some consternation by publishing a letter entitled "Go To Statement Considered Harmful" in the *Communications of the ACM* (vol. 11, pages 147–148). DIJKSTRA has since published several papers and books that are most instructive in programming method. One book of special interest is

EDSGER W. DIJKSTRA, *A Discipline of Programming*, Prentice Hall, Englewood Cliffs, N.J., 1976, 217 pages.

A full treatment of object oriented design is provided by

GRADY BOOCH, *Object-Oriented Analysis and Design with Applications*, Benjamin/Cummings, Redwood City, Calif., 1994.

The Game of Life

The prominent British mathematician J. H. CONWAY has made many original contributions to subjects as diverse as the theory of finite simple groups, logic, and combinatorics. He devised the game of Life by starting with previous technical studies of cellular automata and devising reproduction rules that would make it difficult for a configuration to grow without bound, but for which many configurations would go through interesting progressions. CONWAY, however, did not publish his observations, but communicated them to MARTIN GARDNER. The popularity of the game skyrocketed when it was discussed in

MARTIN GARDNER, "Mathematical Games" (regular column), *Scientific American* 223, no. 4 (October 1970), 120–123; 224, no. 2 (February 1971), 112–117.

The examples at the end of Sections 1.2 and 1.4 are taken from these columns. These columns have been reprinted with further results in

MARTIN GARDNER, *Wheels, Life and Other Mathematical Amusements*, W. H. Freeman, New York and San Francisco, 1983, pp. 214–257.

This book also contains a bibliography of articles on Life. A quarterly newsletter, entitled *Lifeline*, was even published for a few years to keep the real devotees up to date on current developments in Life and related topics.

Software Engineering

A thorough discussion of many aspects of structured programming is found in

EDWARD YOURDON, *Techniques of Program Structure and Design*, Prentice-Hall, Englewood Cliffs, N. J., 1975, 364 pages.

A perceptive discussion (in a book that is also enjoyable reading) of the many problems that arise in the construction of large software systems is provided in

FREDERICK P. BROOKS, JR., *The Mythical Man–Month: Essays on Software Engineering*, Addison-Wesley, Reading, Mass., 1975, 195 pages.

A good textbook on software engineering is

IAN SOMMERVILLE, *Software Engineering*, Addison-Wesley, Wokingham, England, 1985, 334 pages.

algorithm verification   Two books concerned with proving programs and with using assertions and invariants to develop algorithms are

DAVID GRIES, *The Science of Programming*, Springer-Verlag, New York, 1981, 366 pages.

SUAD ALAGIĆ and MICHAEL A. ARBIB, *The Design of Well-Structured and Correct Programs*, Springer-Verlag, New York, 1978, 292 pages.

Keeping programs so simple in design that they can be proved to be correct is not easy, but is very important. C. A. R. HOARE (who invented the quicksort algorithm that we shall study in Chapter 8) writes: "There are two ways of constructing a software design: One way is to make it so simple that there are obviously no deficiencies, and the other way is to make it so complicated that there are no obvious deficiencies. The first method is far more difficult." This quotation is from the 1980 Turing Award Lecture: "The emperor's old clothes," *Communications of the ACM* 24 (1981), 75–83.

Two books concerned with methods of problem solving are

problem solving   GEORGE PÓLYA, *How to Solve It*, second edition, Doubleday, Garden City, N.Y., 1957, 253 pages.

WAYNE A. WICKELGREN, *How to Solve Problems*, W. H. Freeman, San Francisco, 1974, 262 pages.

The programming project on one-dimensional Life is taken from

JONATHAN K. MILLER, "One-dimensional Life," *Byte* 3 (December, 1978), 68–74.

Introduction to Stacks

2

THIS CHAPTER introduces the study of stacks, one of the simplest but most important of all data structures. The application of stacks to the reversal of data is illustrated with a program that calls on the standard-library stack implementation. A contiguous implementation of a stack data structure is then developed and used to implement a reverse Polish calculator and a bracket-checking program. The chapter closes with a discussion of the general principles of abstract data types and data structures.

2.1 STACK SPECIFICATIONS

2.1.1 Lists and Arrays

Soon after the introduction of loops and arrays, every elementary programming class attempts some programming exercise like the following:

> *Read an integer n, which will be at most 25, then read a list of n numbers, and print the list in reverse order.*

This simple exercise will probably cause difficulty for some students. Most will realize that they need to use an array, but some will attempt to set up the array to have n entries and will be confused by the error message resulting from attempting to use a variable rather than a constant to declare the size of the array. Other students will say, "I could solve the problem if I knew that there were 25 numbers, but I don't see how to handle fewer." Or "Tell me before I write the program how large n is, and then I can do it."

lists and arrays

The difficulties of these students come not from stupidity, but from thinking logically. A beginning course sometimes does not draw enough distinction between two quite different concepts. First is the concept of a *list* of n numbers, a list whose size is variable; that is, a list for which numbers can be inserted or deleted, so that, if $n = 3$, then the list contains only 3 numbers, and if $n = 19$, then it contains 19 numbers. Second is the programming feature called an *array* or a vector, which contains a constant number of positions, that is, whose size is fixed when the program is compiled. A list is a *dynamic* data structure because its size can change, while an array is a *static* data structure because it has a fixed size.

implementation

The concepts of a list and an array are, of course, related in that a list of variable size can be implemented in a computer as occupying part of an array of fixed size, with some of the entries in the array remaining unused. We shall later find, however, that there are several different ways to implement lists, and therefore we should not confuse implementation decisions with more fundamental decisions on choosing and specifying data structures.

2.1.2 Stacks

A *stack* is a version of a list that is particularly useful in applications involving reversing, such as the problem of Section 2.1.1. In a stack data structure, all insertions and deletions of entries are made at one end, called the *top* of the stack. A helpful analogy (see Figure 2.1) is to think of a stack of trays or of plates sitting on the counter in a busy cafeteria. Throughout the lunch hour, customers take trays off the top of the stack, and employees place returned trays back on top of the stack. The tray most recently put on the stack is the first one taken off. The bottom tray is the first one put on, and the last one to be used.

Figure 2.1. Stacks

Sometimes this picture is described with plates or trays on a spring-loaded device so that the top of the stack stays near the same height. This imagery is poor and should be avoided. If we were to implement a computer stack in this way, it would mean moving every item in the stack whenever one item was inserted or deleted. It is far better to think of the stack as resting on a firm counter or floor, so that only the top item is moved when it is added or deleted. The spring-loaded imagery, however, has contributed a pair of colorful words that are firmly embedded in computer jargon and that we shall use to name the fundamental

push and pop   operations on a stack. When we add an item to a stack, we say that we ***push*** it onto the stack, and when we remove an item, we say that we *pop* it from the stack. See Figure 2.2. Note that the last item pushed onto a stack is always the first that will be popped from the stack. This property is called ***last in, first out***, or *LIFO* for short.

2.1.3 First Example: Reversing a List

As a simple example of the use of stacks, let us write a program to solve the problem of Section 2.1.1. Our program must read an integer n, followed by n floating-point numbers. It then writes them out in reverse order. We can accomplish this task by pushing each number onto a stack as it is read. When the input is finished, we pop numbers off the stack, and they will come off in the reverse order.

Push box Q onto empty stack:

Push box A onto stack:

Pop a box from stack:

Pop a box from stack: (empty)

Push box R onto stack:

Push box D onto stack:

Push box M onto stack:

Pop a box from stack:

Push box Q onto stack:

Push box S onto stack:

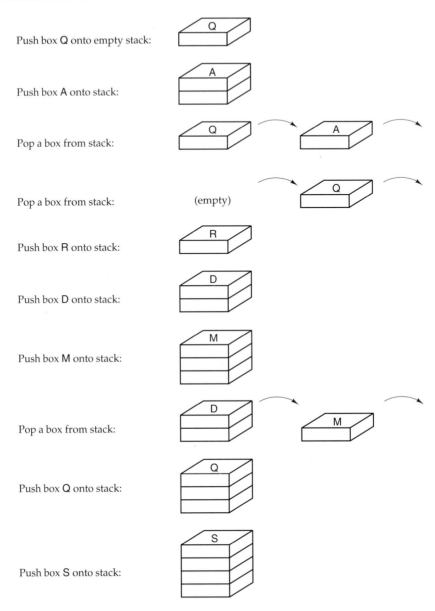

Figure 2.2. Pushing and popping a stack

standard template library   In our program we shall rely on the ***standard template library*** of C++ (usually called the ***STL***) to provide a **class** that implements stacks.[1] The STL is part of the standard library of C++. This standard library contains all kinds of useful information, functions, and classes. The STL is the part of the standard library that

---

[1] If the STL stack implementation is not available, the stack class that we implement in the next section can be used in its place.

provides convenient implementations for many common data structures, including almost all the data structures we shall study in this book.

We can include the STL stack implementation into our programs with the directive #include <stack> (or, on some older, pre-ANSI compilers, the directive #include <stack.h>). Once the library is included, we can define initially empty stack objects, and apply methods called **push**, **pop**, **top**, and **empty**. We will discuss these methods and the STL itself in more detail later, but its application in the following program is quite straightforward.

```
#include <stack>

int main( )
/* Pre:   The user supplies an integer n and n decimal numbers.
    Post:  The numbers are printed in reverse order.
    Uses:  The STL class stack and its methods */
{
  int n;
  double item;
  stack<double> numbers;    //   declares and initializes a stack of numbers
  cout ≪ " Type in an integer n followed by n decimal numbers." ≪ endl
       ≪ " The numbers will be printed in reverse order." ≪ endl;
  cin  ≫ n;
  for (int i = 0;  i < n;  i++) {
    cin ≫ item;
    numbers.push(item);
  }
  cout ≪ endl ≪ endl;
  while (!numbers.empty()) {
    cout ≪ numbers.top() ≪ " ";
    numbers.pop();
  }
  cout ≪ endl;
}
```

initialization

In this number-reversing program, we have used not only the methods push(), top(), and pop() of the **stack** called **numbers**, but we have made crucial use of the implicit initialization of **numbers** as an empty **stack**. That is, when the **stack** called **numbers** is created, it is automatically initialized to be empty. Just as with the standard-library classes, whenever we construct a class we shall be careful to ensure that it is automatically initialized, in contrast to variables and arrays, whose initialization must be given explicitly.

capitalization

We remark that, like the atomic classes **int**, **float**, and so on, the C++ library **class stack** has an identifier that begins with a lowercase letter. As we decided in Section 1.3, however, the classes that we shall create will have identifiers with an initial capital letter.

One important feature of the STL **stack** implementation is that the user can specify the type of entries to be held in a particular stack. For example, in the reversing program, we create a stack of elements of type **double** with the definition stack<**double**> numbers, whereas, if we had required a stack of integers, we would have declared stack<**int**> numbers. The standard library uses a C++ construction known as a *template* to achieve this flexibility. Once we are familiar with more basic implementations of data structures, we shall practice the construction and use of our own templates, starting in Chapter 6.

template

2.1.4 Information Hiding

We have been able to write our program for reversing a line of input without any consideration of how a stack is actually implemented. In this way, we have an example of *information hiding*: The methods for handling stacks are implemented in the C++ standard library, and we can use them without needing to know the details of how stacks are kept in memory or of how the stack operations are actually done.

As a matter of fact, we have already been practicing information hiding in the programs we have previously written, without thinking about it. Whenever we have written a program using an array or a structure, we have been content to use the operations on these structures without considering how the C++ compiler actually represents them in terms of bits or bytes in the computer memory or the machine-language steps it follows to look up an index or select a member.

built-in structures

One important difference between practicing information hiding with regard to arrays and practicing information hiding with regard to stacks is that C++ provides just one built-in implementation of arrays, but the STL has several implementations of stacks. Although the code in a client program that uses stacks should not depend on a particular choice of stack implementation, the performance of the final program may very much depend on the choice of implementation. In order to make an informed decision about which stack implementation should be used in a given application, we need to appreciate the different features and behaviors of the different implementations. In the coming chapters, we shall see that for stacks (as for almost all the data types we shall study) there are several different ways to represent the data in the computer memory, and there are several different ways to do the operations. In some applications, one implementation is better, while in other applications another implementation proves superior.

alternative implementations

Even in a single large program, we may first decide to represent stacks one way and then, as we gain experience with the program, we may decide that another way is better. If the instructions for manipulating a stack have been written out every time a stack is used, then every occurrence of these instructions will need to be changed. If we have practiced information hiding by using separate functions for manipulating stacks, then only the declarations will need to be changed.

change of implementation

Another advantage of information hiding shows up in programs that use stacks where the very appearance of the words *push* and *pop* immediately alert a person reading the program to what is being done, whereas the instructions themselves

clarity of program

top-down design

might be more obscure. We shall find that separating the use of data structures from their implementation will help us improve the top-down design of both our data structures and our programs.

2.1.5 The Standard Template Library

The standard C++ library is available in implementations of ANSI C++. This library provides all kinds of system-dependent information, such as the maximum exponent that can be stored in a floating-point type, input and output facilities, and other functions whose optimal implementation depends on the system. In addition, the standard library provides an extensive set of data structures and their

library of data structures

methods for use in writing programs. In fact, the standard library contains implementations of almost all the data structures that we consider in this text, including stacks, queues, deques, lists, strings, and sets, among others.

To be able to use these library implementations appropriately and efficiently, it is essential that we learn the principles and the alternative implementations of the data structures represented in the standard library. We shall therefore give only a very brief introduction to the standard library, and then we return to our main goal, the study of the data structures themselves. In one sense, however, most of this book can be regarded as an introduction to the STL of C++, since our goal is to learn the basic principles and methods of data structures, knowledge that is essential to the discerning use of the STL.

template parameter

As we have already noted, the STL **stack** implementation is a class template, and therefore a programmer can choose exactly what sort of items will be placed in a stack, by specifying its template parameters between < > symbols. In fact, a programmer can also utilize a second template parameter to control what sort of **stack** implementation will be used. This second parameter has a default value, so that a programmer who is unsure of which implementation to use will get a **stack** constructed from a default implementation; in fact, it will come from a deque—a data structure that we will introduce in Chapter 3. A programmer can choose

alternative implementations

instead to use a vector-based or a list-based implementation of a stack. In order to choose among these implementations wisely, a programmer needs to understand their relative advantages, and this understanding can only come from the sort of general study of data structures that we undertake in this book.

algorithm performance

Regardless of the chosen implementation, however, the STL does guarantee that stack methods will be performed efficiently, operating in constant time, independent of the size of the stack. In Chapter 7, we shall begin a systematic study of the time used by various algorithms, and we shall continue this study in later chapters. As it happens, the constant-time operation of standard stack methods is guaranteed only in an averaged sense known as *amortized* performance. We shall study the amortized analysis of programs in Section 10.5.

The STL provides implementations of many other standard data structures, and, as we progress through this book, we shall note those implementations that correspond to topics under discussion. In general, these library implementations are highly efficient, convenient, and designed with enough default options to allow programmers to use them easily.

Exercises 2.1

E1. Draw a sequence of stack frames like Figure 2.2 showing the progress of each of the following segments of code, each beginning with an empty **stack** s. Assume the declarations

```
#include <stack>
stack<char> s;
char x, y, z;
```

(a) s.push('a');
　　s.push('b');
　　s.push('c');
　　s.pop();
　　s.pop();
　　s.pop();

(b) s.push('a');
　　s.push('b');
　　s.push('c');
　　x = s.top();
　　s.pop();
　　y = s.top();
　　s.pop();
　　s.push(x);
　　s.push(y);
　　s.pop();

(c) s.push('a');
　　s.push('b');
　　s.push('c');
　　while (!s.empty())
　　　　s.pop();

(d) s.push('a');
　　s.push('b');
　　while (!s.empty()) {
　　　　x = s.top();
　　　　s.pop();
　　}
　　s.push('c');
　　s.pop();
　　s.push('a');
　　s.pop();
　　s.push('b');
　　s.pop();

E2. Write a program that makes use of a stack to read in a single line of text and write out the characters in the line in reverse order.

E3. Write a program that reads a sequence of integers of increasing size and prints the integers in decreasing order of size. Input terminates as soon as an integer that does not exceed its predecessor is read. The integers are then printed in decreasing order.

E4. A stack may be regarded as a railway switching network like the one in Figure 2.3. Cars numbered $1, 2, \ldots, n$ are on the line at the left, and it is desired to rearrange (permute) the cars as they leave on the right-hand track. A car that is on the spur (stack) can be left there or sent on its way down the right track, but it can never be sent back to the incoming track. For example, if $n = 3$, and we have the cars $1, 2, 3$ on the left track, then 3 first goes to the spur. We could then send 2 to the spur, then on its way to the right, then send 3 on the way, then 1, obtaining the new order $1, 3, 2$.

stack permutations

(a) For $n = 3$, find all possible permutations that can be obtained.

(b) For $n = 4$, find all possible permutations that can be obtained.

(c) [Challenging] For general n, find how many permutations can be obtained by using this stack.

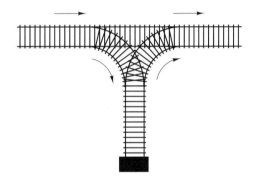

Figure 2.3. Switching network for stack permutations

2.2 IMPLEMENTATION OF STACKS

contiguous implementation

We now turn to the problem of the construction of a stack implementation in C++. We will produce a **contiguous** Stack implementation, meaning that the entries are stored next to each other in an array. In Chapter 4, we shall study a *linked* implementation using pointers in dynamic memory.

classes

In these and all the other implementations we construct, we shall be careful always to use classes to implement the data structures. Thus, we shall now develop a **class** Stack whose data members represent the entries of a stack. Before we implement any class, we should decide on specifications for its methods.

2.2.1 Specification of Methods for Stacks

stack methods

The methods of our **class** Stack must certainly include the fundamental operations called empty(), top(), push(), and pop(). Only one other operation will be essential: This is an *initialization* operation to set up an empty stack. Without such an initialization operation, client code would have to deal with stacks made up of random and probably illegal data, whatever happened beforehand to be in the storage area occupied by the stack.

1. Constructors

The C++ language allows us to define special initialization methods for any class. These methods are called **constructors** for the class. Each constructor is a function with the same name as the corresponding class. A constructor has no return type. Constructors are applied automatically whenever we declare an object of the class. For example, the standard library implementation of a **stack** includes a constructor that initializes each newly created stack as empty: In our earlier program for reversing a line of input, such an initialization was crucial. Naturally, we shall create a similar Stack constructor for the **class** that we develop. Thus, whenever one of our clients declares a Stack object, that object is automatically initialized as empty. The specification of our Stack constructor follows.

initialization

> Stack :: Stack( );
>
> *precondition*: None.
>
> *postcondition*: The Stack exists and is initialized to be empty.

2. Entry Types, Generics

The declarations for the fundamental methods of a stack depend on the type of entries that we intend to store in the stack. To keep as much generality as we can, let us use Stack_entry for the type of entries in our Stack. For one application, Stack_entry might be **int**, for another it might be **char**. A client can select an appropriate entry type with a definition such as

entry type

typedef char Stack_entry;

By keeping the type Stack_entry general, we can use the same stack implementation for many different applications.

The ability to use the same underlying data structure and operations for different entry types is called *generics*. Our use of a **typedef** statement to choose the type of entry in our Stack is a simple way to achieve generic data structures in C++. For complex applications, ones that need stacks with different entry types in a single program, the more sophisticated **template** treatment, which is used in the standard library **class** stack, is more appropriate. After we have gained some experience with simple data structures, we shall also choose to work with templates, beginning with the programs in Chapter 6.

generics

templates

3. Error Processing

In deciding on the parameters and return types of the fundamental Stack methods, we must recognize that a method might be applied illegally by a client. For example, a client might try to pop an empty stack. Our methods will signal any such problems with diagnostic *error codes*. In this book, we shall use a single enumerated type called Error_code to report errors from all of our programs and functions.

error codes

The enumerated type Error_code will be part of our utility package, described in Appendix C. In implementing the Stack methods, we shall make use of three values of an Error_code, namely:

success,   overflow,   underflow

If a method is able to complete its work normally, it will return success as its Error_code; otherwise, it will return a code to indicate what went wrong. Thus, a client that tries to pop from an empty Stack will get back an Error_code of underflow. However, any other application of the pop method is legitimate, and it will result in an Error_code of success.

stack error codes

This provides us with a first example of *error handling*, an important safeguard that we should build into our data structures whenever possible. There are several different ways that we could decide to handle error conditions that are detected in a method of a data structure. We could decide to handle the error directly, by printing

error handling

YOU Make
The**CALL**

out an error message or by halting the execution of the program. Alternatively, since methods are always called from a client program, we can decide to return an error code back to the client and let it decide how to handle the error. We take the view that the client is in the best position to judge what to do when errors are detected; we therefore adopt the second course of action. In some cases, the client code might react to an error code by ceasing operation immediately, but in other cases it might be important to ignore the error condition.

Programming Precept

After a client uses a class method,
it should decide whether to check the resulting error status.
Classes should be designed to allow clients to decide
how to respond to errors.

---

exception handling

We remark that C++ does provide a more sophisticated technique known as *exception handling*: When an error is detected an exception can be thrown. This exception can then be caught by client code. In this way, exception handling conforms to our philosophy that the client should decide how to respond to errors detected in a data structure. The standard library implementations of stacks and other classes use exception handling to deal with error conditions. However, we shall opt instead for the simplicity of returning error codes in all our implementations in this text.

4. Specification for Methods

Stack methods

Our specifications for the fundamental methods of a **Stack** come next.

Error_code Stack :: pop( );

precondition: None.

postcondition: If the **Stack** is not empty, the top of the **Stack** is removed. If the **Stack** is empty, an **Error_code** of underflow is returned and the **Stack** is left unchanged.

Error_code Stack :: push(**const** Stack_entry &item);

precondition: None.

postcondition: If the **Stack** is not full, item is added to the top of the **Stack**. If the **Stack** is full, an **Error_code** of overflow is returned and the **Stack** is left unchanged.

The parameter item that is passed to push is an input parameter, and this is indicated by its declaration as a **const** reference. In contrast, the parameter for the next method, top, is an output parameter, which we implement with call by reference.

Error_code Stack :: top(Stack_entry &item) **const;**

precondition: None.

postcondition: The top of a nonempty Stack is copied to item. A code of **fail** is returned if the Stack is empty.

The modifier **const** that we have appended to the declaration of this method indicates that the corresponding Stack object is not altered by, or during, the method. Just as it is important to specify input parameters as constant, as information for the reader and the compiler, it is important for us to indicate constant methods with this modifier. The last Stack method, **empty**, should also be declared as a constant method.

bool Stack :: empty( ) **const;**

precondition: None.

postcondition: A result of **true** is returned if the Stack is empty, otherwise **false** is returned.

2.2.2 The Class Specification

For a contiguous Stack implementation, we shall set up an array that will hold the entries in the stack and a counter that will indicate how many entries there are. We collect these data members together with the methods in the following definition for a **class** Stack containing items of type Stack_entry. This definition constitutes *stack type*   the file stack.h.

```
const int maxstack = 10;        //   small value for testing

class Stack {
public:
   Stack();
   bool empty( ) const;
   Error_code pop();
   Error_code top(Stack_entry &item) const;
   Error_code push(const Stack_entry &item);
private:
   int count;
   Stack_entry entry[maxstack];
};
```

As we explained in Section 1.2.4, we shall place this class definition in a header file with extension .h, in this case the file stack.h. The corresponding code file, with the method implementations that we shall next develop, will be called stack.c. The code file can then be compiled separately and linked to client code as needed.

2.2.3 Pushing, Popping, and Other Methods

The stack methods are implemented as follows. We must be careful of the extreme cases: We might attempt to pop an entry from an empty stack or to push an entry onto a full stack. These conditions must be recognized and reported with the return of an error code.

```
Error_code Stack :: push(const Stack_entry &item)
/* Pre:   None.
   Post:  If the Stack is not full, item is added to the top of the Stack. If the Stack
          is full, an Error_code of overflow is returned and the Stack is left un-
          changed. */
{
   Error_code outcome = success;
   if (count >= maxstack)
      outcome = overflow;
   else
      entry[count++] = item;
   return outcome;
}
```

```
Error_code Stack :: pop( )
/* Pre:   None.
   Post:  If the Stack is not empty, the top of the Stack is removed. If the Stack is
          empty, an Error_code of underflow is returned. */
{
   Error_code outcome = success;
   if (count ==  0)
      outcome = underflow;
   else  −−count;
   return outcome;
}
```

We note that the data member count represents the number of items in a Stack. Therefore, the top of a Stack occupies entry[count − 1], as shown in Figure 2.4.

```
Error_code Stack :: top(Stack_entry &item) const
/* Pre:   None.
   Post:  If the Stack is not empty, the top of the Stack is returned in item. If the
          Stack is empty an Error_code of underflow is returned. */
{
   Error_code outcome = success;
   if (count ==  0)
      outcome = underflow;
   else
      item = entry[count − 1];
   return outcome;
}
```

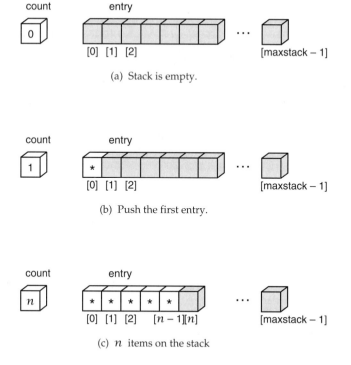

(a) Stack is empty.

(b) Push the first entry.

(c) n items on the stack

Figure 2.4. **Representation of data in a contiguous stack**

```
bool Stack :: empty( ) const
/* Pre:   None.
   Post:  If the Stack is empty, true is returned. Otherwise false is returned. */
{
    bool outcome = true;
    if (count > 0) outcome = false;
    return outcome;
}
```

constructor The other method of our **Stack** is the *constructor*. The purpose of the constructor is to initialize any new **Stack** object as empty.

```
Stack :: Stack( )
/* Pre:   None.
   Post:  The stack is initialized to be empty. */
{
    count = 0;
}
```

2.2.4 Encapsulation

data integrity

Notice that our stack implementation forces client code to make use of information hiding. Our declaration of **private** visibility for the data makes it is impossible for a client to access the data stored in a Stack except by using the official methods push(), pop(), and top(). One important result of this data privacy is that a Stack can never contain illegal or corrupted data. Every Stack object will be initialized to represent a legitimate empty stack and can only be modified by the official Stack methods. So long as our methods are correctly implemented, we have a guarantee that correctly initialized objects must continue to stay free of any data corruption.

encapsulation

We summarize this protection that we have given our Stack objects by saying that they are *encapsulated*. In general, data is said to be encapsulated if it can only be accessed by a controlled set of functions.

The small extra effort that we make to encapsulate the data members of a C++ class pays big dividends. The first advantage of using an encapsulated class shows up when we specify and program the methods: For an encapsulated class, we need never worry about illegal data values. Without encapsulation, the operations on a data structure almost always depend on a precondition that the data members have been correctly initialized and have not been corrupted. We can and should use encapsulation to avoid such preconditions. For our encapsulated **class** Stack, all of the methods have precondition specifications of *None*. This means that a client does not need to check for any special situations, such as an uninitialized stack, before applying a public Stack method. Since we think of data structures as services that will be written once and used in many different applications, it is particularly appropriate that the clients should be spared extra work where possible.

Programming Precept

The public methods for a data structure
should be implemented without preconditions.
The data members should be kept private.

We shall omit the precondition section from public method specifications in all our encapsulated C++ classes.

The private member functions of a data structure cannot be used by clients, so there is no longer a strong case for writing these functions without preconditions. We shall emphasize the distinction between public and private member functions of a data structure, by reserving the term *method* for the former category.

Exercises 2.2   **E1.** Assume the following definition file for a contiguous implementation of an extended stack data structure.

```
class Extended_stack {
public:
   Extended_stack();
   Error_code pop();
   Error_code push(Stack_entry item);
   Error_code top(Stack_entry &item) const;
   bool empty() const;
   void clear();          //  Reset the stack to be empty.
   bool full() const ;    //  If the stack is full, return true; else return false.
   int size() const;      //  Return the number of entries in the stack.
private:
   int top;
   Stack_entry entry[maxstack];
};
```

Write code for the following methods. [Use the private data members in your code.]

   (a) clear   **(b)** full   **(c)** size

E2. Start with the stack methods, and write a function copy_stack with the following specifications:

Error_code copy_stack(Stack &dest, Stack &source);

precondition: None.

postcondition: **Stack dest** has become an exact copy of **Stack source**; **source** is unchanged. If an error is detected, an appropriate code is returned; otherwise, a code of **success** is returned.

Write three versions of your function:

   (a) Simply use an assignment statement: dest = source;

   (b) Use the Stack methods and a temporary Stack to retrieve entries from the Stack source and add each entry to the Stack dest and restore the Stack source.

   (c) Write the function as a friend[2] to the **class** Stack. Use the private data members of the Stack and write a loop that copies entries from source to dest.

---

[2]   Friend functions have access to all members of a C++ class, even private ones.

Which of these is easiest to write? Which will run most quickly if the stack is nearly full? Which will run most quickly if the stack is nearly empty? Which would be the best method if the implementation might be changed? In which could we pass the parameter **source** as a constant reference?

E3. Write code for the following functions. [Your code must use **Stack** methods, but you should not make any assumptions about how stacks or their methods are actually implemented. For some functions, you may wish to declare and use a second, temporary **Stack** object.]

(a) Function **bool** full(Stack &s) leaves the **Stack** s unchanged and returns a value of **true** or **false** according to whether the **Stack** s is or is not full.

(b) Function Error_code pop_top(Stack &s, Stack_entry &t) removes the top entry from the **Stack** s and returns its value as the output parameter t.

(c) Function **void** clear(Stack &s) deletes all entries and returns s as an empty Stack.

(d) Function **int** size(Stack &s) leaves the **Stack** s unchanged and returns a count of the number of entries in the **Stack**.

(e) Function **void** delete_all(Stack &s, Stack_entry x) deletes all occurrences (if any) of x from s and leaves the remaining entries in s in the same relative order.

E4. Sometimes a program requires two stacks containing the same type of entries. If the two stacks are stored in separate arrays, then one stack might overflow while there was considerable unused space in the other. A neat way to avoid this problem is to put all the space in one array and let one stack grow from one end of the array and the other stack start at the other end and grow in the opposite direction, toward the first stack. In this way, if one stack turns out to be large and the other small, then they will still both fit, and there will be no overflow until all the space is actually used. Define a new class **Double_stack** that includes (as private data members) the array and the two indices **top_a** and **top_b**, and write code for the methods **Double_stack()**, **push_a()**, **push_b()**, **pop_a()**, and **pop_b()** to handle the two stacks within one **Double_stack**.

two coexisting stacks

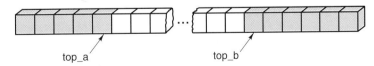

Programming Projects 2.2

prime divisors

P1. Assemble the appropriate declarations from the text into the files stack.h and stack.c and verify that stack.c compiles correctly, so that the **class** Stack can be used by future client programs.

P2. Write a program that uses a **Stack** to read an integer and print all its prime divisors in descending order. For example, with the integer 2100 the output should be

$$7 \quad 5 \quad 5 \quad 3 \quad 2 \quad 2.$$

[*Hint*: The smallest divisor greater than 1 of any integer is guaranteed to be a prime.]

2.3 APPLICATION: A DESK CALCULATOR

reverse Polish calculations

This section outlines a program to imitate the behavior of a simple calculator that does addition, subtraction, multiplication, division, and perhaps some other operations. There are many kinds of calculators available, and we could model our program after any of them. To provide a further illustration of the use of stacks, however, let us choose to model what is often called a *reverse Polish* calculator. In such a calculator, the operands (numbers, usually) are entered *before* an operation is specified. The operands are pushed onto a stack. When an operation is performed, it pops its operands from the stack and pushes its result back onto the stack.

examples

We shall write ? to denote an instruction to read an operand and push it onto the stack; + , − , * , and / represent arithmetic operations; and = is an instruction to print the top of the stack (but not pop it off). Further, we write a, b, c, and d to denote numerical values such as 3.14 or −7. The instructions ? a ? b + = mean read and store the numbers a and b, calculate and store their sum, and then print the sum. The instructions ? a ? b + ? c ? d + * = request four numerical operands, and the result printed is the value of (a + b) * (c + d). Similarly, the instructions ? a ? b ? c − = * ? d + = mean push the numbers a, b, c onto the stack, replace the pair b, c by b − c and print its value, calculate a * (b − c), push d onto the stack, and finally calculate and print (a * (b − c)) + d. The advantage of

no parentheses needed

a reverse Polish calculator is that any expression, no matter how complicated, can be specified without the use of parentheses.

If you have access to a UNIX system, you can experiment with a reverse Polish calculator with the command dc.

Polish notation is useful for compilers as well as for calculators, and its study forms the major topic of Chapter 13. For the present, however, a few minutes' practice with a reverse Polish calculator will make you quite comfortable with its use.

It is clear that we should use a stack in an implementation of a reverse Polish calculator. After this decision, the task of the calculator program becomes simple. The main program declares a stack of entries of type **double**, accepts new commands, and performs them as long as desired.

Plain Simple

In the program, we shall apply our generic Stack implementation. We begin with a **typedef** statement to set the type of Stack_entry. We then include the Stack definition file stack.h.

```
typedef double Stack_entry;
#include "stack.h"
```

int main()
/* **Post:** *The program has executed simple arithmetic commands entered by the user.*
  Uses: *The class* Stack *and the functions* introduction, instructions, do_command, *and* get_command. */

```
{
  Stack stored_numbers;
  introduction();
  instructions();
  while (do_command(get_command(), stored_numbers));
}
```

The auxiliary function **get_command** obtains a command from the user, checking that it is valid and converting it to lowercase by using the string function **tolower()** that is declared in the standard header file **cctype**. (The file **cctype**, or its older incarnation **ctype.h**, can be automatically included via our standard utility package; see Appendix C.)

user commands   In order to implement **get_command**, let us make the decision to represent the commands that a user can type by the characters **?, =, +, −, *, /**, where **?** requests input of a numerical value from the user, **=** prints the result of an operation, and the remaining symbols denote addition, subtraction, multiplication, and division, respectively.

```
char get_command()
{
  char command;
  bool waiting = true;
  cout << "Select command and press < Enter > :";
  while (waiting) {
    cin >> command;
    command = tolower(command);
    if (command == '?' || command == '=' || command == '+' ||
        command == '−' || command == '*' || command == '/'  ||
        command == 'q') waiting = false;
    else {
      cout << "Please enter a valid command:"  << endl
           << "[?]push to stack   [=]print top"   << endl
           << "[+] [−] [*] [/]  are arithmetic operations" << endl
           << "[Q]uit."  << endl;
    }
  }
  return command;
}
```

The work of selecting and performing the commands, finally, is the task of the function **do_command**. We present here an abbreviated form of the function *Do a user command*   **do_command**, in which we have coded only a few of the possible commands in its main switch statement.

```
        bool do_command(char command, Stack &numbers)
        /* Pre:   The first parameter specifies a valid calculator command.
           Post:  The command specified by the first parameter has been applied to the
                  Stack of numbers given by the second parameter.  A result of true is re-
                  turned unless command == 'q'.
           Uses: The class Stack. */
        {
          double p, q;
          switch (command) {
          case '?':
read        cout << "Enter a real number: " << flush;
            cin >> p;
            if (numbers.push(p) == overflow)
              cout << "Warning: Stack full, lost number" << endl;
            break;
          case '=':
print       if (numbers.top(p) == underflow)
              cout << "Stack empty" << endl;
            else
              cout << p << endl;
            break;
          case '+':
add         if (numbers.top(p) == underflow)
              cout << "Stack empty" << endl;
            else {
              numbers.pop();
              if (numbers.top(q) == underflow) {
                cout << "Stack has just one entry" << endl;
                numbers.push(p);
              }
              else {
                numbers.pop();
                if (numbers.push(q + p) == overflow)
                  cout << "Warning: Stack full, lost result" << endl;
              }
            }
            break;

        //   Add options for further user commands.

          case 'q':
quit        cout << "Calculation finished.\n";
            return false;
          }
          return true;
        }
```

In calling this function, we must pass the Stack parameter by reference, because its value might need to be modified. For example, if the command parameter is **+**, then we normally pop two values off the Stack **numbers** and push their sum back onto it: This should certainly change the Stack.

The function do_command allows for an additional user command, **q**, that quits the program.

Exercises 2.3

E1. If we use the standard library **class** stack in our calculator, the method **top()** returns the top entry off the stack as its result. Then the function do_command can then be shortened considerably by writing such statements as

> **case** ′ − ′: numbers.push(numbers.pop() − numbers.pop());

  (a) Assuming that this statement works correctly, explain why it would still be bad programming style.

  (b) It is possible that two different C++ compilers, both adhering strictly to standard C++, would translate this statement in ways that would give different answers when the program runs. Explain how this could happen.

E2. Discuss the steps that would be needed to make the calculator process complex numbers.

Programming Projects 2.3

P1. Assemble the functions developed in this section and make the necessary changes in the code so as to produce a working calculator program.

P2. Write a function that will interchange the top two numbers on the stack, and include this capability as a new command.

P3. Write a function that will add all the numbers on the stack together, and include this capability as a new command.

P4. Write a function that will compute the average of all numbers on the stack, and include this capability as a new command.

2.4 APPLICATION: BRACKET MATCHING

Programs written in C++ contain several different types of brackets. For example, brackets are used to enclose expressions, function arguments, array indices, and blocks of code. As we know, the brackets used within a program must pair off.

For example, the following string

$$\{a = (1 + v(b[3 + c[4]]));$$

cannot possibly have matched brackets, because it has five opening brackets and only four closing brackets: Like the first drafts of many C++ programs, it is missing a final brace. The string

$$\{ a = (b[0] + 1]; \}$$

has equal numbers of opening and closing brackets, but we can see that it has unmatched brackets, because its first closing bracket) does not correspond to the most recent opening bracket [. On the other hand, the bracket sequence

$$\{()[()]\}$$

is matched, although it is not a legitimate part of any C++ program.

specifications   In this section we shall implement a program to check that brackets are correctly matched in an input text file. For simplicity, we will limit our attention to the brackets {, }, (,), [, and]. Moreover, we shall just read a single line of characters, and ignore all input other than bracket characters. In checking the bracketing of an actual C++ program, we would need to apply special rules for brackets within comments and strings, and we would have to recognize that the symbols <, > can also denote brackets (for example, in the declaration **stack**<**double**> numbers; that we used in the program of Section 2.1.3).

algorithm   If we formalize the rules for pairing brackets, we quickly obtain the following algorithm: Read the program file character by character. Each opening bracket (, [, or { that is encountered is considered as unmatched and is stored until a matching bracket can be found. Any closing bracket),], or } must correspond, in bracket style, to the last unmatched opening bracket, which should now be retrieved and removed from storage. Finally, at the end of the program, we must check that no unmatched opening brackets are left over.

data structure: stack   We see that a program to test the matching of brackets needs to process an input file character by character, and, as it works its way through the input, it needs some way to remember any currently unmatched brackets. These brackets must be retrieved in the exact reverse of their input order, and therefore a **Stack** provides an attractive option for their storage.

Once we have made this decision, our program need only loop over the input characters, until either a bracketing error is detected or the input file ends. Whenever a bracket is found, an appropriate **Stack** operation is applied. We thus obtain the following program.

```
int main()
/* Post:  The program has notified the user of any bracket mismatch in the standard
          input file.
   Uses: The class Stack. */
```

```
{
  Stack openings;
  char symbol;
  bool is_matched = true;
  while (is_matched && (symbol = cin.get()) != '\n') {
    if (symbol == '{' || symbol == '(' || symbol == '[')
      openings.push(symbol);
    if (symbol == '}' || symbol == ')' || symbol == ']') {
      if (openings.empty()) {
        cout << "Unmatched closing bracket " << symbol
             << " detected." << endl;
        is_matched = false;
      }
      else {
        char match;
        openings.top(match);
        openings.pop();
        is_matched = (symbol == '}' && match == '{')
                     || (symbol == ')' && match == '(')
                     || (symbol == ']' && match == '[');
        if (!is_matched)
          cout << "Bad match " << match << symbol << endl;
      }
    }
  }
  if (!openings.empty())
    cout << "Unmatched opening bracket(s) detected." << endl;
}
```

Programming Projects 2.4

P1. Modify the bracket checking program so that it reads the whole of an input file.

P2. Modify the bracket checking program so that input characters are echoed to output, and individual unmatched closing brackets are identified in the output file.

P3. Incorporate C++ comments and character strings into the bracket checking program, so that any bracket within a comment or character string is ignored.

2.5 ABSTRACT DATA TYPES AND THEIR IMPLEMENTATIONS ▬▬▬

2.5.1 Introduction

In any of our applications of stacks, we could have used an array and counter in place of the stack. This would entail replacing each stack operation by a group of array and counter manipulations. For example, the bracket checking program might use statements such as:

```
if (counter < max) {
    openings[counter] = symbol;
    counter++;
}
```

In some ways, this may seem like an easy approach, since the code is straightforward, simpler in many ways than setting up a class and declaring all its methods.

A major drawback to this approach, however, is that the writer (and any reader) of the program must spend considerable effort verifying the details of array index manipulations every time the stack is used, rather than being able to concentrate on the ways in which the stack is actually being used. This unnecessary effort is a direct result of the programmer's failure to recognize the general concept of a stack and to distinguish between this general concept and the particular implementation needed for a given application.

Another application might include the following instructions instead of a simple stack operation:

```
if ((xxt == mxx) || (xxt > mxx))
    try_again();
else {
    xx[xxt] = wi;
    xxt++;
}
```

In isolation, it may not even be clear that this section of code has essentially the same function as the earlier one. Both segments are intended to push an item onto the top of a stack.

analogies   Researchers working in different subjects frequently have ideas that are fundamentally similar but are developed for different purposes and expressed in different language. Often years will pass before anyone realizes the similarity of the work, but when the observation is made, insight from one subject can help with the other. In computer science, even so, the same basic idea often appears in quite different disguises that obscure the similarity. But if we can discover and emphasize the similarities, then we may be able to generalize the ideas and obtain easier ways to meet the requirements of many applications.

implementation   The way in which an underlying structure is implemented can have substantial effects on program development and on the capabilities and usefulness of the result. Sometimes these effects can be subtle. The underlying mathematical concept of a real number, for example, is usually (but not always) implemented by computer as a floating-point number with a certain degree of precision, and the inherent limitations in this implementation often produce difficulties with round-off error. Drawing a clear separation between the logical structure of our data and its implementation in computer memory will help us in designing programs. Our first step is to recognize the logical connections among the data and embody these connections in a logical data structure. Later we can consider our data structures and decide what is the best way to implement them for efficiency of programming and execution. By separating these decisions they both become easier, and we avoid pitfalls that attend premature commitment.

To help us clarify this distinction and achieve greater generality, let us now consider data structures from as general a perspective as we can.

2.5.2 General Definitions

1. Mathematical Concepts

Mathematics is the quintessence of generalization and therefore provides the language we need for our definitions. We start with the definition of a type:

Definition | A *type* is a set, and the elements of the set are called the *values* of the type.

We may therefore speak of the type *integer*, meaning the set of all integers, the type *real*, meaning the set of all real numbers, or the type *character*, meaning the set of symbols that we wish to manipulate with our algorithms.

Notice that we can already draw a distinction between an abstract type and its implementation: The C++ type **int**, for example, is not the set of all integers; it consists only of the set of those integers directly represented in a particular computer, the largest of which depends on the word size of the computer. Similarly, the C++ types **float** and **double** generally mean certain sets of floating-point numbers (separate mantissa and exponent) that are only small subsets of the set of all real numbers.

2. Atomic and Structured Types

Types such as **int**, **float**, and **char** are called *atomic* types because we think of their values as single entities only, not something we wish to subdivide. Computer languages like C++, however, provide tools such as arrays, classes, and pointers with which we can build new types, called *structured* types. A single value of a structured type (that is, a single element of its set) is a structured object such as a contiguous stack. A value of a structured type has two ingredients: It is made up of *component* elements, and there is a *structure*, a set of rules for putting the components together.

For our general point of view we shall use mathematical tools to provide the rules for building up structured types. Among these tools are sets, sequences, and *building types* functions. For the study of lists of various kinds the one that we need is the *finite sequence*, and for its definition we use mathematical induction.[3] A definition by induction (like a proof by induction) has two parts: First is an initial case, and second is the definition of the general case in terms of preceding cases.

Definition | A *sequence of length* 0 is empty. A *sequence of length* $n \geq 1$ of elements from a set T is an ordered pair (S_{n-1}, t) where S_{n-1} is a sequence of length $n - 1$ of elements from T, and t is an element of T.

---

[3] See Appendix A for samples of proof by induction.

From this definition we can build up longer and longer sequences, starting with the empty sequence and adding on new elements from T, one at a time.

From now on we shall draw a careful distinction between the word *sequential*, meaning that the elements form a sequence, and the word *contiguous*, which we take to mean that the elements have adjacent addresses in memory. Hence we shall be able to speak of a *sequential* list in a *contiguous* implementation.

sequential versus contiguous

3. Abstract Data Types

definition of list

The definition of a finite sequence immediately makes it possible for us to attempt a definition of a list: a *list* of items of a type T is simply a finite sequence of elements of the set T.

Next we would like to define a stack, but if you consider the definitions, you will realize that there will be nothing regarding the sequence of items to distinguish these structures from a list. The primary characteristic of a stack is the set of *operations* or *methods* by which changes or accesses can be made. Including a statement of these operations with the structural rules defining a finite sequence, we obtain

Definition

A *stack* of elements of type T is a finite sequence of elements of T, together with the following operations:

1. *Create* the stack, leaving it empty.
2. Test whether the stack is *Empty*.
3. *Push* a new entry onto the top of the stack, provided the stack is not full.
4. *Pop* the entry off the top of the stack, provided the stack is not empty.
5. Retrieve the *Top* entry from the stack, provided the stack is not empty.

Note that this definition makes no mention of the way in which the abstract data type *stack* is to be implemented. In the coming chapters we will study several different implementations of stacks, and this new definition fits any of these implementations equally well. This definition produces what is called an ***abstract data type***, often abbreviated as ***ADT***. The important principle is that the definition of any abstract data type involves two parts: First is a description of the way in which the components are related to each other, and second is a statement of the operations that can be performed on elements of the abstract data type.

abstract data type

2.5.3 Refinement of Data Specification

Now that we have obtained such a general definition of an abstract data type, it is time to begin specifying more detail, since the objective of all this work is to find general principles that will help with designing programs, and we need more detail to accomplish this objective.

There is, in fact, a close analogy between the process of top-down refinement of algorithms and the process of top-down specification of data structures that we have now begun. In algorithm design we begin with a general but precise statement of the problem and slowly specify more detail until we have developed a complete

top-down specification

program. In data specification we begin with the selection of the mathematical concepts and abstract data types required for our problem and slowly specify more detail until finally we can implement our data structures as classes.

stages of refinement   The number of stages required in this specification process depends on the application. The design of a large software system will require many more decisions than will the design of a single small program, and these decisions should be taken in several stages of refinement. Although different problems will require different numbers of stages of refinement, and the boundaries between these stages sometimes blur, we can pick out four levels of the refinement process.

conceptual   1. On the *abstract* level we decide how the data are related to each other and what operations are needed, but we decide nothing concerning how the data will actually be stored or how the operations will actually be done.

algorithmic   2. On the *data structures* level we specify enough detail so that we can analyze the behavior of the methods and make appropriate choices as dictated by our problem. This is the level, for example, at which we might choose a contiguous structure where data is stored in an array.

programming   3. On the *implementation* level we decide the details of how the data structures will be represented in computer memory.

4. On the *application* level we settle all details required for our particular application, such as names for variables or special requirements for the operations imposed by the application.

The first two levels are often called **conceptual** because at these levels we are more concerned with problem solving than with programming. The middle two levels can be called **algorithmic** because they concern precise methods for representing data and operating with it. The last two levels are specifically concerned with **programming**.

Our task in implementing a data structure in C++ is to begin with conceptual information, often the definition of an ADT, and refine it to obtain an implementation as a C++ class. The methods of the C++ class correspond naturally to the operations of the ADT, while the data members of the C++ class correspond to the physical data structure that we choose to represent our ADT. In this way, the process of moving from an abstract ADT, to a data structure, and then on to an implementation leads directly to a C++ class definition.

Let us conclude this section by restating its most important principles as programming precepts:

Programming Precept

Let your data structure your program.
Refine your algorithms and data structures at the same time.

Programming Precept

Once your data are fully structured,
your algorithms should almost write themselves.

Exercises 2.5

E1. Give a formal definition of the term *extended stack* as used in Exercise E1 of Section 2.2.

E2. In mathematics the ***Cartesian product*** of sets $T_1, T_2, \ldots, T_n$ is defined as the set of all n-tuples $(t_1, t_2, \ldots, t_n)$, where t_i is a member of T_i for all $i, 1 \le i \le n$. Use the Cartesian product to give a precise definition of a class.

POINTERS AND PITFALLS

1. Use data structures to clarify the logic of your programs.

2. Practice information hiding and encapsulation in implementing data structures: Use functions to access your data structures, and keep these in classes separate from your application program.

3. Postpone decisions on the details of implementing your data structures as long as you can.

4. Stacks are among the simplest kind of data structures; use stacks when possible.

5. In any problem that requires a reversal of data, consider using a stack to store the data.

6. Avoid tricky ways of storing your data; tricks usually will not generalize to new situations.

7. Be sure to initialize your data structures.

8. In designing algorithms, always be careful about the extreme cases and handle them gracefully. Trace through your algorithm to determine what happens in extreme cases, particularly when a data structure is empty or full.

9. Before choosing implementations, be sure that all the data structures and their associated operations are fully specified on the abstract level.

REVIEW QUESTIONS

2.1   **1.** What is the standard library?

2. What are the methods of a stack?

3. What are the advantages of writing the operations on a data structure as methods?

2.2   **4.** What are the differences between information hiding and encapsulation?

5. Describe three different approaches to error handling that could be adopted by a C++ class.

6. Give two different ways of implementing a generic data structure in C++.

2.3   **7.** What is the reason for using the reverse Polish convention for calculators?

2.5   **8.** What two parts must be in the definition of any abstract data type?

9. In an abstract data type, how much is specified about implementation?

10. Name (in order from abstract to concrete) four levels of refinement of data specification.

REFERENCES FOR FURTHER STUDY

stacks

For many topics concerning data structures, such as stacks, the best source for additional information, historical notes, and mathematical analysis is the following series of books, which can be regarded almost like an encyclopædia for the aspects of computing science that they discuss:

encyclopædic reference: KNUTH

DONALD E. KNUTH, *The Art of Computer Programming*, published by Addison-Wesley, Reading, Mass.

Three volumes have appeared to date:

1. *Fundamental Algorithms*, second edition, 1973, 634 pages.

2. *Seminumerical Algorithms*, second edition, 1980, 700 pages.

3. *Sorting and Searching*, 1973, 722 pages.

In future chapters we shall often give references to this series of books, and for convenience we shall do so by specifying only the name KNUTH together with the volume and page numbers. The algorithms are written both in English and in an assembler language, where KNUTH calculates detailed counts of operations to compare various algorithms.

A detailed description of the standard library in C++ occupies a large part of the following important reference:

BJARNE STROUSTRUP, *The C++ Programming Language*, third edition, Addison-Wesley, Reading, Mass., 1997.

The Polish notation is so natural and useful that one might expect its discovery to be hundreds of years ago. It may be surprising to note that it is a discovery of the twentieth century:

JAN ŁUKASIEWICZ, *Elementy Logiki Matematyczny*, Warsaw, 1929; English translation: *Elements of Mathematical Logic*, Pergamon Press, 1963.

Queues

3

A QUEUE is a data structure modeled after a line of people waiting to be served. Along with stacks, queues are one of the simplest kinds of data structures. This chapter develops properties of queues, studies how they are applied, and examines different implementations. The implementations illustrate the use of derived classes in C++ and the important object-oriented technique of class inheritance.

3.1 DEFINITIONS

In ordinary English, a queue is defined as a waiting line, like a line of people waiting to purchase tickets, where the first person in line is the first person served. For computer applications, we similarly define a *queue* to be a list in which all additions to the list are made at one end, and all deletions from the list are made at the other end. Queues are also called *first-in, first-out lists*, or *FIFO* for short. See Figure 3.1.

Figure 3.1. A queue

applications Applications of queues are, if anything, even more common than are applications of stacks, since in performing tasks by computer, as in all parts of life, it is often necessary to wait one's turn before having access to something. Within a computer system there may be queues of tasks waiting for the printer, for access to disk storage, or even, with multitasking, for use of the CPU. Within a single program, there may be multiple requests to be kept in a queue, or one task may create other tasks, which must be done in turn by keeping them in a queue.

front and rear The entry in a queue ready to be served, that is, the first entry that will be removed from the queue, is called the *front* of the queue (or, sometimes, the *head* of the queue). Similarly, the last entry in the queue, that is, the one most recently added, is called the *rear* (or the *tail*) of the queue.

3.1.1 Queue Operations

operations To complete the definition of our queue ADT, we specify all the operations that it permits. We shall do so by giving the method name for each operation, together with the postconditions that complete its specification. As you read these specifications, you should note the similarity with the corresponding operations for a stack. As in our treatment of stacks, we shall implement queues whose entries have a generic type, which we call Queue_entry.

The first step we must perform in working with any queue is to use a constructor to initialize it for further use:

Queue :: Queue( );

postcondition: The Queue has been created and is initialized to be empty.

The declarations for the fundamental operations on a queue come next.

Error_code Queue :: append(**const** Queue_entry &x);

postcondition: If there is space, x is added to the Queue as its rear. Otherwise an Error_code of overflow is returned.

Error_code Queue :: serve( );

postcondition: If the Queue is not empty, the front of the Queue has been removed. Otherwise an Error_code of underflow is returned.

Error_code Queue :: retrieve(Queue_entry &x) **const**;

postcondition: If the Queue is not empty, the front of the Queue has been recorded as x. Otherwise an Error_code of underflow is returned.

---

bool Queue :: empty( ) **const**;

postcondition: Return **true** if the Queue is empty, otherwise return **false**.

The names ***append*** and ***serve*** are used for the fundamental operations on a queue to indicate clearly what actions are performed and to avoid confusion with the terms we shall use for other data types. Other names, however, are also often used for these operations, terms such as *insert* and *delete* or the coined words *enqueue* and *dequeue*.

alternative names:
insert, delete,
enqueue, dequeue

Note that error codes are generated by any attempt to append an entry onto a full **Queue** or to serve an entry from an empty **Queue**. Thus our queues will use the same enumerated **Error_code** declaration as stacks, including the codes

success, underflow, overflow.

The **Queue** method specifications show that our C++ class definition is based on the following skeleton.

```
class Queue {
public:
   Queue( );
   bool empty( ) const;
   Error_code append(const Queue_entry &x);
   Error_code serve( );
   Error_code retrieve(Queue_entry &x) const;
//   Additional members will represent queue data.
};
```

The standard template library provides a **template** for a **class** queue. The operations that we have called empty, append, serve, and retrieve are known in the standard library as empty, push, pop, and front. However, since the operations behave very differently from those of a stack, we prefer to use operation names that highlight these differences. The standard library queue implementation also provides operations called back and size that examine the last entry (that is, the one most recently appended) and the total number of entries in a queue, respectively.

3.1.2 Extended Queue Operations

In addition to the fundamental methods append, serve, retrieve, and empty there are other queue operations that are sometimes helpful. For example, it can be convenient to have a queue method full that checks whether the queue is completely full.

reinitialization

There are three more operations that are very useful for queues. The first is clear, which takes a queue that has already been created and makes it empty. Second is the function size, which returns the number of entries in the queue. The third is the function serve_and_retrieve, which combines the effects of serve and retrieve.

queue size

We could choose to add these functions as additional methods for our basic **class** Queue. However, in object-oriented languages like C++, we can create new classes that reuse the methods and implementations of old classes. In this case, we shall create a new class called an Extended_queue that allows new methods in addition to the basic methods of a Queue. We shall say that the **class** Extended_queue is *derived* from the **class** Queue.

derived classes

inheritance

Derived classes provide a simple way of defining classes by adding methods to an existing class. The ability of a derived class to reuse the members of a *base* class is known as *inheritance*. Inheritance is one of the features that is fundamental to object-oriented programming.

We illustrate the relationship between the **class** Queue and the derived **class** Extended_queue with a *hierarchy diagram*, as shown in part (a) of Figure 3.2. An arrow in a hierarchy diagram points up from a derived class to the base class from which it is derived. Part (b) of Figure 3.2 illustrates how the methods of a base class are inherited by a derived class, which then may also include additional methods.

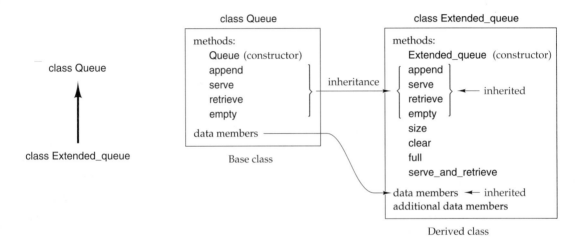

(a) Hierarchy diagram   (b) Derived class Extended_queue from base class Queue

Figure 3.2. Inheritance and derived classes

Extended_queue class

In C++ we use the : operator (colon) to define a derived class. The definition of the **class** Extended_queue is as follows.

```
class Extended_queue: public Queue {
public:
    bool full() const;
    int size() const;
    void clear();
    Error_code serve_and_retrieve(Queue_entry &item);
};
```

The keyword **public** in the first line of the class definition indicates that each inherited member of an Extended_queue has exactly the same visibility (to clients) as it would have as a member of a Queue.

The new operations for our **class** Extended_queue have the following specifications.

status

> **bool** Extended_queue :: full( ) **const;**
>
> *postcondition*: Return **true** if the Extended_queue is full; return **false** otherwise.

other operations

> **void** Extended_queue :: clear( );
>
> *postcondition*: All entries in the Extended_queue have been removed; it is now empty.

> **int** Extended_queue :: size( ) **const;**
>
> *postcondition*: Return the number of entries in the Extended_queue.

> Error_code Extended_queue :: serve_and_retrieve(Queue_entry &item);
>
> *postcondition*: Return underflow if the Extended_queue is empty. Otherwise remove and copy the item at the front of the Extended_queue to item and return success.

is-a relationship   The relationship between the **class** Extended_queue and the **class** Queue is often called an *is-a* relationship. This is because every Extended_queue object "is a" Queue object with other features—namely, the methods serve_and_retrieve, full, size, and clear. Whenever a verbal description of the relationship between two ADTs A and B includes the phrase "Every A is a B ", we should consider implementing a **class** to represent A as derived from a class representing B.

example   As another illustration of the is-a relationship between classes, consider C++ classes that might be used in a program to manage a university budget. Some of these classes are University, Student, University_president, and Person. Every student is a person, and therefore we might create the **class** Student as derived from the **class** Person to reflect the is-a relationship between the corresponding concepts. The **class** University_president could also be implemented as a derived class of Person to reflect another obvious is-a relationship. The classes University and University_president do not reflect an is-a relationship, however the classes are related, because every university does have a president. We shall say that these *has-a relationship* classes reflect a has-a relationship, and in an implementation we would make this *layering* relationship clear by *layering* the classes, that is, by including a data member of type University_president in the definition of the class University.

Exercises 3.1   **E1.** Suppose that q is a Queue that holds characters and that x and y are character variables. Show the contents of q at each step of the following code segments.

(a) Queue q;	(b) Queue q;	(c) Queue q;
q.append('a');	q.append('a');	q.append('a');
q.serve();	q.append('b');	x = 'b';
q.append('b');	q.retrieve(x);	q.append('x');
q.serve();	q.serve();	q.retrieve(y);
q.append('c');	q.append('c');	q.serve();
q.append('d');	q.append(x);	q.append(x);
q.serve();	q.serve();	q.serve();
	q.serve();	q.append(y);

accounting

E2. Suppose that you are a financier and purchase 100 shares of stock in Company X in each of January, April, and September and sell 100 shares in each of June and November. The prices per share in these months were

Jan	Apr	Jun	Sep	Nov
$10	$30	$20	$50	$30

Determine the total amount of your capital gain or loss using **(a)** FIFO (first-in, first-out) accounting and **(b)** LIFO (last-in, first-out) accounting [that is, assuming that you keep your stock certificates in **(a)** a queue or **(b)** a stack]. The 100 shares you still own at the end of the year do not enter the calculation.

E3. Use the methods for stacks and queues developed in the text to write functions that will do each of the following tasks. In writing each function, be sure to check for empty and full structures as appropriate. Your functions may declare other, local structures as needed.

(a) Move all the entries from a Stack into a Queue.

(b) Move all the entries from a Queue onto a Stack.

(c) Empty one Stack onto the top of another Stack in such a way that the entries that were in the first Stack keep the same relative order.

(d) Empty one Stack onto the top of another Stack in such a way that the entries that were in the first Stack are in the reverse of their original order.

(e) Use a local Stack to reverse the order of all the entries in a Queue.

(f) Use a local Queue to reverse the order of all the entries in a Stack.

3.2 IMPLEMENTATIONS OF QUEUES

Now that we have considered definitions of queues and their methods, let us change our point of view and consider how queues can be implemented with computer storage and as a C++ class.

1. The Physical Model

As we did for stacks, we can easily create a queue in computer storage by setting up an ordinary array to hold the entries. Now, however, we must keep track of both the front and the rear of the queue. One strategy would be to keep the front of the queue always in the first location of the array. Then an entry could be appended to the queue simply by increasing the counter showing the rear, in exactly the same way as we added an entry to a stack. To remove an entry from the queue, *fault:* however, would be very expensive indeed, since after the first entry was served, *many moves* all the remaining entries would need to be moved one position up the queue to fill in the vacancy. With a long queue, this process would be prohibitively slow. Although this method of storage closely models a queue of people waiting to be served, it is a poor choice for use in computers.

2. Linear Implementation

For efficient processing of queues, we shall therefore need two indices so that we can keep track of both the front and the rear of the queue without moving any entries. To append an entry to the queue, we simply increase the rear by one and put the entry in that position. To serve an entry, we take it from the position at the front and then increase the front by one. This method, however, still has a major defect: Both the front and rear indices are increased but never decreased. Even *fault:* if there are never more than two entries in the queue, an unbounded amount of *discarded space* storage will be needed for the queue if the sequence of operations is

append, append, serve, append, serve, append, serve, append, ...

The problem, of course, is that, as the queue moves down the array, the storage space at the beginning of the array is discarded and never used again. Perhaps the queue can be likened to a stretchable snake crawling through storage. Sometimes the snake is longer, sometimes shorter, but if it always keeps crawling in a straight line, then it will soon reach the end of the storage space.

Note, however, that for applications where the queue is regularly emptied *advantage* (such as when a series of requests is allowed to build up to a certain point, and then a task is initiated that clears all the requests before returning), then at a time when the queue is empty, the front and rear can both be reset to the beginning of the array, and the simple scheme of using two indices and straight-line storage becomes a very efficient implementation.

3. Circular Arrays

In concept, we can overcome the inefficient use of space simply by thinking of the array as a circle rather than a straight line. See Figure 3.3. In this way, as entries are added and removed from the queue, the head will continually chase the tail around the array, so that the snake can keep crawling indefinitely but stay in a confined circuit. At different times, the queue will occupy different parts of the array, but we never need worry about running out of space unless the array is fully occupied, in which case we truly have overflow.

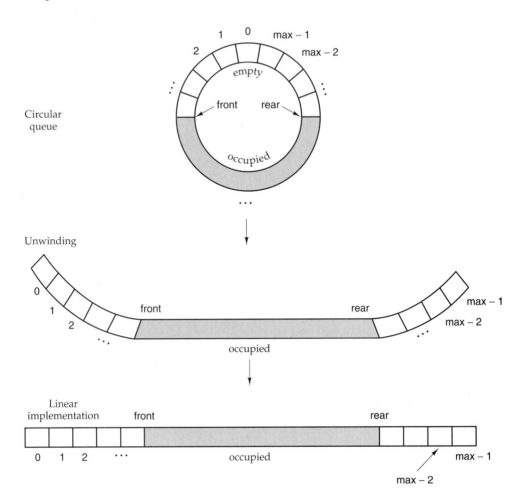

Circular
queue

Unwinding

Linear
implementation

Figure 3.3. Queue in a circular array

4. Implementation of Circular Arrays

Our next problem is to implement a circular array as an ordinary linear (that is, straight-line) array. To do so, we think of the positions around the circle as numbered from 0 to max − 1, where max is the total number of entries in the circular array, and to implement the circular array, we use the same-numbered entries of a linear array. Then moving the indices is just the same as doing modular arithmetic:

modular arithmetic When we increase an index past max − 1, we start over again at 0. This is like doing arithmetic on a circular clock face; the hours are numbered from 1 to 12, and if we add four hours to ten o'clock, we obtain two o'clock.

A very rough analogy of this linear representation is that of a priest serving communion to people kneeling at the front of a church. The communicants do not move until the priest comes by and serves them. When the priest reaches the end of the row, he returns to the beginning and starts again, since by this time a new row of people have come forward.

5. Circular Arrays in C++

ternary operator ? :

In C++, we can increment an index i of a circular array by using the ***ternary operator*** ? : and writing

$$i = ((i + 1) == \ max) ? 0 : (i + 1);$$

This use of the rarely seen ternary operator ? : of C++ has the same meaning as

if ((i + 1) == max) i = 0; **else** i = i + 1;

Or we can use the modulus operator and write

$$i = (i + 1) \% \ max$$

(You should check to verify that the result of the latter expression is always between 0 and max − 1.)

6. Boundary Conditions

empty or full?

Before writing formal algorithms to add to and remove from a queue, let us consider the boundary conditions, that is, the indicators that a queue is empty or full. If there is exactly one entry in the queue, then the front index will equal the rear index. When this one entry is removed, then the front will be increased by 1, so that an empty queue is indicated when the rear is one position before the front. Now suppose that the queue is nearly full. Then the rear will have moved well away from the front, all the way around the circle, and when the array is full the rear will be exactly one position before the front. Thus we have another difficulty: The front and rear indices are in exactly the same relative positions for an empty queue and for a full queue! There is no way, by looking at the indices alone, to tell a full queue from an empty one. This situation is illustrated in Figure 3.4.

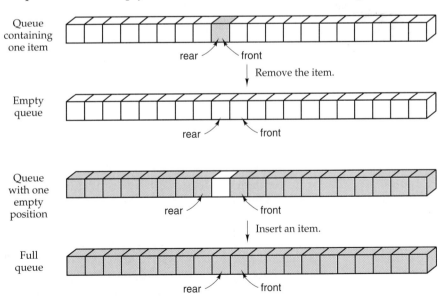

Figure 3.4. Empty and full queues

7. Possible Solutions

1. empty position   There are at least three essentially different ways to resolve this problem. One is to insist on leaving one empty position in the array, so that the queue is considered full when the rear index has moved within two positions of the front. A second *2. flag*   method is to introduce a new variable. This can be a Boolean flag that is set as **true** when the rear comes just before the front to indicate that the queue is full (a flag to indicate emptiness would be just as good) or an integer variable that counts *3. special values*   the number of entries in the queue. The third method is to set one or both of the indices to some value(s) that would otherwise never occur in order to indicate an empty (or full) queue. For example, an empty queue could be indicated by setting the rear index to -1.

8. Summary of Implementations

To summarize the discussion of queues, let us list all the methods we have discussed for implementing queues.

➡ *The physical model:* a linear array with the front always in the first position and all entries moved up the array whenever the front is removed. This is generally a poor method for use in computers.

➡ A *linear array* with two indices always increasing. This is a good method if the queue can be emptied all at once.

➡ A *circular array* with front and rear indices and one position left *vacant*.

➡ A *circular array* with front and rear indices and a *flag* to indicate fullness (or emptiness).

➡ A *circular array* with front and rear indices and an *integer variable* counting entries.

➡ A *circular array* with front and rear indices taking *special values* to indicate emptiness.

postpone implementation decisions   In the next chapter, we shall consider yet one more way to implement queues, by using a linked structure. The most important thing to remember from this list of implementations is that, with so many variations in implementation, we should always keep questions concerning the use of data structures like queues separate from questions concerning their implementation; and, in programming we should always consider only one of these categories of questions at a time. After we have considered how queues will be used in our application, and after we have written the client code employing queues, we will have more information to help us choose the best implementation of queues suited to our application.

Programming Precept

Practice information hiding:
Separate the application of data structures from their implementation.

3.3 CIRCULAR IMPLEMENTATION OF QUEUES IN C++ ▬▬▬

Next, let us write formal methods to implement queues and extended queues. It is clear from the last section that a great many implementations are possible, some of which are but slight variations on others. Let us therefore concentrate on only one implementation, leaving the others as exercises.

The implementation in a circular array which uses a counter to keep track of the number of entries in the queue both illustrates techniques for handling circular arrays and simplifies the programming of some of the extended-queue operations. Let us therefore work only with this implementation.

We shall take the queue as stored in an array indexed with the range

$$0 \text{ to } (\text{maxqueue} - 1)$$

class Queue
definition

and containing entries of a type called Queue_entry. The Queue data members front and rear will record appropriate indices of the array. The data member count is used to keep track of the number of entries in the Queue. The class definition for a Queue thus takes the form

```
const int maxqueue = 10;    //   small value for testing

class Queue {
public:
  Queue();
  bool empty() const;
  Error_code serve();
  Error_code append(const Queue_entry &item);
  Error_code retrieve(Queue_entry &item) const;
protected:
  int count;
  int front, rear;
  Queue_entry entry[maxqueue];
};
```

protected *visibility*

Notice that we have given the data members of a Queue **protected** rather than **private** visibility. For client code, **protected** visibility has the same meaning as **private** visibility, so that our **class** Queue is still encapsulated. However, the member functions of derived classes are allowed to access **protected** members of a base class. Thus, when we write methods for the derived **class** Extended_queue, our code will be able to make use of the data members of the **class** Queue. Without this access, the implementations of some of the methods of an Extended_queue would be very inefficient. The class specification for extended queues is already given in Section 3.1.2.

We begin coding the methods of a Queue with initialization.

```
Queue :: Queue( )
/* Post:  The Queue is initialized to be empty. */
{
   count = 0;
   rear = maxqueue − 1;
   front = 0;
}


bool Queue :: empty( ) const
/* Post:  Return true if the Queue is empty, otherwise retrun false. */
{
   return count ==  0;
}
```

The methods for adding to and removing from a **Queue** follow our preceding discussion closely. Notice that we return an **Error_code** whenever necessary.

```
Error_code Queue :: append(const Queue_entry &item)
/* Post:  item is added to the rear of the Queue.  If the Queue is full return an
          Error_code of overflow and leave the Queue unchanged. */
{
   if (count >= maxqueue) return overflow;
   count++;
   rear = ((rear + 1) ==  maxqueue) ? 0 : (rear + 1);
   entry[rear] = item;
   return success;
}


Error_code Queue :: serve( )
/* Post:  The front of the Queue is removed.  If the Queue is empty return an
          Error_code of underflow. */
{
   if (count <= 0) return underflow;
   count−−;
   front = ((front + 1) ==  maxqueue) ? 0 : (front + 1);
   return success;
}
```

```
Error_code Queue :: retrieve(Queue_entry &item) const
/* Post:  The front of the Queue retrieved to the output parameter item.  If the
          Queue is empty return an Error_code of underflow. */
{
   if (count <= 0) return underflow;
   item = entry[front];
   return success;
}
```

We leave the methods **empty** and **retrieve** as exercises and consider one of the methods for extended queues. The method giving the size of the extended queue is particularly easy to write in our implementation.

```
int Extended_queue :: size( ) const
/* Post: Return the number of entries in the Extended_queue. */
{
    return count;
}
```

Note that in writing the method size, we have used the protected Queue member count. If the data members in the **class** Queue had had **private** visibility, then they would have been unavailable to this function, and our code for the method size would have required a complicated set of calls to the **public** Queue methods serve, retrieve and append. The other Extended_queue methods, full, clear, and serve_and_retrieve, have similar implementations and are left as exercises.

Exercises 3.3

E1. Write the remaining methods for queues as implemented in this section:

    (a) empty   **(b)** retrieve

E2. Write the remaining methods for extended queues as implemented in this section:

    (a) full   **(b)** clear   **(c)** serve_and_retrieve

E3. Write the methods needed for the implementation of a queue in a linear array when it can be assumed that the queue can be emptied when necessary.

E4. Write the methods to implement queues by the simple but slow technique of keeping the front of the queue always in the first position of a linear array.

E5. Write the methods to implement queues in a linear array with two indices **front** and **rear**, such that, when **rear** reaches the end of the array, all the entries are moved to the front of the array.

E6. Write the methods to implement queues, where the implementation does not keep a count of the entries in the queue but instead uses the special conditions

$$\text{rear} = -1 \quad \text{and} \quad \text{front} = 0$$

to indicate an empty queue.

E7. Rewrite the methods for queue processing from the text, using a flag to indicate a full queue instead of keeping a count of the entries in the queue.

E8. Write methods to implement queues in a circular array with one unused entry in the array. That is, we consider that the array is full when the rear is two positions before the front; when the rear is one position before, it will always indicate an empty queue.

deque The word *deque* (pronounced either "deck" or "DQ") is a shortened form of *double-ended queue* and denotes a list in which entries can be added or removed from either the first or the last position of the list, but no changes can be made elsewhere in the list. Thus a deque is a generalization of both a stack and a queue. The fundamental operations on a deque are append_front, append_rear, serve_front, serve_rear, retrieve_front, and retrieve_rear.

E9. Write the class definition and the method implementations needed to implement a deque in a linear array.

E10. Write the methods needed to implement a deque in a circular array. Consider the **class** Deque as derived from the **class** Queue. (Can you hide the Queue methods from a client?)

E11. Is it more appropriate to implement a deque in a linear array or in a circular array? Why?

E12. Note from Figure 2.3 that a stack can be represented pictorially as a spur track on a straight railway line. A queue can, of course, be represented simply as a straight track. Devise and draw a railway switching network that will represent a deque. The network should have only one entrance and one exit.

E13. Suppose that data items numbered 1, 2, 3, 4, 5, 6 come in the input stream in this order. That is, 1 comes first, then 2, and so on. By using (1) a queue and (2) a deque, which of the following rearrangements can be obtained in the output order? The entries also leave the deque in left-to-right order.

(a) 1 2 3 4 5 6   (b) 2 4 3 6 5 1   (c) 1 5 2 4 3 6
(d) 4 2 1 3 5 6   (e) 1 2 6 4 5 3   (f) 5 2 6 3 4 1

Programming Projects 3.3

P1. Write a function that will read one line of input from the terminal. The input is supposed to consist of two parts separated by a colon ':'. As its result, your function should produce a single character as follows:

N   No colon on the line.
L   The left part (before the colon) is longer than the right.
R   The right part (after the colon) is longer than the left.
D   The left and right parts have the same length but are different.
S   The left and right parts are exactly the same.

Examples:	*Input*	*Output*
	Sample Sample	N
	Left:Right	R
	Sample:Sample	S

Use either a queue or an extended queue to keep track of the left part of the line while reading the right part.

3.4 DEMONSTRATION AND TESTING

menu-driven demonstration

After we have written a collection of methods and functions for processing a data structure, we should immediately test the implementation to make sure that every part of it works correctly. One of the simplest ways to do this is to write a ***menu-driven demonstration program*** that will set up the data structure and allow a user to perform all possible operations on the data structure in any desired order, printing out the results whenever the user wishes. Let us now develop such a program for our extended queues. This program will then serve as the basis for similar programs for further data structures throughout the book.

We can make the entries in the extended queue have any type we wish, so for simplicity let us use a queue of characters. Hence the entries will be single letters, digits, punctuation marks, and such.

At each iteration of its main loop, the demonstration program will ask the user to choose an operation. It will then (if possible) perform that operation on the data structure and print the results.

Hence the main program is:

```
int main()
/* Post: Accepts commands from user as a menu-driven demonstration program
          for the class Extended_queue.
    Uses: The class Extended_queue and the functions introduction, get_command,
          and do_command. */

{
    Extended_queue test_queue;
    introduction();
    while (do_command(get_command(), test_queue));
}
```

In this demonstration program, the user will enter a single character to select a command. The meanings of the commands together with the corresponding characters are explained by the help function, which can itself be activated by the appropriate command:

```
void help( )
/* Post: A help screen for the program is printed, giving the meaning of each
         command that the user may enter. */
{
   cout << endl
      << "This program allows the user to enter one command" << endl
      << "(but only one) on each input line." << endl
      << "For example, if the command S is entered, then" << endl
      << "the program will serve the front of the queue." << endl
      << endl
      << " The valid commands are:" << endl
      << "A – Append the next input character to the extended queue" << endl
      << "S – Serve the front of the extended queue" << endl
      << "R – Retrieve and print the front entry." << endl
      << "# – The current size of the extended queue" << endl
      << "C – Clear the extended queue (same as delete)" << endl
      << "P – Print the extended queue" << endl
      << "H – This help screen" << endl
      << "Q – Quit" << endl
      << "Press < Enter >  to continue." << flush;

   char c;
   do {
      cin.get(c);
   } while (c != '\n');
}
```

There is also an introduction function, which is activated only once at the start of the program. The purpose of this function is to explain briefly what the program does and to show the user how to begin. Further instructions that the user may need will come either from help or from get_command.

The function get_command prints the menu and obtains a command from the user. It is but a slight variation on the corresponding function from Section 2.3, so we leave its implementation as a project.

The work of selecting and performing commands, finally, is the task of the function do_command. This function just runs the appropriate case of a **switch** statement. We give a partial version of the function that has an abbreviated form of this **switch** statement.

```
bool do_command(char c, Extended_queue &test_queue)
/* Pre:  c represents a valid command.
   Post: Performs the given command c on the Extended_queue test_queue. Re-
         turns false if c == 'q', otherwise returns true.
   Uses: The class Extended_queue. */

{
  bool continue_input = true;
  Queue_entry x;
  switch (c) {
  case 'r':
    if (test_queue.retrieve(x) ==  underflow)
      cout << "Queue is empty." << endl;
    else
      cout << endl
           << "The first entry is: " << x
           << endl;
    break;
  case 'q':
    cout << "Extended queue demonstration finished." << endl;
    continue_input = false;
    break;

  //   Additional cases will cover other commands.

  }
  return continue_input;
}
```

You should note that, in all our testing functions, we have been careful to maintain the principles of data abstraction. The Extended_queue specification and methods are in files, so, if we wish, we can replace our particular Extended_queue implementation with another, and the program will work with no further change.

We have also written the testing functions so we can use the program to test other data structures later, changing almost nothing other than the valid operations and the introduction and help screens.

Programming Projects 3.4

P1. Complete the menu-driven demonstration program for manipulating an Extended_queue of characters, by implementing the function **get_command** and completing the function **do_command**.

P2. Write a menu-driven demonstration program for manipulating a deque of characters, similar to the Extended_queue demonstration program.

3.5 APPLICATION OF QUEUES: SIMULATION ━━━━━━━━━

3.5.1 Introduction

simulation   ***Simulation*** is the use of one system to imitate the behavior of another system. Simulations are often used when it would be too expensive or dangerous to experiment with the real system. There are physical simulations, such as wind tunnels used to experiment with designs for car bodies and flight simulators used to train airline pilots. Mathematical simulations are systems of equations used to describe some system, and computer simulations use the steps of a program to imitate the behavior of the system under study.

computer simulation   In a computer simulation, the objects being studied are usually represented as data, often as data structures given by classes whose members describe the properties of the objects. Actions being studied are represented as methods of the classes, and the rules describing these actions are translated into computer algorithms. By changing the values of the data or by modifying these algorithms, we can observe the changes in the computer simulation, and then we can draw worthwhile inferences concerning the behavior of the actual system.

While one object in a system is involved in some action, other objects and actions will often need to be kept waiting. Hence queues are important data structures for use in computer simulations. We shall study one of the most common and useful kinds of computer simulations, one that concentrates on queues as its basic data structure. These simulations imitate the behavior of systems (often, in fact, called *queueing systems*) in which there are queues of objects waiting to be served by various processes.

3.5.2 Simulation of an Airport

As a specific example, let us consider a small but busy airport with only one runway (see Figure 3.5). In each unit of time, one plane can land or one plane can take off, but not both. Planes arrive ready to land or to take off at random times, so at any given moment of time, the runway may be idle or a plane may be landing or taking off, and there may be several planes waiting either to land or take off.

class Plane   In simulating the airport, it will be useful to create a class **Plane** whose objects represent individual planes. This class will definitely need an initialization method and methods to represent takeoff and landing. Moreover, when we write the main program for the simulation, the need for other **Plane** methods will become apparent. We will also use a class **Runway** to hold information about the state and operation of the runway. This class will maintain members representing queues of planes waiting to land and take off.

class Random   We shall need one other class in our simulation, a class **Random** to encapsulate the random nature of plane arrivals and departures from the runway. We shall discuss this class in more detail in Section 3.5.3. In our main program, we use a

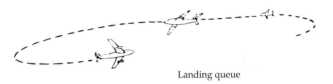

Landing queue

Plane landing

Runway

Takeoff queue

Figure 3.5. An airport

single method, called **poisson**, from the **class** Random. This method uses a floating-point parameter (representing an average outcome) and it returns an integer value. Although the returned value is random, it has the property that over the course of many repeated method calls, the average of the returned values will match our specified parameter.

In our simulation, we shall be especially concerned with the amounts of time that planes need to wait in queues before taking off or landing. Therefore, the measurement of time will be of utmost importance to our program. We shall divide the time period of our simulation into units in such a way that just one plane can use the runway, either to land or take off, in any given unit of time.

The precise details of how we handle the landing and takeoff queues will be dealt with when we program the **Runway** class. Similarly, the precise methods describing the operation of a **Plane** are not needed by our main program.

int main( ) // *Airport simulation program*
/* **Pre:** *The user must supply the number of time intervals the simulation is to run, the expected number of planes arriving, the expected number of planes departing per time interval, and the maximum allowed size for runway queues.*

Post: *The program performs a random simulation of the airport, showing the status of the runway at each time interval, and prints out a summary of airport operation at the conclusion.*

Uses: *Classes* Runway, Plane, Random *and functions* run_idle, initialize. */

```
{
    int end_time;              //   time to run simulation
    int queue_limit;           //   size of Runway queues
    int flight_number = 0;
    double arrival_rate, departure_rate;
    initialize(end_time, queue_limit, arrival_rate, departure_rate);
    Random variable;
    Runway small_airport(queue_limit);
    for (int current_time = 0; current_time < end_time; current_time++) {
                               //   loop over time intervals
        int number_arrivals = variable.poisson(arrival_rate);
                               //   current arrival requests
        for (int i = 0; i < number_arrivals; i++) {
            Plane current_plane(flight_number++, current_time, arriving);
            if (small_airport.can_land(current_plane) != success)
                current_plane.refuse();
        }
        int number_departures = variable.poisson(departure_rate);
                               //   current departure requests
        for (int j = 0; j < number_departures; j++) {
            Plane current_plane(flight_number++, current_time, departing);
            if (small_airport.can_depart(current_plane) != success)
                current_plane.refuse();
        }

        Plane moving_plane;
        switch (small_airport.activity(current_time, moving_plane)) {
            //   Let at most one Plane onto the Runway at current_time.
        case land:
            moving_plane.land(current_time);
            break;
        case takeoff:
            moving_plane.fly(current_time);
            break;
        case idle:
            run_idle(current_time);
        }
    }
    small_airport.shut_down(end_time);
}
```

In this program, we begin with a call to the function initialize that prints instructions
to the user and gathers information about how long the user wishes the simulation
to run and how busy the airport is to be. We then enter a **for** loop, in which
current_time ranges from 0 to the user specified value end_time. In each time unit,
we process random numbers of arriving and departing planes; these planes are
declared and initialized as the objects called current_plane. In each cycle, we also
allow one moving plane to use the runway. If there is no plane to use the runway,

we apply the function run_idle. Note that if our **class** Runway is unable to add an incoming flight to the landing Queue (presumably because the Queue is full), we apply a method called **refuse** to direct the Plane to another airport. Similarly, we sometimes have to refuse a Plane permission to take off.

3.5.3 Random Numbers

A key step in our simulation is to decide, at each time unit, how many new planes become ready to land or take off. Although there are many ways in which these decisions can be made, one of the most interesting and useful is to make a random decision. When the program is run repeatedly with random decisions, the results will differ from run to run, and with sufficient experimentation, the simulation may display a range of behavior not unlike that of the actual system being studied. The Random method poisson in the preceding main program returns a random number of planes arriving ready to land or ready to take off in a particular time unit.

pseudorandom number

Appendix B studies numbers, called ***pseudorandom***, for use in computer programs. Several different kinds of pseudorandom numbers are useful for different applications. For the airport simulation, we need one of the more sophisticated kinds, called *Poisson* random numbers.

To introduce the idea, let us note that saying that an average family has 2.6 children does not mean that each family has 2 children and 0.6 of a third. Instead, it means that, averaged over many families, the mean number of children is 2.6. Hence, for five families with 4, 1, 0, 3, 5 children the mean number is 2.6. Similarly, if the number of planes arriving to land in ten time units is 2, 0, 0, 1, 4, 1, 0, 0, 0, 1, then the mean number of planes arriving in one unit is 0.9.

expected value, Poisson distribution

Let us now start with a fixed number called the ***expected value*** v of the random numbers. Then to say that a sequence of nonnegative integers satisfies a ***Poisson distribution*** with expected value v implies that, over long subsequences, the mean value of the integers in the sequence approaches v. Appendix B describes a C++ class that generates random integers according to a Poisson distribution with a given expected value, and this is just what we need for the airport simulation.

3.5.4 The Runway Class Specification

rules

The Runway class needs to maintain two queues of planes, which we shall call landing and takeoff, to hold waiting planes. It is better to keep a plane waiting on the ground than in the air, so a small airport allows a plane to take off only if there are no planes waiting to land. Hence, our Runway method activity, which controls access to the Runway, will first service the head of the Queue of planes waiting to land, and only if the landing Queue is empty will it allow a Plane to take off.

One aim of our simulation is to gather data about likely airport use. It is natural to use the **class** Runway itself to keep statistics such the number of planes processed, the average time spent waiting, and the number of planes (if any) refused service. These details are reflected in the various data members of the following Runway class definition.

```
enum Runway_activity {idle, land, takeoff};
```

Runway definition

```
class Runway {
public:
    Runway(int limit);
    Error_code can_land(const Plane &current);
    Error_code can_depart(const Plane &current);
    Runway_activity activity(int time, Plane &moving);
    void shut_down(int time) const;
private:
    Extended_queue landing;
    Extended_queue takeoff;
    int queue_limit;
    int num_land_requests;      //   number of planes asking to land
    int num_takeoff_requests;   //   number of planes asking to take off
    int num_landings;           //   number of planes that have landed
    int num_takeoffs;           //   number of planes that have taken off
    int num_land_accepted;      //   number of planes queued to land
    int num_takeoff_accepted;   //   number of planes queued to take off
    int num_land_refused;       //   number of landing planes refused
    int num_takeoff_refused;    //   number of departing planes refused
    int land_wait;              //   total time of planes waiting to land
    int takeoff_wait;           //   total time of planes waiting to take off
    int idle_time;              //   total time runway is idle
};
```

Note that the **class** Runway has two queues among its members. The implementation reflects the has-a relationships in the statement that a runway has a landing queue and has a takeoff queue.

3.5.5 The Plane Class Specification

The **class** Plane needs to maintain data about particular **Plane** objects. This data must include a flight number, a time of arrival at the airport system, and a **Plane** status as either arriving or departing. Since we do not wish a client to be able to change this information, we shall keep it in private data members. When we declare a **Plane** object in the main program, we shall wish to initialize these three pieces of information as the object is constructed. Hence we need a **Plane** class constructor that has three parameters. Other times, however, we shall wish to construct a **Plane** object without initializing this information, because either its values are irrelevant or will otherwise be determined. Hence we really need two constructors for the **Plane** class, one with three parameters and one with none.

multiple versions of functions

The C++ language provides exactly the feature we need; it allows us to use the same identifier to name as many different functions as we like, even within a single block of code, so long as no two of these functions have identically typed parameter lists. When the function is invoked, the C++ compiler can figure out which version of the function to use, by looking at the number of actual parameters and their types. It simply determines which set of formal parameters match the actual parameters in number and types.

function overloading

When we use a single name for several different functions, we say that the name is **overloaded**. Inside the scope of the **class** Plane, we are able to overload the two plane constructors, because the first uses an empty parameter list, whereas the second uses a parameter list of three integer variables.

From now on, class specifications will often contain two constructors, one with parameters for initializing data members, and one without parameters.

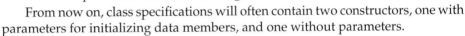

Finally, the Plane class must contain the methods **refuse**, **land**, and **fly** that are explicitly used by the main program. We will also need each Plane to be able to communicate its time of arrival at the airport to the **class** Runway, so a final method called **started** is included with this purpose in mind. We can now give the specification for the **class** Plane.

```
enum Plane_status {null, arriving, departing};
```

Plane *definition*

```
class Plane {
public:
    Plane( );
    Plane(int flt, int time, Plane_status status);
    void refuse( ) const;
    void land(int time) const;
    void fly(int time) const;
    int started( ) const;
private:
    int flt_num;
    int clock_start;
    Plane_status state;
};
```

3.5.6 Functions and Methods of the Simulation

The actions of the functions and methods for doing the steps of the simulation are generally straightforward, so we proceed to write each in turn, with comments only as needed for clarity.

1. Simulation Initialization

```
void initialize(int &end_time, int &queue_limit,
                double &arrival_rate, double &departure_rate)
/* Pre:   The user specifies the number of time units in the simulation, the maximal
         queue sizes permitted, and the expected arrival and departure rates for
         the airport.
   Post: The program prints instructions and initializes the parameters end_time,
         queue_limit, arrival_rate, and departure_rate to the specified values.
   Uses: utility function user_says_yes */
{
   cout  ≪ "This program simulates an airport with only one runway." ≪ endl
         ≪ "One plane can land or depart in each unit of time." ≪ endl;
   cout  ≪ "Up to what number of planes can be waiting to land "
         ≪ "or take off at any time? " ≪ flush;
   cin   ≫ queue_limit;
   cout  ≪ "How many units of time will the simulation run?" ≪ flush;
   cin   ≫ end_time;
   bool acceptable;
   do {
      cout  ≪ "Expected number of arrivals per unit time?" ≪ flush;
      cin   ≫ arrival_rate;
      cout  ≪ "Expected number of departures per unit time?" ≪ flush;
      cin   ≫ departure_rate;
      if (arrival_rate < 0.0 || departure_rate < 0.0)
         cerr ≪ "These rates must be nonnegative." ≪ endl;
      else
         acceptable = true;
      if (acceptable && arrival_rate + departure_rate > 1.0)
         cerr ≪ "Safety Warning: This airport will become saturated. " ≪ endl;
   } while (!acceptable);
}
```

2. Runway Initialization

```
Runway :: Runway(int limit)
/* Post: The Runway data members are initialized to record no prior Runway use
         and to record the limit on queue sizes. */
{
   queue_limit = limit;
   num_land_requests = num_takeoff_requests = 0;
   num_landings = num_takeoffs = 0;
   num_land_refused = num_takeoff_refused = 0;
   num_land_accepted = num_takeoff_accepted = 0;
   land_wait = takeoff_wait = idle_time = 0;
}
```

3. Accepting a New Plane into a Runway Queue

Error_code Runway :: can_land(**const** Plane &current)
/* **Post:** *If possible, the* Plane current *is added to the landing* Queue; *otherwise, an* Error_code *of* overflow *is returned. The* Runway *statistics are updated.*
  Uses: class Extended_queue. */
{
  Error_code result;
  if (landing.size( ) < queue_limit)
    result = landing.append(current);
  else
    result = fail;
  num_land_requests++;
  if (result != success)
    num_land_refused++;
  else
    num_land_accepted++;
  return result;
}

Error_code Runway :: can_depart(**const** Plane &current)
/* **Post:** *If possible, the* Plane current *is added to the takeoff* Queue; *otherwise, an* Error_code *of* overflow *is returned. The* Runway *statistics are updated.*
  Uses: class Extended_queue. */
{
  Error_code result;
  if (takeoff.size( ) < queue_limit)
    result = takeoff.append(current);
  else
    result = fail;
  num_takeoff_requests++;
  if (result != success)
    num_takeoff_refused++;
  else
    num_takeoff_accepted++;
  return result;
}

4. Handling Runway Access

Runway_activity Runway :: activity(**int** time, Plane &moving)
/* **Post:** *If the landing* Queue *has entries, its front* Plane *is copied to the parameter* moving *and a result* land *is returned. Otherwise, if the takeoff* Queue *has entries, its front* Plane *is copied to the parameter* moving *and a result* takeoff *is returned. Otherwise,* idle *is returned. Runway statistics are updated.*
  Uses: class Extended_queue. */

```
{
  Runway_activity in_progress;
  if (!landing.empty()) {
    landing.retrieve(moving);
    land_wait += time − moving.started();
    num_landings++;
    in_progress = land;
    landing.serve();
  }
  else if (!takeoff.empty()) {
    takeoff.retrieve(moving);
    takeoff_wait += time − moving.started();
    num_takeoffs++;
    in_progress = takeoff;
    takeoff.serve();
  }
  else {
    idle_time++;
    in_progress = idle;
  }
  return in_progress;
}
```

5. Plane Initialization

```
Plane :: Plane(int flt, int time, Plane_status status)
/* Post: The Plane data members flt_num, clock_start, and state are set to the
         values of the parameters flt, time and status, respectively. */
{
  flt_num = flt;
  clock_start = time;
  state = status;
  cout << "Plane number " << flt << " ready to ";
  if (status ==  arriving)
    cout << "land." << endl;
  else
    cout << "take off." << endl;
}

Plane :: Plane()
/* Post: The Plane data members flt_num, clock_start, state are set to illegal de-
         fault values. */
{
  flt_num = −1;
  clock_start = −1;
  state = null;
}
```

null initialization The second of these constructors performs a ***null initialization***. In many programs it is not necessary to provide such a constructor for a class. However, in C++, if we ever declare an array of objects that do have a constructor, then the objects must have an explicit default constructor. A ***default constructor*** is a constructor without parameters (or with specified defaults for all parameters). Each **Runway** object contains queues of planes, and each of these queues is implemented using an array of planes. Hence, in our simulation, we really do need the null initialization operation.

6. Refusing a Plane

void Plane :: refuse( ) **const**
/* **Post:** *Processes a* Plane *wanting to use* Runway, *when the* Queue *is full.* */
{
  cout ≪ "Plane number " ≪ flt_num;
  if (state == arriving)
    cout ≪ " directed to another airport" ≪ endl;
  else
    cout ≪ " told to try to takeoff again later" ≪ endl;
}

7. Processing an Arriving Plane

void Plane :: land(**int** time) **const**
/* **Post:** *Processes a* Plane *that is landing at the specified time.* */
{
  int wait = time − clock_start;
  cout ≪ time ≪ ": Plane number " ≪ flt_num ≪ " landed after "
    ≪ wait ≪ " time unit" ≪ ((wait == 1) ? "" : "s")
    ≪ " in the takeoff queue." ≪ endl;
}

In this function we have used the ternary operator ? : to append an "s" where needed to achieve output such as "1 time unit" or "2 time units".

8. Processing a Departing Plane

void Plane :: fly(**int** time) **const**
/* **Post:** *Process a* Plane *that is taking off at the specified time.* */
{
  int wait = time − clock_start;
  cout ≪ time ≪ ": Plane number " ≪ flt_num ≪ " took off after "
    ≪ wait ≪ " time unit" ≪ ((wait == 1) ? "" : "s")
    ≪ " in the takeoff queue." ≪ endl;
}

9. Communicating a Plane's Arrival Data

```
int Plane :: started( ) const
/* Post: Return the time that the Plane entered the airport system. */
{
   return clock_start;
}
```

10. Marking an Idle Time Unit

```
void run_idle(int time)
/* Post: The specified time is printed with a message that the runway is idle. */
{
   cout << time << ": Runway is idle." << endl;
}
```

11. Finishing the Simulation

```
void Runway :: shut_down(int time) const
/* Post: Runway usage statistics are summarized and printed. */
{
   cout << "Simulation has conluded after " << time << " time units." << endl
        << "Total number of planes processed "
        << (num_land_requests + num_takeoff_requests) << endl
        << "Total number of planes asking to land "
        << num_land_requests << endl
        << "Total number of planes asking to take off "
        << num_takeoff_requests << endl
        << "Total number of planes accepted for landing "
        << num_land_accepted << endl
        << "Total number of planes accepted for takeoff "
        << num_takeoff_accepted << endl
        << "Total number of planes refused for landing "
        << num_land_refused << endl
        << "Total number of planes refused for takeoff "
        << num_takeoff_refused << endl
        << "Total number of planes that landed "
        << num_landings << endl
        << "Total number of planes that took off "
        << num_takeoffs << endl
        << "Total number of planes left in landing queue "
        << landing.size( ) << endl
        << "Total number of planes left in takeoff queue "
        << takeoff.size( ) << endl;
```

```
            cout ≪ "Percentage of time runway idle "
                 ≪ 100.0 ∗ ((float) idle_time)/((float) time) ≪ "%" ≪ endl;
            cout ≪ "Average wait in landing queue "
                 ≪ ((float) land_wait)/((float) num_landings) ≪ " time units";
            cout ≪ endl ≪ "Average wait in takeoff queue "
                 ≪ ((float) takeoff_wait)/((float) num_takeoffs)
                 ≪ " time units" ≪ endl;
            cout ≪ "Average observed rate of planes wanting to land "
                 ≪ ((float) num_land_requests)/((float) time)
                 ≪ " per time unit" ≪ endl;
            cout ≪ "Average observed rate of planes wanting to take off "
                 ≪ ((float) num_takeoff_requests)/((float) time)
                 ≪ " per time unit" ≪ endl;
        }
```

3.5.7 Sample Results

We conclude this section with part of the output from a sample run of the airport simulation. You should note that there are some periods when the runway is idle and others when one of the queues is completely full and in which planes must be turned away. If you run this simulation again, you will obtain different results from those given here, but, if the expected values given to the program are the same, then there will be some correspondence between the numbers given in the summaries of the two runs.

This program simulates an airport with only one runway.
One plane can land or depart in each unit of time.
Up to what number of planes can be waiting to land or take off at any time ? 5
How many units of time will the simulation run ? 1000
Expected number of arrivals per unit time ? .48
Expected number of departures per unit time ? .48
       Plane number 0 ready to take off.
   0: Plane 1 landed; in queue 0 units.
       Plane number 0 took off after 0 time units in the takeoff queue.
       Plane number 1 ready to take off.
   1: Plane number 1 took off after 0 time units in the takeoff queue.
       Plane number 2 ready to take off.
       Plane number 3 ready to take off.
   2: Plane number 2 took off after 0 time units in the takeoff queue.
       Plane number 4 ready to land.
       Plane number 5 ready to take off.

3: Plane number 4 landed after 0 time units in the takeoff queue.

Plane number 6 ready to land.

Plane number 7 ready to land.

Plane number 8 ready to take off.

Plane number 9 ready to take off.

4: Plane number 6 landed after 0 time units in the takeoff queue.

Plane number 10 ready to land.

Plane number 11 ready to take off.

5: Plane number 7 landed after 1 time unit in the takeoff queue.

Plane number 12 ready to land.

6: Plane number 10 landed after 1 time unit in the takeoff queue.

7: Plane number 12 landed after 1 time unit in the takeoff queue.

Plane number 13 ready to land.

Plane number 14 ready to take off.

takeoff queue is full   Plane number 14 told to try to takeoff again later.

8: Plane number 13 landed after 0 time units in the takeoff queue.

9: Plane number 3 took off after 7 time units in the takeoff queue.

10: Plane number 5 took off after 7 time units in the takeoff queue.

11: Plane number 8 took off after 7 time units in the takeoff queue.

Plane number 15 ready to take off.

12: Plane number 9 took off after 8 time units in the takeoff queue.

Plane number 16 ready to land.

Plane number 17 ready to land.

13: Plane number 16 landed after 0 time units in the takeoff queue.

Plane number 18 ready to land.

14: Plane number 17 landed after 1 time unit in the takeoff queue.

15: Plane number 18 landed after 1 time unit in the takeoff queue.

Plane number 19 ready to land.

Plane number 20 ready to take off.

16: Plane number 19 landed after 0 time units in the takeoff queue.

17: Plane number 11 took off after 12 time units in the takeoff queue.

18: Plane number 15 took off after 6 time units in the takeoff queue.

19: Plane number 20 took off after 3 time units in the takeoff queue.

both queues are empty   20: Runway is idle.

Eventually, after many more steps of the simulation, we get a statistical summary.

summary

Simulation has concluded after 1000 time units.

Total number of planes processed	970
Total number of planes asking to land	484
Total number of planes asking to take off	486
Total number of planes accepted for landing	484
Total number of planes accepted for takeoff	423
Total number of planes refused for landing	0
Total number of planes refused for takeoff	63
Total number of planes that landed	483
Total number of planes that took off	422
Total number of planes left in landing queue	1
Total number of planes left in takeoff queue	1
Percentage of time runway idle	9.5 %
Average wait in landing queue	0.36646 time units
Average wait in takeoff queue	4.63744 time units
Average observed rate of planes wanting to land	0.484 time units
Average observed rate of planes wanting to take off	0.486 time units

Notice that the last two statistics, giving the observed rates of planes asking for landing and departure permission, do match the expected values put in at the beginning of the run (within a reasonable range): This outcome should give us some confidence that the pseudo-random number algorithm of Appendix B really does simulate an appropriate Poisson distribution.

Programming Projects 3.5

P1. Combine all the functions and methods for the airport simulation into a complete program. Experiment with several sample runs of the airport simulation, adjusting the values for the expected numbers of planes ready to land and take off. Find approximate values for these expected numbers that are as large as possible subject to the condition that it is very unlikely that a plane must be refused service. What happens to these values if the maximum size of the queues is increased or decreased?

P2. Modify the simulation to give the airport two runways, one always used for landings and one always used for takeoffs. Compare the total number of planes that can be served with the number for the one-runway airport. Does it more than double?

P3. Modify the simulation to give the airport two runways, one usually used for landings and one usually used for takeoffs. If one of the queues is empty, then both runways can be used for the other queue. Also, if the landing queue is full and another plane arrives to land, then takeoffs will be stopped and both runways used to clear the backlog of landing planes.

P4. Modify the simulation to have three runways, one always reserved for each of landing and takeoff and the third used for landings unless the landing queue is empty, in which case it can be used for takeoffs.

P5. Modify the original (one-runway) simulation so that when each plane arrives to land, it will have (as one of its data members) a (randomly generated) fuel level, measured in units of time remaining. If the plane does not have enough fuel to wait in the queue, it is allowed to land immediately. Hence the planes in the landing queue may be kept waiting additional units, and so may run out of fuel themselves. Check this out as part of the landing function, and find about how busy the airport can become before planes start to crash from running out of fuel.

P6. Write a stub to take the place of the random-number function. The stub can be used both to debug the program and to allow the user to control exactly the number of planes arriving for each queue at each time unit.

POINTERS AND PITFALLS

1. Before choosing implementations, be sure that all the data structures and their associated operations are fully specified on the abstract level.

2. In choosing between implementations, consider the necessary operations on the data structure.

3. If every object of **class** A has all the properties of an object of **class** B, implement **class** A as a derived class of B.

4. Consider the requirements of derived classes when declaring the members of a base class.

5. Implement is-a relationships between classes by using public inheritance.

6. Implement has-a relationships between classes by layering.

7. Use Poisson random variables to model random event occurrences.

REVIEW QUESTIONS

3.1   **1.** Define the term *queue*. What operations can be done on a queue?

2. How is a circular array implemented in a linear array?

3. List three different implementations of queues.

4. Explain the difference between *has-a* and *is-a* relationships between classes.

3.4   **5.** Define the term *simulation*.

REFERENCES FOR FURTHER STUDY

Queues are a standard topic covered by all data structures books. Most modern texts take the viewpoint of separating properties of data structures and their operations from the implementation of the data structures. Two examples of such books are:

JIM WELSH, JOHN ELDER, and DAVID BUSTARD, *Sequential Program Structures*, Prentice-Hall International, London, 1984, 385 pages.

DANIEL F. STUBBS and NEIL W. WEBRE, *Data Structures with Abstract Data Types and Pascal*, Brooks/Cole Publishing Company, Monterey, Calif., 1985, 459 pages.

For many topics concerning queues, the best source for additional information, historical notes, and mathematical analysis is KNUTH, volume 1 (reference in Chapter 2).

An elementary survey of computer simulations appears in *Byte* 10 (October 1985), 149–251. A simulation of the National Airport in Washington, D.C., appears on pp. 186–190.

A useful discussion of the possible relationships between classes and appropriate C++ implementations of these relationships is given in

SCOTT MEYERS, *Effective C++*, second edition, Addison-Wesley, Reading, Mass., 1997.

Linked Stacks and Queues

4

T HIS chapter introduces linked implementations of data structures. The chapter begins with a review of the use of dynamically allocated memory in C++. Next come implementations of linked stacks and queues. As an application, we derive a class to represent polynomials and use it to implement a reverse-Polish calculator for polynomials. The chapter closes with a review of the principles of abstract data types.

4.1 POINTERS AND LINKED STRUCTURES

4.1.1 Introduction and Survey

1. The Problem of Overflow

If we implement a data structure by storing all the data within arrays, then the arrays must be declared to have some size that is fixed when the program is written, and that therefore cannot be changed while the program is running. When writing a program, we must decide on the maximum amount of memory that will be needed for our arrays and set this aside in the declarations. If we run the program on a small sample, then much of this space will never be used. If we decide to run the program on a large set of data, then we may exhaust the space set aside and encounter overflow, even when the computer memory itself is not fully used, simply because our original bounds on the array were too small.

misallocation of space
Even if we are careful to declare our arrays large enough to use up all the available memory, we can still encounter overflow, since one array may reach its limit while a great deal of unused space remains in others. Since different runs of the same program may cause different structures to grow or shrink, it may be impossible to tell before the program actually executes which structures will overflow.

Modern languages, including C++, provide constructions that allow us to keep data structures in memory without using arrays, whereby we can avoid these difficulties.

2. Pointers

The C++ construction that we use is a pointer. A *pointer*, also called a *link* or a *reference*, is defined to be an object, often a variable, that stores the location (that is the machine address) of some other object, typically of a structure containing data that we wish to manipulate. If we use pointers to locate all the data in which we are interested, then we need not be concerned about where the data themselves are actually stored, since by using a pointer, we can let the computer system itself locate the data when required.

3. Diagram Conventions

Figure 4.1 shows pointers to several objects. Pointers are generally depicted as arrows and the referenced objects as rectangular boxes. In the figures throughout this book, variables containing pointers are generally shown as emanating from colored boxes or circles. Colored circles generally denote ordinary variables that contain pointers; colored boxes contain pointers that are parts of larger objects.

pointers referring nowhere
Hence, in the diagram, r is a pointer to the object "Lynn" and v is a pointer to the object "Jack." As you can see, the use of pointers is quite flexible: Two pointers can refer to the same object, as t and u do in Figure 4.1, or a pointer can refer to no object at all. We denote this latter situation within diagrams by the electrical *ground symbol*, as shown for pointer s.

113

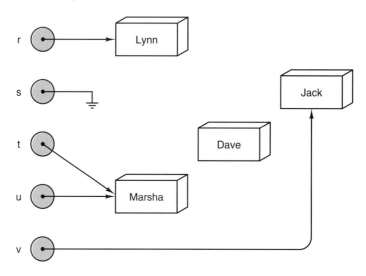

Figure 4.1. Pointers to objects

garbage

Care must be exercised when using pointers, moreover, to be sure that, when they are moved, no object is lost. In the diagram, the object "**Dave**" is lost, with no pointer referring to it, and therefore there is no way to find it. In such a situation, we shall say that the object has become *garbage*. Although a small amount of garbage does little harm, if we allow garbage to mount up, it can eventually occupy all of our available memory in the computer and smother our program. Therefore, in our work, we shall always strive to avoid the creation of garbage.

4. Linked Structures

linked list

In Chapters 2 and 3, we implemented stacks and queues by storing elements of the associated structure in an array. In this chapter, we illustrate how to use pointers to obtain a different implementation, where elements of the structure are linked together. The idea of a *linked list* is to augment every element of a list structure with a pointer giving the location of the next element in the list. This idea is illustrated in Figure 4.2.

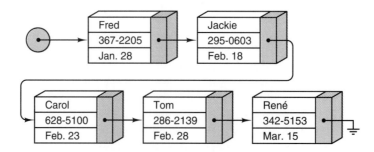

Figure 4.2. A linked list

analogies

As you can see from the illustration, a linked list is simple in concept. It uses the same idea as a children's treasure hunt, where each clue that is found tells where to find the next one. Or consider friends passing a popular cassette around. Fred has it, and has promised to give it to Jackie. Carol asks Jackie if she can borrow it, and then will next share it with Tom. And so it goes. A linked list may be considered analogous to following instructions where each instruction is given out only upon completion of the previous task. There is then no inherent limit on the number of tasks to be done, since each task may specify a new instruction, and there is no way to tell in advance how many instructions there are. The stack implementation studied in Section 2.2, on the other hand, is analogous to a list of instructions written on a single sheet of paper. It is then possible to see all the instructions in advance, but there is a limit to the number of instructions that can be written on the single sheet of paper.

With some practice in their use, you will find that linked structures are as easy to work with as structures implemented within arrays. The methods differ substantially, however, so we must spend some time developing new programming skills. Before we turn to this work, let us consider a few more general observations.

5. Contiguous and Linked Lists

definitions

The word **contiguous** means *in contact, touching, adjoining*. The entries in an array are contiguous, and we speak of a list kept in an array as a **contiguous list**. We can then distinguish as desired between contiguous lists and linked lists, and we use the unqualified word *list* only to include both. The same convention applies to stacks, queues, and other data structures.

6. Dynamic Memory Allocation

multitasking and time sharing

As well as preventing unnecessary overflow problems caused by running out of space in arrays, the use of pointers has advantages in a multitasking or time-sharing environment. If we use arrays to reserve in advance the maximum amount of memory that our task might need, then this memory is assigned to it and will be unavailable for other tasks. If it is necessary to page our task out of memory, then there may be time lost as unused memory is copied to and from a disk. Instead of using arrays to hold all our data, we can begin very small, with space only for the program instructions and simple variables, and whenever we need space for more data, we can request the system for the needed memory. Similarly, when an item is no longer needed, its space can be returned to the system, which can then assign it to another task. In this way, a program can start small and grow only as necessary, so that when it is small, it can run more efficiently, and, when necessary, it can grow to the limits of the computer system.

advantages of dynamic memory allocation

Even with only one task executing at a time, this dynamic control of memory can prove useful. During one part of a task, a large amount of memory may be needed for some purpose, which can later be released and then allocated again for another purpose, perhaps now containing data of a completely different type than before.

4.1.2 Pointers and Dynamic Memory in C++

Most modern programming languages, including C++, provide powerful facilities for processing pointers, as well as standard functions for requesting additional memory and for releasing memory during program execution.

1. Automatic and Dynamic Objects

Objects that can be used during execution of a C++ program come in two varieties. *automatic objects* *Automatic objects* are those that are declared and named, as usual, while writing the program. Space for them is explicitly allocated by the compiler and exists as long as the block of the program in which they are declared is running. The programmer need not worry about whether storage space will exist for an automatic object, or whether the storage used for such an object will be cleaned up after it is used. *Dynamic objects* are created (and perhaps destroyed) during program execution. *dynamic objects* Since dynamic objects do not exist while the program is compiled, but only when it is run, they are not assigned names while it is being written. Moreover, the storage occupied by dynamic objects must be managed entirely by the programmer.

The only way to access a dynamic object is by using pointers. Once it is created, however, a dynamic object does contain data and must have a type like any other object. Thus we can talk about creating a new dynamic object of type x and setting a pointer to point to it, or of moving a pointer from one dynamic object of type x to another, or of returning a dynamic object of type x to the system.

Automatic objects, on the other hand, cannot be explicitly created or destroyed during execution of the block in which they are declared. They come into existence automatically when the block begins execution and disappear when execution ends.

Pointer variables can be used to point to automatic objects: This creates a *aliases* second name, or *alias*, for the object. The object can then be changed using one name and later used with the other name, perhaps without the realization that it had been changed. Aliases are therefore dangerous and should be avoided as much as possible.

2. C++ Notation

C++ uses an asterisk (star) * to denote a pointer. If Item denotes the type of data in *pointer type* which we are interested, then a pointer to such an object has the type Item *. For example, we can make a declaration:

Item *item_ptr;

The verbal translation of any C++ declaration is most easily formed by reading the tokens of the declaration from right to left. In this case, the tokens, read from the right, are item_ptr, *, and Item. Hence, we see that the declaration says that item_ptr is a pointer to an Item object.

Normally, we should only use a pointer of type Item * to store the address of an object of type Item. However, as we shall see later, it is also reasonable to store the address of an object from a derived **class** of Item in a pointer of type Item *.

3. Creating and Destroying Dynamic Objects

We can create dynamic objects with the C++ operator **new**. The operator **new** is invoked with an object type as its argument, and it returns the address of a newly created dynamic object of the appropriate type. If we are ever to use this dynamic object, we should immediately record its address in an appropriate pointer variable: Thus the **new** operator is most often applied on the right-hand side of a pointer assignment. For example, suppose that p has been declared as a pointer to type *creation of dynamic* Item. Then the statement
objects

$$p = \textbf{new } \text{Item};$$

creates a new dynamic object of type Item and assigns its location to the pointer p.

free store The dynamic objects that we create are actually kept in an area of computer memory called the *free store* (or the *heap*). Like all other resources, the free store is finite, and if we create enough dynamic objects, it can be exhausted. If the free store is full, then calls to the **new** operator will fail. In early implementations of C++ this failure was signaled by the return from **new** of a value of 0 rather than a legitimate machine address. In ANSI C++, an exception is generated to signal the failure of the **new** operator. However, the modified statement

$$p = \textbf{new}(\text{nothrow}) \text{ Item};$$

restores the traditional behavior of the **new** operator. In this text, we will assume the older behavior of the **new** operator. Our code should be modified using nothrow to run in an ANSI C++ environment. It follows that we should always check that the result of a call to **new** is nonzero to make sure that the call has succeeded.

deletion of dynamic To help us conserve the free store, C++ provides a second operator called **delete**
objects that disposes of dynamically allocated objects. The storage formerly occupied by such objects is returned to the free store for reuse. The operator **delete** is applied to a pointer that references a dynamic object, and it returns the space used by the referenced object to the system. For example, if p is a pointer to a dynamic object of type Item, the statement

$$\textbf{delete } p;$$

disposes of the object. After this **delete** statement is executed, the pointer variable p is undefined and so should not be used until it is assigned a new value.

The effects of the **new** and **delete** operators are illustrated in Figure 4.3.

4. Following the Pointers

We use a star ∗ to denote a *pointer* not only in the declarations of a C++ program, but also to access the object referenced by a pointer. In this context, the star appears not to the right of a type, but to the left of a pointer. Thus ∗p denotes the object to which *dereferencing pointers* p points. Again, the words *link* and *reference* are often used in this connection. The action of taking ∗p is sometimes called "dereferencing the pointer p."

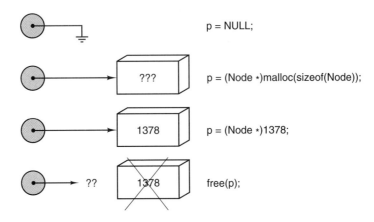

p = NULL;

p = (Node *)malloc(sizeof(Node));

p = (Node *)1378;

free(p);

Figure 4.3. Creating and disposing of dynamic objects

Note that a dereferenced pointer, such as *p, really is just the name of an object. In particular, we can use the expression *p on the left of an assignment. (Techni-

modifiable lvalue   cally, we say that a dereferenced pointer is a ***modifiable lvalue***.) For example, the assignment expression *p = 0 resets the value of the object referenced by p to 0. This assignment is illustrated in Figure 4.4.

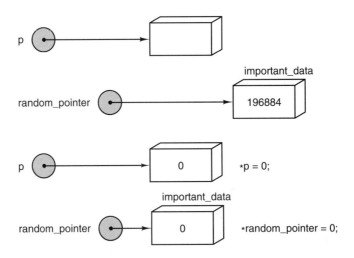

Figure 4.4. Modifying dereferenced pointers

This figure also shows that if a pointer random_pointer stores an illegal or uninitialized memory address, an assignment to the object *random_pointer can cause a particularly insidious type of error. For example, an uninitialized pointer random_pointer might happen to record the address of another variable, impor-

very dangerous   tant_data, say. Any assignment such as *random_pointer = 0, would (acciden-tally) alter the value of important_data. If we are lucky, this error will merely result in our program crashing at some later time. However, because this crash will prob-ably not occur immediately, its origin will be rather hard to explain. Worse still, our program might run to completion and silently produce unreliable results. Or it might destroy some other part of memory, producing effects that do not become apparent until we start some completely unrelated application later.

We shall now consider a useful safeguard against errors of this sort.

5. NULL Pointers

NULL pointer

Sometimes a pointer variable **p** has no dynamic object to which it currently refers. This situation can be established by the assignment

$$p = NULL;$$

and subsequently checked by a condition such as

$$\textbf{if } (p \: != NULL) \: \ldots .$$

In diagrams we reserve the electrical ground symbol

for NULL pointers. The value NULL is used in the same way as a constant for all pointer types and is generic in that the same value can be assigned to a variable of any pointer type. Actually, the value NULL is not part of the C++ language, but it is defined, as 0, in standard header files such as `<cstddef>` that we include in our utility header file.

undefined pointers
versus NULL *pointers*

Note carefully the distinction between a pointer variable whose value is undefined and a pointer variable whose value is NULL. The assertion p == NULL means that **p** currently points to no dynamic object. If the value of **p** is undefined, then **p** might point to any random location in memory.

If **p** is set as NULL, then any attempt to form the expression *p should cause our program to crash immediately. Although it is unpleasant to have to deal with any error, this crash is much easier to understand and correct than the problems that, as we have seen, are likely to result from an assignment through a random pointer.

Programming Precept

Uninitialized or random pointer objects should always be reset to NULL.
After deletion, a pointer object should be reset to NULL.

---

6. Dynamically allocated arrays

dynamic arrays

The **new** and **delete** keywords can be used to assign and delete contiguous blocks of dynamic storage for use as arrays. For example, if **array_size** represents an integer value, the declaration

$$\text{item\_array} = \textbf{new } \text{Item}[\text{array\_size}];$$

creates a dynamic array of Item objects. The entries of this array are indexed from **0** up to **array_size** − 1. We access a typical entry with an expression such as item_array[i].

For example, we can read in an array size from a user and create and use an appropriate array with the following statements. The resulting assignments are illustrated in Figure 4.5.

```
int size, *dynamic_array, i;
cout << "Enter an array size: " << flush;
cin >> size;
dynamic_array = new int[size];
for (i = 0; i < size; i++) dynamic_array[i] = i;
```

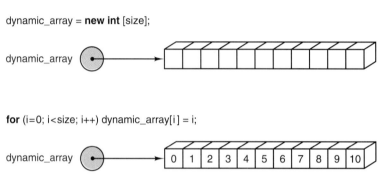

Figure 4.5. Dynamic arrays and pointers

Dynamically allocated array storage is returned with the operator **delete** [ ]. For example, we return the storage in dynamic_array by the statement

delete [ ] dynamic_array;

7. Pointer Arithmetic

pointer arithmetic

A pointer object p of type Item * can participate in assignment statements, can be checked for equality, and (as an argument) can appear in calls to functions. The programmer can also add and subtract integers from pointer values and obtain pointer values as results. For example, if i is an integer value, then p + i is an expression of type Item *. The value of p + i gives the memory address offset from p by i Item objects. That is, the expression p + i actually yields the address $p + n \times i$, where n is the number of bytes of storage occupied by a simple object of type Item.

It is also possible to print out the values of pointers, but since they are addresses assigned while the program is running, they may differ from one run of the program to the next. Moreover, their values (as addresses in the computer memory) are implementation features with which the programmer should not be directly concerned. (During debugging, it is, however, sometimes useful to print pointer values so that a programmer can check that appropriate equalities hold and that appropriate pointer assignments have been made.)

Note that rules and restrictions on using pointers do not apply to the dynamic variables to which the pointers refer. If p is a pointer, then *p is not usually a pointer (although it is legal for pointers to point to pointers) but a variable of some other type Item, and therefore *p can be used in any legitimate way for type Item.

8. Pointer assignment

assignment　With regard to assignment statements, it is important to remember the difference between p = q and *p = *q, both of which are legal (provided that p and q point to objects of the same type), but which have quite different effects. The first statement makes p point to the same object to which q points, but it does not change the value of either that object or of the other object that was formerly *p. The latter object will become garbage unless there is some other pointer variable that still refers to it. The second statement, *p = *q, on the contrary, copies the value of the object *q into the object *p, so that we now have two objects with the same value, with p and q pointing to the two separate copies. Finally, the two assignment statements p = *q and *p = q have mixed types and are illegal (except in the rare case that both p and q point to pointers of their same type!). Figure 4.6 illustrates these assignments.

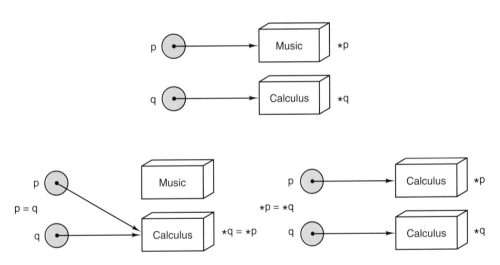

Figure 4.6. Assignment of pointer variables

9. Addresses of Automatic Objects

In C++, automatic objects are usually accessed simply by using their names—just as we have always done. However, at run time, we can recover and use the machine *the address operator*　addresses at which automatic objects are stored. For example, if x is a variable of type Item, then &x is a value of type Item * that gives the address of x. In this case, a declaration and assignment such as Item *ptr = &x would establish a pointer, ptr, to the object x.

We can also look up the address at which the initial element of an array is stored. This address is found by using the array's name without any attached [ ] operators. For example, given a declaration Item x[20] the assignment

$$\text{Item } *\text{ptr} = \text{x}$$

sets up a pointer ptr to the initial element of the array x. Observe that an assignment expression ptr = &(x[0]) could also be used to find this address. In exactly the same way, an assignment expression, p = &(x[i]), locates the address where x[i] is stored. However, since the location of x[i] is offset from that of x[0] by the storage required for i items, the expression x + i uses pointer arithmetic to give a simpler way of finding the address of x[i].

10. Pointers to Structures

Many programs make use of pointers to structures, and the C++ language includes an extra operator to help us access members of such structures. For example, if p is a pointer to an object that has a data member called the_data, then we could access this data member with the expression (*p).the_data. The rules of operator precedence prevent us from omitting the parentheses in this expression, and thus the common operation of following a link and then looking up a member becomes cumbersome. Happily, C++ provides the operator -> as a shorthand, and we can replace the expression (*p).the_data by an equivalent, but more convenient, expression p->the_data.

dereferencing operator

->

For example, given the definitions

```
class Fraction{
public:
    int numerator;
    int denominator;
};
Fraction *p;
```

we can access the members of the Fraction object referenced by p with an expression such as p->numerator = 0 or with a somewhat less convenient, but equivalent, expression (*p).numerator = 0.

4.1.3 The Basics of Linked Structures

With the tools of pointers and pointer types, we can now begin to consider the implementation of linked structures in C++. The place to start is with the definitions we shall need to set up the entries of a linked structure.

1. Nodes and Type Declarations

nodes and links

Recall from Figure 4.2 that a linked structure is made up of nodes, each containing both the information that is to be stored as an entry of the structure and a pointer telling where to find the next node in the structure. We shall refer to these nodes making up a linked structure as the **nodes** of the structure, and the pointers we often call **links**. Since the link in each node tells where to find the next node of the structure, we shall use the name **next** to designate this link.

We shall use a **struct** rather than a **class** to implement nodes. The only difference between a **struct** and a **class** is that, unless modified by the keywords **private** and **public**, members of a **struct** are public whereas members of a **class** are private. Thus, by using modifiers **public** and **private** to adjust the visibility of members, we can implement any structure as either a **struct** or a **class**. We shall adopt the convention of using a **struct** to implement structures that are not encapsulated, all of whose members can be accessed by clients. For example, our node structure is not encapsulated. However, although we can use nodes in their own right, we shall usually consider them as either **private** or **protected** members of other, encapsulated, data structures. In this context it is both safe and convenient to implement nodes without encapsulation. Translating these decisions into C++ yields:

```
struct Node {
//   data members
   Node_entry entry;
   Node *next;
//   constructors
   Node();
   Node(Node_entry item, Node *add_on = NULL);
};
```

use before definition

Note that we have an apparent problem of circularity in this definition. The member **next** of type **Node** * is part of the structure **Node**. On the other hand, it would appear that type **Node** should be defined before **Node** *. To avoid this problem of circular definitions, for pointer types (and only for pointer types) C++ relaxes the fundamental rule that every type identifier must be defined before being used. Instead, the type

$$Some\_type *$$

is valid in type definitions, even if **Some_type** has not yet been defined. (Before the program ends, however, **Some_type** must be defined or it is an error.)

space for pointers: word of storage

The reason why C++ can relax its rule in this way and still compile efficiently is that all pointers take the same amount of space in memory, often the same amount as an integer requires, no matter to what type they refer. We shall call the amount of

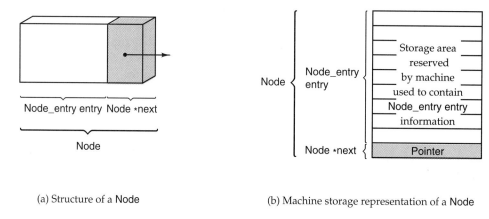

(a) Structure of a **Node**   (b) Machine storage representation of a **Node**

Figure 4.7. Structures containing pointers

space taken by a pointer one *word*.[1] Hence when encountering the declaration of a pointer type, the compiler can set aside the right amount of storage and postpone the problems of checking that all declarations and use of variables are consistent with the rules. For example, Figure 4.7 illustrates the structure and machine storage required to implement our **struct Node** definition.

2. Node Constructors

overloading

In addition to storage for the data, our node specification includes two constructors. These constructors are implemented as two overloaded versions of the function **Node :: Node**. In C++, we say that a function is *overloaded* if two or more different instances of the function are included within the same scope of a program. When a function is overloaded, the different implementations must have different sets or types of parameters, so that the compiler can use the arguments passed by a client to see which version of the function should be used. For example, our overloaded constructor has a first version with an empty parameter list, but the second version requires parameters.

multiple constructors

The first constructor does nothing except to set **next** to NULL as a safeguard for error checking. The second constructor is used to set the data members of a **Node** to the values specified as parameters. Note that in our prototype for the second constructor we have specified a *default* value of NULL for the second parameter. This allows us to call the second constructor with either its usual two arguments or with just a first argument. In the latter situation the second argument is given the default value NULL.

---

[1] More precisely, most computers store an integer as 32 bits, although 16-bit integers and 64-bit integers are also common, and some machines use other sizes, like 24 or 48 bits. Pointers also usually occupy 32 bits, but some compilers use other sizes, like 16, 24, or 64 bits. Some compilers even use two different sizes of pointers, called short and long pointers. Hence a pointer may take space usually called a half word, a word, or a double word, but we shall adopt the convention of always calling the space for a pointer *one word*.

```
Node :: Node( )
{
    next = NULL;
}
```

The second form accepts two parameters for initializing the data members.

```
Node :: Node(Node_entry item, Node *add_on)
{
    entry = item;
    next = add_on;
}
```

These constructors make it easy for us to attach nodes together into linked configurations. For example, the following code will produce the linked nodes illustrated in Figure 4.8.

```
Node first_node('a');         //   Node first_node stores data 'a'.
Node *p0 = &first_node;       //   p0 points to first_Node.
Node *p1 = new Node('b');     //   A second node storing 'b' is created.
p0->next = p1;                //   The second Node is linked after first_node.
Node *p2 = new Node('c', p0); //   A third Node storing 'c' is created.
    //   The third Node links back to the first node, *p0.
p1->next = p2;                //   The third Node is linked after the second Node.
```

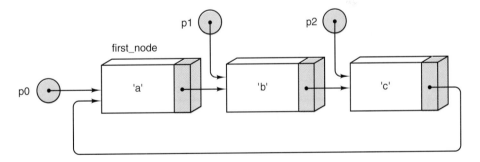

Figure 4.8. Linking nodes

Note that, in Figure 4.8 and in the code, we have given the first **Node** the name first_node, and it can be accessed either by this name or as *p0, since p0 points to it. The second and third nodes, however, are *not* given explicit names, and therefore these nodes can most easily be accessed by using the pointers p1 and p2, respectively.

Exercises 4.1

E1. Draw a diagram to illustrate the configuration of linked nodes that is created by the following statements.

```
Node *p0 = new Node('0');
Node *p1 = p0->next = new Node('1');
Node *p2 = p1->next = new Node('2', p1);
```

E2. Write the C++ statements that are needed to create the linked configuration of nodes shown in each of the following diagrams. For each part, embed these statements as part of a program that prints the contents of each node (both **data** and **next**), thereby demonstrating that the nodes have been correctly linked.

(a)

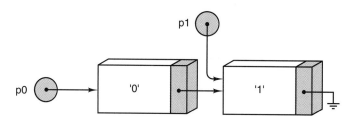

(b)

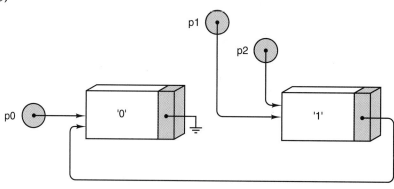

(c)

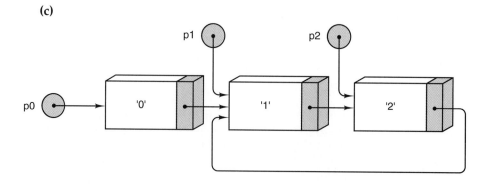

4.2 LINKED STACKS

In Section 2.2, we used an array of entries to create a contiguous implementation of a stack. It is equally easy to implement stacks as linked structures in dynamic memory.

consistency

We would like clients to see our new implementation as interchangeable with our former contiguous implementation. Therefore, our stacks must still contain entries of type **Stack_entry**. Moreover, we intend to build up stacks out of nodes, so we will need a declaration

typedef Stack_entry Node_entry;

to equate the types of the entries stored in stacks and nodes. Moreover, we must provide methods to *push* and *pop* entries of type **Stack_entry** to and from our stacks. Before we can write the operations *push* and *pop*, we must consider some more details of exactly how such a linked stack will be implemented.

The first question to settle is to determine whether the beginning or the end of the linked structure will be the top of the stack. At first glance, it may appear that (as for contiguous stacks) it might be easier to add a node at the end, but this choice makes popping the stack difficult: There is no quick way to find the node immediately before a given one in a linked structure, since the pointers stored in the structure give only one-way directions. Thus, after we remove the last element, finding the new element at the end might require tracing all the way from the head. To pop a linked stack, it is much better to make all additions and deletions at the beginning of the structure. Hence the top of the stack will always be the *first* node of the linked structure, as illustrated in Figure 4.9.

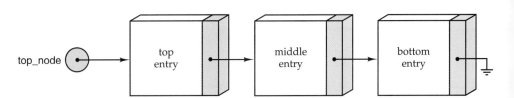

Figure 4.9. The linked form of a stack

declaration of type
Stack

Each linked structure needs to have a header member that points to its first node; for a linked stack this header member will always point to the top of the stack. Since each node of a linked structure points to the next one, we can reach all the nodes of a linked stack by following links from its first node. Thus, the only information needed to keep track of the data in a linked stack is the location of its top. The bottom of a **Stack** can always be identified as the **Node** that contains a NULL link.

We can therefore declare a linked stack by setting up a class having the top of the stack as its only data member:

```
class Stack {
public:
   Stack();
   bool empty() const;
   Error_code push(const Stack_entry &item);
   Error_code pop();
   Error_code top(Stack_entry &item) const;
protected:
   Node *top_node;
};
```

Since this class contains only one data member, we might think of dispensing with the class and referring to the top by the same name that we assign to the stack itself. There are four reasons, however, for using the class we have introduced.

➟ The most important reason is to maintain encapsulation: If we do not use a class to contain our stack, we lose the ability to set up methods for the stack.

➟ The second reason is to maintain the logical distinction between the stack itself, which is made up of all of its entries (each in a node), and the top of the stack, which is a pointer to a single node. The fact that we need only keep track of the top of the stack to find all its entries is irrelevant to this logical structure.

➟ The third reason is to maintain consistency with other data structures and other implementations, where structures are needed to collect several methods and pieces of information.

➟ Finally, keeping a stack and a pointer to its top as incompatible data types helps with debugging by allowing the compiler to perform better type checking.

empty stack   Let us start with an empty stack, which now means **top_node == NULL**, and consider how to add **Stack_entry item** as the first entry. We must create a new **Node** storing a copy of **item**, in dynamic memory. We shall access this **Node** with a pointer variable **new_top**. We must then copy the address stored in **new_top** to the **Stack** member **top_node**. Hence, pushing **item** onto the **Stack** consists of the instructions

Node *new_top = new Node(item);   top_node = new_top;

Notice that the constructor that creates the **Node** *new_top** sets its **next** pointer to the default value NULL.

pushing a linked stack   As we continue, let us suppose that we already have a nonempty **Stack**. In order to push a new entry onto the **Stack**, we need to add a **Stack_entry item** to it. The required adjustments of pointers are shown in Figure 4.10. First, we must create a new **Node**, referenced by a pointer **new_top**, that stores the value of **item**

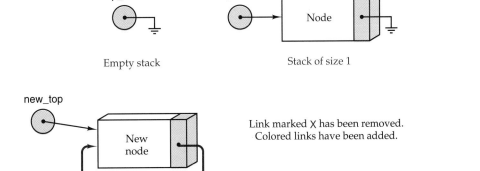

Empty stack

Stack of size 1

Link marked X has been removed.
Colored links have been added.

Figure 4.10. Pushing a node onto a linked stack

and points to the old top of the **Stack**. Then we must change **top_node** to point to the new node. The order of these two assignments is important: If we attempted to do them in the reverse order, the change of the top from its previous value would mean that we would lose track of the old part of the **Stack**. We thus obtain the following function:

```
Error_code Stack :: push(const Stack_entry &item)
/* Post:  Stack_entry item is added to the top of the Stack; returns success or returns
          a code of overflow if dynamic memory is exhausted. */
{
   Node *new_top = new Node(item, top_node);
   if (new_top == NULL) return overflow;
   top_node = new_top;
   return success;
}
```

Of course, our fundamental operations must conform to the earlier specifications, and so it is important to include error checking and to consider extreme cases. In particular, we must return an **Error_code** in the unlikely event that dynamic memory cannot be found for **new_top**.

One extreme case for the function is that of an empty **Stack**, which means **top_node == NULL**. Note that, in this case, the function works just as well to push the first entry onto an empty **Stack** as to push an additional entry onto a nonempty **Stack**.

popping a linked stack   It is equally simple to pop an entry from a linked **Stack**. This process is illustrated in Figure 4.11, whose steps translate to the following C++ code.

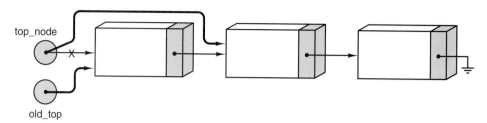

Figure 4.11. Popping a node from a linked stack

```
Error_code Stack :: pop( )
/* Post:  The top of the Stack is removed. If the Stack is empty the method returns
          underflow; otherwise it returns success. */
{
   Node *old_top = top_node;
   if (top_node ==  NULL) return underflow;
   top_node = old_top->next;
   delete old_top;
   return success;
}
```

When we reset the value of **top_node** in the method **pop**, the pointer **old_top** is the only link to the node that used to occupy the top position of the **Stack**. Therefore, once the function ends, and **old_top** goes out of scope, there will be no way for us to access that **Node**. We therefore delete **old_top**; otherwise garbage would be created. Of course, in small applications, the method would work equally well without the use of **delete**. However, if a client repeatedly used such an implementation, the garbage would eventually mount up to occupy all available memory and our client's program would suffocate.

Our linked stack implementation actually suffers from a number of subtle defects that we shall identify and rectify in the next section. We hasten to add that we know of no bugs in the methods that we have presented; however, it is possible for a client to make a **Stack** object malfunction. We must either document the limitations on the use of our **Stack** class, or we must correct the problems by adding in a number of extra features to the class.

Exercises 4.2   **E1.** Explain why we cannot use the following implementation for the method **push** in our linked **Stack**.

```
Error_code Stack :: push(Stack_entry item)
{
   Node new_top(item, top_node);
   top_node = new_top;
   return success;
}
```

E2. Consider a linked stack that includes a method size. This method size requires a loop that moves through the entire stack to count the entries, since the number of entries in the stack is not kept as a separate member in the stack record.

(a) Write a method size for a linked stack by using a loop that moves a pointer variable from node to node through the stack.

(b) Consider modifying the declaration of a linked stack to make a stack into a structure with two members, the top of the stack and a counter giving its size. What changes will need to be made to the other methods for linked stacks? Discuss the advantages and disadvantages of this modification compared to the original implementation of linked stacks.

Programming Project 4.2

P1. Write a demonstration program that can be used to check the methods written in this section for manipulating stacks. Model your program on the one developed in Section 3.4 and use as much of that code as possible. The entries in your stack should be characters. Your program should write a one-line menu from which the user can select any of the stack operations. After your program does the requested operation, it should inform the user of the result and ask for the next request. When the user wishes to push a character onto the stack, your program will need to ask what character to push.

Use the linked implementation of stacks, and be careful to maintain the principles of information hiding.

4.3 LINKED STACKS WITH SAFEGUARDS

Client code can apply the methods of the linked stack that we developed in the last section in ways that lead to the accumulation of garbage or that break the encapsulation of Stack objects. In this section, we shall examine in detail how these insecurities arise, and we shall look at three particular devices that are provided by the C++ language to alleviate these problems. The devices take the form of *destructor,* additional **class** methods, known as *destructors, copy constructors,* and *overloaded copy constructor,* *assignment operators.* These new methods replace compiler generated default *overloaded assignment* behavior and are often called silently (that is, without explicit action by a client). *operator* Thus, the addition of these safety features to our Stack class does not change its appearance to a client.

4.3.1 The Destructor

Suppose that a client runs a simple loop that declares a Stack object and pushes some data onto it. Consider, for example, the following code:

```
for (int i = 0; i < 1000000; i++) {
   Stack small;
   small.push(some_data);
}
```

In each iteration of the loop, a **Stack** object is created, data is inserted into dynamically allocated memory, and then the object goes out of scope. Suppose now that the client is using the linked **Stack** implementation of Section 4.2. As soon as the object **small** goes out of scope, the data stored in **small** becomes garbage. Over the course of a million iterations of the loop, a lot of garbage will accumulate. This problem should not be blamed on the (admittedly peculiar) behavior of our client: The loop would have executed without any problem with a contiguous **Stack** implementation, where all allocated space for member data is released every time a **Stack** object goes out of scope.

accumulation of garbage

It is surely the job of a linked stack implementation either to include documentation to warn the client not to let nonempty **Stack** objects go out of scope, or to clean up **Stack** objects before they go out of scope.

destructors

The C++ language provides class methods known as ***destructors*** that solve our problem. For every class, a destructor is a special method that is executed on objects of the class immediately before they go out of scope. Moreover, a client does not need to call a destructor explicitly and does not even need to know it is present. Thus, from the client's perspective, a class with a destructor can simply be substituted for a corresponding class without one.

Destructors are often used to delete dynamically allocated objects that would otherwise become garbage. In our case, we should simply add such a destructor to the linked **Stack** class. After this modification, clients of our class will be unable to generate garbage by letting nonempty **Stack** objects go out of scope.

The destructor must be declared as a class method without return type and without parameters. Its name is given by adding a ~ prefix to the corresponding class name. Hence, the prototype for a **Stack** destructor is:

destructor prefix ~

$$\text{Stack :: } \sim\text{Stack();}$$

Since the method **pop** is already programmed to delete single nodes, we can implement a **Stack** destructor by repeatedly popping **Stack** entries.

```
Stack :: ~Stack()            //    Destructor
/* Post: The Stack is cleared. */
{
   while (!empty())
      pop();
}
```

We shall adopt the policy that every linked structure should be equipped with a destructor to clear its objects before they go out of scope.

4.3.2 Overloading the Assignment Operator

Even after we add a destructor to our linked stack implementation, a suitably perverse client can still create a tremendous buildup of garbage with a simple loop. For example, the following client code first creates an outer **Stack** object and then runs a loop with instructions to set up and immediately reset an inner **Stack**.

```
Stack outer_stack;
for (int i = 0;  i < 1000000;  i++) {
    Stack inner_stack;
    inner_stack.push(some_data);
    inner_stack = outer_stack;
}
```

The statement inner_stack = outer_stack causes a serious problem for our **Stack** implementation. C++ carries out the resulting assignment by copying the data member **outer_stack.top_node**. This copying overwrites pointer **inner_stack.top_node**, *discarded memory*   so the contents of **inner_stack** are lost. As we illustrate in Figure 4.12, in every iteration of the loop, the previous inner stack data becomes garbage. The blame for the resulting buildup of garbage rests firmly with our **Stack** implementation. As before, no problem occurs when the client uses a contiguous stack implementation.

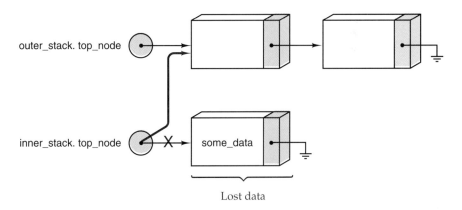

outer_stack. top_node

inner_stack. top_node   some_data

Lost data

Figure 4.12. The application of bitwise copy to a Stack

This figure also shows that the assignment operator has another undesired consequence. After the use of the operator, the two stack objects share their nodes. *alias problem:*   Hence, at the end of each iteration of the loop, any application of a **Stack** destructor *dangling pointers*   on **inner_stack** will result in the deletion of the outer stack. Worse still, such a deletion would leave the pointer **outer_stack.top_node** addressing what has become a random memory location.

The problems caused by using the assignment operator on a linked stack arise because it copies references rather than values: We summarize this situation by *reference semantics*   saying that **Stack** assignment has ***reference semantics***. In contrast, when the assignment operator copies the data in a structure, we shall say that it has ***value*** *value semantics*   ***semantics***. In our linked **Stack** implementation, either we must attach documentation to warn clients that assignment has reference semantics, or we must make the C++ compiler treat assignment differently.

In C++, we implement special methods, known as ***overloaded assignment op-*** *overloaded operators*   ***erators*** to redefine the effect of assignment. Whenever the C++ compiler translates an assignment expression of the form x = y, it first checks whether the class of **x** has an overloaded assignment operator. Only if such a method is absent will the

overloaded assignment

compiler translate the assignment as a bitwise copy of data members. Thus, to provide value semantics for **Stack** assignment, we should overload assignment for our **Stack** class.

There are several options for the declaration and implementation of this overloaded operator. A simple approach is to supply a prototype with **void** return type:

void Stack :: **operator** = (**const** Stack &original);

This declares a **Stack** method called **operator** = , the overloaded assignment operator, that can be invoked with the member selection operator in the usual way.

x.**operator** = (y);

Alternatively, the method can be invoked with the much more natural and convenient operator syntax:

x = y;

operator syntax

By looking at the type(s) of its operands, the C++ compiler can tell that it should use the overloaded operator rather than the usual assignment. We obtain operator syntax by omitting the period denoting member selection, the keyword **operator**, and the parentheses from the ordinary method invocation.

The implementation of the overloaded assignment operator for our **Stack** class proves to be quite tricky.

➡ First, we must make a copy of the data stacked in the calling parameter.

➡ Next, we must clear out any data already in the **Stack** object being assigned to.

➡ Finally, we must move the newly copied data to the **Stack** object.

```
void Stack :: operator = (const Stack &original)  //    Overload assignment
/* Post:  The Stack is reset as a copy of Stack original. */
{
  Node *new_top, *new_copy, *original_node = original.top_node;
  if (original_node ==  NULL) new_top = NULL;
  else {                     //    Duplicate the linked nodes
    new_copy = new_top = new Node(original_node->entry);
    while (original_node->next != NULL) {
      original_node = original_node->next;
      new_copy->next = new Node(original_node->entry);
      new_copy = new_copy->next;
    }
  }
  while (!empty())          //    Clean out old Stack entries
    pop();
  top_node = new_top;       //    and replace them with new entries.
}
```

Note that, in the implementation, we do need to **pop** all of the existing entries out of the **Stack** object whose value we are assigning. As a precaution, we first make a copy of the **Stack** parameter and then repeatedly apply the method **pop**. In this way, we ensure that our assignment operator does not lose objects in assignments such as x = x.

remaining defect:
multiple assignment

Although our overloaded assignment operator does succeed in giving **Stack** assignment value semantics, it still has one defect: A client cannot use the result of an assignment in an expression such as fist_stack = second_stack = third_stack. A very thorough implementation would return a reference of type **Stack &** to allow clients to write such an expression.

4.3.3 The Copy Constructor

One final insecurity that can arise with linked structures occurs when the C++ compiler calls for a copy of an object. For example, objects need to be copied when an argument is passed to a function by value. In C++, the default copy operation copies each data member of a class. Just as illustrated in Figure 4.12, the default copy operation on a linked **Stack** leads to a sharing of data between objects. In other words, the default copy operation on a linked **Stack** has reference semantics. This allows a malicious client to declare and run a function whose sole purpose is to destroy linked **Stack** objects:

```
void destroy_the_stack (Stack copy)
{
}
int main()
{
   Stack vital_data;
   destroy_the_stack(vital_data);
}
```

In this code, a copy of the **Stack** vital_data is passed to the function. The **Stack copy** shares its nodes with the **Stack** vital_data, and therefore when a **Stack** destructor is applied to **copy**, at the end of the function, vital_data is also destroyed.

copy constructor

Again, C++ provides a tool to fix this particular problem. Indeed, if we include a *copy constructor* as a member of our **Stack** class, our copy constructor will be invoked whenever the compiler needs to copy **Stack** objects. We can thus ensure that **Stack** objects are copied using value semantics.

For any class, a standard way to declare a ***copy constructor*** is as a constructor with one argument that is declared as a constant reference to an object of the class. Hence, a **Stack** copy constructor would normally have the following prototype:

Stack :: Stack(const Stack &original);

In our implementation of this constructor, we first deal with the case of copying an empty **Stack**. We then copy the first node, after which we run a loop to copy all of the other nodes.

```
Stack :: Stack(const Stack &original)   //   copy constructor
/* Post: The Stack is initialized as a copy of Stack original. */
{
   Node *new_copy, *original_node = original.top_node;
   if (original_node == NULL) top_node = NULL;
   else {                            //   Duplicate the linked nodes.
      top_node = new_copy = new Node(original_node->entry);
      while (original_node->next != NULL) {
         original_node = original_node->next;
         new_copy->next = new Node(original_node->entry);
         new_copy = new_copy->next;
      }
   }
}
```

This code is similar to our implementation of the overloaded assignment operator. However, in this case, since we are creating a new **Stack** object, we do not need to remove any existing stack entries.

In general, for every linked class, either we should include a copy constructor, or we should provide documentation to warn clients that objects are copied with reference semantics.

4.3.4 The Modified Linked-Stack Specification

We close this section by giving an updated specification for a linked stack. In this specification we include all of our proposed safety features.

```
class Stack {
public:
//   Standard Stack methods
   Stack();
   bool empty() const;
   Error_code push(const Stack_entry &item);
   Error_code pop();
   Error_code top(Stack_entry &item) const;
//   Safety features for linked structures
   ~Stack();
   Stack(const Stack &original);
   void operator = (const Stack &original);
protected:
   Node *top_node;
};
```

Exercises 4.3   **E1.** Suppose that x, y, and z are **Stack** objects. Explain why the overloaded assignment operator of Section 4.3.2 cannot be used in an expression such as x = y = z. Modify the prototype and implementation of the overloaded assignment operator so that this expression becomes valid.

E2. What is wrong with the following attempt to use the copy constructor to implement the overloaded assignment operator for a linked **Stack**?

```
void Stack :: operator = (const Stack &original)
{
    Stack new_copy(original);
    top_node = new_copy.top_node;
}
```

How can we modify this code to give a correct implementation?

4.4 LINKED QUEUES

In contiguous storage, queues were significantly harder to manipulate than were stacks, because it was necessary to treat straight-line storage as though it were arranged in a circle, and the extreme cases of full queues and empty queues caused difficulties. It is for queues that linked storage really comes into its own. Linked queues are just as easy to handle as are linked stacks. We need only keep two pointers, **front** and **rear**, that will point, respectively, to the beginning and the end of the queue. The operations of insertion and deletion are both illustrated in Figure 4.13.

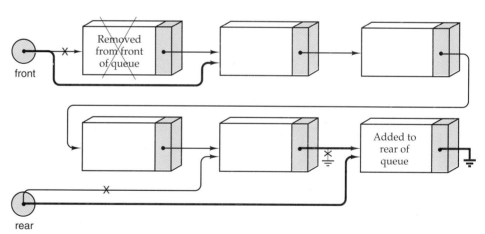

Figure 4.13. Operations on a linked queue

4.4.1 Basic Declarations

For all queues, we denote by **Queue_entry** the type designating the items in the queue. For linked implementations, we declare nodes as we did for linked structures in Section 4.1.3 and use a **typedef** statement to identify the types **Queue_entry** and **Node_entry**. In close analogy to what we have already done for stacks, we obtain the following specification:

type Queue

```
class Queue {
public:
//    standard Queue methods
   Queue();
   bool empty() const;
   Error_code append(const Queue_entry &item);
   Error_code serve();
   Error_code retrieve(Queue_entry &item) const;
//    safety features for linked structures
   ~Queue();
   Queue(const Queue &original);
   void operator = (const Queue &original);
protected:
   Node *front, *rear;
};
```

initialize   The first constructor initializes a queue as empty, as follows:

```
Queue :: Queue()
/* Post: The Queue is initialized to be empty. */
{
   front = rear = NULL;
}
```

Let us now turn to the method to append entries. To add an entry **item** to the rear of a queue, we write:

```
Error_code Queue :: append(const Queue_entry &item)
/* Post: Add item to the rear of the Queue and return a code of success or return
           a code of overflow if dynamic memory is exhausted. */
{
   Node *new_rear = new Node(item);
   if (new_rear == NULL) return overflow;
   if (rear == NULL) front = rear = new_rear;
   else {
      rear->next = new_rear;
      rear = new_rear;
   }
   return success;
}
```

The cases when the **Queue** is empty or not must be treated separately, since the addition of a **Node** to an empty **Queue** requires setting both **front** and **rear** to point to the new **Node**, whereas addition to a nonempty **Queue** requires changing only **rear**.

To serve an entry from the front of a Queue, we use the following function:

```
Error_code Queue :: serve( )
/* Post: The front of the Queue is removed.  If the Queue is empty, return an
        Error_code of underflow. */
{
   if (front ==  NULL) return underflow;
   Node *old_front = front;
   front = old_front->next;
   if (front ==  NULL) rear = NULL;
   delete old_front;
   return success;
}
```

Again the possibility of an empty Queue must be considered separately. Any attempt to delete from an empty Queue should generate an Error_code of underflow. It is, however, not an error for the Queue to become empty after a deletion, but then **rear** and **front** should both become NULL to indicate that the Queue has become empty. We leave the other methods of linked queues as exercises.

If you compare these algorithms for linked queues with those needed for contiguous queues, you will see that the linked versions are both conceptually easier and easier to program. We leave overloading the assignment operator and writing the destructor and copy constructor for a Queue as exercises.

4.4.2 Extended Linked Queues

Our linked implementation of a Queue provides the base class for other sorts of queue classes. For example, extended queues are defined as in Chapter 3. The following C++ code defining a derived **class** Extended_queue is identical to the corresponding code of Chapter 3.

```
class Extended_queue:  public Queue {
public:
   bool full( ) const;
   int size( ) const;
   void clear( );
   Error_code serve_and_retrieve(Queue_entry &item);
};
```

*default method
implementation*
Although this **class** Extended_queue has a linked implementation, there is no need to supply explicit methods for the copy constructor, the overloaded assignment operator, or the destructor. For each of these methods, the compiler generates a default implementation. The default method calls the corresponding method of the base Queue object. For example, the default destructor for an Extended_queue merely calls the linked Queue destructor: This will delete all dynamically allocated Extended_queue nodes. Because our **class** Extended_queue stores no linked data that is not already part of the **class** Queue, the compiler generated-defaults are exactly what we need.

The declared methods for the linked **class** Extended_queue need to be reprogrammed to make use of the linked data members in the base class. For example, the new method size must use a temporary pointer called window that traverses the Queue (in other words, it moves along the Queue and points at each Node in sequence).

```
int Extended_queue :: size( ) const
/* Post: Return the number of entries in the Extended_queue. */
{
   Node *window = front;
   int count = 0;
   while (window != NULL) {
      window = window->next;
      count++;
   }
   return count;
}
```

The other methods for the linked implementation of an extended queue are left as exercises.

Exercises 4.4

E1. Write the following methods for linked queues:

(a) the method **empty**,
(b) the method **retrieve**,
(c) the destructor,
(d) the copy constructor,
(e) the overloaded assignment operator.

E2. Write an implementation of the Extended_queue method full. In light of the simplicity of this method in the linked implementation, why is it still important to include it in the linked **class** Extended_queue?

E3. Write the following methods for the linked **class** Extended_queue:

(a) clear;
(b) serve_and_retrieve;

E4. For a linked Extended_queue, the function size requires a loop that moves through the entire queue to count the entries, since the number of entries in the queue is not kept as a separate member in the class. Consider modifying the declaration of a linked Extended_queue to add a count data member to the class. What changes will need to be made to all the other methods of the class? Discuss the advantages and disadvantages of this modification compared to the original implementation.

E5. A *circularly linked list*, illustrated in Figure 4.13, is a linked list in which the node at the tail of the list, instead of having a NULL pointer, points back to the node at the head of the list. We then need only one pointer tail to access both ends of the list, since we know that tail->next points back to the head of the list.

(a) If we implement a queue as a circularly linked list, then we need only one pointer tail (or rear) to locate both the front and the rear. Write the methods needed to process a queue stored in this way.

(b) What are the disadvantages of implementing this structure, as opposed to using the version requiring two pointers?

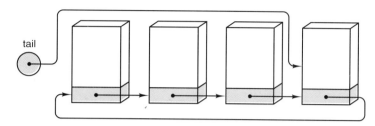

Figure 4.14. A circularly linked list with tail pointer

Programming Projects 4.4

P1. Assemble specification and method files, called queue.h and queue.c, for linked queues, suitable for use by an application program.

P2. Take the menu-driven demonstration program for an Extended_queue of characters in Section 3.4 and substitute the linked Extended_queue implementation files for the files implementing contiguous queues. If you have designed the program and the classes carefully, then the program should work correctly with no further change.

P3. In the airport simulation developed in Section 3.5, replace the implementations of contiguous queues with linked versions. If you have designed the classes carefully, the program should run in exactly the same way with no further change required.

4.5 APPLICATION: POLYNOMIAL ARITHMETIC

4.5.1 Purpose of the Project

In Section 2.3 we developed a program that imitates the behavior of a simple calculator doing addition, subtraction, multiplication, division, and perhaps some other operations. The goal of this section is to develop a similar calculator, but now one that performs these operations for polynomials rather than numbers.

reverse Polish calculator for polynomials

As in Section 2.3, we shall model a *reverse Polish* calculator where the operands (polynomials for us) are entered *before* the operation is specified. The operands are pushed onto a stack. When an operation is performed, it pops its operands from the stack and pushes its result back onto the stack. We reuse the conventions of Section 2.3 (which you may wish to review), so that ? denotes pushing an operand onto the stack, +, −, *, / represent arithmetic operations, and = means printing the top of the stack (but not popping it off). For example, the instructions ? a ? b + = mean to read two operands a and b, then calculate and print their sum.

4.5.2 The Main Program

main program

It is clear that we ought to implement a Polynomial class for use in our calculator. After this decision, the task of the calculator program becomes simple. We need to customize a generic stack implementation to make use of polynomial entries. Then the main program can declare a stack of polynomials, accept new commands, and perform them as long as desired.

```
int main( )
/* Post:  The program has executed simple polynomial arithmetic commands en-
          tered by the user.
   Uses:  The classes Stack and Polynomial and the functions introduction, instruc-
          tions, do_command, and get_command. */
{
   Stack stored_polynomials;
   introduction( );
   instructions( );
   while (do_command(get_command( ), stored_polynomials));
}
```

This program is almost identical to the main program of Section 2.3, and its auxiliary function **get_command** is identical to the earlier version.

1. Polynomial Methods

user commands   As in Section 2.3, we represent the commands that a user can type by the characters ? , = , + , − , * , / , where ? requests input of a polynomial from the user, = prints the result of an operation, and the remaining symbols denote addition, subtraction, multiplication, and division, respectively.

Most of these commands will need to invoke **Polynomial** class methods; hence we must now decide on the form of some of these methods.

We will need a method to add a pair of polynomials. One convenient way to implement this method is as a method, **equals_sum**, of the **Polynomial** class.
polynomial methods   Thus, if **p, q, r** are **Polynomial** objects, the expression **p.equals_sum(q, r)** replaces **p** by the sum of the polynomials **q** and **r**. We shall implement similar methods called **equals_difference**, **equals_product**, and **equals_quotient** to perform other arithmetic operations on polynomials.

The user commands = and ? will lead us to call on **Polynomial** methods to print out and read in polynomials. Thus we shall suppose that **Polynomial** objects have methods without parameters called **print** and **read** to accomplish these tasks.

2. Performing Commands

Given our earlier decisions, we can immediately write the function **do_command**.
Do a user command   We present an abbreviated form of the function, where we have coded only a few of the possibilities in its main switch statement.

```
bool do_command(char command, Stack &stored_polynomials)
/* Pre:  The first parameter specifies a valid calculator command.
   Post:  The command specified by the first parameter has been applied to the
          Stack of Polynomial objects given by the second parameter. A result of
          true is returned unless command == 'q'.
   Uses:  The classes Stack and Polynomial. */
```

```
                    {
                      Polynomial p, q, r;
                      switch (command) {
                      case '?':
 read Polynomial        p.read();
                        if (stored_polynomials.push(p) == overflow)
                          cout << "Warning: Stack full, lost polynomial" << endl;
                        break;
                      case '=':
 print Polynomial       if (stored_polynomials.empty())
                          cout << "Stack empty" << endl;
                        else {
                          stored_polynomials.top(p);
                          p.print();
                        }
                        break;
                      case '+':
 add polynomials        if (stored_polynomials.empty())
                          cout << "Stack empty" << endl;
                        else {
                          stored_polynomials.top(p);
                          stored_polynomials.pop();
                          if (stored_polynomials.empty()) {
                            cout << "Stack has just one polynomial" << endl;
                            stored_polynomials.push(p);
                          }
                          else {
                            stored_polynomials.top(q);
                            stored_polynomials.pop();
                            r.equals_sum(q, p);
                            if (stored_polynomials.push(r) == overflow)
                              cout << "Warning: Stack full, lost polynomial" << endl;
                          }
                        }
                        break;

                      //   Add options for further user commands.
                      case 'q':
 quit                   cout << "Calculation finished." << endl;
                        return false;
                      }
                      return true;
                    }
```

In this function, we need to pass the **Stack** parameter by reference, because its value might need to be modified. For example, if the command parameter is **+**, then we normally pop two polynomials off the stack and push their sum back onto it. The function **do_command** also allows for an additional user command, **q**, that quits the program.

3. Stubs and Testing

We have now designed enough of our program that we should pause to compile it, debug it, and test it to make sure that what has been done so far is correct.

For the task of compiling the program, we must, of course, supply stubs for all the missing elements. Since we can use any of our earlier stack implementations, the only missing part is the class **Polynomial**. At present, however, we have not even decided how to store polynomial objects.

For testing, let us run our program as an ordinary reverse Polish calculator operating on real numbers. Thus we need a stub class declaration that uses real numbers in place of polynomials.

temporary type declaration

```
class Polynomial {
public:
   void read( );
   void print( );
   void equals_sum(Polynomial p, Polynomial q);
   void equals_difference(Polynomial p, Polynomial q);
   void equals_product(Polynomial p, Polynomial q);
   Error_code equals_quotient(Polynomial p, Polynomial q);
private:
   double value;
};
```

Since the method **equals_quotient** must detect attempted division by 0, it has an **Error_code** return type, whereas the other methods do not detect errors and so have **void** return type. The following function is typical of the stub methods that are needed.

```
void Polynomial :: equals_sum(Polynomial p, Polynomial q)
{
   value = p.value + q.value;
}
```

Producing a skeleton program at this time also ensures that the stack and utility packages are properly integrated into the program. The program, together with its stubs, should operate correctly whether we use a contiguous or a linked **Stack** implementation.

4.5.3 The Polynomial Data Structure

Let us now turn to our principal task by deciding how to represent polynomials and writing methods to manipulate them. If we carefully consider a polynomial such as

$$3x^5 - 2x^3 + x^2 + 4$$

essence of a polynomial

we see that the important information about the polynomial is contained in the coefficients and exponents of x; the variable x itself is really just a place holder (a dummy variable). Hence, for purposes of calculation, we may think of a polynomial as made up of *terms*, each of which consists of a *coefficient* and an *exponent*. In a

computer, we could similarly represent a polynomial as a *list* of pairs of coefficients and exponents. Each of these pairs constitutes a structure that we shall call a Term. We implement a Term as a **struct** with a constructor:

Term

```
struct Term {
    int degree;
    double coefficient;
    Term (int exponent = 0, double scalar = 0);
};
Term :: Term(int exponent, double scalar)
/* Post: The Term is initialized with the given coefficient and exponent, or with
          default parameter values of 0. */
{
    degree = exponent;
    coefficient = scalar;
}
```

A polynomial is represented as a list of terms. We must then build into our methods rules for performing arithmetic on two such lists. When we do this work, however, we find that we continually need to remove the first entry from the list, and we find that we need to insert new entries only at the end of the list. In other words, we find that the arithmetic operations treat the list as a queue, or, more precisely, as an *extended queue*, since we frequently need methods such as clear and serve_and_retrieve, as well as deletion from the front and insertion at the rear.

implementation of a polynomial

Should we use a contiguous or a linked queue? If, in advance, we know a bound on the degree of the polynomials that can occur and if the polynomials that occur have nonzero coefficients in almost all their possible terms, then we should probably do better with contiguous queues. But if we do not know a bound on the degree, or if polynomials with only a few nonzero terms are likely to appear, then we shall find linked storage preferable. Let us in fact decide to represent a polynomial as an extended linked queue of *terms*. This representation is illustrated in Figure 4.15.

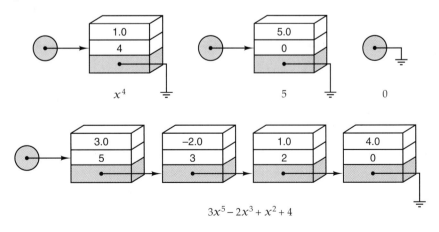

Figure 4.15. Polynomials as linked queues of terms

assumptions   Each node contains one term of a polynomial, and we shall keep only nonzero terms in the queue. The polynomial that is always 0 (that is, it consists of only a 0 term) will be represented by an empty queue. We call this the ***zero polynomial*** or say that it is ***identically 0***.

Our decisions about the Polynomial data structure suggest that we might implement it as a class *derived* from an extended queue. This will allow us to reuse methods for Extended_queue operations, and we can concentrate on coding just those additional methods that are special to polynomials.

As a final check before going ahead with such a derived class implementation, we should ask: Is a Polynomial an Extended_queue?

An Extended_queue allows methods such as **serve** that do not apply directly to polynomials, so we must admit that a Polynomial is not really an Extended_queue. (In coding an implementation this drawback would become clear if we tried to prevent clients from serving entries from Polynomial objects.) Thus, although it would be useful to reuse the data members and function code from the **class** Extended_queue in implementing our **class** Polynomial, we should reject a simple inheritance implementation because the two classes do not exhibit an is-a relationship (see page 83).

private inheritance   The C++ language provides a second form of inheritance, called ***private inheritance***, which is exactly what we need. Private inheritance models an "is implemented in terms of" relationship between classes. We shall therefore define the **class** Polynomial to be privately inherited from the **class** Extended_queue. This means that Extended_queue members and methods are available in the implementation of the class Polynomial, but they are not available to clients using a Polynomial.

Polynomial

```
class Polynomial: private Extended_queue {  //    Use private inheritance.
public:
    void read();
    void print() const;
    void equals_sum(Polynomial p, Polynomial q);
    void equals_difference(Polynomial p, Polynomial q);
    void equals_product(Polynomial p, Polynomial q);
    Error_code equals_quotient(Polynomial p, Polynomial q);
    int degree() const;
private:
    void mult_term(Polynomial p, Term t);
};
```

We have incorporated a useful method, Polynomial :: degree(), that returns the degree of the leading term in a Polynomial, together with an auxiliary function that multiplies a Polynomial by a single Term.

We have not yet considered the order of storing the terms of the polynomial. If we allow them to be stored in any order, then it might be difficult to recognize that

$$x^5 + x^2 - 3 \quad \text{and} \quad -3 + x^5 + x^2 \quad \text{and} \quad x^2 - 3 + x^5$$

restriction   all represent the same polynomial. Hence we adopt the usual convention that the terms of every polynomial are stored in the order of decreasing exponent within the linked queue. We further assume that no two terms have the same exponent and that no term has a zero coefficient. (Recall that the polynomial that is identically 0 is represented as an empty queue.)

4.5.4 Reading and Writing Polynomials

With polynomials implemented as linked queues, writing out a polynomial is a simple matter of looping through the nodes of the queue and printing out data for each node. The intricate nature of the following **print** method is a reflection of the

standard conventions   customary but quite special conventions for writing polynomials, rather than any conceptual difficulty in working with our data structure. In particular, our method suppresses any initial $+$ sign, any coefficients and exponents with value 1, and any reference to x^0: Thus, for example, we are careful to print $3x^2 + x + 5$ and $-3x^2 + 1$ rather than $+3x^2 + 1x^1 + 5x^0$ and $-3x^2 + 1x^0$.

```
void Polynomial :: print( ) const
/* Post:  The Polynomial is printed to cout. */
{
   Node *print_node = front;
   bool first_term = true;
   while (print_node != NULL) {
      Term &print_term = print_node->entry;
      if (first_term) {              //   In this case, suppress printing an initial '+'.
         first_term = false;
         if (print_term.coefficient < 0) cout << " − ";
      }
      else if (print_term.coefficient < 0) cout << " − ";
      else cout << " + ";
      double r = (print_term.coefficient >= 0)
                  ? print_term.coefficient : −(print_term.coefficient);
      if (r != 1) cout << r;
      if (print_term.degree > 1) cout << " X^" << print_term.degree;
      if (print_term.degree == 1) cout << " X";
      if (r == 1 && print_term.degree == 0) cout << " 1";
      print_node = print_node->next;
   }
   if (first_term)
      cout << "0";                    //   Print 0 for an empty Polynomial.
   cout << endl;
}
```

print Polynomial

As we read in a new polynomial, we shall construct a new **Polynomial** object and then append an entry to the object for each term (coefficient-exponent pair) that we read from the input.

Like all functions that accept input directly from the user, our function for reading a new polynomial must carefully check its input to make sure that it meets the requirements of the problem. Making sure that the exponents in the polynomial appear in descending order is one of the larger tasks for our function. To do this, we continually compare the exponent of the current term with that of the previous term.

We shall use the special values of either a coefficient of 0.0 or an exponent of 0 to stop the reading process: Recall that a term with 0.0 as a coefficient is never stored in the polynomial, and, since the exponents are in descending order, any term with an exponent of 0 must always be last. The resulting function follows.

read Polynomial

```
void Polynomial :: read( )
/* Post: The Polynomial is read from cin. */
{
   clear( );
   double coefficient;
   int last_exponent, exponent;
   bool first_term = true;
   cout ≪ "Enter the coefficients and exponents for the polynomial, "
        ≪ "one pair per line.  Exponents must be in descending order." ≪ endl
        ≪ "Enter a coefficient of 0 or an exponent of 0 to terminate." ≪ endl;
   do {
      cout ≪ "coefficient? " ≪ flush;
      cin  ≫ coefficient;
      if (coefficient != 0.0) {
         cout ≪ "exponent? " ≪ flush;
         cin  ≫ exponent;
         if ((!first_term && exponent >= last_exponent) || exponent < 0) {
            exponent = 0;
            cout ≪ "Bad exponent: Polynomial terminates without its last term."
                 ≪ endl;
         }
         else {
            Term new_term(exponent, coefficient);
            append(new_term);
            first_term = false;
         }
         last_exponent = exponent;
      }
   } while (coefficient != 0.0 && exponent != 0);
}
```

4.5.5 Addition of Polynomials

We now study one of the fundamental operations on polynomials, addition of two polynomials.

The requirement that the terms of a **Polynomial** appear with descending exponents in the corresponding **Extended_queue** greatly simplifies their addition. To add two polynomials, we need only scan through them once each. If we find terms with the same exponent in the two polynomials, then we add the coefficients; otherwise, we copy the term with larger exponent into the sum and move on to the next term of that polynomial. We must also be careful not to include terms with zero coefficient in the sum. Our method destroys the data in both parameters, and therefore we pass them both by value.

add polynomials

```
void Polynomial :: equals_sum(Polynomial p, Polynomial q)
/* Post: The Polynomial object is reset as the sum of the two parameters. */
{
  clear();
  while (!p.empty() || !q.empty()) {
    Term p_term, q_term;
    if (p.degree() > q.degree()) {
      p.serve_and_retrieve(p_term);
      append(p_term);
    }

    else if (q.degree() > p.degree()) {
      q.serve_and_retrieve(q_term);
      append(q_term);
    }

    else {
      p.serve_and_retrieve(p_term);
      q.serve_and_retrieve(q_term);
      if (p_term.coefficient + q_term.coefficient != 0) {
        Term answer_term(p_term.degree,
                         p_term.coefficient + q_term.coefficient);
        append(answer_term);
      }
    }
  }
}
```

The method begins by clearing any terms currently stored in the **Polynomial** object that records the answer. We complete the implementation with a loop that peels off a leading term from one or both of the polynomial parameters and adds these terms onto our answer. We first decide which parameter or parameters should provide the next term according to their respective degrees.

Polynomial degrees are calculated by the method **degree()**, which has to retrieve() the leading term and return its degree. We follow one of the standard mathematical conventions and assign a degree of -1 to the zero polynomial.

```
int Polynomial :: degree( ) const
```
/ Post: If the Polynomial is identically 0, a result of −1 is returned. Otherwise the
        degree of the Polynomial is returned. */*

determine degree
```
{
    if (empty( )) return − 1;
    Term lead;
    retrieve(lead);
    return lead.degree;
}
```

4.5.6 Completing the Project

1. The Missing Procedures

At this point, the remaining methods for the **class** Polynomial are sufficiently similar to those already written that they can be left as projects. Methods for the remaining arithmetical operations have the same general form as equals_sum. Some of these are easy: Subtraction is almost identical to addition. For multiplication, we can first write a function that multiplies a Polynomial by a Term. Then we combine use of this function with the addition function to do a general multiplication. Division is more complicated.

2. The Choice of Stack Implementation

Our implementation of the **class** Polynomial makes use of a linked Extended_queue of terms. Therefore, we must declare that a Node contains a Term as its entry. This prevents us from using our linked Stack class to contain Polynomial entries (since that would require nodes that contain Polynomial entries). We must therefore compile our calculator program with our contiguous Stack implementation.

templates

This is the first case where we have been handicapped by our simple treatment of generics. As we have previously observed, however, C++ does provide a more sophisticated approach to generics that makes use of templates. If we had used templates systematically throughout this chapter, our calculator program could have been compiled with either a linked or a contiguous Stack implementation. In the next chapter, we shall begin using templates to achieve truly generic data structures.

3. Group Project

Production of a coherent package of functions for manipulating polynomials makes an interesting group project. Different members of the group can write auxiliary functions or methods for different operations. Some of these are indicated as projects at the end of this section, but you may wish to include additional features as well. Any additional features should be planned carefully to be sure that they can be completed in a reasonable time, without disrupting other parts of the program.

specifications
After deciding on the division of work among its members, the most important decisions of the group relate to the exact ways in which the functions and methods should communicate with each other, and especially with the calling program. If you wish to make any changes in the organization of the program, be certain that the precise details are spelled out clearly and completely for all members of the group.

cooperation
Next, you will find that it is too much to hope that all members of the group will complete their work at the same time, or that all parts of the project can be combined and debugged together. You will therefore need to use program stubs and drivers (see Section 1.4) to debug and test the various parts of the project. One member of the group might take special responsibility for this testing. In any case, you will find it very effective for different members to read, help debug, and test each other's functions.

coordination
Finally, there are the responsibilities of making sure that all members of the group complete their work on time, of keeping track of the progress of various aspects of the project, of making sure that no functions are integrated into the project before they are thoroughly debugged and tested, and then of combining all the work into the finished product.

Exercise 4.5

E1. Discuss the steps that would be needed to extend the polynomial calculator so that it would process polynomials in several variables.

Programming Projects 4.5

P1. Assemble the functions developed in this section and make the necessary changes in the code so as to produce a working skeleton for the calculator program, one that will read, write, and add polynomials. You will need to supply the functions get_command(), introduction(), and instructions().

P2. Write the Polynomial method equals_difference and integrate it into the calculator.

P3. Write an auxiliary function

void Polynomial :: mult_term(Polynomial p, Term t)

that calculates a Polynomial object by multiplying p by the single Term t.

P4. Use the function developed in the preceding problem, together with the Polynomial method equals_sum, to write the Polynomial method equals_product, and integrate the resulting method into the calculator.

P5. Write the Polynomial method equals_quotient and integrate it into the calculator.

P6. Many reverse Polish calculators use not only a stack but also provide memory locations where operands can be stored. Extend the project to provide an array to store polynomials. Provide additional commands to store the top of the stack into an array entry and to push the polynomial in an array entry onto the stack. The array should have 100 entries, and all 100 positions should be initialized to the zero polynomial when the program begins. The functions that access the array should ask the user which entry to use.

P7. Write a function that will discard the top polynomial on the stack, and include this capability as a new command.

P8. Write a function that will interchange the top two polynomials on the stack, and include this capability as a new command.

P9. Write a function that will add all the polynomials on the stack together, and include this capability as a new command.

P10. Write a function that will compute the derivative of a polynomial, and include this capability as a new command.

P11. Write a function that, given a polynomial and a real number, evaluates the polynomial at that number, and include this capability as a new command.

P12. Write a new method equals_remainder that obtains the remainder when a first Polynomial argument is divided by a second Polynomial argument. Add a new user command % to the calculator program to call this method.

4.6 ABSTRACT DATA TYPES AND THEIR IMPLEMENTATIONS

When we first introduced stacks and queues, we considered them only as they are implemented in contiguous storage, and yet upon introduction of linked stacks and queues, we had no difficulty in recognizing the same underlying abstract data types. To clarify the general process of passing from an abstract data type definition to a C++ implementation, let us reflect on these data types and the implementations that we have seen.

We begin by recalling the definition of the stack ADT from Section 2.5.

Definition   A *stack* of elements of type T is a finite sequence of elements of T together with the following operations:

1. *Create* the stack, leaving it empty.
2. Test whether the stack is *Empty*.
3. *Push* a new entry onto the top of the stack, provided the stack is not full.
4. *Pop* the entry off the top of the stack, provided the stack is not empty.
5. Retrieve the *Top* the entry off the stack, provided the stack is not empty.

To obtain the definition of a queue ADT, we replace stack methods by queue methods as follows.

Definition A *queue* of elements of type T is a finite sequence of elements of T together with the following operations:

1. *Create* the queue, leaving it empty.
2. Test whether the queue is *Empty*.
3. *Append* a new entry onto the rear of the queue, provided the queue is not full.
4. *Serve* (and remove) the entry from the front of the queue, provided the queue is not empty.
5. *Retrieve* the front entry off the queue, provided the queue is not empty.

We can also give a precise definition of extended queues as follows.

Definition An *extended queue* of elements of type T is a queue of elements of T together with the following additional operations:

4. Determine whether the queue is *full* or not.
5. Find the *size* of the queue.
6. *Serve and retrieve* the front entry in the queue, provided the queue is not empty.
7. *Clear* the queue to make it empty.

Note that these definitions make no mention of the way in which the abstract data type (stack, queue, or extended queue) is to be implemented. In the past several chapters we have studied different implementations of each of these types, and these new definitions fit any of these implementations equally well.

As we recall from Section 2.5, in the process of implementing an abstract data type we must pass from the abstract level of a type definition, through a data structures level, where we decide on a structure to model our data type, to an implementation level, where we decide on the details of how our data structure will be stored in computer memory. Figure 4.16 illustrates these stages of refinement in the case of a queue. We begin with the mathematical concept of a sequence and then the queue considered as an abstract data type. At the next level, we choose from the various data structures shown in the diagram, ranging from the physical model (in which all items move forward as each one leaves the head of the queue) to the linear model (in which the queue is emptied all at once) to circular arrays and finally linked lists. Some of these data structures allow further variation in their implementation, as shown on the next level. At the final stage, the queue is coded for a specific application.

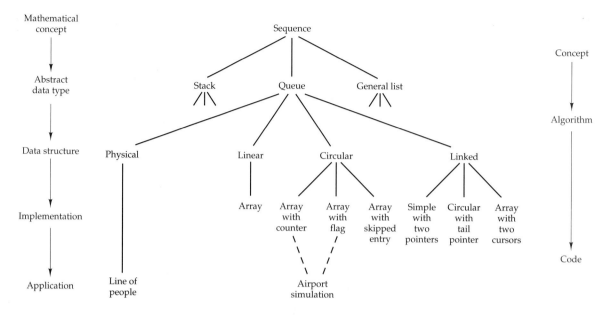

Figure 4.16. Refinement of a queue

Exercises 4.6 **E1.** Draw a diagram similar to that of Figure 4.16 showing levels of refinement for a stack.

E2. Give a formal definition of the term *deque*, using the definitions given for stack and queue as models. Recall that entries may be added to or deleted from either end of a deque, but nowhere except at its ends.

POINTERS AND PITFALLS

1. Before choosing implementations, be sure that all the data structures and their associated operations are fully specified on the abstract level.

2. In choosing between linked and contiguous implementations, consider the necessary operations on the data structure. Linked structures are more flexible in regard to insertions, deletions, and rearrangement; contiguous structures are sometimes faster.

3. Contiguous structures usually require less computer memory, computer time, and programming effort when the items in the structure are small and the algorithms are simple. When the structure holds large records, linked structures usually save space, time, and often programming effort.

4. Dynamic memory and pointers allow a program to adapt automatically to a wide range of application sizes and provide flexibility in space allocation among different data structures. Automatic memory is sometimes more efficient for applications whose size can be completely specified in advance.

5. Before reassigning a pointer, make sure that the object that it references will not become garbage.

6. Set uninitialized pointers to NULL.

7. Linked data structures should be implemented with destructors, copy constructors, and overloaded assignment operators.

8. Use private inheritance to model an "is implemented with" relationship between classes.

9. Draw "before" and "after" diagrams of the appropriate part of a linked structure, showing the relevant pointers and the way in which they should be changed. If they might help, also draw diagrams showing intermediate stages of the process.

10. To determine in what order values should be placed in the pointer fields to carry out the various changes, it is usually better first to assign the values to previously undefined pointers, then to those with value NULL, and finally to the remaining pointers. After one pointer variable has been copied to another, the first is free to be reassigned to its new location.

undefined links   11. Be sure that no links are left undefined at the conclusion of a method of a linked structure, either as links in new nodes that have never been assigned or links in old nodes that have become dangling, that is, that point to nodes that no longer are used. Such links should either be reassigned to nodes still in use or set to the value NULL.

extreme cases   12. Always verify that your algorithm works correctly for an empty structure and for a structure with only one node.

   13. Avoid the use of constructions such as (p->next)->next, even though they are
multiple dereferencing   syntactically correct. A single object should involve only a single pointer dereferencing. Constructions with repeated dereferencing usually indicate that the algorithms can be improved by rethinking what pointer variables should be declared in the algorithm, introducing new ones if necessary.

REVIEW QUESTIONS

4.1   **1.** Give two reasons why dynamic memory allocation is valuable.

   2. What is garbage?

   3. Why should uninitialized pointers be set to NULL?

   4. What is an alias and why is it dangerous?

4.2   **5.** Why is it important to return an Error_code from the push method of a linked Stack?

4.3   **6.** Why should we always add a destructor to a linked data structure?

7. How is a copy constructor used and why should a copy constructor be included in a linked data structure?

8. Why should a linked data structure be implemented with an overloaded assignment operator?

4.5   **9.** Discuss some problems that occur in group programming projects that do not occur in individual programming projects. What advantages does a group project have over individual projects?

4.6   **10.** In an abstract data type, how much is specified about implementation?

11. Name (in order from abstract to concrete) four levels of refinement of data specification.

Recursion

5

THIS CHAPTER introduces the study of recursion, the method in which a problem is solved by reducing it to smaller cases of the same problem. To illustrate recursion we shall study some applications and sample programs, thereby demonstrating some of the variety of problems to which recursion may fruitfully be applied. Some of these examples are simple; others are quite sophisticated. We also analyze how recursion is usually implemented on a computer. In the process, we shall obtain guidelines regarding good and bad uses of recursion, when it is appropriate, and when it should best be avoided.

5.1 INTRODUCTION TO RECURSION

5.1.1 Stack Frames for Subprograms

invocation record

As one important application of stacks, consider what happens within the computer system when functions are called. The system (or the program) must remember the place where the call was made, so that it can return there after the function is complete. It must also remember all the local variables, processor registers, and the like, so that information will not be lost while the function is working. We can think of all this information as one large data structure, a temporary storage area for each function. This structure is sometimes called the ***invocation record*** or the ***activation record*** for the function call.

nested function calls

Suppose now that we have three functions called A, B, and C, and suppose that A invokes B and B invokes C. Then B will not have finished its work until C has finished and returned. Similarly, A is the first to start work, but it is the last to be finished, not until sometime after B has finished and returned. Thus the sequence by which function activity proceeds is summed up as the property *last in, first out*. If we consider the machine's task of assigning temporary storage areas for use by functions, then these areas would be allocated in a list with this same property; that is, in a stack (see Figure 5.1, where M represents an invocation record for the main program, and A, B, and C represent invocation records for the corresponding functions). Hence a stack plays a key role in invoking functions in a computer system.

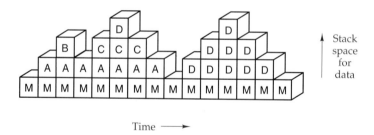

Time $\longrightarrow$

Figure 5.1. Stack frames for function calls

stack frames

Figure 5.1 shows a sequence of ***stack frames***, where each vertical column shows the contents of the stack at a given time, and changes to the stack are portrayed by reading through the frames from left to right. Notice from Figure 5.1 that it makes no difference whether the temporary storage areas pushed on the stack come from different functions or from repeated occurrences of the same function. ***Recursion*** is the name for the case when a function invokes itself or invokes a sequence of other functions, one of which eventually invokes the first function again. In regard to stack frames for function calls, recursion is no different from any other function call.

definition: recursion

5.1.2 Tree of Subprogram Calls

One more picture elucidates the connection between stacks and function calls. This is a *tree* diagram showing the order in which the functions are invoked. Such a tree diagram appears in Figure 5.2, corresponding to the stack frames shown in Figure 5.1.

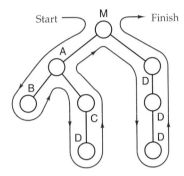

Figure 5.2. Tree of function calls

root, vertex, node   We start at the top of the tree, which is called its *root* and corresponds to the main program. Each circle (called a *vertex* or a *node*) corresponds to a call to a function. All the calls that the main program makes directly are shown as the vertices directly below the root. Each of these functions may, of course, call other functions, which are shown as further vertices on lower levels. In this way, the tree grows into a form like the one in Figure 5.2. We shall call such a tree a *tree of function calls*.

children, parent   We shall frequently use several other terms in reference to trees, recklessly mixing the metaphors of botanical trees and family trees. The vertices immediately below a given vertex are called the *children* of that vertex, and the (unique) vertex immediately above is called its *parent*. The line connecting a vertex with one immediately above or below is called a *branch*. *Siblings* are vertices with the same

branch, sibling, leaf   parent. The root is the only vertex in the tree that has no parent. A vertex with no children is called a *leaf* or, sometimes, an *external vertex*. For example, in Figure 5.2, M is the root; A and D are its children; B and C are children of A; B and the two bottom occurrences of D are leaves. (The other two occurrences of D are not leaves.) We say that two branches of a tree are *adjacent* if the lower vertex of the first branch is the upper vertex of the second. A sequence of branches in which each is adjacent to its successor is called a *path*. The *height* of a tree is the number of

height, depth, level   vertices on a longest-possible path from the root to a leaf. Hence the tree in Figure 5.2 has height 4, and a tree containing only one vertex has height 1. Sometimes (but not for function calls) we allow empty trees (no vertices); an empty tree has height 0. The *depth* or *level* of a vertex is the number of branches on a path from the root to the vertex. Hence the root has depth 0; in Figure 5.2, A has depth 1, B and C have depth 2.

traversal

To trace the function calls made in a program, we start at the root and move around the tree, as shown by the colored path in Figure 5.2. This colored path is called a ***traversal*** of the tree. When we come to a vertex while moving downward, we invoke the function. After we traverse the part of the tree below the vertex, we reach it again on the way up, and this represents termination and return from the function. The leaves represent functions that do not invoke any other functions.

recursion tree

execution trace

We are especially interested in recursion, so that often we draw only the part of the tree showing the recursive calls, and we call it a ***recursion tree***. You should first notice from the diagram that there is no difference in the way a recursive call appears and the way any other function call occurs. Different recursive calls appear simply as different vertices that happen to have the same name of function attached. Second, note carefully that the tree shows the *calls* to functions. Hence a function called from only one place, but within a loop executed more than once, will appear several times in the tree, once for each execution of the loop. Similarly, if a function is called from a conditional statement that is not executed, then the call will not appear in the tree.

stack frames

space requirement

The stack frames like Figure 5.1 show the nesting of recursive calls and also illustrate the storage requirements for recursion. If a function calls itself recursively several times, then separate copies of the variables declared in the function are created for each recursive call. In the usual implementation of recursion, these are kept on a stack. Note that the amount of space needed for this stack is proportional to the height of the recursion tree, *not* to the total number of nodes in the tree. That is, the amount of space needed to implement a recursive function depends on the *depth* of recursion, not on the *number* of times the function is invoked.

The last two figures can, in fact, be interpreted in a broader context than as the process of invoking functions. They thereby elucidate an easy but important observation, providing an intimate connection between arbitrary trees and stacks:

Theorem 5.1

> *During the traversal of any tree, vertices are added to or deleted from the path back to the root in the fashion of a stack. Given any stack, conversely, a tree can be drawn to portray the life history of the stack, as items are pushed onto and popped from it.*

We now turn to the study of several simple examples of recursion. We next analyze how recursion is usually implemented on a computer. In the process, we shall obtain guidelines regarding good and bad uses of recursion, when it is appropriate, and when it should best be avoided. The rest of this chapter includes several more sophisticated applications of recursion.

5.1.3 Factorials: A Recursive Definition

In mathematics, the ***factorial*** function of a positive integer is usually defined by the formula

informal definition

$$n! = n \times (n-1) \times \cdots \times 1.$$

The ellipsis (three dots) in this formula means "continue in the same way." This notation is not precise, since there can be more than one sensible way to fill in the ellipsis. To calculate factorials, we need a more precise definition, such as the following:

formal definition

$$n! = \begin{cases} 1 & \text{if } n = 0 \\ n \times (n-1)! & \text{if } n > 0. \end{cases}$$

This definition tells us exactly how to calculate a factorial, provided we follow the rules carefully and use a piece of paper to help us remember where we are.

example

Suppose that we wish to calculate $4!$. Since $4 > 0$, the definition tells us that $4! = 4 \times 3!$. This may be some help, but not enough, since we do not know what $3!$ is. Since $3 > 0$, the definition again gives us $3! = 3 \times 2!$. Again, we do not know the value of $2!$, but the definition gives us $2! = 2 \times 1!$. We still do not know $1!$, but, since $1 > 0$, we have $1! = 1 \times 0!$. The definition, finally, treats the case $n = 0$ separately, so we know that $0! = 1$. We can substitute this answer into the expression for $1!$ and obtain $1! = 1 \times 0! = 1 \times 1 = 1$. Now comes the reason for using a piece of paper to keep track of partial results. Unless we write the computation down in an organized fashion, by the time we work our way through a definition several times we will have forgotten the early steps of the process before we reach the lowest level and begin to use the results to complete the earlier calculations. For the factorial calculation, it is of course easy to write out all the steps in an organized way:

$$\begin{aligned} 4! &= 4 \times 3! \\ &= 4 \times (3 \times 2!) \\ &= 4 \times (3 \times (2 \times 1!)) \\ &= 4 \times (3 \times (2 \times (1 \times 0!))) \\ &= 4 \times (3 \times (2 \times (1 \times 1))) \\ &= 4 \times (3 \times (2 \times 1)) \\ &= 4 \times (3 \times 2) \\ &= 4 \times 6 \\ &= 24. \end{aligned}$$

problem reduction

This calculation illustrates the essence of the way recursion works. To obtain the answer to a large problem, a general method is used that reduces the large problem to one or more problems of a similar nature but a smaller size. The same general method is then used for these subproblems, and so recursion continues until the size of the subproblems is reduced to some smallest, base case, where the solution is given directly without using further recursion. In other words:

aspects of recursion

Every recursive process consists of two parts:

1. *A smallest, base case that is processed without recursion; and*

2. *A general method that reduces a particular case to one or more of the smaller cases, thereby making progress toward eventually reducing the problem all the way to the base case.*

C++ (like most other modern computer languages) provides easy access to recursion. The factorial calculation in C++ becomes the following function.

recursive program

```
int factorial(int n)
/* Pre:   n is a nonnegative integer.
   Post: Return the value of the factorial of n. */
{
  if (n ==  0)
    return 1;
  else
    return n * factorial(n − 1);
}
```

As you can see from this example of factorials, the recursive definition and recursive solution of a problem can be both concise and elegant, but the computational details can require keeping track of many partial computations before the process is complete.

remembering partial computations

Computers can easily keep track of such partial computations with a stack; the human mind is not at all good for such tasks. It is exceedingly difficult for a person to remember a long chain of partial results and then go back through it to complete the work. Consider, for example, the following nursery rhyme:

> As I was going to St. Ives,
>   I met a man with seven wives.
> Each wife had seven sacks,
>   Each sack had seven cats,
>   Each cat had seven kits:
> Kits, cats, sacks and wives,
>   How many were there going to St. Ives?

Because of the human difficulty in keeping track of many partial computations simultaneously, when we use recursion, it becomes necessary for us to think in somewhat different terms than with other programming methods. Programmers must look at the big picture and leave the detailed computations to the computer.

We must specify in our algorithm the precise form of the general step in reducing a large problem to smaller cases; we must determine the stopping rule (the smallest case) and how it is processed. On the other hand, except for a few simple and small examples, we should generally *not* try to understand a recursive algorithm by working the general case all the way down to the stopping rule or by tracing the action the computer will take on a good-sized case. We would quickly become so confused by all the postponed tasks that we would lose track of the complete problem and the overall method used for its solution.

There are good general methods and tools that allow us to concentrate on the general methods and key steps while at the same time analyzing the amount of work that the computer will do in carrying out all the details. We now turn to an example that illustrates some of these methods and tools.

5.1.4 Divide and Conquer: The Towers of Hanoi

1. The Problem

the story

In the nineteenth century, a game called the ***Towers of Hanoi*** appeared in Europe, together with promotional material (undoubtedly apocryphal) explaining that the game represented a task underway in the Temple of Brahma. At the creation of the world, the priests were given a brass platform on which were 3 diamond needles. On the first needle were stacked 64 golden disks, each one slightly smaller than the one under it. (The less exotic version sold in Europe had 8 cardboard disks and 3 wooden posts.) The priests were assigned the task of moving all the golden disks from the first needle to the third, subject to the conditions that only one disk can be moved at a time and that no disk is ever allowed to be placed on top of a smaller disk. The priests were told that when they had finished moving the 64 disks, it would signify the end of the world. See Figure 5.3.

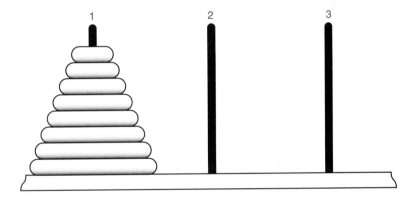

Figure 5.3. The Towers of Hanoi

Our task, of course, is to write a computer program that will type out a list of instructions for the priests. We can summarize our task by the instruction

move(64, 1, 3, 2)

which means

Move 64 disks from tower 1 to tower 3 using tower 2 as temporary storage.

2. The Solution

The idea that gives a solution is to concentrate our attention not on the first step (which must be to move the top disk somewhere), but rather on the hardest step: moving the bottom disk. There is no way to reach the bottom disk until the top 63

disks have been moved, and, furthermore, they must all be on tower 2 so that we can move the bottom disk from tower 1 to tower 3. This is because only one disk can be moved at a time and the bottom (largest) one can never be on top of any other, so that when we move the bottom one, there can be no other disks on towers 1 or 3. Thus we can summarize the steps of our algorithm for the *Towers of Hanoi* problem as

```
move(63, 1, 2, 3);      //   Move 63 disks from tower 1 to 2 (tower 3 temporary).
cout ≪ "Move disk 64 from tower 1 to tower 3." ≪ endl;
move(63, 2, 3, 1);      //   Move 63 disks from tower 2 to 3 (tower 1 temporary).
```

general reduction

We now have a small step toward the solution, only a very small one since we must still describe how to move the 63 disks two times. It is a significant step nonetheless, since there is no reason why we cannot move the 63 remaining disks in the same way. (As a matter of fact, we must indeed do so in the same way, since there is again a largest disk that must be moved last.)

divide and conquer

This is exactly the idea of recursion. We have described how to do the key step and asserted that the rest of the problem is done in essentially the same way. This is also the idea of ***divide and conquer***: To solve a problem, we split the work into smaller and smaller parts, each of which is easier to solve than the original problem.

3. Refinement

To write the algorithm formally, we shall need to know at each step which tower may be used for temporary storage, and thus we will invoke the function with specifications as follows:

---

void move(**int** count, **int** start, **int** finish, **int** temp);

precondition: There are at least count disks on the tower start. The top disk (if any) on each of towers temp and finish is larger than any of the top count disks on tower start.

postcondition: The top count disks on start have been moved to finish; temp (used for temporary storage) has been returned to its starting position.

---

stopping rule

Supposedly our task is to be finished in a finite number of steps (even if it does mark the end of the world!), and thus there must be some way that the recursion stops. The obvious stopping rule is that, when there are no disks to be moved, there is nothing to do. We can now write the complete program to embody these rules. The main program is:

```
const int disks = 64;          //   Make this constant much smaller to run program.
void move(int count, int start, int finish, int temp);
```

```
/* Pre:   None.
    Post:  The simulation of the Towers of Hanoi has terminated. */
main( )
{
   move(disks, 1, 3, 2);
}
```

The recursive function that does the work is:

recursive function
```
void move(int count, int start, int finish, int temp)
{
   if (count > 0) {
      move(count − 1, start, temp, finish);
      cout ≪ "Move disk " ≪ count ≪ " from " ≪ start
           ≪ " to " ≪ finish ≪ "." ≪ endl;
      move(count − 1, temp, finish, start);
   }
}
```

4. Program Tracing

One useful tool in studying a recursive function when applied to a very small example is to construct a trace of its action. Such a trace is shown in Figure 5.4 for the Towers of Hanoi in the case when the number of disks is 2. Each box in the diagram shows what happens in one of the calls. The outermost call **move(2, 1, 3, 2)** (the call made by the main program) results essentially in the execution of the following three statements, shown as the statements in the outer box (colored gray) of the diagram.

```
move(1, 1, 2, 3);             //   Move 1 disk from tower 1 to 2 (using tower 3).
cout ≪ "Move disk 2 from tower 1 to tower 3." ≪ endl;
move(1, 2, 3, 1);             //   Move 1 disk from tower 2 to 3 (using tower 1).
```

The first and third of these statements make recursive calls. The statement

move(1, 1, 2, 3)

starts the function **move** over again from the top, but now with the new parameters. Hence this statement results essentially in the execution of the following three statements, shown as the statements in the first inner box (shown in color):

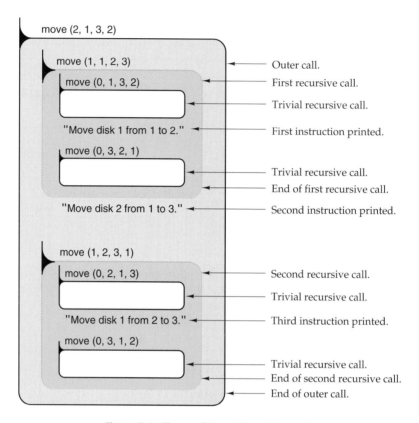

Figure 5.4. Trace of Hanoi for disks == 2

move(0, 1, 3, 2);   //   *Move 0 disks.*
cout ≪ "Move disk 1 from tower 1 to tower 2." ≪ endl;
move(0, 3, 2, 1);   //   *Move 0 disks.*

If you wish, you may think of these three statements as written out in place of the call **move(1, 1, 2, 3)**, but think of them as having a different color from the statements of the outer call, since they constitute a new and different call to the function. These statements are shown as colored print in the figure.

After the box corresponding to this call comes the output statement and then a second box corresponding to the call **move(1, 2, 3, 1)**. But before these statements are reached, there are two more recursive calls coming from the first inner box. That is, we must next expand the call **move(0, 1, 3, 2)**. But the function **move** does nothing when its parameter **count** is 0; hence this call **move(0, 1, 3, 2)** executes no further function calls or other statements. We show it as corresponding to the first empty box in the diagram.

After this empty call comes the output statement shown in the first inner box, and then comes another call that does nothing. This then completes the work for the call **move(1, 1, 2, 3)**, so it returns to the place from which it was called. The following statement is then the output statement in the outer box, and finally the statement **move(1, 2, 3, 1)** is done. This call produces the statements shown in the second inner box, which are then, in turn, expanded as the further empty boxes shown.

sorcerer's apprentice   With all the recursive calls through which we worked our way, the example we have studied may lead you to liken recursion to the fable of the Sorcerer's Apprentice, who, when he had enchanted a broom to fetch water for him, did not know how to stop it and so chopped it in two, whereupon it started duplicating itself until there were so many brooms fetching water that disaster would have ensued had the master not returned.

We now turn to another tool to visualize recursive calls, a tool that manages the multiplicity of calls more effectively than a program trace can. This tool is the recursion tree.

5. Analysis

The recursion tree for the Towers of Hanoi with three disks appears as Figure 5.5, and the progress of execution follows the path shown in color.

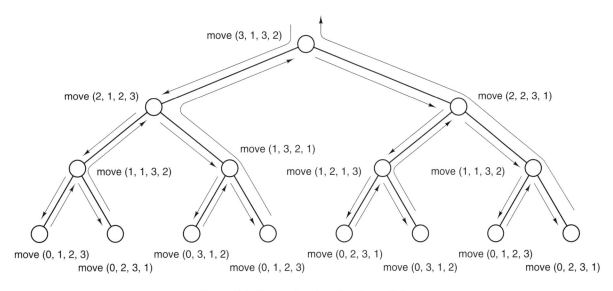

Figure 5.5. Recursion tree for three disks

Note that our program for the Towers of Hanoi not only produces a complete solution to the task, but it produces the best possible solution, and, in fact, the only solution that can be found except for the possible inclusion of redundant and useless sequences of instructions such as

Move disk 1 from tower 1 to tower 2.
Move disk 1 from tower 2 to tower 3.
Move disk 1 from tower 3 to tower 1.

To show the uniqueness of the irreducible solution, note that, at every stage, the task to be done can be summarized as moving a certain number of disks from one tower to another. There is no way of doing this task other than moving all the disks except the bottom one first, then perhaps making some redundant moves, then moving the bottom one, possibly making more redundant moves, and finally moving the upper disks again.

Next, let us find out how many times the recursion will proceed before starting to return and back out. The first time function move is called, it is with count == 64, and each recursive call reduces the value of count by 1. Thus, if we exclude the calls with count == 0, which do nothing, we have a total depth of recursion of 64. *depth of recursion* That is, if we were to draw the tree of recursive calls for the program, it would have 64 levels above its leaves. Except for the leaves, each vertex results in two recursive calls (as well as in writing out one instruction), and so the number of vertices on each level is exactly double that of the level above.

From thinking about its recursion tree (even if it is much too large to draw), we can easily calculate how many instructions are needed to move 64 disks. One instruction is printed for each vertex in the tree, except for the leaves (which are calls with count == 0). The number of non-leaves is

total number of moves

$$1 + 2 + 4 + \cdots + 2^{63} = 2^0 + 2^1 + 2^2 + \cdots + 2^{63} = 2^{64} - 1.$$

Hence the number of moves required altogether for 64 disks is $2^{64} - 1$. We can estimate how large this number is by using the approximation

$$10^3 = 1000 \approx 1024 = 2^{10}.$$

(This easy fact is well worth remembering and is frequently used in discussing computers: The abbreviation K, as in 512K, means 1024.) Thus the number of moves is approximately

$$2^{64} = 2^4 \times 2^{60} \approx 2^4 \times 10^{18} = 1.6 \times 10^{19}.$$

There are about 3.2×10^7 seconds in one year. Suppose that the instructions could be carried out at the rather frenetic rate of one every second. (The priests have plenty of practice.) The total task will then take about 5×10^{11} years. Astronomers estimate the age of the universe at less than 20 billion (2×10^{10}) years, so, according to this story, the world will indeed endure a long time—25 times as long as it already has!

time and space You should note carefully that, although no computer could ever carry out the full Towers of Hanoi program, it would fail for lack of *time*, but certainly not for lack of *space*. The space needed is only that to keep track of 64 recursive calls, but the time needed is that required for 2^{64} calculations.

Exercises 5.1   **E1.** Consider the function $f(n)$ defined as follows, where n is a nonnegative integer:

$$f(n)= \begin{cases} 0 & \text{if } n = 0; \\ f(\tfrac{1}{2}n) & \text{if } n \text{ is even, } n > 0; \\ 1 + f(n-1) & \text{if } n \text{ is odd, } n > 0. \end{cases}$$

Calculate the value of $f(n)$ for the following values of n.

(a) $n = 1$.   (c) $n = 3$.   (e) $n = 100$.
(b) $n = 2$.   (d) $n = 99$.   (f) $n = 128$.

E2. Consider the function $f(n)$ defined as follows, where n is a nonnegative integer:

$$f(n)= \begin{cases} n & \text{if } n \le 1; \\ n + f(\tfrac{1}{2}n) & \text{if } n \text{ is even, } n > 1; \\ f(\tfrac{1}{2}(n + 1)) + f(\tfrac{1}{2}(n - 1)) & \text{if } n \text{ is odd, } n > 1. \end{cases}$$

For each of the following values of n, draw the recursion tree and calculate the value of $f(n)$.

(a) $n = 1$.   (c) $n = 3$.   (e) $n = 5$.
(b) $n = 2$.   (d) $n = 4$.   (f) $n = 6$.

Programming Projects 5.1   **P1.** Compare the running times[1] for the recursive factorial function written in this section with a nonrecursive function obtained by initializing a local variable to 1 and using a loop to calculate the product $n! = 1 \times 2 \times \cdots \times n$. To obtain meaningful comparisons of the CPU time required, you will probably need to write a loop in your driver program that will repeat the same calculation of a factorial several hundred times. Integer overflow will occur if you attempt to calculate the factorial of a large number. To prevent this from happening, you may declare n and the function value to have type **double** instead of **int**.

P2. Confirm that the running time[1] for the program hanoi increases approximately like a constant multiple of 2^n, where n is the number of disks moved. To do this, make disks a variable, comment out the line that writes a message to the user, and run the program for several successive values of disks, such as 10, 11, ..., 15. How does the CPU time change from one value of disks to the next?

---

[1] You will need one of the standard header files `ctime` or `time.h` that accesses a package of functions for calculating the CPU time used by a C or C++ program; see Appendix C for more details of this package.

5.2 PRINCIPLES OF RECURSION

5.2.1 Designing Recursive Algorithms

Recursion is a tool to allow the programmer to concentrate on the key step of an algorithm, without having initially to worry about coupling that step with all the others. As usual with problem solving, the first approach should usually be to consider several simple examples, and as these become better understood, to attempt to formulate a method that will work more generally. Some of the important aspects of designing algorithms with recursion are as follows:

➡ **Find the key step.** Begin by asking yourself, "How can this problem be divided into parts?" or "How will the key step in the middle be done?" Be sure to keep your answer simple but generally applicable. Do not come up with a multitude of special cases that work only for small problems or at the beginning and end of large ones. Once you have a simple, small step toward the solution, ask whether the remainder of the problem can be done in the same or a similar way, and modify your method, if necessary, so that it will be sufficiently general.

➡ **Find a stopping rule.** The stopping rule indicates that the problem or a suitable part of it is done. This stopping rule is usually the small, special case that is trivial or easy to handle without recursion.

➡ **Outline your algorithm.** Combine the stopping rule and the key step, using an **if** statement to select between them. You should now be able to write the main program and a recursive function that will describe how to carry the key step through until the stopping rule applies.

➡ **Check termination.** Next, and of great importance, is a verification that the recursion will always terminate. Start with a general situation and check that, in a finite number of steps, the stopping rule will be satisfied and the recursion terminate. Be sure also that your algorithm correctly handles extreme cases. When called on to do nothing, any algorithm should be able to return gracefully, but it is especially important that recursive algorithms do so, since a call to do nothing is often the stopping rule. Notice, as well, that a call to do nothing is usually *not* an error for a recursive function. It is therefore usually not appropriate for a recursive function to generate a message when it performs an empty call; it should instead simply return silently.

➡ **Draw a recursion tree.** The key tool for the analysis of recursive algorithms is the recursion tree. As we have seen for the Towers of Hanoi, the height of the tree is closely related to the amount of memory that the program will require, and the total size of the tree reflects the number of times the key step will be done, and hence the total time the program will use. It is usually highly instructive to draw the recursion tree for one or two simple examples appropriate to your problem.

5.2.2 How Recursion Works

design versus implementation
The question of how recursion is actually done in a computer should be carefully separated in our minds from the question of using recursion in designing algorithms.

➡ In the design phase, we should use all problem-solving methods that prove to be appropriate, and recursion is one of the most flexible and powerful of these tools.

➡ In the implementation phase, we may need to ask which of several methods is the best under the circumstances.

There are at least two ways to accomplish recursion in computer systems. The first of these, at present, is only available in some large systems, but with changing costs and capabilities of computer equipment, it may soon be more common. Our major point in considering two different implementations is that, although restrictions in space and time do need to be considered, they should be considered separately from the process of algorithm design, since different kinds of computer equipment in the future may lead to different capabilities and restrictions.

1. Multiple Processors: Concurrency

Perhaps the most natural way to think of implementing recursion is to think of each function not as occupying a different part of the same computer, but to think of each function as running on a separate machine. In that way, when one function invokes another, it starts the corresponding machine going, and when the other machine completes its work, then it sends the answer back to the first machine, which can then continue its task. If a function makes two recursive calls to itself, then it will simply start two other machines working with the same instructions that it is using. When these machines complete their work, they will send the answers back to the one that started them going. If they, in turn, make recursive calls, then they will simply start still more machines working.

costs
It used to be that the central processor was the most expensive component of a computer system, and any thought of a system including more than one processor would have been considered extravagant. The price of processing power compared to other computing costs has now dropped radically, and in all likelihood we shall, before long, see large computer systems that will include hundreds, if not thousands, of identical microprocessors among their components. When this occurs, implementation of recursion via multiple processors will become commonplace if not inevitable.

parallel processing

concurrency
With multiple processors, programmers should no longer consider algorithms solely as a linear sequence of actions, but should instead realize that some parts of the algorithm can often be done in parallel (at the same time) as other parts. Processes that take place simultaneously are called **concurrent**. The study of concurrent processes and the methods for communication between them is, at present, an active subject for research in computing science, one in which important developments will undoubtedly improve the ways in which algorithms will be described and implemented in coming years.

2. Single-Processor Implementation: Storage Areas

In order to determine how recursion can be efficiently implemented in a system with only one processor, let us first for the moment leave recursion to consider the question of what steps are needed to call a function, on the primitive level of machine-language instructions in a simple computer.

The hardware of any computer has a limited range of instructions that includes (amongst other instructions) doing arithmetic on specified words of storage or on special locations within the CPU called *registers*, moving data to and from the memory and registers, and branching (jumping) to a specified address. When a calling program branches to the beginning of a function, the address of the place whence the call was made must be stored in memory, or else the function could not remember where to return. The addresses or values of the calling parameters must

return address   also be stored where the function can find them, and where the answers can in turn be found by the calling program after the function returns. When the function starts, it will do various calculations on its local variables and storage areas. Once

local variables   the function finishes, however, these local variables are lost, since they are not available outside the function. The function will, of course, have used the registers within the CPU for its calculations, so normally these would have different values after the function finishes than before it is called. It is traditional, however, to expect that a function will change nothing except its calling parameters or global variables (side effects). Thus it is customary that the function will save all the registers it will use and restore their values before it returns.

In summary, when a function is called, it must have a storage area (perhaps

storage area   scattered as several areas); it must save the registers or whatever else it will change, using the storage area also for its return address, calling parameters, and local variables. As it returns, it will restore the registers and the other storage that it was expected to restore. After the return, it no longer needs anything in its local storage area.

In this way, we implement function calls by changing storage areas, an action that takes the place of changing processors that we considered before. In these considerations, it really makes no difference whether the function is called recursively or not, providing that, in the recursive case, we are careful to regard two recursive calls as being different, so that we do not mix the storage areas for one call with those of another, any more than we would mix storage areas for different functions, one called from within the other. For a nonrecursive function, the storage area can be one fixed area, permanently reserved, since we know that one call to the function will have returned before another one is made, and after the first one returns, the information stored is no longer needed. For recursive functions, however, the information stored must be preserved until the outer call returns, so an inner call must use a different area for its temporary storage.

Note that the once-common practice of reserving a permanent storage area for a nonrecursive function can in fact be quite wasteful, since a considerable amount of memory may be consumed in this way, memory that might be useful for other

 purposes while the function is not active. This is, nevertheless, the way that storage was allocated for functions in older versions of languages like FORTRAN and COBOL, and this is the reason why these older languages did not allow recursion.

3. Re-Entrant Programs

Essentially the same problem of multiple storage areas arises in a quite different context, that of *re-entrant* programs. In a large time-sharing system, there may be many users simultaneously using the C++ compiler, the text-editing system, or database software. Such systems programs are quite large, and it would be very wasteful of high-speed memory to keep thirty or forty copies of exactly the same large set of instructions in memory at once, one for each user. What is often done instead is to write large systems programs like the text editor with the instructions in one area, but the addresses of all variables or other data kept in a separate area. Then, in the memory of the time-sharing system, there will be only one copy of the instructions, but a separate data area for each user.

This situation is somewhat analogous to students writing a test in a room where the questions are written on the blackboard. There is then only one set of questions that all students can read, but each student separately writes answers on different pieces of paper. There is no difficulty for different students to be reading the same or different questions at the same time, and with different pieces of paper, their answers will not be mixed with each other. See Figure 5.6.

Figure 5.6. Example of concurrent, re-entrant processes

4. Data Structures: Stacks and Trees

We have yet to specify the data structure that will keep track of all these storage areas for functions; to do so, let us look at the tree of function calls. So that an inner function can access variables declared in an outer block, and so that we can return properly to the calling program, we must, at every point in the tree, remember all vertices on the path from the given point back to the root. As we move through the tree, vertices are added to and deleted from one end of this path; the other end *stacks* (at the root) remains fixed. Hence the vertices on the path form a stack; the storage areas for functions likewise are to be kept as a stack. This process is illustrated in Figure 5.7.

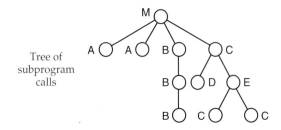

Tree of
subprogram
calls

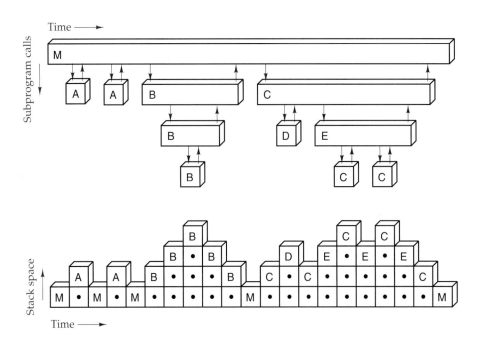

Figure 5.7. A tree of function calls and the associated stack frames

From Figure 5.7 and our discussion, we can immediately conclude that the amount of space needed to implement recursion (which, of course, is related to the number of storage areas in current use) is directly proportional to the height of the recursion tree. Programmers who have not carefully studied recursion sometimes mistakenly think that the space requirement relates to the total number of vertices in the tree. The *time* requirement of the program is related to the number of times functions are done, and therefore to the total number of vertices in the tree, but the *space* requirement is only that of the storage areas on the path from a single vertex back to the root. Thus the space requirement is reflected in the height of the tree. A well-balanced, bushy recursion tree signifies a recursive process that can do much work with little need for extra space.

time and space
requirements

5.2.3 Tail Recursion

Suppose that the very last action of a function is to make a recursive call to itself. In the stack implementation of recursion, as we have seen, the local variables of the function will be pushed onto the stack as the recursive call is initiated. When the recursive call terminates, these local variables will be popped from the stack and thereby restored to their former values. But doing this step is pointless, because the recursive call was the last action of the function, so that the function now terminates and the just-restored local variables are immediately discarded.

discarding stack entries

When the very last action of a function is a recursive call to itself, it is thus unnecessary to use the stack, as we have seen, since no local variables need to be preserved. All that we need to do is to set the dummy calling parameters to their new values (as specified for the inner recursive call) and branch to the beginning of the function. We summarize this principle for future reference.

> *If the last-executed statement of a function is a recursive call to the function itself, then this call can be eliminated by reassigning the calling parameters to the values specified in the recursive call, and then repeating the whole function.*

The process of this transformation is shown in Figure 5.8. Part (a) shows the storage areas used by the calling program **M** and several copies of the recursive function **P**, each invoked by the previous one. The colored arrows show the flow of control from one function call to the next and the blocks show the storage areas maintained by the system. Since each call by **P** to itself is its last action, there is no need to maintain the storage areas after returning from the call. The reduced storage areas are shown in part (b). Part (c), finally, shows the calls to **P** as repeated in iterative fashion on the same level of the diagram.

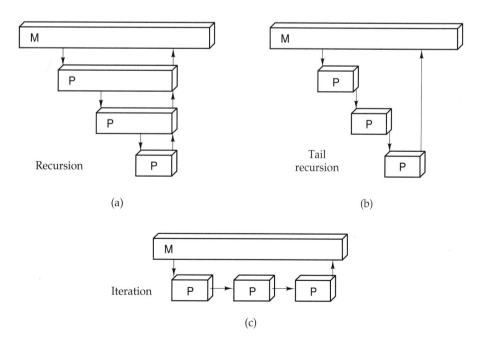

Figure 5.8. Tail recursion

tail recursion

This special case when a recursive call is the last-executed statement of the function is especially important because it frequently occurs. It is called **tail recursion**. You should carefully note that tail recursion means that the *last-executed* statement is a recursive call, not necessarily that the recursive call is the last statement appearing in the function. Tail recursion may appear, for example, within one clause of a **switch** statement or an **if** statement where other program lines appear later.

time and space

With most compilers, there will be little difference in execution *time* whether tail recursion is left in a program or is removed. If *space* considerations are important, however, then tail recursion should often be removed. By rearranging the termination condition, if needed, it is usually possible to repeat the function using a **do while** or a **while** statement.

Consider, for example, a divide-and-conquer algorithm like the Towers of Hanoi. The second recursive call inside function **move** is tail recursion; the first call is not. By removing the tail recursion, function **move** of the original recursive program can be expressed as

Hanoi without tail recursion

```
void move(int count, int start, int finish, int temp)
/* move: iterative version
     Pre:   Disk count is a valid disk to be moved.
     Post:  Moves count disks from start to finish using temp for temporary storage. */
{
  int swap;                   //   temporary storage to swap towers
  while (count > 0) {         //   Replace the if statement with a loop.
    move(count − 1, start, temp, finish);  //   first recursive call
    cout ≪ "Move disk " ≪ count ≪ " from " ≪ start
         ≪ " to " ≪ finish ≪ "." ≪ endl;
    count−−;                  //   Change parameters to mimic the second recursive call.
    swap = start;
    start = temp;
    temp = swap;
  }
}
```

We would have been quite clever had we thought of this version of the function when we first looked at the problem, but now that we have discovered it via other considerations, we can give it a natural interpretation. Think of the two towers **start** and **temp** as in the same class: We wish to use them for intermediate storage as we slowly move all the disks onto **finish**. To move a pile of **count** disks onto **finish**, then, we must move all except the bottom to the other one of **start** and **temp**. Then move the bottom one to **finish**, and repeat after interchanging **start** and **temp**, continuing to shuffle all except the bottom one between **start** and **temp**, and, at each pass, getting a new bottom one onto **finish**.

5.2.4 When Not to Use Recursion

1. Factorials

Consider the following two functions for calculating factorials. We have already seen the recursive one:

```
int factorial(int n)
/* factorial: recursive version
     Pre:  n is a nonnegative integer.
     Post: Return the value of the factorial of n. */
{
  if (n == 0) return 1;
  else        return n * factorial(n − 1);
}
```

There is an almost equally simple iterative version:

```
int factorial(int n)
/* factorial: iterative version
     Pre:  n is a nonnegative integer.
     Post: Return the value of the factorial of n. */
{
  int count, product = 1;
  for (count = 1; count <= n; count++)
    product *= count;
  return product;
}
```

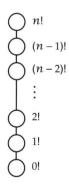

Figure 5.9.
Recursion tree for calculating factorials

Which of these programs uses less storage space? At first glance, it might appear that the recursive one does, since it has no local variables, and the iterative program has two. But actually (see Figure 5.9), the recursive program will set up a stack and fill it with the n numbers

$$n, n − 1, n − 2, \ldots, 2, 1$$

that are its calling parameters before each recursion and will then, as it works its way out of the recursion, multiply these numbers in the same order as does the second program. The progress of execution for the recursive function applied with $n = 5$ is as follows:

```
factorial(5) = 5 * factorial(4)
             = 5 * (4 * factorial(3))
             = 5 * (4 * (3 * factorial(2)))
             = 5 * (4 * (3 * (2 * factorial(1))))
             = 5 * (4 * (3 * (2 * (1 * factorial(0)))))
             = 5 * (4 * (3 * (2 * (1 * 1))))
             = 5 * (4 * (3 * (2 * 1)))
             = 5 * (4 * (3 * 2))
             = 5 * (4 * 6)
             = 5 * 24
             = 120.
```

Thus the recursive program keeps more storage than the iterative version, and it will take more time as well, since it must store and retrieve all the numbers as well as multiply them.

2. Fibonacci Numbers

A far more wasteful example than factorials (one that also appears as an apparently recommended program in some textbooks) is the computation of the *Fibonacci numbers*, which are defined by the recurrence relation

$$F_0 = 0, \quad F_1 = 1, \quad F_n = F_{n-1} + F_{n-2} \text{ for } n \geq 2.$$

The recursive program closely follows the definition:

```
int fibonacci(int n)
/* fibonacci: recursive version
     Pre:   The parameter n is a nonnegative integer.
     Post:  The function returns the nth Fibonacci number. */
{
    if (n <= 0)          return 0;
    else if (n == 1)     return 1;
    else                 return fibonacci(n − 1) + fibonacci(n − 2);
}
```

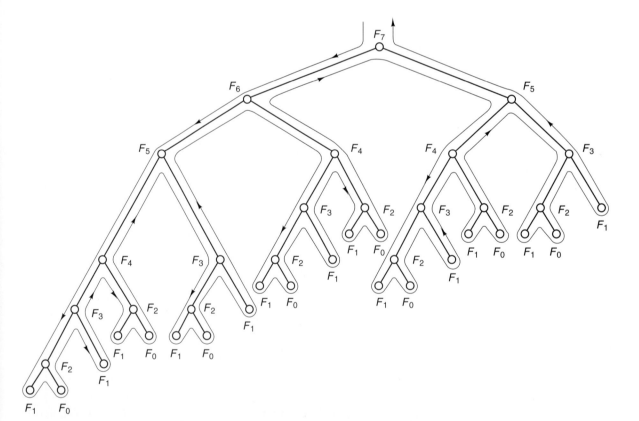

Figure 5.10. Recursion tree for the calculation of F_7

In fact, this program is quite attractive, since it is of the divide-and-conquer form: The answer is obtained by calculating two smaller cases. As we shall see, however, in this example it is not "divide and conquer," but "divide and complicate."

To assess this algorithm, let us consider, as an example, the calculation of F_7, whose recursion tree is shown in Figure 5.10. The function will first have to obtain F_6 and F_5. To get F_6 requires F_5 and F_4, and so on. But after F_5 is calculated on the way to F_6, then it will be lost and unavailable when it is later needed to get F_7. Hence, as the recursion tree shows, the recursive program needlessly repeats the same calculations over and over. Further analysis appears as an exercise. It turns out that the amount of time used by the recursive function to calculate F_n grows exponentially with n.

As with factorials, we can produce a simple iterative program by noting that we can start at 0 and keep only three variables, the current Fibonacci number and its two predecessors.

```
int fibonacci(int n)

/* fibonacci: iterative version
   Pre:   The parameter n is a nonnegative integer.
   Post:  The function returns the nth Fibonacci number. */
{
   int last_but_one;        //   second previous Fibonacci number, F_{i-2}
   int last_value;          //   previous Fibonacci number, F_{i-1}
   int current;             //   current Fibonacci number F_i
   if (n <= 0) return 0;
   else if (n ==  1) return 1;
   else {
      last_but_one = 0;
      last_value = 1;
      for (int i = 2;  i <= n;  i++) {
         current = last_but_one + last_value;
         last_but_one = last_value;
         last_value = current;
      }
      return current;
   }
}
```

The iterative function obviously uses time that increases linearly in (that is, in direct proportion with) n, so that the time difference between this function and the exponential time of the recursive function will be vast.

3. Comparisons between Recursion and Iteration

What is fundamentally different between this last example and the proper uses of recursion? To answer this question, we shall again turn to the examination of recursion trees. It should already be clear that a study of the recursion tree will provide much useful information to help us decide when recursion should or should not be used.

chain

If a function makes only one recursive call to itself, then its recursion tree has a very simple form: It is a chain; that is, each vertex has only one child. This child corresponds to the single recursive call that occurs. Such a simple tree is easy to comprehend. For the factorial function, it is simply the list of requests to calculate the factorials from $(n-1)!$ down to $1!$. By reading the recursion tree from bottom to top instead of top to bottom, we immediately obtain the iterative program from the recursive one. When the tree does reduce to a chain, then transformation from recursion to iteration is often easy, and it will likely save both space and time.

Note that a function's making only one recursive call to itself is not at all the same as having the recursive call made only one place in the function, since this place might be inside a loop. It is also possible to have two places that issue a recursive call (such as both the clauses of an **if** statement) where only one call can actually occur.

duplicate tasks

The recursion tree for calculating Fibonacci numbers is not a chain; instead, it contains a great many vertices signifying duplicate tasks. When a recursive program is run, it sets up a stack to use while traversing the tree, but if the results stored on the stack are discarded rather than kept in some other data structure for future use, then a great deal of duplication of work may occur, as in the recursive calculation of Fibonacci numbers.

change data structures

In such cases, it is preferable to substitute another data structure for the stack, one that allows references to locations other than the top. For the Fibonacci numbers, we needed only two additional temporary variables to hold the information required for calculating the current number.

recursion removal

Finally, by setting up an explicit stack, it is possible to take any recursive program and rearrange it into nonrecursive form. The resulting program, however, is almost always more complicated and harder to understand than is the recursive version. The only reason for translating a program to remove recursion is if you are forced to program in a language that does not support recursion, and fewer and fewer programs are written in such languages.

4. Comparison of Fibonacci and Hanoi: Size of Output

The recursive function for Fibonacci numbers and the recursive procedure for the Towers of Hanoi have a very similar divide-and-conquer form. Each consists essentially of two recursive calls to itself for cases slightly smaller than the original. Why, then, is the Hanoi program as efficient as possible while the Fibonacci program is very inefficient? The answer comes from considering the size of the output. In Fibonacci we are calculating only one number, and we wish to complete this calculation in only a few steps, as the iterative function does but the recursive one does not. For Hanoi, on the other hand, the size of the output is the number of instructions to be printed, which increases exponentially with the number of disks. Hence any procedure for the Towers of Hanoi will necessarily require time that increases exponentially in the number of disks.

5.2.5 Guidelines and Conclusions

In making a decision, then, about whether to write a particular algorithm in recursive or nonrecursive form, a good starting point is to consider the recursion tree.

If it has a simple form, the iterative version may be better. If it involves duplicate tasks, then data structures other than stacks will be appropriate, and the need
for recursion may disappear. If the recursion tree appears quite bushy, with little
duplication of tasks, then recursion is likely the natural method.

The stack used to resolve recursion can be regarded as a list of postponed
obligations for the program. If this list can be easily constructed in advance, then
iteration is probably better; if not, recursion may be. Recursion is something of
top-down design   a top-down approach to problem solving; it divides the problem into pieces or
selects out one key step, postponing the rest. Iteration is more of a bottom-up
approach; it begins with what is known and from this constructs the solution step
by step.

It is always true that recursion can be replaced by iteration and stacks. It is also
stacks or recursion   true, conversely (see the references for the proof), that any (iterative) program that
manipulates a stack can be replaced by a recursive program with no stack. Thus
the careful programmer should not only ask whether recursion should be removed,
but should also ask, when a program involves stacks, whether the introduction of
recursion might produce a more natural and understandable program that could
lead to improvements in the approach and in the results.

Exercises 5.2   **E1.** In the recursive calculation of F_n, determine exactly how many times each
smaller Fibonacci number will be calculated. From this, determine the order-
of-magnitude time and space requirements of the recursive function. [You may
find out either by setting up and solving a recurrence relation (top-down approach), or by finding the answer in simple cases and proving it more generally
by mathematical induction (bottom-up approach).]

E2. The *greatest common divisor* (gcd) of two positive integers is the largest integer
that divides both of them. Thus, for example, the gcd of 8 and 12 is 4, the gcd
of 9 and 18 is 9, and the gcd of 16 and 25 is 1.

(a) Write a nonrecursive function **int gcd(int x, int y)**, where x and y are required
to be positive integers, that searches through the positive integers until it
finds the largest integer dividing both x and y.

(b) Write a recursive function **int gcd(int x, int y)** that implements *Euclid's
algorithm*: If y = 0, then the gcd of x and y is x; otherwise the gcd of x and
y is the same as the gcd of y and x % y.[2]

(c) Rewrite the function of part (b) into iterative form.

(d) Discuss the advantages and disadvantages of each of these methods.

---

[2] Recall that **%** is the *modulus* operator: The result of x % y is the remainder after the integer
division of integer x by nonzero integer y.

E3. The binomial coefficients may be defined by the following recurrence relation, which is the idea of *Pascal's triangle*. The top of Pascal's triangle is shown in Figure 5.11.

$$C(n, 0) = 1 \quad \text{and} \quad C(n, n) = 1 \quad \text{for } n \geq 0.$$
$$C(n, k) = C(n - 1, k) + C(n - 1, k - 1) \quad \text{for } n > k > 0.$$

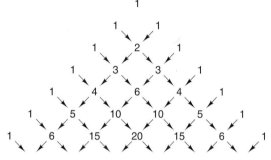

(a) Symmetric form

	0	1	2	3	4	5	6
0	1						
1	1	1					
2	1	2	1				
3	1	3	3	1			
4	1	4	6	4	1		
5	1	5	10	10	5	1	
6	1	6	15	20	15	6	1

(b) In square array

Figure 5.11. The top of Pascal's triangle of binomial coefficients

(a) Write a recursive function to generate $C(n, k)$ by the foregoing formula.
(b) Draw the recursion tree for calculating $C(6, 4)$.
(c) Use a square array with n indicating the row and k the column, and write a nonrecursive program to generate Pascal's triangle in the lower left half of the array, that is, in the entries for which $k \leq n$.
(d) Write a nonrecursive program that uses neither an array nor a stack to calculate $C(n, k)$ for arbitrary $n \geq k \geq 0$.
(e) Determine the approximate space and time requirements for each of the algorithms devised in parts (a), (c), and (d).

E4. *Ackermann's function*, defined as follows, is a standard device to determine how well recursion is implemented on a computer.

$$A(0, n) = n + 1 \quad\quad\quad\quad\quad \text{for } n \geq 0.$$
$$A(m, 0) = A(m - 1, 1) \quad\quad\quad \text{for } m > 0.$$
$$A(m, n) = A(m - 1, A(m, n - 1)) \quad \text{for } m > 0 \text{ and } n > 0.$$

(a) Write a recursive function to calculate Ackermann's function.
(b) Calculate the following values. If it is impossible to obtain any of these values, explain why.

$$A(0, 0) \quad A(0, 9) \quad A(1, 8) \quad A(2, 2) \quad A(2, 0)$$
$$A(2, 3) \quad A(3, 2) \quad A(4, 2) \quad A(4, 3) \quad A(4, 0)$$

(c) Write a nonrecursive function to calculate Ackermann's function.

5.3 BACKTRACKING: POSTPONING THE WORK

As a more complex application of recursion, let us consider the well-known puzzle of how to place eight queens on a chessboard so that no queen can take another. Recall that in the rules for chess a queen can take another piece that lies on the same row, the same column, or the same diagonal (either direction) as the queen. The chessboard has eight rows and eight columns.

It is by no means obvious how to solve this puzzle, and even the great C. F. GAUSS did not obtain a complete solution when he considered it in 1850. It is typical of puzzles that do not seem suitable for completely analytical solutions, but require either luck coupled with trial and error, or else much exhaustive (and exhausting) computation. To convince you that solutions to this problem really do exist, two of them are shown in Figure 5.12.

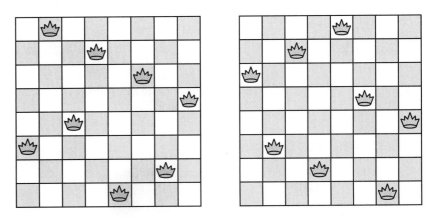

Figure 5.12. **Two configurations showing eight nonattacking queens**

In this section, we shall develop two programs to solve the eight-queens problem that will illustrate how the choice of data structures can affect a recursive program.

5.3.1 Solving the Eight-Queens Puzzle

A person attempting to solve the eight-queens problem will usually soon abandon attempts to find all (or even one) of the solutions by being clever and will start to put queens on the board, perhaps randomly or perhaps in some logical order, but always making sure that no queen placed can take another already on the board. If the person is lucky enough to place eight queens on the board by proceeding in this way, then this is a solution; if not, then one or more of the queens must be removed and placed elsewhere to continue the search for a solution. To start formulating a program, let us sketch this technique, which we think of as a recursive function that locates all solutions that begin from a given configuration of queens on a chessboard. We call the function **solve_from**. We imagine using a class called **Queens** to represent a partial configuration of queens. Thus, we can pass a **Queens** configuration as the parameter for our recursive function, solve_from. In the initial call to solve_from, from a main program, the parameter Queens configuration is empty.

outline

solve_from (Queens configuration)
    if Queens configuration *already contains eight queens*
        print configuration
    else
        for *every chessboard square* p *that is unguarded by* configuration {
            add a queen on square p *to* configuration;
            solve_from(configuration);
            remove the queen from square p *of* configuration;
        }

This sketch illustrates the use of recursion to mean "Continue to the next stage and repeat the task." Placing a queen in square p is only tentative; we leave it there only if we can continue adding queens until we have eight. Whether we reach eight or not, the procedure will return when it finds that it has finished or there are no further possibilities to investigate. After the inner call has returned, then, our program goes back to investigate the addition of other possible unguarded squares to the Queens configuration.

5.3.2 Example: Four Queens

Let us see how this algorithm works for a simpler problem, that of placing four queens on a 4×4 board, as illustrated in Figure 5.13.

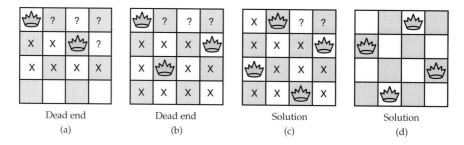

Dead end
(a)

Dead end
(b)

Solution
(c)

Solution
(d)

Figure 5.13. Solution to the four-queens problem

We shall need to put one queen in each row of the board. Let us first try to place the queen as far to the left in the row as we can. Such a choice is shown in the first row of part (a) of Figure 5.13. The question marks indicate other legitimate choices that we have not yet tried. Before we investigate these choices, we move on to the second row and try to insert a queen. The first two columns are guarded by the queen in row 1, as shown by the crossed-off squares. Columns 3 and 4 are free, so we first place the queen in column 3 and mark column 4 with a question mark. Next we move on to row 3, but we find that all four squares are guarded by one of the queens in the first two rows. We have now reached a dead end.

When we reach a dead end, we must *backtrack* by going back to the most recent choice we have made and trying another possibility. This situation is shown in part (b) of Figure 5.13, which shows the queen in row 1 unchanged, but the queen in row 2 moved to the second possible position (and the previously occupied position crossed off as no longer possible). Now we find that column 2 is the only possible position for a queen in row 3, but all four positions in row 4 are guarded. Hence we have again reached a point where no other queens can be added, and we must backtrack.

At this point, we no longer have another choice for row 2, so we must move all the way back to row 1 and move the queen to the next possible position, column 2. This situation is shown in part (c) of Figure 5.13. Now we find that, in row 2, only column 4 is unguarded, so a queen must go there. In row 3, then, column 1 is the only possibility, and, in row 4, only column 3 is possible. This placement of queens, however, does lead to a solution to the problem of four nonattacking queens on the same 4×4 board.

If we wish to find *all* the solutions, we can continue in the same way, backtracking to the last choice we made and changing the queen to the next possible move. In part (c) we had no choice in rows 4, 3, or 2, so we now back up to row 1 and move the queen to column 3. This choice leads to the unique solution shown in part (d).

Finally, we should investigate the possibilities with a queen in column 4 of row 1, but, as in part (a), there will be no solution in this case. In fact, the configurations with a queen in either column 3 or column 4 of row 1 are just the mirror images of those with a queen in column 2 or column 1, respectively. If you do a left-right reflection of the board shown in part (c), you will obtain the board shown in (d), and the boards with a queen in column 4, row 1, are just the reflections of those shown in parts (a) and (b).

5.3.3 Backtracking

This method is typical of a broad class called *backtracking algorithms*, which attempt to complete a search for a solution to a problem by constructing partial solutions, always ensuring that the partial solutions remain consistent with the requirements of the problem. The algorithm then attempts to extend a partial solution toward completion, but when an inconsistency with the requirements of the problem occurs, the algorithm backs up (*backtracks*) by removing the most recently constructed part of the solution and trying another possibility.

Backtracking proves useful in situations where many possibilities may first appear, but few survive further tests. In scheduling problems (like arranging a sports tournament), for example, it will likely be easy to assign the first few matches, but as further matches are made, the constraints drastically reduce the number of possibilities. Or take the problem of designing a compiler. In some languages, it is impossible to determine the meaning of a statement until almost all of it has been read. Consider, for example, the pair of FORTRAN statements

DO 17 K = 1, 6
DO 17 K = 1. 6

OUCH!

Both of these are legal: The first starts a loop, and the second assigns the number 1.6 to a variable called DO17K. (FORTRAN ignores all spaces, even spaces inside identifiers.) In such cases where the meaning cannot be deduced immediately, backtracking is a useful method in *parsing* (that is, splitting apart to decipher) the text of a program.

parsing

5.3.4 Overall Outline

1. The Main Program

Although we still need to fill in a great many details about the data structure that we will need to represent positions of queens on the chessboard, we can provide a main program to drive the recursive method already outlined.

We first print information about what the program does. Since it will be useful to test the program by solving smaller problems such as the four-queens problem, we allow the user to specify the number (called board_size) of queens to use. We use a global constant max_board (declared in the header file queens.h) to limit the maximum number of queens that the program can try to place.

```
int main()
/* Pre:   The user enters a valid board size.
   Post:  All solutions to the n-queens puzzle for the selected board size are printed.
   Uses:  The class Queens and the recursive function solve_from. */
{
  int board_size;
  print_information();
  cout  << "What is the size of the board? " << flush;
  cin   >> board_size;
  if (board_size < 0 || board_size > max_board)
    cout << "The number must be between 0 and " << max_board << endl;
  else {
    Queens configuration(board_size);   //   Initialize empty configuration.
    solve_from(configuration);  //   Find all solutions extending configuration.
  }
}
```

2. The Queens Class

The variable definition

Queens configuration(board_size)

uses a constructor, with a parameter, for the **class** Queens to set the user-selected board size and to initialize the empty Queens object called configuration. This empty configuration is passed as a parameter to our recursive function that will place queens on the board.

The outline of Section 5.3.1 shows that our **class** Queens will need methods to print a configuration, to add a queen at a particular square of the chessboard to a configuration, to remove this queen, and to test whether a particular square is unguarded by a configuration. Moreover, any attempt to program our function solve_from quickly shows the need for Queens data members board_size (to keep track of the size of the board) and count (to keep track of the number of queens already inserted).

After we have started building a configuration, how do we find the next square to try? Once a queen has been put into a given row, no person would waste time searching to find a place to put another queen in the same row, since the row is fully guarded by the first queen. There can never be more than one queen in each row. But our goal is to put board_size queens on the board, and there are only board_size rows. It follows that there must be a queen, exactly one queen, in *every* one of the rows. (This is called the ***pigeonhole principle***: If you have n pigeons and n pigeonholes, and no more than one pigeon ever goes in the same hole, then there must be a pigeon in every hole.) Thus, we can proceed by placing the queens on the board one row at a time, starting with row 0, and we can keep track of where they are with the single data member count, which therefore not only gives the total number of queens in the configuration so far but also gives the index of the first unoccupied row. Hence we shall always attempt to insert the next queen into the row count of a Queens configuration.

pigeonhole principle

The specifications for the major methods of the **class** Queens are as follows:

---

bool Queens :: unguarded(**int** col) **const**;

postcondition: Returns **true** or **false** according as the square in the first unoccupied row (row count) and column col is not guarded by any queen.

---

void Queens :: insert(**int** col);

precondition: The square in the first unoccupied row (row count) and column col is not guarded by any queen.

postcondition: A queen has been inserted into the square at row count and column col; count has been incremented by 1.

---

void Queens :: remove(**int** col);

precondition: There is a queen in the square in row count − 1 and column col.

postcondition: The above queen has been removed; count has been decremented by 1.

---

bool Queens :: is_solved( ) **const**;

postcondition: The function returns **true** if the number of queens already placed equals board_size; otherwise, it returns **false**.

---

3. The Backtracking Function solve_from

With these decisions, we can now write C++ code for the first version of a recursive function that places the queens on the board. Note that we pass the function's parameter by reference to save the time used to copy a **Queens** object. Unfortunately, although this parameter is just an input parameter, we do make and undo changes to it in the function, and therefore we cannot pass it as a constant reference.

```
void solve_from(Queens &configuration)
/* Pre:   The Queens configuration represents a partially completed arrangement
          of nonattacking queens on a chessboard.
   Post:  All n-queens solutions that extend the given configuration are printed.
          The configuration is restored to its initial state.
   Uses:  The class Queens and the function solve_from, recursively. */
{
  if (configuration.is_solved()) configuration.print();
  else
    for (int col = 0;  col < configuration.board_size;  col++)
      if (configuration.unguarded(col)) {
        configuration.insert(col);
        solve_from(configuration);   //   Recursively continue to add queens.
        configuration.remove(col);
      }
}
```

5.3.5 Refinement: The First Data Structure and Its Methods

An obvious way to represent a **Queens** configuration is to store the chessboard as a square array with entries indicating where the queens have been placed. Such an array will be our first choice for the data structure. The header file for this representation is thus:

```
const int max_board = 30;

class Queens {
public:
  Queens(int size);
  bool is_solved() const;
  void print() const;
  bool unguarded(int col) const;
  void insert(int col);
  void remove(int col);
  int board_size;          //   dimension of board = maximum number of queens
private:
  int count;               //   current number of queens = first unoccupied row
  bool queen_square[max_board] [max_board];
};
```

With this data structure, the method for adding a new queen is trivial:

```
void Queens :: insert(int col)
/* Pre:   The square in the first unoccupied row (row count) and column col is not
          guarded by any queen.
   Post:  A queen has been inserted into the square at row count and column col;
          count has been incremented by 1. */
{
  queen_square[count++][col] = true;
}
```

The methods is_solved, remove, and print are also very easy; these are left as exercises.

To initialize a Queens configuration, we have a constructor that uses its parameter to set the size of the board:

```
Queens :: Queens(int size)
/* Post:  The Queens object is set up as an empty configuration on a chessboard
          with size squares in each row and column. */
{
  board_size = size;
  count = 0;
  for (int row = 0;  row < board_size;  row++)
    for (int col = 0;  col < board_size;  col++)
      queen_square[row][col] = false;
}
```

We have set the count of placed queens to 0. This constructor is executed whenever we declare a Queens object and at the same time specify one integer parameter, as in our main program.

Finally, we must write the method that checks whether or not the square, located at a particular column in the first unoccupied row of the chessboard, is guarded by one (or more) of the queens already in a configuration. To do this we must search the column and both of the diagonals on which the square lies. Searching the column is straightforward, but finding the diagonals requires more delicate index calculations. See Figure 5.14 for the case of a 4×4 chessboard.

We can identify up to four diagonal directions emerging from a square of a chessboard. We shall call these the *lower-left* diagonal (which points downwards and to the left from the original square), the *lower-right* diagonal, the *upper-left* diagonal, and the *upper-right* diagonal.

First consider the upper-left diagonal, as shown in part (c) of Figure 5.14. If we start at a square of the chessboard with position [row][col], then the squares belonging to the upper-left diagonal have positions of the form [row − i][col − i], where i is a positive integer. This upper-left diagonal must end on either the upper

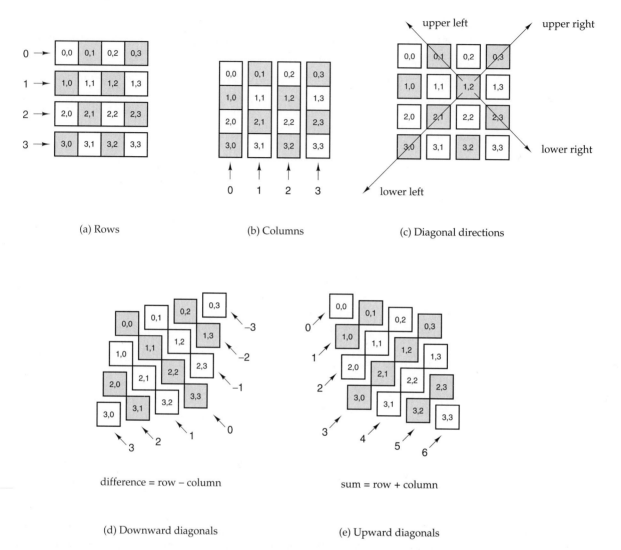

(a) Rows

(b) Columns

(c) Diagonal directions

difference = row − column

sum = row + column

(d) Downward diagonals

(e) Upward diagonals

Figure 5.14. Chessboard separated into components

edge of the board, where row − i == 0, or the left-hand edge of the board, where col − i == 0. Therefore, we can list the squares on the upper-left diagonal by using a **for** loop to increment i from 1 until one of the conditions row − i >= 0 and col − i >= 0 fails.

Similar loops delineate the other three diagonals that emerge from a given square of the board. However, when we come to check whether a particular square in the first unoccupied row of the chessboard is unguarded, we need never check the two lower diagonals, since lower squares are automatically unoccupied. Therefore, only the cases of upper diagonals are reflected in the code for the method **unguarded**, which follows.

```
bool Queens :: unguarded(int col) const
/* Post: Returns true or false according as the square in the first unoccupied row
         (row count) and column col is not guarded by any queen. */
{
    int i;
    bool ok = true;         //    turns false if we find a queen in column or diagonal
    for (i = 0; ok && i < count; i++)
        ok = !queen_square[i][col];   //   Check upper part of column
    for (i = 1; ok && count − i >= 0 && col − i >= 0; i++)
        ok = !queen_square[count − i][col − i];   //   Check upper-left diagonal
    for (i = 1; ok && count − i >= 0 && col + i < board_size; i++)
        ok = !queen_square[count − i][col + i];   //   Check upper-right diagonal
    return ok;
}
```

5.3.6 Review and Refinement

The program we have just finished is quite adequate for the problem of 8 queens; it turns out that there are 92 solutions for placing 8 queens on an 8×8 chessboard. If, however, you try running the program on larger sizes of chessboards, you will find that it quickly starts to consume huge amounts of time. For example, one run produced the following numbers:

Size	8	9	10	11	12	13
Number of solutions	92	352	724	2680	14200	73712
Time (seconds)	0.05	0.21	1.17	6.62	39.11	243.05
Time per solution (ms.)	0.54	0.60	1.62	2.47	2.75	3.30

rapidly increasing time

As you can see, the number of solutions increases rapidly with the size of the board, and the time increases even more rapidly, since even the time per solution increases with the size. If we wish to obtain results for larger-sized chessboards, we must either find a more efficient program or use large amounts of computer time.

Let us therefore ask where our program spends most of its time. Making the recursive calls and backtracking takes a great deal of time, but this time reflects the basic method by which we are solving the problem and the existence of a large number of solutions. The several loops in the method unguarded( ) will also require considerable time. Let us see if these loops can be eliminated, that is, whether it is possible to determine whether or not a square is guarded without searching its row, column, and diagonals.

first refinement

One way to do this is to change the data we keep in the square array representing the chessboard. Rather than keeping track only of which squares are occupied by queens, we can use the array to keep track of all the squares that are guarded by queens. It is then easy to check if a square is unguarded. A small change helps with the backtracking, since a square may be guarded by more than one queen. For each square, we can keep a count of the number of queens guarding the square. Then, when a queen is inserted, we increase the counts by 1 for all squares on the same row, column, and diagonals. When a queen is deleted, we simply decrease all these counts by 1.

Programming this method is left as a project. Let us note that this method, while faster than the previous one, still requires loops to update the guard counts for each square. Instead, with a little more thought, we can eliminate all these loops.

second refinement

The key idea is to notice that each row, column, and diagonal on the chessboard can contain at most one queen. (The pigeonhole principle shows that, in a solution, *all* the rows and *all* the columns are occupied, but not all the diagonals will be occupied, since there are more diagonals than rows or columns.)

We can thus keep track of unguarded squares by using three **bool** arrays: col_free, upward_free, and downward_free, where diagonals from the lower left to the upper right are considered upward and those from the upper left to lower right are considered downward. (See parts (d) and (e) of Figure 5.14.) Since we place queens on the board one row at a time, starting at row 0, we do not need an explicit array to find which rows are free.

Finally, for the sake of printing the configuration, we need to know the column number for the queen in each row, and this we can do with an integer-valued array indexed by the rows.

loopless program

Note that we can now solve the entire problem without even keeping a square array representing the chessboard, and without any loops at all except for initializing the "free" arrays. Hence the time that our revised program will need will closely reflect the number of steps investigated in backtracking.

How do we identify the squares along a single diagonal? Along the longest upward diagonal, the entry indices are

[board_size − 1] [0], [board_size − 2] [1], ..., [0] [board_size − 1].

These have the property that the row and column indices always sum to the value board_size − 1. It turns out that (as shown in part (e) of Figure 5.14) along any upward diagonal, the row and column indices will have a *constant sum*. This sum ranges from 0 for the upward diagonal of length 1 in the upper left corner, to $2 \times$ board_size − 2, for the upward diagonal of length 1 in the lower right corner. Thus we can number the upward diagonals from 0 to $2 \times$ board_size − 2, so that the square in row i and column j is in upward diagonal number $i + j$.

Similarly, along downward diagonals (as shown in part(d) of Figure 5.14), the *difference* of the row and column indices is constant, ranging from −board_size + 1 to board_size − 1. Hence, we can number the downward diagonals from 0 to $2 \times$ board_size − 1, so that the square in row i and column j is in downward diagonal number $i − j +$ board_size − 1.

After making all these decisions, we can now specify our revised **Queens** data structure formally.

```
class Queens {
public:
   Queens(int size);
   bool is_solved() const;
   void print() const;
   bool unguarded(int col) const;
   void insert(int col);
   void remove(int col);
   int board_size;
private:
   int count;
   bool col_free[max_board];
   bool upward_free[2 * max_board − 1];
   bool downward_free[2 * max_board − 1];
   int queen_in_row[max_board];   //   column number of queen in each row
};
```

We complete our program by supplying the methods for the revised class **Queens**. We begin with the constructor:

Queens :: Queens(int size)
/* **Post:** *The* Queens *object is set up as an empty configuration on a chessboard with* size *squares in each row and column.* */

```
{
   board_size = size;
   count = 0;
   for (int i = 0; i < board_size; i++) col_free[i] = true;
   for (int j = 0; j < (2 * board_size − 1); j++) upward_free[j] = true;
   for (int k = 0; k < (2 * board_size − 1); k++) downward_free[k] = true;
}
```

This is similar to the constructor for the first version, except that now we have marked all columns and diagonals as unguarded, rather than initializing a square array.

The method **insert()** encodes our conventions about the numbering of diagonals.

void Queens :: insert(**int** col)
/* **Pre:** *The square in the first unoccupied row (row* count*) and column* col *is not guarded by any queen.*
   Post: *A queen has been inserted into the square at row* count *and column* col*; count has been incremented by 1.* */

```
{
   queen_in_row[count] = col;
   col_free[col] = false;
   upward_free[count + col] = false;
   downward_free[count − col + board_size − 1] = false;
   count++;
}
```

Finally, the method unguarded() needs only to test whether the column and two diagonals that contain a particular square are unguarded.

bool Queens :: unguarded(**int** col) **const**
/* **Post:** *Returns* **true** *or* **false** *according as the square in the first unoccupied row (row* count) *and column* col *is not guarded by any queen.* */
{
  return col_free[col]
      && upward_free[count + col]
      && downward_free[count − col + board_size − 1];
}

Note how much simpler unguarded() is than it was in the first version. Indeed you will note that there are no loops in any of the methods, only in the initialization code in the constructor.

The remaining methods is_solved(), remove(), and print() can safely be left as exercises.

The following table gives information about the performance of our new program for the n-queens problem. For comparison purposes, we produced the data on the same machine under the same conditions as in the testing of our earlier program. The timing data shows that for the 8-queens problem the new program runs about 5 times as fast as the older program. As the board size increases, we would expect the new program to gain even more on the old program. Indeed for the 13-queens problem, our new program is faster by a factor of about 7.

Size	8	9	10	11	12	13
Number of solutions	92	352	724	2680	14200	73712
Time (seconds)	0.01	0.05	0.22	1.06	5.94	34.44
Time per solution (ms.)	0.11	0.14	0.30	0.39	0.42	0.47

5.3.7 Analysis of Backtracking

Let us conclude this section by estimating the amount of work that our program will do.

1. Effectiveness of Backtracking

We begin by looking at how much work backtracking saves when compared with enumerating all possibilities. To obtain numerical results, we look only at the 8×8 case. If we had taken the naïve approach by writing a program that first placed all eight queens on the board and then rejected the illegal configurations, we would be investigating as many configurations as choosing 8 places out of 64, which is

$$\binom{64}{8} = 4,426,165,368.$$

The observation that there can be only one queen in each row immediately cuts this number to

$$8^8 = 16,777,216.$$

This number is still large, but our program will not investigate nearly this many squares. Instead, it rejects squares whose column or diagonals are guarded. The requirement that there be only one queen in each column reduces the number to

reduced count

$$8! = 40,320,$$

which is quite manageable by computer, and the actual number of cases the program considers will be much less than this, since squares with guarded diagonals in the early rows will be rejected immediately, with no need to make the fruitless attempt to fill the later rows.

effectiveness of backtracking

This behavior summarizes the effectiveness of backtracking: positions that are discovered to be impossible prevent the later investigation of fruitless paths.

Another way to express this behavior of backtracking is to consider the tree of recursive calls to the recursive function solve_from, part of which is shown in Figure 5.15. The two solutions shown in this tree are the same as the solutions shown in Figure 5.12. It appears formally that each node in the tree might have up to eight children corresponding to the recursive calls to solve_from for the eight possible values of new_col. Even at levels near the root, however, most of these branches are found to be impossible, and the removal of one node on an upper level removes a multitude of its descendents. Backtracking is a most effective tool to prune a recursion tree to manageable size.

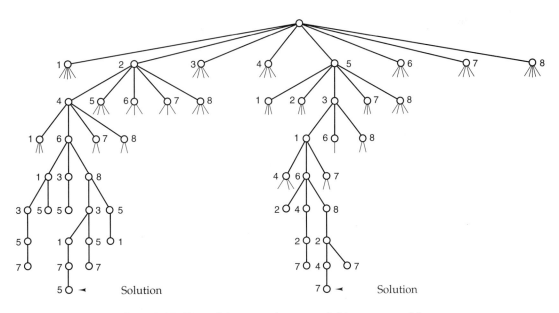

Figure 5.15. Part of the recursion tree, eight-queens problem

2. Lower Bounds

On the other hand, for the n-queens problem, the amount of work done by backtracking still grows very rapidly with n. Let us obtain a very rough idea of how fast. When we place a queen in one row of the chessboard, notice that it excludes at most 3 positions (its column, upper diagonal, and lower diagonal) from each following row of the board. For the first row, backtracking will investigate n positions for the queen. For the second row it must investigate at least $n - 3$ positions, for the third row $n - 6$, and so on. Hence, to place a queen in each of the first $n/4$ rows, backtracking investigates a minimum of

$$n(n - 3)(n - 6)\ldots(n - 3n/4)$$

positions. The last of these factors is $n/4$; the others are all larger, and there are $n/4$ factors. Hence, just to fill the first $n/4$ rows, backtracking must investigate more than $(n/4)^{n/4}$ positions.

To obtain an idea how rapidly this number grows with n, recall that the Towers of Hanoi requires 2^n steps for n disks, and notice that $(n/4)^{n/4}$ grows even more rapidly than 2^n as n increases. To see this, we need only observe that $\log((n/4)^{n/4})/\log(2^n) = \log(n/4)/4\log(2)$. This ratio clearly increases without *exponential growth* bound as n increases. We say that 2^n increases *exponentially*, and $(n/4)^{n/4}$ increases even more rapidly. Hence backtracking for the n-queens problem becomes impossibly slow as n increases.

3. Number of Solutions

Notice that we have *not* proved that it is impossible to print out all solutions to the n-queens problem by computer for large n, but only that backtracking will not do so. Perhaps there might exist some other, very clever, algorithm that would display the solutions much more quickly than backtracking does. This is, however, not the case. It is possible (see the references) to prove that the number of solutions of the n-queens problem cannot be bounded by any polynomial in n. In fact, it appears that the number of solutions cannot even be bounded by any expression *unsolved problem* of the exponential form k^n, where k is a constant, but to prove this is an unsolved problem.

Exercises 5.3

E1. What is the maximum depth of recursion in the function solve_from?

E2. Starting with the following partial configuration of five queens on the board, construct the recursion tree of all situations that the function solve_from will consider in trying to add the remaining three queens. Stop drawing the tree at the point where the function will backtrack and remove one of the original five queens.

E3. By performing backtracking by hand, find all solutions to the problem of placing five queens on a 5 × 5 board. You may use the left-right symmetry of the first row by considering only the possibilities when the queen in row 1 is in one of columns 1, 2, or 3.

Programming Projects 5.3

P1. Run the eight-queens program on your computer:

(a) Write the missing Queens methods.

(b) Find out exactly how many board positions are investigated by including a counter that is incremented every time function solve_from is started. [Note that a method that placed all eight queens before it started checking for guarded squares would be equivalent to eight calls to solve_from.]

(c) Run the program for the number of queens ranging from 4 to 15. Try to find a mathematical function that approximates the number of positions investigated as a function of the number of queens.

P2. A *superqueen* can make not only all of a queen's moves, but it can also make a knight's move. (See Project P4.) Modify Project P1 so it uses superqueens instead of ordinary queens.

P3. Describe a rectangular maze by indicating its paths and walls within an array. Write a backtracking program to find a way through the maze.

P4. Another chessboard puzzle (this one reputedly solved by GAUSS at the age of four) is to find a sequence of moves by a knight that will visit every square of the board exactly once. Recall that a knight's move is to jump two positions either vertically or horizontally and one position in the perpendicular direction. Such a move can be accomplished by setting x to either 1 or 2, setting y to $3 - x$, and then changing the first coordinate by $\pm x$ and the second by $\pm y$ (provided that the resulting position is still on the board). Write a backtracking program that will input an initial position and search for a knight's tour starting at the given position and going to every square once and no square more than once. If you find that the program runs too slowly, a good method is to order the list of squares to which it can move from a given position so that it will first try to go to the squares with the least accessibility, that is, to the squares from which there are the fewest knight's moves to squares not yet visited.

P5. Modify the program from Project P4 so that it numbers the squares of the chessboard in the order they are visited by the knight, starting with 1 in the square where the knight starts. Modify the program so that it finds a *magic* knight's tour, that is, a tour in which the resulting numbering of the squares produces a magic square. [See Section 1.6, Project P1(a) for the definition of a magic square.]

5.4 TREE-STRUCTURED PROGRAMS: LOOK-AHEAD IN GAMES ─────

In games of mental skill the person who can anticipate what will happen several moves in advance has an advantage over a competitor who looks only for immediate gain. In this section we develop a computer algorithm to play games by looking at moves several steps in advance. This algorithm can be described in terms of a tree; afterward we show how recursion can be used to program this structure.

5.4.1 Game Trees

We can picture the sequences of possible moves by means of a *game tree*, in which the root denotes the initial situation and the branches from the root denote the legal moves that the first player could make. At the next level down, the branches correspond to the legal moves by the second player in each situation, and so on, with branches from vertices at even levels denoting moves by the first player, and from vertices at odd levels denoting moves by the second player.

Eight   The complete game tree for the trivial game of *Eight* is shown in Figure 5.16. In this game the first player chooses one of the numbers 1, 2, or 3. At each later turn the appropriate player chooses one of 1, 2, or 3, but the number chosen by the previous player is not allowed. The branches of the tree are labeled with the number chosen. A running sum of the numbers chosen is kept, and if a player brings this sum to exactly eight, then the player wins. If the player takes the sum over eight, then the other player wins. No draws are possible. In the diagram, **F** denotes a win by the first player, and **S** a win by the second player.

Even a trivial game like Eight produces a good-sized tree. Games of real interest like Chess or Go have trees so huge that there is no hope of investigating all the branches, and a program that runs in reasonable time can examine only a few levels below the current vertex in the tree. People playing such games are also unable to see every possibility to the end of the game, but they can make intelligent choices, because, with experience, a person comes to recognize that some situations in a game are much better than others, even if they do not guarantee a win.

evaluation function   For any interesting game that we propose to play by computer, therefore, we shall need some kind of *evaluation function* that will examine the current situation and return an integer assessing its benefits. To be definite, we shall assume that large numbers reflect favorable situations for the first player, and therefore small (or more negative) numbers show an advantage for the second player.

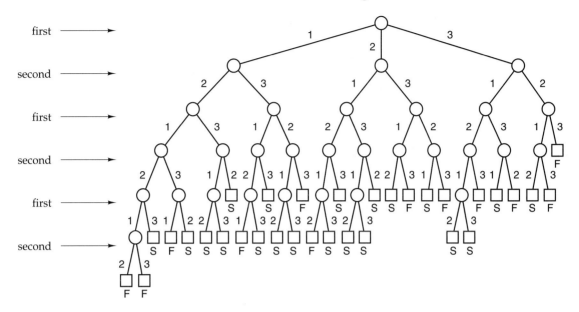

Figure 5.16. Tree for the game of Eight

5.4.2 The Minimax Method

Part of the tree for a fictitious game appears in Figure 5.17. Since we are looking ahead, we need the evaluation function only at the leaves of the tree (that is, the positions from which we shall not look further ahead in the game), and, from this information, we wish to select a move. We shall draw the leaves of the game tree as squares and the remaining nodes as circles. Hence Figure 5.16 provides values only for the nodes drawn as squares.

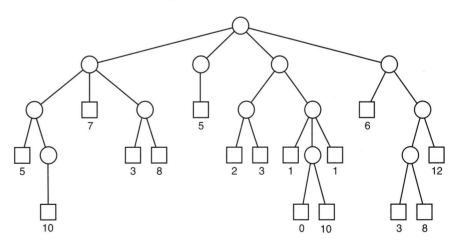

Figure 5.17. A game tree with values assigned at the leaves

The move we eventually select is one of the branches coming directly from the root, at the top level of the tree. We take the evaluation function from the perspective of the player who must make the first move, which means that this player selects the maximum value possible. At the next level down, the other player will select the smallest value possible, and so on.

tracing the tree   By working up from the bottom of the tree, we can assign values to all the vertices. Let us trace this process part of the way through Figure 5.17, starting at the lower left side of the tree. The first unlabeled node is the circle above the square labeled 10. Since there is no choice for the move made at this node, it must also have the value 10. Its parent node has two children now labeled 5 and 10. This parent node is on the third level of the tree. That is, it represents a move by the first player, who wishes to maximize the value. Hence, this player will choose the move with value 10, and so the value for the parent node is also 10.

Next let us move up one level in the tree to the node with three children. We now know that the leftmost child has value 10, and the second child has value 7. The value for the rightmost child will be the maximum of the values of its two children, 3 and 8. Hence its value is 8. The node with three children is on the second level; that is, it represents a move by the player who wishes to minimize the value. Thus this player will choose the center move of the three possibilities, and the value at this node is therefore 7.

And thus the process continues. You should take a moment to complete the evaluation of all the nodes in Figure 5.17. The result is shown in Figure 5.18. The value of the current situation turns out to be 7, and the current (first) player will choose the leftmost branch as the best move.

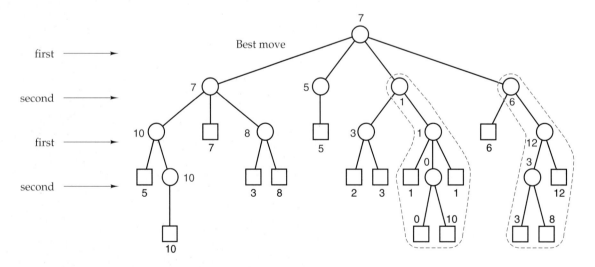

Figure 5.18. Minimax evaluation of a game tree

The dotted lines shown in color will be explained later, in one of the Projects. It turns out that, by keeping track of the minimum and maximum found so far, it is not necessary to evaluate every node in a game tree, and, in Figure 5.18, the nodes enclosed in the dotted lines need not be evaluated. Since in evaluating a game tree we alternately take minima and maxima, this process is called a ***minimax*** method.

minimax method

5.4.3 Algorithm Development

Next let us see how the minimax method can be embodied in a formal algorithm for looking ahead in a game-playing program. We wish to write a general-purpose algorithm that can be used with any two-player game.

Our program will need access to information about the particular game that we want it to play. We shall assume that this information is collected in the implementation of classes called **Move** and **Board**. An object of type **Move** will represent a single game move, and an object of type **Board** will represent a single game position. Later we will implement versions of these classes for the game of tic-tac-toe (noughts and crosses).

For the **class Move**, we shall only require constructor methods. We shall need one constructor to create **Move** objects that might be specified by a client and a second, default constructor to create empty **Move** objects. We shall also assume that **Move** objects (as well as **Board** objects) can be passed as value parameters to functions and can be copied safely with the assignment operator (that is, the operator =).

For the class **Board**, we shall clearly require methods to initialize the **Board**, to detect whether the game is over, to play a move that is passed as a parameter, to evaluate a position, and to supply a list of all current legal moves.

The method **legal_moves** that gives current move options will need a list parameter to communicate its results. We have our choice of several list data structures to hold these moves. The order in which they are investigated in later stages of look-ahead is unimportant, so they could be kept as any form of list. For simplicity of programming, let us use a stack. The entries in the stack are moves; so that, in order to use our earlier **Stack** implementation, we require the definition:

legal moves

typedef Move Stack_entry;

We shall also need two other methods, which are useful in our selection of the most favorable move for the ***mover***, defined to be the player who must make the next move. The first of these is the method called **better**: It uses two integer parameters and returns a nonzero result if the mover would prefer a game value given by the first rather than the second parameter.

compare value of moves

The other method, **worst_case**, returns a predetermined constant value that the mover would definitely like less than the value of any possible game position. Although we will be able to analyze the game without communicating with a user, any program that uses our analysis to play the game will need **Board** methods to print a stored position and to print game instructions.

find worst-case value

leave Board
unchanged

Just as a chess player may not touch the pieces on a chessboard except to make a move, we shall require that the Board methods (other than the one to **play** a move) leave Board data members unchanged. The touch-move rule in chess helps to reassure an arbiter or observer that the game is proceeding fairly, and, in a similar way, the protection that we give our **class** Board reassures a programmer who uses the class. As we have already seen, in C++, we attach the modifier **const** after the parameter list of a method or member function to guarantee that the function will not change data members of the corresponding object. Thus our definition for the **class** Board will take the form:

```
class Board {
public:
   Board();                               //   constructor for initialization
   int done() const;                      //   Test whether the game is over.
   void play(Move try_it);
   int evaluate() const;
   int legal_moves(Stack &moves) const;
   int worst_case() const;
   int better(int value, int old_value) const;
                                          //   Which parameter does the mover prefer?
   void print() const;
   void instructions() const;
   /* Additional methods, functions, and data will depend on the game under con-
      sideration. */
};
```

Observe that the data members of the class **Board** will need to keep track of both the board position and which player is the mover.

termination

Before we write a function that looks ahead to evaluate a game tree, we should decide when our look-ahead algorithm is to stop looking further. For a game of reasonable complexity, we must establish a number of levels **depth** beyond which the search will not go. The other condition for termination is that the game is over: this is detected by a return of **true** from Board::done(). The basic task of looking ahead in the tree can now be described with the following recursive algorithm.

outline

```
look_ahead at game (a Board object);
   if the recursion terminates (i.e. depth == 0 or game.done())
      return an evaluation of the position
   else
      for each legal Move
         create a new Board by making the Move
            and recursively look_ahead for the game value corresponding
            to the best follow-up Move for the other player;
         select the best option for the mover among values found in the loop;
         return the corresponding Move and value as the result;
```

5.4.4 Refinement

The outline of Section 5.4.3 leads to the following recursive function.

```
int look_ahead(const Board &game, int depth, Move &recommended)
/* Pre:   Board game represents a legal game position.
   Post:  An evaluation of the game, based on looking ahead depth moves, is re-
          turned. The best move that can be found for the mover is recorded as
          Move recommended.
   Uses:  The classes Stack, Board, and Move, together with function look_ahead
          recursively. */
{
  if (game.done( ) || depth ==  0)
    return game.evaluate( );

  else {
    Stack moves;
    game.legal_moves(moves);
    int value, best_value = game.worst_case( );

    while (!moves.empty( )) {
      Move try_it, reply;
      moves.top(try_it);
      Board new_game = game;
      new_game.play(try_it);
      value = look_ahead(new_game, depth − 1, reply);
      if (game.better(value, best_value)) {
                            //    try_it is the best move yet found
        best_value = value;
        recommended = try_it;
      }
      moves.pop( );
    }
    return best_value;
  }
}
```

The reference parameter **Move recommended** is used to return a recommended move (unless the game is over or the depth of search is 0). The reference parameter **Board game** could be specified as a value parameter, since we do not want to change the **Board** in the function. However, to avoid a possibly expensive copying operation, we pass **game** as a constant reference parameter. Observe that the compiler can guarantee that the object **Board game** is unchanged by the function look_ahead, because the only **Board** methods that are applied have been declared with the modifier **const**. Without this earlier care in our definition of the **class Board**, it would have been illegal to pass the parameter **Board game** as a constant.

5.4.5 Tic-Tac-Toe

We shall finish this section by giving implementations of the classes **Board** and **Move** for use in the game of tic-tac-toe (noughts and crosses). Here, the classes consist of little more than a formal implementation of the rules of the game.

main program
We leave the writing of a main program that harnesses these classes with the function **look_ahead** to play a game of tic-tac-toe as a project. A number of options could be followed in such a program: the computer could play against a human opponent, give a complete analysis of a position, or give its assessments of the moves of two human players.

We shall represent the grid for a tic-tac-toe game as a 3×3 array of integers, and we shall use the value 0 to denote an empty square and the values 1 and 2 to denote squares occupied by the first and second players, respectively.

In a **Move** object, we shall just store the coordinates of a square on the grid. For legal moves, these coordinates will be between 0 and 2. We shall not try to encapsulate **Move** objects, because they act as little more than holders for a collection of data values. We thus arrive at the following implementation of the **class Move**.

```
//   class for a tic-tac-toe move
class Move {
public:
   Move();
   Move(int r, int c);
   int row;
   int col;
};


Move :: Move()
/* Post:  The Move is initialized to an illegal, default value. */
{
   row = 3;
   col = 3;
}
Move :: Move(int r, int c)
/* Post:  The Move is initialized to the given coordinates. */
{
   row = r;
   col = c;
}
```

We have seen that the class **Board** needs a constructor (to initialize a game), methods **print** and **instructions** (which print out information for a user), methods **done**, **play**, and legal_moves (which implement rules of the game), and methods evaluate, better, and worst_case (which make judgments about the values of various moves). We shall find it useful to have an auxiliary function the_winner, which returns a result to indicate whether the game has been won and, if it has, by which player.

The Board class must also store data members to record the current game state in a 3×3 array and to record how many moves have been played. We thus arrive at the following **class** definition.

```
class Board {
public:
    Board();
    bool done() const;
    void print() const;
    void instructions() const;
    bool better(int value, int old_value) const;
    void play(Move try_it);
    int worst_case() const;
    int evaluate() const;
    int legal_moves(Stack &moves) const;
private:
    int squares[3][3];
    int moves_done;
    int the_winner() const;
};
```

constructor   The constructor simply fills the array squares with the value 0 to indicate that neither player has made any moves.

```
Board :: Board()
/* Post:  The Board is initialized as empty. */
{
    for (int i = 0;  i < 3;  i++)
        for (int j = 0;  j < 3;  j++)
            squares[i][j] = 0;
    moves_done = 0;
}
```

making a move   We shall leave the methods that print information for the user as exercises; instead we concentrate next on methods that apply the rules of the game. To make a move, we need only reset the value of one of the squares and update the counter moves_done to record that another move has been played. The value of the counter moves_done is used to calculate whether player 1 or player 2 should be credited with the move.

```
void Board :: play(Move try_it)
/* Post:  The Move try_it is played on the Board. */
{
   squares[try_it.row] [try_it.col] = moves_done % 2 + 1;
   moves_done++;
}
```

determine a winner

The auxiliary function the_winner returns a nonzero result if either player has won. It tests all eight possible lines of the Board in turn.

```
int Board :: the_winner() const
/* Post:  Return either a value of 0 for a position where neither player has won, a
          value of 1 if the first player has won, or a value of 2 if the second player
          has won. */
{
   int i;
   for (i = 0; i < 3; i++)
     if (squares[i] [0]  && squares[i] [0] ==  squares[i] [1]
                          && squares[i] [0] ==  squares[i] [2])
         return squares[i] [0];
   for (i = 0; i < 3; i++)
     if (squares[0] [i]  && squares[0] [i] ==  squares[1] [i]
                          && squares[0] [i] ==  squares[2] [i])
         return squares[0] [i];
   if (squares[0] [0]  && squares[0] [0] ==  squares[1] [1]
                        && squares[0] [0] ==  squares[2] [2])
       return squares[0] [0];
   if (squares[0] [2]  && squares[0] [2] ==  squares[1] [1]
                        && squares[2] [0] ==  squares[0] [2])
       return squares[0] [2];
   return 0;
}
```

The game is finished either after nine moves have been played or when one or the other player has won. (Our program will not recognize that the game is guaranteed to be a draw until all nine squares are filled.)

```
bool Board :: done() const
/* Post:  Return true if the game is over; either because a player has already won
          or because all nine squares have been filled. */
{
   return moves_done == 9 || the_winner() > 0;
}
```

The legal moves available for a player are just the **squares** with a value of 0.

```
int Board :: legal_moves(Stack &moves) const
/* Post: The parameter Stack moves is set up to contain all possible legal moves
         on the Board. */
{
  int count = 0;
  while (!moves.empty()) moves.pop();
  for (int i = 0;  i < 3;  i++)
    for (int j = 0;  j < 3;  j++)
      if (squares[i] [j] == 0) {
        Move can_play(i, j);
        moves.push(can_play);
        count++;
      }
  return count;
}
```

evaluating a position   We now come to the methods that must make a judgment about the value of a **Board** position or of a potential **Move**. We shall initially evaluate a **Board** position as 0 if neither player has yet won; however, if one or other player has won, we shall evaluate the position according to the rule that quick wins are considered very good, and quick losses are considered very bad. Of course, this evaluation will only ever be applied at the end of a **look_ahead** and, so long as we look far enough ahead, its crude nature will not be a drawback.

```
int Board :: evaluate( ) const
/* Post: Return either a value of 0 for a position where neither player has won, a
         positive value between 1 and 9 if the first player has won, or a negative
         value between −1 and −9 if the second player has won, */
{
  int winner = the_winner( );
  if (winner == 1) return 10 − moves_done;
  else if (winner == 2) return moves_done − 10;
  else return 0;
}
```

The method **worst_case** can simply return a value of either 10 or −10, since **evaluate** always produces a value between −9 and 9. Hence, the comparison method **better** needs only to compare a pair of integers with values between −10 and 10. We leave these methods as exercises.

We have now sketched out most of a program to play tic-tac-toe. A program that sets the depth of look-ahead to a value of 9 will play a perfect game, since it will always be able to look ahead to a situation where its evaluation of the position is exact. A program with shallower depth can make mistakes, because it might finish its look-ahead with a collection of positions that misleadingly evaluate as zero.

Exercises 5.4   **E1.** Assign values of +1 for a win by the first player and −1 for a win by the second player in the game of Eight, and evaluate its game tree by the minimax method, as shown in Figure 5.16.

E2. A variation of the game of *Nim* begins with a pile of sticks, from which a player can remove 1, 2, or 3 sticks at each turn. The player must remove at least 1 (but no more than remain on the pile). The player who takes the last stick loses. Draw the complete game tree that begins with

(a) 5 sticks   **(b)** 6 sticks.

Assign appropriate values for the leaves of the tree, and evaluate the other nodes by the minimax method.

E3. Draw the top three levels (showing the first two moves) of the game tree for the game of tic-tac-toe (noughts and crosses), and calculate the number of vertices that will appear on the fourth level. You may reduce the size of the tree by taking advantage of symmetries: At the first move, for example, show only three possibilities (the center square, a corner, or a side square) rather than all nine. Further symmetries near the root will reduce the size of the game tree.

Programming Projects 5.4   **P1.** Write a main program and the **Move** and **Board** class implementations to play Eight against a human opponent.

P2. If you have worked your way through the tree in Figure 5.17 in enough detail, you may have noticed that it is not necessary to obtain the values for all the vertices while doing the minimax process, for there are some parts of the tree in which the best move certainly cannot appear.

Let us suppose that we work our way through the tree starting at the lower left and filling in the value for a parent vertex as soon as we have the values for all its children. After we have done all the vertices in the two main branches on the left, we find values of 7 and 5, and therefore the maximum value will be at least 7. When we go to the next vertex on level 1 and its left child, we find that the value of this child is 3. At this stage, we are taking minima, so the value to be assigned to the parent on level 1 cannot possibly be more than 3 (it is actually 1). Since 3 is less than 7, the first player will take the leftmost branch instead, and we can exclude the other branch. The vertices that, in this way, need never be evaluated are shown within dotted lines in color in Figure 5.18.

The process of eliminating vertices in this way is called ***alpha-beta pruning***. The Greek letters α (alpha) and β (beta) are generally used to denote the cutoff points found.

alpha-beta pruning

Modify the function **look_ahead** so that it uses alpha-beta pruning to reduce the number of branches investigated. Compare the performance of the two versions in playing several games.

POINTERS AND PITFALLS

1. Recursion should be used freely in the initial design of algorithms. It is especially appropriate where the main step toward solution consists of reducing a problem to one or more smaller cases.

2. Study several simple examples to see whether recursion should be used and how it will work.

3. Attempt to formulate a method that will work more generally. Ask, "How can this problem be divided into parts?" or "How will the key step in the middle be done?"

4. Ask whether the remainder of the problem can be done in the same or a similar way, and modify your method if necessary so that it will be sufficiently general.

5. Find a stopping rule that will indicate that the problem or a suitable part of it is done.

6. Be very careful that your algorithm always terminates and handles trivial cases correctly.

7. The key tool for the analysis of recursive algorithms is the recursion tree. Draw the recursion tree for one or two simple examples appropriate to your problem.

8. The recursion tree should be studied to see whether the recursion is needlessly repeating work, or if the tree represents an efficient division of the work into pieces.

9. A recursive function can accomplish exactly the same tasks as an iterative function using a stack. Consider carefully whether recursion or iteration with a stack will lead to a clearer program and give more insight into the problem.

10. Tail recursion may be removed if space considerations are important.

11. Recursion can always be translated into iteration, but the general rules will often produce a result that greatly obscures the structure of the program. Such obscurity should be tolerated only when the programming language makes it unavoidable, and even then it should be well documented.

12. Study your problem to see if it fits one of the standard paradigms for recursive algorithms, such as divide and conquer, backtracking, or tree-structured algorithms.

13. Let the use of recursion fit the structure of the problem. When the conditions of the problem are thoroughly understood, the structure of the required algorithm will be easier to see.

14. Always be careful of the extreme cases. Be sure that your algorithm terminates gracefully when it reaches the end of its task.

15. Do as thorough error checking as possible. Be sure that every condition that a function requires is stated in its preconditions, and, even so, defend your function from as many violations of its preconditions as conveniently possible.

REVIEW QUESTIONS

5.1   **1.** Define the term *divide and conquer*.

5.2   **2.** Name two different ways to implement recursion.

3. What is a *re-entrant* program?

4. How does the time requirement for a recursive function relate to its recursion tree?

5. How does the space requirement for a recursive function relate to its recursion tree?

6. What is *tail* recursion?

7. Describe the relationship between the shape of the recursion tree and the efficiency of the corresponding recursive algorithm.

8. What are the major phases of designing recursive algorithms?

9. What is *concurrency*?

10. What important kinds of information does the computer system need to keep while implementing a recursive function call?

11. Is the removal of tail recursion more important for saving time or for saving space?

5.3   **12.** Describe *backtracking* as a problem-solving method.

13. State the *pigeonhole* principle.

5.4   **14.** Explain the *minimax* method for finding the value of a game.

15. Determine the value of the following game tree by the *minimax* method.

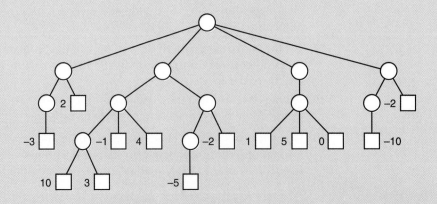

REFERENCES FOR FURTHER STUDY

Two books giving thorough introductions to recursion, with many examples, and serving as excellent supplements to this book are:

ERIC S. ROBERTS, *Thinking Recursively*, John Wiley & Sons, New York, 1986, 179 pages.

The Towers of Hanoi is quite well known and appears in many textbooks. A survey of related papers is

D. WOOD, "The Towers of Brahma and Hanoi revisited," *Journal of Recreational Math* 14 (1981–82), 17–24.

The proof that stacks may be eliminated by the introduction of recursion appears in

S. BROWN, D. GRIES and T. SZYMANSKI, "Program schemes with pushdown stores," *SIAM Journal on Computing* 1 (1972), 242–268.

Consult the references at the end of the previous chapter for several good sources for examples and applications of recursion. One of the earlier books containing algorithms for both the knight's tour and eight-queens problems is

N. WIRTH, *Algorithms + Data Structures = Programs*, Prentice Hall, Englewood Cliffs, N.J., 1976.

For a general discussion of the n-queens problem, including a proof that the number of solutions cannot be bounded by any polynomial in n, see

IGOR RIVIN, ILAN VARDI, and PAUL ZIMMERMANN, "The n-Queens Problem," *The American Mathematical Monthly* 101(7) (1994), 629–639.

Many other applications of recursion appear in books such as

E. HOROWITZ and S. SAHNI, *Fundamentals of Computer Algorithms*, Computer Science Press, 1978, 626 pages.

This book (pp. 290–302) contains more extensive discussion and analysis of game trees and look-ahead programs. The general theory of recursion forms a research topic. A readable presentation from a theoretical approach is

R. S. BIRD, *Programs and Machines*, John Wiley, New York, 1976.

Lists and Strings

6

THIS CHAPTER turns from restricted lists, like stacks and queues, in which changes occur only at the ends of the list, to more general lists in which insertions, deletions, and retrievals may occur at any point of the list. After examining the specification and implementation of such lists, we study lists of characters, called strings, develop a simple text editor as an application, and finally consider the implementation of linked lists within arrays.

6.1 LIST DEFINITION

Let us begin with our definition of an abstract data type that we call a *list*. Like a stack or a queue, a list has a sequence of entries as its data value. However, unlike a stack or a queue, a list permits operations that alter arbitrary entries of the sequence.

Definition   A *list* of elements of type T is a finite sequence of elements of T together with the following operations:

1. *Construct* the list, leaving it empty.
2. Determine whether the list is *empty* or not.
3. Determine whether the list is *full* or not.
4. Find the *size* of the list.
5. *Clear* the list to make it empty.
6. *Insert* an entry at a specified position of the list.
7. *Remove* an entry from a specified position in the list.
8. *Retrieve* the entry from a specified position in the list.
9. *Replace* the entry at a specified position in the list.
10. *Traverse* the list, performing a given operation on each entry.

There are many other operations that are also useful to apply to sequences of elements. Thus we can form a wide variety of similar ADTs by utilizing different packages of operations. Any one of these related ADTs could reasonably go by the name of list. However, we fix our attention on one particular list ADT whose operations give a representative sampling of the ideas and problems that arise in working with lists.

standard template   The standard template library provides a rather different data structure called a
library list. The STL list provides only those operations that can be implemented efficiently in a List implementation known as doubly linked, which we shall study shortly. In particular, the STL list does not allow random access to an arbitrary list position, as provided by our List operations for insertion, removal, retrieval, and replacement. Another STL **template class**, called a vector, does provide some random access to a sequence of data values. An STL vector bears some similarity to our List ADT, in particular, it provides the operations that can be implemented efficiently in the List implementation that we shall call contiguous. In this way, our study of the List ADT provides an introduction to the STL classes list and vector.

6.1.1 Method Specifications

*operations,
information hiding,
and implementations*

When we first studied stacks, we applied *information hiding* by separating our uses for stacks from the actual programming of these operations. In studying queues, we continued this practice and soon saw that many variations in *implementation* are possible. With general lists, we have much more flexibility and freedom in accessing and changing entries in any part of the list. The principles of information hiding are hence even more important for general lists than for stacks or queues. Let us therefore begin by enumerating postconditions for all the methods that we wish to have available for lists.

A constructor is required before a list can be used:

constructor

> List :: List( );
>
> *postcondition*: The List has been created and is initialized to be empty.

The next operation takes a list that already exists and empties it:

reinitialization

> **void** List :: clear( );
>
> *postcondition*: All List entries have been removed; the List is empty.

Next come the operations for checking the status of a list:

status operations

> **bool** List :: empty( ) **const**;
>
> *postcondition*: The function returns **true** or **false** according to whether the List is empty or not.

> **bool** List :: full( ) **const**;
>
> *postcondition*: The function returns **true** or **false** according to whether the List is full or not.

> **int** List :: size( ) **const**;
>
> *postcondition*: The function returns the number of entries in the List.

We now consider operations that access entries of a list. As in our earlier treatment of stacks and queues, we shall suppose that, whenever necessary, our methods will report problems by returning an Error_code. We shall use a generic type called List_entry to stand for entries of our list.

position in a list

To find an entry in a list, we use an integer that gives its *position* within the list. We shall number the positions in a list so that the first entry in the list has position 0, the second position 1, and so on. Hence, locating an entry of a list by its position is superficially like indexing an array, but there are important differences. First, if we insert an entry at a particular position, then the position numbers of all later entries increase by 1. If we remove an entry, then the positions of all following entries decrease by 1. Moreover, the position number for a list is defined without regard to the implementation. For a contiguous list, implemented in an array, the position will indeed be the index of the entry within the array. But we will also use the position to find an entry within linked implementations of a list, where no indices or arrays are used at all.

implementation independence

We can now give precise specifications for the methods of a list that access a single entry.

Error_code List :: insert(**int** position, **const** List_entry &x);

postcondition: If the List is not full and $0 \leq$ position $\leq n$, where n is the number of entries in the List, the function succeeds: Any entry formerly at position and all later entries have their position numbers increased by 1, and x is inserted at position in the List.
Else: The function fails with a diagnostic error code.

Note that **insert** allows **position** $==n$, since it is permissible to insert an entry after the last entry of the list. The following methods, however, require **position** $< n$, since they refer to a position that must already be in the list.

Error_code List :: remove(**int** position, List_entry &x);

postcondition: If $0 \leq$ position $< n$, where n is the number of entries in the List, the function succeeds: The entry at position is removed from the List, and all later entries have their position numbers decreased by 1. The parameter x records a copy of the entry formerly at position.
Else: The function fails with a diagnostic error code.

Error_code List :: retrieve(**int** position, List_entry &x) **const**;

postcondition: If $0 \leq$ position $< n$, where n is the number of entries in the List, the function succeeds: The entry at position is copied to x; all List entries remain unchanged.
Else: The function fails with a diagnostic error code.

> Error_code List :: replace(**int** position, **const** List_entry &x);
>
> *postcondition*: If $0 \le$ position $< n$, where n is the number of entries in the List, the function succeeds: The entry at position is replaced by x; all other entries remain unchanged.
> Else: The function fails with a diagnostic error code.

traverse A method to traverse a list, performing a task on entries, often proves useful: It is especially useful for testing purposes. A client using this traverse method specifies the action to be carried out on individual entries of the list; the action is applied in turn to each entry of the list. For example, a client that has two functions,

void update(List_entry &x)   and   **void** modify(List_entry &x),

and an object List the_list, could use a command

the_list.traverse(update)   or   the_list.traverse(modify)

to perform one or the other of the operations on every entry of the list. If, as scaffolding, the client desires to print out all the entries of a list, then all that is needed is a statement

the_list.traverse(print);

where **void** print(List_entry &x) is a function that prints a single List_entry.

In these calls to the method traverse, the client merely supplies the name of the function to be performed as a parameter. In C++, a function's name, without any parentheses, is evaluated as a pointer to the function. The formal parameter, *pointers to functions* visit, for the method traverse must therefore be declared as a pointer to a function. Moreover, this pointer declaration must include the information that the function ∗visit has **void** return type and a List_entry reference parameter. Hence, we obtain the following specification for the method traverse:

> **void** List :: traverse(**void** (∗visit)(List_entry &));
>
> *postcondition*: The action specified by function ∗visit has been performed on every entry of the List, beginning at position 0 and doing each in turn.

As with all parameters, visit is only a formal name that is initialized with a pointer value when the traverse method is used. The expression ∗visit stands for the function that will be used during traversal to process each entry in the list.

In the next section, we shall turn to implementation questions.

Exercises 6.1 Given the methods for lists described in this section, write functions to do each of the following tasks. Be sure to specify the preconditions and postconditions for each function. You may use local variables of types List and List_entry, but do not write any code that depends on the choice of implementation. Include code to detect and report an error if a function cannot complete normally.

E1. Error_code insert_first(**const** List_entry &x, List &a_list) inserts entry x into position 0 of the List a_list.

E2. Error_code remove_first(List_entry &x, List &a_list) removes the first entry of the List a_list, copying it to x.

E3. Error_code insert_last(**const** List_entry &x, List &a_list) inserts x as the last entry of the List a_list.

E4. Error_code remove_last(List_entry &x, List &a_list) removes the last entry of a_list, copying it to x.

E5. Error_code median_list(List_entry &x, List &a_list) copies the central entry of the List a_list to x if a_list has an odd number of entries; otherwise, it copies the left-central entry of a_list to x.

E6. Error_code interchange(**int** pos1, **int** pos2, List &a_list) interchanges the entries at positions pos1 and pos2 of the List a_list.

E7. **void** reverse_traverse_list(List &a_list, **void** (*visit)(List_entry &)) traverses the List a_list in reverse order (from its last entry to its first).

E8. Error_code copy(List &dest, List &source) copies all entries from source into dest; source remains unchanged. You may assume that dest already exists, but any entries already in dest are to be discarded.

E9. Error_code join(List &list1, List &list2) copies all entries from list1 onto the end of list2; list1 remains unchanged, as do all the entries previously in list2.

E10. **void** reverse(List &a_list) reverses the order of all entries in a_list.

E11. Error_code split(List &source, List &oddlist, List &evenlist) copies all entries from source so that those in odd-numbered positions make up oddlist and those in even-numbered positions make up evenlist. You may assume that oddlist and evenlist already exist, but any entries they may contain are to be discarded.

6.2 IMPLEMENTATION OF LISTS

At this point, we have specified how we wish the operations of our list ADT to behave. It is now time to turn to the details of implementing lists in C++. In our previous study of stacks and queues, we programmed two kinds of implementations: contiguous implementations using arrays, and linked implementations using pointers. For lists we have the same division, but we shall find several variations of further interest.

We shall implement our lists as generic *template classes* rather than as classes; we therefore begin with a brief review of templates.

6.2.1 Class Templates

Suppose that a client program needs three lists: a list of integers, a list of characters, and a list of real numbers. The implementation tools we have developed so far are inadequate, since, if we use a **typedef** to set the type List_entry to one of **int**, **char**, or **double**, then we cannot use the same List class to set up lists with the other two types of entries. We need to set up a *generic* list, one whose entry type is not yet specified, but one that the client program can specialize in order to declare lists with the three different entry types.

template

In C++, we accomplish this aim with a ***template*** construction, which allows us to write code, often code to implement a class, that uses objects of a generic type. In template code we utilize a parameter to denote the generic type, and later, when a client uses our code, the client can substitute an actual type for the template parameter. The client can thus obtain several actual pieces of code from our template, using different actual types in place of the template parameter.

For example, we shall implement a **template class** List that depends on one generic type parameter. A client can then use our template to declare a list of integers with a declaration of the following form:

List<**int**> first_list;

Moreover, in the same program, the client could also set up a list of characters with a declaration:

List<**char**> second_list;

In these declaration statements, our client customizes the class template by specifying the value of the template's parameter between angled brackets.

generics

We see that templates provide a new mechanism for creating generic data structures. One advantage of using templates rather than our prior, simple treatment of generics is that a client can make many different specializations of a given data structure template in a single application. For example, the lists first_list and second_list that we declared earlier have different entry types but can coexist in the same client program. The lack of precisely this flexibility, in our earlier treatment of generics, restricted our choice of Stack implementation in the polynomial project of Section 4.5.

The added generality that we get by using templates comes at the price of slightly more complicated class specifications and implementations. For the most part, we just need to prefix templated code with the keyword **template** and a declaration of template parameters. Thus our later **template class** List, which uses a generic entry type called List_entry, is defined by adding members to the following specification:

```
template <class List_entry>
class List{
    //   Add in member information for the class.
};
```

6.2.2 Contiguous Implementation

In a contiguous list implementation, we store list data in an array with max_list entries of type List_entry. Just as we did for contiguous stacks, we must keep a count of how much of the array is actually taken up with list data. Thus, we must define a class with all of the methods of our list ADT together with two data members.

```
template <class List_entry>
class List {
public:
//    methods of the List ADT
   List( );
   int size( ) const;
   bool full( ) const;
   bool empty( ) const;
   void clear( );
   void traverse(void (*visit)(List_entry &));
   Error_code retrieve(int position, List_entry &x) const;
   Error_code replace(int position, const List_entry &x);
   Error_code remove(int position, List_entry &x);
   Error_code insert(int position, const List_entry &x);

protected:
//    data members for a contiguous list implementation
   int count;
   List_entry entry[max_list];
};
```

Many of the methods (List, clear, empty, full, size, retrieve) have very simple implementations. However, these methods all depend on the template parameter List_entry, and so must be implemented as templates too. For example, the method size can be written with the following function template:

```
template <class List_entry>
int List<List_entry>::size( ) const
/* Post: The function returns the number of entries in the List. */
{
   return count;
}
```

We leave the other simple methods as exercises and concentrate on those methods that access data in the list. To add entries to the list, we must move entries within the array to make space to insert the new one. The resulting function template is:

```
template <class List_entry>
Error_code List<List_entry> :: insert(int position, const List_entry &x)
/* Post: If the List is not full and 0 ≤ position ≤ n, where n is the number of
         entries in the List, the function succeeds: Any entry formerly at position
         and all later entries have their position numbers increased by 1 and x is
         inserted at position of the List.
         Else: The function fails with a diagnostic error code. */
{
  if (full())
    return overflow;
  if (position < 0 || position > count)
    return range_error;
  for (int i = count − 1; i >= position; i−−)
    entry[i + 1] = entry[i];
  entry[position] = x;
  count++;
  return success;
}
```

How much work does this function do? If we insert an entry at the end of the list, then the function executes only a small, constant number of commands. If, at the other extreme, we insert an entry at the beginning of the list, then the function must move every entry in the list to make room, so, if the list is long, it will do much more work. In the average case, where we assume that all possible insertions are equally likely, the function will move about half the entries of the list. Thus we say that the amount of work the function does is approximately **proportional** to n, the length of the list.

Deletion, similarly, must move entries in the list to fill the hole left by the removed entry. Hence deletion also requires time approximately proportional to n, the number of entries. Most of the remaining operations, on the other hand, do not use any loops and do their work in constant time. In summary,

> *In processing a contiguous list with n entries:*
>
> ➡ insert *and* remove *require time approximately proportional to n.*
>
> ➡ List, clear, empty, full, size, replace, *and* retrieve *operate in constant time.*

We have not included traverse in this discussion, since its time depends on the time used by its parameter visit, something we do not know in general. The implementation of traverse must include a loop through all n elements of the list, so we cannot hope that its time requirement is ever less than proportional to n. However, for traversal with a fixed parameter visit, the time requirement is approximately proportional to n.

```
template <class List_entry>
void List<List_entry> :: traverse(void (*visit)(List_entry &))
/* Post:  The action specified by function (*visit) has been performed on every entry
           of the List, beginning at position 0 and doing each in turn. */
{
   for (int i = 0;  i < count;  i++)
      (*visit)(entry[i]);
}
```

6.2.3 Simply Linked Implementation

1. Declarations

For a linked implementation of a list, we can begin with declarations of nodes. Our nodes are similar to those we used for linked stacks and queues, but we now make them depend on a template parameter.

```
template <class Node_entry>
struct Node {
//   data members
   Node_entry entry;
   Node<Node_entry> *next;
//   constructors
   Node();
   Node(Node_entry, Node<Node_entry> *link = NULL);
};
```

We have included two constructors, the choice of which depends on whether or not the contents of the **Node** are to be initialized. The implementations of these constructors are almost identical to those for the linked nodes that we used in Section 4.1.3. Once we have defined the **struct Node**, we can give the definition for a linked list by filling in the following skeleton:

```
template <class List_entry>
class List {
public:
//   Specifications for the methods of the list ADT go here.

//   The following methods replace compiler-generated defaults.
   ~List();
   List(const List<List_entry> &copy);
   void operator = (const List<List_entry> &copy);
protected:
//   Data members for the linked list implementation now follow.
   int count;
   Node<List_entry> *head;
//   The following auxiliary function is used to locate list positions
   Node<List_entry> *set_position(int position) const;
};
```

In the definition we have omitted the method prototypes, because these are identical to those used in the contiguous implementation. As well as protected data members, we have included a protected member function set_position that will prove useful in our implementations of the methods.

2. Examples

To illustrate some of the kinds of actions we need to perform with linked lists, let us consider for a moment the problem of editing text, and suppose that each node holds one word as well as the link to the next node. The sentence "Stacks are Lists" appears as in (a) of Figure 6.1. If we *insert* the word "simple" before the word "Lists" we obtain the list in (b). Next we decide to *replace* "Lists" by "structures" and *insert* the three nodes "but important data" to obtain (c). Afterward, we decide to *remove* "simple but" and so arrive at list (d). Finally, we *traverse* the list to print its contents.

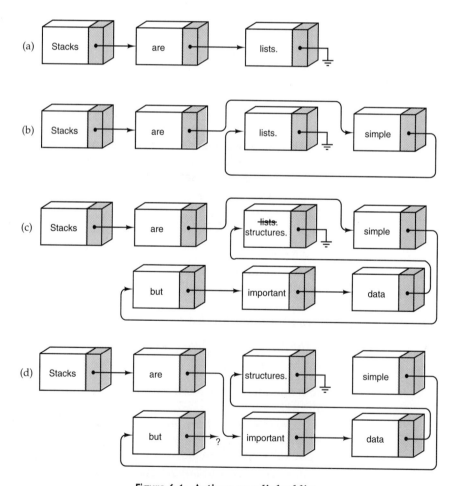

Figure 6.1. Actions on a linked list

3. Finding a List Position

Several of the methods for lists make use of a function called **set_position** that takes as its parameter a *position* (that is, an integer index into the list) and returns a *pointer* to the corresponding node of the list.

    We should declare the visibility of **set_position** as protected. This is because **set_position** returns a pointer to, and therefore gives access to, a **Node** in the **List**. Any client with access to **set_position** would have access to all of the data in the corresponding **List**. Therefore, to maintain an encapsulated data structure, we must restrict the visibility of **set_position**. By giving it a protected visibility we ensure that it is only available as a tool for constructing other methods of the **List**.

    The easiest way, conceptually, to construct **set_position** is to start at the beginning of the **List** and traverse it until we reach the desired node:

```
template <class List_entry>
Node<List_entry> *List<List_entry> :: set_position(int position) const
/* Pre:   position is a valid position in the List; 0 ≤ position < count.
   Post: Returns a pointer to the Node in position. */
{
   Node<List_entry> *q = head;
   for (int i = 0;  i < position;  i++) q = q->next;
   return q;
}
```

Since we control exactly which functions can use **set_position**, there is no need to include error checking: Instead, we impose preconditions. Indeed the functions that call **set_position** will include their own error checking so it would be inefficient to repeat the process in **set_position**.

    If all nodes are equally likely, then, on average, the **set_position** function must move halfway through the **List** to find a given position. Hence, on average, its time requirement is approximately proportional to n, the size of the **List**.

4. Insertion

Next let us consider the problem of inserting a new entry into a linked **List**. If we have a new entry that we wish to insert into the middle of a linked **List**, then, as shown in Figure 6.2, we set up pointers to the nodes *preceding* and *following* the place where the new entry is to be inserted. If we let **new_node** point to the new node to be inserted, **previous** point to the preceding node, and **following** point to the following node, then this action consists of the two statements

```
new_node->next = following;
previous->next = new_node;
```

    We can now build this code into a function for inserting a new entry into a linked **List**. Observe that the assignment **new_node->next = following** is carried out by the constructor that initializes **new_node**. Insertion at the beginning of the **List** must be treated as a special case, since the new entry then does not follow any other.

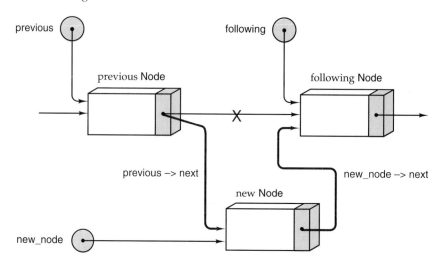

Figure 6.2. Insertion into a linked list

```
template <class List_entry>
Error_code List<List_entry> :: insert(int position, const List_entry &x)
/* Post: If the List is not full and 0 ≤ position ≤ n, where n is the number of
          entries in the List, the function succeeds: Any entry formerly at position
          and all later entries have their position numbers increased by 1, and x is
          inserted at position of the List.
          Else: The function fails with a diagnostic error code. */
{
   if (position < 0 || position > count)
      return range_error;
   Node<List_entry> *new_node, *previous, *following;
   if (position > 0) {
      previous = set_position(position − 1);
      following = previous->next;
   }
   else following = head;
   new_node = new Node<List_entry>(x, following);
   if (new_node == NULL)
      return overflow;
   if (position ==  0)
      head = new_node;
   else
      previous->next = new_node;
   count++;
   return success;
}
```

Apart from the call to **set_position** the steps performed by **insert** do not depend on
the length of the List. Therefore, it operates, like **set_position**, in time approximately
proportional to n, the size of the List.

5. Other Operations

The remaining operations for linked lists will all be left as exercises. Those that access a particular position in the List all need to use the function **set_position**, sometimes for the current position and sometimes, as in **insert**, for the previous position. All these functions turn out to perform at most a constant number of steps other than those in **set_position**, except for **clear** (and **traverse**), which go through all entries of the List. We therefore have the conclusion:

> *In processing a linked* List *with n entries:*
>
> ➡ **clear**, **insert**, **remove**, **retrieve**, *and* **replace** *require time approximately proportional to n.*
> ➡ List, **empty**, **full**, *and* **size** *operate in constant time.*

Again, we have not included **traverse** in this discussion, since its time depends on the time used by its parameter **visit**, something we do not know in general. However, as before, for a fixed parameter **visit**, the time required by **traverse** is approximately proportional to n.

6.2.4 Variation: Keeping the Current Position

Many applications process the entries of a list in order, moving from one entry to the next. Many other applications refer to the same entry several times, doing **retrieve** or **replace** operations before moving to another entry. For all these applications, our current implementation of linked lists is very inefficient, since every operation that accesses an entry of the list begins by tracing through the list from its start until the desired position is reached. It would be much more efficient if, instead, we were able to *remember* the last-used position in the list and, if the next operation refers to the same or a later position, start tracing through the list from this last-used position.

Note, however, that remembering the last-used position will not speed up *every* application using lists. If, for example, some program accesses the entries of a linked list in reverse order, starting at its end, then every access will require tracing from the start of the list, since the links give only one-way directions and so remembering the last-used position gives no help in finding the one preceding it.

One problem arises with the method **retrieve**. This method is defined as a constant method, but its implementation will need to alter the last-used position of a List. We recognize that although this operation does change some data members of a List object, it does not change the sequence of entries that represents the actual value of the object. In order to make sure that the C++ compiler agrees, we must define the data members that record the last-used position of a List with a storage modifier of **mutable**. The keyword **mutable** is a relatively recent addition to C++, and it is not yet available in all implementations of the language. Mutable data members of a **class** can be changed, even by constant methods.

The enlarged definition for a list is obtained by adding method specifications to the following skeleton:

```
template <class List_entry>
class List {
public:
//    Add specifications for the methods of the list ADT.
//    Add methods to replace the compiler-generated defaults.
protected:
//    Data members for the linked-list implementation with
//    current position follow:
   int count;
   mutable int current_position;
   Node<List_entry> *head;
   mutable Node<List_entry> *current;
//    Auxiliary function to locate list positions follows:
   void set_position(int position) const;
};
```

Observe that although we have added extra members to our earlier class definition, all of the new members have protected visibility. This means that, from the perspective of a client, the class looks exactly like our earlier implementation.

We can rewrite set_position to use and change the new data members of this class. The current position is now a member of the **class** List, so there is no longer a need for set_position to return a pointer; instead, the function can simply reset the pointer current directly within the List.

```
template <class List_entry>
void List<List_entry> :: set_position(int position) const
/* Pre:   position is a valid position in the List: 0 ≤ position < count.
   Post:  The current Node pointer references the Node at position. */
{
   if (position < current_position) {  //    must start over at head of list
      current_position = 0;
      current = head;
   }
   for (; current_position != position; current_position++)
      current = current->next;
}
```

Note that, for repeated references to the same position, neither the body of the **if** statement nor the body of the **for** statement will be executed, and hence the function will take almost no time. If we move forward only one position, the body of the **for** statement will be executed only once, so again the function will be very fast. On the other hand, when it is necessary to move backwards through the List, then the function operates in almost the same way as the version of **set_position** used in the previous implementation.

With this revised version of **set_position** we can now revise the linked-list implementation to improve its efficiency. The changes needed to the various methods are minor, and they will all be left as exercises.

6.2.5 Doubly Linked Lists

Some applications of linked lists require that we frequently move both forward and backward through the list. In the last section we solved the problem of moving backwards by traversing the list from its beginning until the desired node was found, but this solution is generally unsatisfactory. Its programming is difficult, and the running time of the program will depend on the length of the list, which may be quite long.

There are several strategies that can be used to overcome this problem of finding the node preceding the given one. In this section, we shall study the simplest and, in many ways, the most flexible and satisfying strategy.

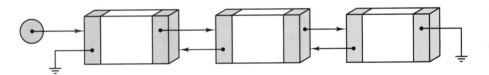

Figure 6.3. A doubly linked list

1. Declarations for a Doubly Linked List

doubly linked list

The idea, as shown in Figure 6.3, is to keep *two* links in each node, pointing in opposite directions. Hence, by following the appropriate link, we can move in either direction through the linked list with equal ease. We call such a list a *doubly linked list*.

In a doubly linked list, the definition of a **Node** becomes

```
template <class Node_entry>
struct Node {
//   data members
   Node_entry entry;
   Node<Node_entry> *next;
   Node<Node_entry> *back;
//   constructors
   Node();
   Node(Node_entry, Node<Node_entry> *link_back = NULL,
                    Node<Node_entry> *link_next = NULL);
};
```

The **Node** constructor implementations are just minor modifications of the constructors for the singly linked nodes of Section 4.1.3. We therefore proceed straight to a skeleton definition of a doubly-linked list class.

```
template <class List_entry>
class List {
public:

//    Add specifications for methods of the list ADT.
//    Add methods to replace compiler generated defaults.
protected:
//    Data members for the doubly-linked list implementation follow:
    int count;
    mutable int current_position;
    mutable Node<List_entry> *current;
//    The auxiliary function to locate list positions follows:
    void set_position(int position) const;
};
```

In this implementation, it is possible to move in either direction through the List while keeping only one pointer into the List. Therefore, in the declaration, we keep only a pointer to the current node of the List. We do not even need to keep pointers to the head or the tail of the List, since they, like any other nodes, can be found by tracing back or forth from any given node.

2. Methods for Doubly Linked Lists

With a doubly linked list, retrievals in either direction, finding a particular position, insertions, and deletions from arbitrary positions in the list can be accomplished without difficulty. Some of the methods that make changes in the list are longer than those for simply linked lists because it is necessary to update both forward and backward links when a node is inserted or removed from the list.

First, to find a particular location within the list, we need only decide whether to move forward or backward from the initial position. Then we do a partial traversal of the list until we reach the desired position. The resulting function is:

```
template <class List_entry>
void List<List_entry> :: set_position(int position) const
/* Pre:   position is a valid position in the List: 0 ≤ position < count.
   Post:  The current Node pointer references the Node at position. */
{
    if (current_position <= position)
        for ( ; current_position != position; current_position++)
            current = current->next;
    else
        for ( ; current_position != position; current_position--)
            current = current->back;
}
```

Given this function, we can now write the insertion method, which is made some-what longer by the need to adjust multiple links. The action of this function is shown in Figure 6.4.

Special care must be taken when the insertion is at one end of the List or into a previously empty List.

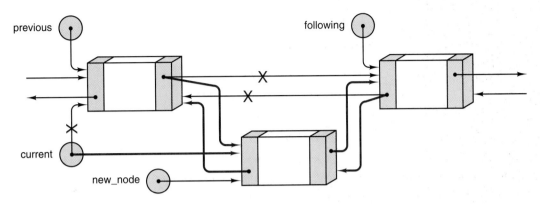

Figure 6.4. Insertion into a doubly linked list

```
template <class List_entry>
Error_code List<List_entry>::insert(int position, const List_entry &x)
/* Post: If the List is not full and 0 ≤ position ≤ n, where n is the number of
         entries in the List, the function succeeds: Any entry formerly at position
         and all later entries have their position numbers increased by 1 and x is
         inserted at position of the List.
         Else: the function fails with a diagnostic error code. */
{
   Node<List_entry> *new_node, *following, *preceding;
   if (position < 0 || position > count) return range_error;

   if (position ==  0) {
      if (count ==  0) following = NULL;
      else {
         set_position(0);
         following = current;
      }
      preceding = NULL;
   }
   else {
      set_position(position − 1);
      preceding = current;
      following = preceding->next;
   }
   new_node = new Node<List_entry>(x, preceding, following);

   if (new_node ==  NULL) return overflow;
   if (preceding != NULL) preceding->next = new_node;
   if (following != NULL) following->back = new_node;
   current = new_node;
   current_position = position;
   count++;
   return success;
}
```

The cost of a doubly linked list, of course, is the extra space required in each **Node** for a second link. For most applications, however, the amount of space needed for the information member, **entry**, in each **Node** is much larger than the space needed for a link, so the second link member in each **Node** does not significantly increase the total amount of storage space required for the **List**.

6.2.6 Comparison of Implementations

Now that we have seen several algorithms for manipulating linked lists and several variations in their structure and implementation, let us pause to assess some relative advantages of linked and of contiguous implementation of lists.

advantages

The foremost advantage of linked lists in dynamic storage is flexibility. Overflow is no problem until the computer memory is actually exhausted. Especially when the individual entries are quite large, it may be difficult to determine the

overflow

amount of contiguous static storage that might be needed for the required arrays while keeping enough free for other needs. With dynamic allocation, there is no need to attempt to make such decisions in advance.

changes

Changes, especially insertions and deletions, can be made in the middle of a linked list more quickly than in the middle of a contiguous list. If the structures are large, then it is much quicker to change the values of a few pointers than to copy the structures themselves from one location to another.

disadvantages

The first drawback of linked lists is that the links themselves take space—space that might otherwise be needed for additional data. In most systems, a pointer requires the same amount of storage (one word) as does an integer. Thus a list of integers will require double the space in linked storage that it would require in contiguous storage.

space use

On the other hand, in many practical applications, the nodes in the list are quite large, with data members taking hundreds of words altogether. If each node contains 100 words of data, then using linked storage will increase the memory requirement by only one percent, an insignificant amount. In fact, if extra space is allocated to arrays holding contiguous lists to allow for additional insertions, then linked storage will probably require less space altogether. If each entry takes 100 words, then contiguous storage will save space only if all the arrays can be filled to more than 99 percent of capacity.

random access

The major drawback of linked lists is that they are not suited to random access. With contiguous storage, a client can refer to any position within a list as quickly as to any other position. With a linked list, it may be necessary to traverse a long path to reach the desired node. Access to a single node in linked storage may even take slightly more computer time, since it is necessary, first, to obtain the pointer and then go to the address. This last consideration, however, is usually of

programming

no importance. Similarly, you may find at first that writing methods to manipulate linked lists takes a bit more programming effort, but, with practice, this discrepancy will decrease.

In summary, therefore, we can conclude as follows:

Contiguous storage is generally preferable

➡ *when the entries are individually very small;*
➡ *when the size of the list is known when the program is written;*
➡ *when few insertions or deletions need to be made except at the end of the list; and*
➡ *when random access is important.*

Linked storage proves superior

➡ *when the entries are large;*
➡ *when the size of the list is not known in advance; and*
➡ *when flexibility is needed in inserting, deleting, and rearranging the entries.*

Finally, to help choose one of the many possible variations in structure and implementation, the programmer should consider which of the operations will actually be performed on the list and which of these are the most important. Is there *locality* of reference? That is, if one entry is accessed, is it likely that it will next be accessed again? Are the entries processed in order or not? If so, then it may be worthwhile to maintain the last-used position as part of the list structure. Is it necessary to move both directions through the list? If so, then doubly linked lists may prove advantageous.

Exercises 6.2

E1. Write C++ functions to implement the remaining operations for the contiguous implementation of a **List**, as follows:

(a) The constructor List
(b) clear
(c) empty
(d) full

(e) replace
(f) retrieve
(g) remove

E2. Write C++ functions to implement the constructors (both forms) for singly linked and doubly linked **Node** objects.

E3. Write C++ functions to implement the following operations for the (first) simply linked implementation of a list:

(a) The constructor List   (g) empty
(b) The copy constructor   (h) full
(c) The overloaded assignment   (i) replace
     operator   (j) retrieve
(d) The destructor ~List   (k) remove
(e) clear   (l) traverse
(f) size

E4. Write **remove** for the (second) implementation of simply linked lists that remembers the last-used position.

E5. Indicate which of the following functions are the same for doubly linked lists (as implemented in this section) and for simply linked lists. For those that are different, write new versions for doubly linked lists. Be sure that each function conforms to the specifications given in Section 6.1.

(a) The constructor List   (g) empty
(b) The copy constructor   (h) full
(c) The overloaded assignment   (i) replace
     operator   (j) insert
(d) The destructor ~List   (k) retrieve
(e) clear   (l) remove
(f) size   (m) traverse

Programming Projects 6.2

P1. Prepare a collection of files containing the declarations for a contiguous list and all the functions for list processing.

P2. Write a menu-driven demonstration program for general lists, based on the one in Section 3.4. The list entries should be characters. Use the declarations and the functions for contiguous lists developed in Project P1.

P3. Create a collection of files containing declarations and functions for processing linked lists.

(a) Use the simply linked lists as first implemented.
(b) Use the simply linked lists that maintain a pointer to the last-used position.
(c) Use doubly linked lists as implemented in this section.

P4. In the menu-driven demonstration program of Project P2, substitute the collection of files with declarations and functions that support linked lists (from Project P3) for the files that support contiguous lists (Project P1). If you have designed the declarations and the functions carefully, the program should operate correctly with no further change required.

P5. (a) Modify the implementation of doubly linked lists so that, along with the pointer to the last-used position, it will maintain pointers to the first node and to the last node of the list.

(b) Use this implementation with the menu-driven demonstration program of Project P2 and thereby test that it is correct.

(c) Discuss the advantages and disadvantages of this variation of doubly linked lists in comparison with the doubly linked lists of the text.

P6. (a) Write a program that will do addition, subtraction, multiplication, and division for arbitrarily large integers. Each integer should be represented as a list of its digits. Since the integers are allowed to be as large as you like, linked lists will be needed to prevent the possibility of overflow. For some operations, it is useful to move backwards through the list; hence, doubly linked lists are appropriate. Multiplication and division can be done simply as repeated addition and subtraction.

(b) Rewrite multiply so that it is not based on repeated addition but on standard multiplication where the first multiplicand is multiplied with each digit of the second multiplicand and then added.

(c) Rewrite the divide operation so that it is not based on repeated subtraction but on long division. It may be necessary to write an additional function that determines if the dividend is larger than the divisor in absolute value.

6.3 STRINGS

definition

In this section, we shall implement a class to represent strings of characters. A *string* is defined as a sequence of characters. Examples of strings are "This is a string" or "Name?", where the double quotes (" ") are not part of the string. There is an *empty string*, denoted "". Since strings store sequences of data (characters), a string ADT is a kind of list. However, because the operations that are normally applied to a string differ considerably from the operations of our list ADT, we will not base our strings on any of our earlier list structures.

We begin with a review of the string processing capabilities supplied by the C++ language.

6.3.1 Strings in C++

C-strings

The C++ language provides a pair of implementations of strings. The more primitive of these is just a C implementation of strings. Like other parts of the C language, it is available in all implementations of C++. We shall refer to the string objects provided by this implementation as *C-strings*. C-strings reflect the strengths and weaknesses of the C language: They are widely available, they are very efficient, but they are easy to misuse with disastrous consequences. C-strings must conform to a collection of conventions that we now review.

conventions

Every C-string has type **char** *. Hence, a C-string references an address in memory; the referenced address is the first of a contiguous set of bytes that store the characters making up the string. The storage occupied by the string must terminate with the special character value '\0'. The compiler cannot enforce any of these conventions, but any deviation from the rules is likely to result in a run-time crash. In other words, C-string objects are not encapsulated.

The standard header file <cstring> contains a library of functions that manipulate C-strings. In older C++ compilers, this header file is sometimes called <string.h>. These library functions are convenient, efficient, and represent almost every string operation that we could ever wish to use. For example, suppose that s and t are C-strings. Then the operation strlen(s) returns the length of s, str-cmp(s, t) reveals the lexicographic order of s and t, and strstr(s, t) returns a pointer to the first occurrence of the string t in s. Moreover, in C++ the output operator ≪ is overloaded to apply to C-strings, so that a simple instruction cout ≪ s prints the string s.

drawbacks   Although the implementation of C-strings has many excellent features, it has some serious drawbacks too. In fact, it suffers from exactly the problems that we identified in studying linked data structures in Section 4.3. It is easy for a client to create either garbage or aliases for string data. For example, in Figure 6.5, we illustrate how the C-string assignment s = t leads to both of these problems.

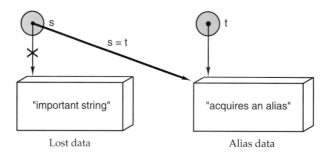

Figure 6.5. Insecurities of C-string objects

Another problem often arises in applications that use C-strings. Uninitialized C-strings should store the value NULL. However, many of the string library functions fail (with a run-time crash) when presented with a NULL string object. For example, the statements

char ∗x = NULL;
cout ≪ strlen(x);

are accepted by the compiler, but, for many implementations of the C-string library, they generate a fatal run-time error. Thus, client code needs to test preconditions for C-string functions very carefully.

In C++, it is easy to use encapsulation to embed C-strings into safer class-based implementations of strings. Indeed, the standard template library includes a safe string implementation in the header file <string>. This library implements a class called std::string that is convenient, safe, and efficient. Since this library is not included with older C++ compilers, we shall develop our own safe String ADT that uses encapsulation and object-oriented techniques to overcome the problems that we have identified in C-strings.

6.3.2 Implementation of Strings

class String   In order to create a safer string implementation, we embed the C-string representation as a member of a **class** String. It is very convenient to add the string length as a second data member in our class. Moreover, our **class** String can avoid the problems of aliases, garbage creation, and uninitialized objects by including an overloaded assignment operator, a copy constructor, a destructor, and a constructor.

comparison operators

For later applications, it will be extremely convenient to be able to apply the comparison operators <, >, <=, >=, == , != to determine the lexicographic relationship between a pair of strings. Therefore, our **class** String will include overloaded comparison operators.

String constructor

We shall also equip the **class** String with a constructor that uses a parameter of type **char** *. This constructor provides a convenient translator from C-string objects to String objects. The translator can be called explicitly with code such as:

String s("some_string");

In this statement, the String s is constructed by translating the C-string

"some_string".

Our constructor is also called implicitly, by the compiler, whenever client code requires a type cast from type **char** * to String. For instance, the constructor is invoked in running the following statements:

String s;
s = "some_string";

To translate the second statement, the C++ compiler first calls our new constructor to cast "some_string" to a temporary String object. It then calls the overloaded String assignment operator to copy the temporary String to s. Finally, it calls the destructor for the temporary String.

It is very useful to have a similar constructor to convert from a List of characters to a String. For example, when we read a String from a user, it is most convenient to read characters into a linked list. Once the list is read, we can apply our translator to turn the linked list into a String.

conversion from
String to C-string

Finally, it is useful to be able to convert String objects to corresponding C-string objects. For example, such a conversion allows us to apply many of the C-string library functions to String data. We shall follow the example of the standard template library and implement this conversion as a String method called c_str(). The method should return a value of type **const char** *, which is a pointer to constant character data that represents the String. The method c_str() can be used as follows:

String s = "some_string";
const char *new_s = s.c_str();

It is important that the method c_str() returns a C-string of constant characters. We can see the need for this precaution if we consider the computer memory occupied by the string in new_s. This memory is certainly allocated by the **class** String. Once allocated, the memory must be looked after and ultimately deleted — either by client code or by the **class** String. We shall take the view that the **class** String should accept these responsibilities, since this will allow us to write a very efficient implementation of the conversion function, and it will avoid the possibility that a client forgets to delete C-strings created by the String class. However, the price that we must pay for this decision is that the client should not use the returned pointer to alter referenced character data. Hence, our conversion returns a constant C-string.

Highlights

The few features that we have described combine to give us very flexible, powerful, and yet safe string processing. Our own **String** class is a fully encapsulated ADT, but it provides a complete interface both to C-strings and to lists of characters. We have now arrived at the following class specification:

```
class String {
public:                          //    methods of the string ADT
    String();
    ~String();
    String (const String &copy);  //   copy constructor
    String (const char * copy);   //   conversion from C-string
    String (List<char> &copy);    //   conversion from List
    void operator = (const String &copy);
    const char *c_str() const;    //   conversion to C-style string
protected:
    char *entries;
    int length;
};

bool operator == (const String &first, const String &second);
bool operator >  (const String &first, const String &second);
bool operator <  (const String &first, const String &second);
bool operator >= (const String &first, const String &second);
bool operator <= (const String &first, const String &second);
bool operator != (const String &first, const String &second);
```

constructors

The constructors that convert C-string and List data to **String** objects are implemented as follows:

```
String :: String (const char *in_string)
/* Pre:   The pointer in_string references a C-string.
   Post:  The String is initialized by the C-string in_string. */
{
    length = strlen(in_string);
    entries = new char[length + 1];
    strcpy(entries, in_string);
}


String :: String (List<char> &in_list)
/* Post:  The String is initialized by the character List in_list. */
{
    length = in_list.size();
    entries = new char[length + 1];
    for (int i = 0; i < length; i++) in_list.retrieve(i, entries[i]);
    entries[length] = '\0';
}
```

We shall choose to implement the conversion method c_str( ), that converts a **String** to type **const char** ∗ as follows:

```
const char∗String :: c_str( ) const
/∗ Post:  A pointer to a legal C-string object matching the String is returned. ∗/
{
    return (const char ∗) entries;
}
```

compromise for efficiency

This implementation is not entirely satisfactory, because it gives access to internal **String** data; however, as we shall explain, other implementation strategies also have problems, and our implementation has the advantage of supreme efficiency. We note that the standard template library makes a similar compromise in its implementation of c_str( ).

alias problem

The method c_str( ) returns a pointer to an array of characters that can be read but not modified by clients: In this situation, we choose to return access to the C-string data member of the **String**. We use a cast to make sure that the returned pointer references a constant C-string. However, an irresponsible client could similarly cast away the constancy of the returned C-string and thus break the encapsulation of our class. A more serious problem is the alias created by our function. This means that clients of either our **class** String or the STL **class** string should use the result of c_str( ) only immediately after application of the method. Otherwise, even responsible clients could run into the problem exhibited by the following code.

```
String s = "abc";
const char ∗new_string = s.c_str( );
s = "def";
cout ≪ new_string;
```

The statement

```
s = "def";
```

results in the deletion of the former **String** and C-string data, so that the final statement has unpredictable results.

alternative implementation

An alternative implementation strategy for c_str( ) is to allocate dynamic memory for a copy of **String** data and copy characters into this storage. A pointer to the dynamic C-string is turned over to the client as the return value from the function. This alternative is clearly much less efficient, especially when converting long strings. However, it has another serious drawback: It is very likely to lead to the creation of garbage. The client has to remember to delete the C-string object after its use. For example, the following statements cause no problems for our earlier implementation of the method c_str( ) but would create some garbage if we adopted the alternative implementation.

```
String s = "Some very long string";
cout ≪ s.c_str( );        //   creates garbage from a temporary C-string object
```

Finally, we turn to the overloaded comparison operators. The following implementation of the overloaded operator == is short and extremely efficient precisely because of the convenience and efficiency of our method String :: c_str( ).

```
bool operator == (const String &first, const String &second)
/* Post: Return true if the String first agrees with String second. Else: Return
         false. */
{
   return strcmp(first.c_str( ), second.c_str( )) == 0;
}
```

The syntax that we use in overloading the **operator ==** is similar to that used in implementing an overloaded assignment operator in Section 4.3.2. The other overloaded comparison operators have almost identical implementations.

6.3.3 Further String Operations

We now develop a number of functions that work with **String** objects. Since users are likely to know the methods in the library for C-strings, we shall create an analogous library for **String** objects.

In many cases, the C-string functions can be applied directly to converted **String** objects. For example, with no extra programming effort, we can legally write:

```
String s = "some_string";
cout ≪ s.c_str( ) ≪ endl;
cout ≪ strlen(s.c_str( )) ≪ endl;
```

overloaded functions For C-string functions such as **strcpy** that do change string arguments, we shall write overloaded versions that operate with **String** parameters instead of **char *** parameters. As we have already mentioned, in C++: a function is overloaded if two or more different versions of the function are included in a single scope within a program. Of course, we have already overloaded constructors and operator functions, such as the assignment operator, several times. When a function is overloaded, the different function implementations must have different sets or types of parameters, so that the compiler can use the arguments passed by a client to see which version of the function should be used.

Our overloaded version of **strcat** is a function with prototype

void strcat(String &add_to, **const** String &add_on)

A client can concatenate strings s and t with the call **strcat(s, t)**; if the parameter s is a **String**, the parameter t could be either a C-string or a **String**. The overloaded function **strcat** is implemented as follows:

```
void strcat(String &add_to, const String &add_on)
/* Post:  The function concatenates String add_on onto the end of String add_to. */
{
    const char *cfirst = add_to.c_str( );
    const char *csecond = add_on.c_str( );
    char *copy = new char[strlen(cfirst) + strlen(csecond) + 1];
    strcpy(copy, cfirst);
    strcat(copy, csecond);
    add_to = copy;
    delete [ ] copy;
}
```

Observe that the function strcat, called in this implementation, uses arguments of
type **char** * and **const char** *. The C++ compiler recognizes this as a call to the
C-string function strcat, because of the exact match in argument types. Thus, our
overloaded function contains a call to the corresponding library function, rather
than a recursive call to itself. The statement add_to = copy calls for a cast from the
C-string copy to a String, and then an application of our overload String assignment
operator: In other words, it leads to two complete string copying operations. In
order to avoid the cost of these operations, we could consider recoding the statement. For example, one simple solution is to make the function strcat a *friend* of
friend function   the class String, we can then simply copy the address of copy to add_to.entries.

We shall need a function to read String objects. One way to achieve this, which
would maintain an analogy with operations for C-strings, is to overload the stream
input operator ≪ to accept String parameters. However, we shall adopt the alternative approach of creating a String library function called read_in.

Our String reading function uses a temporary List of characters to collect its input from a stream specified as a parameter. The function then calls the appropriate
constructor to translate this List into a String. The function assumes that input is
terminated by either a new line or an end-of-file character.

```
String read_in(istream &input)
/* Post:  Return a String read (as characters terminated by a newline or an end-of-
           file character) from an istream parameter. */
{
    List<char> temp;
    int size = 0;
    char c;
    while ((c = input.peek( )) != EOF && (c = input.get( )) != '\n')
        temp.insert(size++, c);
    String answer(temp);
    return answer;
}
```

It will be useful to have another version of the function read_in that uses a second reference parameter to record the input terminator. The specification for this
overloaded function follows:

> String read_in(istream &input, **int** &terminator);
>
> *postcondition*: Return a **String** read (as characters terminated by a newline or an end-of-file character) from an **istream** parameter. The terminating character is recorded as the output parameter **terminator**.

We shall also find it useful to apply the following **String** output function as an alternative to the operator ≪ .

void write(String &s)
/* **Post**: *The* String *parameter s is written to* cout. */
{
    cout ≪ s.c_str() ≪ endl;
}

In the next section, and in later sections, we shall use the following additional **String** *library functions*, whose implementations are left as exercises.

specifications

> **void** strcpy(String &copy, **const** String &original);
>
> *postcondition*: The function copies **String** original to **String** copy.

> **void** strncpy(String &copy, **const** String &original, **int** n);
>
> *postcondition*: The function copies at most n characters from **String** original to **String** copy.

These overloaded string handling functions have been designed to have behavior that matches that of the original C-string functions. However, the corresponding C-string library functions both return a value. This return value has type **char** ∗ and is set to point at the first string parameter. We have omitted any return values from our **String** library analogues.

The final C-string function for which we shall need an analogue is **strstr**. This function returns a pointer to the first occurrence of a target C-string in a text C-string. The returned pointer is normally used to calculate an offset from the start of the text. Our overloaded version of **strstr** uses two **String** parameters and returns an integer giving the index of the first occurrence of the **target** parameter in the **text** parameter.

> **int** strstr(**const** String &text, **const** String &target);
>
> *postcondition*: If **String** target is a substring of **String** text, the function returns the array index of the first occurrence of the string stored in target in the string stored in **text**.
> Else: The function returns a code of −1.

Exercises 6.3   **E1.** Write implementations for the remaining String methods.

    (a) The constructor String()

    (b) The destructor ~String()

    (c) The copy constructor String(**const** String &copy)

    (d) The overloaded assignment operator.

E2. Write implementations for the following String comparison operators:

$$>\quad <\quad >=\quad <=\quad !=$$

E3. Write implementations for the remaining String processing functions.

    (a) **void** strcpy(String &copy, **const** String &original);

    (b) **void** strncpy(String &copy, **const** String &original, **int** n);

    (c) **int** strstr(**const** String &text, **const** String &target);

palindromes

E4. A *palindrome* is a string that reads the same forward as backward; that is, a string in which the first character equals the last, the second equals the next to last, and so on. Examples of palindromes include 'radar' and

'ABLE WAS I ERE I SAW ELBA'.

Write a C++ function to test whether a String object passed as a reference parameter represents a palindrome.

Programming Projects 6.3

P1. Prepare a file containing implementations of the String methods and the functions for String processing. This file should be suitable for inclusion in any application program that uses strings.

P2. Different authors tend to employ different vocabularies, sentences of different lengths, and paragraphs of different lengths. This project is intended to analyze a text file for some of these properties.

    (a) Write a program that reads a text file and counts the number of words of each length that occurs, as well as the total number of words. The program should then print the mean (average) length of a word and the percentage of words of each length that occurs. For this project, assume that a word

text analysis

        consists entirely of (uppercase and lowercase) letters and is terminated by the first non-letter that appears.

    (b) Modify the program so that it also counts sentences and prints the total number of sentences and the mean number of words per sentence. Assume that a sentence terminates as soon as one of the characters period (.), question mark (?), or exclamation point (!) appears.

    (c) Modify the program so that it counts paragraphs and prints the total number of paragraphs and the mean number of words per paragraph. Assume that a paragraph terminates when a blank line or a line beginning with a blank character appears.

6.4 APPLICATION: A TEXT EDITOR

This section develops an application showing the use of both lists and strings. Our project is the development of a miniature text-editing program. This program will allow only a few simple commands and is, therefore, quite primitive in comparison with a modern text editor or word processor. Even so, it illustrates some of the basic ideas involved in the construction of much larger and more sophisticated text editors.

6.4.1 Specifications

Our text editor will allow us to read a file into memory, where we shall say that it is stored in a *buffer*. The buffer will be implemented as an object of a class that we call Editor. We shall consider each line of text in an Editor object to be a *string*. Hence, the Editor class will be based on a List of strings. We shall devise editing commands that will do list operations on the lines in the buffer and will do string operations on the characters in a single line.

Since, at any moment, the user may be typing either characters to be inserted into a line or commands to apply to existing text, a text editor should always be written to be as forgiving of invalid input as possible, recognizing illegal commands, and asking for confirmation before taking any drastic action like deleting the entire buffer.

We shall supply arguments, known as command line arguments to the main program of our editor implementation. These arguments allow us to run a compiled program, edit, with a standard invocation: edit infile outfile. Here is the list of commands to be included in our text editor. Each command is given by typing the letter shown in response to the editor's prompt '??'. The command letter may be typed in either uppercase or lowercase.

commands

'R' Read the text file, whose name is given in the command line, into the buffer. Any previous contents of the buffer are lost. At the conclusion, the current line will be the first line of the file.

'W' Write the contents of the buffer to the text file whose name is given in the command line. Neither the current line nor the buffer is changed.

'I' Insert a single new line. The user must type in the new line and supply its line number in response to appropriate prompts.

'D' Delete the current line and move to the next line.

'F' Find the first line, starting from the current line, that contains a target string that will be requested from the user.

'L' Show the length in characters of the current line and the length in lines of the buffer.

'C' Change a string requested from the user to a replacement text, also requested from the user, working within the current line only.

'Q' Quit the editor: Terminate immediately.

'H' Print out help messages explaining all the commands. The program will also accept '?' as an alternative to 'H'.

'N' Next line: Advance one line through the buffer.

'P' Previous line: Back up one line in the buffer.

'B' Beginning: Go to the first line of the buffer.

'E' End: go to the last line of the buffer.

'G' Go to a user-specified line number in the buffer.

'S' Substitute a line typed in by the user for the current line. The function should print out the line for verification and then request the new line.

'V' View the entire contents of the buffer, printed out to the terminal.

6.4.2 Implementation

1. The Main Program

The first task of the main program is to use the command-line arguments to open input and output files. If the files can be opened, the program should then declare an **Editor** object called **buffer** and repeatedly run the **Editor** methods of **buffer** to get commands from a user and process these commands. The resulting program follows.

```
int main(int argc, char *argv[])  //   count, values of command-line arguments
/* Pre:  Names of input and output files are given as command-line arguments.
   Post: Reads an input file that contains lines (character strings), performs simple
         editing operations on the lines, and writes the edited version to the output
         file.
   Uses: methods of class Editor */
{
  if (argc != 3) {
    cout << "Usage:\n\t edit  inputfile  outputfile" << endl;
    exit (1);
  }
  ifstream file_in(argv[1]);   //   Declare and open the input stream.
  if (file_in == 0) {
    cout << "Can't open input file " << argv[1] << endl;
    exit (1);
  }
  ofstream file_out(argv[2]);   //   Declare and open the output stream.
  if (file_out == 0) {
    cout << "Can't open output file " << argv[2] << endl;
    exit (1);
  }
  Editor buffer( &file_in,  &file_out);
  while (buffer.get_command())
    buffer.run_command();
}
```

2. The Editor Class Specification

The class **Editor** must contain a List of String objects, and it should permit efficient operations to move in both directions through the List. To meet these requirements, since we do not know in advance how large the buffer will be, let us decide that the **class Editor** will be derived from a doubly linked implementation of the **class** List<String>. This derived class needs the additional methods get_command and run_command that we have called from our main program. It also needs private data members to store a user command and links to the input and output streams.

```
class Editor: public List<String> {
public:
   Editor(ifstream *file_in, ofstream *file_out);
   bool get_command( );
   void run_command( );
private:
   ifstream *infile;
   ofstream *outfile;
   char user_command;
//   auxiliary functions
   Error_code next_line( );
   Error_code previous_line( );
   Error_code goto_line( );
   Error_code insert_line( );
   Error_code substitute_line( );
   Error_code change_line( );
   void read_file( );
   void write_file( );
   void find_string( );
};
```

The class specification sets up a number of auxiliary member functions. These will be used to implement various editor commands.

The constructor links input and output streams to the editor.

```
Editor :: Editor(ifstream *file_in, ofstream *file_out)
/* Post: Initialize the Editor members infile and outfile with the parameters. */
{
   infile = file_in;
   outfile = file_out;
}
```

3. Receiving a Command

We now turn to the method that requests a command from the user. Since a text editor must be tolerant of invalid input, we must carefully check the commands typed in by the user and make sure that they are legal. Since the user cannot be expected to be consistent in typing uppercase or lowercase letters, our first step is to translate an uppercase letter into lowercase, as is done by the standard routine **tolower** from the library <**cctype**>. The method **get_command** needs to print the current line, print a prompt, obtain a response from the user, translate a letter to lowercase, and check that the response is valid.

```
bool Editor :: get_command( )
/* Post:  Sets member user_command; returns true unless the user's command is q.
   Uses:  C library function tolower. */
{
  if (current != NULL)
    cout << current_position << " : "
         << current->entry.c_str() << "\n??" << flush;
  else
    cout << "File is empty.\n??" << flush;
  cin >> user_command;        //   ignores white space and gets command
  user_command = tolower(user_command);
  while (cin.get() != '\n')
    ;                         //   ignore user's enter key
  if (user_command == 'q')
    return false;
  else
    return true;
}
```

4. Performing Commands

The method **run_command** that does the commands as specified consists essentially of one large **switch** statement that sends the work out to a different function for each command. Some of these functions (like **remove**) are just members of the class List. Others are closely based on corresponding list-processing functions but have additional processing to handle user selections and erroneous cases. The functions that find and change strings require considerable new programming effort.

```
void Editor :: run_command( )
/* Post:  The command in user_command has been performed.
   Uses:  methods and auxiliary functions of the class Editor, the class String, and
          the String processing functions. */
```

```
                        {
                        String temp_string;
                        switch (user_command) {
beginning of buffer     case 'b':
                          if (empty())
                            cout ≪ " Warning: empty buffer " ≪ endl;
                          else
                            while (previous_line() == success)
                              ;
                          break;

change a line           case 'c':
                          if (empty())
                            cout ≪ " Warning: Empty file" ≪ endl;
                          else if (change_line() != success)
                            cout ≪ " Error: Substitution failed " ≪ endl;
                          break;

delete a line           case 'd':
                          if (remove(current_position, temp_string) != success)
                            cout ≪ " Error: Deletion failed " ≪ endl;
                          break;

go to end of buffer     case 'e':
                          if (empty())
                            cout ≪ " Warning: empty buffer " ≪ endl;
                          else
                            while (next_line() == success)
                              ;
                          break;

find a target string    case 'f':
                          if (empty())
                            cout ≪ " Warning: Empty file" ≪ endl;
                          else
                            find_string();
                          break;

go to a specified line  case 'g':
                          if (goto_line() != success)
                            cout ≪ " Warning: No such line" ≪ endl;
                          break;

print a help message    case '?':
                        case 'h':
                          cout ≪ "Valid commands are: b(egin) c(hange) d(el) e(nd)" ≪ endl
                                ≪ "f(ind) g(o) h(elp) i(nsert) l(ength) n(ext) p(rior) " ≪ endl
                                ≪ "q(uit) r(ead) s(ubstitue) v(iew) w(rite) " ≪ endl;
```

```
insert a new line       case 'i':
                            if (insert_line( ) != success)
                                cout << " Error: Insertion failed " << endl;
                            break;

show buffer length      case 'l':
and line length             cout << "There are " << size( ) << " lines in the file." << endl;
                            if (!empty( ))
                                cout << "Current line length is "
                                        << strlen((current->entry).c_str( )) << endl;
                            break;

go to next line         case 'n':
                            if (next_line( ) != success)
                                cout << " Warning: at end of buffer" << endl;
                            break;

go to previous line     case 'p':
                            if (previous_line( ) != success)
                                cout << " Warning: at start of buffer" << endl;
                            break;

read a file             case 'r':
                            read_file( );
                            break;

substitute a new line   case 's':
                            if (substitute_line( ) != success)
                                cout << " Error: Substitution failed " << endl;
                            break;

view entire buffer      case 'v':
                            traverse(write);
                            break;

write buffer to file    case 'w':
                            if (empty( ))
                                cout << " Warning: Empty file" << endl;
                            else
                                write_file( );
                            break;

invalid input           default :
                            cout << "Press h or ? for help or enter a valid command: ";
                        }
                    }
```

To complete the project, we must, in turn, write each of the auxiliary **Editor** functions invoked by **do_command**.

5. Reading and Writing Files

Since reading destroys any previous contents of the buffer, it requests confirmation before proceeding unless the buffer is empty when it begins.

```
void Editor :: read_file()
/* Pre:   Either the Editor is empty or the user authorizes the command.
   Post:  The contents of *infile are read to the Editor. Any prior contents of the
          Editor are overwritten.
   Uses: String and Editor methods and functions. */
{
  bool proceed = true;
  if (!empty()) {
    cout << "Buffer is not empty; the read will destroy it." << endl;
    cout << " OK to proceed? " << endl;
    if (proceed = user_says_yes()) clear();
  }
  int line_number = 0, terminal_char;
  while (proceed) {
    String in_string = read_in(*infile, terminal_char);
    if (terminal_char == EOF) {
      proceed = false;
      if (strlen(in_string.c_str()) > 0) insert(line_number, in_string);
    }
    else insert(line_number++, in_string);
  }
}
```

writing a file   The function write_file is somewhat simpler than read_file, and it is left as an exercise.

6. Inserting a Line

For insertion of a new line at the current line number, we first read a string with the auxiliary String function read_in that we discussed in Section 6.3. After reading in the string, we insert it with the List method insert. There is no need for us to check directly whether the buffer is full since this is carried out by the List operations.

```
Error_code Editor :: insert_line()
/* Post:  A string entered by the user is inserted as a user-selected line number.
   Uses: String and Editor methods and functions. */
{
  int line_number;
  cout << " Insert what line number? " << flush;
  cin  >> line_number;
  while (cin.get() != '\n');
  cout << " What is the new line to insert? " << flush;
  String to_insert = read_in(cin);
  return insert(line_number, to_insert);
}
```

7. Searching for a String

Now we come to a more difficult task, that of searching for a line that contains a target string that the user will provide. We use our String function strstr to check whether the current line contains the target. If the target does not appear in the current line, then we search the remainder of the buffer. If and when the target is found, we highlight it by printing out the line where it was found, which now becomes the current line, together with a series of upward arrows (∧) showing where in the line the target appears.

```
void Editor :: find_string( )
/* Pre:   The Editor is not empty.
   Post:  The current line is advanced until either it contains a copy of a user-selected
          string or it reaches the end of the Editor. If the selected string is found,
          the corresponding line is printed with the string highlighted.
   Uses: String and Editor methods and functions. */
{
    int index;
    cout << "Enter string to search for:" << endl;
    String search_string = read_in(cin);
    while ((index = strstr(current->entry, search_string)) == −1)
        if (next_line( ) != success) break;
    if (index == −1) cout << "String was not found.";
    else {
        cout << (current->entry).c_str( ) << endl;
        for (int i = 0;  i < index;  i++)
            cout << " ";
        for (int j = 0;  j < strlen(search_string.c_str( ));  j++)
            cout << "^";
    }
    cout << endl;
}
```

8. Changing One String to Another

In accordance with the practice of several text editors, we shall allow the searches instituted by the find command to be global, starting at the present position and continuing to the end of the buffer. We shall, however, treat the change_string command differently, so that it will make changes only in the current line. It is very easy for the user to make a mistake while typing a target or its replacement text. The find_string command changes nothing, so such a mistake is not too serious. If the change_string command were to work globally, a spelling error might cause changes in far different parts of the buffer from the previous location of the current line.

The function change_line first obtains the target from the user and then locates it in the current string. If it is not found, the user is informed; otherwise, the user is requested to give the replacement text, after which a series of String and C-string operations remove the target from the current line and replace it with the replacement text.

```
Error_code Editor :: change_line( )
/* Pre:   The Editor is not empty.
   Post: If a user-specified string appears in the current line, it is replaced by a new
         user-selected string. Else: an Error_code is returned.
   Uses: String and Editor methods and functions. */
{
   Error_code result = success;
   cout ≪ " What text segment do you want to replace? " ≪ flush;
   String old_text = read_in(cin);
   cout ≪ " What new text segment do you want to add in? " ≪ flush;
   String new_text = read_in(cin);

   int index = strstr(current->entry, old_text);
   if (index == −1) result = fail;
   else {
      String new_line;
      strncpy(new_line, current->entry, index);
      strcat(new_line, new_text);
      const char *old_line = (current->entry).c_str( );
      strcat(new_line, (String)(old_line + index + strlen(old_text.c_str( ))));
      current->entry = new_line;
   }
   return result;
}
```

The tricky statement

$$\text{strcat(new\_line, (String)(old\_line + index + strlen(old\_text.c\_str( ))));}$$

calculates a temporary pointer to the part of the C-string old_line that follows the replaced string. The C-string referenced by this temporary pointer is cast to a String that is immediately concatenated onto new_line.

Programming Projects 6.4

P1. Supply the following functions; test and exercise the text editor.

    (a) next_line   (d) substitute_line

    (b) previous_line   (e) write_file

    (c) goto_line

P2. Add a feature to the text editor to put text into two columns, as follows. The user will select a range of line numbers, and the corresponding lines from the buffer will be placed into two queues, the first half of the lines in one, and the second half in the other. The lines will then be removed from the queues, one at a time from each, and combined with a predetermined number of blanks between them to form a line of the final result. (The white space between the columns is called the *gutter*.)

6.5 LINKED LISTS IN ARRAYS

old languages

Several of the older but widely-used computer languages, such as FORTRAN, COBOL, and BASIC, do not provide facilities for dynamic storage allocation or pointers. Even when implemented in these languages, however, there are many problems where the methods of linked lists are preferable to those of contiguous lists, where, for example, the ease of changing a pointer rather than copying a large entry proves advantageous. We will even find that in C++ applications, it is sometimes best to use an array-based implementation of linked lists. This section shows how to implement linked lists using only integer variables and arrays.

1. The Method

The idea is to begin with a large workspace array (or several arrays to hold different parts of each list entry, in the case when the programming language does not support structures) and regard the array as our allocation of unused space. We then set up our own functions to keep track of which parts of the array are unused and to link entries of the array together in the desired order.

dynamic memory

The one feature of linked lists that we must invariably lose in this implementation method is the dynamic allocation of storage, since we must decide in advance how much space to allocate to each array. All the remaining advantages of linked lists, such as flexibility in rearranging large entries or ease in making insertions or deletions anywhere in the list, will still apply, and linked lists still prove a valuable method.

Highlights

The implementation of linked lists within arrays even proves valuable in languages like C++ that do provide pointers and dynamic memory allocation. The applications where arrays may prove preferable are those where

advantages

➥ the number of entries in a list is known in advance,

➥ the links are frequently rearranged, but relatively few additions or deletions are made, or

➥ the same data are sometimes best treated as a linked list and other times as a contiguous list.

multiple linkages

An example of such an application is illustrated in Figure 6.6, which shows a small part of a student record system. Identification numbers are assigned to students first come, first served, so neither the names nor the marks in any particular course are in any special order. Given an identification number, a student's records may be found immediately by using the identification number as an index to look in the arrays. Sometimes, however, it is desired to print out the student records alphabetically by name, and this can be done by following the links stored in the

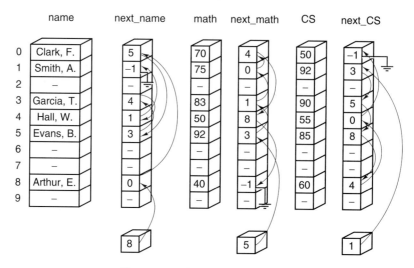

Figure 6.6. Linked lists in arrays

array **next_name**. Similarly, student records can be ordered by marks in any course by following the links in the appropriate array.

To show how this implementation of linked lists works, let us traverse the linked list **next_name** shown in the first part of Figure 6.6. The list header (shown below the table) contains the value 8, which means that the entry in position 8, **Arthur, E.**, is the first entry on the list. Position 8 of **next_name** then contains the value 0, which means that the name in position 0, **Clark, F.**, comes next. In position 0, **next_name** contains 5, so **Evans, B.** comes next. Position 5 points to position 3 (**Garcia, T.**), which points to position 4 (**Hall, W.**), and position 4 points to position 1 (**Smith, A.**). In position 1, **next_name** contains a −1, which means that position 1 is the last entry on the linked list.

The array **next_math**, similarly, describes a linked list giving the scores in the array **math** in descending order. The first entry is 5, which points to entry 3, and the following nodes in the order of the linked list are 1, 0, 4, and 8.

In the same way, the order in which the nodes appear in the linked list described by **next_CS** is 1, 3, 5, 8, 4, and 0.

As the example in Figure 6.6 shows, implementation of linked lists in arrays can achieve the *flexibility* of linked lists for making changes, the ability to *share* the same information fields (such as the names in Figure 6.6) among several linked lists, and, by using indices to access entries directly, the advantage of *random access* otherwise available only for contiguous lists.

In the implementation of linked lists in arrays, pointers become indices relative to the start of arrays, and the links of a list are stored in an array, each entry of which gives the index where, within the array, the next entry of the list is stored. To distinguish these indices from the pointers of a linked list in dynamic storage, we

shared lists and random access

indices

shall refer to links within arrays as *indices* and reserve the word *pointer* for links in dynamic storage.

For the sake of writing programs we could declare two arrays for each linked list, entry[ ] to hold the information in the nodes and next_node[ ] to give the index of the next node. For most applications, entry is an array of structured entries, or it is split into several arrays in the case when the programming language does not provide for structures. Both the arrays entry and next_node would be indexed from 0 to max_list − 1, where max_list is a symbolic constant.

null indices   Since we begin the indices with 0, we make another arbitrary choice and use the index value −1 to indicate the end of the list, just as the pointer value NULL is used in dynamic storage. This choice is also illustrated in Figure 6.6.

You should take a moment to trace through Figure 6.6, checking that the index values as shown correspond to the colored arrows shown from each entry to its successor.

2. Operations: Space Management

To obtain the flavor of implementing linked lists in arrays, let us rewrite some of the functions of this chapter with this implementation.

Our first task is to set up a list of available space and write auxiliary functions to obtain a new node and to return a node to available space. For the sake of programming consistently with Section 6.2, we shall change our point of view *workspace for linked* slightly. All the space that we use will come from a single array called workspace, *lists*   whose entries correspond to the nodes of the linked list. To emphasize this analogy, we shall refer to entries of workspace as nodes, and we shall design a data type called Node to store entry data. Each Node will be a structure with two members, entry of type List_entry and next of type index. The type index is implemented as an integer, but its values are interpreted as array locations so that it replaces the pointer type of other linked lists.

The available space in workspace comes in two varieties.

➡ First, there are nodes that have never been allocated.

➡ Second, there are nodes that have previously been used but have now been released.

count of used positions   We shall initially allocate space starting at the beginning of the array; hence we can keep track of how much space has been used at some time by an index last_used that indicates the position of the last node that has been used at some time. Locations with indices greater than last_used have never been allocated.

linked stack of   For the nodes that have been used and then returned to available space, we *previously-used space*   need to use some kind of linked structure to allow us to go from one to the next. Since linked stacks are the simplest kind of such structure, we shall use a linked stack to keep track of the nodes that have been previously used and then returned to available space. This stack will be linked by means of the next indices in the nodes of the array workspace.

To keep track of the stack of available space, we need an integer variable available that gives the index of its top. If this stack is empty (which will be represented by available == −1), then we will need to obtain a new Node, that is, a position within the array that has not yet been used for any Node. We do so by increasing the index variable last_used that will count the total number of positions within our array that have been used to hold list entries. When last_used reaches max_list − 1 (the bound we have assumed for array size) and available == −1, the workspace is full and no further space can be allocated.

protected members   We declare the array workspace and the indices available and last_used as protected data members of our List class. When a List object is initialized, both members available and last_used should be initialized to −1, available to indicate that the stack of space previously used but now available is empty, and last_used to indicate that no space from the array has yet been assigned.

The available-space list is illustrated in Figure 6.7. The arrows shown on the left of the array next_node describe a linked list that produces the names in the list in alphabetical order. The arrows on the right side of array next_node, with header variable available, show the nodes in the stack of (previously used but now) available space. Notice that the indices that appear in the available-space list are precisely the indices in positions 10 or earlier that are not assigned to names in the array workspace. Finally, none of the entries in positions 11 or later has been assigned. This fact is indicated by the value last_used = 10. If we were to insert additional names into the List, we would first pop nodes from the stack with top available, and only when the stack is empty would we increase last_used to insert a name in previously unused space.

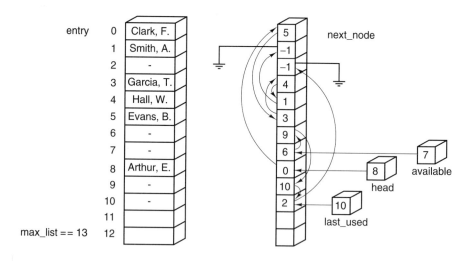

Figure 6.7. The array and stack of available space

The decisions we have made translate into the following declarations to be placed in the linked list specification file:

```
typedef int index;
const int max_list = 7;          //   small value for testing purposes


template <class List_entry>
class Node {
public:
   List_entry entry;
   index next;
};


template <class List_entry>
class List {
public:
//   Methods of the list ADT
   List();
   int size() const;
   bool full() const;
   bool empty() const;
   void clear();
   void traverse(void (*visit)(List_entry &));
   Error_code retrieve(int position, List_entry &x) const;
   Error_code replace(int position, const List_entry &x);
   Error_code remove(int position, List_entry &x);
   Error_code insert(int position, const List_entry &x);

protected:
//   Data members
   Node<List_entry> workspace[max_list];
   index available, last_used, head;
   int count;
//   Auxiliary member functions
   index new_node();
   void delete_node(index n);
   int current_position(index n) const;
   index set_position(int position) const;
};
```

compatibility

We observe that the publicly available methods are exactly the same as those of our other list implementations. This means that our new implementation is interchangeable with any of our earlier List ADT implementations. We have added a number of protected member functions. Most of these functions manage the nodes in workspace. We use them as tools for building the methods; however, they are not accessible to a client. With these declarations, we can now write the functions for keeping track of unused space. The functions new_node and delete_node play the roles of the C++ operators **new** and **delete**. Thus, for example, new_node returns a previously unallocated index from workspace. These functions take the form:

```
template <class List_entry>
index List<List_entry> :: new_node( )
/* Post: The index of the first available Node in workspace is returned; the data
         members available, last_used, and workspace are updated as necessary. If
         the workspace is already full, −1 is returned. */
{
  index new_index;
  if (available != −1) {
    new_index = available;
    available = workspace[available].next;
  } else if (last_used < max_list − 1) {
    new_index = ++last_used;
  } else return −1;
  workspace[new_index].next = −1;
  return new_index;
}
```

```
template <class List_entry>
void List<List_entry> :: delete_node(index old_index)
/* Pre:  The List has a Node stored at index old_index.
   Post: The List index old_index is pushed onto the linked stack of available space;
         available, last_used, and workspace are updated as necessary. */
{
  index previous;
  if (old_index == head) head = workspace[old_index].next;
  else {
    previous = set_position(current_position(old_index) − 1);
    workspace[previous].next = workspace[old_index].next;
  }
  workspace[old_index].next = available;
  available = old_index;
}
```

These two functions, of course, simply pop and push a stack. We could, if we wished, write functions for processing stacks and use those functions.

The other protected member functions are **set_position** and **current_position**. As in our earlier implementations, the **set_position** operation is used to locate the index of **workspace** that stores the element of our list with a given position number. The **current_position** operation uses an index in **workspace** as its parameter; it calculates the position of any list entry stored there. We leave these operations as exercises; their specifications are as follows:

---

index List<List_entry>::set_position(int position) **const;**

precondition: position is a valid position in the list; $0 \le$ position $<$ count.

postcondition: Returns the index of the node at position in the list.

---

int List<List_entry>::current_position(index n) **const;**

postcondition: Returns the position number of the node stored at index n, or
                 -1 if there no such node.

---

3. Other Operations

The coding of all methods to manipulate linked lists implemented within arrays
proceeds by translating linked list methods, and most of these will be left as exercises. To provide models, however, let us write translations of the functions to
traverse a List and to insert a new entry into a List.

```
template <class List_entry>
void List<List_entry>::traverse(void (*visit)(List_entry &))
/* Post: The action specified by function *visit has been performed on every entry
         of the List, beginning at position 0 and doing each in turn. */
{
   for (index n = head; n != -1; n = workspace[n].next)
     (*visit)(workspace[n].entry);
}
```

Compare this method with the corresponding one for simply linked lists with
pointers and dynamic memory presented in Section 6.2. You will quickly see that
each statement in this implementation is a simple translation of a corresponding
statement in our earlier implementation. A similar translation process turns our
earlier insertion method into an insertion method for the array-based linked-list
implementation.

```
template <class List_entry>
Error_code List<List_entry>::insert(int position, const List_entry &x)
/* Post: If the List is not full and 0 ≤ position ≤ n, where n is the number of
         entries in the List, the function succeeds: Any entry formerly at position
         and all later entries have their position numbers increased by 1 and x is
         inserted at position of the List.
         Else: the function fails with a diagnostic error code. */
```

```
{
    index new_index, previous, following;
    if (position < 0 || position > count) return range_error;
    if (position > 0) {
        previous = set_position(position − 1);
        following = workspace[previous].next;
    }
    else following = head;
    if ((new_index = new_node()) == −1) return overflow;
    workspace[new_index].entry = x;
    workspace[new_index].next = following;
    if (position ==  0)
        head = new_index;
    else
        workspace[previous].next = new_index;
    count++;
    return success;
}
```

4. Linked-List Variations

Arrays with indices are not restricted to the implementation of simply linked lists. They are equally effective with doubly linked lists or with any other variation. For doubly linked lists, in fact, the ability to do arithmetic with indices allows an implementation (which uses negative as well as positive values for the indices) in which both forward and backward links can be included in a single index field. (See Exercise E5.)

Exercises 6.5   **E1.** Draw arrows showing how the list entries are linked together in each of the following **next** node tables.

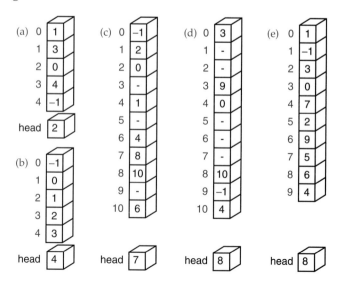

E2. Construct **next** tables showing how each of the following lists is linked into alphabetical order. Also, in each case, give the value of the variable **head** that starts the list.

(a)			(c)			(d)		
	1	array		1	the		1	London
	2	stack		2	of		2	England
	3	queue		3	and		3	Rome
	4	list		4	to		4	Italy
	5	deque		5	a		5	Madrid
	6	scroll		6	in		6	Spain
				7	that		7	Oslo
(b)	1	push		8	is		8	Norway
	2	pop		9	I		9	Paris
	3	add		10	it		10	France
	4	remove		11	for		11	Warsaw
	5	insert		12	as		12	Poland

E3. For the list of cities and countries in part (d) of the previous question, construct a **next** node table that produces a linked list, containing all the cities in alphabetical order followed by all the countries in alphabetical order.

E4. Write versions of each of the following functions for linked lists in arrays. Be sure that each function conforms to the specifications given in Section 6.1 and the declarations in this section.

   (a) set_position   **(e)** full   **(h)** remove
   (b) List (a constructor)   **(f)** size   **(i)** replace
   (c) clear   **(g)** retrieve   **(j)** current_position
   (d) empty

E5. It is possible to implement a doubly linked list in a workspace array by using only one index **next**. That is, we do not need to keep a separate field **back** in the nodes that make up the workspace array to find the backward links. The idea is to put into workspace[current] not the index of the next entry on the list but, instead, a member workspace[current].difference giving the index of the next entry *minus* the index of the entry preceding **current**. We also must maintain two pointers to successive nodes in the list, the **current** index and the index **previous** of the node just before **current** in the linked list. To find the next entry of the list, we calculate

$$\text{workspace[current].difference + previous;}$$

Similarly, to find the entry preceding **previous**, we calculate

$$\text{current} - \text{workspace[previous].difference;}$$

An example of such a list is shown in the first part of the following diagram. Inside each box is shown the value stored in **difference**; on the right is the corresponding calculation of index values.

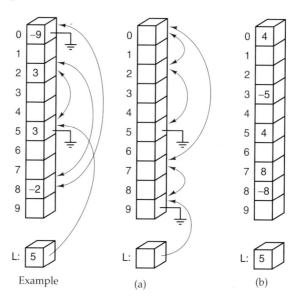

Example (a) (b)

(a) For the doubly linked list shown in the second part of the preceding diagram, show the values that will be stored in list.head and in the difference fields of occupied nodes of the workspace.

(b) For the values of list.head and difference shown in the third part of the preceding diagram, draw links showing the corresponding doubly linked list.

(c) With this implementation, write the function set_position.

(d) With this implementation, write the function insert.

(e) With this implementation, write the function remove.

6.6 APPLICATION: GENERATING PERMUTATIONS

Our final sample project in this chapter illustrates the use both of general lists and of linked lists in arrays in a highly application-specific way. This project is to generate all the $n!$ permutations of n objects as efficiently as possible. Recall that the permutations of n different objects are all the ways to put them in different orders.[1]

The reason why there are $n!$ permutations of n objects is that we can choose any of the n objects to be first, then choose any of the $n - 1$ remaining objects second, and so on. These choices are independent, so the number of choices multiply. If we think of the number $n!$ as the product

$$n! = 1 \times 2 \times 3 \times \cdots \times n,$$

then the process of multiplication can be pictured as the tree in Figure 6.8. (Ignore the labels for the moment.)

---

[1] For more information on permutations, see Appendix A.

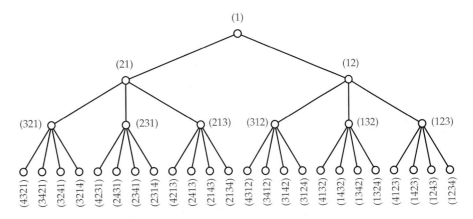

Figure 6.8. Permutation generation by multiplication, $n = 4$

1. The Idea

We can identify permutations with the nodes as given by the labels in Figure 6.8. At the top is 1 by itself. We can obtain the two permutations of $\{1, 2\}$ by writing 2 first on the left, then on the right of 1. Similarly, the six permutations of $\{1, 2, 3\}$ can be obtained by starting with one of the permutations $(2, 1)$ or $(1, 2)$ and inserting 3 into one of the three possible positions (left, center, or right). The task of generating permutations of $\{1, 2, \ldots, k\}$ can now be summarized as

> *Take a given permutation of $\{1, 2, \ldots, k - 1\}$ and put its entries into a list. Insert k, in turn, into each of the k possible positions in this list, thereby obtaining k distinct permutations of $\{1, 2, \ldots, k\}$.*

This algorithm illustrates the use of recursion to complete tasks that have been temporarily postponed. That is, we shall write a function that will first insert 1 into an empty list, and then use a recursive call to insert the remaining numbers from 2 to n into the list. This first recursive call will insert 2 into the list containing only 1 and postpone further insertions to a recursive call. On the nth recursive call, finally, the integer n will be inserted. In this way, having begun with a tree structure as motivation, we have now developed an algorithm for which the given tree becomes the recursion tree.

2. Refinement

Let us restate the algorithm in slightly more formal terms. We shall invoke our function as

permute(1, n)

which will mean to insert all integers from 1 to n to build all the $n!$ permutations. When it is time to insert the integer k, the remaining task is

```
void permute(int k, int n)
/* Pre:   1 through k − 1 are already in the permutation list;
    Post:  inserts the integers from k through n into the permutation list */
{
    for                              //   each of the k possible positions in the list
    {
        //   Insert k into the given position.
        if (k ==  n) process_permutation;
        else permute(k + 1, n);
        //   Remove k from the given position.
    }
}
```

outline

The function process_permutation will make whatever disposition is desired of a complete permutation of $\{1, 2, \dots, n\}$. We might wish only to print it out, or we might wish to send it as input to some other task.

3. The General Procedure

To translate this algorithm into C++, we shall change some of the notation. We shall create permutations in a variable **permutation** of type **List<int>**. Instead of k we shall let new_entry denote the integer being inserted, and write **degree** instead of n for the total number of objects being permuted. We then obtain the following function:

```
void permute(int new_entry, int degree, List<int> &permutation)
/* Pre:   permutation contains a permutation with entries in positions 1 through
              new_entry − 1.
    Post: All permutations with degree entries, built from the given permutation,
              have been constructed and processed.
    Uses: permute recursively, process_permutation, and List functions. */
{
    for (int current = 0;  current < permutation.size() + 1;  current++) {
        permutation.insert(current, new_entry);
        if (new_entry ==  degree)
            process_permutation(permutation);
        else
            permute(new_entry + 1, degree, permutation);
        permutation.remove(current, new_entry);
    }
}
```

Embedding this function into a working program is left as a project. For the required list functions, any of the implementations from Section 6.2 will be acceptable.

4. Data Structures: Optimization

The number $n!$ increases very rapidly with n; the number of permutations goes up very quickly indeed with n. Hence this project is one of the few applications where optimization to increase the speed may be worth the effort, especially if we wish to use the program to study interesting questions concerning generating permutations.

Let us now make some decisions regarding representation of the data with the view of increasing the program's speed as much as possible, even at the expense of readability. We use a list to hold the numbers being permuted. This list is available to the recursive invocations of the function as **permutation**, and each recursive call updates the entries in this list. Since we must continually insert and remove entries into and from the list, linked storage will be more flexible than keeping the entries in a contiguous list. But the total number of entries in the list never exceeds n, so we can (probably) improve efficiency by keeping the linked list within an array, rather than using dynamic memory allocation. Our links are thus integer
linked list in array   indices relative to the start of the array. With an array, furthermore, the index of each entry, as it is assigned, will happen to be the same as the value of the number being inserted, so there is no longer any need to keep this numerical value. Hence only the links need to be kept in the array.

This representation of a permutation as a linked list within an array is illustrated in Figure 6.9. The top diagram shows the permutation $(3, 2, 1, 4)$ as a linked list, and the second diagram shows it as a linked list inside an array. The third diagram omits the actual entries being permuted, since they are the same as the locations in the array, and keeps only the links describing the linked list.

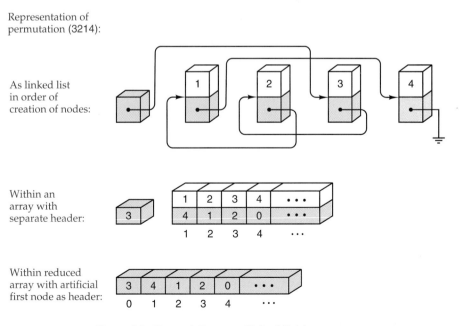

Figure 6.9. Permutation as a linked list in an array

artificial node   Insertions and deletions are further simplified if we put an artificial first node at the beginning of the list, so that insertions and deletions at the beginning of the (actual) list can be treated in the same way as those at other positions, always as insertions or deletions after a node. Hence we can obtain increased efficiency by using all these special conditions and writing the insertions and deletions into the function **permute**, instead of using a generic list implementation.

5. Final Program

With these decisions we can write an optimized version of **permute**.

```
void permute(int new_entry, int degree, int *permutation)
/* Pre:   permutation contains a linked permutation with entries in positions 1
             through new_entry − 1.
     Post: All permutations with degree entries, built from the given permutation,
             have been constructed and processed.
     Uses: Functions permute (recursively) and process_permutation. */
{
  int current = 0;
  do {
    permutation[new_entry] = permutation[current];
    permutation[current] = new_entry;
    if (new_entry ==  degree)
      process_permutation(permutation);
    else
      permute(new_entry + 1, degree, permutation);
    permutation[current] = permutation[new_entry];
    current = permutation[current];
  } while (current != 0);
}
```

The main program does little except to establish the declarations and initiate the process.

```
main( )
/* Pre:   The user specifies the degree of permutations to construct.
     Post: All permutations of a user-supplied degree are printed to the terminal. */
{
  int degree;
  int permutation[max_degree + 1];
  cout ≪ "Number of elements to permute? ";
  cin  ≫ degree;
  if (degree < 1 || degree > max_degree)
    cout ≪ "Number must be between 1 and " ≪ max_degree ≪ endl;
  else {
    permutation[0] = 0;
    permute(1, degree, permutation);
  }
}
```

Recall that the array **permutation** describes a linked list of pointers and does not contain the objects being permuted. If, for example, it is desired to print the integers $1, \ldots, n$ being permuted, then the auxiliary function becomes

```
void process_permutation(int *permutation)
/* Pre:   permutation is in linked form.
   Post:  The permutation has been printed to the terminal. */
{
   int current = 0;
   while (permutation[current] != 0) {
      cout << permutation[current] << " ";
      current = permutation[current];
   }
   cout << endl;
}
```

With this, we have a complete program, and, in fact, one of the most efficient available programs for generating permutations at high speed.

Programming Projects 6.6

P1. Complete a version of the permutation-generation program that uses one of the general list implementations by writing its main program and a function **process_permutation** that prints the permutation at the terminal. After testing your program, suppress printing the permutations and include the CPU timer functions provided with your compiler. Compare the performance of your program with each of the list implementations in Section 6.2. Also compare the performance with that of the optimized program written in the text.

P2. Modify the general version of **permute** so that the position occupied by each number does not change by more than one to the left or to the right from any permutation to the next one generated. [This is a simplified form of one rule for *campanology* (ringing changes on church bells).]

POINTERS AND PITFALLS

1. Use C++ templates to implement generic data structures.

2. Don't confuse contiguous lists with arrays.

3. Choose your data structures as you design your algorithms, and avoid making premature decisions.

4. Always be careful about the extreme cases and handle them gracefully. Trace through your algorithm to determine what happens when a data structure is empty or full.

5. Don't optimize your code until it works perfectly, and then only optimize it if improvement in efficiency is definitely required. First try a simple implementation of your data structures. Change to a more sophisticated implementation only if the simple one proves too inefficient.

6. When working with general lists, first decide exactly what operations are needed, and then choose the implementation that enables those operations to be done most easily.

7. In choosing between linked and contiguous implementations of lists, consider the necessary operations on the lists. Linked lists are more flexible in regard to insertions, deletions, and rearrangement; contiguous lists allow random access.

8. Contiguous lists usually require less computer memory, computer time, and programming effort when the items in the list are small and the algorithms are simple. When the list holds large data entries, linked lists usually save space, time, and often programming effort.

9. Dynamic memory and pointers allow a program to adapt automatically to a wide range of application sizes and provide flexibility in space allocation among different data structures. Static memory (arrays and indices) is sometimes more efficient for applications whose size can be completely specified in advance.

10. For advice on programming with linked lists in dynamic memory, see the guidelines in Chapter 4.

11. Avoid sophistication for sophistication's sake. If a simple method is adequate for your application, use it.

12. Don't reinvent the wheel. If a ready-made class template or function is adequate for your application, consider using it.

REVIEW QUESTIONS

6.1 **1.** Which of the operations possible for general lists are also possible for queues? for stacks?

2. List three operations possible for general lists that are not allowed for either stacks or queues.

6.2 **3.** If the items in a list are integers (one word each), compare the amount of space required altogether if (a) the list is kept contiguously in an array 90 percent full, (b) the list is kept contiguously in an array 40 percent full, and (c) the list is kept as a linked list (where the pointers take one word each).

4. Repeat the comparisons of the previous exercise when the items in the list are entries taking 200 words each.

5. What is the major disadvantage of linked lists in comparison with contiguous lists?

6.3   **6.** What are the major disadvantages of C-strings?

6.5   **7.** What are some reasons for implementing linked lists in arrays with indices instead of in dynamic memory with pointers?

REFERENCES FOR FURTHER STUDY

The references given for stacks and queues continue to be appropriate for the current chapter. In particular, for many topics concerning list manipulation, the best source for additional information, historical notes, and mathematical analysis is KNUTH, volume 1. This book, however, does not take the principles of data abstraction into account.

For details regarding the C++ standard string implementation and library, see Chapter 20 of

> B. STROUSTRUP, *The C++ Programming Language*, third edition, Addison-Wesley, Reading, Mass., 1997.

For a careful discussion of the advantages and drawbacks of the various implementation strategies for a conversion from strings to C-strings, see:

> SCOTT MEYERS, *Effective C++*, second edition, Addison-Wesley, Reading, Mass., 1997.

The algorithm that generates permutations by insertion into a linked list was published in the ACM *SIGCSE Bulletin* 14 (February 1982), 92–96. Useful surveys of many methods for generating permutations are

> R. SEDGEWICK, "Permutation generation methods," *Computing Surveys* 9 (1977), 137–164; addenda, ibid., 314–317.

> R. W. TOPOR, "Functional programs for generating permutations," *Computer Journal* 25 (1982), 257–263.

The applications of permutations to campanology (change ringing of bells) produce interesting problems amenable to computer study. An excellent source for further information is

> F. J. BUDDEN, *The Fascination of Groups*, Cambridge University Press, Cambridge, England, 1972, pp. 451–479.

Searching

7

THIS CHAPTER introduces the problem of searching a list to find a particular entry. Our discussion centers on two well-known algorithms: sequential search and binary search. We shall develop several sophisticated mathematical tools, used both to demonstrate the correctness of algorithms and to calculate how much work they must do. These mathematical tools include invariant assertions, comparison trees, and the big-O, Θ, and Ω notations. Finally, we shall obtain lower bounds showing conditions under which any searching algorithm must do at least as much work as binary search.

7.1 SEARCHING: INTRODUCTION AND NOTATION

Information retrieval is one of the most important applications of computers. We are given a name and are asked for an associated telephone listing. We are given an account number and are asked for the transactions occurring in that account. We are given an employee name or number and are asked for the personnel records of the employee.

1. Keys

keys and records

In these examples and a host of others, we are given one piece of information, which we shall call a *key*, and we are asked to find a record that contains other information associated with the key. We shall allow both the possibility that there is more than one record with the same key and that there is no record at all with a given key. See Figure 7.1.

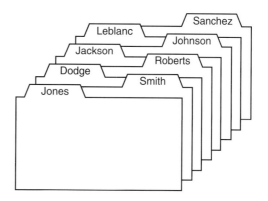

Figure 7.1. Records and their keys

2. Analysis

Searching for the keys that locate records is often the most time-consuming action in a program, and, therefore, the way the records are arranged and the choice of method used for searching can make a substantial difference in the program's performance. For this reason, we shall spend some time in this chapter studying how much work is done by each of the algorithms we develop. We shall find that counting the number of times that one key is compared with another gives us an excellent measure of the total amount of work that the algorithm will do and of the total amount of computer time it will require when it is run.

3. External and Internal Searching

The searching problem falls naturally into two cases. If there are many records, perhaps each one quite large, then it will be necessary to store the records in files on disk or tape, external to the computer memory. This case is called *external* searching. In the other case, the records to be searched are stored entirely within the computer memory. This case is called *internal* searching. In this book, we consider only internal searching. Although many of the methods we shall develop in this and later chapters are useful for external searching, a comprehensive study of methods for external searching lies beyond the scope of this book.

4. Implementation in C++

To implement our programs in C++, we establish some conventions.

Certain searching algorithms are inefficient when applied to linked list implementations. Thus, in this chapter, we shall tacitly assume that any lists have contiguous implementations. Searching a linked structure is the major concern of Chapter 10, and we postpone consideration of linked structures until then.

We shall be concerned only with searches of lists in this chapter. Some of our programs search lists that meet the ADT specifications of Chapter 6, while other programs apply to a slightly different category of lists. However, in every case, *contiguous only* we shall always search a contiguous list of records that we generally call the_list. The records that are stored in a list being searched must conform to the following minimal standards:

➡ Every record is associated to a key.

➡ Keys can be compared for equality or relative ordering.

➡ Records can be compared to each other or to keys by first converting records to their associated keys.

We shall therefore implement searching programs to work with objects of a type Record that reflects this behavior. In particular, there is an associated type called Key (that might be the same as Record) and a conversion operation to turn a Record into its associated Key. In applications the conversion operation could be one of the following:

➡ A method of the **class** Record, with the declaration **operator** Key( ) **const;**

➡ A constructor for the class Key, with the declaration Key(**const** Record &);

➡ Or, if the classes Key and Record are identical, no conversion needs to be defined, since any Record is automatically a Key.

comparison operators We shall require that any pair of objects of type Key can be compared with the standard operators: == , != , <, >, <= , >= . Further, since any Record can be converted by the compiler to a Key, the Key comparison operators apply to compare records or to compare records to keys.

For example, to select existing types as records and keys, a client could use type definition statements such as:

typedef int Key;
typedef int Record;

Alternatively, a client can design new classes that display appropriate behavior based on the following skeletons:

```
//   Definition of a Key class:
  class Key{
    public:
      //   Add any constructors and methods for key data.
    private:
      //   Add declaration of key data members here.
  };
//   Declare overloaded comparison operators for keys.
  bool operator ==  (const Key &x, const Key &y);
  bool operator >   (const Key &x, const Key &y);
  bool operator <   (const Key &x, const Key &y);
  bool operator >=  (const Key &x, const Key &y);
  bool operator <=  (const Key &x, const Key &y);
  bool operator != (const Key &x, const Key &y);
//   Definition of a Record class:
  class Record{
    public:
      operator Key();              //   implicit conversion from Record to Key.
      //   Add any constructors and methods for Record objects.
    private:
      //   Add data components.
  };
```

We note that we do not assume that a Record necessarily has a Key object as a data member, although this will often be the case. We merely assume that the compiler is able to turn a Record into its corresponding Key.

5. Parameters

parameters Each searching function that we write will have two input parameters. The first parameter gives the *list* to be searched. The second parameter gives the key for
target which we are searching. This key is always called the **target** of the search.

The search function will also have an output parameter and a returned value. The returned value has type Error_code and indicates whether or not the search is successful in finding an entry with the target key. If the search is successful, then the output parameter called position will locate the target within the list. If the search is unsuccessful, then this output parameter may have an undefined value or a value that will differ from one method to another.

7.2 SEQUENTIAL SEARCH

1. Algorithm and Procedure

Plain&Simple

Beyond doubt, the simplest way to do a search is to begin at one end of the list and scan down it until the desired key is found or the other end is reached. This is our first method.

```
Error_code sequential_search(const List<Record> &the_list,
                             const Key &target, int &position)
/* Post:  If an entry in the_list has key equal to target, then return success and the
          output parameter position locates such an entry within the list.
          Otherwise return not_present and position becomes invalid. */
{
    int s = the_list.size();
    for (position = 0; position < s; position++) {
        Record data;
        the_list.retrieve(position, data);
        if (data == target) return success;
    }
    return not_present;
}
```

The **for** loop in this function keeps moving through the list as long as the key **target** has not been found in a Record but terminates as soon as the target is found. If the search is unsuccessful, then the value **not_present** is returned, and at the conclusion **position** has moved beyond the end of the list (recall that for an unsuccessful search the value of **position** may be left undefined).

2. Analysis

Let us now estimate the amount of work that sequential search will do, so that we can make comparisons with other techniques later. Suppose that sequential search was run on a long list. The statements that appear outside the **for** loop are done only once, and therefore take insignificant computer time compared to the work done inside the loop. For each pass through the loop, one key is compared with the target key, several other statements are executed, and several expressions are checked. But all these other statements and expressions are executed in lock step with the comparison of keys: They are all done once for each iteration of the loop.

Hence all the actions that we need to count relate directly to the comparison of keys. If someone else, using the same method, had written the functions, then differences in programming approach would likely make a difference in the running time. But all these cases still produce the same number of comparisons of keys. If the length of the list changes, then the work done by any implementation of the searching method will also change proportionately.

We shall study the way in which the number of comparisons of keys depends on the length of the list. Doing this study will give us the most useful information about the algorithm, information that can be applied equally well no matter what implementation or programming technique we decide to use when we actually write the program.

importance of comparison count   Hence, if we wish to estimate how much computer time sequential search is likely to require, or if we wish to compare it with some other method, then knowing the number of comparisons of keys that it makes will give us the most useful information—information actually more useful than the total running time, which is too dependent on programming variations and on the particular machine being used.

No matter what algorithm for searching we develop, we can make a similar statement that we take as our fundamental premise in analyzing searching algorithms: The total work is reflected by the number of comparisons of keys that the algorithm makes.

> *To analyze the behavior of an algorithm that makes comparisons of keys, we shall use the count of these key comparisons as our measure of the work done.*

How many comparisons of keys does sequential search make when it is applied to a list of n entries? Since sequential search compares the target to each key in the list in turn, the answer depends on if and where the target may be. If the function finds the target in the first position of the list, it does only one key comparison. If the target is second, the function does two key comparisons. If it is the last entry on the list, then the function does n key comparisons. If the search is unsuccessful, then the target will have been compared to all entries in the list, for a total of n comparisons of keys.

Our question, then, has several answers depending on if and where the target is found. If the search is unsuccessful, then the answer is n key comparisons. The best performance for a successful search is 1 comparison, and the worst is n comparisons.

We have obtained very detailed information about the performance of sequential search, information that is really too detailed for most uses, in that we generally will not know exactly where in a list a particular key may appear. Instead, it will *average behavior* generally be much more helpful if we can determine the *average* behavior of an algorithm. But what do we mean by average? One reasonable assumption, the one that we shall always make, is to take each possibility once and average the results.

Note, however, that this assumption may be very far from the actual situation. *provisos* Not all English words, for example, appear equally often in a typical essay. The telephone operator receives far more requests for the number of a large business than for that of an average family. The C++ compiler encounters the keywords **if**, **class**, and **return** far more often than the keywords **switch**, **continue**, and **auto**.

There are a great many interesting, but exceedingly difficult, problems associated with analyzing algorithms where the input is chosen according to some statistical distribution. These problems, however, would take us too far afield to be considered here. We shall therefore limit our attention to the most important case, the one where all the possibilities are equally likely.

Under the assumption of equal likelihood we can find the average number of key comparisons done in a successful sequential search. We simply add the number needed for all the successful searches, and divide by n, the number of items in the list. The result is

$$\frac{1 + 2 + 3 + \cdots + n}{n}.$$

The first formula established in Appendix A is

$$1 + 2 + 3 + \cdots + n = \tfrac{1}{2}n(n + 1).$$

average number of key
comparisons

Hence the average number of key comparisons done by sequential search in the successful case is

$$\frac{n(n+1)}{2n} = \tfrac{1}{2}(n+1).$$

3. Testing

An appropriate balance to the theoretical analysis of algorithms is empirical testing of the resulting functions. We set up sample data, run the functions, and compare the results with those of the analysis.

For searching functions, there are at least two numbers worth calculating, the average number of key comparisons done over many searches, and the amount of CPU time required. Let us now develop a function that can be used to test our sequential search routine.

For test purposes, we shall use integer keys, and we need not store any data other than a key in a record. In our tests, we need to keep a count of all key comparison operations. One way to do this is to modify the sequential search function, to increment a global counter whenever it makes a key comparison. However, we prefer an approach that avoids any alteration of the search function being tested. We shall instead modify the overloaded key comparison operations to increment a counter whenever they are called. This counter must be available to all **Key** objects: Thus, it should be declared as a **static** class member. In C++, static class members provide data objects that are shared by every instance of the class.[1] Thus, no matter where keys are compared, the same instance of the counter **comparisons** will be incremented.

static *class member*

We have now arrived at the following definition of the class **Key** for our testing program.

```
class Key {
    int key;
public:
    static int comparisons;
    Key (int x = 0);
    int the_key() const;
};
bool operator == (const Key &x, const Key &y);
bool operator >  (const Key &x, const Key &y);
bool operator <  (const Key &x, const Key &y);
bool operator >= (const Key &x, const Key &y);
bool operator <= (const Key &x, const Key &y);
bool operator != (const Key &x, const Key &y);
```

---

[1] See a C++ textbook for a fuller explanation of **static class** members.

We use the method the_key to inspect a copy of a key's value. The static counter comparisons is incremented by any call to a Key comparison operator. For example, the test for equality of keys can be implemented as follows:

```
bool operator == (const Key &x, const Key &y)
{
   Key :: comparisons++;
   return x.the_key() == y.the_key();
}
```

Static data members must be defined and initialized outside of a class definition. Accordingly, we place the following definition statement, along with the class methods, in the Key implementation file key.c.

int Key :: comparisons = 0;

Since our program is merely used for testing purposes, there is no reason for a Record to contain any more data than its Key. Accordingly, we define:

typedef Key Record;

choice of test data

Most of the searching methods later in this chapter require the data to be ordered, so, in our testing functions, let us use a list with keys in increasing order. We are interested in both successful and unsuccessful searches, so let us insert only keys containing odd integers into the list, and then look for odd integers for successful searches and even integers for unsuccessful searches. If the list has n entries, then the targets for successful searches will be $1, 3, 5, \ldots, 2n - 1$. For unsuccessful searches, we look for the integers $0, 2, 4, 6, \ldots, 2n$. In this way we test all possible failures, including targets less than the smallest key in the list, between each pair, and greater than the largest. To make the test more realistic, we use pseudo-random numbers to choose the target, by employing the method Random :: random_integer from Appendix B.

CPU timing

In our testing, we use the **class** Timer from Appendix C to provide CPU timing information. Objects of **class** Timer have methods including a constructor and a method reset, which both start a timer going, and a method elapsed_time, which reads the timer. We use the Timer clock to time first a set number of successful searches and then a similar number of unsuccessful searches. The user supplies a value for searches as the number of trials to be made. With these decisions, the following test function results:

```
void test_search(int searches, List<Record> &the_list)
/* Pre:   None.
   Post:  The number of key comparisons and CPU time for a sequential searching
          funtion have been calculated.
   Uses:  Methods of the classes List, Random, and Timer, together with an output
          function print_out */
```

```
{
    int list_size = the_list.size();
    if (searches <= 0 || list_size < 0) {
        cout << " Exiting test: " << endl
            << " The number of searches must be positive." << endl
            << " The number of list entries must exceed 0." << endl;
        return;
    }
    int i, target, found_at;
    Key :: comparisons = 0;
    Random number;
    Timer clock;
    for (i = 0;  i < searches;  i++) {
        target = 2 * number.random_integer(0, list_size − 1) + 1;
        if (sequential_search(the_list, target, found_at) == not_present)
            cout << "Error: Failed to find expected target " << target << endl;
    }
    print_out("Successful", clock.elapsed_time(), Key :: comparisons, searches);
    Key :: comparisons = 0;
    clock.reset();
    for (i = 0;  i < searches;  i++) {
        target = 2 * number.random_integer(0, list_size);
        if (sequential_search(the_list, target, found_at) == success)
            cout << "Error: Found unexpected target " << target
                << " at " << found_at << endl;
    }
    print_out("Unsuccessful", clock.elapsed_time(), Key :: comparisons, searches);
}
```

The details of embedding this function into a working program and writing the output function, print_out, are left as a project.

Exercises 7.2   **E1.** One good check for any algorithm is to see what it does in extreme cases. Determine what sequential search does when

   (a) there is only one item in the list.

   (b) the list is empty.

   (c) the list is full.

E2. Trace sequential search as it searches for each of the keys present in a list containing three items. Determine how many comparisons are made, and thereby check the formula for the average number of comparisons for a successful search.

E3. If we can assume that the keys in the list have been arranged in order (for example, numerical or alphabetical order), then we can terminate unsuccessful searches more quickly. If the smallest keys come first, then we can terminate the search as soon as a key greater than or equal to the target key has been found. If we assume that it is equally likely that a target key not in the list is in any one of the $n + 1$ intervals (before the first key, between a pair of successive keys, or after the last key), then what is the average number of comparisons for unsuccessful search in this version?

E4. At each iteration, sequential search checks two inequalities, one a comparison of keys to see if the target has been found, and the other a comparison of indices to see if the end of the list has been reached. A good way to speed up the algorithm by eliminating the second comparison is to make sure that eventually key **target** will be found, by increasing the size of the list and inserting an extra *sentinel* item at the end with key **target**. Such an item placed in a list to ensure that a process terminates is called a ***sentinel***. When the loop terminates, the search will have been successful if **target** was found before the last item in the list and unsuccessful if the final sentinel item was the one found.

Write a C++ function that embodies the idea of a sentinel in the contiguous version of sequential search using lists developed in Section 6.2.2.

E5. Find the number of comparisons of keys done by the function written in Exercise E4 for

   (a) unsuccessful search.

   (b) best successful search.

   (c) worst successful search.

   (d) average successful search.

Programming Projects 7.2

P1. Write a program to test sequential search and, later, other searching methods using lists developed in Section 6.2.2. You should make the appropriate declarations required to set up the list and put keys into it. The keys are the odd integers from 1 to n, where the user gives the value of n. Then successful searches can be tested by searching for odd integers, and unsuccessful searches can be tested by searching for even integers. Use the function **test_search** from the text to do the actual testing of the search function. Overload the key comparison operators so that they increment the **counter**. Write appropriate **introduction** and **print_out** functions and a menu driver. For now, the only options are to fill the list with a user-given number of entries, to test **sequential_search**, and to quit. Later, other searching methods could be added as further options.

Find out how many comparisons are done for both unsuccessful and successful searches, and compare these results with the analyses in the text.

Run your program for representative values of n, such as $n = 10$, $n = 100$, $n = 1000$.

sentinel search   **P2.** Take the driver program written in Project P1 to test searching functions, and insert the version of sequential search that uses a sentinel (see Exercise E4). For various values of n, determine whether the version with or without a sentinel is faster. By experimenting, find the cross-over point between the two versions, if there is one. That is, for what value of n is the extra time needed to insert a sentinel at the end of a list of size n about the same as the time needed for extra comparisons of indices in the version without a sentinel?

linked sequential   **P3.** What changes are required to our sequential search function and testing pro-
search   gram in order to operate on simply linked lists as developed in Section 6.2.3? Make these changes and apply the testing program from Project P1 for linked lists to test linked sequential search.

7.3 BINARY SEARCH

Sequential search is easy to write and efficient for short lists, but a disaster for long ones. Imagine trying to find the name "Amanda Thompson" in a large telephone book by reading one name at a time starting at the front of the book! To find any entry in a long list, there are far more efficient methods, provided that the keys in the list are already sorted into order.

method   One of the best methods for a list with keys in order is first to compare the target key with one in the center of the list and then restrict our attention to only the first or second half of the list, depending on whether the target key comes before or after the central one. With one comparison of keys we thus reduce the list to half its original size. Continuing in this way, at each step, we reduce the length of the list to be searched by half. In only twenty steps, this method will locate any requested key in a list containing more than a million keys.

restrictions   The method we are discussing is called **binary search**. This approach of course requires that the keys in the list be of a scalar or other type that can be regarded as having an order and that the list already be completely in order.

7.3.1 Ordered Lists

What we are really doing here is introducing a new abstract data type, which is defined in the following way.

Definition   An **ordered list** is a list in which each entry contains a key, such that the keys are in order. That is, if entry i comes before entry j in the list, then the key of entry i is less than or equal to the key of entry j.

The only List operations that do not apply, without modification, to an ordered list are insert and replace. These standard List operations must fail when they would otherwise disturb the order of a list. We shall therefore implement an ordered list as a class *derived* from a contiguous List. In this derived class, we shall override the methods insert and replace with new implementations. Hence, we use the following class specification:

```
class Ordered_list: public List<Record>{
public:
  Ordered_list();
  Error_code insert(const Record &data);
  Error_code insert(int position, const Record &data);
  Error_code replace(int position, const Record &data);
};
```

As well as overriding the methods insert and replace, we have overloaded the method insert so that it can be used with a single parameter. This overloaded method places an entry into the correct position, determined by the order of the keys. We shall study this operation further in Chapter 8, but here is a simple, implementation-independent version of the overloaded method.

If the list already contains keys equal to the new one being inserted, then the new key will be inserted as the *first* of those that are equal.

```
Error_code Ordered_list :: insert(const Record &data)
/* Post: If the Ordered_list is not full, the function succeeds: The Record data is
         inserted into the list, following the last entry of the list with a strictly lesser
         key (or in the first list position if no list element has a lesser key).
         Else: the function fails with the diagnostic Error_code overflow. */
{
  int s = size();
  int position;
  for (position = 0; position < s; position++) {
    Record list_data;
    retrieve(position, list_data);
    if (data >= list_data) break;
  }
  return List<Record> :: insert(position, data);
}
```

scope resolution

Here, we apply the original insert method of the base List class by using the scope resolution operator. The scope resolution is necessary, because we have overridden this original insertion method with a new Ordered_list method that is coded as follows:

```
Error_code Ordered_list :: insert(int position, const Record &data)
/* Post: If the Ordered_list is not full, 0 ≤ position ≤ n, where n is the number
         of entries in the list, and the Record data can be inserted at position in
         the list, without disturbing the list order, then the function succeeds: Any
         entry formerly in position and all later entries have their position numbers
         increased by 1 and data is inserted at position of the List.
         Else: the function fails with a diagnostic Error_code. */
{
    Record list_data;
    if (position > 0) {
        retrieve(position − 1, list_data);
        if (data < list_data)
            return fail;
    }
    if (position < size()) {
        retrieve(position, list_data);
        if (data > list_data)
            return fail;
    }
    return List<Record> :: insert(position, data);
}
```

Note the distinction between overridden and overloaded methods in a derived class: The *overridden* methods replace methods of the base class by methods with matching names and parameter lists, whereas the *overloaded* methods merely match existing methods in name but have different parameter lists.

7.3.2 Algorithm Development

dangers

OUCH!

Simple though the idea of binary search is, it is exceedingly easy to program it incorrectly. The method dates back at least to 1946, but the first version free of errors and unnecessary restrictions seems to have appeared only in 1962. One study (see the references at the end of the book) showed that about 90 percent of professional programmers fail to code binary search correctly, even after working on it for a full hour. Another study[2] found correct solutions in only five out of twenty textbooks.

Let us therefore take special care to make sure that we make no mistakes. To do this, we must state exactly what our variables designate; we must state precisely what conditions must be true before and after each iteration of the loop contained in the program; and we must make sure that the loop will terminate properly.

Our binary search algorithm will use two indices, **top** and **bottom**, to enclose the part of the list in which we are looking for the target key. At each iteration, we

---

[2] Richard E. Pattis, "Textbook errors in binary searching," *SIGCSE Bulletin*, 20 (1988), 190–194.

shall reduce the size of this part of the list by about half. To help us keep track of the progress of the algorithm, let us write down an assertion that we shall require to be true before every iteration of the process. Such a statement is called an ***invariant*** of the process.

invariant
> *The target key, provided it is present in the list, will be found between the indices* **bottom** *and* **top**, *inclusive.*

We establish the initial correctness of this assertion by setting **bottom** to 0 and **top** to the_list.size() − 1.

To do binary search, we first calculate the index **mid** halfway between **bottom** and **top** as

$$\text{mid} = (\text{bottom} + \text{top})/2$$

Next, we compare the target key against the key at position **mid** and then we change the appropriate one of the indices **top** or **bottom** so as to reduce the list to either its bottom or top half.

termination
Next, we note that binary search should terminate when **top** ≤ **bottom**; that is, when the remaining part of the list contains at most one item, providing that we have not terminated earlier by finding the target.

progress
Finally, we must make progress toward termination by ensuring that the number of items remaining to be searched, **top** − **bottom** + 1, strictly decreases at each iteration of the process.

Several slightly different algorithms for binary search can be written.

7.3.3 The Forgetful Version

Perhaps the simplest variation is to forget the possibility that the **Key target** might be found quickly and continue, whether **target** has been found or not, to subdivide the list until what remains has length 1.

This method is implemented as the following function, which, for simplicity in programming, we write in recursive form. The bounds on the sublist are given as additional parameters for the recursive function.

Error_code recursive_binary_1(**const** Ordered_list &the_list, **const** Key &target,
          int bottom, **int** top, **int** &position)
/* **Pre:** *The indices* bottom *to* top *define the range in the list to search for the target.*
  Post: *If a* Record *in the range of locations from* bottom *to* top *in* the_list *has key equal to* target, *then* position *locates one such entry and a code of success is returned. Otherwise, the* Error_code *of* not_present *is returned and* position *becomes undefined.*
  Uses: recursive_binary_1 *and methods of the classes* List *and* Record. */

```
{
  Record data;
  if (bottom < top) {            //   List has more than one entry.
    int mid = (bottom + top)/2;
    the_list.retrieve(mid, data);
    if (data < target)           //   Reduce to top half of list.
      return recursive_binary_1(the_list, target, mid + 1, top, position);
    else                         //   Reduce to bottom half of list.
      return recursive_binary_1(the_list, target, bottom, mid, position);
  }
  else if (top < bottom)
    return not_present;          //   List is empty.
  else {                         //   List has exactly one entry.
    position = bottom;
    the_list.retrieve(bottom, data);
    if (data ==  target) return success;
    else return not_present;
  }
}
```

The division of the list into sublists is described in the following diagram:

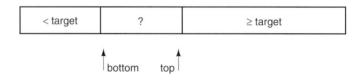

Note that this diagram shows only entries *strictly* less than **target** in the first part of the list, whereas the last part contains entries greater than or *equal* to **target**. In this way, when the middle part of the list is reduced to size 1 and hits the target, it will be guaranteed to be the first occurrence of the target if it appears more than once in the list.

If the list is empty, the function fails; otherwise it first calculates the value of **mid**. As their average, **mid** is between **bottom** and **top**, and so **mid** indexes a legitimate entry of the list.

termination   Note that the **if** statement that invokes the recursion is not symmetrical, since the condition tested puts **mid** into the lower of the two intervals. On the other hand, integer division of nonnegative integers always truncates downward. It is only these two facts together that ensure that the recursion always terminates. Let us determine what occurs toward the end of the search. The recursion will continue only as long as **top** > **bottom**. But this condition implies that when **mid** is calculated we always have

$$\text{bottom} <= \text{mid} < \text{top}$$

since integer division truncates downward. Next, the **if** statement reduces the size of the interval from **top** − **bottom** either to **top** − (**mid** + 1) or to **mid** − **bottom**, both of which, by the inequality, are strictly less than **top** − **bottom**. Thus at each iteration the size of the interval strictly decreases, so the recursion will eventually terminate.

After the recursion terminates, we must finally check to see if the target key has been found, since all previous comparisons have tested only inequalities.

To adjust the parameters to our standard search function conventions, we produce the following search function:

Error_code run_recursive_binary_1(**const** Ordered_list &the_list,
                                     const Key &target, **int** &position)

main call to
recursive_binary1

```
{
   return recursive_binary_1(the_list, target, 0, the_list.size() − 1, position);
}
```

Since the recursion used in the function recursive_binary_1 is tail recursion, we can easily convert it into an iterative loop. At the same time, we can make the parameters consistent with other searching methods.

Error_code binary_search_1 (**const** Ordered_list &the_list,
                            const Key &target, **int** &position)
/* **Post:** *If a Record in* the_list *has* Key *equal to* target, *then* position *locates one such entry and a code of success is returned. Otherwise,* not_present *is returned and* position *is undefined.*
    Uses: *Methods for classes* List *and* Record. */

```
{
   Record data;
   int bottom = 0, top = the_list.size() − 1;
   while (bottom < top) {
      int mid = (bottom + top)/2;
      the_list.retrieve(mid, data);
      if (data < target)
         bottom = mid + 1;
      else
         top = mid;
   }
   if (top < bottom) return not_present;
   else {
      position = bottom;
      the_list.retrieve(bottom, data);
      if (data == target) return success;
      else return not_present;
   }
}
```

7.3.4 Recognizing Equality

Although binary_search_1 is a simple form of binary search, it seems that it will often make unnecessary iterations because it fails to recognize that it has found the target before continuing to iterate. Thus we might hope to save computer time with a variation that checks at each stage to see if it has found the target.

In recursive form this method becomes:

```
Error_code recursive_binary_2(const Ordered_list &the_list, const Key &target,
                              int bottom, int top, int &position)
/* Pre:  The indices bottom to top define the range in the list to search for the
         target.
   Post: If a Record in the range from bottom to top in the_list has key equal
         to target, then position locates one such entry, and a code of success is
         returned. Otherwise, not_present is returned, and position is undefined.
   Uses: recursive_binary_2, together with methods from the classes Ordered_list
         and Record. */
{
   Record data;
   if (bottom <= top) {
      int mid = (bottom + top)/2;
      the_list.retrieve(mid, data);
      if (data == target) {
         position = mid;
         return success;
      }
      else if (data < target)
         return recursive_binary_2(the_list, target, mid + 1, top, position);
      else
         return recursive_binary_2(the_list, target, bottom, mid − 1, position);
   }
   else return not_present;
}
```

As with run_recursive_binary_1, we need a function run_recursive_binary_2 to adjust the parameters to our standard conventions.

```
Error_code run_recursive_binary_2(const Ordered_list &the_list,
                                  const Key &target, int &position)
{
   return recursive_binary_2(the_list, target, 0, the_list.size() − 1, position);
}
```

main call to
recursive_binary2

Again, this function can be translated into nonrecursive form with only the standard parameters:

```
Error_code binary_search_2(const Ordered_list &the_list,
                           const Key &target, int &position)
/* Post: If a Record in the_list has key equal to target, then position locates one
         such entry and a code of success is returned. Otherwise, not_present is
         returned and position is undefined.
   Uses: Methods for classes Ordered_list and Record. */
{
   Record data;
   int bottom = 0, top = the_list.size() − 1;
   while (bottom <= top) {
      position = (bottom + top)/2;
      the_list.retrieve(position, data);
      if (data ==  target) return success;
      if (data < target) bottom = position + 1;
      else top = position − 1;
   }
   return not_present;
}
```

The operation of this version is described in the following diagram:

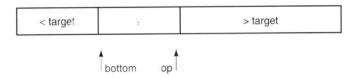

Notice that this diagram (in contrast to that for the first method) is symmetrical in that the first part contains only entries strictly less than **target**, and the last part contains only entries strictly greater than **target**. With this method, therefore, if **target** appears more than once in the list, then the algorithm may return any instance of the target.

loop termination   Proving that the loop in **binary_search_2** terminates is easier than the proof for **binary_search_1**. In **binary_search_2**, the form of the **if** statement within the loop guarantees that the length of the interval is reduced by at least half in each iteration.

comparison of methods   Which of these two versions of binary search will do fewer comparisons of keys? Clearly **binary_search_2** will, if we happen to find the target near the beginning of the search. But each iteration of **binary_search_2** requires two comparisons of keys, whereas **binary_search_1** requires only one. Is it possible that if many iterations are needed, then **binary_search_1** may do fewer comparisons? To answer this question we shall develop new analytic tools in the next section.

Exercises 7.3   **E1.** Suppose that the_list contains the integers $1, 2, \ldots, 8$. Trace through the steps of binary_search_1 to determine what comparisons of keys are done in searching for each of the following targets: **(a)** 3, **(b)** 5, **(c)** 1, **(d)** 9, **(e)** 4.5.

E2. Repeat Exercise E1 using binary_search_2.

E3. [*Challenging*] Suppose that L_1 and L_2 are ordered lists containing n_1 and n_2 integers, respectively.

   (a) Use the idea of binary search to describe how to find the median of the $n_1 + n_2$ integers in the combined lists.

   (b) Write a function that implements your method.

Programming Projects 7.3

P1. Take the driver program of Project P1 of Section 7.2 (page 277), and make binary_search_1 and binary_search_2 the search options. Compare their performance with each other and with sequential search.

P2. Incorporate the recursive versions of binary search (both variations) into the testing program of Project P1 of Section 7.2 (page 277). Compare the performance with the nonrecursive versions of binary search.

7.4 COMPARISON TREES

definitions

The *comparison tree* (also called *decision tree* or *search tree*) of an algorithm is obtained by tracing through the action of the algorithm, representing each comparison of keys by a *vertex* of the tree (which we draw as a circle). Inside the circle we put the index of the key against which we are comparing the target key. *Branches* (lines) drawn down from the circle represent the possible outcomes of the comparison and are labeled accordingly. When the algorithm terminates, we put either F (for failure) or the position where the target is found at the end of the appropriate branch, which we call a *leaf*, and draw as a square. Leaves are also sometimes called *end vertices* or *external vertices* of the tree. The remaining vertices are called the *internal vertices* of the tree.

The comparison tree for sequential search is especially simple; it is drawn in Figure 7.2.

definitions

The number of comparisons done by an algorithm in a particular search is the number of internal (circular) vertices traversed in going from the top of the tree (which is called its *root*) down the appropriate path to a leaf. The number of branches traversed to reach a vertex from the root is called the *level* of the vertex. Thus the root itself has level 0, the vertices immediately below it have level 1, and so on.

The number of vertices in the longest path that occurs is called the *height* of the tree. Hence a tree with only one vertex has height 1. In future chapters we shall sometimes allow trees to be empty (that is, to consist of no vertices at all), and we adopt the convention that an empty tree has height 0.

To complete the terminology we use for trees we shall now, as is traditional, mix our metaphors by thinking of family trees as well as botanical trees: We call the vertices immediately below a vertex v the *children* of v and the vertex immediately above v the *parent* of v. Hence we can use oxymorons like "the parent of a leaf" or "a child of the root."

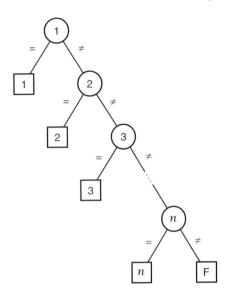

Figure 7.2. Comparison tree for sequential_search

7.4.1 Analysis for $n = 10$

1. Shape of Trees

That sequential search on average does far more comparisons than binary search is obvious from comparing the shape of its tree with the shape of the trees for binary_search_1 and binary_search_2, which for $n = 10$ are drawn in Figures 7.3 and 7.4, respectively. Sequential search has a long, narrow tree, which means many comparisons, whereas the trees for binary search are much wider and shorter.

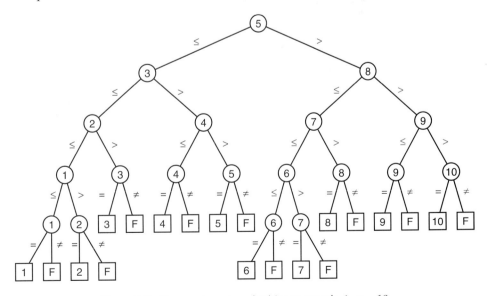

Figure 7.3. Comparison tree for binary_search_1, $n = 10$

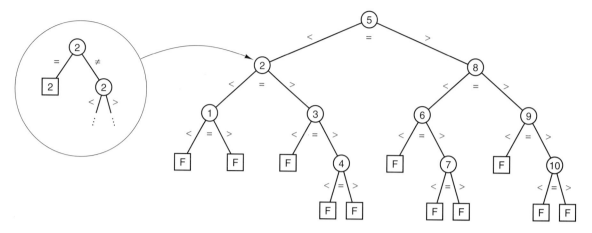

Figure 7.4. Comparison tree for binary_search_2, $n = 10$

2. Three-Way Comparisons and Compact Drawings

expanded and condensed trees

In the tree drawn for binary_search_2 we have shown the algorithm structure more clearly (and reduced the space needed) by combining two comparisons to obtain one three-way comparison for each pass through the loop. Drawing the tree this way means that every vertex that is not a leaf terminates some successful search and the leaves correspond to unsuccessful searches. Thus the drawing in Figure 7.4 is more compact, but remember that two comparisons are really done for each of the vertices shown, except that only one comparison is done at the vertex at which the search succeeds in finding the target.

It is this compact way of drawing comparison trees that will become our standard method in future chapters.

schematic tree

It is also often convenient to show only part of a comparison tree. Figure 7.5 shows the top of a comparison tree for the recursive version of binary_search_2, with all the details of the recursive calls hidden in the subtrees. The comparison tree and the recursion tree for a recursive algorithm are often two ways of considering the same thing.

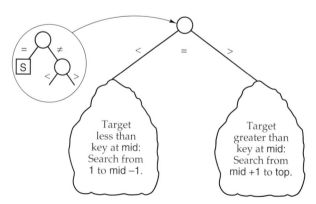

Figure 7.5. Top of the comparison tree, recursive binary_search_2

From the trees shown for binary_search_1 and binary_search_2 with $n = 10$, it is easy to read off how many comparisons will be done by each algorithm. In the worst case search, this number is simply one more than the height of the tree; in fact, for every search it is the number of interior vertices lying between the root and the vertex that terminates the search.

3. Comparison Count for binary_search_1

external path length

In binary_search_1, every search terminates at a leaf; to obtain the average number of comparisons for both successful and unsuccessful searches, we need what is called the **external path length** of the tree: the sum of the number of branches traversed in going from the root once to every leaf in the tree. For the tree in Figure 7.3, the external path length is

$$(4 \times 5)+(6 \times 4)+(4 \times 5)+(6 \times 4)= 88.$$

Half the leaves correspond to successful searches, and half to unsuccessful searches. Hence the average number of comparisons needed for either a successful or unsuccessful search by binary_search_1 is $\frac{44}{10} = 4.4$ when $n = 10$.

4. Comparison Count for binary_search_2

internal path length

In the tree as it is drawn for binary_search_2, all the leaves correspond to unsuccessful searches; hence the external path length leads to the number of comparisons for an unsuccessful search. For successful searches, we need the **internal path length**, which is defined to be the sum, over all vertices that are not leaves, of the number of branches from the root to the vertex. For the tree in Figure 7.4, the internal path length is

$$0 + 1 + 2 + 2 + 3 + 1 + 2 + 3 + 2 + 3 = 19.$$

Recall that binary_search_2 does two comparisons for each non-leaf except for the vertex that finds the target, and note that the number of these internal vertices traversed is one more than the number of branches (for each of the $n = 10$ internal vertices). We thereby obtain the average number of comparisons for a successful search to be

average successful count

$$2 \times \left(\frac{19}{10} + 1\right) - 1 = 4.8.$$

The subtraction of 1 corresponds to the fact that one fewer comparison is made when the target is found.

For an unsuccessful search by binary_search_2, we need the external path length of the tree in Figure 7.4. This is

$$(5 \times 3)+(6 \times 4)= 39.$$

average unsuccessful count

We shall assume for unsuccessful searches that the $n + 1$ intervals (less than the first key, between a pair of successive keys, or greater than the largest) are all equally likely; for the diagram we therefore assume that any of the 11 failure leaves are equally likely. Thus the average number of comparisons for an unsuccessful search is

$$\frac{2 \times 39}{11} \approx 7.1.$$

5. Comparison of Algorithms

For $n = 10$, binary_search_1 does slightly fewer comparisons both for successful and for unsuccessful searches. To be fair, however, we should note that the two comparisons done by binary_search_2 at each internal vertex are closely related (the same keys are being compared), so that an optimizing compiler may not do as much work as two full comparisons. In that case, in fact, binary_search_2 may be a slightly better choice than binary_search_1 for successful searches when $n = 10$.

7.4.2 Generalization

What happens when n is larger than 10? For longer lists, it may be impossible to draw the complete comparison tree, but from the examples with $n = 10$, we can make some observations that will always be true.

1. 2-Trees

Let us define a **2-tree** as a tree in which every vertex except the leaves has exactly two children. Both versions of comparison trees that we have drawn fit this definition and are 2-trees. We can make several observations about 2-trees that will provide information about the behavior of binary search methods for all values of n.

terminology

Other terms for 2-tree are **strictly binary tree** and **extended binary tree**, but we shall not use these terms, because they are too easily confused with the term *binary tree*, which (when introduced in Chapter 10) has a somewhat different meaning.

number of vertices in a 2-tree

In a 2-tree, the number of vertices on any level can be no more than twice the number on the level above, since each vertex has either 0 or 2 children (depending on whether it is a leaf or not). Since there is one vertex on level 0 (the root), the number of vertices on level t is at most 2^t for all $t \geq 0$. We thus have the facts:

Lemma 7.1

> *The number of vertices on each level of a 2-tree is at most twice the number on the level immediately above. Hence, in a 2-tree, the number of vertices on level t is at most 2^t for $t \geq 0$.*

If we wish, we can turn this last observation around by taking logarithms. Let us assume that we have k vertices on level t. Since (by the second half of Lemma 7.1) $k \leq 2^t$, we obtain $t \geq \lg k$, where $\lg$ denotes a logarithm with base 2.[3]

Lemma 7.2

> *If a 2-tree has k vertices on level t, then $t \geq \lg k$, where $\lg$ denotes a logarithm with base 2.*

---

[3] For a review of properties of logarithms, see Appendix A.

The notation for base 2 logarithms just used will be our standard notation throughout this book. In analyzing algorithms we shall also sometimes need natural logarithms (taken with base $e = 2.71828\dots$). We shall denote a natural logarithm by ln.
logarithms   We shall rarely need logarithms to any other base. We thus summarize as follows:

Conventions

Unless stated otherwise, all logarithms will be taken with base 2.
The symbol lg *denotes a logarithm with base* 2,
and the symbol ln *denotes a natural logarithm.*
When the base for logarithms is not specified (or is not important),
then the symbol log *will be used.*

---

floor and ceiling   After we take logarithms, we frequently need to move either up or down to the
next integer. To specify this action, we define the **floor** of a real number x to be
the largest integer less than or equal to x, and the **ceiling** of x to be the smallest
integer greater than or equal to x. We denote the floor of x by $\lfloor x \rfloor$ and the ceiling
of x by $\lceil x \rceil$.

For an integer n, note that

$$\lfloor n/2 \rfloor + \lceil n/2 \rceil = n$$
$$(n-1)/2 \le \lfloor n/2 \rfloor \le n/2$$
$$n/2 \le \lceil n/2 \rceil \le (n+1)/2.$$

2. Analysis of binary_search_1

We can now turn to the general analysis of binary_search_1 on a list of n entries.
The final step done in binary_search_1 is always a check for equality with the target;
hence both successful and unsuccessful searches terminate at leaves, and so there
are exactly $2n$ leaves altogether. As illustrated in Figure 7.3 for $n = 10$, all these
leaves must be on the same level or on two adjacent levels. (This observation can
be proved by using mathematical induction to establish the following stronger
statement: If T_1 and T_2 are the comparison trees of binary_search_1 operating on
lists L_1 and L_2 whose lengths differ by at most 1, then all leaves of T_1 and T_2 are
on the same or adjacent levels. The statement is clearly true when L_1 and L_2 are
lists with length at most 2. Moreover, if binary_search_1 divides two larger lists
whose sizes differ by at most one, the sizes of the four halves also differ by at
most 1, and the induction hypothesis shows that their leaves are all on the same or
adjacent levels.) From Lemma 7.2 it follows that the maximum level t of leaves in
the comparison tree satisfies $t = \lceil \lg 2n \rceil$.

Since one comparison of keys is done at the root (which is level 0), but no
comparisons are done at the leaves (level t), it follows that the maximum number
of key comparisons is also $t = \lceil \lg 2n \rceil$. Furthermore, the maximum number is at
most one more than the average number, since all leaves are on the same or adjacent
levels.

Hence we have:

comparison count,
binary_search_1

> *The number of comparisons of keys done by* binary_search_1 *in searching a list of n items is approximately*
>
> $$\lg n + 1$$
>
> *in the worst case and*
>
> $$\lg n$$
>
> *in the average case. The number of comparisons is essentially independent of whether the search is successful or not.*

3. Analysis of binary_search_2, Unsuccessful Search

To count the comparisons made by binary_search_2 for a general value of n for an unsuccessful search, we shall examine its comparison tree. For reasons similar to those given for binary_search_1, this tree is again full at the top, with all its leaves on at most two adjacent levels at the bottom. For binary_search_2, all the leaves correspond to unsuccessful searches, so there are exactly $n + 1$ leaves, corresponding to the $n + 1$ unsuccessful outcomes: less than the smallest key, between a pair of keys, and greater than the largest key. Since these leaves are all at the bottom of the tree, Lemma 7.1 implies that the number of leaves is approximately 2^h, where *comparison count for* h is the height of the tree. Taking (base 2) logarithms, we obtain that $h \approx \lg(n + 1)$. binary_search_2, This value is the approximate distance from the root to one of the leaves. Since, *unsuccessful case* in binary_search_2, two comparisons of keys are performed for each internal vertex, the number of comparisons done in an unsuccessful search is approximately $2\lg(n + 1)$.

> *The number of comparisons done in an unsuccessful search by* binary_search_2 *is approximately* $2\lg(n + 1)$.

4. The Path-Length Theorem

To calculate the average number of comparisons for a successful search by binary_search_2, we first obtain an interesting and important relationship that holds for any 2-tree.

Theorem 7.3

> *Denote the external path length of a 2-tree by* E, *the internal path length by* I, *and let* q *be the number of vertices that are not leaves. Then*
>
> $$E = I + 2q.$$

Proof   To prove the theorem we use the method of mathematical induction, using the number of vertices in the tree to do the induction.

If the tree contains only its root, and no other vertices, then $E = I = q = 0$, and the base case of the theorem is trivially correct.

Now take a larger tree, and let v be some vertex that is not a leaf, but for which both the children of v are leaves. Let k be the number of branches on the path from the root to v. See Figure 7.6.

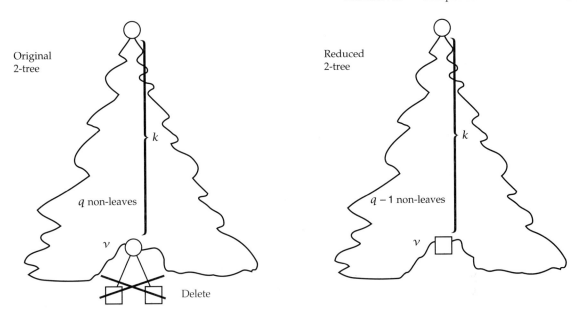

Figure 7.6. Path length in a 2-tree

Now let us delete the two children of v from the 2-tree. Since v is not a leaf but its children are, the number of non-leaves goes down from q to $q - 1$. The internal path length I is reduced by the distance to v; that is, to $I - k$. The distance to each child of v is $k + 1$, so the external path length is reduced from E to $E - 2(k + 1)$, but v is now a leaf, so its distance, k, must be added, giving a new external path length of

$$E - 2(k + 1) + k = E - k - 2.$$

Since the new tree has fewer vertices than the old one, by the induction hypothesis we know that

$$E - k - 2 = (I - k) + 2(q - 1).$$

end of proof   Rearrangement of this equation gives the desired result.   ∎

5. Analysis of binary_search_2, Successful Search

In the comparison tree of binary_search_2, the distance to the leaves is $\lg(n + 1)$, as we have seen. The number of leaves is $n + 1$, so the external path length is about

$$(n + 1)\lg(n + 1).$$

Theorem 7.3 then shows that the internal path length is about

$$(n + 1)\lg(n + 1) - 2n.$$

To obtain the average number of comparisons done in a successful search, we must first divide by n (the number of non-leaves) and then add 1 and double, since two comparisons were done at each internal node. Finally, we subtract 1, since only one comparison is done at the node where the target is found. The result is:

> *In a successful search of a list of n entries,* binary_search_2 *does approximately*
>
> $$\frac{2(n + 1)}{n} \lg(n + 1) - 3$$
>
> *comparisons of keys.*

7.4.3 Comparison of Methods

simplified counts

Note the similarities and differences in the formulas for the two versions of binary search. Recall, first, that we have already made some approximations in our calculations, and hence our formulas are only approximate. For large values of n the difference between $\lg n$ and $\lg(n + 1)$ is insignificant, and $(n + 1)/n$ is very nearly 1. Hence we can simplify our results as follows:

	Successful search	Unsuccessful search
binary_search_1	$\lg n + 1$	$\lg n + 1$
binary_search_2	$2\lg n - 3$	$2\lg n$

In all four cases the times are proportional to $\lg n$, except for small constant terms, and the coefficients of $\lg n$ are, in all cases, the number of comparisons inside the loop. The fact that the loop in binary_search_2 can terminate early contributes disappointingly little to improving its speed for a successful search; it does not reduce the coefficient of $\lg n$ at all, but only reduces the constant term from $+1$ to -3.

A moment's examination of the comparison trees will show why. More than half of the vertices occur at the bottom level, and so their loops cannot terminate early. More than half the remaining ones could terminate only one iteration early. Thus, for large n, the number of vertices relatively high in the tree, say, in the top half of the levels, is negligible in comparison with the number at the bottom level. It is only for this negligible proportion of the vertices that binary_search_2 can achieve better results than binary_search_1, but it is at the cost of nearly doubling the number of comparisons for all searches, both successful and unsuccessful.

With the smaller coefficient of $\lg n$, binary_search_1 will do fewer comparisons when n is sufficiently large, but with the smaller constant term, binary_search_2 may do fewer comparisons when n is small. But for such a small value of n, the overhead in setting up binary search and the extra programming effort probably make it a more expensive method to use than sequential search. Thus we arrive at the conclusion, quite contrary to what we would intuitively conclude, that binary_search_2 is probably not worth the effort, since for large problems binary_search_1 is better, and for small problems, sequential_search is better. To be fair, however, with some computers and optimizing compilers, the two comparisons needed in binary_search_2 will not take double the time of the one in binary_search_1, so in such a situation binary_search_2 might prove the better choice.

Our object in doing analysis of algorithms is to help us decide which may be better under appropriate circumstances. Disregarding the foregoing provisos, we have now been able to make such a decision, and have available to us information that might otherwise not be obvious.

The numbers of comparisons of keys done in the average successful case by sequential_search, binary_search_1, and binary_search_2 are graphed in Figure 7.7. The numbers shown in the graphs are from test runs of the functions; they are not approximations. The first graph in Figure 7.7 compares the three functions for small values of n, the number of items in the list. In the second graph we compare *logarithmic graphs* the numbers over a much larger range by employing a ***log-log graph*** in which each unit along an axis represents doubling the corresponding coordinate. In the third graph we wish to compare the two versions of binary search; a ***semilog graph*** is appropriate here, so that the vertical axis maintains linear units while the horizontal axis is logarithmic.

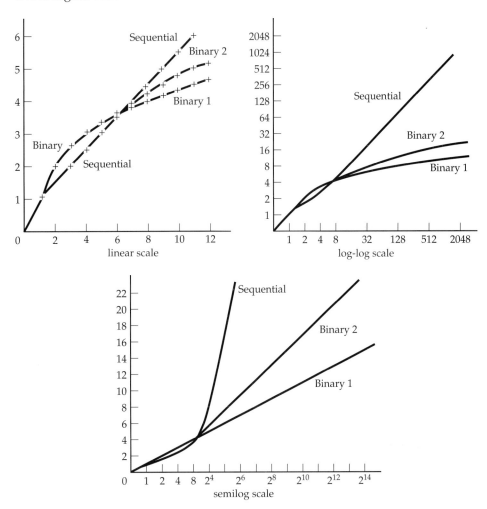

Figure 7.7. Numbers of comparisons for average successful searches

7.4.4 A General Relationship

hypotheses

Before leaving this section, let us use Theorem 7.3 to obtain a relationship between the average number of key comparisons for successful and for unsuccessful
searches, a relationship that holds for any searching method for which the comparison tree can be drawn as we did for binary_search_2. That is, we shall assume
that the leaves of the comparison tree correspond to unsuccessful searches, that the
internal vertices correspond to successful searches, and that two comparisons of
keys are made for each internal vertex, except that only one is made at the vertex
where the target is found. If I and E are the internal and external path lengths of
the tree, respectively, and n is the number of items in the list, so that n is also the
number of internal vertices in the tree, then, as in the analysis of binary_search_2,
we know that the average number of comparisons in a successful search is

$$S = 2\left(\frac{I}{n} + 1\right) - 1 = \frac{2I}{n} + 1$$

and the average number for an unsuccessful search is $U = 2E/(n+1)$. By Theorem
7.3, $E = I + 2n$. Combining these expressions, we can therefore conclude that

Theorem 7.4

*Under the specified conditions, the average numbers of key comparisons done in suc-
cessful and unsuccessful searches are related by*

$$S = \left(1 + \frac{1}{n}\right)U - 3.$$

In other words, the average number of comparisons for a successful search is almost
exactly the same as that for an unsuccessful search. Knowing that an item is in the
list is very little help in finding it, if you are searching by means of comparisons of
keys.

Exercises 7.4

E1. Draw the comparison trees for (i) binary_search_1 and (ii) binary_search_2
when **(a)** $n = 5$, **(b)** $n = 7$, **(c)** $n = 8$, **(d)** $n = 13$. Calculate the external
and internal path lengths for each of these trees, and verify that the conclusion
of Theorem 7.3 holds.

E2. Sequential search has less overhead than binary search, and so may run faster
for small n. Find the break-even point where the same number of comparisons
of keys is made between sequential_search and binary_search_1. Compute in
terms of the formulas for the number of comparisons done in the average
successful search.

E3. Suppose that you have a list of 10,000 names in alphabetical order in an array
and you must frequently look for various names. It turns out that 20 percent
of the names account for 80 percent of the retrievals. Instead of doing a binary
search over all 10,000 names every time, consider the possibility of splitting the

list into two: a high-frequency list of 2000 names and a low-frequency list of the remaining 8000 names. To look up a name, you will first use binary search on the high-frequency list, and 80 percent of the time you will not need to go on to the second stage, where you use binary search on the low-frequency list. Is this scheme worth the effort? Justify your answer by finding the number of comparisons done by binary_search_1 for the average successful search, both in the new scheme and in a binary search of a single list of 10,000 names.

E4. Use mathematical induction on n to prove that, in the comparison tree for binary_search_1 on a list of n entries, $n > 0$, all the leaves are on levels $\lfloor \lg 2n \rfloor$ and $\lceil \lg 2n \rceil$. [Hence, if n is a power of 2 (so that $\lg 2n$ is an integer), then all the leaves are on one level; otherwise, they are all on two adjacent levels.]

E5. If you modified binary search so that it divided the list not essentially in half at each pass, but instead into two pieces of sizes about one-third and two-thirds of the remaining list, then what would be the approximate effect on its average count of comparisons?

Programming Projects 7.4

P1. (a) Write a "ternary" search function analogous to binary_search_2 that examines the key one-third of the way through the list, and if the target key is greater, then examines the key two-thirds of the way through, and thus in any case at each pass reduces the length of the list by a factor of three. **(b)** Include your function as an additional option in the testing program of Project P1 of Section 7.2 (page 277), and compare its performance with other methods.

P2. (a) Write a program that will do a "hybrid" search, using binary_search_1 for large lists and switching to sequential search when the search is reduced to a sufficiently small sublist. (Because of different overhead, the best switch-over point is not necessarily the same as your answer to Exercise E2.) **(b)** Include your function as an additional option in the testing program of Project P1 of Section 7.2 (page 277), and compare its performance to other methods.

7.5 LOWER BOUNDS

We know that for an ordered contiguous list, binary search is much faster than sequential search. It is only natural to ask if we can find another method that is much faster than binary search.

1. Polishing Programs

One approach is to attempt to polish and refine our programs to make them run faster. By being clever we may be able to reduce the work done in each iteration by a bit and thereby speed up the algorithm. One method, called *Fibonacci search*, even manages to replace the division inside the loop of binary search by certain subtractions (with no auxiliary table needed), which on some computers will speed up the function.

basic algorithms and
small variations

Fine tuning of a program may be able to cut its running time in half, or perhaps reduce it even more, but limits will soon be reached if the underlying algorithm remains the same. The reason why binary search is so much faster than sequential search is not that there are fewer steps within its loop (there are actually more) or that the code is optimized, but that the loop is iterated fewer times, about $\lg n$ times instead of n times, and as the number n increases, the value of $\lg n$ grows much more slowly than does the value of n.

In the context of comparing underlying methods, the differences between binary_search_1 and binary_search_2 become insignificant in comparison with the difference between either binary search and sequential search. For large lists, binary_search_2 may require nearly double the time of binary_search_1, but the difference between $2 \lg n$ and $\lg n$ is negligible compared to the difference between $2 \lg n$ comparisons and the n comparisons sometimes needed by sequential search.

2. Arbitrary Searching Algorithms

Let us now ask whether it is possible for any search algorithm to exist that will, in the worst and the average cases, be able to find its target using significantly fewer comparisons of keys than binary search. We shall see that the answer is *no*, providing that we stay within the class of algorithms that rely only on comparisons of keys to determine where to look within an ordered list.

general algorithms
and comparison trees

Let us start with an arbitrary algorithm that searches an ordered list by making comparisons of keys, and imagine drawing its comparison tree in the same way as we drew the tree for binary_search_1. That is, each internal node of the tree will correspond to one comparison of keys and each leaf to one of the possible final outcomes. (If the algorithm is formulated as three-way comparisons like those of binary_search_2, then we expand each internal vertex into two, as shown for one vertex in Figure 7.4.) The possible outcomes to which the leaves correspond include not only the successful discovery of the target but also the different kinds of failure that the algorithm may distinguish. Binary search of a list of length n produces $k = 2n + 1$ outcomes, consisting of n successful outcomes and $n + 1$ different kinds of failure (less than the smallest key, between each pair of keys, or larger than the largest key). On the other hand, our sequential search function produced only $k = n + 1$ possible outcomes, since it distinguished only one kind of failure.

height and external
path length

As with all search algorithms that compare keys, the height of our tree will equal the number of comparisons that the algorithm does in its worst case, and (since all outcomes correspond to leaves) the external path length of the tree divided by the number of possible outcomes will equal the average number of comparisons done by the algorithm. We therefore wish to obtain lower bounds on the height and the external path length in terms of k, the number of leaves.

3. Observations on 2-Trees

Here is the result on 2-trees that we shall need:

Lemma 7.5   *Let T be a 2-tree with k leaves. Then the height h of T satisfies $h \geq \lceil \lg k \rceil$ and the external path length $E(T)$ satisfies $E(T) \geq k \lg k$. The minimum values for h and $E(T)$ occur when all the leaves of T are on the same level or on two adjacent levels.*

Proof We begin the proof by establishing the assertion in the last sentence. For suppose that some leaves of T are on level r and some are on level s, where $r > s + 1$. Now take two leaves on level r that are both children of the same vertex v, detach them from v, and attach them as children of some (former) leaf on level s. Then we have changed T into a new 2-tree T' that still has k leaves, the height of T' is certainly no more than that of T, and the external path length of T' satisfies

$$E(T') = E(T) - 2r + (r - 1) - s + 2(s + 1) = E(T) - r + s + 1 < E(T)$$

since $r > s + 1$. The terms in this expression are obtained as follows. Since two leaves at level r are removed, $E(T)$ is reduced by $2r$. Since vertex v has become a leaf, $E(T)$ is increased by $r - 1$. Since the vertex on level s is no longer a leaf, $E(T)$ is reduced by s. Since the two leaves formerly on level r are now on level $s + 1$, the term $2(s + 1)$ is added to $E(T)$. This process is illustrated in Figure 7.8.

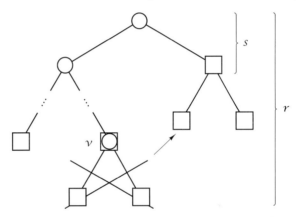

Figure 7.8. Moving leaves higher in a 2-tree

We can continue in this way to move leaves higher up the tree, reducing the external path length and possibly the height each time, until finally all the leaves are on the same or adjacent levels, and then the height and the external path length will be minimal amongst all 2-trees with k leaves.

proof of $h \geq \lceil \lg k \rceil$ To prove the remaining assertions in Lemma 7.5, let us from now on assume that T has minimum height and path length amongst the 2-trees with k leaves, so all leaves of T occur on levels h and (possibly) $h - 1$, where h is the height of T. By Lemma 7.2, the number of vertices on level h (which are necessarily leaves) is at most 2^h. If all the leaves are on level h, then $k \leq 2^h$. If some of the leaves are on level $h - 1$, then each of these (since it has no children) reduces the number of possible vertices on level h by 2, so the bound $k \leq 2^h$ continues to hold. We take logarithms to obtain $h \geq \lg k$ and, since the height is always an integer, we move up to the ceiling $h \geq \lceil \lg k \rceil$.

proof of $E(T) \geq k \lg k$ For the bound on the external path length, let x denote the number of leaves of T on level $h - 1$, so that $k - x$ leaves are on level h. These vertices are children of exactly $\frac{1}{2}(k - x)$ vertices on level $h - 1$, which, with the x leaves, comprise all vertices on level $h - 1$. Hence, by Lemma 7.2,

$$\tfrac{1}{2}(k - x) + x \leq 2^{h-1},$$

which becomes $x \leq 2^h - k$. We now have

$$
\begin{aligned}
E(T) &= (h-1)x + h(k-x) \\
&= kh - x \\
&\geq kh - (2^h - k) \\
&= k(h+1) - 2^h.
\end{aligned}
$$

From the bound on the height, we already know that $2^{h-1} < k \leq 2^h$. If we set $h = \lg k + \epsilon$, then ϵ satisfies $0 \leq \epsilon < 1$, and substituting ϵ into the bound for $E(T)$ we obtain

$$
E(T) \geq k(\lg k + 1 + \epsilon - 2^\epsilon).
$$

It turns out that, for $0 \leq \epsilon < 1$, the quantity $1 + \epsilon - 2^\epsilon$ is between 0 and 0.0861. Thus the minimum path length is quite close to $k \lg k$ and, in any case, is at least $k \lg k$, *end of proof*   as was to be shown. With this, the proof of Lemma 7.5 is complete.   ∎

4. Lower Bounds for Searching

Finally, we return to the study of our arbitrary searching algorithm. Its comparison tree may not have all leaves on two adjacent levels, but, even if not, the bounds in Lemma 7.5 will still hold. Hence we may translate these bounds into the language of comparisons, as follows.

Theorem 7.6   *Suppose that an algorithm uses comparisons of keys to search for a target in a list. If there are k possible outcomes, then the algorithm must make at least $\lceil \lg k \rceil$ comparisons of keys in its worst case and at least $\lg k$ in its average case.*

Observe that there is very little difference between the worst-case bound and the average-case bound. By Theorem 7.4, moreover, for many algorithms it does not much matter whether the search is successful or not, in determining the bound in the preceding theorem. When we apply Theorem 7.6 to algorithms like binary search for which, on an ordered list of length n, there are n successful and $n+1$ unsuccessful outcomes, we obtain a worst-case bound of

$$
\lceil \lg(2n+1) \rceil \geq \lceil \lg(2n) \rceil = \lceil \lg n \rceil + 1
$$

and an average-case bound of $\lg n + 1$ comparisons of keys. When we compare these numbers with those obtained in the analysis of binary_search_1, we obtain

Corollary 7.7   *binary_search_1 is optimal in the class of all algorithms that search an ordered list by making comparisons of keys. In both the average and worst cases, binary_search_1 achieves the optimal bound.*

An informal way to see why Corollary 7.7 is true is to start with an arbitrary searching algorithm and imagine drawing its comparison tree for a list of length n. Since the algorithm is arbitrary, we can't really draw the tree, but it still would exist, and we can imagine working with it. If this tree happens to have some leaves that are at least two levels higher in the tree than other leaves, then we could modify the tree by deleting a pair of sibling leaves from the lowest level and reattaching them as the children of a former leaf at least two levels higher. (This process is illustrated in Figure 7.8.) Doing this will shorten the path length of the tree. Now imagine that we can even modify the arbitrary algorithm so that its comparison tree becomes the modified tree. Doing this will improve the performance of the algorithm, since the number of key comparisons is closely related to the path length of the tree. Now let us keep on optimizing the algorithm in the same way, as long as there are any leaves at least two levels higher than other leaves in the comparison tree. Doing so will make the algorithm better and better, until finally it cannot be optimized any further in this way because all the leaves in its comparison tree are on one level or two adjacent levels. But binary_search_1 already has a tree like that. In other words, by starting with an arbitrary searching algorithm and optimizing it as much as possible, we might be able to bring its performance up to that of binary_search_1, and that is therefore as good as we can ever get.

5. Other Ways to Search

The bounds in Theorem 7.6 do not imply that no algorithm can run faster than binary search, only those that rely only on comparisons of keys. As a simple example, suppose that the keys are the integers from 0 to $n - 1$ themselves. If we know that the target key x is an integer in this range, then we would never perform a search algorithm to locate its entry; we would simply store the entries in an array of size n and immediately look in index x to find the desired entry.

interpolation search

This idea can be extended to obtain another method called ***interpolation search***. We assume that the keys are either numerical or are information, such as words, that can be readily encoded as numbers. The method also assumes that the keys in the list are uniformly distributed, that is, that the probability of a key being in a particular range equals its probability of being in any other range of the same size. To find the target key target, interpolation search then estimates, according to the magnitude of the number target relative to the first and last entries of the list, about where target would be in the list and looks there. It then reduces the size of the list according as target is less than or greater than the key examined. It can be shown that on average, with uniformly distributed keys, interpolation search will take about $\lg \lg n$ comparisons of keys, which, for large n, is somewhat fewer than binary search requires. If, for example, $n = 1,000,000$, then binary_search_1 will require about $\lg 10^6 + 1 \approx 21$ comparisons, while interpolation search may need only about $\lg \lg 10^6 \approx 4.32$ comparisons.

Interpolation sort is the method a person would normally use to find a specific page in a book. If you guess that a book is about 500 pages long and you want to find page 345, you would normally first look about two-thirds of the way through the book, and search from there. If you wished to find page 10, you would start near the beginning, or near the end for page 487.

Finally, we should repeat that, even for search by comparisons, our assumption that requests for all keys are equally likely may be far from correct. If one or two keys are much more likely than the others, then even sequential search, if it looks for those keys first, may be faster than any other method. The importance of search or, more generally, information retrieval is so fundamental that much research has been applied to its methods. In later chapters we shall return to these problems again and again.

Exercise 7.5

E1. Suppose that, like binary_search_2, a search algorithm makes three-way comparisons. Let each internal node of its comparison tree correspond to a successful search and each leaf to an unsuccessful search.

(a) Use Lemma 7.5 to obtain a theorem like Theorem 7.6 giving lower bounds for worst and average case behavior for an unsuccessful search by such an algorithm.

(b) Use Theorem 7.4 to obtain a similar result for successful searches.

(c) Compare the bounds you obtain with the analysis of binary_search_2.

Programming Project 7.5

P1. (a) Write a program to do interpolation search and verify its correctness (especially termination). See the references at the end of the chapter for suggestions and program analysis. **(b)** Include your function as another option in the testing program of Project P1 of Section 7.2 (page 277) and compare its performance with the other methods.

7.6 ASYMPTOTICS

7.6.1 Introduction

The time has come to distill important generalizations from our analyses of searching algorithms. As we have progressed, we have been able to see more clearly which aspects of algorithm analysis are of great importance and which parts can safely be neglected. If a section of a program is performed only once outside any loops or recursion, for example, then the amount of time it uses is negligible compared to the amount of time used inside loops or recursion. We have found that, although binary search is more difficult to program and to analyze than sequential search, and even though it runs more slowly when applied to a very short list, for a longer list it will run far faster than sequential search.

designing algorithms
for small problems
The design of efficient methods to work on small problems is an important subject to study, because a large program may need to do the same or similar small tasks many times during its execution. As we have discovered, however, for small problems, the large overhead of a sophisticated method may make it inferior to a simpler method. For a list of three or four entries, sequential search is certainly superior to binary search. To improve efficiency in the algorithm for a

small problem, the programmer must necessarily devote attention to details specific to the computer system and programming language, and there are few general observations that will help with this task.

choice of method for large problems

The design of efficient algorithms for large problems is an entirely different matter, and it is this matter that concerns us now. In studying search methods, for example, we have seen that the overhead becomes relatively unimportant as the size of the list increases; it is the basic idea that will make all the difference between an efficient algorithm and one that runs too slowly to be practical.

asymptotics

The word ***asymptotics*** that titles this section means the study of functions of a parameter n, as n becomes larger and larger without bound. Typically, we study a function $f(n)$ that gives the amount of work done by an algorithm in solving a problem of size n, as the parameter n increases. In comparing searching algorithms on a list of n entries, for example, we have seen that the count $f(n)$ of the number of comparisons of keys accurately reflects the total running time for large problems, since it has generally been true that all the other operations (such as incrementing and comparing indices) have gone in lock step with comparison of keys.

basic actions

In fact, the frequency of such basic actions is much more important than is a total count of all operations, including the housekeeping. The total including housekeeping is too dependent on the choice of programming language and on the programmer's particular style, so dependent that it tends to obscure the general methods. Variations in housekeeping details or programming technique can easily triple the running time of a program, but such a change probably will not make the difference between whether the computation is feasible or not. If we wait a little while or invest a little more money, we can obtain a computer three times as fast and so will not be inconvenienced by a program that takes three times as long as it might.

program variation

choice of method

A change in fundamental method, on the other hand, can make a vital difference in the resources required to solve a problem. If the number of basic actions done by an algorithm is proportional to the size n of the input, then doubling n will about double the running time, no matter how the housekeeping is done. If the number of basic actions is proportional to $\lg n$, then doubling n will hardly change the running time at all. If the number of basic actions is proportional to n^2, then the running time will quadruple, and the computation may still be feasible, but it may be uncomfortably long. But now suppose that the number of basic actions is proportional to 2^n, that is, is an *exponential* function of n. In this case, doubling n will square the number of basic actions that the program must do. A computation that took 1 second might involve a million (10^6) basic actions, and doubling the size of the input would then require 10^{12} basic actions, increasing the running time from 1 second to $11\frac{1}{2}$ days. Doubling the input again raises the count of basic actions to 10^{24} and the time to about 30 billion years. The function 2^n grows very rapidly indeed as n increases.

generalization

Our desire in formulating general principles that will apply to the analysis of many classes of algorithms, then, is to have a notation that will accurately reflect the way in which the computation time will increase with the size, but that will ignore superfluous details with little effect on the total. We wish to concentrate on one or two basic operations within the algorithm, without too much concern for all the housekeeping operations that will accompany them. If an algorithm does $f(n)$ basic operations when the size of its input is n, then its total running time will be at most $cf(n)$, where c is a constant that depends on the way the algorithm is programmed and on the computer used, but c does not depend on the size n of the input as n increases.

Our goal is now to obtain a concise, easy-to-understand notation that will tell us how rapidly a function $f(n)$ grows as n increases, a notation that will give us useful information about the amount of work an algorithm does.

7.6.2 Orders of Magnitude

1. Definitions

The idea is for us to compare our function $f(n)$ with some well-known function $g(n)$ whose behavior we already understand. In fact, some of the most common choices for the function $g(n)$ against which we compare $f(n)$ are:

➥ $g(n) = 1$	Constant function
➥ $g(n) = \log n$	Logarithmic function
➥ $g(n) = n$	Linear function
➥ $g(n) = n^2$	Quadratic function
➥ $g(n) = n^3$	Cubic function
➥ $g(n) = 2^n$	Exponential function

To compare $f(n)$ against $g(n)$, we take their quotient $f(n)/g(n)$ and take the limit of this quotient as n increases without bound. Depending on the outcome, we have one of the following cases:

Definition

If $\lim\limits_{n \to \infty} \dfrac{f(n)}{g(n)} = 0$ then:

$f(n)$ has **strictly smaller order of magnitude** than $g(n)$.

If $\lim\limits_{n \to \infty} \dfrac{f(n)}{g(n)}$ is finite and nonzero then:

$f(n)$ has **the same order of magnitude** as $g(n)$.

If $\lim\limits_{n \to \infty} \dfrac{f(n)}{g(n)} = \infty$ then:

$f(n)$ has **strictly greater order of magnitude** than $g(n)$.

The term *order of magnitude* is often shortened to *order* when the context makes the meaning clear.

Note that the second case, when $f(n)$ and $g(n)$ have the same order of magnitude, includes all values of the limit except 0 and ∞. In this way, changing the running time of an algorithm by any nonzero constant factor will not affect its order of magnitude.

2. Assumptions

In this definition, and always throughout this book, we make two assumptions:

➥ We assume that $f(n) > 0$ and $g(n) > 0$ for all sufficiently large n.

➥ We assume that $\lim\limits_{n \to \infty} \dfrac{f(n)}{g(n)}$ exists.

The reason for assuming that $f(n)$ and $g(n)$ are strictly positive (for large n) is to avoid the possibility of division by 0 and the need to worry about whether limits are positive or negative. Since operation counts and timings for algorithms are always positive, this is really no restriction.

The assumption that the limit exists avoids the possibility that the quotient might turn out to be a function like $x \sin x$, part of whose graph is shown in Figure 7.9. This function takes on every possible value an infinite number of times, and, no matter how large you require x to be, it still takes on every possible value an infinite number of times for even larger values of x. Hence there is no way that $x \sin x$ can be considered to be approaching any fixed limit as x tends to infinity.

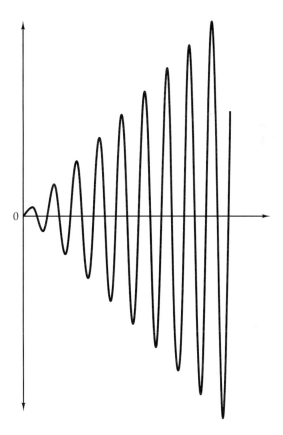

Figure 7.9. Graph of $x \sin x$

Note that we are following the convention that the limit of a function that grows larger and larger without bound *does* exist and is infinite. (Some mathematicians consider that such a limit does not exist.) The following defines an infinite limit in terms of finite limits:

Definition

$$\lim_{n \to \infty} \frac{f(n)}{g(n)} = \infty \qquad \text{means the same as} \qquad \lim_{n \to \infty} \frac{g(n)}{f(n)} = 0.$$

3. Polynomials

For our first example, let us take a polynomial

$$f(n) = 3n^2 - 100n - 25.$$

First, let us note that, for small values of n, $f(n)$ is negative; for example, $f(1) = 3 - 100 - 25 = -122$. This is because $3n^2 < 100n$ for small n. However, as n increases—anytime, in fact, after $n \geq 34$—$3n^2$ *dominates* $100n$, and, in fact, $f(n) > 0$ for all $n \geq 34$.

Suppose $g(n) = n^3$. Then

$$\lim_{n \to \infty} \frac{f(n)}{g(n)} = \lim_{n \to \infty} \frac{3n^2 - 100n - 25}{n^3} = \lim_{n \to \infty} \left(\frac{3}{n} - \frac{100}{n^2} - \frac{25}{n^3} \right) = 0$$

since each term goes to 0 as $n \to \infty$. Hence $3n^2 - 100n - 25$ has strictly smaller order than n^3.

On the other hand, for $g(n) = n$ we have

$$\lim_{n \to \infty} \frac{f(n)}{g(n)} = \lim_{n \to \infty} \frac{3n^2 - 100n - 25}{n} = \lim_{n \to \infty} \left(3n - 100 - \frac{25}{n} \right) = \infty$$

since the first term goes to ∞ as $n \to \infty$, whereas the second term does not change and the third goes to 0. Hence $3n^2 - 100n - 25$ has strictly greater order than n.

If we choose $g(n) = n^2$ we obtain the same order as $f(n)$, since

$$\lim_{n \to \infty} \frac{f(n)}{g(n)} = \lim_{n \to \infty} \frac{3n^2 - 100n - 25}{n} = \lim_{n \to \infty} \left(3 - \frac{100}{n} - \frac{25}{n^2} \right) = 3.$$

It is easy to generalize this example to obtain:

polynomials

> If $f(n)$ is any polynomial in n with degree r, then $f(n)$ has the same order of magnitude as n^r.

We can also see that

powers of n

> If $r < s$, then n^r has strictly smaller order of magnitude than n^s.

4. Logarithms and L'Hôpital's Rule

Logarithms form a second class of functions that appear frequently in studying algorithms. We have already used logarithms in the analysis of binary search, and we have seen that the logarithm of n grows much more slowly than n itself. We shall now generalize this observation, but first let us note the following:

change of base

> *The order of magnitude of a logarithm does not depend on the base for the logarithms.*

To see why this is true, let $\log_a n$ and $\log_b n$ be logarithms to two different bases $a > 1$ and $b > 1$. As observed in Section A.2.6, $\log_b n = (\log_b a)(\log_a n)$. Hence,

$$\lim_{n \to \infty} \frac{\log_b n}{\log_a n} = \lim_{n \to \infty} \frac{(\log_b a)(\log_a n)}{\log_a n} = \log_b a,$$

which is a nonzero constant, so $\log_b n$ has the same order of magnitude as $\log_a a$, which was to be shown.

Since the base for logarithms makes no difference to the order of magnitude, we shall generally write log rather than lg or ln in any order-of-magnitude expression.

Next, let us compare the order of magnitude of $\log n$ with a power of n, say n^r where $r > 0$ is any positive real number. When we take the quotient we see that both $\log n \to \infty$ and $n^r \to \infty$ as $n \to \infty$. The limit of the quotient is called **indeterminate** because it is not possible to determine the limit without further information. We shall borrow an important tool from calculus, called **L'Hôpital's Rule**, to help with this problem.

Theorem 7.8

> **L'Hôpital's Rule** *Suppose that:*
>
> ➡ *$f(x)$ and $g(x)$ are differentiable functions for all sufficiently large x, with derivatives $f'(x)$ and $g'(x)$, respectively.*
>
> ➡ *$\lim_{x \to \infty} f(x) = \infty$ and $\lim_{x \to \infty} g(x) = \infty$.*
>
> ➡ *$\lim_{x \to \infty} \dfrac{f'(x)}{g'(x)}$ exists.*
>
> *Then $\lim_{x \to \infty} \dfrac{f(x)}{g(x)}$ exists and $\lim_{x \to \infty} \dfrac{f(x)}{g(x)} = \lim_{x \to \infty} \dfrac{f'(x)}{g'(x)}.$*

When we apply L'Hôpital's Rule to $f(x) = \ln x$ and $g(x) = x^r$, $r > 0$, we have $f'(x) = 1/x$ and $g'(x) = rx^{r-1}$, and hence

$$\lim_{x \to \infty} \frac{\ln x}{x^r} = \lim_{x \to \infty} \frac{1/x}{rx^{r-1}} = \lim_{x \to \infty} \frac{1}{rx^r} = 0$$

since $r > 0$. Since the base for logarithms doesn't matter, we have:

logarithms

> $\log n$ *has strictly smaller order of magnitude than any positive power n^r of n, $r > 0$.*

5. Exponential Functions

We can again apply L'Hôpital's Rule to try verifying that an exponential function has strictly greater order of magnitude than a power of n. Specifically, let $f(x) = a^x$, where $a > 1$ is a real number, and let $g(x) = x^r$, where r is a positive integer. Since $f(x) \to \infty$ and $g(x) \to \infty$ as $x \to \infty$, we calculate the derivatives

$$f'(x) = \frac{d}{dx} a^x = \frac{d}{dx} \left(e^{\ln a} \right)^x = \frac{d}{dx} e^{(\ln a)x} = (\ln a) e^{(\ln a)x} = (\ln a) a^x$$

and $g'(x) = r x^{r-1}$.

Unfortunately, both $f'(x) \to \infty$ and (if $r > 1$) $g'(x) \to \infty$ as $x \to \infty$, so L'Hôpital's Rule does not immediately provide the solution. We can, however, apply L'Hôpital's Rule to $f'(x)$ and $g'(x)$. Again, the quotient $f'(x)/g'(x)$ may be indeterminate, but we can continue all the way to the rth derivative, where we find

$$f^{(r)}(x) = (\ln a)^r a^x \qquad \text{and} \qquad g^{(r)}(x) = r!.$$

This quotient, finally, is no longer indeterminate: $f^{(r)}(x) \to \infty$ and $g^{(r)}(x)$ is the constant $r!$. Hence

$$\lim_{x \to \infty} \frac{f(x)}{g(x)} = \lim_{x \to \infty} \frac{f'(x)}{g'(x)} = \cdots = \lim_{x \to \infty} \frac{f^{(r)}(x)}{g^{(r)}(x)} = \lim_{x \to \infty} \frac{(\ln a)^r a^x}{r!} = \infty.$$

Therefore:

exponentials

> *Any exponential function a^n for any real number $a > 1$ has strictly greater order of magnitude than any power n^r of n, for any positive integer r.*

Finally, let us compare exponential functions for two different bases, a^n and b^n. Again, we could try to apply L'Hôpital's Rule, but now we would find that the derivatives always tend to infinity as $x \to \infty$. Fortunately, we can determine the limit directly. We assume $0 \le a < b$.

$$\lim_{n \to \infty} \frac{a^n}{b^n} = \lim_{n \to \infty} \left(\frac{a}{b} \right)^n = 0$$

since $a < b$. Hence:

two exponentials

> *If $0 \le a < b$ then a^n has strictly smaller order of magnitude than b^n.*

6. Common Orders

We could continue to compare many other functions for order of magnitude, but, fortunately, for almost algorithm analyses that we need, a very short list of functions is all we need. We have already seen six of these functions, the functions 1 (constant), $\log n$ (logarithmic), n (linear), n^2 (quadratic), n^3 (cubic), and 2^n (exponential). From the work we have done, we can conclude that these six functions are listed in strictly increasing order of magnitude.

Starting in Section 8.5, we shall see that one more function is important, the function $g(n) = n \log n$. In order of magnitude, where does this function fit in this list? To answer, we shall use the following easy fact:

product with a
function

> If $h(n)$ is any function for which $h(n) > 0$ for all sufficiently large n, then the order of magnitude of $f(n)h(n)$ is related to the order of $g(n)h(n)$ in the same way (less than, equal to, or greater than) as the order of $f(n)$ is related to the order of $g(n)$.

The proof of this is simply the observation that

$$\lim_{n \to \infty} \frac{f(x)h(x)}{g(x)h(x)} = \lim_{n \to \infty} \frac{f(x)}{g(x)}.$$

First, let us compare the order of $n \log n$ with n. We let $h(n) = n$, and we see that the comparison is the same as between $\log n$ and 1, so we conclude that $n \log n$ has strictly greater order than n. But, if we take any $\epsilon > 0$, $\log n$ has strictly smaller order than n^ϵ, so (again with $h(n) = n$) $n \log n$ has strictly smaller order than $n^{1+\epsilon}$.

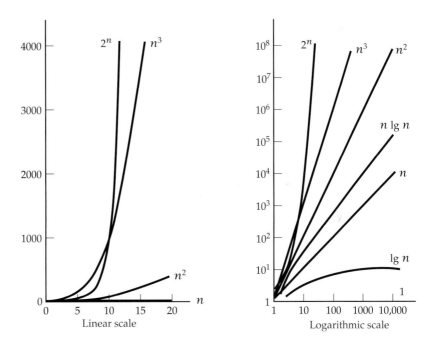

Figure 7.10. Growth rates of common functions

Figure 7.10 shows how these seven functions (with constant 1 and base 2 for logarithms) grow with n, and the relative sizes of some of these numbers are shown in Figure 7.11. The number in the lower right corner of the table in Figure 7.11 is beyond comprehension: If every electron in the universe (10^{50} of them) were a supercomputer doing a hundred million (10^8) operations per second since the creation of the universe (perhaps 30 billion years, or about 10^{18} seconds), then a computation requiring 2^{1000} operations would have done only about 10^{76} operations, so it would have to go 10^{225} *times* as long! A computation requiring 2^n operations is feasible only for *very* small values of n.

n	1	$\lg n$	n	$n \lg n$	n^2	n^3	2^n
1	1	0.00	1	0	1	1	2
10	1	3.32	10	33	100	1000	1024
100	1	6.64	100	664	10,000	1,000,000	1.268×10^{30}
1000	1	9.97	1000	9970	1,000,000	10^9	1.072×10^{301}

Figure 7.11. Relative sizes of functions

Notice especially how much slower $\lg n$ grows than n; this is essentially the reason why binary search is superior to sequential search for large lists. Notice how the functions 1 and $\lg n$ become farther and farther below all the others for large n.

7.6.3 The Big-O and Related Notations

To use orders of magnitude effectively in calculations, we need a notation more compact than writing phrases like

strictly smaller order of magnitude than.

We compare magnitudes in the same way as numbers are compared with the standard comparison symbols $<$, $\leq$, $=$, $\geq$, and $>$. Unfortunately, no such system of comparison symbols for orders of magnitude is in common use. Instead, a system of certain greek and latin letters is used. And, as we shall see, this system does have its own advantages, even though it takes a bit of practice at first to learn its use.

Here are the four terms commonly used:

Notation: $f(n)$ *is*	*Pronounce:* $f(n)$ *is*	*Meaning:* Order of f compared to g is		*Value of* $\lim\limits_{n \to \infty} (f(n)/g(n))$
$o(g(n))$	*little oh of* $g(n)$	$<$	*strictly smaller*	0
$O(g(n))$	*Big Oh of* $g(n)$	$\leq$	*smaller or equal*	*finite*
$\Theta(g(n))$	*Big Theta of* $g(n)$	$=$	*equal*	*nonzero finite*
$\Omega(g(n))$	*Big Omega of* $g(n)$	$\geq$	*larger or equal*	*nonzero*

To illustrate how these notations are used, let us recast some of the algorithm analyses we have done into the new notation:

➡ On a list of length n, sequential search has running time $\Theta(n)$.

➡ On an ordered list of length n, binary search has running time $\Theta(\log n)$.

➡ Retrieval from a contiguous list of length n has running time $O(1)$.

➡ Retrieval from a linked list of length n has running time $O(n)$.

➡ Any algorithm that uses comparisons of keys to search a list of length n must make $\Omega(\log n)$ comparisons of keys (Theorem 7.6).

➡ Any algorithm for the Towers of Hanoi (see Section 5.1.4) requires time $\Omega(2^n)$ in order to move n disks.

The general observations we have made about order of magnitude can also be recast as follows:

polynomials ➡ *If $f(n)$ is a polynomial in n of degree r, then $f(n)$ is $\Theta(n^r)$.*

powers of n ➡ *If $r < s$, then n^r is $o(n^s)$.*

change of base ➡ *If $a > 1$ and $b > 1$ then $\log_a(n)$ is $\Theta(\log_b(n))$.*

logarithms ➡ *$\log n$ is $o(n^r)$ for any $r > 0$.*

exponentials ➡ *For any real number $a > 1$ and any positive integer r, n^r is $o(a^n)$.*

two exponentials ➡ *If $0 \le a < b$ then a^n is $o(b^n)$.*

7.6.4 Keeping the Dominant Term

Note that, in all three notations O, Θ, and Ω where the limit may have a finite, nonzero value, the notations make no distinction between one nonzero value and another. This is usually appropriate for algorithm analyses, since multiplying the result by a constant may reflect only a change in programming style or a change in computer speed.

Sometimes, however, we would like to have a more precise measure of the amount of work done by an algorithm, and we can obtain one by using the big-O notation within an expression, as follows. We define

$$f(n) = g(n) + O(h(n))$$

to mean that $f(n) - g(n)$ is $O(h(n))$. Instead of thinking of $O(h(n))$ as the class of all functions growing no faster than $ch(n)$ for some constant c, we think of $O(h(n))$ as a single but arbitrary such function. We then use this function to represent all the terms of our calculation in which we are not interested, generally
search comparisons all the terms except the one that grows the most quickly.

The results of some of our algorithm analyses can now be summarized as follows:

➡ For a successful search in a list of length n, sequential search has running time $\frac{1}{2}n + O(1)$.

➡ For a successful search in an ordered list of length n, binary search has running time $2\lg n + O(1)$.

➡ Retrieval from a contiguous list of length n has running time $O(1)$.

➡ Retrieval from a simply linked list of length n has average running time $\frac{1}{2}n + O(1)$.

danger

In using the big-O notation in expressions, it is necessary always to remember that $O(h(n))$ does not stand for a well-defined function, but for an arbitrary function from a large class. Hence ordinary algebra cannot be done with $O(h(n))$. For example, we might have two expressions

$$n^2 + 4n - 5 = n^2 + O(n) \text{ and } n^2 - 9n + 7 = n^2 + O(n)$$

but $O(n)$ represents different functions in the two expressions, so we cannot equate the right sides or conclude that the left sides are equal.

Exercises 7.6

E1. For each of the following pairs of functions, find the smallest integer value of $n > 1$ for which the first becomes larger than the second. [For some of these, use a calculator to try various values of n.]

(a) n^2 and $15n + 5$ 　　　　(c) $0.1n$ and $10\lg n$
(b) 2^n and $8n^4$ 　　　　　(d) $0.1n^2$ and $100n\lg n$

E2. Arrange the following functions into increasing order; that is, $f(n)$ should come before $g(n)$ in your list if and only if $f(n)$ is $O(g(n))$.

100000	$(\lg n)^3$	2^n
$n\lg n$	$n^3 - 100n^2$	$n + \lg n$
$\lg\lg n$	$n^{0.1}$	n^2

E3. Divide the following functions into classes so that two functions $f(n)$ and $g(n)$ are in the same class if and only if $f(n)$ is $\Theta(g(n))$. Arrange the classes from the lowest order of magnitude to the highest. [A function may be in a class by itself, or there may be several functions in the same class.]

5000	$(\lg n)^5$	3^n
$\lg n$	$n + \lg n$	n^3
$n^2\lg n$	$n^2 - 100n$	$4n + \sqrt{n}$
$\lg\lg n^2$	$n^{0.3}$	n^2
$\lg n^2$	$\sqrt{n^2 + 4}$	2^n

E4. Show that each of the following is correct.

    (a) $3n^2 - 10n \lg n - 300$ is $\Theta(n^2)$.

    (b) $4n \lg n + 100n - \sqrt{n+5}$ is $\Omega(n)$.

    (c) $4n \lg n + 100n - \sqrt{n+5}$ is $o(\sqrt{n^3})$.

    (d) $(n-5)(n + \lg n + \sqrt{n})$ is $O(n^2)$.

    (e) $\sqrt{n^2 + 5n + 12}$ is $\Theta(n)$.

E5. Decide whether each of the following is correct or not.

    (a) $(3 \lg n)^3 - 10\sqrt{n} + 2n$ is $O(n)$.

    (b) $(3 \lg n)^3 - 10\sqrt{n} + 2n$ is $\Omega(\sqrt{n})$.

    (c) $(3 \lg n)^3 - 10\sqrt{n} + 2n$ is $o(n \log n)$.

    (d) $\sqrt{n^2 - 10n + 100}$ is $\Omega(n)$.

    (e) $3n - 10\sqrt{n} + \sqrt{n \lg n}$ is $O(n)$.

    (f) $2^n - n^3$ is Ωn^4.

    (g) $\sqrt{3n - 12n \lg n - 2n^3 + n^4}$ is $\Theta(n^2)$.

    (h) $(n+10)^3$ is $O((n-10)^3)$.

E6. Suppose you have programs whose running times in microseconds for an input of size n are $1000 \lg n$, $100n$, $10n^2$, and 2^n. Find the largest size n of input that can be processed by each of these programs in **(a)** one second, **(b)** one minute, **(c)** one day, and **(d)** one year.

E7. Prove that a function $f(n)$ is $\Theta(g(n))$ if and only if $f(n)$ is $O(g(n))$ and $f(n)$ is $\Omega(g(n))$

E8. Suppose that $f(n)$ is $\Theta(g(n))$ and $h(n)$ is $o(g(n))$. Prove that $f(n)+h(n)$ is $\Theta(g(n))$.

E9. Find functions $f(n)$ and $h(n)$ that are both $\Theta(n)$ but $f(n)+h(n)$ is *not* $\Theta(n)$.

E10. Suppose that $f(n)$ is $O(g(n))$ and $h(n)$ is $O(g(n))$. Prove that $f(n)+h(n)$ is $O(g(n))$.

E11. Show that the relation O is *transitive*; that is, from the assumption that $f(n)$ is $O(g(n))$ and $g(n)$ is $O(h(n))$, prove that $f(n)$ is $O(h(n))$. Are any of the other relations o, Θ, and Ω transitive? If so, which one(s)?

E12. Show that the relation Θ is *symmetric*; that is, from the assumption that $f(n)$ is $\Theta(g(n))$ prove that $g(n)$ is $O(f(n))$. Are any of the other relations o, O, and Ω transitive? If so, which one(s)?

E13. Show that the relation Ω is *reflexive*; that is, prove that any function $f(n)$ is $\Omega(f(n))$. Are any of the other relations o, O, and Θ transitive? If so, which one(s)?

E14. A relation is called an *equivalence relation* if it is reflexive, symmetric, and transitive. On the basis of the three preceding exercises, which (if any) of o, O, Θ, and Ω is an equivalence relation?

E15. Suppose you are evaluating computer programs by running them without seeing the source code. You run each program for several sizes n of input and obtain the operation counts or times shown. In each case, on the basis of the numbers given, find a constant c and a function $g(n)$ (which should be one of the seven common functions shown in Figure 7.10) so that $cg(n)$ closely approximates the given numbers.

(a)

n:	10	50	200	1000
count:	201	998	4005	19987

(b)

n:	10	100	1000	10000
count:	3	6	12	24

(c)

n:	10	20	40	80
count:	10	40	158	602

(d)

n:	10	11	12	13
count:	3	6	12	24

E16. Two functions f and $g(n)$ are called *asymptotically equal* if

$$\lim_{n \to \infty} \frac{f(n)}{g(n)} = 1;$$

in which case we write $f(n) \asymp g(n)$. Show each of the following:
(a) $3x^2 - 12x + 7 \asymp 3x^2$.
(b) $\sqrt{x^2 + 1} \asymp x$.
(c) If $f(n) \asymp g(n)$ then $f(n)$ is $\Theta(g(n))$.
(d) If $f(n) \asymp g(n)$ and $g(n) \asymp h(n)$, then $f(n) \asymp h(n)$.

Programming Project 7.6

P1. Write a program to test on your computer how long it takes to do $n \lg n$, n^2, n^5, 2^n, and $n!$ additions for $n = 5, 10, 15, 20$.

POINTERS AND PITFALLS

1. In designing algorithms be very careful of the extreme cases, such as empty lists, lists with only one item, or full lists (in the contiguous case).

2. Be sure that all your variables are properly initialized.

3. Double check the termination conditions for your loops, and make sure that progress toward termination always occurs.

4. In case of difficulty, formulate statements that will be correct both before and after each iteration of a loop, and verify that they hold.

5. Avoid sophistication for sophistication's sake. If a simple method is adequate for your application, use it.

6. Don't reinvent the wheel. If a ready-made function is adequate for your application, use it.

7. Sequential search is slow but robust. Use it for short lists or if there is any doubt that the keys in the list are properly ordered.

8. Be extremely careful if you must reprogram binary search. Verify that your algorithm is correct and test it on all the extreme cases.

9. Drawing trees is an excellent way both to trace the action of an algorithm and to analyze its behavior.

10. Rely on the big-O analysis of algorithms for large applications but not for small applications.

REVIEW QUESTIONS

7.4 **1.** Name three conditions under which sequential search of a list is preferable to binary search.

7.5 **2.** In searching a list of n items, how many comparisons of keys are done, on average, by **(a)** sequential_search, **(b)** binary_search_1, and **(c)** binary_search_2?

3. Why was binary search implemented only for contiguous lists, not for linked lists?

4. Draw the comparison tree for binary_search_1 for searching a list of length **(a)** 1, **(b)** 2, and **(c)** 3.

5. Draw the comparison tree for binary_search_2 for searching a list of length **(a)** 1, **(b)** 2, and **(c)** 3.

6. If the height of a 2-tree is 3, what are **(a)** the largest and **(b)** the smallest number of vertices that can be in the tree?

7. Define the terms *internal* and *external path length* of a 2-tree. State the path length theorem.

7.6 **8.** What is the smallest number of comparisons that any method relying on comparisons of keys must make, on average, in searching a list of n items?

9. If binary_search_2 does 20 comparisons for the average successful search, then about how many will it do for the average unsuccessful search, assuming that the possibilities of the target less than the smallest key, between any pair of keys, or larger than the largest key are all equally likely?

7.7 **10.** What is the purpose of the big-O notation?

REFERENCES FOR FURTHER STUDY

The primary reference for this chapter is KNUTH, Volume 3. (See the end of Chapter 2 for bibliographic details.) Sequential search occupies pp. 389–405; binary search is covered in pp. 406–414; then comes Fibonacci search, and a section on history. KNUTH studies every method we have touched, and many others besides. He does algorithm analysis in considerably more detail than we have, writing his algorithms in a pseudo-assembly language and counting operations in detail there.

Proving the correctness of the binary search algorithm is the topic of

> JON BENTLEY, "Programming pearls: Writing correct programs" (regular column), *Communications of the ACM* 26 (1983), 1040–1045.

In this column BENTLEY shows how to formulate a binary search algorithm from its requirements, points out that about 90 percent of professional programmers whom he has taught were unable to write the program correctly in one hour, and gives a formal verification of correctness.

The following paper studies 26 published versions of binary search, pointing out correct and erroneous reasoning and drawing conclusions applicable to other algorithms:

> R. LESUISSE, "Some lessons drawn from the history of the binary search algorithm," *The Computer Journal* 26 (1983), 154–163.

Theorem 7.4 (successful and unsuccessful searches take almost the same time on average) is due to

> T. N. HIBBARD, *Journal of the ACM* 9 (1962), 16–17.

Interpolation search is presented in

> C. C. GOTLIEB and L. R. GOTLIEB, *Data Types and Structures*, Prentice Hall, Englewood Cliffs, N. J., 1978, pp. 133–135.

The following book gives further information on the asymptotic relations o, O, Θ, and Ω, presented in entertaining style:

> GREGORY J. E. RAWLINS, *Compared to What? An Introduction to the Analysis of Algorithms*, Computer Science Press (imprint of W. H. Freeman), New York, 1992, pp. 38–77.

Sorting

8

T HIS CHAPTER studies several important methods for sorting lists, both contiguous lists and linked lists. At the same time, we shall develop further tools that help with the analysis of algorithms and apply these to determine which sorting methods perform better under different circumstances.

8.1 INTRODUCTION AND NOTATION

We live in a world obsessed with keeping information, and to find it, we must keep it in some sensible order. Librarians make sure that no one misplaces a book; income tax authorities trace down every dollar we earn; credit bureaus keep track of almost every detail of our actions. I once saw a cartoon in which a keen filing clerk, anxious to impress the boss, said frenetically, "Let me make sure these files are in alphabetical order before we throw them out." If we are to be the masters of this explosion instead of its victims, we had best learn how to keep track of it all!

practical importance　Several years ago, it was estimated, more than half the time on many commercial computers was spent in sorting. This is perhaps no longer true, since sophisticated methods have been devised for organizing data, methods that do not require that the data be kept in any special order. Eventually, nonetheless, the information does go out to people, and then it must often be sorted in some way.

Because sorting is so important, a great many algorithms have been devised for doing it. In fact, so many good ideas appear in sorting methods that an entire course could easily be built around this one theme. Amongst the differing environments that require different methods, the most important is the distinction between *external and internal* *external and internal*; that is, whether there are so many records to be sorted that *sorting* they must be kept in external files on disks, tapes, or the like, or whether they can all be kept internally in high-speed memory. In this chapter, we consider only internal sorting.

reference　It is not our intention to present anything close to a comprehensive treatment of internal sorting methods. For such a treatment, see Volume 3 of the monumental work of D. E. KNUTH (reference given at end of Chapter 2). KNUTH expounds about twenty-five sorting methods and claims that they are "only a fraction of the algorithms that have been devised so far." We shall study only a few methods in detail, chosen because:

➥ They are good—each one can be the best choice under some circumstances.

➥ They illustrate much of the variety appearing in the full range of methods.

➥ They are relatively easy to write and understand, without too many details to complicate their presentation.

A considerable number of variations of these methods also appear as exercises.

notation　Throughout this chapter we use the notation and classes set up in Chapters 6 and 7. Thus we shall sort lists of records into the order determined by keys associated with the records. The declarations for a list and the names assigned to various types and operations will be the same as in previous chapters.

In one case we must sometimes exercise special care: Two or more of the entries in a list may have the same key. In this case of duplicate keys, sorting might produce different orders of the entries with duplicate keys. If the order of entries with duplicate keys makes a difference to an application, then we must be especially careful in constructing sorting algorithms.

basic operations   In studying searching algorithms, it soon became clear that the total amount of work done was closely related to the number of comparisons of keys. The same observation is true for sorting algorithms, but sorting algorithms must also either change pointers or move entries around within the list, and therefore time spent this way is also important, especially in the case of large entries kept in a contiguous list. Our analyses will therefore concentrate on these two basic actions.

analysis   As before, both the worst-case performance and the average performance of a sorting algorithm are of interest. To find the average, we shall consider what would happen if the algorithm were run on all possible orderings of the list (with n entries, there are $n!$ such orderings altogether) and take the average of the results.

8.1.1 Sortable Lists

Throughout this chapter we shall be particularly concerned with the performance of our sorting algorithms. In order to optimize performance of a program for sorting a list, we shall need to take advantage of any special features of the list's implementation. For example, we shall see that some sorting algorithms work very efficiently on contiguous lists, but different implementations and different algorithms are needed to sort linked lists efficiently. Hence, to write efficient sorting programs, we shall need access to the private data members of the lists being sorted. Therefore, we shall add sorting functions as methods of our basic **List** data structures. The augmented list structure forms a new ADT that we shall call a **Sortable_List**. The class definition for a **Sortable_List** takes the following form.

```
template <class Record>
class Sortable_list: public List<Record> {
public:          //  Add prototypes for sorting methods here.
private:         //  Add prototypes for auxiliary functions here.
};
```

This definition shows that a **Sortable_list** is a **List** with extra sorting methods. As usual, the auxiliary functions of the class are functions, used to build up the methods, that are unavailable to client code. The base list class can be any of the **List** implementations of Chapter 6.

Record and Key   We use a template parameter class called **Record** to stand for entries of the **Sortable_list**. As in Chapter 7, we assume that the class **Record** has the following properties:

requirements   *Every **Record** has an associated key of type **Key**. A **Record** can be implicitly converted to the corresponding **Key**. Moreover, the keys (hence also the records) can be compared under the operations ' < ,' ' > ,' ' >= ,' ' <= ,' ' == ,' and ' != .'*

Any of the **Record** implementations discussed in Chapter 7 can be supplied, by a client, as the template parameter of a **Sortable_list**. For example, a program for testing our **Sortable_list** might simply declare:

Sortable_list<**int**> test_list;

Here, the client uses the type **int** to represent both records and their keys.

8.2 INSERTION SORT

8.2.1 Ordered Insertion

When first introducing binary search in Section 7.3, we mentioned that an ***ordered list*** is just a new abstract data type, which we defined as a list in which each entry has a key, and such that the keys are in order; that is, if entry i comes before entry j in the list, then the key of entry i is less than or equal to the key of entry j. We assume that the keys can be compared under the operations '<' and '>' (for example, keys could be numbers or instances of a class with overloaded comparison operators).

For ordered lists, we shall often use two new operations that have no counterparts for other lists, since they use keys rather than positions to locate the entry.

retrieval by key ➡ One operation *retrieves* an entry with a specified key from the ordered list.

insertion by key ➡ The second operation *inserts* a new entry into an ordered list by using the key in the new entry to determine where in the list to insert it.

Note that insertion is not uniquely specified if the list already contains an entry with the same key as the new entry, since the new entry could go into more than one position.

Retrieval by key from an ordered list is exactly the same as searching. We have already studied this problem in Chapter 7. Ordered insertion will serve as the basis for our first sorting method.

ordered insertion, contiguous list First, let us consider a contiguous list. In this case, it is necessary to move entries in the list to make room for the insertion. To find the position where the insertion is to be made, we must search. One method for performing ordered insertion into a contiguous list is first to do a binary search to find the correct location, then move the entries as required and insert the new entry. This method is left as an exercise. Since so much time is needed to move entries no matter how the search is done, it turns out in many cases to be just as fast to use sequential search as binary search. By doing sequential search from the *end* of the list, the search and the movement of entries can be combined in a single loop, thereby reducing the overhead required in the function.

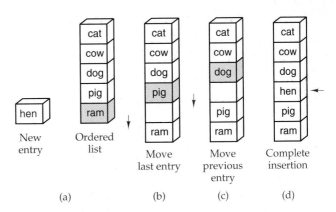

Figure 8.1. Ordered insertion

example An example of ordered insertion appears in Figure 8.1. We begin with the ordered list shown in part (a) of the figure and wish to insert the new entry **hen**. In contrast to the implementation-independent version of **insert** from Section 7.3, we shall start comparing keys at the *end* of the list, rather than at its beginning. Hence we first compare the new key **hen** with the last key **ram** shown in the colored box in part (a). Since **hen** comes before **ram**, we move **ram** one position down, leaving the empty position shown in part (b). We next compare **hen** with the key **pig** shown in the colored box in part (b). Again, **hen** belongs earlier, so we move **pig** down and compare **hen** with the key **dog** shown in the colored box in part (c). Since **hen** comes after **dog**, we have found the proper location and can complete the insertion as shown in part (d).

8.2.2 Sorting by Insertion

Our first sorting method for a list is based on the idea of insertion into an ordered list. To sort an unordered list, we think of removing its entries one at a time and then inserting each of them into an initially empty new list, always keeping the entries in the new list in the proper order according to their keys.

example This method is illustrated in Figure 8.2, which shows the steps needed to sort a list of six words. At each stage, the words that have not yet been inserted into the sorted list are shown in colored boxes, and the sorted part of the list is shown in white boxes. In the initial diagram, the first word **hen** is shown as sorted, since a list of length 1 is automatically ordered. All the remaining words are shown as unsorted at this stage. At each step of the process, the first unsorted word (shown in the uppermost gray box) is inserted into its proper position in the sorted part of the list. To make room for the insertion, some of the sorted words must be moved down the list. Each move of a word is shown as a colored arrow in Figure 8.2. By starting at the end of the sorted part of the list, we can move entries at the same time as we do comparisons to find where the new entry fits.

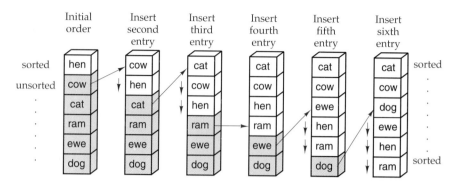

Figure 8.2. Example of insertion sort

The main step required to insert an entry denoted **current** into the sorted part of the list is shown in Figure 8.3. In the method that follows, we assume that the **class Sorted_list** is based on the contiguous **List** implementation of Section 6.2.2. Both the sorted list and the unsorted list occupy the same **List**, member array, which we recall from Section 6.2.2 is called **entry**. The variable **first_unsorted** marks the division between the sorted and unsorted parts of this array. Let us now write the algorithm.

```
template <class Record>
void Sortable_list<Record> :: insertion_sort( )
/* Post:  The entries of the Sortable_list have been rearranged so that the keys in
          all the entries are sorted into nondecreasing order.
   Uses:  Methods for the class Record; the contiguous List implementation of Chap-
          ter 6 */
{
   int first_unsorted;        //  position of first unsorted entry
   int position;              //  searches sorted part of list
   Record current;            //  holds the entry temporarily removed from list
   for (first_unsorted = 1; first_unsorted < count; first_unsorted++)
      if (entry[first_unsorted] < entry[first_unsorted − 1]) {
         position = first_unsorted;
         current = entry[first_unsorted];  //  Pull unsorted entry out of the list.
         do {                 //  Shift all entries until the proper position is found.
            entry[position] = entry[position − 1];
            position−−;                    //  position is empty.
         } while (position > 0 && entry[position − 1] > current);
         entry[position] = current;
      }
}
```

The action of the program is nearly self-explanatory. Since a list with only one entry is automatically sorted, the loop on **first_unsorted** starts with the second entry. If it is in the correct position, nothing needs to be done. Otherwise, the new entry

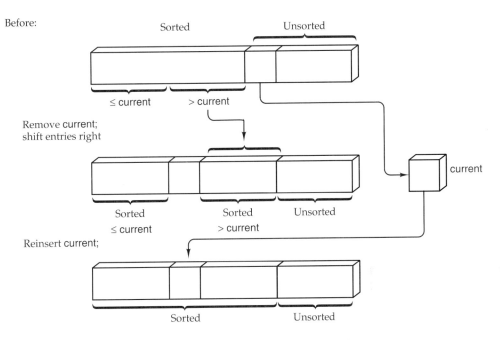

Figure 8.3. The main step of contiguous insertion sort

is pulled out of the list into the variable current, and the **do** ... **while** loop pushes entries one position down the list until the correct position is found, and finally current is inserted there before proceeding to the next unsorted entry. The case when current belongs in the first position of the list must be detected specially, since in this case there is no entry with a smaller key that would terminate the search. We treat this special case as the first clause in the condition of the **do** ... **while** loop.

8.2.3 Linked Version

algorithm

For a linked version of insertion sort, since there is no movement of data, there is no need to start searching at the *end* of the sorted sublist. Instead, we shall traverse the original list, taking one entry at a time and inserting it in the proper position in the sorted list. The pointer variable last_sorted will reference the end of the sorted part of the list, and last_sorted->next will reference the first entry that has not yet been inserted into the sorted sublist. We shall let first_unsorted also point to this entry and use a pointer current to search the sorted part of the list to find where to insert *first_unsorted. If *first_unsorted belongs before the current head of the list, then we insert it there. Otherwise, we move current down the list until first_unsorted->entry <= current->entry and then insert *first_unsorted before *current. To enable insertion before *current we keep a second pointer trailing in lock step one position closer to the head than current.

stopping the loop

A *sentinel* is an extra entry added to one end of a list to ensure that a loop will terminate without having to include a separate check. Since we have

$$last\_sorted\text{->}next = first\_unsorted,$$

the node *first_unsorted is already in position to serve as a sentinel for the search, and the loop moving current is simplified.

Finally, let us note that a list with 0 or 1 entry is already sorted, so that we can check these cases separately and thereby avoid trivialities elsewhere. The details appear in the following function and are illustrated in Figure 8.4.

```
template <class Record>
void Sortable_list<Record> :: insertion_sort()
/* Post:  The entries of the Sortable_list have been rearranged so that the keys in
          all the entries are sorted into nondecreasing order.
   Uses:  Methods for the class Record. The linked List implementation of Chapter
          6. */
{
   Node <Record> *first_unsorted,  //   the first unsorted node to be inserted
                 *last_sorted,     //   tail of the sorted sublist
                 *current,         //   used to traverse the sorted sublist
                 *trailing;        //   one position behind current
   if (head != NULL) {          //   Otherwise, the empty list is already sorted.
      last_sorted = head;       //   The first node alone makes a sorted sublist.
      while (last_sorted->next != NULL) {
         first_unsorted = last_sorted->next;
         if (first_unsorted->entry < head->entry) {
            //   Insert *first_unsorted at the head of the sorted list:
            last_sorted->next = first_unsorted->next;
            first_unsorted->next = head;
            head = first_unsorted;
         }
         else {
            //   Search the sorted sublist to insert *first_unsorted:
            trailing = head;
            current = trailing->next;
            while (first_unsorted->entry > current->entry) {
               trailing = current;
               current = trailing->next;
            }
            //   *first_unsorted now belongs between *trailing and *current.
            if (first_unsorted ==  current)
               last_sorted = first_unsorted;   //   already in right position
            else {
               last_sorted->next = first_unsorted->next;
               first_unsorted->next = current;
               trailing->next = first_unsorted;
            }
         }
      }
   }
}
```

Partially sorted:

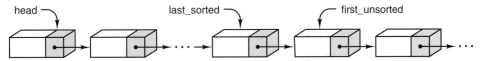

Case 1:   **first_unsorted* belongs at head of list

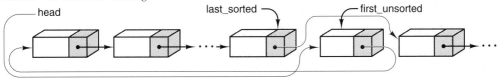

Case 2:   **first_unsorted* belongs between **trailing* and **current*

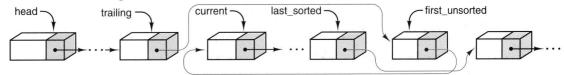

Figure 8.4. Trace of linked insertion sort

Even though the mechanics of the linked version are quite different from those of the contiguous version, you should be able to see that the basic method is the same. The only real difference is that the contiguous version searches the sorted sublist in reverse order, while the linked version searches it in increasing order of position within the list.

8.2.4 Analysis

assumptions

Since the basic ideas are the same, let us analyze only the performance of the contiguous version of the program. We also restrict our attention to the case when the list is initially in random order (meaning that all possible orderings of the keys are equally likely). When we deal with entry i, how far back must we go to insert it? There are i possible ways to move it: not moving it at all, moving it one position, up to moving it $i-1$ positions to the front of the list. Given randomness, these are equally likely. The probability that it need not be moved is thus $1/i$, in which case only one comparison of keys is done, with no moving of entries.

inserting one entry

The remaining case, in which entry i must be moved, occurs with probability $(i-1)/i$. Let us begin by counting the average number of iterations of the **do** ... **while** loop. Since all of the $i-1$ possible positions are equally likely, the average number of iterations is

$$\frac{1+2+\cdots+(i-1)}{i-1} = \frac{(i-1)i}{2(i-1)} = \frac{i}{2}.$$

(This calculation uses Theorem A.1 on page 647.) One key comparison and one assignment are done for each of these iterations, with one more key comparison done outside the loop, along with two assignments of entries. Hence, in this second case, entry i requires, on average, $\frac{1}{2}i + 1$ comparisons and $\frac{1}{2}i + 2$ assignments.

When we combine the two cases with their respective probabilities, we have

$$\frac{1}{i} \times 1 + \frac{i-1}{i} \times \left(\frac{i}{2} + 1\right) = \frac{i+1}{2}$$

comparisons and

$$\frac{1}{i} \times 0 + \frac{i-1}{i} \times \left(\frac{i}{2} + 2\right) = \frac{i+3}{2} - \frac{2}{i}$$

assignments.

inserting all entries   We wish to add these numbers from $i = 2$ to $i = n$, but to avoid complications in the arithmetic, we first use the big-O notation (see Section 7.6.3) to approximate each of these expressions by suppressing the terms bounded by a constant; that is, terms that are $O(1)$. We thereby obtain $\frac{1}{2}i + O(1)$ for both the number of comparisons and the number of assignments of entries. In making this approximation, we are really concentrating on the actions within the main loop and suppressing any concern about operations done outside the loop or variations in the algorithm that change the amount of work only by some bounded amount.

To add $\frac{1}{2}i + O(1)$ from $i = 2$ to $i = n$, we apply Theorem A.1 on page 647 (the sum of the integers from 1 to n). We also note that adding n terms, each of which is $O(1)$, produces as result that is $O(n)$. We thus obtain

$$\sum_{i=2}^{n} \left(\tfrac{1}{2}i + O(1)\right) = \tfrac{1}{2} \sum_{i=2}^{n} i + O(n) = \tfrac{1}{4}n^2 + O(n)$$

for both the number of comparisons of keys and the number of assignments of entries.

So far we have nothing with which to compare this number, but we can note that as n becomes larger, the contributions from the term involving n^2 become much larger than the remaining terms collected as $O(n)$. Hence as the size of the list grows, the time needed by insertion sort grows like the square of this size.

best and worst cases   The worst-case analysis of insertion sort will be left as an exercise. We can observe quickly that the best case for contiguous insertion sort occurs when the list is already in order, when insertion sort will do nothing except $n - 1$ comparisons of keys. We can now show that there is no sorting method that can possibly do better in its best case.

Theorem 8.1.   *Verifying that a list of n entries is in the correct order requires at least $n - 1$ comparisons of keys.*

Proof   Consider an arbitrary program that checks whether a list of n entries is in order or not (and perhaps sorts it if it is not). The program will first do some comparison of keys, and this comparison will involve some two entries from the list. Sometime later, at least one of these two entries must be compared with a third, or else there would be no way to decide where these two should be in the list relative to the third. Thus this second comparison involves only one new entry not previously in a comparison. Continuing in this way, we see that there must be another comparison involving some one of the first three entries and one new entry. Note that we are not necessarily selecting the comparisons in the order in which the algorithm does them. Thus, except for the first comparison, each one that we select involves only one new entry not previously compared. All n of the entries must enter some comparison, for there is no way to decide whether an entry is in the right position unless it is compared to at least one other entry. Thus to involve all n entries

end of proof   requires at least $n - 1$ comparisons, and the proof is complete.   ∎

With this theorem we find one of the advantages of insertion sort: It verifies that a list is correctly sorted as quickly as can be done. Furthermore, insertion sort remains an excellent method whenever a list is nearly in the correct order and few entries are many positions away from their correct locations.

Exercises 8.2

E1. By hand, trace through the steps insertion sort will use on each of the following lists. In each case, count the number of comparisons that will be made and the number of times an entry will be moved.

  (a) The following three words to be sorted alphabetically:

triangle   square   pentagon

  (b) The three words in part (a) to be sorted according to the number of sides of the corresponding polygon, in increasing order

  (c) The three words in part (a) to be sorted according to the number of sides of the corresponding polygon, in decreasing order

  (d) The following seven numbers to be sorted into increasing order:

26 33 35 29 19 12 22

  (e) The same seven numbers in a different initial order, again to be sorted into increasing order:

12 19 33 26 29 35 22

  (f) The following list of 14 names to be sorted into alphabetical order:

Tim Dot Eva Roy Tom Kim Guy Amy Jon Ann Jim Kay Ron Jan

E2. What initial order for a list of keys will produce the worst case for insertion sort in the contiguous version? In the linked version?

E3. How many key comparisons and entry assignments does contiguous insertion sort make in its worst case?

E4. Modify the linked version of insertion sort so that a list that is already sorted, or nearly so, will be processed rapidly.

Programming Projects 8.2

P1. Write a program that can be used to test and evaluate the performance of insertion sort and, later, other methods. The following outline should be used.

(a) Create several files of integers to be used to test sorting methods. Make files of several sizes, for example, sizes 20, 200, and 2000. Make files that are in order, in reverse order, in random order, and partially in order. By keeping all this test data in files (rather than generating it with random numbers each time the testing program is run), the same data can be used to test different sorting methods, and hence it will be easier to compare their performance.

test program for sorting

(b) Write a menu-driven program for testing various sorting methods. One option is to read a file of integers into a list. Other options will be to run one of various sorting methods on the list, to print the unsorted or the sorted list, and to quit. After the list is sorted and (perhaps) printed, it should be discarded so that testing a later sorting method will start with the same input data. This can be done either by copying the unsorted list to a second list and sorting that one, or by arranging the program so that it reads the data file again before each time it starts sorting.

(c) Include code in the program to calculate and print (1) the CPU time, (2) the number of comparisons of keys, and (3) the number of assignments of list entries during sorting a list. Counting comparisons can be achieved, as in Section 7.2, by overloading the comparison operators for the class **Key** so that they increment a counter. In a similar way we can overload the assignment operator for the class **Record** to keep a count of assignments of entries.

(d) Use the contiguous list package as developed in Section 6.2.2, include the contiguous version of insertion sort, and assemble statistics on the performance of contiguous insertion sort for later comparison with other methods.

(e) Use the linked list package as developed in Section 6.2.3, include the linked version of insertion sort, assemble its performance statistics, and compare them with contiguous insertion sort. Why is the count of entry assignments of little interest for this version?

binary insertion sort

P2. Rewrite the contiguous version of the function insertion_sort so that it uses binary search to locate where to insert the next entry. Compare the time needed to sort a list with that of the original function insertion_sort. Is it reasonable to use binary search in the linked version of insertion_sort? Why or why not?

P3. There is an even easier sorting method, which, instead of using two pointers to

scan sort

move through the list, uses only one. We can call it *scan sort*, and it proceeds by starting at one end and moving forward, comparing adjacent pairs of keys, until it finds a pair out of order. It then swaps this pair of entries and starts moving the other way, continuing to swap pairs until it finds a pair in the correct order. At this point it knows that it has moved the one entry as far back as necessary, so that the first part of the list is sorted, but, unlike insertion sort, it has forgotten how far forward has been sorted, so it simply reverses direction and sorts forward again, looking for a pair out of order. When it reaches the far end of the list, then it is finished.

(a) Write a C++ program to implement scan sort for contiguous lists. Your program should use only one position variable (other than the list's count member), one variable of type entry to be used in making swaps, and no other local variables.

(b) Compare the timings for your program with those of insertion_sort.

bubble sort

P4. A well-known algorithm called ***bubble sort*** proceeds by scanning the list from left to right, and whenever a pair of adjacent keys is found to be out of order, then those entries are swapped. In this first pass, the largest key in the list will have "bubbled" to the end, but the earlier keys may still be out of order. Thus the pass scanning for pairs out of order is put in a loop that first makes the scanning pass go all the way to count, and at each iteration stops it one position sooner. **(a)** Write a C++ function for bubble sort. **(b)** Find the performance of bubble sort on various kinds of lists, and compare the results with those for insertion sort.

8.3 SELECTION SORT

Insertion sort has one major disadvantage. Even after most entries have been sorted properly into the first part of the list, the insertion of a later entry may require that many of them be moved. All the moves made by insertion sort are moves of only one position at a time. Thus to move an entry 20 positions up the list requires 20 separate moves. If the entries are small, perhaps a key alone, or if the entries are in linked storage, then the many moves may not require excessive time. But if the entries are very large, records containing hundreds of components like personnel files or student transcripts, and the records must be kept in contiguous storage, then it would be far more efficient if, when it is necessary to move an entry, it could be moved immediately to its final position. Our next sorting method accomplishes this goal.

8.3.1 The Algorithm

An example of this sorting method appears in Figure 8.5, which shows the steps needed to sort a list of six words alphabetically. At the first stage, we scan the list to find the word that comes last in alphabetical order. This word, ram, is shown in a colored box. We then exchange this word with the word in the last position, as shown in the second part of Figure 8.5. Now we repeat the process on the shorter list obtained by omitting the last entry. Again the word that comes last is shown in a colored box; it is exchanged with the last entry still under consideration; and so we continue. The words that are not yet sorted into order are shown in gray boxes at each stage, except for the one that comes last, which is shown in a colored box. When the unsorted list is reduced to length 1, the process terminates.

Initial order   Sorted

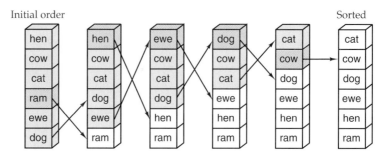

Colored box denotes largest unsorted key.
Gray boxes denote other unsorted keys.

Figure 8.5. Example of selection sort

This method translates into an algorithm called *selection sort*. The general
step in selection sort is illustrated in Figure 8.6. The entries with large keys will
be sorted in order and placed at the end of the list. The entries with smaller keys
are not yet sorted. We then look through the unsorted entries to find the one with
the largest key and swap it with the last unsorted entry. In this way, at each pass
through the main loop, one more entry is placed in its final position.

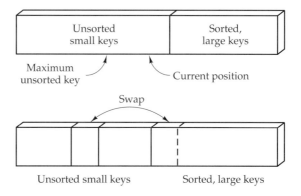

Figure 8.6. The general step in selection sort

8.3.2 Contiguous Implementation

Since selection sort minimizes data movement by putting at least one entry in its
final position at every pass, the algorithm is primarily useful for contiguous lists
with large entries for which movement of entries is expensive. If the entries are
small, or if the list is linked, so that only pointers need be changed to sort the list,
then insertion sort is usually faster than selection sort. We therefore give only a
contiguous version of selection sort. The algorithm uses an auxiliary Sortable_list
member function called max_key, which finds the maximum key on a part of the
list that is specified by parameters. The auxiliary function swap simply swaps the
two entries with the given indices. For convenience in the discussion to follow, we
write these two as separate auxiliary member functions:

```
template <class Record>
void Sortable_list<Record>::selection_sort()
/* Post:  The entries of the Sortable_list have been rearranged so that the keys in
          all the entries are sorted into nondecreasing order.
   Uses: max_key, swap. */
{
   for (int position = count - 1; position > 0; position--) {
      int max = max_key(0, position);
      swap(max, position);
   }
}
```

Note that when all entries but one are in the correct position in a list, then the remaining one must be also. Thus the **for** loop stops at 1.

```
template <class Record>
int Sortable_list<Record>::max_key(int low, int high)
/* Pre:   low and high are valid positions in the Sortable_list and low <= high.
   Post:  The position of the entry between low and high with the largest key is
          returned.
   Uses: The class Record. The contiguous List implementation of Chapter 6. */
{
   int largest, current;
   largest = low;
   for (current = low + 1; current <= high; current++)
      if (entry[largest] < entry[current])
         largest = current;
   return largest;
}
```

```
template <class Record>
void Sortable_list<Record>::swap(int low, int high)
/* Pre:   low and high are valid positions in the Sortable_list.
   Post:  The entry at position low is swapped with the entry at position high.
   Uses: The contiguous List implementation of Chapter 6. */
{
   Record temp;
   temp = entry[low];
   entry[low] = entry[high];
   entry[high] = temp;
}
```

8.3.3 Analysis

À propos of algorithm analysis, the most remarkable fact about this algorithm is that both of the loops that appear are **for** loops with completely predictable ranges, which means that we can calculate in advance exactly how many times they will iterate. In the number of comparisons it makes, selection sort pays no attention to

ordering unimportant the original ordering of the list. Hence for a list that is in nearly correct order to begin with, selection sort is likely to be much slower than insertion sort. On the other hand, selection sort does have the advantage of predictability: Its worst-case time will differ little from its best.

advantage of selection sort The primary advantage of selection sort regards data movement. If an entry is in its correct final position, then it will never be moved. Every time any pair of entries is swapped, then at least one of them moves into its final position, and therefore at most $n - 1$ swaps are done altogether in sorting a list of n entries. This is the very best that we can expect from any method that relies entirely on swaps to move its entries.

analysis We can analyze the performance of function selection_sort in the same way that it is programmed. The main function does nothing except some bookkeeping and calling the subprograms. The function swap is called $n - 1$ times, and each call does 3 assignments of entries, for a total count of $3(n - 1)$. The function max_key is called $n - 1$ times, with the length of the sublist ranging from n down to 2. If t is the number of entries on the part of the list for which it is called, then max_key does

comparison count for selection sort exactly $t - 1$ comparisons of keys to determine the maximum. Hence, altogether, there are $(n - 1) + (n - 2) + \cdots + 1 = \frac{1}{2}n(n - 1)$ comparisons of keys, which we approximate to $\frac{1}{2}n^2 + O(n)$.

8.3.4 Comparisons

Let us pause for a moment to compare the counts for selection sort with those for insertion sort. The results are:

	Selection	Insertion (average)
Assignments of entries	$3.0n + O(1)$	$0.25n^2 + O(n)$
Comparisons of keys	$0.5n^2 + O(n)$	$0.25n^2 + O(n)$

The relative advantages of the two methods appear in these numbers. When n becomes large, $0.25n^2$ becomes much larger than $3n$, and if moving entries is a slow process, then insertion sort will take far longer than will selection sort. But the amount of time taken for comparisons is, on average, only about half as much for insertion sort as for selection sort. If the list entries are small, so that moving them is not slow, then insertion sort will be faster than selection sort.

Exercises 8.3

E1. By hand, trace through the steps selection sort will use on each of the following lists. In each case, count the number of comparisons that will be made and the number of times an entry will be moved.

(a) The following three words to be sorted alphabetically:

triangle   square   pentagon

(b) The three words in part (a) to be sorted according to the number of sides of the corresponding polygon, in increasing order

(c) The three words in part (a) to be sorted according to the number of sides of the corresponding polygon, in decreasing order

(d) The following seven numbers to be sorted into increasing order:

$$26 \quad 33 \quad 35 \quad 29 \quad 19 \quad 12 \quad 22$$

(e) The same seven numbers in a different initial order, again to be sorted into increasing order:

$$12 \quad 19 \quad 33 \quad 26 \quad 29 \quad 35 \quad 22$$

(f) The following list of 14 names to be sorted into alphabetical order:

Tim Dot Eva Roy Tom Kim Guy Amy Jon Ann Jim Kay Ron Jan

count sort

E2. There is a simple algorithm called *count sort* that begins with an unsorted list and constructs a new, sorted list in a new array, provided we are guaranteed that all the keys in the original list are different from each other. Count sort goes through the list once, and for each record scans the list to count how many records have smaller keys. If c is this count, then the proper position in the sorted list for this key is c. Determine how many comparisons of keys will be done by count sort. Is it a better algorithm than selection sort?

Programming Projects 8.3

P1. Run the test program written in Project P1 of Section 8.2 (page 328), to compare selection sort with insertion sort (contiguous version). Use the same files of test data used with insertion sort.

P2. Write and test a linked version of selection sort.

8.4 SHELL SORT

As we have seen, in some ways insertion sort and selection sort behave in opposite ways. Selection sort moves the entries very efficiently but does many redundant comparisons. In its best case, insertion sort does the minimum number of comparisons, but it is inefficient in moving entries only one position at a time. Our goal now is to derive another method that avoids, as much as possible, the problems with both of these. Let us start with insertion sort and ask how we can reduce the number of times it moves an entry.

The reason why insertion sort can move entries only one position is that it compares only adjacent keys. If we were to modify it so that it first compares keys far apart, then it could sort the entries far apart. Afterward, the entries closer together would be sorted, and finally the increment between keys being compared would be reduced to 1, to ensure that the list is completely in order. This is the idea implemented in 1959 by D. L. SHELL in the sorting method bearing his name. This

diminishing increments

method is also sometimes called *diminishing-increment sort*. Before describing the algorithm formally, let us work through a simple example of sorting names.

example

Figure 8.7 shows what will happen when we first sort all names that are at distance 5 from each other (so there will be only two or three names on each such list), then re-sort the names using increment 3, and finally perform an ordinary insertion sort (increment 1).

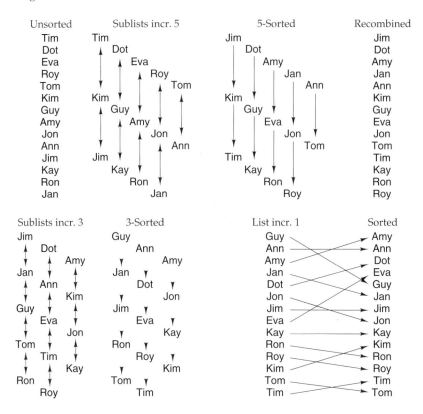

Figure 8.7. Example of Shell sort

You can see that, even though we make three passes through all the names, the early passes move the names close to their final positions, so that at the final pass (which does an ordinary insertion sort), all the entries are very close to their final positions so the sort goes rapidly.

choice of increments   There is no magic about the choice of 5, 3, and 1 as increments. Many other choices might work as well or better. It would, however, probably be wasteful to choose powers of 2, such as 8, 4, 2, and 1, since then the same keys compared on one pass would be compared again at the next, whereas by choosing numbers that are not multiples of each other, there is a better chance of obtaining new information from more of the comparisons. Although several studies have been made of Shell sort, no one has been able to prove that one choice of the increments is greatly superior to all others. Various suggestions have been made. If the increments are chosen close together, as we have done, then it will be necessary to make more passes, but each one will likely be quicker. If the increments decrease rapidly, then fewer but longer passes will occur. The only essential feature is that the final increment be 1, so that at the conclusion of the process, the list will be checked to be completely in order. For simplicity in the following algorithm, we start with increment == count, where we recall from Section 6.2.2 that count represents the size of the List being sorted, and at each pass reduce the increment with a statement

$$increment = increment/3 + 1;$$

Thus the increments used in the algorithm are not the same as those used in Figure 8.7.

　　We can now outline the algorithm for contiguous lists.

```
template <class Record>
void Sortable_list<Record>::shell_sort()
/* Post: The entries of the Sortable_list have been rearranged so that the keys in
         all the entries are sorted into nondecreasing order.
   Uses: sort_interval */
{
   int increment,              //   spacing of entries in sublist
       start;                  //   starting point of sublist
   increment = count;
   do {
      increment = increment/3 + 1;
      for (start = 0; start < increment; start++)
         sort_interval(start, increment);   //   modified insertion sort
   } while (increment > 1);
}
```

The auxiliary member function sort_interval(**int** start, **int** increment) is exactly the function insertion_sort, except that the list starts at the variable start instead of 0 and the increment between successive values is as given instead of 1. The details of modifying insertion_sort into sort_interval are left as an exercise.

optimized insertion sort　　Since the final pass through Shell sort has increment 1, Shell sort really is insertion sort optimized by the preprocessing stage of first sorting sublists using larger increments. Hence the proof that Shell sort works correctly is exactly the same as the proof that insertion sort works correctly. And, although we have good reason to think that the preprocessing stage will speed up the sorting considerably by eliminating many moves of entries by only one position, we have not actually proved that Shell sort will ever be faster than insertion sort.

analysis　　The analysis of Shell sort turns out to be exceedingly difficult, and to date, good estimates on the number of comparisons and moves have been obtained only under special conditions. It would be very interesting to know how these numbers depend on the choice of increments, so that the best choice might be made. But even without a complete mathematical analysis, running a few large examples on a computer will convince you that Shell sort is quite good. Very large empirical studies have been made of Shell sort, and it appears that the number of moves, when n is large, is in the range of $n^{1.25}$ to $1.6n^{1.25}$. This constitutes a substantial improvement over insertion sort.

Exercises 8.4

E1. By hand, sort the list of 14 names in the "unsorted" column of Figure 8.7 using Shell sort with increments of **(a)** 8, 4, 2, 1 and **(b)** 7, 3, 1. Count the number of comparisons and moves that are made in each case.

E2. Explain why Shell sort is ill suited for use with linked lists.

Programming Projects 8.4

P1. Rewrite the method insertion_sort to serve as the function sort_interval embedded in shell_sort.

P2. Test shell_sort with the program of Project P1 of Section 8.2 (page 328), using the same data files as for insertion sort, and compare the results.

8.5 LOWER BOUNDS

Now that we have seen a method that performs much better than our first attempts, it is appropriate to ask,

> *How fast is it possible to sort?*

To answer, we shall limit our attention (as we did when answering the same question for searching) to sorting methods that rely entirely on comparisons between pairs of keys to do the sorting.

comparison tree   Let us take an arbitrary sorting algorithm of this class and consider how it sorts a list of n entries. Imagine drawing its comparison tree. Sample comparison trees for insertion sort and selection sort applied to three numbers a, b, c are shown in Figure 8.8. As each comparison of keys is made, it corresponds to an interior vertex (drawn as a circle). The leaves (square nodes) show the order that the numbers have after sorting.

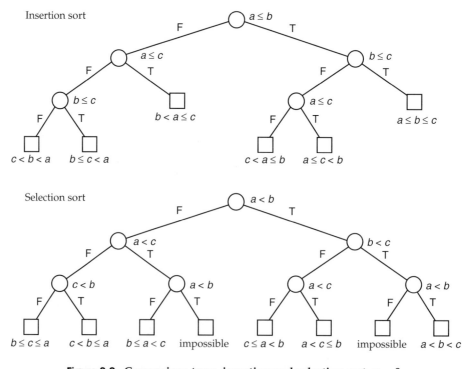

Figure 8.8. Comparison trees, insertion and selection sort, $n = 3$

Note that the diagrams show clearly that, on average, selection sort makes more comparisons of keys than insertion sort. In fact, selection sort makes redundant comparisons, repeating comparisons that have already been made.

The comparison tree of an arbitrary sorting algorithm displays several features *comparison trees:* of the algorithm. Its height is the largest number of comparisons that will be made *height and path length* and hence gives the worst-case behavior of the algorithm. The external path length, after division by the number of leaves, gives the average number of comparisons that the algorithm will do. The comparison tree displays all the possible sequences of comparisons that can be made as all the different paths from the root to the leaves. Since these comparisons control how the entries are rearranged during sorting, any two different orderings of the list must result in some different decisions, and hence different paths through the tree, which must then end in different leaves. The number of ways that the list containing n entries could originally have been ordered is $n!$ (see Section A.3.1), and thus the number of leaves in the tree must be at least $n!$. Lemma 7.5 now implies that the height of the tree is at least $\lceil \lg n! \rceil$ and its external path length is at least $n! \lg n!$. (Recall that $\lceil k \rceil$ means the smallest integer not less than k.) Translating these results into the number of comparisons, we obtain

Theorem 8.2   *Any algorithm that sorts a list of n entries by use of key comparisons must, in its worst case, perform at least $\lceil \lg n! \rceil$ comparisons of keys, and, in the average case, it must perform at least $\lg n!$ comparisons of keys.*

Stirling's formula (Theorem A.5 on page 658) gives an approximation to the factorial of an integer, which, after taking the base 2 logarithm, is

$$\lg n! \approx (n + \tfrac{1}{2})\lg n - (\lg e)n + \lg \sqrt{2\pi} + \frac{\lg e}{12n}.$$

approximating $\lg n!$ The constants in this expression have the approximate values

$$\lg e \approx 1.442695041 \quad \text{and} \quad \lg \sqrt{2\pi} \approx 1.325748069.$$

Stirling's approximation to $\lg n!$ is very close indeed, much closer than we shall ever need for analyzing algorithms. For almost all purposes, the following rough approximation will prove quite satisfactory:

$$\lg n! \approx (n + \tfrac{1}{2})(\lg n - 1\tfrac{1}{2}) + 2$$

and often we use only the approximation $\lg n! = n \lg n + O(n)$.

Before ending this section we should note that there are sometimes methods *other methods* for sorting that do not use comparisons and can be faster. For example, if you know in advance that you have 100 entries and that their keys are exactly the integers between 1 and 100 in some order, with no duplicates, then the best way to sort them is not to do any comparisons, but simply, if a particular entry has key i, then place it in location i. With this method we are (at least temporarily) regarding the entries to be sorted as being in a table rather than a list, and then we can use the key as an index to find the proper position in the table for each entry. Project P1 suggests an extension of this idea to an algorithm.

Exercises 8.5

E1. Draw the comparison trees for **(a)** insertion sort and **(b)** selection sort applied to four objects.

E2. **(a)** Find a sorting method for four keys that is optimal in the sense of doing the smallest possible number of key comparisons in its worst case. **(b)** Find how many comparisons your algorithm does in the average case (applied to four keys). Modify your algorithm to make it come as close as possible to achieving the lower bound of $\lg 4! \approx 4.585$ key comparisons. Why is it impossible to achieve this lower bound?

E3. Suppose that you have a shuffled deck of 52 cards, 13 cards in each of 4 suits, and you wish to sort the deck so that the 4 suits are in order and the 13 cards within each suit are also in order. Which of the following methods is fastest?

(a) Go through the deck and remove all the clubs; then sort them separately. Proceed to do the same for the diamonds, the hearts, and the spades.

(b) Deal the cards into 13 piles according to the rank of the card. Stack these 13 piles back together and deal into 4 piles according to suit. Stack these back together.

(c) Make only one pass through the cards, by placing each card in its proper position relative to the previously sorted cards.

Programming Projects 8.5

The sorting projects for this section are specialized methods requiring keys of a particular type, pseudorandom numbers between 0 and 1. Hence they are not intended to work with the testing program devised for other methods, nor to use the same data as the other methods studied in this chapter.

P1. Construct a list of n pseudorandom numbers strictly between 0 and 1. Suitable values for n are 10 (for debugging) and 500 (for comparing the results with other methods). Write a program to sort these numbers into an array via the following *interpolation sort*. First, clear the array (to all 0). For each number from the old list, multiply it by n, take the integer part, and look in that position of the table. If that position is 0, put the number there. If not, move left or right (according to the relative size of the current number and the one in its place) to find the position to insert the new number, moving the entries in the table over if necessary to make room (as in the fashion of insertion sort). Show that your algorithm will really sort the numbers correctly. Compare its running time with that of the other sorting methods applied to randomly ordered lists of the same size.

interpolation sort

P2. [suggested by B. Lee] Write a program to perform a linked distribution sort, as follows. Take the keys to be pseudorandom numbers between 0 and 1, as in the previous project. Set up an array of linked lists, and distribute the keys into the linked lists according to their magnitude. The linked lists can either be kept sorted as the numbers are inserted or sorted during a second pass, during which the lists are all connected together into one sorted list. Experiment to determine the optimum number of lists to use. (It seems that it works well to have enough lists so that the average length of each list is about 3.)

linked distribution sort

8.6 DIVIDE-AND-CONQUER SORTING

8.6.1 The Main Ideas

Making a fresh start is often a good idea, and we shall do so by forgetting (temporarily) almost everything that we know about sorting. Let us try to apply only one important principle that has shown up in the algorithms we have previously studied and that we already know from common experience: It is much easier to sort short lists than long ones. If the number of entries to be sorted doubles, then the work more than doubles (with insertion or selection sort it quadruples, roughly). Hence if we can find a way to divide the list into two roughly equal-sized lists and sort them separately, then we will save work. If, for example, you were working in a library and were given a thousand index cards to put in alphabetical order, then a good way would be to distribute them into piles according to the first letter and sort the piles separately.

shorter is easier

divide and conquer

Here again we have an application of the idea of dividing a problem into smaller but similar subproblems; that is, of *divide and conquer*.

First, we note that comparisons by computer are usually two-way branches, so we shall divide the entries to sort into two lists at each stage of the process.

What method, you may ask, should we use to sort the reduced lists? Since we have (temporarily) forgotten all the other methods we know, let us simply use the same method, divide and conquer, again, repeatedly subdividing the list. But we won't keep going forever: Sorting a list with only one entry doesn't take any work, even if we know no formal sorting methods.

In summary, let us informally outline divide-and-conquer sorting:

```
void Sortable_list :: sort( )
{
  if the list has length greater than 1 {
    partition the list into lowlist, highlist;
    lowlist.sort( );
    highlist.sort( );
    combine(lowlist, highlist);
  }
}
```

We still must decide how we are going to partition the list into two sublists and, after they are sorted, how we are going to combine the sublists into a single list. There are two methods, each of which works very well in different circumstances.

➡ *Mergesort*: In the first method, we simply chop the list into two sublists of sizes as nearly equal as possible and then sort them separately. Afterward, we carefully merge the two sorted sublists into a single sorted list. Hence this method is called ***mergesort***.

mergesort

➡ *Quicksort*: The second method does more work in the first step of partitioning the list into two sublists, and the final step of combining the sublists then becomes trivial. This method was invented and christened ***quicksort***

quicksort

by C. A. R. HOARE. To partition the list, we first choose some key from the list for which, we hope, about half the keys will come before and half after. We shall use the name *pivot* for this selected key. We next partition the entries so that all those with keys less than the pivot come in one sublist, and all those with greater keys come in another. Finally, then, we sort the two reduced lists separately, put the sublists together, and the whole list will be in order.

pivot

8.6.2 An Example

Before we refine our methods into detailed functions, let us work through a specific example. We take the following seven numbers to sort:

26   33   35   29   19   12   22.

1. Mergesort Example

convention: left list may be longer

The first step of mergesort is to chop the list into two. When (as in this example) the list has odd length, let us establish the convention of making the left sublist one entry larger than the right sublist. Thus we divide the list into

26   33   35   29   and   19   12   22

first half

and first consider the left sublist. It is again chopped in half as

26   33   and   35   29.

For each of these sublists, we again apply the same method, chopping each of them into sublists of one number each. Sublists of length one, of course, require no sorting. Finally, then, we can start to merge the sublists to obtain a sorted list. The sublists 26 and 33 merge to give the sorted list 26 33, and the sublists 35 and 29 merge to give 29 35. At the next step, we merge these two sorted sublists of length two to obtain a sorted sublist of length four,

26   29   33   35.

second half

Now that the left half of the original list is sorted, we do the same steps on the right half. First, we chop it into the sublists

19   12   and   22.

The first of these is divided into two sublists of length one, which are merged to give 12 19. The second sublist, 22, has length one, so it needs no sorting. It is now merged with 12 19 to give the sorted list

12   19   22.

Finally, the sorted sublists of lengths four and three are merged to produce

12   19   22   26   29   33   35.

The way that all these sublists and recursive calls are put together is shown by the recursion tree for mergesort drawn in Figure 8.9. The order in which the recursive calls occur is shown by the colored path. The numbers in each sublist passed to a recursive call are shown in black, and the numbers in their order after the merge is done are shown in color. The calls for which no further recursion is required (sublists of length 1) are the leaves of the tree and are drawn as squares.

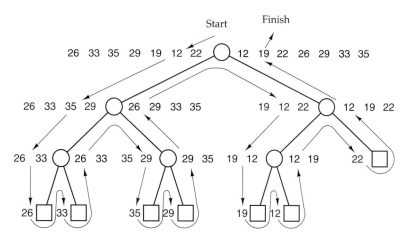

Figure 8.9. Recursion tree, mergesort of 7 numbers

2. Quicksort Example

Let us again work through the same example, this time applying quicksort and keeping careful account of the execution of steps from our outline of the method. *choice of pivot* To use quicksort, we must first decide, in order to partition the list into two pieces, what key to choose as the pivot. We are free to choose any number we wish, but, for consistency, we shall adopt a definite rule. Perhaps the simplest rule is to choose the first number in a list as the pivot, and we shall do so in this example. For practical applications, however, other choices are usually better than the first number.

partition Our first pivot, then, is 26, and the list partitions into sublists

$$19 \quad 12 \quad 22 \quad\quad \text{and} \quad\quad 33 \quad 35 \quad 29$$

consisting, respectively, of the numbers less than and greater than the pivot. We have left the order of the entries in the sublists unchanged from that in the original list, but this decision also is arbitrary. Some versions of quicksort put the pivot into one of the sublists, but we choose to place the pivot into neither sublist.

We now arrive at the next line of the outline, which tells us to sort the first sublist. We thus start the algorithm over again from the top, but this time applied to the shorter list

$$19 \quad 12 \quad 22.$$

lower half The pivot of this list is 19, which partitions its list into two sublists of one number each, 12 in the first and 22 in the second. With only one entry each, these sublists do not need sorting, so we arrive at the last line of the outline, whereupon we combine the two sublists with the pivot between them to obtain the sorted list

$$12 \quad 19 \quad 22.$$

Now the call to the sort function is finished for this sublist, so it returns whence it was called. It was called from within the sort function for the full list of seven numbers, so we now go on to the next line of that function.

inner and outer
function calls   We have now used the function twice, with the second instance occurring within the first instance. Note carefully that the two instances of the function are working on different lists and are as different from each other as is executing the same code twice within a loop. It may help to think of the two instances as having different colors, so that the instructions in the second (inner) call could be written out in full in place of the call, but in a different color, thereby clearly distinguishing them as a separate instance of the function. The steps of this process are illustrated in Figure 8.10.

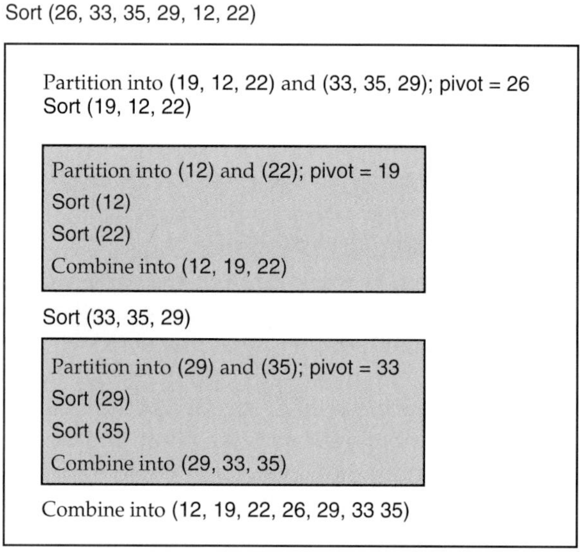

Sort (26, 33, 35, 29, 12, 22)

Partition into (19, 12, 22) and (33, 35, 29); pivot = 26
Sort (19, 12, 22)

Partition into (12) and (22); pivot = 19
Sort (12)
Sort (22)
Combine into (12, 19, 22)

Sort (33, 35, 29)

Partition into (29) and (35); pivot = 33
Sort (29)
Sort (35)
Combine into (29, 33, 35)

Combine into (12, 19, 22, 26, 29, 33 35)

Figure 8.10. Execution trace of quicksort

Returning to our example, we find the next line of the first instance of the function to be another call to sort another list, this time the three numbers

33   35   29.

upper half   As in the previous (inner) call, the pivot 33 immediately partitions the list, giving sublists of length one that are then combined to produce the sorted list

29   33   35.

Finally, this call to sort returns, and we reach the last line of the (outer) instance that sorts the full list. At this point, the two sorted sublists of length three are combined with the original pivot of 26 to obtain the sorted list

12   19   22   26   29   33   35.

recombine   After this step, the process is complete.

The easy way to keep track of all the calls in our quicksort example is to draw its recursion tree, as shown in Figure 8.11. The two calls to **sort** at each level are shown as the children of the vertex. The sublists of size 1 or 0, which need no sorting, are drawn as the leaves. In the other vertices (to avoid cluttering the diagram), we include only the pivot that is used for the call. It is, however, not hard to read all the numbers in each sublist (but not necessarily in their original order). The numbers in the sublist at each recursive call are the number at the corresponding vertex and those at all descendents of the vertex.

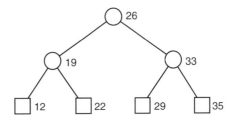

Figure 8.11. Recursion tree, quicksort of 7 numbers

example

If you are still uneasy about the workings of recursion, then you will find it helpful to pause and work through sorting the list of 14 names introduced in previous sections, using both mergesort and quicksort. As a check, Figure 8.12 provides the tree of calls for quicksort in the same abbreviated form used for the previous example. This tree is given for two versions, one where the pivot is the first key in each sublist, and one where the central key (center left for even-sized lists) is the pivot.

Exercises 8.6

E1. Apply quicksort to the list of seven numbers considered in this section, where the pivot in each sublist is chosen to be **(a)** the last number in the sublist and **(b)** the center (or left-center) number in the sublist. In each case, draw the tree of recursive calls.

E2. Apply mergesort to the list of 14 names considered for previous sorting methods:

> Tim Dot Eva Roy Tom Kim Guy Amy Jon Ann Jim Kay Ron Jan

E3. Apply quicksort to this list of 14 names, and thereby sort them by hand into alphabetical order. Take the pivot to be **(a)** the first key in each sublist and **(b)** the center (or left-center) key in each sublist. See Figure 8.12.

E4. In both divide-and-conquer methods, we have attempted to divide the list into two sublists of approximately equal size, but the basic outline of sorting by divide-and-conquer remains valid without equal-sized halves. Consider dividing the list so that one sublist has size 1. This leads to two methods, depending on whether the work is done in splitting one element from the list or in combining the sublists.

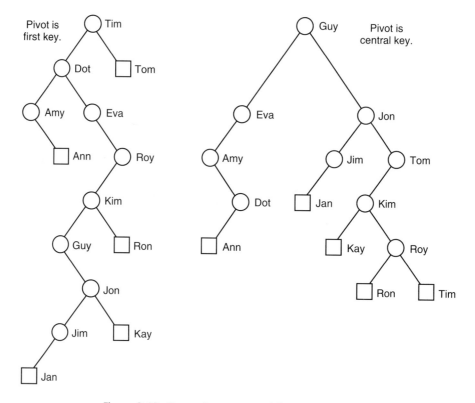

Figure 8.12. Recursion trees, quicksort of 14 names

(a) Split the list by finding the entry with the largest key and making it the sublist of size 1. After sorting the remaining entries, the sublists are combined easily by placing the entry with largest key last.

(b) Split off the last entry from the list. After sorting the remaining entries, merge this entry into the list.

Show that one of these methods is exactly the same method as insertion sort and the other is the same as selection sort.

8.7 MERGESORT FOR LINKED LISTS

Let us now turn to the writing of formal functions for each of our divide-and-conquer sorting methods. In the case of mergesort, we shall write a version for linked lists and leave the case of contiguous lists as an exercise. For quicksort, we shall do the reverse, writing the code only for contiguous lists. Both of these methods, however, work well for both contiguous and linked lists.

Mergesort is also an excellent method for *external sorting*; that is, for problems in which the data are kept on disks, not in high-speed memory.

8.7.1 The Functions

When we sort a linked list, we work by rearranging the links of the list and we avoid the creation and deletion of new nodes. In particular, our mergesort program must call a recursive function that works with subsets of nodes of the list being sorted. We call this recursive function recursive_merge_sort. Our primary implementation of mergesort simply passes a pointer to the first node of the list in a call to recursive_merge_sort.

main function

```
template <class Record>
void Sortable_list<Record>::merge_sort()
/* Post:  The entries of the sortable list have been rearranged so that their keys are
          sorted into nondecreasing order.
    Uses: The linked List implementation of Chapter 6 and recursive_merge_sort. */
{
  recursive_merge_sort(head);
}
```

Our outline of the basic method for mergesort translates directly into the following recursive sorting function.

```
template <class Record>
void Sortable_list<Record>::recursive_merge_sort(Node<Record> * &sub_list)
/* Post:  The nodes referenced by sub_list have been rearranged so that their keys
          are sorted into nondecreasing order. The pointer parameter sub_list is
          reset to point at the node containing the smallest key.
    Uses: The linked List implementation of Chapter 6; the functions divide_from,
          merge, and recursive_merge_sort. */
{
  if (sub_list != NULL && sub_list->next != NULL) {
    Node<Record> *second_half = divide_from(sub_list);
    recursive_merge_sort(sub_list);
    recursive_merge_sort(second_half);
    sub_list = merge(sub_list, second_half);
  }
}
```

Observe that the parameter sub_list in the function recursive_merge_sort is a reference to a pointer to a node. The reference is needed to allow the function to make a change to the calling argument.

The first subsidiary function called by recursive_merge_sort,

divide_from(Node<Record> *sub_list)

takes the list referenced by the parameter sub_list and divides it in half, by replacing its middle link by a NULL pointer. The function returns a pointer to the first node of the second half of the original sublist.

template <**class** Record>
Node<Record> *Sortable_list<Record> :: divide_from(Node<Record> *sub_list)
/* **Post:** *The list of nodes referenced by* sub_list *has been reduced to its first half,
          and a pointer to the first node in the second half of the sublist is returned.
          If the sublist has an odd number of entries, then its first half will be one
          entry larger than its second.*
    Uses: *The linked* List *implementation of Chapter 6.* */
{
    Node<Record> *position,   //   *traverses the entire list*
                 *midpoint,   //   *moves at half speed of* position *to midpoint*
                 *second_half;
    if ((midpoint = sub_list) == NULL) **return** NULL;   //   *List is empty.*
    position = midpoint->next;
    while (position != NULL) { //   *Move* position *twice for* midpoint's *one move.*
        position = position->next;
        if (position != NULL) {
            midpoint = midpoint->next;
            position = position->next;
        }
    }
    second_half = midpoint->next;
    midpoint->next = NULL;
    return second_half;
}

The second auxiliary function,

Node<Record> *merge(Node<Record> *first, Node<Record> *second)

merges the lists of nodes referenced by first and second, returning a pointer to
the node of the merged list that has the smallest key. Most of the work in this
function consists of comparing a pair of keys, one from each list, and adjoining
the appropriate one to the merged list. Special care, however, is required at both

the start and the end of the list. At the end, one of the lists first and second may
be exhausted before the other, in which case we need only adjoin the rest of the
remaining list to the merged list. At the start, we must remember a pointer to the
first node of the merged list, which is to be returned as the function value.

To keep track of the start of the merged list without needing to consider several
special cases, our merge function declares a temporary Node called combined,
which we place at the start of the merged list before we look at any actual keys.
(That is, we force the merged list to begin with one node already in it.) Then the
actual nodes can be inserted without considering special cases. At the conclusion,
combined will contain a pointer to the first actual node of the merged list, so we can

then return this pointer. The temporary node combined is called a *dummy node*
since it contains no actual data, it is used only to simplify the pointer manipulations.
        The action of function merge is illustrated in Figure 8.13.

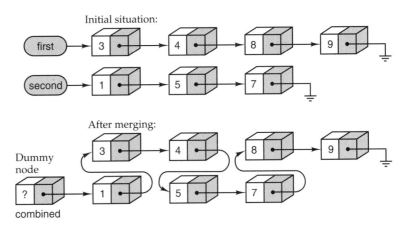

Figure 8.13. Merging two sorted linked lists

merge two sorted
linked lists

```
template <class Record>
Node<Record> *Sortable_list<Record> :: merge(Node<Record> *first,
                                             Node<Record> *second)
/* Pre:   first and second point to ordered lists of nodes.
   Post:  A pointer to an ordered list of nodes is returned. The ordered list contains
          all entries that were referenced by first and second. The original lists of
          nodes referenced by first and second are no longer available.
   Uses: Methods for Record class; the linked List implementation of Chapter 6. */
{
   Node<Record> *last_sorted;    //   points to the last node of sorted list
   Node<Record> combined;        //   dummy first node, points to merged list
   last_sorted = &combined;
   while (first != NULL && second != NULL) {  //   Attach node with smaller key
      if (first->entry <= second->entry) {
         last_sorted->next = first;
         last_sorted = first;
         first = first->next;     //   Advance to the next unmerged node.
      }
      else {
         last_sorted->next = second;
         last_sorted = second;
         second = second->next;
      }
   }
   //   After one list ends, attach the remainder of the other.
   if (first == NULL)
      last_sorted->next = second;
   else
      last_sorted->next = first;
   return combined.next;
}
```

8.7.2 Analysis of Mergesort

Now that we have a working function for mergesort, it is time to pause and determine its behavior, so that we can make reasonable comparisons with other sorting methods. As with other algorithms on linked lists, we need not be concerned with the time needed to move entries. We concentrate instead on the number of comparisons of keys that the function will do.

1. Counting Comparisons

merge function

Comparison of keys is done at only one place in the complete mergesort function. This place is within the main loop of the merge function. After each comparison, one of the two nodes is sent to the output list. Hence the number of comparisons certainly cannot exceed the number of entries being merged. To find the total lengths of these lists, let us again consider the recursion tree of the algorithm, which for simplicity we show in Figure 8.14 for a case when $n = 2^m$ is a power of 2.

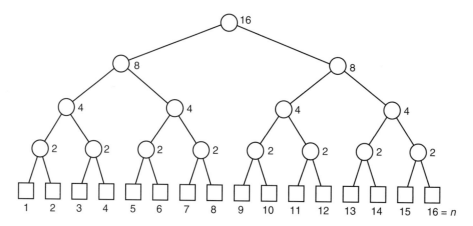

Figure 8.14. Lengths of sublist merges

It is clear from the tree of Figure 8.14 that the total lengths of the lists on each level is precisely n, the total number of entries. In other words, every entry is treated in precisely one merge on each level. Hence the total number of comparisons done on each level cannot exceed n. The number of levels, excluding the leaves (for which no merges are done), is $\lg n$ rounded up to the next smallest integer, the ceiling $\lceil \log n \rceil$. The number of comparisons of keys done by mergesort on a list of n entries, therefore, is no more than $\lceil n \lg n \rceil$.

2. Contrast with Insertion Sort

Recall (Section 8.2.4) that insertion sort does more than $\frac{1}{4}n^2$ comparisons of keys, on average, in sorting n entries. As soon as n becomes greater than 16, $\lg n$ becomes less than $\frac{1}{4}n$. When n is of practical size for sorting a list, $\lg n$ is far less than $\frac{1}{4}n$, and therefore the number of comparisons done by mergesort is far less than the number done by insertion sort. When $n = 1024$, for example, $\lg n = 10$, so that the bound on comparisons for mergesort is 10,240, whereas the average number that insertion sort will do is more than 250,000. A problem requiring a minute of computer time using insertion sort will probably require only a second or two using mergesort.

n lg n

The appearance of the expression $n \lg n$ in the preceding calculation is by no means accidental, but relates closely to the lower bounds established in Section 8.5, where it was proved that any sorting method that uses comparisons of keys must do at least

$$\lg n! \approx n \lg n - 1.44n + O(\log n)$$

comparisons of keys. When n is large, the first term of this expression becomes more important than what remains. We have now found, in mergesort, an algorithm that comes within reach of this lower bound.

3. Improving the Count

By being somewhat more careful we can, in fact, obtain a more accurate count of comparisons made by mergesort, which will show that its actual performance comes even closer to the best possible number of comparisons of keys allowed by the lower bound.

First, let us observe that merging two lists of combined size k never requires k comparisons, but instead at most $k - 1$, since after the second largest key has been put out, there is nothing left to which to compare the largest key, so it goes out without another comparison. Hence we should reduce our total count of comparisons by 1 for each merge that is performed. The total number of merges is essentially

$$\frac{n}{2} + \frac{n}{4} + \frac{n}{8} + \cdots + 1 = n - 1.$$

(This calculation is exact when n is a power of 2 and is a good approximation otherwise.) The total number of key comparisons done by mergesort is therefore less than

$$n \lg n - n + 1.$$

Second, we should note that it is possible for one of the two lists being merged to be finished before the other, and then all entries in the second list will go out with no further comparisons, so that the number of comparisons may well be less than we have calculated. Every element of one list, for example, might precede every element of the second list, so that all elements of the second list would come out using no comparisons. The exercises outline a proof that the total count can be reduced, on average, to

improved count

$$n \lg n - 1.1583n + 1,$$

and the correct coefficient of n is likely close to -1.25. We thus see that, not only is the leading term as small as the lower bound permits, but the second term is also quite close. By refining the merge function even more, the method can be brought within a few percent of the theoretically optimal number of comparisons (see the references).

4. Conclusions

advantages of linked mergesort

From these remarks, it may appear that mergesort is the ultimate sorting method, and, indeed, for linked lists in random order, it is difficult to surpass. We must remember, however, that considerations other than comparing keys are important. The program we have written spends significant time finding the center of the list, so that it can break it in half. The exercises discuss one method for saving some of this time. The linked version of mergesort uses space efficiently. It needs no large auxiliary arrays or other lists, and since the depth of recursion is only $\lg n$, the amount of space needed to keep track of the recursive calls is very small.

5. Contiguous Mergesort

For contiguous lists, unfortunately, mergesort is not such an unqualified success. The difficulty is in merging two contiguous lists without substantial expense in one of

three-way trade-off for merging

➡ space,

➡ computer time, or

➡ programming effort.

The first and most straightforward way to merge two contiguous lists is to use an auxiliary array large enough to hold the combined list and copy the entries into the array as the lists are merged. This method requires extra space that is $\Theta(n)$. For a second method, we could put the sublists to be merged next to each other, forget the amount of order they already have, and use a method like insertion sort to put the combined list into order. This approach uses almost no extra space but uses computer time proportional to n^2, compared to time proportional to n for a good merging algorithm. Finally (see the references), algorithms have been invented that will merge two contiguous lists in time proportional to n while using only a small, fixed amount of extra space. These algorithms, however, are quite complicated.

Exercises 8.7

E1. An article in a professional journal stated, "This recursive process [mergesort] takes time $O(n \log n)$, and so runs 64 times faster than the previous method [insertion sort] when sorting 256 numbers." Criticize this statement.

E2. The count of key comparisons in merging is usually too high, since it does not account for the fact that one list may be finished before the other. It might happen, for example, that all entries in the first list come before any in the second list, so that the number of comparisons is just the length of the first list. For this exercise, assume that all numbers in the two lists are different and that all possible arrangements of the numbers are equally likely.

    (a) Show that the average number of comparisons performed by our algorithm to merge two ordered lists of length 2 is $\frac{8}{3}$. [*Hint:* Start with the ordered list 1, 2, 3, 4. Write down the six ways of putting these numbers into two ordered lists of length 2, and show that four of these ways will use 3 comparisons, and two will use 2 comparisons.]

(b) Show that the average number of comparisons done to merge two ordered lists of length 3 is 4.5.

(c) Show that the average number of comparisons done to merge two ordered lists of length 4 is 6.4.

(d) Use the foregoing results to obtain the improved total count of key comparisons for mergesort.

(e) Show that, as m tends to infinity, the average number of comparisons done to merge two ordered lists of length m approaches $2m - 2$.

fixed-space linear-time merging

E3. [*Very challenging*] The straightforward method for merging two contiguous lists, by building the merged list in a separate array, uses extra space proportional to the number of entries in the two lists but can be written to run efficiently, with time proportional to the number of entries. Try to devise a merging method for contiguous lists that will require as little extra space as possible but that will still run in time (linearly) proportional to the number of entries in the lists. [There is a solution using only a small, constant amount of extra space. See the references.]

Programming Projects 8.7

P1. Implement mergesort for linked lists on your computer. Use the same conventions and the same test data used for implementing and testing the linked version of insertion sort. Compare the performance of mergesort and insertion sort for short and long lists, as well as for lists nearly in correct order and in random order.

P2. Our mergesort program for linked lists spends significant time locating the center of each sublist, so that it can be broken in half. Implement the following modification that will save some of this time. Rewrite the divide_from function to use a second parameter giving the length of original list of nodes. Use this to simplify and speed up the subdivision of the lists. What modifications are needed in the functions merge_sort() and recursive_merge_sort()?

natural mergesort

P3. Our mergesort function pays little attention to whether or not the original list was partially in the correct order. In ***natural mergesort*** the list is broken into sublists at the end of an increasing sequence of keys, instead of arbitrarily at its halfway point. This exercise requests the implementation of two versions of natural mergesort.

one sorted list

(a) In the first version, the original list is traversed only once, and only two sublists are used. As long as the order of the keys is correct, the nodes are placed in the first sublist. When a key is found out of order, the first sublist is ended and the second started. When another key is found out of order, the second sublist is ended, and the second sublist merged into the first. Then the second sublist is repeatedly built again and merged into the first. When the end of the original list is reached, the sort is finished. This first version is simple to program, but as it proceeds, the first sublist is likely to become much longer than the second, and the performance of the function will degenerate toward that of insertion sort.

several sorted lists

(b) The second version ensures that the lengths of sublists being merged are closer to being equal and, therefore, that the advantages of divide and conquer are fully used. This method keeps a (small) auxiliary array containing (1) the lengths and (2) pointers to the heads of the ordered sublists that are not yet merged. The entries in this array should be kept in order according to the length of sublist. As each (naturally ordered) sublist is split from the original list, it is put into the auxiliary array. If there is another list in the array whose length is between half and twice that of the new list, then the two are merged, and the process repeated. When the original list is exhausted, any remaining sublists in the array are merged (smaller lengths first) and the sort is finished.

YOU Make The CALL

There is nothing sacred about the ratio of 2 in the criterion for merging sublists. Its choice merely ensures that the number of entries in the auxiliary array cannot exceed $\lg n$ (prove it!). A smaller ratio (required to be greater than 1) will make the auxiliary table larger, and a larger ratio will lessen the advantages of divide and conquer. Experiment with test data to find a good ratio to use.

contiguous mergesort   **P4.** Devise a version of mergesort for contiguous lists. The difficulty is to produce a function to merge two sorted lists in contiguous storage. It is necessary to use some additional space other than that needed by the two lists. The easiest solution is to use two arrays, each large enough to hold all the entries in the two original lists. The two sorted sublists occupy different parts of the same array. As they are merged, the new list is built in the second array. After the merge is complete, the new list can, if desired, be copied back into the first array. Otherwise, the roles of the two arrays can be reversed for the next stage.

8.8 QUICKSORT FOR CONTIGUOUS LISTS

We now turn to the method of quicksort, in which the list is first partitioned into lower and upper sublists for which all keys are, respectively, less than some pivot key or greater than the pivot key. Quicksort can be developed for linked lists with little difficulty, and doing so will be pursued as a project. The most important applications of quicksort, however, are to contiguous lists, where it can prove to be very fast and where it has the advantage over contiguous mergesort of not requiring a choice between using substantial extra space for an auxiliary array or investing great programming effort in implementing a complicated and difficult merge algorithm.

8.8.1 The Main Function

Our task in developing contiguous quicksort consists of writing an algorithm for partitioning entries in a list by use of a pivot key, swapping the entries within the list so that all those with keys before the pivot come first, then the entry with the pivot key, and then the entries with larger keys. We shall let the variable pivot_position store the position of the pivot in the partitioned list.

Since the partitioned sublists are kept in the same array, in the proper relative positions, the final step of combining sorted sublists is completely vacuous and thus is omitted from the function.

To apply the sorting function recursively to sublists, the bounds **low** and **high** of the sublists need to be parameters for the function. Our prior sorting functions, however, have no parameters, so for consistency of notation we do the recursion in a function **recursive_quick_sort** that is invoked by the method **quick_sort**, which has no parameters.

main function
quick_sort

```
template <class Record>
void Sortable_list<Record> :: quick_sort( )
/* Post: The entries of the Sortable_list have been rearranged so that their keys
         are sorted into nondecreasing order.
    Uses: The contiguous List implementation of Chapter 6, recursive_quick_sort. */
{
   recursive_quick_sort(0, count − 1);
}
```

The actual quicksort function for contiguous lists is then

recursive function,
recursive_quick_sort

```
template <class Record>
void Sortable_list<Record> :: recursive_quick_sort(int low, int high)
/* Pre:  low and high are valid positions in the Sortable_list.
   Post: The entries of the Sortable_list have been rearranged so that their keys
         are sorted into nondecreasing order.
   Uses: The contiguous List implementation of Chapter 6, recursive_quick_sort,
         and partition. */
{
   int pivot_position;
   if (low < high) {              //   Otherwise, no sorting is needed.
      pivot_position = partition(low, high);
      recursive_quick_sort(low, pivot_position − 1);
      recursive_quick_sort(pivot_position + 1, high);
   }
}
```

8.8.2 Partitioning the List

Now we must construct the function **partition**. There are several strategies that we might use (one of which is suggested as an exercise), strategies that sometimes are faster than the algorithm we develop but that are more intricate and difficult to get correct. The algorithm we develop is much simpler and easier to understand, and it is certainly not slow; in fact, it does the smallest possible number of key comparisons of any partitioning algorithm.

1. Algorithm Development

Given a pivot value, we must rearrange the entries of the list and compute an index, pivot_position, so that pivot is at pivot_position, all entries to its left have keys less than **pivot**, and all entries to its right have larger keys. To allow for the possibility that more than one entry has key equal to **pivot**, we insist that the entries to the left of **pivot_position** have keys strictly less than **pivot**, and the entries to its right have keys greater than or equal to **pivot**, as shown in the following diagram:

goal (postcondition)

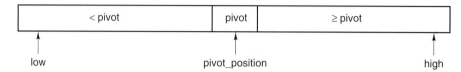

To reorder the entries this way, we must compare each key to the pivot. We shall use a **for** loop (running on a variable i) to do this. We shall use a second variable **last_small** such that all entries at or before location **last_small** have keys less than **pivot**. Suppose that **pivot** starts in the first position, and let us leave it there temporarily. Then in the middle of the loop the list has the following property:

loop invariant

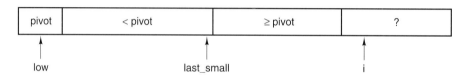

When the function inspects entry i, there are two cases. If the entry is greater than or equal to **pivot**, then i can be increased and the list still has the required property. If the entry is less than **pivot**, then we restore the property by increasing **last_small** and swapping that entry (the first of those at least **pivot**) with entry i, as shown in the following diagrams:

restore the invariant

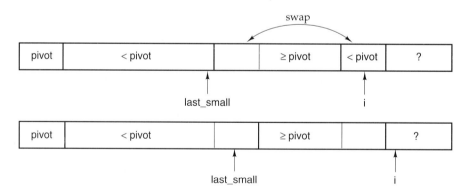

When the loop terminates, we have the situation:

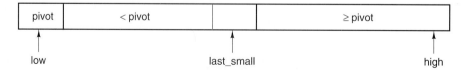

final position   and we then need only swap the pivot from position **low** to position **last_small** to obtain the desired final arrangement.

2. Choice of Pivot

We are not bound to the choice of the first entry in the list as the pivot; we can choose any entry we wish and swap it with the first entry before beginning the loop that partitions the list. In fact, the first entry is often a poor choice for pivot, since if the list is already sorted, then the first key will have no others less than it, and so one of the sublists will be empty. Hence, let us instead choose a pivot near the center of the list, in the hope that our choice will partition the keys so that about half come on each side of the pivot.

pivot from center

3. Coding

With these decisions, we obtain the following function, in which we use the **swap** function from Section 8.3.2 (page 331). For convenience of reference we also include the property that holds during iteration of the loop as an assertion (loop invariant) in the function.

```
template <class Record>
int Sortable_list<Record> :: partition(int low, int high)
/* Pre:   low and high are valid positions of the Sortable_list, with low <= high.
   Post:  The center (or left center) entry in the range between indices low and
          high of the Sortable_list has been chosen as a pivot. All entries of the
          Sortable_list between indices low and high, inclusive, have been rear-
          ranged so that those with keys less than the pivot come before the pivot
          and the remaining entries come after the pivot. The final position of the
          pivot is returned.
   Uses:  swap(int i, int j) (interchanges entries in positions i and j of a Sortable_list),
          the contiguous List implementation of Chapter 6, and methods for the
          class Record. */
{
  Record pivot;
  int i,                     //  used to scan through the list
      last_small;            //  position of the last key less than pivot
  swap(low, (low + high)/2);
  pivot = entry[low];        //  First entry is now pivot.
  last_small = low;
  for (i = low + 1; i <= high; i++)
/* At the beginning of each iteration of this loop, we have the following conditions:
          If low < j <= last_small then entry[j].key < pivot.
          If last_small < j < i then entry[j].key >= pivot. */
    if (entry[i] < pivot) {
      last_small = last_small + 1;
      swap(last_small, i);   //  Move large entry to right and small to left.
    }
  swap(low, last_small);     //  Put the pivot into its proper position.
  return last_small;
}
```

8.8.3 Analysis of Quicksort

It is now time to examine the quicksort algorithm carefully, to determine when it works well, when it does not, and how much computation it performs.

1. Choice of Pivot

Our choice of a key at the center of the list to be the pivot is arbitrary. This choice may succeed in dividing the list nicely in half, or we may be unlucky and find that one sublist is much larger than the other. Some other methods for choosing the pivot are considered in the exercises. An extreme case for our method occurs for the following list, where every one of the pivots selected turns out to be the largest *worst case* key in its sublist:

$$2 \quad 4 \quad 6 \quad 7 \quad 3 \quad 1 \quad 5$$

Check it out, using the **partition** function in the text. When quicksort is applied to this list, its label will appear to be quite a misnomer, since at the first recursion the nonempty sublist will have length 6, at the second 5, and so on.

If we were to choose the pivot as the first key or the last key in each sublist, then the extreme case would occur when the keys are in their natural order or in their reverse order. These orders are more likely to happen than some random order, and therefore choosing the first or last key as pivot is likely to cause problems.

2. Count of Comparisons and Swaps

Let us determine the number of comparisons and swaps that contiguous quicksort makes. Let $C(n)$ be the number of comparisons of keys made by quicksort when applied to a list of length n, and let $S(n)$ be the number of swaps of entries. We have $C(1) = C(0) = 0$. The partition function compares the pivot with every other key in the list exactly once, and thus the function **partition** accounts for exactly $n - 1$ key comparisons. If one of the two sublists it creates has length r, then the other sublist will have length exactly $n - r - 1$. The number of comparisons done in the two recursive calls will then be $C(r)$ and $C(n - r - 1)$. Thus we have

total number of comparisons

$$C(n) = n - 1 + C(r) + C(n - r - 1).$$

To solve this equation we need to know r. In fact, our notation is somewhat deceptive, since the values of $C(\ )$ depend not only on the length of the list but also on the exact ordering of the entries in it. Thus we shall obtain different answers in different cases, depending on the ordering.

3. Comparison Count, Worst Case

First, consider the worst case for comparisons. We have already seen that this occurs when the pivot fails to split the list at all, so that one sublist has $n - 1$ entries and the other is empty. In this case, since $C(0) = 0$, we obtain $C(n) = n - 1 + C(n - 1)$. An *recurrence relation* expression of this form is called a ***recurrence relation*** because it expresses its answer in terms of earlier cases of the same result. We wish to solve the recurrence, which means to find an equation for $C(n)$ that does not involve $C(\ )$ on the other side.

Various (sometimes difficult) methods are needed to solve recurrence relations, but in this case we can do it easily by starting at the bottom instead of the top:

$$
\begin{aligned}
C(1) &= 0. \\
C(2) &= 1 + C(1) &&= 1. \\
C(3) &= 2 + C(2) &&= 2 + 1. \\
C(4) &= 3 + C(3) &&= 3 + 2 + 1. \\
&\ \ \vdots &&\ \ \vdots \\
C(n) &= n - 1 + C(n - 1) &&= (n - 1) + (n - 2) + \cdots + 2 + 1 \\
& &&= \tfrac{1}{2}(n - 1)n = \tfrac{1}{2}n^2 - \tfrac{1}{2}n.
\end{aligned}
$$

In this calculation we have applied Theorem A.1 on page 647 to obtain the sum of the integers from 1 to $n - 1$.

selection sort   Recall that selection sort makes about $\tfrac{1}{2}n^2 - \tfrac{1}{2}n$ key comparisons, and making too many comparisons was the weak point of selection sort (as compared with insertion sort). Hence in its worst case, quicksort is as bad as the worst case of selection sort.

4. Swap Count, Worst Case

Next let us determine how many times quicksort will swap entries, again in its worst case. The partition function does one swap inside its loop for each key less than the pivot and two swaps outside its loop. In its worst case, the pivot is the largest key in the list, so the partition function will then make $n + 1$ swaps. With $S(n)$ the total number of swaps on a list of length n, we then have the recurrence

$$S(n) = n + 1 + S(n - 1)$$

in the worst case. The partition function is called only when $n \geq 2$, and $S(2) = 3$ in the worst case. Hence, as in counting comparisons, we can solve the recurrence by working downward, and we obtain

answer $S(n) = (n + 1) + n + \cdots + 3 = \tfrac{1}{2}(n + 1)(n + 2) - 3 = 0.5n^2 + 1.5n - 1$

swaps in the worst case.

5. Comparison with Insertion Sort and Selection Sort

In its worst case, contiguous insertion sort must make about twice as many comparisons and assignments of entries as it does in its average case, giving a total of $0.5n^2 + O(n)$ for each operation. Each swap in quicksort requires three assignments of entries, so quicksort in its worst case does $1.5n^2 + O(n)$ assignments, or, for large n, about three times as many as insertion sort. But moving entries was the weak point of insertion sort in comparison to selection sort. Hence, in its worst case, quicksort (so-called) is worse than the poor aspect of insertion sort, and, in *poor worst-case* regard to key comparisons, it is also as bad as the poor aspect of selection sort. *behavior* Indeed, in the worst-case analysis, quicksort is a disaster, and its name is nothing less than false advertising.

It must be for some other reason that quicksort was not long ago consigned to the scrap heap of programs that never worked. The reason is the *average* behavior of quicksort when applied to lists in random order, which turns out to be one of the best of any sorting methods (using key comparisons and applied to contiguous lists) yet known!

excellent average-case behavior

8.8.4 Average-Case Analysis of Quicksort

To do the average-case analysis, we shall assume that all possible orderings of the list are equally likely, and for simplicity, we take the keys to be just the integers from 1 to n.

1. Counting Swaps

When we select the pivot in the function **partition**, it is equally likely to be any one of the keys. Denote by p whatever key is selected as pivot. Then after the partition, key p is guaranteed to be in position p, since the keys $1, \ldots, p - 1$ are all to its left and $p + 1, \ldots, n$ are to its right.

The number of swaps that will have been made in one call to **partition** is $p + 1$, consisting of one swap in the loop for each of the $p - 1$ keys less than p and two swaps outside the loop. Let us denote by $S(n)$ the average number of swaps done by quicksort on a list of length n and by $S(n, p)$ the average number of swaps on a list of length n where the pivot for the first partition is p. We have now shown that, for $n \geq 2$,

$$S(n, p) = (p + 1) + S(p - 1) + S(n - p).$$

We must now take the average of these expressions, since p is random, by adding them from $p = 1$ to $p = n$ and dividing by n. The calculation uses the formula for the sum of the integers (Theorem A.1), and the result is

$$S(n) = \frac{n}{2} + \frac{3}{2} + \frac{2}{n}\left(S(0) + S(1) + \cdots + S(n - 1)\right).$$

2. Solving the Recurrence Relation

The first step toward solving this recurrence relation is to note that, if we were sorting a list of length $n - 1$, we would obtain the same expression with n replaced by $n - 1$, provided that $n \geq 2$:

$$S(n - 1) = \frac{n - 1}{2} + \frac{3}{2} + \frac{2}{n - 1}\left(S(0) + S(1) + \cdots + S(n - 2)\right).$$

Multiplying the first expression by n, the second by $n - 1$, and subtracting, we obtain

$$nS(n) - (n - 1)S(n - 1) = n + 1 + 2S(n - 1),$$

or

$$\frac{S(n)}{n + 1} = \frac{S(n - 1)}{n} + \frac{1}{n}.$$

We can solve this recurrence relation as we did a previous one by starting at the bottom. The result is

$$\frac{S(n)}{n+1} = \frac{S(2)}{3} + \frac{1}{3} + \cdots + \frac{1}{n}.$$

The sum of the reciprocals of integers is studied in Section A.2.8, where it is shown that

$$1 + \frac{1}{2} + \cdots + \frac{1}{n} = \ln n + O(1).$$

The difference between this sum and the one we want is bounded by a constant, so we obtain

$$S(n)/(n+1) = \ln n + O(1),$$

or, finally,

$$S(n) = n \ln n + O(n).$$

To compare this result with those for other sorting methods, we note that

$$\ln n = (\ln 2)(\lg n)$$

and $\ln 2 \approx 0.69$, so that

$$S(n) \approx 0.69(n \lg n) + O(n).$$

3. Counting Comparisons

Since a call to the partition function for a list of length n makes exactly $n - 1$ comparisons, the recurrence relation for the number of comparisons made in the average case will differ from that for swaps in only one way: Instead of $p + 1$ swaps in the partition function, there are $n - 1$ comparisons. Hence the first recurrence for the number $C(n, p)$ of comparisons for a list of length n with pivot p is

$$C(n, p) = n - 1 + C(p - 1) + C(n - p).$$

When we average these expressions for $p = 1$ to $p = n$, we obtain

$$C(n) = n + \frac{2}{n}\left(C(0) + C(1) + \cdots + C(n - 1)\right).$$

Since this recurrence for the number $C(n)$ of key comparisons differs from that for $S(n)$ only by the factor of $\frac{1}{2}$ in the latter, the same steps used to solve for $S(n)$ will yield

$$C(n) \approx 2n \ln n + O(n) \approx 1.39n \lg n + O(n).$$

8.8.5 Comparison with Mergesort

key comparisons

The calculation just completed shows that, on average, quicksort does about 39 percent more comparisons of keys than required by the lower bound and, therefore, also about 39 percent more than does mergesort. The reason, of course, is that mergesort is carefully designed to divide the list into halves of essentially equal size, whereas the sizes of the sublists for quicksort cannot be predicted in advance. Hence it is possible that quicksort's performance can be seriously degraded, but such an occurrence is unlikely in practice, so that averaging the times of poor performance with those of good performance yields the result just obtained.

data movement

Concerning data movement, we did not derive detailed information for mergesort since we were primarily interested in the linked version. If, however, we consider the version of contiguous mergesort that builds the merged sublists in a second array, and reverses the use of arrays at each pass, then it is clear that, at each level of the recursion tree, all n entries will be copied from one array to the other. The number of levels in the recursion tree is $\lg n$, and it therefore follows that the number of assignments of entries in contiguous mergesort is $n \lg n$. For quicksort, on the other hand, we obtained a count of about $0.69n \lg n$ swaps, on average. A good (machine-language) implementation should accomplish a swap of entries in two assignments. Therefore, again, quicksort does about 39 percent more assignments of entries than does mergesort. The exercises, however, outline another

optimization

partition function that does, on average, only about one-third as many swaps as the version we developed. With this refinement, therefore, contiguous quicksort may perform fewer than half as many assignments of data entries as contiguous mergesort.

Exercises 8.8

E1. How will the quicksort function (as presented in the text) function if all the keys in the list are equal?

E2. [Due to KNUTH] Describe an algorithm that will arrange a contiguous list whose keys are real numbers so that all the entries with negative keys will come first, followed by those with nonnegative keys. The final list need not be completely sorted. Make your algorithm do as few movements of entries and as few comparisons as possible. Do not use an auxiliary array.

E3. [Due to HOARE] Suppose that, instead of sorting, we wish only to find the mth smallest key in a given list of size n. Show how quicksort can be adapted to this problem, doing much less work than a complete sort.

E4. Given a list of integers, develop a function, similar to the partition function, that will rearrange the integers so that either all the integers in even-numbered positions will be even or all the integers in odd-numbered positions will be odd. (Your function will provide a proof that one or the other of these goals can always be attained, although it may not be possible to establish both at once.)

E5. A different method for choosing the pivot in quicksort is to take the median of the first, last, and central keys of the list. Describe the modifications needed to the function quick_sort to implement this choice. How much extra computation will be done? For $n = 7$, find an ordering of the keys

$$1, 2, \ldots, 7$$

that will force the algorithm into its worst case. How much better is this worst case than that of the original algorithm?

meansort

E6. A different approach to the selection of pivot is to take the mean (average) of all the keys in the list as the pivot. The resulting algorithm is called **meansort**.

    (a) Write a function to implement meansort. The partition function must be modified, since the mean of the keys is not necessarily one of the keys in the list. On the first pass, the pivot can be chosen any way you wish. As the keys are then partitioned, running sums and counts are kept for the two sublists, and thereby the means (which will be the new pivots) of the sublists can be calculated without making any extra passes through the list.

    (b) In meansort, the relative *sizes* of the keys determine how nearly equal the sublists will be after partitioning; the initial *order* of the keys is of no importance, except for counting the number of swaps that will take place. How bad can the worst case for meansort be in terms of the relative sizes of the two sublists? Find a set of n integers that will produce the worst case for meansort.

E7. [Requires elementary probability theory] A good way to choose the pivot is to use a random-number generator to choose the position for the next pivot at each call to recursive_quick_sort. Using the fact that these choices are independent, find the probability that quicksort will happen upon its worst case. **(a)** Do the problem for $n = 7$. **(b)** Do the problem for general n.

optimize partition

E8. At the cost of a few more comparisons of keys, the partition function can be rewritten so that the number of swaps is reduced by a factor of about 3, from $\frac{1}{2}n$ to $\frac{1}{6}n$ on average. The idea is to use two indices moving from the ends of the lists toward the center and to perform a swap only when a large key is found by the low position and a small key by the high position. This exercise outlines the development of such a function.

    (a) Establish two indices i and j, and maintain the invariant property that all keys before position i are less than or equal to the pivot and all keys after position j are greater than the pivot. For simplicity, swap the pivot into the first position, and start the partition with the second element. Write a loop that will increase the position i as long as the invariant holds and another loop that will decrease j as long as the invariant holds. Your loops must also ensure that the indices do not go out of range, perhaps by checking that i ≤ j. When a pair of entries, each on the wrong side, is found, then they should be swapped and the loops repeated. What is the termination condition of this outer loop? At the end, the pivot can be swapped into its proper place.

(b) Using the invariant property, verify that your function works properly.

(c) Show that each swap performed within the loop puts two entries into their final positions. From this, show that the function does at most $\frac{1}{2}n + O(1)$ swaps in its worst case for a list of length n.

(d) If, after partitioning, the pivot belongs in position p, then the number of swaps that the function does is approximately the number of entries originally in one of the p positions at or before the pivot, but whose keys are greater than or equal to the pivot. If the keys are randomly distributed, then the probability that a particular key is greater than or equal to the pivot is $\frac{1}{n}(n - p - 1)$. Show that the average number of such keys, and hence the average number of swaps, is approximately $\frac{p}{n}(n-p)$. By taking the average of these numbers from $p = 1$ to $p = n$, show that the number of swaps is approximately $\frac{n}{6} + O(1)$.

(e) The need to check to make sure that the indices i and j in the partition stay in bounds can be eliminated by using the pivot key as a sentinel to stop the loops. Implement this method in your function. Be sure to verify that your function works correctly in all cases.

(f) [Due to WIRTH] Consider the following simple and "obvious" way to write the loops using the pivot as a sentinel:

```
do {
    do { i = i + 1; } while (entry[i] < pivot);
    do { j = j − 1; } while (entry[j] > pivot);
    swap(i, j)
} while (j > i);
```

Find a list of keys for which this version fails.

Programming Projects 8.8

P1. Implement quicksort (for contiguous lists) on your computer, and test it with the program from Project P1 of Section 8.2 (page 328). Compare its performance with that of all the other sorting methods you have studied.

P2. Write a version of quicksort for linked lists, integrate it into the linked version of the testing program from Project P1 of Section 8.2 (page 328), and compare its performance with that of other sorting methods for linked lists.

linked quicksort   Use the first entry of a sublist as the pivot for partitioning. The partition function for linked lists is somewhat simpler than for contiguous lists, since minimization of data movement is not a concern. To partition a sublist, you need only traverse it, deleting each entry as you go, and then add the entry to one of two lists depending on the size of its key relative to the pivot.

Since **partition** now produces two new lists, you will, however, require a short additional function to recombine the sorted sublists into a single linked list.

P3. Because it may involve more overhead, quicksort may be inferior to simpler methods for short lists. Through experiment, find a value where, on average for lists in random order, quicksort becomes more efficient than insertion sort. Write a hybrid sorting function that starts with quicksort and, when the sublists are sufficiently short, switches to insertion sort. Determine if it is better to do the switch-over within the recursive function or to terminate the recursive calls when the sublists are sufficiently short to change methods and then at the very end of the process run through insertion sort once on the whole list.

8.9 HEAPS AND HEAPSORT

Quicksort has the disadvantage that, even though its usual performance is excellent, some kinds of input can make it misbehave badly. In this section we study another sorting method that overcomes this problem. This algorithm, called *heapsort*, sorts a contiguous list of length n with $O(n \log n)$ comparisons and movements of entries, even in its worst case. Hence it achieves worst-case bounds better than those of quicksort, and for contiguous lists it is better than mergesort, since it needs only a small and constant amount of space apart from the list being sorted.

corporate hierarchy   Heapsort is based on a tree structure that reflects the pecking order in a corporate hierarchy. Imagine the organizational structure of corporate management as a tree, with the president at the top. When the president retires, the vice-presidents compete for the top job; one then wins promotion and creates a vacancy. The junior executives are thus always competing for promotion whenever a vacancy arises. Now (quite unrealistically) imagine that the corporation always does its "downsizing" by pensioning off its most expensive employee, the president. Hence a vacancy continually appears at the top, employees are competing for promotion, and as each employee reaches the "top of the heap" that position again becomes vacant. With this, we have the essential idea of our sorting method.

8.9.1 Two-Way Trees as Lists

Let us begin with a complete 2-tree such as the one shown in Figure 8.15, and number the vertices, beginning with the root, labeled 0, from left to right on each level.

We can now put the 2-tree into a list by storing each node in the position shown by its label. We conclude that

finding the children   *If the root of the tree is in position 0 of the list, then the left and right children of the node in position k are in positions $2k + 1$ and $2k + 2$ of the list, respectively. If these positions are beyond the end of the list, then these children do not exist.*

With this idea, we can define what we mean by a heap.

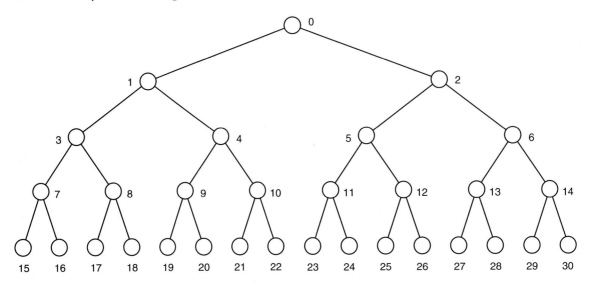

Figure 8.15. Complete 2-tree with 31 vertices

Definition	A *heap* is a list in which each entry contains a key, and, for all positions k in the list, the key at position k is at least as large as the keys in positions $2k$ and $2k + 1$, provided these positions exist in the list.

In this way, a heap is analogous to a corporate hierarchy in which each employee (except those at the bottom of the heap) supervises two others.

In explaining the use of heaps, we shall draw trees like Figure 8.16 to show the hierarchical relationships, but algorithms operating on heaps always treat them as a particular kind of list.

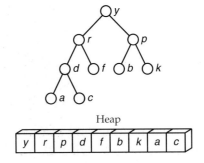

Figure 8.16. A heap as a tree and as a list

Note that a heap is definitely *not* an ordered list. The first entry, in fact, must have the largest key in the heap, whereas the first key is smallest in an ordered list. In a heap, there is no necessary ordering between the keys in locations k and $k + 1$ if $k > 1$.

Remark   Many C++ manuals and textbooks refer to the area used for dynamic memory as the "heap"; this use of the word *heap* has nothing to do with the present definition.

8.9.2 Development of Heapsort

1. Method

two-phase function   Heapsort proceeds in two phases. First, we must arrange the entries in the list so that they satisfy the requirements for a heap (analogous to organizing a corporate hierarchy). Second, we repeatedly remove the top of the heap and promote another entry to take its place.

For this second phase, we recall that the root of the tree (which is the first entry of the list as well as the top of the heap) has the largest key. This key belongs at the end of the list. We therefore move the first entry to the last position, replacing an entry current. We then decrease a counter last_unsorted that keeps track of the size of the unsorted part of the list, thereby excluding the largest entry from further sorting. The entry current that has been removed from the last position, however, may not belong on the top of the heap, and therefore we must insert current into the proper position to restore the heap property before continuing to loop in the same way.

From this description, you can see that heapsort requires random access to all parts of the list. We must therefore decide:

> *Heapsort is suitable only for contiguous lists.*

2. The Main Function

Let us now crystallize heapsort by writing it in C++, using our standard conventions.

```
template <class Record>
void Sortable_list<Record>::heap_sort()
/* Post: The entries of the Sortable_list have been rearranged so that their keys
         are sorted into nondecreasing order.
   Uses: The contiguous List implementation of Chapter 6, build_heap, and in-
         sert_heap. */
{
    Record current;              //   temporary storage for moving entries
    int last_unsorted;           //   Entries beyond last_unsorted have been sorted.
    build_heap();                //   First phase: Turn the list into a heap.
    for (last_unsorted = count − 1; last_unsorted > 0; last_unsorted−−) {
        current = entry[last_unsorted];  //   Extract the last entry from the list.
        entry[last_unsorted] = entry[0]; //   Move top of heap to the end
        insert_heap(current, 0, last_unsorted − 1);  //   Restore the heap
    }
}
```

3. An Example

Before we begin work on the two functions build_heap and insert_heap, let us see what happens in the first few stages of sorting the heap shown in Figure 8.16. These stages are shown in Figure 8.17. In the first step, the largest key, *y*, is moved from the first to the last entry of the list. The first diagram shows the resulting tree, with *y* removed from further consideration, and the entry that was formerly last, *c*, put aside as the temporary variable current. To find how to rearrange the heap and insert *c*, we look at the two children of the root. Each of these is guaranteed to have a larger key than any other entry in its subtree, and hence the largest of these two entries and *c* belongs in the root. We therefore promote *r* to the top of the heap, and repeat the process on the subtree whose root has just been removed. Hence the larger of *d* and *f* is now inserted where *r* was formerly. At the next step, we would compare current = *c* with the two children of *f*, but these do not exist, so the promotion of entries through the tree ceases, and current = *c* is inserted in the empty position formerly occupied by *f*.

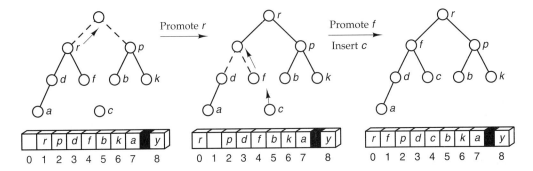

Figure 8.17. First stage of heap_sort

At this point, we are ready to repeat the algorithm, again moving the top of the heap to the end of the list and restoring the heap property. The sequence of actions that occurs in the complete sort of the list is shown in Figure 8.18.

4. The Function insert_heap

It is only a short step from this example to a formal function for inserting the entry current into the heap.

```
template <class Record>
void Sortable_list<Record> :: insert_heap(const Record &current, int low, int high)
/* Pre:  The entries of the Sortable_list between indices low + 1 and high, inclu-
         sive, form a heap. The entry in position low will be discarded.
   Post: The entry current has been inserted into the Sortable_list and the entries
         rearranged so that the entries between indices low and high, inclusive,
         form a heap.
   Uses: The class Record, and the contiguous List implementation of Chapter 6. */
```

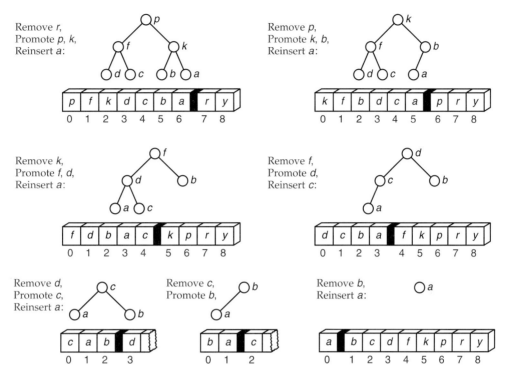

Figure 8.18. Trace of heap_sort

```
    {
        int large;                    //   position of child of entry[low] with the larger key
        large = 2 * low + 1;          //   large is now the left child of low.
        while (large <= high) {
            if (large < high && entry[large] < entry[large + 1])
                large++;              //   large is now the child of low with the largest key.
            if (current >= entry[large])
                break;                //   current belongs in position low.
            else {                    //   Promote entry[large] and move down the tree.
                entry[low] = entry[large];
                low = large;
                large = 2 * low + 1;
            }
        }
        entry[low] = current;
    }
```

5. Building the Initial Heap

initialization　The remaining task that we must specify is to build the initial heap from a list in arbitrary order. To do so, we first note that a 2-tree with only one node automatically satisfies the properties of a heap, and therefore we need not worry about any of the leaves of the tree; that is, about any of the entries in the second half of the list. If we begin at the midpoint of the list and work our way back toward the start, we can use the function insert_heap to insert each entry into the partial heap consisting of all later entries, and thereby build the complete heap. The desired function is therefore simply:

```
template <class Record>
void Sortable_list<Record> :: build_heap( )
/* Post:  The entries of the Sortable_list have been rearranged so that it becomes
          a heap.
    Uses: The contiguous List implementation of Chapter 6, and insert_heap. */
{
    int low;                        //   All entries beyond the position low form a heap.
    for (low = count/2 − 1; low >= 0; low−−) {
        Record current = entry[low];
        insert_heap(current, low, count − 1);
    }
}
```

8.9.3 Analysis of Heapsort

From the example we have worked out, it is not at all clear that heapsort is efficient, and, in fact, heapsort is not a good choice for short lists. It seems quite strange that we can sort by moving large keys slowly toward the beginning of the list before finally putting them away at the end. When n becomes large, however, such small quirks become unimportant, and heapsort proves its worth as one of very few sorting algorithms for contiguous lists that is guaranteed to finish in time $O(n \log n)$ with minimal space requirements.

worst-case insertion   First, let us determine how much work insert_heap does in its worst case. At each pass through the loop, the value of $low + 1$ is at least doubled; hence the number of passes cannot exceed $\lg((\text{high} + 1)/(\text{low} + 1))$; this is also the height of the subtree rooted at entry[low]. Each pass through the loop does two comparisons of keys (usually) and one assignment of entries. Therefore, the number of comparisons done in insert_heap is at most $2 \lg((\text{high} + 1)/(\text{low} + 1))$ and the number of assignments $\lg((\text{high} + 1)/(\text{low} + 1))$.

Let $m = \lfloor \frac{1}{2}n \rfloor$ (that is, the greatest integer that does not exceed $\frac{1}{2}n$). In build_heap we make m calls to insert_heap, for values of $k = low$ ranging from
first phase $m - 1$ down to 0. Hence the total number of comparisons is about

$$2 \sum_{k=1}^{m} \lg \left(\frac{n}{k} \right) = 2(m \lg n - \lg m!) \approx 5m \approx 2.5n,$$

since, by Stirling's approximation (Theorem A.5 on page 658) and $\lg m = \lg n - 1$, we have

$$\lg m! \approx m \lg m - 1.5m \approx m \lg n - 2.5m.$$

second phase   Similarly, in the sorting and insertion phase, we have about

$$2 \sum_{k=2}^{n} \lg k = 2 \lg n! \approx 2n \lg n - 3n$$

comparisons. This term dominates that of the initial phase, and hence we conclude

total worst-case   that the number of comparisons is $2n \lg n + O(n)$.

counts   One assignment of entries is done in insert_heap for each two comparisons (approximately). Therefore the total number of assignments is $n \lg n + O(n)$.

In summary, we can state:

> In its worst case for sorting a list of length n, heapsort performs $2n \lg n + O(n)$ comparisons of keys and $n \lg n + O(n)$ assignments of entries.

From Section 8.8.4 we can see that the corresponding numbers for quicksort in the average case are $1.39n \lg n + O(n)$ comparisons and $0.69n \lg n + O(n)$ swaps, which would be at least $1.39n \lg n + O(n)$ assignments of entries. Hence the worst case for heapsort is somewhat poorer than is the average case for quicksort in regard to comparisons of keys, and somewhat better in regard to assignments of

comparison with   entries. Quicksort's worst case, however, is $\Theta(n^2)$, which is far worse than the

quicksort   worst case of heapsort for large n. An average-case analysis of heapsort appears to be very complicated, but empirical studies show that (as for selection sort) there is relatively little difference between the average and worst cases, and heapsort usually takes about twice as long as quicksort.

Heapsort, therefore, should be regarded as something of an insurance policy: On average, heapsort costs somewhat more than quicksort, but heapsort avoids the slight possibility of a catastrophic degradation of performance.

8.9.4 Priority Queues

To conclude this section, we briefly mention another application of heaps.

Definition   A *priority queue* consists of entries, each of which contains a key called the *priority* of the entry. A priority queue has only two operations other than the usual creation, clearing, size, full, and empty operations:

➡ Insert an entry.

➡ Remove the entry having the largest (or smallest) key.

If entries have equal keys, then any entry with the largest key may be removed first.

applications   In a time-sharing computer system, for example, a large number of tasks may be waiting for the CPU. Some of these tasks have higher priority than others. Hence the set of tasks waiting for the CPU forms a priority queue. Other applications of priority queues include simulations of time-dependent events (like the airport simulation in Section 3.5) and solution of sparse systems of linear equations by row reduction.

implementations   We could represent a priority queue as a sorted contiguous list, in which case removal of an entry is immediate, but insertion would take time proportional to n, the number of entries in the queue. Or we could represent it as an unsorted list, in which case insertion is rapid but removal is slow.

Now consider the properties of a heap. The entry with largest key is on the top and can be removed immediately. It will, however, take time $O(\log n)$ to restore the heap property for the remaining keys. If, however, another entry is to be inserted immediately, then some of this time may be combined with the $O(\log n)$ time needed to insert the new entry. Thus the representation of a priority queue as a heap proves advantageous for large n, since it is represented efficiently in contiguous storage and is guaranteed to require only logarithmic time for both insertions and deletions.

Exercises 8.9

E1. Show the list corresponding to each of the following trees under the representation that the children of the entry in position k are in positions $2k + 1$ and $2k + 2$. Which of these are heaps? For those that are not, state the position in the list at which the heap property is violated.

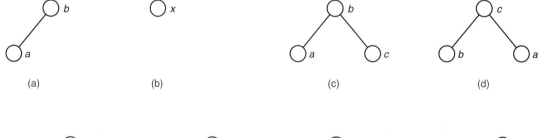

(a)   (b)   (c)   (d)

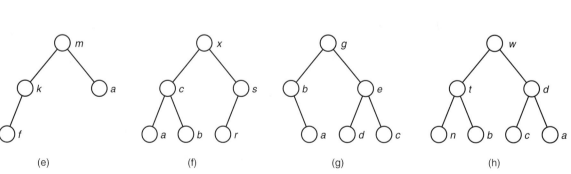

(e)   (f)   (g)   (h)

E2. By hand, trace the action of **heap_sort** on each of the following lists. Draw the initial tree to which the list corresponds, show how it is converted into a heap, and show the resulting heap as each entry is removed from the top and the new entry inserted.

(a) The following three words to be sorted alphabetically:

triangle   square   pentagon

(b) The three words in part (a) to be sorted according to the number of sides of the corresponding polygon, in increasing order

(c) The three words in part (a) to be sorted according to the number of sides of the corresponding polygon, in decreasing order

(d) The following seven numbers to be sorted into increasing order:

26   33   35   29   19   12   22

(e) The same seven numbers in a different initial order, again to be sorted into increasing order:

12   19   33   26   29   35   22

(f) The following list of 14 names to be sorted into alphabetical order:

Tim Dot Eva Roy Tom Kim Guy Amy Jon Ann Jim Kay Ron Jan

E3. (a) Design a function that will insert a new entry into a heap, obtaining a new heap. (The function insert_heap in the text requires that the root be unoccupied, whereas, for this exercise, the root will already contain the entry with largest key, which must remain in the heap. Your function will increase the count of entries in the list.)

(b) Analyze the time and space requirements of your function.

E4. (a) Design a function that will delete the entry with the largest key (the root) from the top of the heap and restore the heap properties of the resulting, smaller list.

(b) Analyze the time and space requirements of your function.

E5. (a) Design a function that will delete the entry with index i from a heap and restore the heap properties of the resulting, smaller list.

(b) Analyze the time and space requirements of your function.

E6. Consider a heap of n keys, with x_k being the key in position k (in the contiguous representation) for $0 \le k < n$. Prove that the height of the subtree rooted at x_k is the greatest integer not exceeding $\lg((n+1)/(k+1))$, for all k satisfying $0 \le k < n$. [*Hint*: Use "backward" induction on k, starting with the leaves and working back toward the root, which is x_0.]

E7. Define the notion of a *ternary heap*, analogous to an ordinary heap except that each node of the tree except the leaves has three children. Devise a sorting method based on ternary heaps, and analyze the properties of the sorting method.

Programming Project 8.9

P1. Implement heapsort (for contiguous lists) on your computer, integrate it into the test program of Project P1 of Section 8.2 (page 328), and compare its performance with all the previous sorting algorithms.

8.10 REVIEW: COMPARISON OF METHODS

CONCLUSION

In this chapter we have studied and carefully analyzed quite a variety of sorting methods. Perhaps the best way to summarize this work is to emphasize in turn each of the three important efficiency criteria:

➥ Use of storage space;

➥ Use of computer time; and

➥ Programming effort.

1. Use of space

stack space for recursion

In regard to space, most of the algorithms we have discussed use little space other than that occupied by the original list, which is rearranged in its original place to be in order. The exceptions are quicksort and mergesort, where the recursion does require a small amount of extra storage to keep track of the sublists that have not yet been sorted. But in a well-written function, the amount of extra space used for recursion is $O(\log n)$ and will be trivial in comparison with that needed for other purposes.

Finally, we should recall that a major drawback of mergesort for contiguous lists is that the straightforward version requires extra space $\Theta(n)$, in fact, space equal to that occupied by the original list.

external sorting

In many applications the list to be sorted is much too large to be kept in high-speed memory, and when this is the case, other methods become necessary. A frequent approach is to divide the list into sublists that can be sorted internally within high-speed memory and then merge the sorted sublists externally. Hence *external sorting and merging* much work has been invested in developing merging algorithms, primarily when it is necessary to merge many sublists at once. We shall not discuss this topic further.

2. Computer Time

The second efficiency criterion is use of computer time, which we have already carefully analyzed for each of the methods we have developed. In summary, the simple methods insertion sort and selection sort have time that is $\Theta(n^2)$ for a list of length n. Shell sort is much faster; and the remaining methods are usually the fastest, with time that is $\Theta(n \log n)$. Quicksort, however, has a worst-case time that is $\Theta(n^2)$. Heapsort is something of an insurance policy. It usually is more costly than quicksort, but it avoids the slight possibility of a serious degradation in performance.

3. Programming Effort

The third efficiency criterion is often the most important of all: This criterion is the efficient and fruitful use of the programmer's time.

If a list is small, the sophisticated sorting techniques designed to minimize computer time requirements are usually worse or only marginally better in achieving their goal than are the simpler methods. If a program is to be run only once or twice and there is enough machine time, then it would be foolish for a programmer to spend days or weeks investigating many sophisticated algorithms that might, in the end, only save a few seconds of computer time.

old languages   When programming in languages like most dialects of FORTRAN, COBOL, or BASIC that do not support recursion, implementation of mergesort and quicksort becomes considerably more complicated, although it can be done by using stacks to hold the values of variables, as we observed in Chapter 5.

Shell sort comes not far behind mergesort and quicksort in performance, does not require recursion, and is easy to program. One should therefore never sell Shell sort short.

The saving of programming time is an excellent reason for choosing a simple algorithm, even if it is inefficient, but two words of caution should always be remembered. First, saving programming time is never an excuse for writing an incorrect program, one that may usually work but can sometimes misbehave. Murphy's law will then inevitably come true. Second, simple programs, designed to be run only a few times and then be discarded, often instead find their way into applications not imagined when they were first written. Lack of care in the early stages will then prove exceedingly costly later.

For many applications, insertion sort can prove to be the best choice. It is easy to write and maintain, and it runs efficiently for short lists. Even for long lists, if they are nearly in the correct order, insertion sort will be very efficient. If the list is completely in order, then insertion sort verifies this condition as quickly as can be done.

4. Statistical Analysis

The final choice of algorithm will depend not only on the length of list, the size of records, and their representation in storage, but very strongly on the way in which the records can be expected to be ordered before sorting. The analysis of algorithms from the standpoint of probability and statistics is of great importance. For most algorithms, we have been able to obtain results on the mean (average)
mean   performance, but the experience of quicksort shows that the amount by which this performance changes from one possible ordering to another is also an important factor to consider.

standard deviation   The **standard deviation** is a statistical measure of this variability. Quicksort has an excellent mean performance, and the standard deviation is small, which signifies that the performance is likely to differ little from the mean. For algorithms like selection sort, heapsort, and mergesort, the best-case and worst-case performances differ little, which means that the standard deviation is quite small. Other algorithms, like insertion sort, will have a much larger standard deviation in their performance. The particular distribution of the orderings of the incoming lists is therefore an important consideration in choosing a sorting method. To enable intelligent decisions, the professional computer scientist needs to be knowledgeable about important aspects of mathematical statistics as they apply to algorithm analysis.

5. Empirical Testing

Finally, in all these decisions, we must be careful to temper the theoretical analysis of algorithms with empirical testing. Different computers and compilers will produce different results. It is most instructive, therefore, to see by experiment how the different algorithms behave in different circumstances.

Exercises 8.10

E1. Classify the sorting methods we have studied into one of the following categories: (a) The method does not require access to the entries at one end of the list until the entries at the other end have been sorted; (b) The method does not require access to the entries that have already been sorted; (c) The method requires access to all entries in the list throughout the process.

E2. Some of the sorting methods we have studied are not suited for use with linked lists. Which ones, and why not?

E3. Rank the sorting methods we have studied (both for linked and contiguous lists) according to the amount of extra storage space that they require for indices or pointers, for recursion, and for copies of the entries being sorted.

E4. Which of the methods we studied would be a good choice in each of the following applications? Why? If the representation of the list in contiguous or linked storage makes a difference in your choice, state how.

   (a) You wish to write a general-purpose sorting program that will be used by many people in a variety of applications.

   (b) You wish to sort 1000 numbers once. After you finish, you will not keep the program.

   (c) You wish to sort 50 numbers once. After you finish, you will not keep the program.

   (d) You need to sort 5 entries in the middle of a long program. Your sort will be called hundreds of times by the long program.

   (e) You have a list of 1000 keys to sort in high-speed memory, and key comparisons can be made quickly, but each time a key is moved, a corresponding 500 block file on disk must also be moved, and doing so is a slow process.

   (f) There is a twelve foot long shelf full of computer science books all catalogued by number. A few of these have been put back in the wrong places by readers, but rarely are the books more than one foot from where they belong.

   (g) You have a stack of 500 library index cards in random order to sort alphabetically.

   (h) You are told that a list of 5000 words is already in alphabetical order, but you wish to check it to make sure, and sort any words found out of order.

E5. Discuss the advantages and disadvantages of designing a general sorting function as a hybrid between quicksort and Shell sort. What criteria would you use to switch from one to the other? Which would be the better choice for what kinds of lists?

E6. Summarize the results of the test runs of the sorting methods of this chapter for your computer. Also include any variations of the methods that you have written as exercises. Make charts comparing the following:

(a) the number of key comparisons.

(b) the number of assignments of entries.

(c) the total running time.

(d) the working storage requirements of the program.

(e) the length of the program.

(f) the amount of programming time required to write and debug the program.

E7. Write a one-page guide to help a user of your computer system select one of our sorting algorithms according to the desired application.

stable sorting methods

E8. A sorting function is called *stable* if, whenever two entries have equal keys, then on completion of the sorting function, the two entries will be in the same order in the list as before sorting. Stability is important if a list has already been sorted by one key and is now being sorted by another key, and it is desired to keep as much of the original ordering as the new one allows. Determine which of the sorting methods of this chapter are stable and which are not. For those that are not, produce a list (as short as possible) containing some entries with equal keys whose orders are not preserved. In addition, see if you can discover simple modifications to the algorithm that will make it stable.

POINTERS AND PITFALLS

1. Many computer systems have a general-purpose sorting utility. If you can access this utility and it proves adequate for your application, then use it rather than writing a sorting program from scratch.

2. In choosing a sorting method, take into account the ways in which the keys will usually be arranged before sorting, the size of the application, the amount of time available for programming, the need to save computer time and space, the way in which the data structures are implemented, the cost of moving data, and the cost of comparing keys.

3. Divide-and-conquer is one of the most widely applicable and most powerful methods for designing algorithms. When faced with a programming problem, see if its solution can be obtained by first solving the problem for two (or more) problems of the same general form but of a smaller size. If so, you may be able to formulate an algorithm that uses the divide-and-conquer method and program it using recursion.

4. Mergesort, quicksort, and heapsort are powerful sorting methods, more difficult to program than the simpler methods, but much more efficient when applied to large lists. Consider the application carefully to determine whether the extra effort needed to implement one of these sophisticated algorithms will be justified.

5. Priority queues are important for many applications, and heaps provide an excellent implementation of priority queues.

6. Heapsort is like an insurance policy: It is usually slower than quicksort, but it guarantees that sorting will be completed in $O(n \log n)$ comparisons of keys, as quicksort cannot always do.

REVIEW QUESTIONS

8.2   **1.** How many comparisons of keys are required to verify that a list of n entries is in order?

2. Explain in twenty words or less how insertion sort works.

8.3   **3.** Explain in twenty words or less how selection sort works.

4. On average, about how many more comparisons does selection sort do than insertion sort on a list of 20 entries?

5. What is the advantage of selection sort over all the other methods we studied?

8.4   **6.** What disadvantage of insertion sort does Shell sort overcome?

8.5   **7.** What is the lower bound on the number of key comparisons that any sorting method must make to put n keys into order, if the method uses key comparisons to make its decisions? Give both the average- and worst-case bounds.

8. What is the lower bound if the requirement of using comparisons to make decisions is dropped?

8.6   **9.** Define the term *divide and conquer*.

10. Explain in twenty words or less how mergesort works.

11. Explain in twenty words or less how quicksort works.

8.7   **12.** Explain why mergesort is better for linked lists than for contiguous lists.

8.8   **13.** In quicksort, why did we choose the pivot from the center of the list rather than from one of the ends?

14. On average, about how many more comparisons of keys does quicksort make than the optimum? About how many comparisons does it make in the worst case?

8.9   **15.** What is a heap?

16. How does heapsort work?

17. Compare the worst-case performance of heapsort with the worst-case performance of quicksort, and compare it also with the average-case performance of quicksort.

8.10   **18.** When are simple sorting algorithms better than sophisticated ones?

REFERENCES FOR FURTHER STUDY

The primary reference for this chapter is the comprehensive series by D. E. KNUTH (bibliographic details on page 77). Internal sorting occupies Volume 3, pp. 73–180. KNUTH does algorithm analysis in considerably more detail than we have. He writes all algorithms in a pseudo-assembly language and does detailed operation counts there. He studies all the methods we have, several more, and many variations.

The original references to Shell sort and quicksort are, respectively,

D. L. SHELL, "A high-speed sorting function," *Communications of the ACM* 2 (1959), 30–32.

C. A. R. HOARE, "Quicksort," *Computer Journal* 5 (1962), 10–15.

The unified derivation of mergesort and quicksort, one that can also be used to produce insertion sort and selection sort, is based on the work

JOHN DARLINGTON, "A synthesis of several sorting algorithms," *Acta Informatica* 11 (1978), 1–30.

Mergesort can be refined to bring its performance very close to the optimal lower bound. One example of such an improved algorithm, whose performance is within 6 percent of the best possible, is

R. MICHAEL TANNER, "Minimean merging and sorting: An algorithm," *SIAM J. Computing* 7 (1978), 18–38.

A relatively simple contiguous merge algorithm that operates in linear time with a small, constant amount of additional space appears in

BING-CHAO HUANG and MICHAEL A. LANGSTON, "Practical in-place merging," *Communications of the ACM* 31 (1988), 348–352.

The algorithm for partitioning the list in quicksort was discovered by NICO LOMUTO and was published in

JON L. BENTLEY, "Programming pearls: How to sort," *Communications of the ACM* 27 (1984), 287–291.

The "Programming pearls" column contains many elegant algorithms and helpful suggestions for programming that have been collected into the following two books:

JON L. BENTLEY, *Programming Pearls*, Addison-Wesley, Reading, Mass., 1986, 195 pages.

JON L. BENTLEY, *More Programming Pearls: Confessions of a Coder*, Addison-Wesley, Reading, Mass., 1988, 224 pages.

An extensive analysis of the quicksort algorithm is given in

ROBERT SEDGEWICK, "The analysis of quicksort programs," *Acta Informatica* 7 (1976–77), 327–355.

The exercise on meansort (taking the mean of the keys as pivot) comes from

DALIA MOTZKIN, "MEANSORT," *Communications of the ACM* 26 (1983), 250–251; 27 (1984), 719–722.

Heapsort was discovered and so named by

J. W. J. WILLIAMS, *Communications of the ACM* 7 (1964), 347–348.

A simple but complete development of algorithms for heaps and priority queues appears in

JON L. BENTLEY, "Programming pearls: Thanks, heaps," *Communications of the ACM* 28 (1985), 245–250.

There is, of course, a vast literature in probability and statistics with potential applications to computers. A classic treatment of elementary probability and statistics is

W. FELLER, *An Introduction to Probability Theory and Its Applications*, Vol. 1, second edition, Wiley–Interscience, New York, 1957.

Tables and Information Retrieval

9

THIS CHAPTER continues the study of information retrieval that was started in Chapter 7, but now concentrating on tables instead of lists. We begin with ordinary rectangular arrays, then we consider other kinds of arrays, and then we generalize to the study of hash tables. One of our major purposes in this chapter is to analyze and compare various algorithms, to see which are preferable under different conditions. Applications in the chapter include a sorting method based on tables and a version of the Life game using a hash table.

9.1 INTRODUCTION: BREAKING THE lg n BARRIER

In Chapter 7 we showed that, by use of key comparisons alone, it is impossible to complete a search of n items in fewer than $\lg n$ comparisons, on average. But this result speaks only of searching by key comparisons. If we can use some other method, then we may be able to arrange our data so that we can locate a given item even more quickly.

table lookup

In fact, we commonly do so. If we have 500 different records, with an index between 0 and 499 assigned to each, then we would never think of using sequential or binary search to locate a record. We would simply store the records in an array of size 500, and use the index n to locate the record of item n by ordinary table lookup.

functions for information retrieval

Both table lookup and searching share the same essential purpose, that of *information retrieval*. We begin with a key (which may be complicated or simply an index) and wish to find the location of the entry (if any) with that key. In other words, both table lookup and our searching algorithms provide *functions* from the set of keys to locations in a list or array. The functions are in fact one-to-one from the set of keys that actually occur to the set of locations that actually occur, since we assume that each entry has only one key, and there is only one entry with a given key.

tables

In this chapter we study ways to implement and access tables in contiguous storage, beginning with ordinary rectangular arrays and then considering tables with restricted location of nonzero entries, such as triangular tables. We turn afterward to more general problems, with the purpose of introducing and motivating the use first of access arrays and then hash tables for information retrieval.

We shall see that, depending on the shape of the table, several steps may be needed to retrieve an entry, but, even so, the time required remains $O(1)$—that is, it is bounded by a constant that does not depend on the size of the table—and thus table lookup can be more efficient than any searching method.

table indices

The entries of the tables that we consider will be indexed by sequences of integers, just as array entries are indexed by such sequences. Indeed, we shall implement abstractly defined tables with arrays. In order to distinguish between the abstract concept and its implementation, we introduce the following notation:

Convention

*The index defining an entry of an abstractly defined table
is enclosed in parentheses,
whereas the index of an entry of an array
is enclosed in square brackets.*

---

example

Thus $T(1,2,3)$ denotes the entry of the table T that is indexed by the sequence $1,2,3$, and A[1][2][3] denotes the correspondingly indexed entry of the C++ array A.

9.2 RECTANGULAR TABLES

Because of the importance of rectangular tables, almost all high-level languages provide convenient and efficient 2-dimensional arrays to store and access them, so that generally the programmer need not worry about the implementation details. Nonetheless, computer storage is fundamentally arranged in a contiguous sequence (that is, in a straight line with each entry next to another), so for every access to a rectangular table, the machine must do some work to convert the location within a rectangle to a position along a line. Let us take a closer look at this process.

1. Row-Major and Column-Major Ordering

row-major ordering

A natural way to read a rectangular table is to read the entries of the first row from left to right, then the entries of the second row, and so on until the last row has been read. This is also the order in which most compilers store a rectangular array, and is called *row-major ordering*. Suppose, for example, that the rows of a table are numbered from 1 to 2 and the columns are numbered from 5 to 7. (Since we are working with general tables, there is no reason why we must be restricted by the requirement in C and C++ that all array indexing begins at 0.) The order of indices in the table with which the entries are stored in row-major ordering is

$$(1, 5) \quad (1, 6) \quad (1, 7) \quad (2, 5) \quad (2, 6) \quad (2, 7).$$

FORTRAN: column-major ordering

This is the ordering used by C++ and most high-level languages for storing the elements of a two dimensional array. Standard FORTRAN instead uses *column-major ordering*, in which the entries of the first column come first, and so on. This example in column-major ordering is

$$(1, 5) \quad (2, 5) \quad (1, 6) \quad (2, 6) \quad (1, 7) \quad (2, 7).$$

Figure 9.1 further illustrates row- and column-major orderings for a table with three rows and four columns.

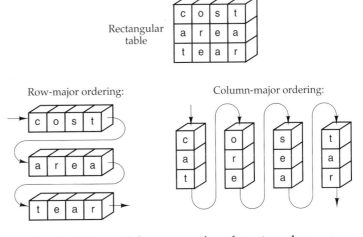

Figure 9.1. Sequential representation of a rectangular array

2. Indexing Rectangular Tables

In the general problem, the compiler must be able to start with an index (i, j) and calculate where in a sequential array the corresponding entry of the table will be stored. We shall derive a formula for this calculation. For simplicity we shall use only row-major ordering and suppose that the rows are numbered from 0 to $m - 1$ and the columns from 0 to $n - 1$. The general case is treated as an exercise. Altogether, the table will have mn entries, as must its sequential implementation in an array. We number the entries in the array from 0 to $mn - 1$. To obtain the formula calculating the position where (i, j) goes, we first consider some special cases. Clearly $(0, 0)$ goes to position 0, and, in fact, the entire first row is easy: $(0, j)$ goes to position j. The first entry of the second row, $(1, 0)$, comes after $(0, n - 1)$, and thus goes into position n. Continuing, we see that $(1, j)$ goes to position $n + j$. Entries of the next row will have two full rows (that is, $2n$ entries) preceding them. Hence entry $(2, j)$ goes to position $2n + j$. In general, the entries of row i are preceded by ni earlier entries, so the desired formula is

index function, rectangular array

> *Entry (i, j) in a rectangular table goes to position $ni + j$ in a sequential array.*

A formula of this kind, which gives the sequential location of a table entry, is called an *index function*.

3. Variation: An Access Array

The index function for rectangular tables is certainly not difficult to calculate, and the compilers of most high-level languages will simply write into the machine-language program the necessary steps for its calculation every time a reference is made to a rectangular table. On small machines, however, multiplication can be relatively slow, so a slightly different method can be used to eliminate the multiplications.

access array, rectangular table

This method is to keep an auxiliary array, a part of the multiplication table for n. The array will contain the values

$$0, \quad n, \quad 2n, \quad 3n, \quad \ldots, \quad (m - 1)n.$$

Note that this array is much smaller (usually) than the rectangular table, so that it can be kept permanently in memory without losing too much space. Its entries then need be calculated only once (and note that they can be calculated using only addition). For all later references to the rectangular table, the compiler can find the position for (i, j) by taking the entry in position i of the auxiliary table, adding j, and going to the resulting position.

This auxiliary array provides our first example of an *access array* (see Figure 9.2). In general, an access array is an auxiliary array used to find data stored elsewhere. An access array is also sometimes called an *access vector*.

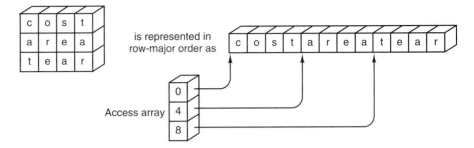

Figure 9.2. Access array for a rectangular table

Exercises 9.2

E1. What is the index function for a two-dimensional rectangular table whose rows are indexed from 0 to $m - 1$ and whose columns are indexed from 0 ot $n - 1$, inclusive, under column-major ordering?

E2. Give the index function, with row-major ordering, for a two-dimensional table with arbitrary bounds r to s, inclusive, for the row indices, and t to u, inclusive, for the column indices.

E3. Find the index function, with the generalization of row-major ordering, for a table with d dimensions and arbitrary bounds for each dimension.

9.3 TABLES OF VARIOUS SHAPES

matrix

Information that is usually stored in a rectangular table may not require every position in the rectangle for its representation. If we define a ***matrix*** to be a rectangular table of numbers, then often some of the positions within the matrix will be required to be 0. Several such examples are shown in Figure 9.3. Even when the entries in a table are not numbers, the positions actually used may not be all of those in a rectangle, and there may be better implementations than using a rectangular array and leaving some positions vacant. In this section, we examine ways to implement tables of various shapes, ways that will not require setting aside unused space in a rectangular array.

9.3.1 Triangular Tables

Let us consider the representation of a lower triangular table as shown in Figure 9.3. Such a table can be defined formally as a table in which all indices (i, j) are required to satisfy $i \geq j$. We can implement a triangular table in a contiguous array by sliding each row out after the one above it, as shown in Figure 9.4.

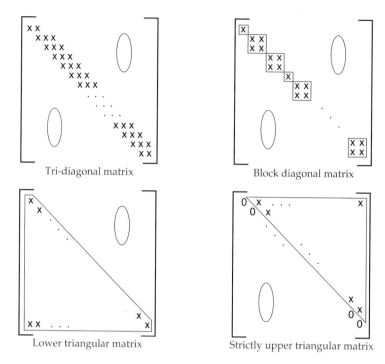

Tri-diagonal matrix

Block diagonal matrix

Lower triangular matrix

Strictly upper triangular matrix

Figure 9.3. Matrices of various shapes

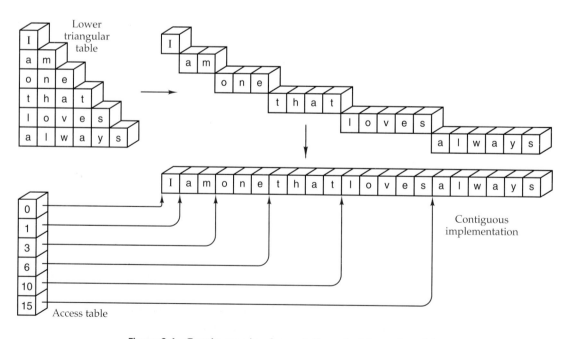

Figure 9.4. Contiguous implementation of a triangular table

To construct the index function that describes this mapping, we again make the slight simplification of assuming that the rows and the columns are numbered starting with 0. To find the position where (i, j) goes, we now need to find where row i starts, and then to locate column j we need only add j to the starting point of row i. If the entries of the contiguous array are also numbered starting with 0, then the index of the starting point will be the same as the number of entries that precede row i. Clearly there are 0 entries before row 0, and only the one entry of row 0 precedes row 1. For row 2 there are $1 + 2 = 3$ preceding entries, and in general we see that preceding row i there are exactly

$$1 + 2 + \cdots + i = \tfrac{1}{2}i(i + 1)$$

entries.[1] Hence the desired function is that entry (i, j) of the triangular table cor-

index function, rectangular table

responds to entry

$$\tfrac{1}{2}i(i + 1) + j$$

of the contiguous array.

As we did for rectangular arrays, we can again avoid all multiplications and divisions by setting up an access array whose entries correspond to the row indices

access array, triangular table

of the triangular table. Position i of the access array will permanently contain the value $\tfrac{1}{2}i(i + 1)$. The access array will be calculated only once at the start of the program, and then used repeatedly at each reference to the triangular table. Note that even the initial calculation of this access array requires no multiplication or division, but only addition to calculate its entries in the order

$$0, \quad 1, \quad 1 + 2, \quad (1 + 2) + 3, \quad \ldots.$$

9.3.2 Jagged Tables

In both of the foregoing examples we have considered a rectangular table as made up from its rows. In ordinary rectangular arrays all the rows have the same length; in triangular tables, the length of each row can be found from a simple formula. We now consider the case of jagged tables such as the one in Figure 9.5, where there is no predictable relation between the position of a row and its length.

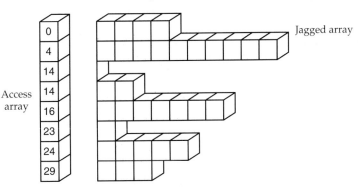

Figure 9.5. Access array for jagged table

---

[1] See Appendix A for a proof of this equality.

It is clear from the diagram that, even though we are not able to give an *a priori* function to map the jagged table into contiguous storage, the use of an access array remains as easy as in the previous examples, and elements of the jagged table can be referenced just as quickly. To set up the access array, we must construct the jagged table in its natural order, beginning with its first row. Entry 0 of the access array is, as before, the start of the contiguous array. After each row of the jagged table has been constructed, the index of the first unused position of the contiguous storage should then be entered as the next entry in the access array and used to start constructing the next row of the jagged table.

9.3.3 Inverted Tables

Next let us consider an example illustrating multiple access arrays, by which we can refer to a single table of records by several different keys at once.

Consider the problem faced by the telephone company in accessing the records of its customers. To publish the telephone book, the records must be sorted alphabetically by the name of the subscriber, but to process long-distance charges, the accounts must be sorted by telephone number. To do routine maintenance, the company also needs to have its subscribers sorted by address, so that a repairman may be able to work on several lines with one trip. Conceivably, the telephone company could keep three (or more) sets of its records, one sorted by name, one by number, and one by address. This way, however, would not only be very wasteful of storage space, but would introduce endless headaches if one set of records were updated but another was not, and erroneous and unpredictable information might be used.

multiple records

By using access arrays we can avoid the multiple sets of records, and we can still find the records by any of the three keys almost as quickly as if the records were fully sorted by that key. For the names we set up one access array. The first entry in this table is the position where the records of the subscriber whose name is first in alphabetical order are stored, the second entry gives the location of the second (in alphabetical order) subscriber's records, and so on. In a second access array, the first entry is the location of the subscriber's records whose telephone number happens to be smallest in numerical order. In yet a third access array the entries give the locations of the records sorted lexicographically by address.

multiple access arrays

An example of this scheme for a small number of accounts is shown in Figure 9.6.

Notice that in this method all the members that are treated as keys are processed in the same way. There is no particular reason why the records themselves need to be sorted according to one key rather than another, or, in fact, why they need to be sorted at all. The records themselves can be kept in an arbitrary order— say, the order in which they were first entered into the system. It also makes no difference whether the records are in an array, with entries in the access arrays being indices of the array, or whether the records are in dynamic storage, with the access arrays holding pointers to individual records. In any case, it is the access arrays that are used for information retrieval, and, as ordinary contiguous arrays, they may be used for table lookup, or binary search, or any other purpose for which a contiguous implementation is appropriate.

unordered records for ordered access arrays

Index	Name	Address	Phone
1	Hill, Thomas M.	High Towers #317	2829478
2	Baker, John S.	17 King Street	2884285
3	Roberts, L. B.	53 Ash Street	4372296
4	King, Barbara	High Towers #802	2863386
5	Hill, Thomas M.	39 King Street	2495723
6	Byers, Carolyn	118 Maple Street	4394231
7	Moody, C. L.	High Towers #210	2822214

Access Arrays

Name	Address	Phone
2	3	5
6	7	7
1	1	1
5	4	4
4	2	2
7	5	3
3	6	6

Figure 9.6. Multikey access arrays: an inverted table

Exercises 9.3

E1. The *main diagonal* of a square matrix consists of the entries for which the row and column indices are equal. A *diagonal matrix* is a square matrix in which all entries not on the main diagonal are 0. Describe a way to store a diagonal matrix without using space for entries that are necessarily 0, and give the corresponding index function.

E2. A *tri-diagonal matrix* is a square matrix in which all entries are 0 except possibly those on the main diagonal and on the diagonals immediately above and below it. That is, T is a tri-diagonal matrix means that $T(i, j) = 0$ unless $|i - j| \le 1$.

(a) Devise a space-efficient storage scheme for tri-diagonal matrices, and give the corresponding index function.

(b) The *transpose* of a matrix is the matrix obtained by interchanging its rows with the corresponding columns. That is, matrix B is the transpose of matrix A means that $B(j, i) = A(i, j)$ for all indices i and j corresponding to positions in the matrix. Design an algorithm that transposes a tri-diagonal matrix using the storage scheme devised in the previous part of the exercise.

E3. An *upper triangular matrix* is a square matrix in which all entries below the main diagonal are 0. Describe the modifications necessary to use the access array method to store an upper triangular matrix.

E4. Consider a table of the triangular shape shown in Figure 9.7, where the columns are indexed from $-n$ to n and the rows from 0 to n.

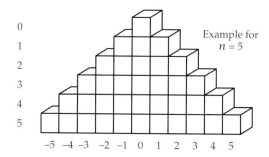

Figure 9.7. A table symmetrically triangular around 0

(a) Devise an index function that maps a table of this shape into a sequential array.
(b) Write a function that will generate an access array for finding the first entry of each row of a table of this shape within the contiguous array.
(c) Write a function that will reflect the table from left to right. The entries in column 0 (the central column) remain unchanged, those in columns -1 and 1 are swapped, and so on.

Programming Projects 9.3

Implement the method described in the text that uses an access array to store a lower triangular table, as applied in the following projects.

P1. Write a function that will read the entries of a lower triangular table from the terminal. The entries should be of type **double**.

P2. Write a function that will print a lower triangular table at the terminal.

P3. Suppose that a lower triangular table is a table of distances between cities, as often appears on a road map. Write a function that will check the triangle rule: The distance from city A to city C is never more than the distance from A to city B, plus the distance from B to C.

P4. Embed the functions of the previous projects into a complete program for demonstrating lower triangular tables.

9.4 TABLES: A NEW ABSTRACT DATA TYPE

At the beginning of this chapter we studied several *index functions* used to locate entries in tables, and then we turned to *access arrays*, which were arrays used for the same purpose as index functions. The analogy between functions and table lookup is indeed very close: With a function, we start with an argument and calculate a corresponding value; with a table, we start with an index and look up a corresponding value. Let us now use this analogy to produce a formal definition of the term *table*, a definition that will, in turn, motivate new ideas that come to fruition in the following section.

1. Functions

In mathematics a *function* is defined in terms of two sets and a correspondence from elements of the first set to elements of the second. If f is a function from a set A to a set B, then f assigns to each element of A a unique element of B. The set A is called the *domain* of f, and the set B is called the *codomain* of f. The subset of B containing just those elements that occur as values of f is called the *range* of f. This definition is illustrated in Figure 9.8.

domain, codomain, and range

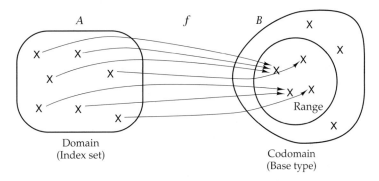

Figure 9.8. The domain, codomain, and range of a function

index set, value type

Table access begins with an index and uses the table to look up a corresponding value. Hence for a table we call the domain the *index set*, and we call the codomain the *base type* or *value type*. (Recall that in Section 4.6 a *type* was defined as a set of values.) If, for example, we have the array declaration

$$\textbf{double } \text{array}[\text{n}];$$

then the index set is the set of integers between 0 and $n - 1$, and the base type is the set of all real numbers. As a second example, consider a triangular table with m rows whose entries have type Item. The base type is then simply type Item and the index type is the set of ordered pairs of integers

$$\{(i, j) \mid 0 \leq j \leq i < \text{m}\}.$$

2. An Abstract Data Type

We are now well on the way toward defining *table* as a new abstract data type, but recall from Section 4.6 that to complete the definition, we must also specify the operations that can be performed. Before doing so, let us summarize what we know.

Definition

A *table* with index set I and base type T is a function from I into T together with the following operations.

the ADT table

1. *Table access*: Evaluate the function at any index in I.

2. *Table assignment*: Modify the function by changing its value at a specified index in I to the new value specified in the assignment.

These two operations are all that are provided for arrays in C++ and some other languages, but that is no reason why we cannot allow the possibility of further operations for our abstract tables. If we compare the definition of a list, we find that we allowed insertion and deletion as well as access and assignment. We can do the same with tables.

3. *Creation*: Set up a new function from I to T.

4. *Clearing*: Remove all elements from the index set I, so the remaining domain is empty.

5. *Insertion*: Adjoin a new element x to the index set I and define a corresponding value of the function at x.

6. *Deletion*: Delete an element x from the index set I and restrict the function to the resulting smaller domain.

Even though these last operations are not available directly for arrays in C++, they remain very useful for many applications, and we shall study them further in the next section. In some other languages, such as APL and SNOBOL, tables that change size while the program is running are an important feature. In any case, we should always be careful to program *into* a language and never allow our thinking to be limited by the restrictions of a particular language.

3. Implementation

index functions and access arrays

The definition just given is that of an abstract data type and in itself says nothing about implementation, nor does it speak of the index functions or access arrays studied earlier. Index functions and access arrays are, in fact, implementation methods for more general tables. An index function or access array starts with a general index set of some specified form and produces as its result an index in some subscript range, such as a subrange of the integers. This range can then be used directly as subscripts for arrays provided by the programming language. In this way, the implementation of a table is divided into two smaller problems: finding an access array or index function and programming an array. You should note that both of these are special cases of tables, and hence we have an example of solving a

divide and conquer

problem by dividing it into two smaller problems of the same nature. This process is illustrated in Figure 9.9.

4. Comparisons

lists and tables

Let us compare the abstract data types *list* and *table*. The underlying mathematical construction for a list is the sequence, and for a table, it is the set and the function. Sequences have an implicit order; a first element, a second, and so on, but sets and functions have no such order. (If the index set has some natural order, then sometimes this order is reflected in the table, but this is not a necessary aspect of using tables.) Hence information retrieval from a list naturally involves a search

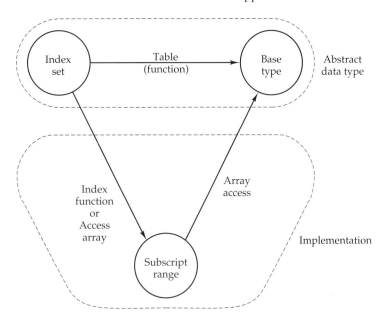

Figure 9.9. Implementation of a table

retrieval

like the ones studied in the previous chapter, but information retrieval from a table requires different methods, access methods that go directly to the desired entry. The time required for searching a list generally depends on the number n of entries in the list and is at least $\lg n$ (see Theorem 7.6), but the time for accessing a table does not usually depend on the number of entries in the table; that is, it is usually $O(1)$. For this reason, in many applications, table access is significantly faster than list searching.

traversal

On the other hand, traversal is a natural operation for a list but not for a table. It is generally easy to move through a list performing some operation with every entry in the list. In general, it may not be nearly so easy to perform an operation on every entry in a table, particularly if some special order for the entries is specified in advance.

tables and arrays

Finally, we should clarify the distinction between the terms *table* and *array*. In general, we shall use *table* as we have defined it in this section and restrict the term *array* to mean the programming feature available in C++ and most high-level languages and used for implementing both tables and contiguous lists.

9.5 APPLICATION: RADIX SORT

A formal sorting algorithm predating computers was first devised for use with punched cards but can be developed into a very efficient sorting method for linked lists that uses a table and queues. The algorithm is applied to records that use character string objects as keys.

9.5.1 The Idea

The idea is to consider the key one character at a time and to divide the entries, not into two sublists, but into as many sublists as there are possibilities for the given character from the key. If our keys, for example, are words or other alphabetic strings, then we divide the list into 26 sublists at each stage. That is, we set up a *table* of 26 lists and distribute the entries into the lists according to one of the characters in the key.

Old fashioned punched cards have 12 rows; hence mechanical card sorters were designed to work on only one column at a time and divide the cards into 12 piles.

A person sorting words by this method might first distribute the words into 26 lists according to the initial letter (or distribute punched cards into 12 piles), then divide each of these sublists into further sublists according to the second letter, and so on. The following idea eliminates this multiplicity of sublists: Partition the items into the table of sublists first by the *least* significant position, not the most significant. After this first partition, the sublists from the table are put back together as a single list, in the order given by the character in the least significant position. The list is then partitioned into the table according to the second least significant position and recombined as one list. When, after repetition of these steps, the list has been partitioned by the most significant place and recombined, it will be completely sorted.

example   This process is illustrated by sorting the list of nine three-letter words in Figure 9.10. The words are in the initial order shown in the left column. They are first divided into three lists according to their third letter, as shown in the second column, where the colored boxes indicate the resulting sublists. The order of the words in each sublist remains the same as it was before the partition. Next, the sublists are put back together as shown in the second column of the diagram, and they are now distributed into two sublists according to the second letter. The result is shown in the colored boxes of the third column. Finally, these sublists are recombined and distributed into four sublists according to the first letter. When these sublists are recombined, the whole list is sorted.

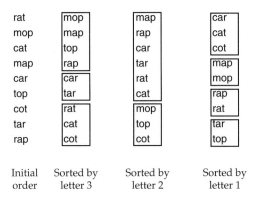

Figure 9.10. Trace of a radix sort

9.5.2 Implementation

We shall implement this method in C++ for lists of records whose keys are alphanumeric strings. After each time the items have been partitioned into sublists in a table, the sublists must be recombined into a single list so that the items can be redistributed according to the next most significant position in the key. We shall treat the sublists as queues, since entries are always inserted at the end of a sublist and, when recombining the sublists, removed from the beginning.

For clarity of presentation, we use our general list and queue packages for this processing. Doing so, however, entails some unnecessary data movement. For example, if we worked with suitably implemented linked lists and queues, we could recombine the linked queues into one list, by merely connecting the rear of each queue to the front of the next queue. This process is illustrated in Figure 9.11

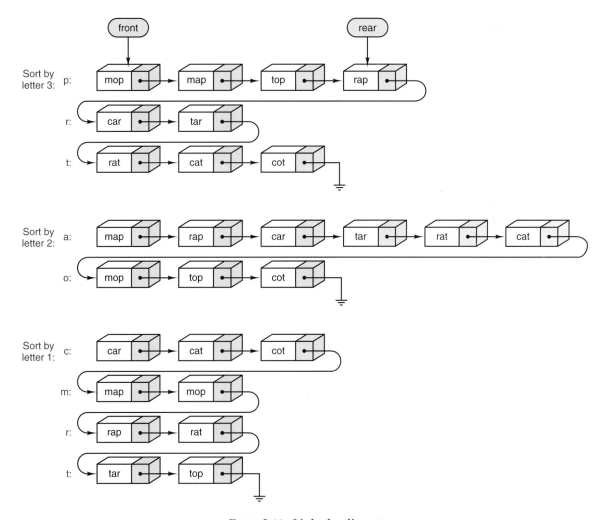

Figure 9.11. Linked radix sort

for the same list of nine words used previously. At each stage, the links shown in black are those within one of the queues, and the links shown in color are those added to recombine the queues into a single list. Programming this optimization of radix sort requires the implementation of a derived linked list class that allows concatenation, and it is left as a project.

In order to allow for missing or nonalphabetic characters, we shall set up an array of max_chars = 28 queues. Position 0 corresponds to a blank character, positions 1 through 26 correspond to the letters (with upper- and lowercase regarded as the same), and position 27 corresponds to any other character that appears in the key. Within a loop running from the least to most significant positions of the key, we shall traverse the linked list and add each item to the end of the appropriate queue. After the list has been thus partitioned, we recombine the queues into one list. At the end of the major loop on positions in the key, the list will be completely sorted.

Finally, with regard to declarations and notation, let us implement radix_sort as a new method for a Sortable_list (see Chapter 8). Thus the list definition now takes the form:

```
template <class Record>
class Sortable_list: public List<Record> {
public:                          //   sorting methods
   void radix_sort( );
   //   Specify any other sorting methods here.
private:                         //   auxiliary functions
   void rethread(Queue queues[ ]);
};
```

Here, the base **class** List can be any one of the implementations studied in Chapter 6. The auxiliary function rethread will be used to recombine the queues.

The requirements for the class Record are similar to those used in Chapter 8: Here, however, every Record uses an alphanumeric string as its Key. We shall use a Record method, **char** key_letter(**int** position), that returns the character in a particular position of the key (or returns a blank, if the key has length less than position). Thus the definition of a Record is based on the following skeleton:

```
class Record {
public:
   char key_letter(int position) const;
   Record( );                   //   default constructor
   operator Key( ) const;       //   cast to Key
//   Add other methods and data members for the class.
};
```

1. The Sorting Method

The sorting method takes the following form:

```
const int max_chars = 28;
template <class Record>
void Sortable_list<Record>::radix_sort()
/* Post: The entries of the Sortable_list have been sorted so all their keys are in
         alphabetical order.
   Uses: Methods from classes List, Queue, and Record;
         functions position and rethread. */
{
  Record data;
  Queue queues[max_chars];
  for (int position = key_size − 1; position >= 0; position−−) {
    //    Loop from the least to the most significant position.
    while (remove(0, data) == success) {
      int queue_number = alphabetic_order(data.key_letter(position));
      queues[queue_number].append(data);   //   Queue operation.
    }
    rethread(queues);                        //   Reassemble the list.
  }
}
```

This function uses two subsidiary subprograms: alphabetic_order to determine which **Queue** corresponds to a particular character, and Sortable_list :: rethread() to recombine the queues as the reordered Sortable_list. We can make use of the **Queue** operations from any of our implementations of the **Queue** ADT in Chapters 3 and 4.

2. Selecting a Queue

The function alphabetic_order checks whether a particular character is in the alphabet and assigns it to the appropriate position, where all nonalphabetical characters other than blanks go to position 27. Blanks are assigned to position 0. The function is also adjusted to make no distinction between upper- and lowercase.

```
int alphabetic_order(char c)
/* Post: The function returns the alphabetic position of character c, or it returns 0
         if the character is blank. */
{
  if (c == ' ') return 0;
  if ('a' <= c && c <= 'z') return c − 'a' + 1;
  if ('A' <= c && c <= 'Z') return c − 'A' + 1;
  return 27;
}
```

3. Connecting the Queues

The function rethread connects the 28 queues back together into one updated Sortable_list. The function also empties out all of these queues so they will be ready for reuse in the next iteration of our sorting procedure. One of the projects at the end of the section requests rewriting this function in an implementation-dependent way that will operate much more quickly than the current version.

```
template <class Record>
void Sortable_list<Record>::rethread(Queue queues[ ])
/* Post: All the queues are combined back to the Sortable_list, leaving all the
          queues empty.
    Uses: Methods of classes List, and Queue. */
{
  Record data;
  for (int i = 0; i < max_chars; i++)
    while (!queues[i].empty()) {
      queues[i].retrieve(data);
      insert(size(), data);
      queues[i].serve();
    }
}
```

9.5.3 Analysis

Note that the time used by radix sort is $\Theta(nk)$, where n is the number of items being sorted and k is the number of characters in a key. The time for all our other sorting methods depends on n but not directly on the length of a key. The best time was that of mergesort, which was $n \lg n + O(n)$.

The relative performance of the methods will therefore relate in some ways to the relative sizes of nk and $n \lg n$; that is, of k and $\lg n$. If the keys are long but there are relatively few of them, then k is large and $\lg n$ relatively small, and other methods (such as mergesort) will outperform radix sort; but if k is small (the keys are short) and there are a large number of keys, then radix sort will be faster than any other method we have studied.

Exercises 9.5

E1. Trace the action of radix sort on the list of 14 names used to trace other sorting methods:

Tim Dot Eva Roy Tom Kim Guy Amy Jon Ann Jim Kay Ron Jan

E2. Trace the action of radix sort on the following list of seven numbers considered as two-digit integers:

26   33   35   29   19   12   22

E3. Trace the action of radix sort on the preceding list of seven numbers considered as six-digit binary integers.

| **Programming Projects 9.5** | **P1.** Design, program, and test a version of radix sort that is implementation independent, with alphabetic keys. |

P2. The radix-sort program presented in the book is very inefficient, since its implementation-independent features force a large amount of data movement. Design a project that is implementation dependent and saves all the data movement. In **rethread** you need only link the rear of one queue to the front of the next. This linking requires access to protected **Queue** data members; in other words we need a modified **Queue** class. A simple way to achieve this is to add a method

Sortable_list :: concatenate(**const** Sortable_list &add_on);

to our derived linked list implementation and use lists instead of queues in the code for radix sort. Compare the performance of this version with that of other sorting methods for linked lists.

9.6 HASHING

9.6.1 Sparse Tables

1. Index Functions

We can continue to exploit table lookup even in situations where the key is no longer an index that can be used directly as in array indexing. What we can do is to set up a one-to-one correspondence between the keys by which we wish to retrieve information and indices that we can use to access an array. The index function that we produce will be somewhat more complicated than those of previous sections, since it may need to convert the key from, say, alphabetic information to an integer, but in principle it can still be done.

The only difficulty arises when the number of possible keys exceeds the amount of space available for our table. If, for example, our keys are alphabetical words of eight letters, then there are $26^8 \approx 2 \times 10^{11}$ possible keys, a number likely greater than the number of positions that will be available in high-speed memory. In practice, however, only a small fraction of these keys will actually occur. That is, the table is *sparse*. Conceptually, we can regard it as indexed by a very large set, but with relatively few positions actually occupied. Abstractly, we might think in terms of conceptual declarations such as

class   ... { **private:** sparse table(Key) of Record; };

Even though it may not be possible to implement a specification such as this directly, it is often helpful in problem solving to begin with such a picture, and only slowly tie down the details of how it is put into practice.

2. Hash Tables

index function not one to one

The idea of a *hash table* (such as the one shown in Figure 9.12) is to allow many of the different possible keys that might occur to be mapped to the same location in an array under the action of the index function. Then there will be a possibility that two records will want to be in the same place, but if the number of records that actually occur is small relative to the size of the array, then this possibility will cause little loss of time. Even when most entries in the array are occupied, hash methods can be an effective means of information retrieval.

1	2	3	4	5	6	7	8	9	10	11	12	13	14	15	16	17	18	19	20	21	22	23	24
class	public	private		do	operator	explicit	switch		return	unsigned	new			protected	enum	register	float	else	continue	typedef			

continued below

25	26	27	28	29	30	31	32	33	34	35	36	37	38	39	40	41	42	43	44	45	46	47
	static	short	template		int	struct			for		auto		signed	this			extern	sizeof		throw		

Figure 9.12. A hash table

hash function

We begin with a *hash function* that takes a key and maps it to some index in the array. This function will generally map several different keys to the same index. If the desired record is in the location given by the index, then our problem is solved; otherwise we must use some method to resolve the *collision* that may have occurred between two records wanting to go to the same location. There are thus two questions we must answer to use hashing:

collision

➥ First, we must find good hash functions.

➥ Second, we must determine how to resolve collisions.

Before approaching these questions, let us pause to outline informally the steps needed to implement hashing.

3. Algorithm Outlines

initialization

First, an array must be declared that will hold the hash table. Next, all locations in the array must be initialized to show that they are empty. How this is done depends on the application; often it is accomplished by setting the **Record** members to have

insertion

a key that is guaranteed never to occur as an actual key. With alphanumeric keys, for example, a key consisting of all blanks might represent an empty position.

To insert a record into the hash table, the hash function of its key is first calculated. If the corresponding location is empty, then the record can be inserted, else if the keys are equal, then insertion of the new record would not be allowed, and in the remaining case (a record with a different key is in the location), it becomes necessary to resolve the collision.

retrieval

To retrieve the record with a given key is entirely similar. First, the hash function for the key is computed. If the desired record is in the corresponding location, then the retrieval has succeeded; otherwise, while the location is nonempty and not all locations have been examined, follow the same steps used for collision resolution. If an empty position is found, or all locations have been considered, then no record with the given key is in the table, and the search is unsuccessful.

9.6.2 Choosing a Hash Function

The two principal criteria in selecting a hash function are as follows:

➡ It should be easy and quick to compute.

➡ It should achieve an even distribution of the keys that actually occur across the range of indices.

method

If we know in advance exactly what keys will occur, then it is possible to construct hash functions that will be very efficient, but generally we do not know in advance what keys will occur. Therefore, the usual way is for the hash function to take the key, chop it up, mix the pieces together in various ways, and thereby obtain an index that (like the pseudorandom numbers generated by computer) will be uniformly distributed over the range of indices.

Note, however, that there is nothing random about a hash function. If the function is evaluated more than once on the same key, then it must give the same result every time, so the key can be retrieved without fail.

It is from this process that the word *hash* comes, since the process produces a result with little resemblance to the original key. At the same time, it is hoped that any patterns or regularities that may occur in the keys will be destroyed, so that the results will be uniformly distributed. Even though the term *hash* is very descriptive, in some books the more technical terms **scatter-storage** or **key-transformation** are used in its place.

We shall consider three methods that can be put together in various ways to build a hash function.

1. Truncation

Ignore part of the key, and use the remaining part directly as the index (considering non-numeric members as their numerical codes). If the keys, for example, are eight-digit integers and the hash table has 1000 locations, then the first, second, and fifth digits from the right might make the hash function, so that 21296876 maps to 976. Truncation is a very fast method, but it often fails to distribute the keys evenly through the table.

2. Folding

Partition the key into several parts and combine the parts in a convenient way (often using addition or multiplication) to obtain the index. For example, an eight-digit integer can be divided into groups of three, three, and two digits, the groups added together, and truncated if necessary to be in the proper range of indices. Hence 21296876 maps to $212 + 968 + 76 = 1256$, which is truncated to 256. Since all information in the key can affect the value of the function, folding often achieves a better spread of indices than does truncation by itself.

3. Modular Arithmetic

prime modulus

Convert the key to an integer (using the aforementioned devices as desired), divide by the size of the index range, and take the remainder as the result. This amounts to using the C++ operator % . The spread achieved by taking a remainder depends very much on the modulus (in this case, the size of the hash array). If the modulus is a power of a small integer like 2 or 10, then many keys tend to map to the same index, while other indices remain unused. The best choice for modulus is often, but not always, a prime number, which usually has the effect of spreading the keys quite uniformly. (We shall see later that a prime modulus also improves an important method for collision resolution.) Hence, rather than choosing a hash table size of 1000, it is often better to choose either 997 or 1009; $2^{10} = 1024$ would usually be a poor choice. Taking the remainder is usually the best way to conclude calculating the hash function, since it can achieve a good spread and at the same time it ensures that the result is in the proper range.

4. C++ Example

alphanumeric strings

As a simple example, let us write a hash function in C++ for transforming a key consisting of eight alphanumeric characters into an integer in the range

$$0 .. hash\_size - 1.$$

Therefore, we shall assume that we have a class **Key** with the methods and functions of the following definition:

```
class Key: public String{
public:
    char key_letter(int position) const;
    void make_blank();
    //   Add constructors and other methods.
};
```

In order to save some programming effort in implementing the class, we have chosen to inherit the methods of our **class** String from Chapter 6. In particular, this saves us from programming the comparison operators. The method key_letter(**int** position) must return the character in a particular position of the Key, or return a blank if the Key has length less than n. The final method make_blank sets up an empty Key.

We can now write a simple hash function as follows:

sample hash function

```
int hash(const Key &target)
/* Post: target has been hashed, returning a value between 0 and hash_size − 1.
   Uses: Methods for the class Key. */
{
   int value = 0;
   for (int position = 0; position < 8; position++)
      value = 4 * value + target.key_letter(position);
   return value % hash_size;
}
```

We have simply added the integer codes corresponding to each of the eight characters, multiplying by 4 each time. There is no reason to believe that this method will be better (or worse), however, than any number of others. We could, for example, subtract some of the codes, multiply them in pairs, or ignore every other character. Sometimes an application will suggest that one hash function is better than another; sometimes it requires experimentation to settle on a good one.

9.6.3 Collision Resolution with Open Addressing

1. Linear Probing

The simplest method to resolve a collision is to start with the hash address (the location where the collision occurred) and do a sequential search through the table for the desired key or an empty location. Hence this method searches in a straight line, and it is therefore called *linear probing*. The table should be considered circular, so that when the last location is reached, the search proceeds to the first location of the table.

2. Clustering

The major drawback of linear probing is that, as the table becomes about half full, there is a tendency toward *clustering*; that is, records start to appear in long strings of adjacent positions with gaps between the strings. Thus the sequential searches needed to find an empty position become longer and longer. Consider the example in Figure 9.13, where the occupied positions are shown in color. Suppose that there are n locations in the array and that the hash function chooses any of them with equal probability $1/n$. Begin with a fairly uniform spread, as shown in the top diagram. If a new insertion hashes to location b, then it will go there, but if it hashes to location a (which is full), then it will also go into b. Thus the probability that b will be filled has doubled to $2/n$. At the next stage, an attempted insertion into any of locations a, b, c, or d will end up in d, so the probability of filling d is $4/n$. After this, e has probability $5/n$ of being filled, and so, as additional insertions are made, the most likely effect is to make the string of full positions beginning at location a longer and longer. Hence the performance of the hash table starts to degenerate toward that of sequential search.

example of clustering

OUCH!

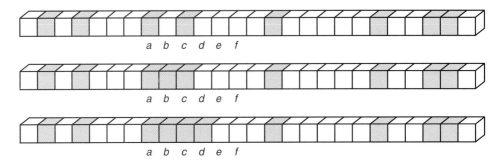

Figure 9.13. Clustering in a hash table

instability The problem of clustering is essentially one of instability; if a few keys happen randomly to be near each other, then it becomes more and more likely that other keys will join them, and the distribution will become progressively more unbalanced.

3. Increment Functions

If we are to avoid the problem of clustering, then we must use some more sophisticated way to select the sequence of locations to check when a collision occurs. There are many ways to do so. One, called *rehashing*, uses a second hash function *rehashing* to obtain the second position to consider. If this position is filled, then some other method is needed to get the third position, and so on. But if we have a fairly good spread from the first hash function, then little is to be gained by an independent second hash function. We will do just as well to find a more sophisticated way of determining the distance to move from the first hash position and apply this method, whatever the first hash location is. Hence we wish to design an increment function that can depend on the key or on the number of probes already made and that will avoid clustering.

4. Quadratic Probing

If there is a collision at hash address h, **quadratic probing** probes the table at locations $h + 1$, $h + 4$, $h + 9$, $\ldots$; that is, at locations $h + i^2$. (In other words, the increment function is i^2.)

Quadratic probing substantially reduces clustering, but it is not obvious that it will probe all locations in the table, and in fact it does not. For some values of hash_size the function will probe relatively few positions in the array. For example, when hash_size is a large power of 2, approximately one sixth of the positions are probed. When hash_size is a prime number, however, quadratic probing reaches half the locations in the array.

proof To prove this observation, suppose that hash_size is a prime number. Also suppose that we reach the same location at probe i and at some later probe that we can take as $i + j$ for some integer $j > 0$. Suppose that j is the smallest such integer. Then the values calculated by the function at i and at $i + j$ differ by a multiple of hash_size. In other words,

$$h + i^2 \equiv h + (i + j)^2 \pmod{\text{hash\_size}}.$$

When this expression is simplified, we obtain

$$j^2 + 2ij = j(j + 2i) \equiv 0 \ (\text{mod hash\_size}).$$

This last expression means that hash_size divides (with no remainder) the product $j(j + 2i)$. The only way that a prime number can divide a product is to divide one of its factors. Hence hash_size either divides j or it divides $j + 2i$. If the first case occurred, then we would have made hash_size probes before duplicating probe i. (Recall that j is the smallest positive integer such that probe $i + j$ duplicates probe i.) The second case, however, will occur sooner, when $j = \text{hash\_size} - 2i$, or, if this expression is negative, at this expression increased by hash_size. Hence the total number of distinct positions that will be probed is exactly

$$(\text{hash\_size} + 1)/2.$$

It is customary to regard the table as full when this number of positions has been probed, and the results are quite satisfactory.

calculation Note that quadratic probing can be accomplished without doing multiplications: After the first probe at position h, the increment is set to 1. At each successive probe, the increment is increased by 2 after it has been added to the previous location. Since

$$1 + 3 + 5 + \cdots + (2i - 1) = i^2$$

for all $i \geq 1$ (you can prove this fact by mathematical induction), probe i will look in position $h + 1 + 3 + \cdots + (2i - 1) = h + i^2$, as desired.

5. Key-Dependent Increments

Rather than having the increment depend on the number of probes already made, we can let it be some simple function of the key itself. For example, we could truncate the key to a single character and use its code as the increment. In C++, we might write

increment = (**int**) the_data.key_letter(0);

A good approach, when the remainder after division is taken as the hash function, is to let the increment depend on the quotient of the same division. An optimizing compiler should specify the division only once, so the calculation will be fast. In this method, the increment, once determined, remains constant. If hash_size is a prime, it follows that the probes will step through all the entries of the array before any repetitions. Hence overflow will not be indicated until the array is completely full.

6. Random Probing

A final method is to use a pseudorandom number generator to obtain the increment. The generator used should be one that always generates the same sequence provided it starts with the same seed.[2] The seed, then, can be specified as some function of the key. This method is excellent in avoiding clustering, but is likely to be slower than the others.

---

[2] See Appendix B for a discussion of pseudo-random number generators.

7. C++ Algorithms

To conclude the discussion of open addressing, we continue to study the C++ example already introduced (page 401), which uses alphanumeric keys. We suppose that the classes Key and Record have the properties that we have used in the last two sections. In particular, we assume these classes have methods key_letter(**int position**), that extract the character in a particular **position** of a key, and that there is a conversion operator that provides the Key of a Record.

We set up the hash table with the declarations

```
const int hash_size = 997;      //   a prime number of appropriate size
class Hash_table {
public:
    Hash_table( );
    void clear( );
    Error_code insert(const Record &new_entry);
    Error_code retrieve(const Key &target, Record &found) const;
private:
    Record table[hash_size];
};
```

initialization   The hash table must be created by initializing each entry in the array **table** to contain the special key that consists of eight blanks. This is the task of the constructor, whose specifications are:

Hash_table :: Hash_table( );

postcondition: The hash table has been created and initialized to be empty.

There should also be a method **clear** that removes all entries from a table that already exists.

---

void Hash_table :: clear( );

postcondition: The hash table has been cleared and is empty.

Although we have started to specify hash-table operations, we shall not continue to develop a complete and general package. Since the choice of a good hash function depends strongly on the kind of keys used, hash-table operations are usually too dependent on the particular application to be assembled into a general package.

To show how the code for further functions might be written, we shall continue to follow the example of the hash function already written in Section 9.6.2, page 401, and we shall use quadratic probing for collision resolution. We have shown that the maximum number of probes that can be made this way is (hash_size + 1)/2, and accordingly we keep a counter **probe_count** to check this upper bound.

With these conventions, let us write a method to insert a Record new_entry into the hash table.

insertion

```
Error_code Hash_table :: insert(const Record &new_entry)
/* Post: If the Hash_table is full, a code of overflow is returned. If the table already
           contains an item with the key of new_entry a code of duplicate_error is re-
           turned. Otherwise: The Record new_entry is inserted into the Hash_table
           and success is returned.
     Uses: Methods for classes Key, and Record. The function hash. */
{
    Error_code result = success;
    int probe_count,          //   Counter to be sure that table is not full.
        increment,            //   Increment used for quadratic probing.
        probe;                //   Position currently probed in the hash table.
    Key null;                 //   Null key for comparison purposes.
    null.make_blank();
    probe = hash(new_entry);
    probe_count = 0;
    increment = 1;
    while (table[probe] != null  //   Is the location empty?
            && table[probe] != new_entry  //   Duplicate key?
            && probe_count < (hash_size + 1)/2) {  //   Has overflow occurred?
        probe_count++;
        probe = (probe + increment) % hash_size;
        increment += 2;        //   Prepare increment for next iteration.
    }
    if (table[probe] == null) table[probe] = new_entry;   //   Insert new entry.
    else if (table[probe] == new_entry) result = duplicate_error;
    else result = overflow;    //   The table is full.
    return result;
}
```

A method to retrieve the record (if any) with a given key will have a similar form and is left as an exercise. The retrieval method should return the full Record associated with a Key target. Its specifications are as follows:

Error_code Hash_table :: retrieve(**const** Key &target, Record &found) **const**;

postcondition: If an entry in the hash table has key equal to target, then found takes on the value of such an entry, and success is returned. Otherwise, not_present is returned.

---

8. Deletions

Up to now, we have said nothing about deleting entries from a hash table. At first glance, it may appear to be an easy task, requiring only marking the deleted location with the special key indicating that it is empty. This method will not work.

The reason is that an empty location is used as the signal to stop the search for a target key. Suppose that, before the deletion, there had been a collision or two and that some entry whose hash address is the now-deleted position is actually stored elsewhere in the table. If we now try to retrieve that entry, then the now-empty position will stop the search, and it is impossible to find the entry, even though it is still in the table.

special key   One method to remedy this difficulty is to invent another special key, to be placed in any deleted position. This special key would indicate that this position is free to receive an insertion when desired but that it should not be used to terminate the search for some other entry in the table. Using this second special key will, however, make the algorithms somewhat more complicated and a bit slower. With the methods we have so far studied for hash tables, deletions are indeed awkward and should be avoided as much as possible.

9.6.4 Collision Resolution by Chaining

Up to now we have implicitly assumed that we are using only contiguous storage while working with hash tables. Contiguous storage for the hash table itself is, in fact, the natural choice, since we wish to be able to refer quickly to random positions *linked storage*   in the table, and linked storage is not suited to random access. There is, however, no reason why linked storage should not be used for the records themselves. We can take the hash table itself as an array of linked lists. An example appears in Figure 9.14.

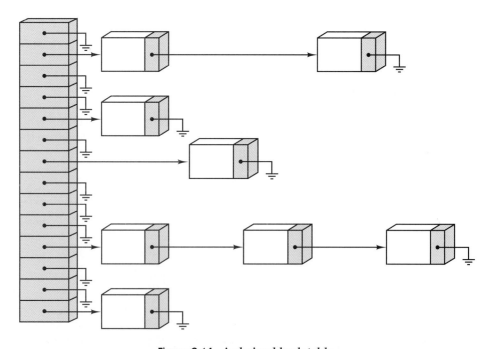

Figure 9.14. A chained hash table

chaining   It is traditional to refer to the linked lists from the hash table as ***chains*** and call this method collision resolution by ***chaining***.

1. Advantages of Chaining

Highlights

space saving

There are several advantages to this point of view. The first, and the most important when the records themselves are quite large, is that considerable space may be saved. Since the hash table is a contiguous array, enough space must be set aside at compilation time to avoid overflow. If the records themselves are in the hash table, then if there are many empty positions (as is desirable to help avoid the cost of collisions), these will consume considerable space that might be needed elsewhere. If, on the other hand, the hash table contains only pointers to the records, pointers that require only one word each, then the size of the hash table may be reduced by a large factor (essentially by a factor equal to the size of the records), and will become small relative to the space available for the records, or for other uses.

collision resolution   The second major advantage of keeping only linked lists in the hash table is that it allows simple and efficient collision handling. With a good hash function, few keys will give the same hash address, so the linked lists will be short and can be searched quickly. Clustering is no problem at all, because keys with distinct hash addresses always go to distinct lists.

overflow   A third advantage is that it is no longer necessary that the size of the hash table exceed the number of records. If there are more records than entries in the table, it means only that some of the linked lists are now sure to contain more than one record. Even if there are several times more records than the size of the table, the average length of the linked lists will remain small and sequential search on the appropriate list will remain efficient.

deletion   Finally, deletion becomes a quick and easy task in a chained hash table. Deletion proceeds in exactly the same way as deletion from a simple linked list.

2. Disadvantage of Chaining

use of space

These advantages of chained hash tables are indeed powerful. Lest you believe that chaining is always superior to open addressing, however, let us point out one important disadvantage: All the links require space. If the records are large, then this space is negligible in comparison with that needed for the records themselves; but if the records are small, then it is not.

small records   Suppose, for example, that the links take one word each and that the entries themselves take only one word (which is the key alone). Such applications are quite common, where we use the hash table only to answer some yes-no question about the key. Suppose that we use chaining and make the hash table itself quite small, with the same number n of entries as the number of entries. Then we shall use $3n$ words of storage altogether: n for the hash table, n for the keys, and n for the links to find the next node (if any) on each chain. Since the hash table will be nearly full, there will be many collisions, and some of the chains will have several entries. Hence searching will be a bit slow. Suppose, on the other hand, that we use open addressing. The same $3n$ words of storage put entirely into the hash table will mean that it will be only one-third full, and therefore there will be relatively few collisions and the search for any given entry will be faster.

3. C++ Algorithms

A chained hash table in C++ has the simple definition:

```
class Hash_table {
public:
    //   Specify methods here.
private:
    List<Record> table[hash_size];
};
```

Here the **class** List can be any one of the generic linked implementations of a list studied in Chapter 6. For consistency, the methods for a chained hash table include all methods of our earlier hash table implementation. The implementation of the constructor simply calls the constructor for each list in the array. To clear a chained hash table is a very different task. To clear the table, we must clear the linked list in each of the table positions. This task can be done by using the List method **clear( )**.

We can even use methods from the list package to access the hash table. The hash function itself is no different from that used with open addressing; for data retrieval, we can simply use a linked version of function **sequential_search** of Section 7.2. The essence of the method **Hash_table :: retrieve** is

sequential_search(table[hash(target)], target, position);

The details of converting this into a full function are left as an exercise.

Similarly, the essence of insertion is the one line

table[hash(new_entry)].insert(0, new_entry);

Here we have chosen to insert the new entry as the first node of its list, since that is the easiest. As you can see, both insertion and retrieval are simpler than the versions for open addressing, since collision resolution is not a problem and we can make use of the previous work done for lists.

deletion   Deletion from a chained hash table is also much simpler than it is from a table with open addressing. To delete the entry with a given key, we need only use sequential search to find the entry where it is located within its chain in the hash table, and then we delete this entry from its linked list. The specifications for this method are as follows:

Error_code Hash_table :: remove(**const** Key_type &target, Record &x);

postcondition: If the table has an entry with key equal to **target**, a code of **success** is returned, the entry is deleted from the hash table and recorded in x. Otherwise a code of **not_present** is returned.

Writing the corresponding function is left as an exercise.

Exercises 9.6

E1. Prove by mathematical induction that $1+3+5+\cdots+(2i-1)=i^2$ for all integers $i > 0$.

E2. Write a C++ function to insert an entry into a hash table with open addressing using linear probing.

E3. Write a C++ function to retrieve an entry from a hash table with open addressing using **(a)** linear probing; **(b)** quadratic probing.

E4. In a student project for which the keys were integers, one student thought that he could mix the keys well by using a trigonometric function, which had to be converted to an integer index, so he defined his hash function as

(int) sin(n).

What was wrong with this choice? He then decided to replace the function sin(n) by exp(n). Criticize this choice.

E5. Devise a simple, easy to calculate hash function for mapping three-letter words to integers between 0 and $n-1$, inclusive. Find the values of your function on the words

PAL   LAP   PAM   MAP   PAT   PET   SET   SAT   TAT   BAT

for $n = 11, 13, 17, 19$. Try for as few collisions as possible.

E6. Suppose that a hash table contains hash_size = 13 entries indexed from 0 through 12 and that the following keys are to be mapped into the table:

10   100   32   45   58   126   3   29   200   400   0

  (a) Determine the hash addresses and find how many collisions occur when these keys are reduced by applying the operation % hash_size.

  (b) Determine the hash addresses and find how many collisions occur when these keys are first folded by adding their digits together (in ordinary decimal representation) and then applying % hash_size.

perfect hash functions

  (c) Find a hash function that will produce no collisions for these keys. (A hash function that has no collisions for a fixed set of keys is called *perfect*.)

  (d) Repeat the previous parts of this exercise for hash_size = 11. (A hash function that produces no collision for a fixed set of keys that completely fill the hash table is called *minimal perfect*.)

E7. Another method for resolving collisions with open addressing is to keep a separate array called the *overflow table*, into which are put all entries that collide with an occupied location. They can either be inserted with another hash function or simply inserted in order, with sequential search used for retrieval. Discuss the advantages and disadvantages of this method.

E8. Write the following functions for processing a chained hash table, using the function sequential_search() of Section 7.2 and the list-processing operations of Section 6.1 to implement the operations.

    (a) Hash_table :: Hash_table( )

    (b) Hash_table :: clear( )

    (c) Hash_table :: insert(**const** Record &new_entry)

    (d) Hash_table :: retrieve(**const** Key &target, Record &found) **const;**

    (e) Hash_table :: remove(**const** Key_type &target, Record &x)

E9. Write a deletion algorithm for a hash table with open addressing using linear probing, using a second special key to indicate a deleted entry (see Part 8 of Section 9.6.3 on page 405). Change the retrieval and insertion algorithms accordingly.

E10. With linear probing, it is possible to delete an entry without using a second special key, as follows. Mark the deleted entry empty. Search until another empty position is found. If the search finds a key whose hash address is at or before the just-emptied position, then move it back there, make its previous position empty, and continue from the new empty position. Write an algorithm to implement this method. Do the retrieval and insertion algorithms need modification?

Programming Projects 9.6

P1. Consider the set of all C++ reserved words.[3] Consider these words as strings of 16 characters, where words less than 16 characters long are filled with blanks on the right.

    (a) Devise an integer-valued function that will produce different values when applied to all the reserved words. [You may find it helpful to write a short program that reads the words from a file, applies the function you devise, and determines what collisions occur.]

    (b) Find the smallest integer hash_size such that, when the values of your function are reduced by applying % hash_size, all the values remain distinct.

    (c) [*Challenging*] Modify your function as necessary until you can achieve hash_size in the preceding part to be the same as the number of reserved words. (You will then have discovered a *minimal perfect* hash function for the C++ reserved words, mapping these words onto a table with no empty positions.)

P2. Write a program that will read a molecular formula such as H_2SO_4 and will write out the molecular weight of the compound that it represents. Your program should be able to handle bracketed radicals such as in $Al_2(SO_4)_3$. [*Hint*: Use recursion to find the molecular weight of a bracketed radical. *Simplifications:* You may find it helpful to enclose the whole formula in parentheses (...). You will need to set up a hash table of atomic weights of elements, indexed by their abbreviations. For simplicity, the table may be restricted to the more common elements. Some elements have one-letter abbreviations, and some two. For uniformity you may add blanks to the one-letter abbreviations.]

molecular weight

---

[3] Any textbook on C++ will contain a list of the reserved words. Different versions of C++, however, support different sets of reserved words.

9.7 ANALYSIS OF HASHING

1. The Birthday Surprise

The likelihood of collisions in hashing relates to the well-known mathematical diversion: How many randomly chosen people need to be in a room before it becomes likely that two people will have the same birthday (month and day)? Since (apart from leap years) there are 365 possible birthdays, most people guess that the answer will be in the hundreds, but in fact, the answer is only 23 people.

We can determine the probabilities for this question by answering its opposite: With m randomly chosen people in a room, what is the probability that no two have the same birthday? Start with any person, and check that person's birthday off on a calendar. The probability that a second person has a different birthday is $364/365$. Check it off. The probability that a third person has a different birthday is now $363/365$. Continuing this way, we see that if the first $m - 1$ people have different birthdays, then the probability that person m has a different birthday is $(365 - m + 1)/365$. Since the birthdays of different people are independent, the probabilities multiply, and we obtain that the probability that m people all have different birthdays is

probability

$$\frac{364}{365} \times \frac{363}{365} \times \frac{362}{365} \times \cdots \times \frac{365 - m + 1}{365}.$$

This expression becomes less than 0.5 whenever $m \geq 23$.

collisions likely

In regard to hashing, the birthday surprise tells us that with any problem of reasonable size, we are almost certain to have some collisions. Our approach, therefore, should not be only to try to minimize the number of collisions, but also to handle those that occur as expeditiously as possible.

2. Counting Probes

As with other methods of information retrieval, we would like to know how many comparisons of keys occur on average during both successful and unsuccessful attempts to locate a given target key. We shall use the word **probe** for looking at one entry and comparing its key with the target.

The number of probes we need clearly depends on how full the table is. Therefore (as for searching methods), we let n be the number of entries in the table, and we let t (which is the same as hash_size) be the number of positions in the array holding the hash table. The *load factor* of the table is $\lambda = n/t$. Thus $\lambda = 0$ signifies an empty table; $\lambda = 0.5$ a table that is half full. For open addressing, λ can never exceed 1, but for chaining there is no limit on the size of λ. We consider chaining and open addressing separately.

load factor

3. Analysis of Chaining

With a chained hash table we go directly to one of the linked lists before doing any probes. Suppose that the chain that will contain the target (if it is present) has k entries. Note that k might be 0.

If the search is unsuccessful, then the target will be compared with all k of the corresponding keys. Since the entries are distributed uniformly over all t lists (equal probability of appearing on any list), the expected number of entries on the one being searched is $\lambda = n/t$. Hence the average number of probes for an unsuccessful search is λ.

Now suppose that the search is successful. From the analysis of sequential search, we know that the average number of comparisons is $\frac{1}{2}(k + 1)$, where k is the length of the chain containing the target. But the expected length of this chain is no longer λ, since we know in advance that it must contain at least one node (the target). The $n - 1$ nodes other than the target are distributed uniformly over all t chains; hence the expected number on the chain with the target is $1 + (n - 1)/t$. Except for tables of trivially small size, we may approximate $(n - 1)/t$ by $n/t = \lambda$. Hence the average number of probes for a successful search is very nearly

$$\tfrac{1}{2}(k + 1) \approx \tfrac{1}{2}(1 + \lambda + 1) = 1 + \tfrac{1}{2}\lambda.$$

In summary:

> *Retrieval from a chained hash table with load factor λ requires, on average, approximately $1 + \frac{1}{2}\lambda$ probes in the successful case and λ probes in the unsuccessful case.*

4. Analysis of Open Addressing

For our analysis of the number of probes done in open addressing, let us first ignore the problem of clustering by assuming that not only are the first probes random, but after a collision, the next probe will be random over all remaining positions of

the table. In fact, let us assume that the table is so large that all the probes can be regarded as independent events.

Let us first study an unsuccessful search. The probability that the first probe hits an occupied cell is λ, the load factor. The probability that a probe hits an empty cell is $1 - \lambda$. The probability that the unsuccessful search terminates in exactly two probes is therefore $\lambda(1 - \lambda)$, and, similarly, the probability that exactly k probes are made in an unsuccessful search is $\lambda^{k-1}(1 - \lambda)$. The expected number $U(\lambda)$ of probes in an unsuccessful search is therefore

$$U(\lambda) = \sum_{k=1}^{\infty} k\lambda^{k-1}(1 - \lambda).$$

This sum is evaluated in Section A.1; we obtain thereby

$$U(\lambda) = \frac{1}{(1 - \lambda)^2}(1 - \lambda) = \frac{1}{1 - \lambda}.$$

To count the probes needed for a successful search, we note that the number needed will be exactly one more than the number of probes in the unsuccessful search made before inserting the entry. Now let us consider the table as beginning empty, with each entry inserted one at a time. As these entries are inserted, the load factor grows slowly from 0 to its final value, λ. It is reasonable for us to approximate this step-by-step growth by continuous growth and replace a sum with an integral. We conclude that the average number of probes in a successful search is approximately

successful retrieval

$$S(\lambda) = \frac{1}{\lambda} \int_0^\lambda U(\mu) d\mu \; = \; \frac{1}{\lambda} \ln \frac{1}{1-\lambda}.$$

In summary:

> *Retrieval from a hash table with open addressing, random probing, and load factor λ requires, on average, approximately*
>
> $$\frac{1}{\lambda} \ln \frac{1}{1-\lambda}$$
>
> *probes in the successful case and $1/(1-\lambda)$ probes in the unsuccessful case.*

linear probing

Similar calculations may be done for open addressing with linear probing, where it is no longer reasonable to assume that successive probes are independent. The details, however, are rather more complicated, so we present only the results. For the complete derivation, consult the references at the end of the chapter.

> *Retrieval from a hash table with open addressing, linear probing, and load factor λ requires, on average, approximately*
>
> $$\frac{1}{2}\left(1 + \frac{1}{1-\lambda}\right)$$
>
> *probes in the successful case and*
>
> $$\frac{1}{2}\left(1 + \frac{1}{(1-\lambda)^2}\right)$$
>
> *probes in the unsuccessful case.*

5. Theoretical Comparisons

Figure 9.15 gives the values of the preceding expressions for different values of the load factor.

We can draw several conclusions from this table. First, it is clear that chaining consistently requires fewer probes than does open addressing. On the other hand, traversal of the linked lists is usually slower than array access, which can reduce the advantage, especially if key comparisons can be done quickly. Chaining comes

Load factor	0.10	0.50	0.80	0.90	0.99	2.00
Successful search, expected number of probes:						
Chaining	1.05	1.25	1.40	1.45	1.50	2.00
Open, random probes	1.05	1.4	2.0	2.6	4.6	—
Open, linear probes	1.06	1.5	3.0	5.5	50.5	—
Unsuccessful search, expected number of probes:						
Chaining	0.10	0.50	0.80	0.90	0.99	2.00
Open, random probes	1.1	2.0	5.0	10.0	100.	—
Open, linear probes	1.12	2.5	13.	50.	5000.	—

Figure 9.15. Theoretical comparison of hashing methods

into its own when the records are large, and comparison of keys takes significant time. Chaining is also especially advantageous when unsuccessful searches are common, since with chaining, an empty list or very short list may be found, so that often no key comparisons at all need be done to show that a search is unsuccessful.

For successful searches in a table with open addressing, the simpler method of linear probing is not significantly slower than more sophisticated methods of collision resolution, at least until the table is almost completely full. For unsuccessful searches, however, clustering quickly causes linear probing to degenerate into a long sequential search. We might conclude, therefore, that if searches are quite likely to be successful, and the load factor is moderate, then linear probing is quite satisfactory, but in other circumstances another method (such as quadratic probing) should be used.

6. Empirical Comparisons

It is important to remember that the computations giving Figure 9.15 are only approximate, and also that in practice nothing is completely random, so that we can always expect some differences between the theoretical results and actual computations. For sake of comparison, therefore, Figure 9.16 gives the results of one empirical study, using 900 keys that are pseudorandom numbers between 0 and 1.

comparisons   If you compare the numbers in Figures 9.15 and 9.16, you will find that the empirical results for chaining are essentially identical to the theoretical results. Those for quadratic probing are quite close to the theoretical results for random probing; the differences can easily be explained by the fact that quadratic probing is not really random. For linear probing, the results are similar when the table is relatively empty, but for nearly full tables the approximations made in the theoretical calculations produce results quite different from those of experiments. This shows the effects of making simplifying assumptions in the mathematics.

Load factor	0.1	0.5	0.8	0.9	0.99	2.0
Successful search, average number of probes:						
Chaining	1.04	1.2	1.4	1.4	1.5	2.0
Open, quadratic probes	1.04	1.5	2.1	2.7	5.2	—
Open, linear probes	1.05	1.6	3.4	6.2	21.3	—
Unsuccessful search, average number of probes:						
Chaining	0.10	0.50	0.80	0.90	0.99	2.00
Open, quadratic probes	1.13	2.2	5.2	11.9	126.	—
Open, linear probes	1.13	2.7	15.4	59.8	430.	—

Figure 9.16. Empirical comparison of hashing methods

conclusions

In comparison with other methods of information retrieval, the important thing to note about all these numbers is that they depend only on the load factor, not on the absolute number of entries in the table. Retrieval from a hash table with 20,000 entries in 40,000 possible positions is no slower, on average, than is retrieval from a table with 20 entries in 40 possible positions. With sequential search, a list 1000 times the size will take 1000 times as long to search. With binary search, this ratio is reduced to 10 (more precisely, to lg 1000), but still the time needed increases with the size, which it does not with hashing.

We can summarize these observations for retrieval from n entries as follows:

➡ Sequential search is $\Theta(n)$.

➡ Binary search is $\Theta(\log n)$.

➡ Hash-table retrieval is $\Theta(1)$.

Finally, we should emphasize the importance of devising a good hash function, one that executes quickly and maximizes the spread of keys. If the hash function is poor, the performance of hashing can degenerate to that of sequential search.

Exercises 9.7

E1. Suppose that each entry in a hash table occupies s words of storage (exclusive of the pointer member needed if chaining is used), where we take one *word* as the amount of space needed for a pointer. Also suppose that there are n occupied entries in the hash table, and the hash table has a total of t possible positions (t is the same as hash_size), including occupied and empty positions.

(a) If open addressing is used, determine how many words of storage will be required for the hash table.

(b) If chaining is used, then each node will require $s + 1$ words, including the pointer member. How many words will be used altogether for the n nodes?

(c) If chaining is used, how many words will be used for the hash table itself? (Recall that with chaining the hash table itself contains only pointers requiring one word each.)

(d) Add your answers to the two previous parts to find the total storage requirement for chaining.

(e) If s is small (that is, the entries have a small size), then open addressing requires less total memory for a given load factor $\lambda = n/t$, but for large s (large entries), chaining requires less space altogether. Find the break-even value for s, at which both methods use the same total storage. Your answer will be a formula for s that depends on the load factor λ, but it should not involve the numbers t or n directly.

(f) Evaluate and graph the results of your formula for values of λ ranging from 0.05 to 0.95.

E2. One reason why the answer to the birthday problem is surprising is that it differs from the answers to apparently related questions. For the following, suppose that there are n people in the room, and disregard leap years.

(a) What is the probability that someone in the room will have a birthday on a random date drawn from a hat?

(b) What is the probability that at least two people in the room will have that same random birthday?

(c) If we choose one person and find that person's birthday, what is the probability that someone else in the room will share the birthday?

E3. In a chained hash table, suppose that it makes sense to speak of an order for the keys, and suppose that the nodes in each chain are kept in order by key. *ordered hash table* Then a search can be terminated as soon as it passes the place where the key should be, if present. How many fewer probes will be done, on average, in an unsuccessful search? In a successful search? How many probes are needed, on average, to insert a new node in the right place? Compare your answers with the corresponding numbers derived in the text for the case of unordered chains.

E4. In our discussion of chaining, the hash table itself contained only lists, one for each of the chains. One variant method is to place the first actual entry of each chain in the hash table itself. (An empty position is indicated by an impossible key, as with open addressing.) With a given load factor, calculate the effect on space of this method, as a function of the number of words (except links) in each entry. (A link takes one word.)

Programming
Project 9.7

P1. Produce a table like Figure 9.16 for your computer, by writing and running test programs to implement the various kinds of hash tables and load factors.

9.8 CONCLUSIONS: COMPARISON OF METHODS

In this chapter and Chapter 7, we have explored four quite different methods of information retrieval:

➡ Sequential search,

➡ Binary search,

➡ Table lookup, and

➡ Hashing.

choice of data structures

If we are to ask which of these is best, we must first select the criteria by which to answer, and these criteria will include both the requirements imposed by the application and other considerations that affect our choice of data structures, since the first two methods are applicable only to lists and the second two to tables. In many applications, however, we are free to choose either lists or tables for our data structures.

table lookup

In regard both to speed and convenience, ordinary lookup in contiguous tables is certainly superior, but there are many applications to which it is inapplicable, such as when a list is preferred or the set of keys is sparse. It is also inappropriate whenever insertions or deletions are frequent, since such actions in contiguous storage may require moving large amounts of information.

Which of the other three methods is best depends on other criteria, such as the form of the data.

other methods

Sequential search is certainly the most flexible of our methods. The data may be stored in any order, with either contiguous or linked representation. Binary search is much more demanding. The keys must be in order, and the data must be in random-access representation (contiguous storage). Hashing requires even more, a peculiar ordering of the keys well suited to retrieval from the hash table, but generally useless for any other purpose. If the data are to be available immediately for human inspection, then some kind of order is essential, and a hash table is inappropriate.

near miss

Finally, there is the question of the unsuccessful search. Sequential search and hashing, by themselves, say nothing except that the search was unsuccessful. Binary search can determine which data have keys closest to the target, and perhaps thereby can provide useful information. In Chapter 10 we shall study tree-based methods for storing data that combine the efficiency of binary search with the flexibility of linked structures.

9.9 APPLICATION: THE LIFE GAME REVISITED

At the end of Chapter 1 we noted that the bounds we used for the arrays in CONWAY's game of Life were highly restrictive and artificial. The Life cells are supposed to be on an unbounded grid. In other words, we would really like to have the C++ declaration

```
class Life {
public:
  //   methods
private:
  bool map[int] [int];
  //   other data and auxiliary functions
};
```

unbounded array
sparse table

which is, of course, illegal. Since only a limited number of the cells in an unbounded grid would actually be occupied at any one time, we should really regard the grid for the Life game as a sparse table, and therefore a hash table proves an attractive way to represent the grid.

9.9.1 Choice of Algorithm

Before we specify our data structures more precisely, let us consider the basic algo-rithm that we might use. In our original implementation, the **main** function makes no reference to the way that a Life configuration is stored in the computer, and therefore we need not change this function at all:

```
int main()                     //   Program to play Conway's game of Life.
/* Pre:   The user supplies an initial configuration of living cells.
   Post:  The program prints a sequence of pictures showing the changes in the
          configuration of living cells according to the rules for the game of Life.
   Uses:  The class Life and its methods initialize(), print() and update().
          The functions  instructions(), user_says_yes(). */
{
  Life configuration;
  instructions();
  configuration.initialize();
  configuration.print();
  cout << "Continue viewing new generations? " << endl;
  while (user_says_yes()) {
    configuration.update();
    configuration.print();
    cout << "Continue viewing new generations? " << endl;
  }
}
```

We shall need to rewrite the Life method **update** so that it uses a table to look up the status of cells. For any given cell in a configuration, we can determine the number of living neighbors by looking up the status of each neighboring cell. Thus, if we settle on a small set of candidates that might live in the coming generation, the method **update** can use the table to determine exactly which of them should become alive. In any **update**, we must examine the cells that are already alive and also their neighbors. Therefore, in our implementation of **update** we traverse these cells, determine their neighbor counts by using the table, and select those cells that will live in the next generation.

9.9.2 Specification of Data Structures

We have already decided that a Life configuration will include a hash table to look up the status of cells. However, we will need to traverse the living cells in a configuration. As we have seen, it is usually inefficient to traverse the entries of a hash table. Let us therefore incorporate a List of living cells as a second data member of a Life configuration. The objects stored in the list and table of a Life configuration carry information about individual cells. We shall represent these cells as instances of a structure called **Cell**: Each **Cell** must contain a pair of grid coordinates. Thus we arrive at the following definition:

```
struct Cell {
    Cell() { row = col = 0; }          // constructors
    Cell(int x, int y) { row = x; col = y; }
    int row, col;                       //  grid coordinates
};
```

In this structure definition we have supplied inline implementations of the constructors and therefore no corresponding code file is needed. In C++, we can place inline method implementations into a header file without jeopardizing separate compilation of our program.

creation of a Cell

As a Life configuration expands, cells on its fringes will be encountered for the first time. Whenever a new **Cell** is needed, it must be created dynamically. Therefore, because **Cell** objects are created dynamically, they can only be accessed through pointers.

indirect linked list

Moreover, to be able to dispose of a **Cell** object, at the end of its lifetime, we must retain a record of the corresponding pointer. Therefore, we shall implement the list member of a Life configuration to store pointers to cells. The result is illustrated in Figure 9.17.

Each node of the list thus contains two pointers: one to a cell and one to the next node of the list.

finding Cell *coordinates*

Notice that, given a pointer to a cell, we can determine the corresponding cell coordinates: We simply follow the pointer to the **Cell** object and its **row** and **col** data members. Thus, we can conveniently store pointers to cells as the records in a hash table; the coordinates of the cells, which are determined by the pointers, are the corresponding keys.

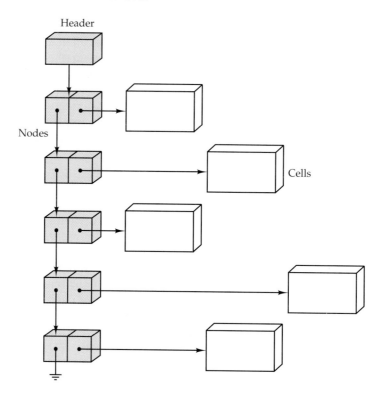

Figure 9.17. An indirect linked list

Now that we have an idea of how a hash table will be used in our new Life program, we can make an informed choice about its implementation. We must decide between open addressing and chaining. The entries to be stored in the

use of space   table need little space: Each entry need only store a pointer to a **Cell**. Since the table entries are small, there are few space considerations to advise our decision. With chaining, the size of each record will increase 100 percent to accommodate the necessary pointer, but the hash table itself will be smaller and can take a higher load factor than with open addressing. With open addressing, the records will be smaller, but more room must be left vacant in the hash table to avoid long searches and possible overflow.

specification   For flexibility, therefore, let us decide to use a chained hash table with the following class definition:

```
class Hash_table {
public:
   Error_code insert(Cell *new_entry);
   bool retrieve(int row, int col) const;
private:
   List<Cell *> table[hash_size];
};
```

Here, we have specified just two methods: insert and retrieve. The only use that we shall make of retrieval is to enquire whether the hash table contains a pointer to a Cell with particular coordinates. Accordingly, the method retrieve uses a pair of coordinates as its parameters and returns a **bool** result to indicate whether such a Cell is represented in the table. We leave the implementation of the methods for this hash table as a project, since they are very similar to those discussed in Section 9.6.

We remark that a Hash_table does come with default constructor and destructor methods. For example, the destructor, which we shall rely on, applies the List destructor to each element of the array table.

9.9.3 The Life Class

pointer manipulations

With these decisions made, we can now tie down the representation and notation for the **class** Life. In order to facilitate the replacement of a configuration by an updated version, we shall store the data members indirectly, as pointers. Therefore, the **class** Life needs a constructor and a destructor to allocate and dispose of dynamic storage for these structures. The other Life methods—initialize, print, and update—are all explicitly used by the main function.

```
class Life {
public:
   Life( );
   void initialize( );
   void print( );
   void update( );
    ~Life( );
private:
   List<Cell *> *living;
   Hash_table *is_living;
   bool retrieve(int row, int col) const;
   Error_code insert(int row, int col);
   int neighbor_count(int row, int col) const;
};
```

The auxiliary member functions retrieve and neighbor_count determine the status of a cell by applying hash-table retrieval. The other auxiliary function, insert, creates a dynamic Cell object and inserts it into both the hash table and the list of cells of a Life object.

9.9.4 The Life Functions

Let us now write several of the Life methods and functions, to show how processing of the cells, lists, and tables transpires. The remaining functions will be left as exercises.

1. Updating the Configuration

review of first Life
program

The crucial **Life** method is **update**, whose task is to start with one **Life** configuration and determine what the configuration will become at the next generation. In Section 1.4.4, we did this by examining every possible cell in the **grid** configuration, calculating its neighbor count to determine whether or not it should live in the coming generation. This information was stored in a local variable **new_grid** that was eventually copied to **grid**.

Let us to continue to follow this outline, except that, with an unbounded grid, we must not try to examine every possible cell in the configuration. Instead, we must limit our attention to the cells that may possibly be alive in the coming generation. Which cells are these? Certainly, we should examine all the living cells to determine which of them remain alive. We must also examine some of the dead cells. For a dead cell to become alive, it must have exactly three living neighbors (according to the rules in Section 1.2.1). Therefore, we will include all these cells (and likely others besides) if we examine all the cells that are neighbors of living cells. All such neighbors are shown as the shaded fringe in the configuration of Figure 9.18.

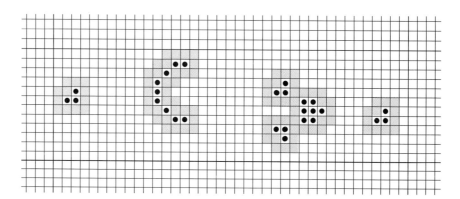

Figure 9.18. A Life configuration with fringe of dead cells

In the method **update**, a local variable **Life new_configuration** is thereby gradually built up to represent the upcoming configuration: We loop over all the (living) cells from the current configuration, and we also loop over all the (dead) cells that are neighbors of these (living) cells. For each cell, we must first determine whether it has already been added to **new_configuration**, since we must be careful not to add duplicate copies of any cell. If the cell does not already belong to **new_configuration**, we use the function **neighbor_count** to decide whether it should be added, and if appropriate we **insert** it into **new_configuration**.

At the end of the method, we must swap the **List** and **Hash_table** members between the current configuration and **new_configuration**. This exchange ensures that the **Life** object now represents an updated configuration. Moreover, it ensures that the destructor that will automatically be applied to the local variable **Life new_configuration** will dispose of the cells, the **List**, and the **Hash_table** that represent the former configuration.

We thus obtain the following implementation:

```
void Life :: update( )
/* Post:  The Life object contains the next generation of configuration.
   Uses:  The class Hash_table and the class Life and its auxiliary functions. */
{
   Life new_configuration;
   Cell *old_cell;
   for (int i = 0;  i < living->size( ); i++) {
      living->retrieve(i, old_cell);   //   Obtain a living cell.
      for (int row_add = −1; row_add < 2; row_add ++)
         for (int col_add = −1; col_add < 2; col_add++) {
            int new_row = old_cell->row + row_add,
               new_col = old_cell->col + col_add;
//   new_row, new_col is now a living cell or a neighbor of a living cell,
            if (!new_configuration.retrieve(new_row, new_col))
               switch (neighbor_count(new_row, new_col)) {
               case 3:             //   With neighbor count 3, the cell becomes alive.
                  new_configuration.insert(new_row, new_col);
                  break;
               case 2:             //   With count 2, cell keeps the same status.
                  if (retrieve(new_row, new_col))
                     new_configuration.insert(new_row, new_col);
                  break;
               default:            //   Otherwise, the cell is dead.
                  break;
               }
         }
   }
//   Exchange data of current configuration with data of new_configuration.
   List<Cell *> *temp_list = living;
   living = new_configuration.living;
   new_configuration.living = temp_list;
   Hash_table *temp_hash = is_living;
   is_living = new_configuration.is_living;
   new_configuration.is_living = temp_hash;
}
```

2. Printing

printing window We recognize that it is impossible to display more than a small piece of the now unbounded Life configuration on a user's screen. Therefore, we shall merely print a rectangular window, showing the status of a 20×80 central portion of a Life configuration. For each cell in the window, we **retrieve** its status from the hash table and print either a blank or non-blank character accordingly.

```
void Life :: print( )
/* Post:  A central window onto the Life object is displayed.
   Uses:  The auxiliary function Life :: retrieve. */
{
  int row, col;
  cout ≪ endl ≪ "The current Life configuration is:" ≪ endl;
  for (row = 0;  row < 20;  row++) {
    for (col = 0;  col < 80;  col++)
      if (retrieve(row, col)) cout ≪ '*';
      else cout ≪ ' ';
    cout ≪ endl;
  }
  cout ≪ endl;
}
```

3. Creation and Insertion of new Cells

task

We now turn to the function insert that creates a Cell object and explicitly references the hash table. The task of the function is to create a new cell, with the given coordinates and put it in both the hash table and the List living. This outline translates into the following C++ function.

```
Error_code Life :: insert(int row, int col)
/* Pre:   The cell with coordinates row and col does not belong to the Life config-
          uration.
   Post:  The cell has been added to the configuration. If insertion into either the
          List or the Hash_table fails, an error code is returned.
   Uses:  The class List, the class Hash_table, and the struct Cell */
{
  Error_code outcome;
  Cell *new_cell = new Cell(row, col);
  int index = living->size( );
  outcome = living->insert(index, new_cell);
  if (outcome ==  success)
    outcome = is_living->insert(new_cell);
  if (outcome != success)
    cout ≪ " Warning: new Cell insertion failed" ≪ endl;
  return outcome;
}
```

4. Construction and Destruction of Life Objects

We must provide a constructor and destructor for our **class** Life to allocate and dispose of its dynamically allocated members. The constructor need only apply the new operator.

```
Life :: Life( )
/* Post:  The members of a Life object are dynamically allocated and initialized.
     Uses:  The class Hash_table and the class List. */
{
   living = new List<Cell *>;
   is_living = new Hash_table;
}
```

The destructor must dispose of any object that might ever be dynamically defined by a method of the **class** Life. In addition to the List *living and the Hash_table *is_living that are dynamically created by the constructor, the Cell objects that they reference are dynamically created by the method insert. The following implementation begins by disposing of these Cell objects:

```
Life :: ~Life( )
/* Post:  The dynamically allocated members of a Life object and all Cell objects
          that they reference are deleted.
     Uses:  The class Hash_table and the class List. */
{
   Cell *old_cell;
   for (int i = 0;  i < living->size( );  i++) {
      living->retrieve(i, old_cell);
      delete old_cell;
   }
   delete is_living;           //   Calls the Hash_table destructor
   delete living;              //   Calls the List destructor
}
```

5. The Hash Function

Our hash function will differ slightly from those earlier in this chapter, in that its argument already comes in two parts (row and column), so that some kind of folding can be done easily. Before deciding how, let us for a moment consider the special case of a small array, where the function is one-to-one and is exactly the index function. When there are exactly maxrow entries in each row, the index i, j maps to

index function

$$i + \text{maxrow} * j$$

to place the rectangular array into contiguous, linear storage, one row after the next.

It should prove effective to use a similar mapping for our hash function, where we replace maxrow by some convenient number (like a prime) that will maximize the spread and reduce collisions. Hence we obtain

```
const int factor = 101;

int hash(int row, int col)
/* Post:  The function returns the hashed valued between 0 and hash_size − 1 that
          corresponds to the given Cell parameter. */
{
  int value;
  value = row + factor * col;
  value %= hash_size;
  if (value < 0) return value + hash_size;
  else return value;
}
```

6. Other Subprograms

The remaining Life member functions initialize, retrieve, and neighbor_count all
bear considerable resemblance either to one of the preceding functions or to the
corresponding function in our earlier Life program. These functions can therefore
safely be left as projects.

**Programming
Projects 9.9**

P1. Write the Life methods **(a)** neighbor_count, **(b)** retrieve, and **(c)** initialize.

P2. Write the Hash_table methods **(a)** insert and **(b)** retrieve for the chained implementation that stores pointers to cells of a Life configuration.

P3. Modify **update** so that it uses a second local Life object to store cells that have
been considered for insertion, but rejected. Use this object to make sure that
no cell is considered twice.

POINTERS AND PITFALLS

1. Use top-down design for your data structures, just as you do for your algorithms. First determine the logical structure of the data, then slowly specify
   more detail, and delay implementation decisions as long as possible.

2. Before considering detailed structures, decide what operations on the data
   will be required, and use this information to decide whether the data belong
   in a *list* or a *table*. Traversal of the data structure or access to all the data in
   a prespecified order generally implies choosing a list. Access to any entry in
   time $O(1)$ generally implies choosing a table.

3. For the design and programming of lists, see Chapter 6.

4. Use the logical structure of the data to decide what kind of table to use: an
   ordinary array, a table of some special shape, a system of inverted tables, or a
   hash table. Choose the simplest structure that allows the required operations
   and that meets the space requirements of the problem. Don't write complicated
   functions to save space that will then remain unused.

5. Let the structure of the data help you decide whether an index function or an access array is better for accessing a table of data. Use the features built into your programming language whenever possible.

6. In using a hash table, let the nature of the data and the required operations help you decide between chaining and open addressing. Chaining is generally preferable if deletions are required, if the records are relatively large, or if overflow might be a problem. Open addressing is usually preferable when the individual records are small and there is no danger of overflowing the hash table.

7. Hash functions usually need to be custom designed for the kind of keys used for accessing the hash table. In designing a hash function, keep the computations as simple and as few as possible while maintaining a relatively even spread of the keys over the hash table. There is no obligation to use every part of the key in the calculation. For important applications, experiment by computer with several variations of your hash function, and look for rapid calculation and even distribution of the keys.

8. Recall from the analysis of hashing that some collisions will almost inevitably occur, so don't worry about the existence of collisions if the keys are spread nearly uniformly through the table.

9. For open addressing, clustering is unlikely to be a problem until the hash table is more than half full. If the table can be made several times larger than the space required for the records, then linear probing should be adequate; otherwise more sophisticated collision resolution may be required. On the other hand, if the table is many times larger than needed, then initialization of all the unused space may require excessive time.

REVIEW QUESTIONS

9.1   **1.** In terms of the Θ and Ω notations, compare the difference in time required for table lookup and for list searching.

9.2   **2.** What are *row-major* and *column-major* ordering?

9.3   **3.** Why do *jagged tables* require access arrays instead of index functions?

    4. For what purpose are *inverted tables* used?

    5. What is the difference in purpose, if any, between an *index function* and an *access array*?

9.4   **6.** What operations are available for an abstract table?

    7. What operations are usually easier for a list than for a table?

9.5   **8.** In 20 words or less, describe how *radix sort* works.

    9. In radix sort, why are the keys usually partitioned first by the least significant position, not the most significant?

9.6   **10.** What is the difference in purpose, if any, between an *index function* and a *hash function*?

     11. What objectives should be sought in the design of a hash function?

     12. Name three techniques often built into hash functions.

     13. What is *clustering* in a hash table?

     14. Describe two methods for minimizing clustering.

     15. Name four advantages of a chained hash table over open addressing.

     16. Name one advantage of open addressing over chaining.

9.7   **17.** If a hash function assigns 30 keys to random positions in a hash table of size 300, about how likely is it that there will be no collisions?

REFERENCES FOR FURTHER STUDY

The primary reference for this chapter is KNUTH, Volume 3. (See page 77 for bibliographic details.) Hashing is the subject of Volume 3, pp. 506–549. KNUTH studies every method we have touched, and many others besides. He does algorithm analysis in considerably more detail than we have, writing his algorithms in a pseudo-assembly language, and counting operations in detail there.

The following book (pp. 156–185) considers arrays of various kinds, index functions, and access arrays in considerable detail:

C. C. GOTLIEB and L. R. GOTLIEB, *Data Types and Structures*, Prentice Hall, Englewood Cliffs, N.J., 1978.

An interesting study of hash functions and the choice of constants used is:

B. J. McKENZIE, R. HARRIES, and T. C. BELL, "Selecting a hashing algorithm," *Software Practice and Experience* 20 (1990), 209–224.

Extensions of the birthday surprise are considered in

M. S. KLAMKIN and D. J. NEWMAN, *Journal of Combinatorial Theory* 3 (1967), 279–282.

A thorough and informative analysis of hashing appears in Chapter 8 of

ROBERT SEDGEWICK and PHILIPPE FLAJOLET, *An Introduction to the Analysis of Algorithms*, Addison-Wesley, Reading, Mass., 1996.

Binary Trees

10

L INKED LISTS have great advantages of flexibility over the contiguous representation of data structures, but they have one weak feature: They are sequential lists; that is, they are arranged so that it is necessary to move through them only one position at a time. In this chapter we overcome these disadvantages by studying trees as data structures, using the methods of pointers and linked lists for their implementation. Data structures organized as trees will prove valuable for a range of applications, especially for problems of information retrieval.

10.1 BINARY TREES

For some time, we have been drawing trees to illustrate the behavior of algorithms. We have drawn comparison trees showing the comparisons of keys in searching and sorting algorithms; we have drawn trees of subprogram calls; and we have drawn recursion trees. If, for example, we consider applying binary search to the following list of names, then the order in which comparisons will be made is shown in the comparison tree of Figure 10.1.

Amy Ann Dot Eva Guy Jan Jim Jon Kay Kim Ron Roy Tim Tom

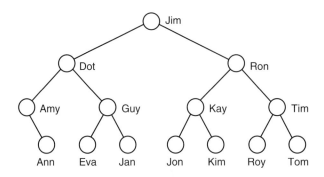

Figure 10.1. Comparison tree for binary search

10.1.1 Definitions

In binary search, when we make a comparison with a key, we then move either left or right depending on the outcome of the comparison. It is thus important to keep the relation of *left* and *right* in the structure we build. It is also possible that the part of the tree on one side or both below a given node is empty. In the example of Figure 10.1, the name Amy has an empty left subtree. For all the leaves, both subtrees are empty.

We can now give the formal definition of a new data structure.

Definition   A *binary tree* is either empty, or it consists of a node called the *root* together with two binary trees called the *left subtree* and the *right subtree* of the root.

ADT   Note that this definition is that of a mathematical structure. To specify binary trees as an abstract data type, we must state what operations can be performed on binary trees. Rather than doing so at once, we shall develop the operations as the chapter progresses.

Note also that this definition makes no reference to the way in which binary trees will be implemented in memory. As we shall presently see, a linked representation is natural and easy to use, but other implementations are possible as well. Note, finally, that this definition makes no reference to keys or the way in which

430

they are ordered. Binary trees are used for many purposes other than searching; hence we have kept the definition general.

Before we consider general properties of binary trees further, let us return to the general definition and see how its recursive nature works out in the construction of small binary trees.

small binary trees

The first case, the base case that involves no recursion, is that of an empty binary tree. For other kinds of trees, we might never think of allowing an empty one, but for binary trees it is convenient, not only in the definition, but in algorithms, to allow for an empty tree. The empty tree will usually be the base case for recursive algorithms and will determine when the algorithm stops.

The only way to construct a binary tree with one node is to make that node into the root and to make both the left and right subtrees empty. Thus a single node with no branches is the one and only binary tree with one node.

With two nodes in the tree, one of them will be the root and the other will be in a subtree. Thus either the left or right subtree must be empty, and the other will contain exactly one node. Hence there are two different binary trees with two nodes.

left and right

At this point, you should note that the concept of a binary tree differs from some of the examples of trees that we have previously seen, in that left and right are important for binary trees. The two binary trees with two nodes can be drawn as

　and　

which are different from each other. We shall never draw any part of a binary tree to look like

since there is no way to tell if the lower node is the left or the right child of its parent.

comparison trees

We should, furthermore, note that binary trees are not the same class as the 2-trees we studied in the analysis of algorithms in Chapters 7 and 8. Each node in a 2-tree has either 0 or 2 children, never 1, as can happen with a binary tree. Left and right are not fundamentally important for studying the properties of comparison trees, but they are crucial in working with binary trees.[1]

---

[1] In Section 10.3.6 we shall, however, see that binary trees can be converted into 2-trees and *vice versa*.

binary trees with three nodes   For the case of a binary tree with three nodes, one of these will be the root, and the others will be partitioned between the left and right subtrees in one of the ways

$$2 + 0 \qquad 1 + 1 \qquad 0 + 2.$$

Since there are two binary trees with two nodes and only one empty tree, the first case gives two binary trees. The third case, similarly, gives two more binary trees. In the second case the left and right subtrees both have one node, and there is only one binary tree with one node, so there is one binary tree in the second case. Altogether, then, there are five binary trees with three nodes.

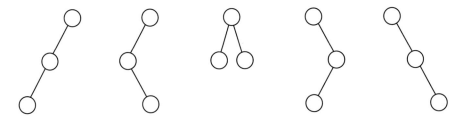

Figure 10.2. The binary trees with three nodes

The binary trees with three nodes are all shown in Figure 10.2. The steps that we went through to construct these binary trees are typical of those needed for larger cases. We begin at the root and think of the remaining nodes as partitioned between the left and right subtrees. The left and right subtrees are then smaller cases for which we know the results from earlier work.

Before proceeding, you should pause to construct all fourteen binary trees with four nodes. This exercise will further help you establish the ideas behind the definition of binary trees.

10.1.2 Traversal of Binary Trees

One of the most important operations on a binary tree is *traversal*, moving through all the nodes of the binary tree, visiting each one in turn. As for traversal of other data structures, the action we shall take when we *visit* each node will depend on the application.

For lists, the nodes came in a natural order from first to last, and traversal followed the same order. For trees, however, there are many different orders in which we could traverse all the nodes. When we write an algorithm to traverse a binary tree, we shall almost always wish to proceed so that the same rules are applied at each node, and we thereby adhere to a general pattern.

At a given node, then, there are three tasks we shall wish to do in some order: We shall visit the node itself; we shall traverse its left subtree; and we shall traverse its right subtree. The key distinction in traversal orders is to decide if we are to visit the node itself before traversing either subtree, between the subtrees, or after traversing both subtrees.

If we name the tasks of visiting a node V, traversing the left subtree L, and traversing the right subtree R, then there are six ways to arrange them:

$$V\,L\,R \qquad L\,V\,R \qquad L\,R\,V \qquad V\,R\,L \qquad R\,V\,L \qquad R\,L\,V.$$

1. Standard Traversal Orders

By standard convention, these six are reduced to three by considering only the ways in which the left subtree is traversed before the right. The three mirror images are clearly similar. The three ways with left before right are given special names that we shall use from now on:

$V\,L\,R$	$L\,V\,R$	$L\,R\,V$
preorder	*inorder*	*postorder*

preorder, inorder, and postorder These three names are chosen according to the step at which the given node is visited. With **preorder traversal**, the node is visited before the subtrees; with **inorder traversal**, it is visited between them; and with **postorder traversal**, the root is visited after both of the subtrees.

Inorder traversal is also sometimes called **symmetric order**, and postorder traversal was once called **endorder**. We shall not use these terms.

2. Simple Examples

As a first example, consider the following binary tree:

preorder Under preorder traversal, the root, labeled 1, is visited first. Then the traversal moves to the left subtree. The left subtree contains only the node labeled 2, and it is visited second. Then preorder traversal moves to the right subtree of the root, finally visiting the node labeled 3. Thus preorder traversal visits the nodes in the order 1, 2, 3.

inorder   Before the root is visited under inorder traversal, we must traverse its left subtree. Hence the node labeled 2 is visited first. This is the only node in the left subtree of the root, so the traversal moves to the root, labeled 1, next, and finally to the right subtree. Thus inorder traversal visits the nodes in the order 2, 1, 3.

postorder   With postorder traversal, we must traverse both the left and right subtrees before visiting the root. We first go to the left subtree, which contains only the node labeled 2, and it is visited first. Next, we traverse the right subtree, visiting the node 3, and, finally, we visit the root, labeled 1. Thus postorder traversal visits the nodes in the order 2, 3, 1.

As a second, slightly more complicated example, let us consider the following binary tree:

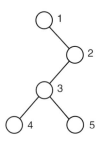

preorder   First, let us determine the preorder traversal. The root, labeled 1, is visited first. Next, we traverse the left subtree. But this subtree is empty, so its traversal does nothing. Finally, we must traverse the right subtree of the root. This subtree contains the vertices labeled 2, 3, 4, and 5. We must therefore traverse this subtree, again using the preorder method. Hence we next visit the root of this subtree, labeled 2, and then traverse the left subtree of 2. At a later step, we shall traverse the right subtree of 2, which is empty, so nothing will be done. But first we traverse the left subtree, which has root 3. Preorder traversal of the subtree with root 3 visits the nodes in the order 3, 4, 5. Finally, we do the empty right subtree of 2. Thus the complete preorder traversal of the tree visits the nodes in the order 1, 2, 3, 4, 5.

inorder   For inorder traversal, we must begin with the left subtree of the root, which is empty. Hence the root, labeled 1, is the first node visited, and then we traverse its right subtree, which is rooted at node 2. Before we visit node 2, we must traverse its left subtree, which has root 3. The inorder traversal of this subtree visits the nodes in the order 4, 3, 5. Finally, we visit node 2 and traverse its right subtree, which does nothing since it is empty. Thus the complete inorder traversal of the tree visits the nodes in the order 1, 4, 3, 5, 2.

postorder   For postorder traversal, we must traverse both the left and right subtrees of each node before visiting the node itself. Hence we first would traverse the empty left subtree of the root 1, then the right subtree. The root of a binary tree is always the last node visited by a postorder traversal. Before visiting the node 2, we traverse its left and right (empty) subtrees. The postorder traversal of the subtree rooted at 3 gives the order 4, 5, 3. Thus the complete postorder traversal of the tree visits the nodes in the order 4, 5, 3, 2, 1.

3. Expression Trees

The choice of the names *preorder*, *inorder*, and *postorder* for the three most important traversal methods is not accidental, but relates closely to a motivating example of considerable interest, that of expression trees.

expression tree

An **expression tree** is built up from the simple operands and operators of an (arithmetical or logical) expression by placing the simple operands as the leaves of a binary tree and the operators as the interior nodes. For each binary operator, the left subtree contains all the simple operands and operators in the left operand of the given operator, and the right subtree contains everything in the right operand.

operators

For a unary operator, one of the two subtrees will be empty. We traditionally write some unary operators to the left of their operands, such as '−' (unary negation) or the standard functions like log( ) and cos( ). Other unary operators are written on the right, such as the factorial function ( )! or the function that takes the square of a number, ( )². Sometimes either side is permissible, such as the derivative operator, which can be written as d/dx on the left, or as ( )' on the right, or the incrementing operator ++ (where the actions on the left and right are different). If the operator is written on the left, then in the expression tree we take its left subtree as empty, so that the operands appear on the right side of the operator in the tree, just as they do in the expression. If the operator appears on the right, then its right subtree will be empty, and the operands will be in the left subtree of the operator.

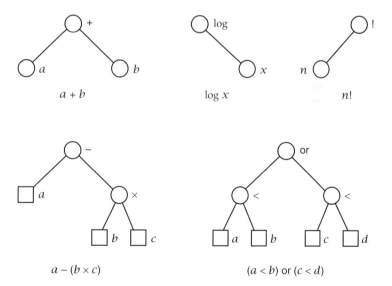

Figure 10.3. Expression trees

The expression trees of a few simple expressions are shown in Figure 10.3, together with the slightly more complicated example of the quadratic formula in Figure 10.4, where we denote exponentiation by ↑.

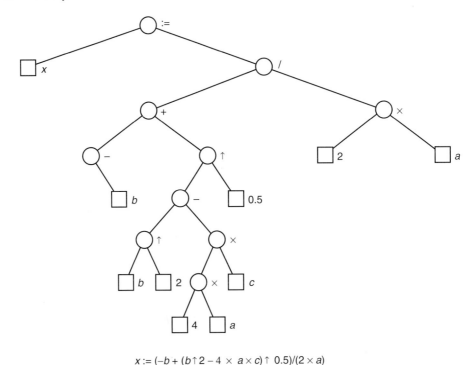

$$x := (-b + (b \uparrow 2 - 4 \times a \times c) \uparrow 0.5)/(2 \times a)$$

Figure 10.4. Expression tree of the quadratic formula

You should take a few moments to traverse each of these expression trees in preorder, inorder, and postorder. To help you check your work, the results of such traversals are shown in Figure 10.5.

Expression:	$a + b$	$\log x$	$n!$	$a - (b \times c)$	$(a < b)$ or $(c < d)$
preorder :	$+ \, a \, b$	$\log \, x$	$! \, n$	$- \, a \times b \, c$	or $< \, a \, b \, < \, c \, d$
inorder :	$a + b$	$\log \, x$	$n \, !$	$a \, - \, b \times c$	$a \, < \, b$ or $c \, < \, d$
postorder :	$a \, b \, +$	$x \, \log$	$n \, !$	$a \, b \, c \times \, -$	$a \, b \, < \, c \, d \, < \,$ or

Figure 10.5. Traversal orders for expression trees

Polish form   The names of the traversal methods are related to the **Polish forms** of the expressions: Traversal of an expression tree in preorder yields the **prefix form**, in which every operator is written before its operand(s); inorder traversal gives the **infix form** (the customary way to write the expression); and postorder traversal gives the **postfix form**, in which all operators appear after their operand(s). A moment's consideration will convince you of the reason: The left and right subtrees of each node are its operands, and the relative position of an operator to its operands in the three Polish forms is the same as the relative order of visiting the components in each of the three traversal methods. The Polish notation is the major topic of Chapter 13.

4. Comparison Trees

As a further example, let us take the binary tree of 14 names from Figure 10.1 (the comparison tree for binary search) and write them in the order given by each traversal method:

preorder:

        Jim Dot Amy Ann Guy Eva Jan Ron Kay Jon Kim Tim Roy Tom

inorder:

        Amy Ann Dot Eva Guy Jan Jim Jon Kay Kim Ron Roy Tim Tom

postorder:

        Ann Amy Eva Jan Guy Dot Jon Kim Kay Roy Tom Tim Ron Jim

It is no accident that inorder traversal produces the names in alphabetical order. The way that we constructed the comparison tree in Figure 10.1 was to move to the left whenever the target key preceded the key in the node under consideration, and to the right otherwise. Hence the binary tree is set up so that all the nodes in the left subtree of a given node come before it in the ordering, and all the nodes in its right subtree come after it. Hence inorder traversal produces all the nodes before a given one first, then the given one, and then all the later nodes.

    In the next section, we shall study binary trees with this property. They are called *binary search trees*, since they are very useful and efficient for problems requiring searching.

10.1.3 Linked Implementation of Binary Trees

A binary tree has a natural implementation in linked storage. As usual for linked structures, we shall link together nodes, created in dynamic storage, so we shall need a separate pointer variable to enable us to find the tree. Our name for this

root   pointer variable will be **root**, since it will point to the root of the tree. Hence, the specification for a generic template for the binary-tree class takes the form:

```
template <class Entry>
class Binary_tree {
public:
//   Add methods here.
protected:
   //   Add auxiliary function prototypes here.
   Binary_node<Entry> *root;
};
```

As usual, the template parameter, class **Entry**, is specified as an actual type by client code.

    We now consider the representation of the nodes that make up a tree.

1. Definitions

Each node of a binary tree (as the root of some subtree) has both a left and a right subtree. These subtrees can be located by pointers to their root nodes. Hence we arrive at the following specification:

```
template <class Entry>
struct Binary_node {
//   data members:
   Entry data;
   Binary_node<Entry> *left;
   Binary_node<Entry> *right;
//   constructors:
   Binary_node();
   Binary_node(const Entry &x);

};
```

The Binary_node class includes two constructors that set the pointer members left and right to NULL in any newly constructed node.

Our specifications for nodes and trees turn the comparison tree for the 14 names from the first tree diagram of this section, Figure 10.1, into the linked binary tree of Figure 10.6. As you can see, the only difference between the comparison tree and the linked binary tree is that we have explicitly shown the NULL links in the latter, whereas it is customary in drawing trees to omit all empty subtrees and the branches going to them.

2. Basic Methods for a Binary Tree

With the root pointer, it is easy to recognize an empty binary tree with the expression

$$root == NULL;$$

and to create a new, empty binary tree we need only assign root to NULL. The Binary_tree constructor should simply make this assignment.

```
template <class Entry>
Binary_tree<Entry> :: Binary_tree()
/* Post: An empty binary tree has been created. */
{
   root = NULL;
}
```

The method empty tests whether root is NULL to determine whether a Binary_tree is empty.

```
template <class Entry>
bool Binary_tree<Entry> :: empty() const
/* Post: A result of true is returned if the binary tree is empty. Otherwise, false is
          returned. */
{
   return root == NULL;
}
```

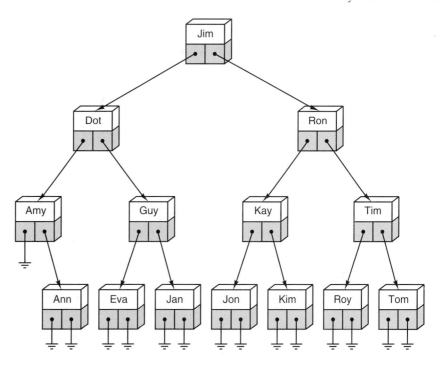

Figure 10.6. A linked binary tree

3. Traversal

We now develop methods that traverse a linked binary tree in each of the three ways we have studied. As usual, we shall assume the existence of another function *visit that does the desired task for each node. As with traversal functions defined for other data structures, we shall make the function pointer visit a formal parameter for the traversal functions.

visit *a node*

In our traversal functions, we need to visit the root node and traverse its sub-trees. Recursion will make it especially easy for us to traverse the subtrees. The subtrees are located by following pointers from the root, and therefore these point-ers must be passed to the recursive traversal calls. It follows that each traversal method should call a recursive function that carries an extra pointer parameter. For example, inorder traversal is written as follows:

recursive traversal

```
template <class Entry>
void Binary_tree<Entry> :: inorder(void (*visit)(Entry &))
/* Post: The tree has been been traversed in inorder sequence.
   Uses: The function recursive_inorder */
{
   recursive_inorder(root, visit);
}
```

We shall generally find that any method of a Binary_tree that is naturally described by a recursive process can be conveniently implemented by calling an auxiliary recursive function that applies to subtrees. The auxiliary inorder traversal function is implemented with the following simple recursion:

```
template <class Entry>
void Binary_tree<Entry> :: recursive_inorder(Binary_node<Entry> *sub_root,
                                             void (*visit)(Entry &))
/* Pre:  sub_root is either NULL or points to a subtree of the Binary_tree.
   Post: The subtree has been been traversed in inorder sequence.
   Uses: The function recursive_inorder recursively */
{
  if (sub_root != NULL) {
    recursive_inorder(sub_root->left, visit);
    (*visit)(sub_root->data);
    recursive_inorder(sub_root->right, visit);
  }
}
```

The other traversal methods are similarly constructed as calls to auxiliary recursive functions. The auxiliary functions have the following implementations:

```
template <class Entry>
void Binary_tree<Entry> :: recursive_preorder(Binary_node<Entry> *sub_root,
                                              void (*visit)(Entry &))
/* Pre:  sub_root is either NULL or points to a subtree of the Binary_tree.
   Post: The subtree has been been traversed in preorder sequence.
   Uses: The function recursive_preorder recursively */
{
  if (sub_root != NULL) {
    (*visit)(sub_root->data);
    recursive_preorder(sub_root->left, visit);
    recursive_preorder(sub_root->right, visit);
  }
}
```

```
template <class Entry>
void Binary_tree<Entry> :: recursive_postorder(Binary_node<Entry> *sub_root,
                                               void (*visit)(Entry &))
/* Pre:  sub_root is either NULL or points to a subtree of the Binary_tree.
   Post: The subtree has been been traversed in postorder sequence.
   Uses: The function recursive_postorder recursively */
{
  if (sub_root != NULL) {
    recursive_postorder(sub_root->left, visit);
    recursive_postorder(sub_root->right, visit);
    (*visit)(sub_root->data);
  }
}
```

We leave the coding of standard Binary_tree methods such as height, size, and clear as exercises. These other methods are also most easily implemented by calling recursive auxiliary functions. In the exercises, we shall develop a method to insert entries into a Binary_tree. This insertion method is useful for testing our basic Binary_tree class.

Later in this chapter, we shall create several more specialized, and more useful derived tree classes: these derived classes will have efficient overridden insertion methods. The derived classes will also possess efficient methods for removing entries, but for the moment we will not add such a method to our basic binary tree class. These decisions lead to a Binary_tree class with the following specification:

```
template <class Entry>
class Binary_tree {
public:
    Binary_tree();
    bool empty() const;
    void preorder(void (*visit)(Entry &));
    void inorder(void (*visit)(Entry &));
    void postorder(void (*visit)(Entry &));

    int size() const;
    void clear();
    int height() const;
    void insert(const Entry &);

    Binary_tree (const Binary_tree<Entry> &original);
    Binary_tree & operator = (const Binary_tree<Entry> &original);
    ~Binary_tree();
protected:
    //   Add auxiliary function prototypes here.
    Binary_node<Entry> *root;
};
```

Although our Binary_tree class appears to be a mere shell whose methods simply pass out their work to auxiliary functions, it serves an important purpose. The class collects together the various tree functions and provides a very convenient client interface that is analogous to our other ADTs. Moreover, the class provides encapsulation: without it, tree data would not be protected and could easily be corrupted. Finally, we shall see that the class serves as the base for other, more useful, derived binary tree classes.

Exercises 10.1

E1. Construct the 14 binary trees with four nodes.

E2. Determine the order in which the vertices of the following binary trees will be visited under **(1)** preorder, **(2)** inorder, and **(3)** postorder traversal.

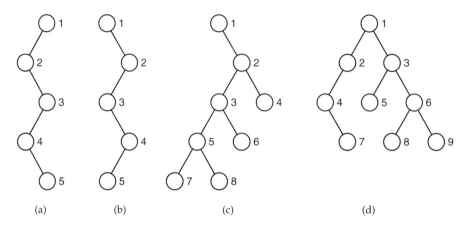

(a)   (b)   (c)   (d)

E3. Draw expression trees for each of the following expressions, and show the order of visiting the vertices in **(1)** preorder, **(2)** inorder, and **(3)** postorder:

(a) $\log n!$

(b) $(a - b) - c$

(c) $a - (b - c)$

(d) $(a < b)$ and $(b < c)$ and $(c < d)$

Binary_tree size

E4. Write a method and the corresponding recursive function to count all the nodes of a linked binary tree.

E5. Write a method and the corresponding recursive function to count the leaves (i.e., the nodes with both subtrees empty) of a linked binary tree.

E6. Write a method and the corresponding recursive function to find the height of a linked binary tree, where an empty tree is considered to have height 0 and a tree with only one node has height 1.

Binary_tree insert

E7. Write a method and the corresponding recursive function to insert an **Entry**, passed as a parameter, into a linked binary tree. If the **root** is empty, the new entry should be inserted into the root, otherwise it should be inserted into the shorter of the two subtrees of the root (or into the left subtree if both subtrees have the same height).

Binary_tree clear
Binary_tree
destructor

E8. Write a method and the corresponding recursive function to traverse a binary tree (in whatever order you find convenient) and dispose of all its nodes. Use this method to implement a **Binary_tree** destructor.

E9. Write a copy constructor

Binary_tree<Entry> :: Binary_tree(**const** Binary_tree<Entry> &original)

Binary_tree copy
constructor

that will make a copy of a linked binary tree. The constructor should obtain the necessary new nodes from the system and copy the data from the nodes of the old tree to the new one.

Binary_tree
assignment operator

E10. Write an overloaded binary tree assignment operator

$$\text{Binary\_tree<Entry> \& Binary\_tree<Entry>::\textbf{operator} =}$$
$$\text{(\textbf{const} Binary\_tree<Entry> \&original)\}.}$$

E11. Write a function to perform a *double-order traversal* of a binary tree, meaning
that at each node of the tree, the function first visits the node, then traverses
double-order traversal its left subtree (in double order), then visits the node again, then traverses its
right subtree (in double order).

E12. For each of the binary trees in Exercise E2, determine the order in which the
nodes will be visited in the mixed order given by invoking method A:

```
void Binary_tree<Entry>::           void Binary_tree<Entry>::
  A(void (*visit)(Entry &))            B(void (*visit)(Entry &))
{                                    {
  if (root != NULL) {                  if (root != NULL) {
    (*visit)(root->data);                root->left.A(visit);
    root->left.B(visit);                 (*visit)(root->data);
    root->right.B(visit);                root->right.A(visit)
  }                                    }
}                                    }
```

printing a binary tree

E13. (a) Suppose that Entry is the type **char**. Write a function that will print all the
entries from a binary tree in the *bracketed form* (data: LT, RT) where **data**
is the Entry in the root, LT denotes the left subtree of the root printed in
bracketed form, and RT denotes the right subtree in bracketed form. For
example, the first tree in Figure 10.3 will be printed as

$$(+ : (a: (:,), (:,)), (b: (:,), (:,)))$$

(b) Modify the function so that it prints nothing instead of (: ,) for an empty
subtree, and x instead of (x: ,) for a subtree consisting of only one node
with the Entry x. Hence the preceding tree will now print as (+ : a, b).

E14. Write a function that will interchange all left and right subtrees in a linked
binary tree. See the example in Figure 10.7.

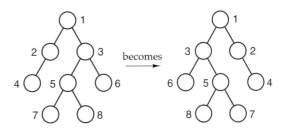

Figure 10.7. Reversal of a binary tree

level-by-level traversal

E15. Write a function that will traverse a binary tree level by level. That is, the root is visited first, then the immediate children of the root, then the grandchildren of the root, and so on. [*Hint*: Use a queue to keep track of the children of a node until it is time to visit them. The nodes in the first tree of Figure 10.7 are numbered in level-by-level ordering.]

width   **E16.** Write a function that will return the width of a linked binary tree, that is, the maximum number of nodes on the same level.

traversal sequences   For the following exercises, it is assumed that the data stored in the nodes of the binary trees are all distinct, but it is not assumed that the trees are binary *search* trees. That is, there is no necessary connection between any ordering of the data and their location in the trees. If a tree is traversed in a particular order, and each key is printed when its node is visited, the resulting sequence is called the sequence corresponding to that traversal.

E17. Suppose that you are given two sequences that supposedly correspond to the preorder and inorder traversals of a binary tree. Prove that it is possible to reconstruct the binary tree uniquely.

E18. Either prove or disprove (by finding a counterexample) the analogous result for inorder and postorder traversal.

E19. Either prove or disprove the analogous result for preorder and postorder traversal.

E20. Find a pair of sequences of the same data that could not possibly correspond to the preorder and inorder traversals of the same binary tree. [*Hint*: Keep your sequences short; it is possible to solve this exercise with only three items of data in each sequence.]

10.2 BINARY SEARCH TREES

Consider the problem of searching a linked list for some target key. There is no way to move through the list other than one node at a time, and hence searching through the list must always reduce to a sequential search. As you know, sequential search is usually very slow in comparison with binary search. Hence, assuming we can keep the keys in order, searching becomes much faster if we use a contiguous

the dilemma   list and binary search. Suppose we also frequently need to make changes in the list, inserting new entries or deleting old entries. Then it is much slower to use a contiguous list than a linked list, because insertion or removal in a contiguous list requires moving many of the entries every time, whereas a linked list requires only adjusting a few pointers.

The pivotal problem for this section is:

> *Can we find an implementation for ordered lists in which we can search quickly (as with binary search on a contiguous list) and in which we can make insertions and removals quickly (as with a linked list)?*

Binary trees provide an excellent solution to this problem. By making the entries of an ordered list into the nodes of a binary tree, we shall find that we can search for a target key in $O(\log n)$ steps, just as with binary search, and we shall obtain algorithms for inserting and deleting entries also in time $O(\log n)$.

comparison trees

When we studied binary search, we drew comparison trees showing the progress of binary search by moving either left (if the target key is smaller than the one in the current node of the tree) or right (if the target key is larger). An example of such a comparison tree appears in Figure 10.1 and again in Figure 10.6, where it is shown as a linked binary tree. From these diagrams, it may already be clear that the way in which we can keep the advantages of linked storage and obtain the speed of binary search is to store the nodes as a binary tree with the structure of the comparison tree itself, with links used to describe the relations of the tree.

The essential feature of the comparison tree is that, when we move to the left subtree, we move to smaller keys, and, when we move to the right subtree, we move to larger keys. This special condition on keys of the nodes of a binary tree is the essential part of the following important definition:

Definition

A **binary search tree** is a binary tree that is either empty or in which every node has a key (within its data entry) and satisfies the following conditions:

1. The key of the root (if it exists) is greater than the key in any node in the left subtree of the root.
2. The key of the root (if it exists) is less than the key in any node in the right subtree of the root.
3. The left and right subtrees of the root are again binary search trees.

The first two properties describe the ordering relative to the key of the root node, and the third property extends them to all nodes of the tree; hence we can continue to use the recursive structure of the binary tree. After we examine the root of the tree, we shall move to either its left or right subtree, and this subtree is again a binary search tree. Thus we can use the same method again on this smaller tree.

no equal keys

We have written this definition in a way that ensures that no two entries in a binary search tree can have equal keys, since the keys of the left subtree are strictly smaller than the key of the root, and those of the right subtree are strictly greater. It is possible to change the definition to allow entries with equal keys, but doing so makes the algorithms somewhat more complicated. Therefore, we always assume:

> *No two entries in a binary search tree may have equal keys.*

The tree shown in Figures 10.1 and 10.6 is automatically a binary search tree, since the decision to move left or right at each node is based on the same comparisons of keys used in the definition of a search tree.

10.2.1 Ordered Lists and Implementations

When the time comes to start formulating C++ methods to manipulate binary search trees, there are at least three different points of view that we might take:

three views

➡ We can regard binary search trees as a new abstract data type with its own definition and its own methods;

➡ Since binary search trees are special kinds of binary trees, we may consider their methods as special kinds of binary tree methods;

➡ Since the entries in binary search trees contain keys, and since they are applied for information retrieval in the same way as ordered lists, we may study binary search trees as a new implementation of the abstract data type *ordered list*.

In practice, programmers sometimes take each of these points of view, and so shall we. We shall specify our binary search tree class as derived from our binary tree class. Thus, our binary tree class does represent a distinct ADT. However, the new class inherits the methods of the former binary tree class. In this way, the use of a derived class emphasizes the first two points of view. The third point of view often shows up in applications of binary search trees. Client code can use our class to solve the same searching and sorting problems that are otherwise tackled with an ordered list.

1. Declarations

We have already introduced C++ declarations that allow us to manipulate binary trees. We use this implementation of binary trees as the base for our binary search tree class template.

```
template <class Record>
class Search_tree: public Binary_tree<Record> {
public:
    Error_code insert(const Record &new_data);
    Error_code remove(const Record &old_data);
    Error_code tree_search(Record &target) const;
private:                    //   Add auxiliary function prototypes here.
};
```

Since binary search trees are derived from the binary tree class, we can apply the methods already defined for general binary trees to binary search trees. These methods include the constructors, the destructor, clear, empty, size, height, and the traversals preorder, inorder, and postorder. In addition to the methods of an ordinary binary tree, a binary search tree also admits specialized methods called insert, remove, and tree_search.

Record

We have used the term Record for the template parameter of a Search_tree to emphasize that the entries in a binary search tree must have keys that can be compared. Thus the class Record has the behavior outlined in Chapter 7: Each Record

Key

is associated with a Key. The keys can be compared with the usual comparison operators, moreover, because we suppose that records can be cast to their corresponding keys, the comparison operators apply to records as well as to keys. For example, all of the Record and Key classes that we have used since Chapter 7 have these properties. Hence, the entries in our binary search tree become compatible with those in an ordered list.

As we have previously observed, for testing purposes it is often convenient to use the type **int** for both the **class** Record and the **class** Key. In this way, our testing programs can make a declaration:

Binary_tree<**int**> test_tree;

and apply Binary_tree methods without any further worry about records and keys.

10.2.2 Tree Search

The first important new method for binary search trees is the one from which their name comes: a function to search through a linked binary search tree for an entry with a particular target key. The method must meet the following specifications:

specifications

> Error_code Search_tree<Record> :: tree_search(Record &target) **const;**
>
> *postcondition*: If there is an entry in the tree whose key matches that in **target**, the parameter **target** is replaced by the corresponding record from the tree and a code of **success** is returned. Otherwise a code of **not_present** is returned.

In applications, this method will often be called with a parameter **target** that contains only a key value. The method will add the complete data belonging to any corresponding Record into **target**.

1. Strategy

To search for the target, we first compare it with the entry at the root of the tree. If their keys match, then we are finished. Otherwise, we go to the left subtree or right subtree as appropriate and repeat the search in that subtree.

Let us, for example, search for the name Kim in the binary search tree of Figures 10.1 and 10.6. We first compare Kim with the entry in the root, Jim. Since Kim comes after Jim in alphabetical order, we move to the right and next compare Kim with Ron. Since Kim comes before Ron, we move left and compare Kim with Kay. Now Kim comes later, so we move to the right and find the desired target.

This is clearly a recursive process, and therefore we shall implement it by calling an auxiliary recursive function. What event will be the termination condition for the recursive search? Clearly, if we find the target, the function finishes successfully. If not, then we continue searching until we hit an empty subtree, in which case the search fails.

From the auxiliary search function, we shall return a pointer to the node that contains the target back to the calling program. Although the returned pointer can be used to gain access to the data stored in a tree object, the only functions that can call the auxiliary search must be tree methods, since only the methods are able to pass the root as a parameter. Thus, returning a node pointer from the auxiliary function will not compromise tree encapsulation. We arrive at the following specification for the auxiliary search function:

Binary_node<Record> *Search_tree<Record> :: search_for_node(
    Binary_node<Record>* sub_root, **const** Record &target) **const;**

precondition: sub_root is either NULL or points to a subtree of a Search_tree

postcondition: If the key of **target** is not in the subtree, a result of NULL is re-
                turned. Otherwise, a pointer to the subtree node containing the
                target is returned.

2. Recursive Version

The simplest way to write the function for searching is to use recursion:

```
template <class Record>
Binary_node<Record> *Search_tree<Record> :: search_for_node(
    Binary_node<Record>* sub_root, const Record &target) const
{
    if (sub_root == NULL || sub_root->data == target) return sub_root;
    else if (sub_root->data < target)
        return search_for_node(sub_root->right, target);
    else return search_for_node(sub_root->left, target);
}
```

3. Recursion Removal

tail recursion

Recursion occurs in this function only as *tail recursion,* that is, as the last statement executed in the function. By using a loop, it is always possible to change tail recursion into iteration. In this case, we need to write a loop in place of the first **if** statement, and we modify the parameter **root** to move through the tree.

nonrecursive tree search

```
template <class Record>
Binary_node<Record> *Search_tree<Record> :: search_for_node(
    Binary_node<Record> *sub_root, const Record &target) const
{
    while (sub_root != NULL && sub_root->data != target)
        if (sub_root->data < target) sub_root = sub_root->right;
        else sub_root = sub_root->left;
    return sub_root;
}
```

4. The Method tree_search

The method tree_search simply calls the auxiliary function search_for_node to locate the node of a binary search tree that contains a record matching a particular key. It then extracts a copy of the record from the tree and returns an appropriate Error_code to the user.

```
template <class Record>
Error_code Search_tree<Record> :: tree_search(Record &target) const
```
/* **Post**: *If there is an entry in the tree whose key matches that in* target, *the parameter* target *is replaced by the corresponding record from the tree and a code of* success *is returned. Otherwise a code of* not_present *is returned.*
     Uses: *function* search_for_node */
```
{
  Error_code result = success;
  Binary_node<Record> *found = search_for_node(root, target);
  if (found ==  NULL)
    result = not_present;
  else
    target = found->data;
  return result;
}
```

5. Behavior of the Algorithm

Recall that **tree_search** is based closely on binary search. If we apply binary search to an ordered list and draw its comparison tree, then we see that binary search does exactly the same comparisons as **tree_search** will do if it is applied to this same tree. We already know from Section 7.4 that binary search performs $O(\log n)$ comparisons for a list of length n. This performance is excellent in comparison to other methods, since $\log n$ grows very slowly as n increases.

example   Suppose, as an example, that we apply binary search to the list of seven letters *a*, *b*, *c*, *d*, *e*, *f*, and *g*. The resulting tree is shown in part (a) of Figure 10.8. If **tree_search** is applied to this tree, it will do the same number of comparisons as binary search.

It is quite possible, however, that the same letters may be built into a binary search tree of a quite different shape, such as any of those shown in the remaining parts of Figure 10.8.

optimal tree   The tree shown as part (a) of Figure 10.8 is the best possible for searching. It is as "bushy" as possible: It has the smallest possible height for a given number of vertices. The number of vertices between the root and the target, inclusive, is the number of comparisons that must be done to find the target. The bushier the tree, therefore, the smaller the number of comparisons that will usually need to be done.

typical tree   It is not always possible to predict (in advance of building it) what shape of binary search tree we will have, and the tree shown in part (b) of Figure 10.8 is more typical of what happens than is the tree in part (a). In the tree of part (b), a search for the target *c* requires four comparisons, but only three in that of part (a). The tree in part (b), however, remains fairly bushy and its performance is only a little poorer than that of the optimal tree of part (a).

poor tree   In part (c) of Figure 10.8, however, the tree has degenerated quite badly, so that a search for target *c* requires six comparisons. In parts (d) and (e), the tree reduces

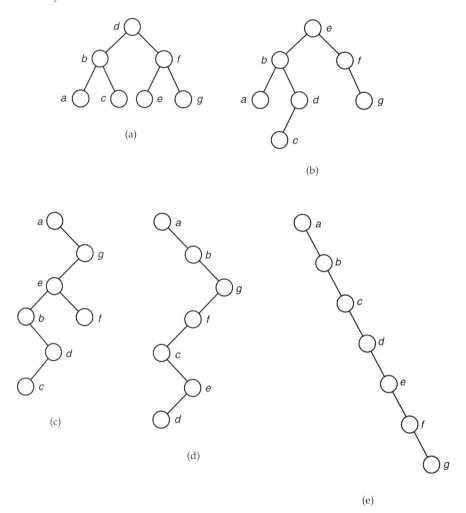

Figure 10.8. Several binary search trees with the same keys

chain:
sequential search

to a single chain. When applied to chains like these, tree_search can do nothing except go through the list entry by entry. In other words, tree_search, when applied to such a chain, degenerates to sequential search. In its worst case on a tree with n nodes, therefore, tree_search may require as many as n comparisons to find its target.

In practice, if the keys are built into a binary search tree in random order, then it is extremely unlikely that a binary search tree degenerates as badly as the trees shown in parts (d) and (e) of Figure 10.8. Instead, trees like those of parts (a) and (b) are much more likely. Hence tree_search almost always performs nearly as well as binary search. In Section 10.2.4, in fact, we shall see that, for random binary search trees, the performance of tree_search is only about 39 percent slower than the optimum of $\lg n$ comparisons of keys, and it is therefore far superior to the n comparisons of keys needed by sequential search.

10.2.3 Insertion into a Binary Search Tree

1. The Problem

The next important operation for us to consider is the insertion of a new node into a binary search tree in such a way that the keys remain properly ordered; that is, so that the resulting tree satisfies the definition of a binary search tree. The formal specifications for this operation are:

specifications

Error_code Search_tree<Record> :: insert(**const** Record &new_data);

postcondition: If a Record with a key matching that of **new_data** already belongs to the Search_tree a code of **duplicate_error** is returned. Otherwise, the Record new_data is inserted into the tree in such a way that the properties of a binary search tree are preserved, and a code of **success** is returned.

---

2. Examples

Before we turn to writing this function, let us study some simple examples. Figure 10.9 shows what happens when we insert the keys *e, b, d, f, a, g, c* into an initially empty tree in the order given.

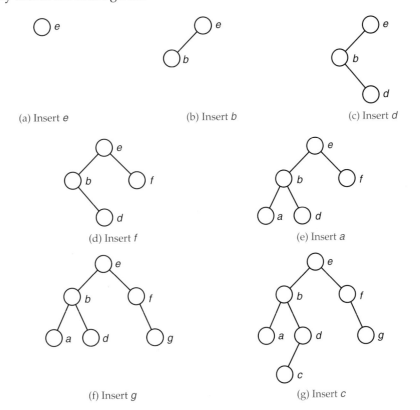

Figure 10.9. Insertions into a binary search tree

When the first entry, *e*, is inserted, it becomes the root, as shown in part (a). Since *b* comes before *e*, its insertion goes into the left subtree of *e*, as shown in part (b). Next we insert *d*, first comparing it to *e* and going left, then comparing it to *b* and going right. The next insertion, *f*, goes to the right of the root, as shown in part (d) of Figure 10.9. Since *a* is the earliest key inserted so far, it moves left from *e* and then from *b*. The key *g*, similarly, comes last in alphabetical order, so its insertion moves as far right as possible, as shown in part (f). The insertion of *c*, finally, compares first with *e*, goes left, then right from *b* and left from *d*. Hence we obtain the binary search tree shown in the last part of Figure 10.9.

It is quite possible that a different order of insertion can produce the same binary search tree. The final tree in Figure 10.9, for example, can be obtained by inserting the keys in either of the orders

different orders,
same tree

$$e, f, g, b, a, d, c \qquad \text{or} \qquad e, b, d, c, a, f, g,$$

as well as several other orders.

One case is of special importance. Suppose that the keys are inserted into an initially empty tree in their natural order *a*, *b*, ..., *g*. Then *a* will go into the root, *b* will become its right child, *c* will move to the right of *a* and *b*, and so on. The insertions will produce a chain for the binary search tree, as shown in the final part of Figure 10.8. Such a chain, as we have already seen, is very inefficient for searching. Hence we conclude:

natural order

> *If the keys to be inserted into an empty binary search tree are in their natural order, then the method* insert *will produce a tree that degenerates into an inefficient chain. The method* insert *should never be used with keys that are already sorted into order.*

The same conclusion holds if the keys are in reverse order or if they are nearly but not quite sorted into order.

3. Method

It is only a small step from the example we have worked to the general method for inserting a new node into a binary search tree.

The first case, inserting a node into an empty tree, is easy. We need only make root point to the new node. If the tree is not empty, then we must compare the key with the one in the root. If it is less, then the new node must be inserted into the left subtree; if it is more, then it must be inserted into the right subtree. It is an error for the keys to be equal.

Note that we have described insertion by using recursion. After we compare the new key with the one in the root, we use exactly the same insertion method either on the left or right subtree that we previously used at the root.

4. Recursive Function

From this outline, we can now write our function, using the declarations from the beginning of this section. As usual, the tree method calls an auxiliary recursive function.

```
template <class Record>
Error_code Search_tree<Record>::insert(const Record &new_data)
{
    return search_and_insert(root, new_data);
}
```

Note that the auxiliary function might need to make a permanent change to the root of a Search_tree, for example, if the tree is initially empty. Therefore, the

recursive insertion   implementation of the auxiliary function must use a reference parameter.

```
template <class Record>
Error_code Search_tree<Record>::search_and_insert(
        Binary_node<Record> * &sub_root, const Record &new_data)
{
  if (sub_root == NULL) {
    sub_root = new Binary_node<Record>(new_data);
    return success;
  }
  else if (new_data < sub_root->data)
    return search_and_insert(sub_root->left, new_data);
  else if (new_data > sub_root->data)
    return search_and_insert(sub_root->right, new_data);
  else return duplicate_error;
}
```

We recall that one of our first requirements on binary search trees was that no two entries should share a key. Accordingly, the function search_and_insert rejects entries with duplicate keys.

The use of recursion in the function insert is not essential, since it is tail recursion. We leave translation of insert into nonrecursive form as an exercise.

In regard to performance, insert makes the same comparisons of keys that tree_search would make in looking for the key being inserted. The method insert also changes a single pointer, but does not move entries or do any other operations that take a large amount of space or time. Therefore, the performance of insert will be very much the same as that of tree_search:

The method insert can usually insert a new node into a random binary search tree with n nodes in $O(\log n)$ steps. It is possible, but extremely unlikely, that a random tree may degenerate so that insertions require as many as n steps. If the keys are inserted in sorted order into an empty tree, however, this degenerate case will occur.

10.2.4 Treesort

Recall from our discussion of traversing binary trees that, when we traverse a binary search tree in inorder, the keys will come out in sorted order. The reason is that all the keys to the left of a given key precede it, and all those that come to its right follow it. By recursion, the same facts are applied again and again until the subtrees have only one key. Hence inorder traversal always gives the sorted order for the keys.

1. The Procedure

treesort   This observation is the basis for an interesting sorting procedure, called **treesort**. We simply take the entries to be sorted, use the method insert to build them into a binary search tree, and use inorder traversal to put them out in order.

2. Comparison with Quicksort

Let us briefly study what comparisons of keys are done by treesort. The first node goes into the root of the binary search tree, with no key comparisons. As each succeeding node comes in, its key is first compared to the key in the root and then it goes either into the left subtree or the right subtree. Notice the similarity with quicksort, where at the first stage every key is compared with the first pivot key, and then put into the left or the right sublist. In treesort, however, as each node comes in it goes into its final position in the linked structure. The second node becomes the root of either the left or right subtree (depending on the comparison of its key with the root key). From then on, all keys going into the same subtree are compared to this second one. Similarly, in quicksort all keys in one sublist are compared to the second pivot, the one for that sublist. Continuing in this way, we can make the following observation:

Theorem 10.1   *Treesort makes exactly the same comparisons of keys as does quicksort when the pivot for each sublist is chosen to be the first key in the sublist.*

As we know, quicksort is usually an excellent method. On average, among the methods we studied, only mergesort makes fewer key comparisons. Hence, on *advantages*   average, we can expect treesort also to be an excellent sorting method in terms of key comparisons. In fact, from Section 8.8.4 we can conclude:

Corollary 10.2   *In the average case, on a randomly ordered list of length n, treesort performs*

$$2n \ln n + O(n) \approx 1.39n \lg n + O(n)$$

comparisons of keys.

Treesort has one advantage over quicksort. Quicksort needs to have access to all the items to be sorted throughout the sorting process. With treesort, the nodes need not all be available at the start of the process, but are built into the tree one by one as they become available. Hence treesort is preferable for applications where the nodes are received one at a time. The major advantage of treesort is that its search tree remains available for later insertions and removals, and that the tree can subsequently be searched in logarithmic time, whereas all our previous sorting methods either required contiguous lists, for which insertions and removals are difficult, or produced linked lists for which only sequential search is available.

drawbacks   The major drawback of treesort is already implicit in Theorem 10.1. Quicksort has a very poor performance in its worst case, and, although a careful choice of pivots makes this case extremely unlikely, the choice of pivot to be the first key in each sublist makes the worst case appear whenever the keys are already sorted. If the keys are presented to treesort already sorted, then treesort too will be a disaster—the search tree it builds will reduce to a chain. Treesort should never be used if the keys are already sorted, or are nearly so.

There are few other reservations about treesort that are not equally applicable to all linked structures. For small problems with small items, contiguous storage is usually the better choice, but for large problems and bulky records, linked storage comes into its own.

10.2.5 Removal from a Binary Search Tree

In the discussion of treesort, we mentioned the ability to make changes in the binary search tree as an advantage. We have already obtained an algorithm that inserts a new node into the binary search tree, and it can be used to update the tree as easily as to build it from scratch. But we have not yet considered how to remove an entry and the node that contains it from the tree. If the node to be removed is a leaf, then the process is easy: We need only replace the link to the removed node by NULL. The process remains easy if the removed node has only one nonempty subtree: We adjust the link from the parent of the removed node to point to the root of its nonempty subtree.

When the node to be removed has both left and right subtrees nonempty, however, the problem is more complicated. To which of the subtrees should the parent of the removed node now point? What is to be done with the other subtree? This problem is illustrated in Figure 10.10, together with the solution we shall implement. First, we find the immediate predecessor of the node under inorder traversal *removal* by moving to its left child and then as far right as possible. (The immediate successor would work just as well.) The immediate predecessor has no right child (since we went as far right as possible), so it can be removed from its current position without difficulty. It can then be placed into the tree in the position formerly occupied by the node that was supposed to be removed, and the properties of a binary search tree will still be satisfied, since there were no keys in the original tree whose ordering comes between the removed key and its immediate predecessor.

We can now implement this plan. We begin with an auxiliary function that removes a particular node from a binary tree. As a calling parameter this function uses a pointer to the node to be removed. Moreover, this parameter is passed by *requirements* reference so that any changes to it are reflected in the calling environment. Since the purpose is to update a binary search tree, we must assume that in the calling program, the actual parameter is one of the links of the tree, and not just a copy, or

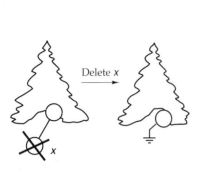

Case: deletion of a leaf   Case: one subtree empty

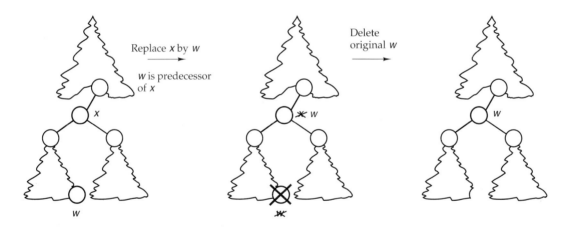

Case: neither subtree empty

Figure 10.10. Deletion of a node from a binary search tree

else the tree structure itself will not be changed as it should. In other words, if the node at the left of x is to be removed, the call should be

remove_root(x->left),

and, if the root is to be removed, the call should be

remove_root(root).

On the other hand, the following call will not work properly, since, although the pointer y would be adjusted, the pointer x->left would be left unchanged:

$$y = x\text{->left; remove\_root}(y);$$

The auxiliary function **remove_root** is implemented as follows:

template <**class** Record>
Error_code Search_tree<Record> :: remove_root(Binary_node<Record>
* &sub_root)
/* **Pre:** sub_root *is either* NULL *or points to a subtree of the* Search_tree.
  Post: *If* sub_root *is* NULL, *a code of* not_present *is returned. Otherwise, the root of the subtree is removed in such a way that the properties of a binary search tree are preserved. The parameter* sub_root *is reset as the root of the modified subtree, and* success *is returned.* */

removal
```
{
    if (sub_root ==  NULL) return not_present;
    Binary_node<Record> *to_delete = sub_root;
                                        //    Remember node to delete at end.
    if (sub_root->right ==  NULL) sub_root = sub_root->left;
    else if (sub_root->left ==  NULL) sub_root = sub_root->right;
    else {                              //    Neither subtree is empty.
      to_delete = sub_root->left;       //    Move left to find predecessor.
      Binary_node<Record> *parent = sub_root;  //    parent of to_delete
      while (to_delete->right != NULL) {     //    to_delete is not the predecessor.
        parent = to_delete;
        to_delete = to_delete->right;
      }
      sub_root->data = to_delete->data;    //    Move from to_delete to root.
      if (parent ==  sub_root) sub_root->left = to_delete->left;
      else parent->right = to_delete->left;
    }
    delete to_delete;                   //    Remove to_delete from tree.
    return success;
}
```

You should trace through this function to check that all pointers are updated properly, especially in the cases when neither subtree is empty. We must carefully distinguish between the case where the left child of the root is its predecessor and the case where it is necessary to move right to find the predecessor. Note the steps needed in this final case to make the loop stop at a node with an empty right subtree, but not to end at the empty subtree itself.

In calling the remove method of a **Search_tree**, a client passes the entry to be removed, rather than a pointer to the node that needs to be removed. To accomplish such a removal from the tree, we combine a recursive search through the tree with the preceding removal function. The resulting **Search_tree** method follows.

```
template <class Record>
Error_code Search_tree<Record>::remove(const Record &target)
/* Post: If a Record with a key matching that of target belongs to the Search_tree
         a code of success is returned and the corresponding node is removed from
         the tree. Otherwise, a code of not_present is returned.
   Uses: Function search_and_destroy */
{
    return search_and_destroy(root, target);
}
```

As usual, this method uses an auxiliary recursive function that refers to the actual nodes in the tree.

```
template <class Record>
Error_code Search_tree<Record>::search_and_destroy(
        Binary_node<Record>* &sub_root, const Record &target)
/* Pre:  sub_root is either NULL or points to a subtree of the Search_tree.
   Post: If the key of target is not in the subtree, a code of not_present is returned.
         Otherwise, a code of success is returned and the subtree node containing
         target has been removed in such a way that the properties of a binary
         search tree have been preserved.
   Uses: Functions search_and_destroy recursively and remove_root */
{
    if (sub_root == NULL || sub_root->data == target)
        return remove_root(sub_root);
    else if (target < sub_root->data)
        return search_and_destroy(sub_root->left, target);
    else
        return search_and_destroy(sub_root->right, target);
}
```

Exercises 10.2

The first several exercises are based on the following binary search tree. Answer each part of each exercise independently, using the original tree as the basis for each part.

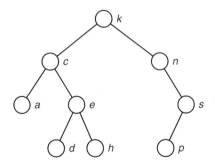

E1. Show the keys with which each of the following targets will be compared in a search of the preceding binary search tree.

(a) *c*	(d) *a*	(g) *f*
(b) *s*	(e) *d*	(h) *b*
(c) *k*	(f) *m*	(i) *t*

E2. Insert each of the following keys into the preceding binary search tree. Show the comparisons of keys that will be made in each case. Do each part independently, inserting the key into the original tree.

(a) *m*	(c) *b*	(e) *c*
(b) *f*	(d) *t*	(f) *s*

E3. Delete each of the following keys from the preceding binary search tree, using the algorithm developed in this section. Do each part independently, deleting the key from the original tree.

(a) *a*	(c) *n*	(e) *e*
(b) *p*	(d) *s*	(f) *k*

E4. Draw the binary search trees that function insert will construct for the list of 14 names presented in each of the following orders and inserted into a previously empty binary search tree.

(a) Jan Guy Jon Ann Jim Eva Amy Tim Ron Kim Tom Roy Kay Dot

(b) Amy Tom Tim Ann Roy Dot Eva Ron Kim Kay Guy Jon Jan Jim

(c) Jan Jon Tim Ron Guy Ann Jim Tom Amy Eva Roy Kim Dot Kay

(d) Jon Roy Tom Eva Tim Kim Ann Ron Jan Amy Dot Guy Jim Kay

E5. Consider building two binary search trees containing the integer keys 1 to 63, inclusive, received in the orders

(a) all the odd integers in order (1, 3, 5, ..., 63), then 32, 16, 48, then the remaining even integers in order (2, 4, 6, ...).

(b) 32, 16, 48, then all the odd integers in order (1, 3, 5, ..., 63), then the remaining even integers in order (2, 4, 6, ...).

Which of these trees will be quicker to build? Explain why. [Try to answer this question without actually drawing the trees.]

E6. All parts of this exercise refer to the binary search trees shown in Figure 10.8 and concern the different orders in which the keys *a, b, ..., g* can be inserted into an initially empty binary search tree.

(a) Give four different orders for inserting the keys, each of which will yield the binary search tree shown in part (a).

(b) Give four different orders for inserting the keys, each of which will yield the binary search tree shown in part (b).

(c) Give four different orders for inserting the keys, each of which will yield the binary search tree shown in part (c).

(d) Explain why there is only one order for inserting the keys that will produce a binary search tree that reduces to a given chain, such as the one shown in part (d) or in part (e).

E7. The use of recursion in function **insert** is not essential, since it is tail recursion. Rewrite function **insert** in nonrecursive form. [You will need a local pointer variable to move through the tree.]

Programming Projects 10.2

P1. Prepare a package containing the declarations for a binary search tree and the functions developed in this section. The package should be suitable for inclusion in any application program.

demonstration program

P2. Produce a menu-driven demonstration program to illustrate the use of binary search trees. The entries may consist of keys alone, and the keys should be single characters. The minimum capabilities that the user should be able to demonstrate include constructing the tree, inserting and removing an entry with a given key, searching for a target key, and traversing the tree in the three standard orders. The project may be enhanced by the inclusion of additional capabilities written as exercises in this and the previous section. These include determining the size of the tree, printing out all entries arranged to show the shape of the tree, and traversing the tree in various ways.

Keep the functions in your project as modular as possible, so that you can later replace the package of operations for a binary search tree by a functionally equivalent package for another kind of tree.

treesort

P3. Write a function for treesort that can be added to Project P1 of Section 8.2 (page 328). Determine whether it is necessary for the list structure to be contiguous or linked. Compare the results with those for the other sorting methods in Chapter 8.

sentinel search

P4. Write a function for searching, using a binary search tree with **sentinel** as follows: Introduce a new sentinel node, and keep a pointer called **sentinel** to it. See Figure 10.11. Replace all the NULL links within the binary search tree with **sentinel** links (links to the sentinel). Then, for each search, store the target key into the sentinel node before starting the search. Delete the test for an unsuccessful search from **tree_search**, since it cannot now occur. Instead, a search that now finds the sentinel is actually an unsuccessful search. Run this function on the test data of the preceding project to compare the performance of this version with the original function **tree_search**.

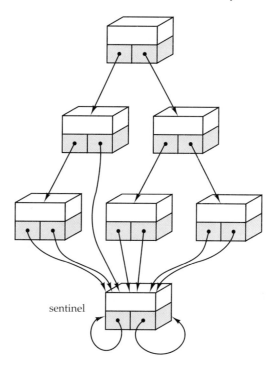

Figure 10.11. Binary search tree with sentinel

information retrieval **P5.** Different authors tend to use different vocabularies and to use common words
program with differing frequencies. Given an essay or other text, it is interesting to find
what distinct words are used and how many times each is used. The purpose of
this project is to compare several different kinds of binary search trees useful
for this information retrieval problem. The current, first part of the project
is to produce a driver program and the information-retrieval package using
ordinary binary search trees. Here is an outline of the main driver program:

1. Create the data structure (binary search tree).

2. Ask the user for the name of a text file and open it to read.

3. Read the file, split it apart into individual words, and insert the words into
the data structure. With each word will be kept a frequency count (how
many times the word appears in the input), and when duplicate words are
encountered, the frequency count will be increased. The same word will
not be inserted twice in the tree.

4. Print the number of comparisons done and the CPU time used in part 3.

5. If the user wishes, print out all the words in the data structure, in alphabetical order, with their frequency counts.

6. Put everything in parts 2–5 into a **do ... while** loop that will run as many
times as the user wishes. Thus the user can build the data structure with
more than one file if desired. By reading the same file twice, the user can
compare time for retrieval with the time for the original insertion.

Here are further specifications for the driver program:

➡ The input to the driver will be a file. The program will be executed with several different files; the name of the file to be used should be requested from the user while the program is running.

➡ A word is defined as a sequence of letters, together with apostrophes (') and hyphens (-), provided that the apostrophe or hyphen is both immediately preceded and followed by a letter. Uppercase and lowercase letters should be regarded as the same (by translating all letters into either uppercase or lowercase, as you prefer). A word is to be truncated to its first 20 characters (that is, only 20 characters are to be stored in the data structure) but words longer than 20 characters may appear in the text. Nonalphabetic characters (such as digits, blanks, punctuation marks, control characters) may appear in the text file. The appearance of any of these terminates a word, and the next word begins only when a letter appears.

➡ Be sure to write your driver so that it will not be changed at all when you change implementation of data structures later.

Here are specifications for the functions to be implemented first with binary search trees.

---

void update(**const** String &word,
              Search_tree<Record> &structure, **int** &num_comps);

postcondition: If **word** was not already present in **structure**, then **word** has been inserted into **structure** and its frequency count is 1. If **word** was already present in **structure**, then its frequency count has been increased by 1. The variable parameter **num_comps** is set to the number of comparisons of words done.

---

void print(**const** Search_tree<Record> &structure);

postcondition: All words in **structure** are printed at the terminal in alphabetical order together with their frequency counts.

---

void write_method();

postcondition: The function has written a short string identifying the abstract data type used for **structure**.

10.3 BUILDING A BINARY SEARCH TREE

Suppose that we have a list of data that is already sorted into order, or perhaps a file of records, with keys already sorted alphabetically. If we wish to use this data to look up information, add additional information, or make other changes, then we would like to take the list or file and make it into a binary search tree.

goal
We could, of course, start out with an empty binary tree and simply use the tree insertion algorithm to insert each entry into it. But the entries are given already sorted into order, so the resulting search tree will become one long chain, and using it will be too slow—with the speed of sequential search rather than binary search. We wish instead, therefore, to take the entries and build them into a tree that will be as bushy as possible, so as to reduce both the time to build the tree and all subsequent search time. When the number of entries, n, is 31, for example, we wish to build the tree of Figure 10.12.

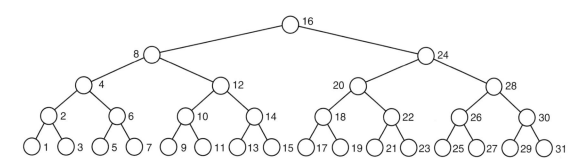

Figure 10.12. Complete binary tree with 31 nodes

In Figure 10.12 the entries are numbered in their natural order, that is, in inorder sequence, which is the order in which they will be received and built into the tree, since they are received in sorted order. We will also use this numbering to label the nodes of the tree.

If you examine the diagram for a moment, you may notice an important property of the labels. The labels of the leaves are all odd numbers; that is, they are not divisible by 2. The labels of the nodes one level above the leaves are 2, 6, 10, 14, 18, 22, 26, and 30. These numbers are all double an odd number; that is, they are all even, but are not divisible by 4. On the next level up, the labels are 4, 12, 20, and 28, numbers that are divisible by 4, but not by 8. Finally, the nodes just below the root are labeled 8 and 24, and the root itself is 16. The crucial observation is:

crucial property
> *If the nodes of a complete binary tree are labeled in inorder sequence, starting with 1, then each node is exactly as many levels above the leaves as the highest power of 2 that divides its label.*

Let us now put one more constraint on our problem: Let us suppose that we do not know in advance how many entries will be built into the tree. If the entries are coming from a file or a linked list, then this assumption is quite reasonable, since we may not have any convenient way to count the entries before receiving them.

This assumption also has the advantage that it will stop us from worrying about the fact that, when the number of entries is not exactly one less than a power of 2, the resulting tree will not be complete and cannot be as symmetrical as the one in Figure 10.12. Instead, we shall design our algorithm as though it were completely symmetrical, and after receiving all entries we shall determine how to tidy up the tree.

10.3.1 Getting Started

There is no doubt what to do with entry number 1 when it arrives. It will be placed in a leaf node whose left and right pointers should both be set to NULL. Node number 2 goes above node 1, as shown in Figure 10.13. Since node 2 links to node 1, we obviously must keep some way to remember where node 1 is until entry 2 arrives. Node 3 is again a leaf, but it is in the right subtree of node 2, so we must remember a pointer to node 2.

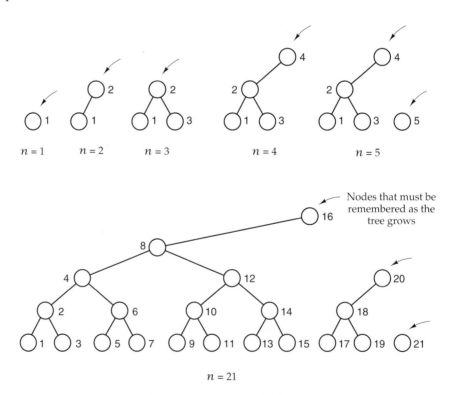

Figure 10.13. Building the first nodes into a binary search tree

Does this mean that we must keep a list of pointers to all nodes previously processed, to determine how to link in the next one? The answer is no, since when node 2 is added, all connections for node 1 are complete. Node 2 must be remembered until node 4 is added, to establish the left link from node 4, but then a pointer to node 2 is no longer needed. Similarly, node 4 must be remembered until node 8 has been processed. In Figure 10.13, colored arrows point to each node that must be remembered as the tree grows.

It should now be clear that to establish future links, we need only remember pointers to one node on each level, the last node processed on that level. We keep these pointers in a List called last_node that will be quite small. For example, a tree with 20 levels (hence 20 entries in last_node) can accommodate $2^{20} - 1 > 1,000,000$ nodes.

As each new node is added, it is clearly the last one received in the order, so we can set its right pointer to NULL (at least temporarily). The left pointer of the new node is NULL if it is a leaf. Otherwise it is the entry in last_node one level lower than the new node. So that we can treat the leaves in the same way as other nodes, we consider the leaves to be on level 1, and we set up the initial element of last_node, in position 0, to have the pointer value NULL permanently. This convention means that we shall always count levels above the leaves *inclusively*, so the leaves themselves are on level 1, and so on.

10.3.2 Declarations and the Main Function

We can now write down declarations of the variables needed for our task. We first note that, while we build up a tree, we need access to the internal structure of the tree in order to create appropriate links. Therefore, the new function will be implemented as a class method. Moreover, it is to be applied to Search_tree objects, and thus it will be a method for a class of search trees. We will therefore create a new class called a Buildable_tree that is derived from the class Search_tree and possesses a new method, the function build_tree. The specification for a buildable tree is thus:

```
template <class Record>
class Buildable_tree: public Search_tree<Record> {
public:
   Error_code build_tree(const List<Record> &supply);
private:                        //   Add auxiliary function prototypes here.
};
```

The first step of build_tree will be to receive the entries. For simplicity, we shall assume that these entries are found in a List of Record data called supply. However, it is an easy matter to rewrite the function to receive its data from a Queue or a file or even from another Search_tree that we wish to rebalance.

As we receive new entries to insert into the tree, we update a variable count to keep track of how many entries we have already added. The value of count is clearly needed to extract data from the List supply. More importantly, the value of count determines the level in the tree that will accommodate a new entry, and therefore it must be passed to any function that needs to calculate this level.

After all the entries from the List supply have been inserted into the new binary search tree, we must find the root of the tree and then connect any right subtrees that may be dangling (see Figure 10.13 in the case of 5 or 21 nodes).

The function thus becomes

```
template <class Record>
Error_code Buildable_tree<Record> :: build_tree(const List<Record> &supply)
/* Post: If the entries of supply are in increasing order, a code of success is returned
         and the Search_tree is built out of these entries as a balanced tree. Oth-
         erwise, a code of fail is returned and a balanced tree is constructed from
         the longest increasing sequence of entries at the start of supply.
   Uses: The methods of class List and the functions build_insert, connect_subtrees,
         and find_root */
{
   Error_code ordered_data = success;   //   Set this to fail if keys do not increase.
   int count = 0;                       //   number of entries inserted so far
   Record x, last_x;
   List < Binary_node<Record> * > last_node;
                                        //   pointers to last nodes on each level
   Binary_node<Record> *none = NULL;
   last_node.insert(0, none);  //   permanently NULL (for children of leaves)
   while (supply.retrieve(count, x) ==  success) {
      if (count > 0 && x <= last_x) {
         ordered_data = fail;
         break;
      }
      build_insert(++count, x, last_node);
      last_x = x;
   }
   root = find_root(last_node);
   connect_trees(last_node);
   return ordered_data;     //   Report any data-ordering problems back to client.
}
```

10.3.3 Inserting a Node

The discussion in the previous section shows how to set up the left links of each node correctly, but, at the conclusion of the process developed so far, some of the nodes will still have NULL right links that must be changed. When a new node arrives, it cannot yet have a nonempty right subtree, since it is the latest node (under the ordering) so far received. The node, however, may be the right child of some previous node. On the other hand, it may instead turn out to be the left child of some node with a larger key, in which case its parent node has not yet arrived. We can tell which case occurs by looking in the list last_node. If level denotes the level above the leaves, inclusive, of the new node, then its parent is at level + 1. We look at the entry of last_node in position level + 1. If its right link is still NULL, then its right child must be the new node; if not, then its right child has already arrived, and the new node must be the left child of some future node.

We can now write a function to insert a new node into the tree.

```
template <class Record>
void Buildable_tree<Record> :: build_insert(int count,
                                const Record &new_data,
                                List < Binary_node<Record>* > &last_node)
/* Post: A new node, containing the Record new_data, has been inserted as the
         rightmost node of a partially completed binary search tree.  The level
         of this new node is one more than the highest power of 2 that divides
         count.
   Uses: Methods of class List */
{
   int level;           //    level of new node above the leaves, counting inclusively
   for (level = 1; count % 2 == 0; level++)
      count /= 2;                 //    Use count to calculate level of next_node.
   Binary_node<Record> *next_node = new Binary_node<Record>(new_data),
                  *parent;  //    one level higher in last_node
   last_node.retrieve(level − 1, next_node->left);
   if (last_node.size() <= level)
      last_node.insert(level, next_node);
   else
      last_node.replace(level, next_node);
   if (last_node.retrieve(level + 1, parent) == success && parent->right == NULL)
      parent->right = next_node;
}
```

10.3.4 Finishing the Task

Finding the root of the tree is easy: The root is the highest node in the tree; hence its pointer is the last entry the List last_node. The partial tree for $n = 21$ shown in Figure 10.13, for example, has its highest node, 16, on level 5, and this will be the root of the finished tree. The pointers to the last node encountered on each level are stored in the list last_node as shown in Figure 10.14.

We thereby obtain the function:

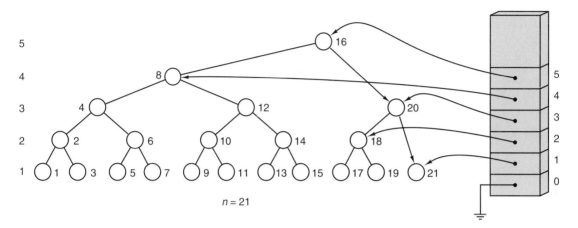

Figure 10.14. Finishing the binary search tree

finding the root

```
template <class Record>
Binary_node<Record> *Buildable_tree<Record>::find_root(
                    List < Binary_node<Record>* > &last_node)
/* Pre:   The list last_node contains pointers to the last node on each occupied level
          of the binary search tree.
   Post:  A pointer to the root of the newly created binary search tree is returned.
   Uses:  Methods of class List */
{
   Binary_node<Record> *high_node;
   last_node.retrieve(last_node.size() − 1, high_node);
      //   Find root in the highest occupied level in last_node.
   return high_node;
}
```

Finally, we must determine how to tie in any subtrees that may not yet be connected properly after all the nodes have been received. For example, if $n = 21$, we must connect the three components shown in Figure 10.13 into a single tree. In programming terms, the problem is that some nodes in the upper part of the tree may still have their right links set to NULL, even though further nodes have been inserted that now belong in their right subtrees.

Any one of these nodes (a node, not a leaf, for which the right child is still NULL) will be one of the nodes in last_node. For $n = 21$, these will be nodes 16 and 20 (in positions 5 and 3 of last_node, respectively), as shown in Figure 10.14.

In the following function we refer to a node with NULL right subtree by using the pointer high_node. We need to determine a pointer, lower_node, to the right child of high_node. The pointer lower_node can be determined as the highest node in last_node that is not already in the left subtree of high_node. To determine whether a node is in the left subtree, we need only compare its key with that of high_node.

tying subtrees
together

```
template <class Record>
void Buildable_tree<Record>::connect_trees(
    const List < Binary_node<Record>* > &last_node)
/* Pre:  The nearly-completed binary search tree has been initialized.  The List
         last_node has been initialized and contains links to the last node on each
         level of the tree.
   Post: The final links have been added to complete the binary search tree.
   Uses: Methods of class List */
{
    Binary_node<Record> *high_node,  //   from last_node with NULL right child
                         *low_node;
                                     //  candidate for right child of high_node
    int high_level = last_node.size() - 1,
        low_level;
    while (high_level > 2) {       //   Nodes on levels 1 and 2 are already OK.
      last_node.retrieve(high_level, high_node);
      if (high_node->right != NULL)
        high_level --;             //   Search down for highest dangling node.
      else {                       //   Case: undefined right tree
        low_level = high_level;
        do {                       //   Find the highest entry not in the left subtree.
          last_node.retrieve(--low_level, low_node);
        } while (low_node != NULL && low_node->data < high_node->data);
        high_node->right = low_node;
        high_level = low_level;
      }
    }
}
```

10.3.5 Evaluation

The algorithm of this section produces a binary search tree that is not always completely balanced. See, for example, the tree with 21 nodes in Figure 10.14. if the tree has 31 nodes, then it will be completely balanced, but if 32 nodes come in, then node 32 will become the root of the tree, and all 31 remaining nodes will be in its left subtree. In this case, the leaves are five steps removed from the root. If the root were chosen optimally, then most of the leaves would be four steps from it, and only one would be five steps. Hence one comparison more than necessary will usually be done in the tree with 32 nodes.

One extra comparison in a binary search is not really a very high price, and it is easy to see that a tree produced by our method is never more than one level away from optimality. There are sophisticated methods for building a binary search tree that is as balanced as possible, but much remains to recommend a simpler method, one that does not need to know in advance how many nodes are in the tree.

The exercises outline ways in which our algorithm can be used to take an arbitrary binary search tree and rearrange the nodes to bring it into better balance, so as to improve search times. Again, there are more sophisticated methods (which, however, will likely be slower) for rebalancing a tree. In Section 10.4 we shall study AVL trees, in which we perform insertions and removals in such a way as always to maintain the tree in a state of near balance. For many practical purposes, however, the simpler algorithm described in this section should prove sufficient.

10.3.6 Random Search Trees and Optimality

To conclude this section, let us ask whether it is worthwhile, on average, to keep a binary search tree balanced or to rebalance it. If we assume that the keys have arrived in random order, then, on average, how many more comparisons are needed in a search of the resulting tree than would be needed in a completely balanced tree?

extended binary tree

In answering the question we first convert the binary search tree into a 2-tree, as follows. Think of all the vertices of the binary tree as drawn as circles, and add on new, square vertices replacing all the empty subtrees (NULL links). This process is shown in Figure 10.15. All the vertices of the original binary tree become internal vertices of the 2-tree, and the new vertices are all external (leaves).

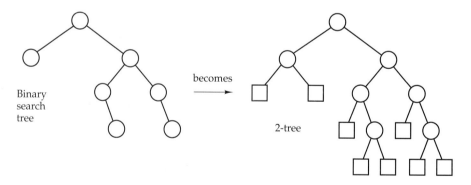

Figure 10.15. Extension of a binary tree into a 2-tree

one-to-one correspondence

We can also apply Figure 10.15 in the reverse direction: By pruning all the leaves (drawn as square vertices) from a 2-tree, it becomes a binary tree. In fact, we can observe:

There is a one-to-one correspondence between binary search trees and 2-trees in which left and right are considered different from each other.

We must draw this left-right distinction, because in binary search trees, the left-right distinction reflects the ordering of the keys, whereas in arbitrary 2-trees (without the left-right distinction), the branching might represent any two-way decision.

path lengths   A successful search in a binary search tree terminates at an interior vertex of the corresponding 2-tree, and an unsuccessful search terminates at a leaf. Hence the internal path length of the 2-tree leads us to the number of comparisons for a successful search, and the external path length of the 2-tree leads us to the number for an unsuccessful search. Since two comparisons are done at each internal node, the number of comparisons done in searching once for each key in the tree is, in fact, twice the internal path length.

We shall assume that the $n!$ possible orderings of keys are equally likely in building the binary search tree. When there are n nodes in the tree, we denote by $S(n)$ the number of comparisons done in the average successful search and by $U(n)$ the number in the average unsuccessful search.

counting comparisons   The number of comparisons needed to find any key in the tree is exactly one more than the number of comparisons that were needed to insert it in the first place, and inserting it required the same comparisons as the unsuccessful search showing that it was not yet in the tree. We therefore have the relationship

$$S(n) = 1 + \frac{U(0) + U(1) + \cdots + U(n-1)}{n}.$$

The relation between internal and external path length, as presented in Theorem 7.4, states that

$$S(n) = \left(1 + \frac{1}{n}\right) U(n) - 3.$$

recurrence relation   The last two equations together give

$$(n+1)U(n) = 4n + U(0) + U(1) + \cdots + U(n-1).$$

We solve this recurrence by writing the equation for $n-1$ instead of n:

$$nU(n-1) = 4(n-1) + U(0) + U(1) + \cdots + U(n-2),$$

and subtracting, to obtain

$$U(n) = U(n-1) + \frac{4}{n+1}.$$

The sum

$$H_n = 1 + \frac{1}{2} + \frac{1}{3} + \cdots + \frac{1}{n}$$

harmonic number   is called the nth **harmonic number**, and it is shown in Theorem A.4 on page 656 that this number is approximately the natural logarithm $\ln n$. Since $U(0) = 0$, we can now evaluate $U(n)$ by starting at the bottom and adding:

$$U(n) = 4\left[\frac{1}{2} + \frac{1}{3} + \cdots + \frac{1}{n+1}\right] = 4H_{n+1} - 4 \approx 4\ln n.$$

By Theorem 7.4, the number of comparisons for a successful search is also approximately $4\ln n$. Since searching any binary search tree requires two comparisons per node and the optimal height is $\lg n$, the optimal number of comparisons is $2\lg n$. But (see Section A.2)

$$\ln n = (\ln 2)(\lg n).$$

Converting natural logarithms to base 2 logarithms, we finally obtain:

Theorem 10.3   *The average number of nodes visited in a search of the average binary search tree with n nodes is approximately $2\ln n = (2\ln 2)(\lg n) \approx 1.39\lg n$, and the number of key comparisons is approximately $4\ln n = (4\ln 2)(\lg n) \approx 2.77\lg n$.*

Corollary 10.4   *The average binary search tree requires approximately $2\ln 2 \approx 1.39$ times as many comparisons as a completely balanced tree.*

cost of not balancing   In other words, the average cost of not balancing a binary search tree is approximately 39 percent more comparisons. In applications where optimality is important, this cost must be weighed against the extra cost of balancing the tree, or of maintaining it in balance. Note especially that these latter tasks involve not only the cost of computer time, but the cost of the extra programming effort that will be required.

Exercises 10.3

E1. Draw the sequence of partial binary search trees (like Figure 10.13) that the method in this section will construct for the following values of n. **(a)** 6, 7, 8; **(b)** 15, 16, 17; **(c)** 22, 23, 24; **(d)** 31, 32, 33.

E2. Write function build_tree for the case when supply is a queue.

E3. Write function build_tree for the case when the input structure is a binary search tree. [This version gives a function to rebalance a binary search tree.]

E4. Write a version of function build_tree that will read keys from a file, one key per line. [This version gives a function that reads a binary search tree from an ordered file.]

E5. Extend each of the binary search trees shown in Figure 10.8 into a 2-tree.

E6. There are $6 = 3!$ possible ordered sequences of the three keys 1, 2, 3, but only 5 distinct binary trees with three nodes. Therefore, these binary trees are not equally likely to occur as search trees. Find which one of the five binary search trees corresponds to each of the six possible ordered sequences of 1, 2, 3. Thereby find the probability for building each of the binary search trees from randomly ordered input.

E7. There are 24 = 4! possible ordered sequences of the four keys 1, 2, 3, 4, but only 14 distinct binary trees with four nodes. Therefore, these binary trees are not equally likely to occur as search trees. Find which one of the 14 binary search trees corresponds to each of the 24 possible ordered sequences of 1, 2, 3, 4. Thereby find the probability for building each of the binary search trees from randomly ordered input.

E8. If T is an arbitrary binary search tree, let $S(T)$ denote the number of ordered sequences of the keys in T that correspond to T (that is, that will generate T if they are inserted, in the given order, into an initially-empty binary search tree). Find a formula for $S(T)$ that depends only on the sizes of L and R and on $S(L)$ and $S(R)$, where L and R are the left and right subtrees of the root of T.

10.4 HEIGHT BALANCE: AVL TREES

The algorithm of Section 10.3 can be used to build a nearly balanced binary search tree, or to restore balance when it is feasible to restructure the tree completely. In many applications, however, insertions and removals occur continually, with no predictable order. In some of these applications, it is important to optimize search times by keeping the tree very nearly balanced at all times. The method in this section for achieving this goal was described in 1962 by two Russian mathematicians, G. M. ADEL'SON-VEL'SKIĬ and E. M. LANDIS, and the resulting binary search trees are called **AVL trees** in their honor.

nearly optimal height   AVL trees achieve the goal that searches, insertions, and removals in a tree with n nodes can all be achieved in time that is $O(\log n)$, even in the worst case. The height of an AVL tree with n nodes, as we shall establish, can never exceed $1.44 \lg n$, and thus even in the worst case, the behavior of an AVL tree could not be much below that of a random binary search tree. In almost all cases, however, the actual length of a search is very nearly $\lg n$, and thus the behavior of AVL trees closely approximates that of the ideal, completely balanced binary search tree.

10.4.1 Definition

In a completely balanced tree, the left and right subtrees of any node would have the same height. Although we cannot always achieve this goal, by building a search tree carefully we can always ensure that the heights of every left and right subtree never differ by more than 1. We accordingly make the following definition:

Definition   An **AVL tree** is a binary search tree in which the heights of the left and right subtrees of the root differ by at most 1 and in which the left and right subtrees are again AVL trees.

     With each node of an AVL tree is associated a **balance factor** that is **left-higher**, **equal-height**, or **right-higher** according, respectively, as the left subtree has height greater than, equal to, or less than that of the right subtree.

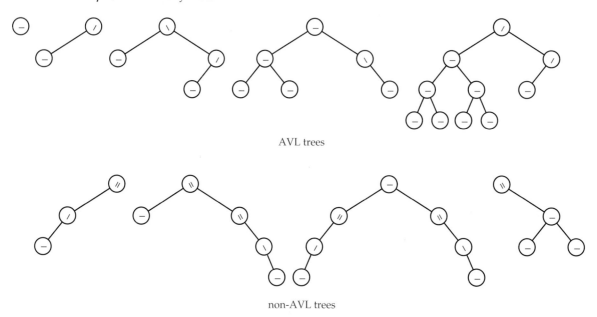

AVL trees

non-AVL trees

Figure 10.16. Examples of AVL trees and other binary trees

In drawing diagrams, we shall show a left-higher node by '/,' a node whose balance factor is equal by '−,' and a right-higher node by '\.' Figure 10.16 shows several small AVL trees, as well as some binary trees that fail to satisfy the definition.

Note that the definition does not require that all leaves be on the same or adjacent levels. Figure 10.17 shows several AVL trees that are quite skewed, with right subtrees having greater height than left subtrees.

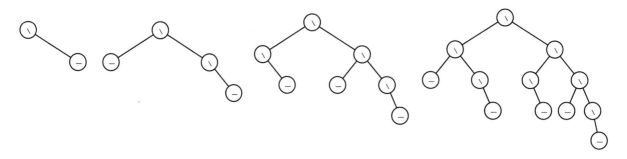

Figure 10.17. AVL trees skewed to the right

1. C++ Conventions

We employ an enumerated data type to record balance factors.

enum Balance_factor { left_higher, equal_height, right_higher };

Balance factors must be included in all the nodes of an AVL tree, and we must adapt our former node specification accordingly.

```
template <class Record>
struct AVL_node: public Binary_node<Record> {
//   additional data member:
  Balance_factor balance;
//   constructors:
  AVL_node();
  AVL_node(const Record &x);
//   overridden virtual functions:
  void set_balance(Balance_factor b);
  Balance_factor get_balance() const;
};
```

One slightly tricky point about this specification is that the left and right pointers of a Binary_node have type Binary_node *. Therefore, the inherited pointer members of an AVL_node have this type too. However, in an AVL tree, we obviously need to use AVL nodes that point to other AVL nodes. The apparent pointer type incompatibility is not a serious problem, because a pointer to an object from a base class can also point to an object of a derived class. In our situation, the left and right

benefit pointers of an AVL_node can legitimately point to other AVL nodes. The benefit that we get in return for implementing AVL nodes with a derived structure is the reuse of all of our functions for processing nodes of binary trees and search trees. However, we shall have to make sure that when we insert new nodes into an AVL tree, we do only insert genuine AVL nodes.

We shall use the AVL_node methods get_balance and set_balance to examine and adjust the balance factor of an AVL node.

```
template <class Record>
void AVL_node<Record> :: set_balance(Balance_factor b)
{
  balance = b;
}
template <class Record>
Balance_factor AVL_node<Record> :: get_balance() const
{
  return balance;
}
```

For the most part, we shall call set_balance and get_balance through a pointer to a node, with a call such as left->get_balance(). However, this particular call can create a problem for the C++ compiler which regards left as merely pointing to a Binary_node rather than to a specialized AVL_node. The compiler must therefore reject the expression left->get_balance() because it cannot be sure whether there

dummy methods is such a method attached to the object *left. We shall resolve this difficulty by including dummy versions of get_balance() and set_balance() in our Binary_node structure. These dummy functions are included as Binary_node methods solely to allow for implementations of derived AVL tree implementations.

After we add appropriate dummy methods to the **struct** Binary_node, the compiler will allow the expression left->set_balance(). However, there is still a problem that cannot be resolved by the compiler: Should it use the AVL version or the dummy version of the method? The correct choice can only be made at run time, when the type of the object *left is known. Accordingly, we must declare the Binary_node versions of set_balance and get_balance as **virtual** methods. This means that the choice of whether to use the dummy version or the more useful AVL_node version is made at run time. For example, if **set_balance( )** is called as a method of an AVL_node, then the AVL version will be used, whereas if it is called as a method of a Binary_node then the dummy version will be used.

Here is our modified specification of binary nodes, together with an implementation of appropriate dummy methods.

```
template <class Entry>
struct Binary_node {
//    data members:
   Entry data;
   Binary_node<Entry> *left;
   Binary_node<Entry> *right;
//    constructors:
   Binary_node( );
   Binary_node(const Entry &x);
//    virtual methods:
   virtual void set_balance(Balance_factor b);
   virtual Balance_factor get_balance( ) const;
};

template <class Entry>
void Binary_node<Entry>::set_balance(Balance_factor b)
{
}
template <class Entry>
Balance_factor Binary_node<Entry>::get_balance( ) const
{
   return equal_height;
}
```

No other related changes are needed to any of our earlier classes and functions, and all of our prior node processing functions are now available for use with AVL nodes.

We can now specify our AVL tree class. We shall only need to override our earlier insertion and deletion functions with versions that maintain a balanced tree structure. The other binary search tree methods can be inherited without any changes. Hence we arrive at the following specification:

```
template <class Record>
class AVL_tree: public Search_tree<Record> {
public:
   Error_code insert(const Record &new_data);
   Error_code remove(const Record &old_data);
private:                        //    Add auxiliary function prototypes here.
};
```

The inherited data member of this class is the pointer root. This pointer has type Binary_node<Record> * and therefore, as we have seen, it can store the address of either an ordinary binary tree node or an AVL tree node. We must ensure that the overridden insert method only creates nodes of type AVL_node; doing so will guarantee that all nodes reached via the root pointer of an AVL tree are AVL nodes.

10.4.2 Insertion of a Node

1. Introduction

usual algorithm

We can insert a new node into an AVL tree by first following the usual binary tree insertion algorithm: comparing the key of the new node with that in the root, and inserting the new node into the left or right subtree as appropriate. It often turns out that the new node can be inserted without changing the height of the subtree, in which case neither the height nor the balance of the root will be changed. Even when the height of a subtree does increase, it may be the shorter subtree that has grown, so only the balance factor of the root will change. The only case that can cause difficulty occurs when the new node is added to a subtree of the root that is

problem

strictly taller than the other subtree, and the height is increased. This would cause one subtree to have height 2 more than the other, whereas the AVL condition is that the height difference is never more than 1. Before we consider this situation more carefully, let us illustrate in Figure 10.18 the growth of an AVL tree through several insertions, and then we shall tie down the ideas by coding our algorithm in C++.

example

The insertions in Figure 10.18 proceed in exactly the same way as insertions into an ordinary binary search tree, except that the balance factors must be adjusted. Note, however, that the balance factors can only be determined *after* the insertion is made. When v is inserted in Figure 10.18, for example, the balance factor in the root, k, changes, but it does not change when p is next inserted. Both v and p are inserted (recursively) into the right subtree, t, of the root, and it is only after the insertion is finished that the balance factor of the root, k, can be determined.

The basic structure of our algorithm will thus be the same as the ordinary recursive binary tree insertion algorithm of Section 10.2.3 (page 452), but with significant additions to accommodate the processing of balance factors and other structure of AVL trees.

We must keep track of whether an insertion (after recursion) has increased the tree height or not, so that the balance factors can be changed appropriately. This we do by including an additional calling parameter taller of type **bool** in the auxiliary recursive function called by the insertion method. The task of restoring balance when required will be done in the subsidiary functions left_balance and right_balance.

With these decisions, we can now write the method and auxiliary function to insert new data into an AVL tree.

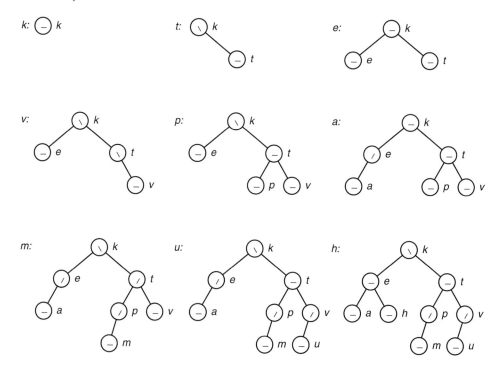

Figure 10.18. Simple insertions of nodes into an AVL tree

```
template <class Record>
Error_code AVL_tree<Record> :: insert(const Record &new_data)
/* Post:  If the key of new_data is already in the AVL_tree, a code of duplicate_error
          is returned.  Otherwise, a code of success is returned and the Record
          new_data is inserted into the tree in such a way that the properties of
          an AVL tree are preserved.
   Uses: avl_insert. */
{
   bool taller;
   return avl_insert(root, new_data, taller);
}
```

```
template <class Record>
Error_code AVL_tree<Record> :: avl_insert(Binary_node<Record> * &sub_root,
            const Record &new_data, bool &taller)
/* Pre:   sub_root is either NULL or points to a subtree of the AVL_tree
   Post:  If the key of new_data is already in the subtree, a code of duplicate_error
          is returned.  Otherwise, a code of success is returned and the Record
          new_data is inserted into the subtree in such a way that the properties of
          an AVL tree have been preserved.  If the subtree is increased in height, the
          parameter taller is set to true; otherwise it is set to false.
   Uses: Methods of struct AVL_node; functions avl_insert recursively,
          left_balance, and right_balance. */
```

```
{
  Error_code result = success;
  if (sub_root ==  NULL) {
    sub_root = new AVL_node<Record>(new_data);
    taller = true;
  }
  else if (new_data ==  sub_root->data) {
    result = duplicate_error;
    taller = false;
  }
  else if (new_data < sub_root->data) { //    Insert in left subtree.
    result = avl_insert(sub_root->left, new_data, taller);
    if (taller ==  true)
      switch (sub_root->get_balance()) { //    Change balance factors.
      case left_higher:
        left_balance(sub_root);
        taller = false;         //    Rebalancing always shortens the tree.
        break;
      case equal_height:
        sub_root->set_balance(left_higher);
        break;
      case right_higher:
        sub_root->set_balance(equal_height);
        taller = false;
        break;
      }
  }
  else {                              //    Insert in right subtree.
    result = avl_insert(sub_root->right, new_data, taller);
    if (taller ==  true)
      switch (sub_root->get_balance()) {
      case left_higher:
        sub_root->set_balance(equal_height);
        taller = false;
        break;
      case equal_height:
        sub_root->set_balance(right_higher);
        break;
      case right_higher:
        right_balance(sub_root);
        taller = false;         //    Rebalancing always shortens the tree.
        break;
      }
  }
  return result;
}
```

2. Rotations

Let us now consider the case when a new node has been inserted into the taller subtree of a root node and its height has increased, so that now one subtree has height 2 more than the other, and the tree no longer satisfies the AVL requirements. We must now rebuild part of the tree to restore its balance. To be definite, let us assume that we have inserted the new node into the right subtree, its height has increased, and the original tree was right higher. That is, we wish to consider the case covered by the function right_balance. Let root denote the root of the tree and right_tree the root of its right subtree.

There are three cases to consider, depending on the balance factor of right_tree.

3. Case 1: Right Higher

left rotation

The first case, when right_tree is right higher, is illustrated in Figure 10.19. The action needed in this case is called a ***left rotation***; we have rotated the node right_tree upward to the root, dropping root down into the left subtree of right_tree; the subtree T_2 of nodes with keys between those of root and right_tree now becomes the right subtree of root rather than the left subtree of right_tree. A left rotation is succinctly described in the following C++ function. Note especially that, when done in the appropriate order, the steps constitute a rotation of the values in three pointer variables. Note also that, after the rotation, the height of the rotated tree has decreased by 1; it had previously increased because of the insertion; hence the height finishes where it began.

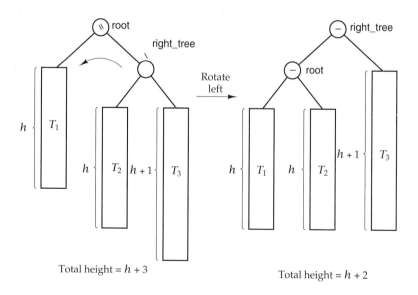

Figure 10.19. First case: Restoring balance by a left rotation

```
template <class Record>
void AVL_tree<Record> :: rotate_left(Binary_node<Record> * &sub_root)
/* Pre:   sub_root points to a subtree of the AVL_tree. This subtree has a nonempty
             right subtree.
   Post:  sub_root is reset to point to its former right child, and the former sub_root
             node is the left child of the new sub_root node. */
{
   if (sub_root == NULL || sub_root->right == NULL)  //   impossible cases
      cout << "WARNING: program error detected in rotate_left" << endl;
   else {
      Binary_node<Record> *right_tree = sub_root->right;
      sub_root->right = right_tree->left;
      right_tree->left = sub_root;
      sub_root = right_tree;
   }
}
```

4. Case 2: Left Higher

double rotation

The second case, when the balance factor of right_tree is left higher, is slightly more complicated. It is necessary to move two levels, to the node **sub_tree** that roots the left subtree of **right_tree**, to find the new root. This process is shown in Figure 10.20 and is called a ***double rotation***, because the transformation can be obtained in two steps by first rotating the subtree with root **right_tree** to the right (so that **sub_tree** becomes its root), and then rotating the tree pointed to by **root** to the left (moving **sub_tree** up to become the new root).

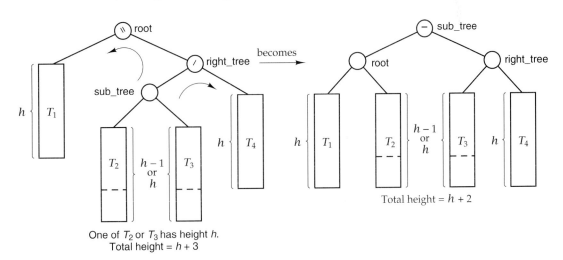

One of T_2 or T_3 has height h.
Total height = $h + 3$

Total height = $h + 2$

Figure 10.20. Second case: Restoring balance by a double rotation

In this second case, the new balance factors for root and right_tree depend on the previous balance factor for sub_tree. (The new balance factor for sub_tree will always be equal_height.) Figure 10.20 shows the subtrees of sub_tree as having equal heights, but it is possible that sub_tree may be either left or right higher. The resulting balance factors are

old sub_tree	*new* root	*new* right_tree	*new* sub_tree
–	–	–	–
/	–	\	–
\	/	–	–

5. Case 3: Equal Height

It would appear, finally, that we must consider a third case, when the two subtrees of right_tree have equal heights, but this case, in fact, can never happen. To see why, let us recall that we have just inserted a new node into the subtree rooted at right_tree, and this subtree now has height 2 more than the left subtree of the root. The new node went either into the left or right subtree of right_tree. Hence its insertion increased the height of only one subtree of right_tree. If these subtrees had equal heights after the insertion, then the height of the full subtree rooted at right_tree was not changed by the insertion, contrary to what we already know.

6. C++ Function for Balancing

It is now straightforward to incorporate these transformations into a C++ function. The forms of functions rotate_right and left_balance are clearly similar to those of rotate_left and right_balance, respectively, and are left as exercises.

```
template <class Record>
void AVL_tree<Record> :: right_balance(Binary_node<Record> * &sub_root)
/* Pre:   sub_root points to a subtree of an AVL_tree that is doubly unbalanced on
          the right.
   Post:  The AVL properties have been restored to the subtree.
   Uses:  Methods of struct AVL_node;
          functions rotate_right and rotate_left. */
{
  Binary_node<Record> * &right_tree = sub_root->right;
  switch (right_tree->get_balance()) {
  case right_higher:          //    single rotation left
    sub_root->set_balance(equal_height);
    right_tree->set_balance(equal_height);
    rotate_left(sub_root);
    break;
```

```
case equal_height:            //   impossible case
  cout << "WARNING: program error detected in right_balance" << endl;
case left_higher:            //   double rotation left
  Binary_node<Record> *sub_tree = right_tree->left;
  switch (sub_tree->get_balance()) {
  case equal_height:
    sub_root->set_balance(equal_height);
    right_tree->set_balance(equal_height);
    break;
  case left_higher:
    sub_root->set_balance(equal_height);
    right_tree->set_balance(right_higher);
    break;
  case right_higher:
    sub_root->set_balance(left_higher);
    right_tree->set_balance(equal_height);
    break;
  }
  sub_tree->set_balance(equal_height);
  rotate_right(right_tree);
  rotate_left(sub_root);
  break;
  }
}
```

Examples of insertions requiring single and double rotations are shown in Figure 10.21.

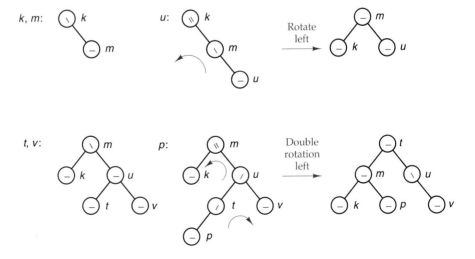

Figure 10.21. AVL insertions requiring rotations

7. Behavior of the Algorithm

counting rotations

The number of times that function avl_insert calls itself recursively to insert a new node can be as large as the height of the tree. At first glance it may appear that each one of these calls might induce either a single or double rotation of the appropriate subtree, but, in fact, at most only one (single or double) rotation will ever be done. To see this, let us recall that rotations are done only in functions right_balance and left_balance and that these functions are called only when the height of a subtree has increased. When these functions return, however, the rotations have removed the increase in height, so, for the remaining (outer) recursive calls, the height has not increased, so no further rotations or changes of balance factors are done.

Most of the insertions into an AVL tree will induce no rotations. Even when rotations are needed, they will usually occur near the leaf that has just been inserted. Even though the algorithm to insert into an AVL tree is complicated, it is reasonable to expect that its running time will differ little from insertion into an ordinary search tree of the same height. Later we shall see that we can expect the height of AVL trees to be much less than that of random search trees, and therefore both insertion and retrieval will be significantly more efficient in AVL trees than in random binary search trees.

10.4.3 Removal of a Node

Removal of a node x from an AVL tree requires the same basic ideas, including single and double rotations, that are used for insertion. We shall give only the steps of an informal outline of the method, leaving the writing of complete algorithms as a programming project.

method

1. Reduce the problem to the case when the node x to be removed has at most one child. For suppose that x has two children. Find the immediate predecessor y of x under inorder traversal (the immediate successor would be just as good), by first taking the left child of x, and then moving right as far as possible to obtain y. The node y is guaranteed to have no right child, because of the way it was found. Place y (or a copy of y) into the position in the tree occupied by x (with the same parent, left and right children, and balance factor that x had). Now remove y from its former position, by proceeding as follows, using y in place of x in each of the following steps.

2. Delete the node x from the tree. Since we know (by step 1) that x has at most one child, we remove x simply by linking the parent of x to the single child of x (or to NULL, if no child). The height of the subtree formerly rooted at x has been reduced by 1, and we must now trace the effects of this change on height through all the nodes on the path from x back to the root of the tree. We use a **bool** variable shorter to show if the height of a subtree has been shortened. The action to be taken at each node depends on the value of shorter, on the balance factor of the node, and sometimes on the balance factor of a child of the node.

3. The **bool** variable shorter is initially true. The following steps are to be done for each node p on the path from the parent of x to the root of the tree, provided shorter remains true. When shorter becomes false, then no further changes are needed, and the algorithm terminates.

4. *Case 1:* The current node p has balance factor equal. The balance factor of p is changed accordingly as its left or right subtree has been shortened, and shorter becomes false.

5. *Case 2:* The balance factor of p is not equal, and the taller subtree was shortened. Change the balance factor of p to equal, and leave shorter as true.

6. *Case 3:* The balance factor of p is not equal, and the shorter subtree was shortened. The height requirement for an AVL tree is now violated at p, so we apply a rotation, as follows, to restore balance. Let q be the root of the taller subtree of p (the one not shortened). We have three cases according to the balance factor of q.

7. *Case 3a:* The balance factor of q is equal. A single rotation (with changes to the balance factors of p and q) restores balance, and shorter becomes false.

8. *Case 3b:* The balance factor of q is the same as that of p. Apply a single rotation, set the balance factors of p and q to equal, and leave shorter as true.

9. *Case 3c:* The balance factors of p and q are opposite. Apply a double rotation (first around q, then around p), set the balance factor of the new root to equal and the other balance factors as appropriate, and leave shorter as true.

In cases 3a, b, c, the direction of the rotations depends on whether a left or right subtree was shortened. Some of the possibilities are illustrated in Figure 10.22, and an example of removal of a node appears in Figure 10.23.

10.4.4 The Height of an AVL Tree

It turns out to be very difficult to find the height of the average AVL tree, and thereby to determine how many steps are done, on average, by the algorithms of this section. It is much easier, however, to find what happens in the worst case, and these results show that the worst-case behavior of AVL trees is essentially no worse than the behavior of random trees. Empirical evidence suggests that the average behavior of AVL trees is much better than that of random trees, almost as good as that which could be obtained from a perfectly balanced tree.

worst-case analysis   To determine the maximum height that an AVL tree with n nodes can have, we can instead ask what is the minimum number of nodes that an AVL tree of height h can have. If F_h is such a tree, and the left and right subtrees of its root are F_l and F_r, then one of F_l and F_r must have height $h - 1$, say F_l, and the other has height either $h - 1$ or $h - 2$. Since F_h has the minimum number of nodes among AVL trees of height h, it follows that F_l must have the minimum number of nodes among AVL trees of height $h - 1$ (that is, F_l is of the form F_{h-1}), and F_r must have height $h - 2$ with minimum number of nodes (so that F_r is of the form F_{h-2}).

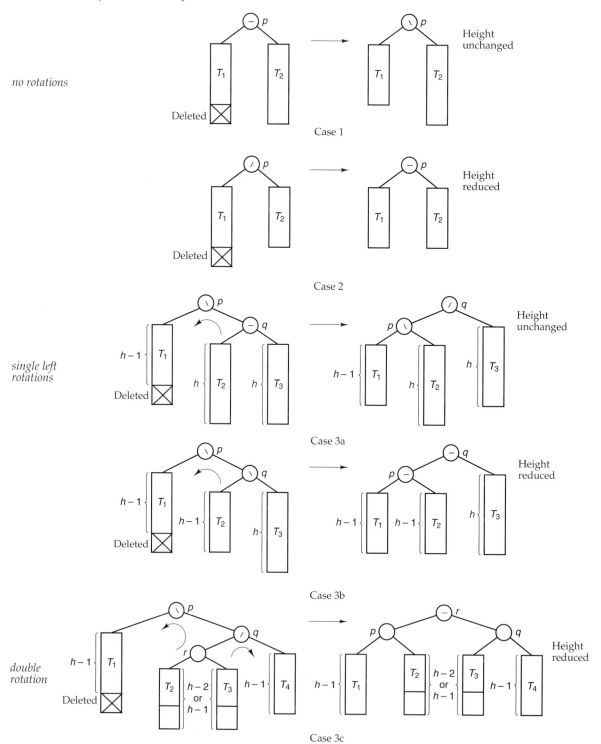

Figure 10.22. Sample cases, removal from an AVL tree

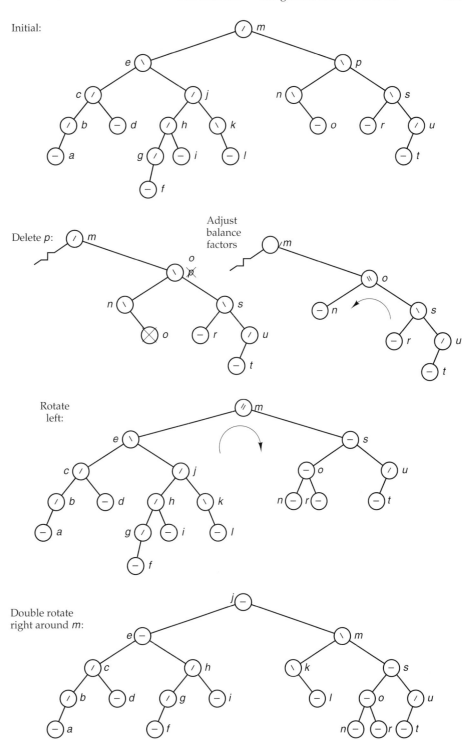

Figure 10.23. Example of removal from an AVL tree

Fibonacci trees   The trees built by the preceding rule, which are therefore as sparse as possible for AVL trees, are called **Fibonacci trees**. The first few are shown in Figure 10.24.

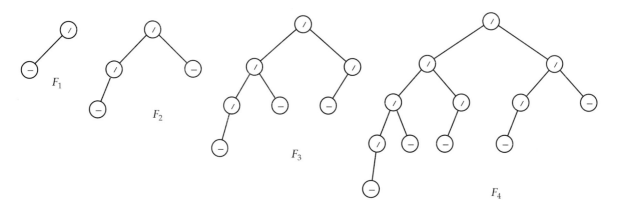

Figure 10.24. Fibonacci trees

counting nodes of a Fibonacci tree   If we write $|T|$ for the number of nodes in a tree T, we then have (counting the root as well as the subtrees) the recurrence relation

$$|F_h| = |F_{h-1}| + |F_{h-2}| + 1,$$

where $|F_0| = 1$ and $|F_1| = 2$. By adding 1 to both sides, we see that the numbers $|F_h| + 1$ satisfy the definition of the Fibonacci numbers (see Section A.4), with the subscripts changed by 3. By the evaluation of Fibonacci numbers in Section A.4, we therefore see that

$$|F_h| + 1 \approx \frac{1}{\sqrt{5}} \left[\frac{1 + \sqrt{5}}{2} \right]^{h+2}$$

Next, we solve this relation for h by taking the logarithms of both sides, and *height of a Fibonacci tree* discarding all except the largest terms. The approximate result is that

$$h \approx 1.44 \lg |F_h|.$$

worst-case bound   This means that the sparsest possible AVL tree with n nodes has height approximately $1.44 \lg n$. A perfectly balanced binary tree with n nodes has height about $\lg n$, and a degenerate tree has height as large as n. Hence the algorithms for manipulating AVL trees are guaranteed to take no more than about 44 percent more time than the optimum. In practice, AVL trees do much better than this. It can be shown that, even for Fibonacci trees, which are the worst case for AVL trees, the average search time is only 4 percent more than the optimum. Most AVL trees are not nearly as sparse as Fibonacci trees, and therefore it is reasonable to expect that average search times for average AVL trees are very close indeed to the optimum. *average-case* Empirical studies, in fact, show that the average number of comparisons seems to be about $\lg n + 0.25$ when n is large.

Exercises
10.4

E1. Determine which of the following binary search trees are AVL trees. For those that are not, find all nodes at which the requirements are violated.

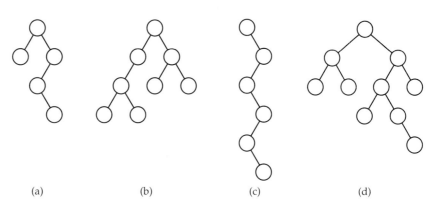

(a)   (b)   (c)   (d)

E2. In each of the following, insert the keys, in the order shown, to build them into an AVL tree.

(a) A, Z, B, Y, C, X.

(b) A, B, C, D, E, F.

(c) M, T, E, A, Z, G, P.

(d) A, Z, B, Y, C, X, D, W, E, V, F.

(e) A, B, C, D, E, F, G, H, I, J, K, L.

(f) A, V, L, T, R, E, I, S, O, K.

E3. Delete each of the keys inserted in Exercise E2 from the AVL tree, in LIFO order (last key inserted is first removed).

E4. Delete each of the keys inserted in Exercise E2 from the AVL tree, in FIFO order (first key inserted is first removed).

E5. Start with the following AVL tree and remove each of the following keys. Do each removal independently, starting with the original tree each time.

(a) *k*   (d) *a*   (f) *m*

(b) *c*   (e) *g*   (g) *h*

(c) *j*

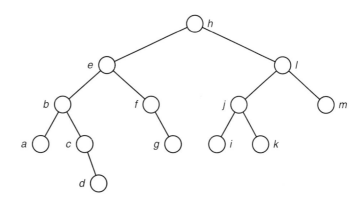

E6. Write a method that returns the height of an AVL tree by tracing only one path to a leaf, not by investigating all the nodes in the tree.

E7. Write a function that returns a pointer to the leftmost leaf closest to the root of a nonempty AVL tree.

E8. Prove that the number of (single or double) rotations done in deleting a key from an AVL tree cannot exceed half the height of the tree.

Programming Projects 10.4

P1. Write a C++ method to remove a node from an AVL tree, following the steps outlined in the text.

P2. Substitute the AVL tree class into the menu-driven demonstration program for binary search trees in Section 10.2, Project P2 (page 460), thereby obtaining a demonstration program for AVL trees.

P3. Substitute the AVL tree class into the information-retrieval project of Project P5 of Section 10.2 (page 461). Compare the performance of AVL trees with ordinary binary search trees for various combinations of input text files.

10.5 SPLAY TREES: A SELF-ADJUSTING DATA STRUCTURE

10.5.1 Introduction

hospital records

Consider the problem of maintaining patient records in a hospital. The records of a patient who is in hospital are extremely active, being consulted and updated continually by the attending physicians and nurses. When the patient leaves hospital, the records become much less active, but are still needed occasionally by the patient's physician or others. If, later, the patient is readmitted to hospital, then suddenly the records become extremely active again. Since, moreover, this readmission may be as an emergency, even the inactive records should be quickly available, not kept only as backup archives that would be slow to access.

access time

If we use an ordinary binary search tree, or even an AVL tree, for the hospital records, then the records of a newly admitted patient will go into a leaf position, far from the root, and therefore will be slow to access. Instead, we wish to keep records that are newly inserted or frequently accessed very close to the root, while records that are inactive may be placed far off, near or in the leaves. But we cannot shut down the hospital's record system even for an hour to rebuild the tree into the desired shape. Instead, we need to make the tree into a *self-adjusting* data structure that *automatically* changes its shape to bring records closer to the root as they are more frequently accessed, allowing inactive records to drift slowly out toward the leaves.

self-adjusting trees

Splay trees are binary search trees that achieve our goals by being self-adjusting in a quite remarkable way: Every time we access a node of the tree, whether for insertion or retrieval, we perform radical surgery on the tree, lifting the newly-accessed node all the way up, so that it becomes the root of the modified tree. Other nodes are pushed out of the way as necessary to make room for this new root. Nodes that are frequently accessed will frequently be lifted up to become the root, and they will never drift too far from the top position. Inactive nodes, on the other hand, will slowly be pushed farther and farther from the root.

It is possible that splay trees can become highly unbalanced, so that a single access to a node of the tree can be quite expensive. Later in this section, however, we shall prove that, over a long sequence of accesses, splay trees are not at all expensive and are guaranteed to require not many more operations even than AVL *amortized analysis* trees. The analytical tool used is called ***amortized algorithm analysis***, since, like insurance calculations, the few expensive cases are averaged in with many less expensive cases to obtain excellent performance over a long sequence of operations.

We perform the radical surgery on splay trees by using rotations of a similar form to those used for AVL trees, but now with *many* rotations done for *every* insertion or retrieval in the tree. In fact, rotations are done all along the path from the root to the target node that is being accessed. Let us now discuss precisely how these rotations proceed.

10.5.2 Splaying Steps

When a single rotation is performed in a binary search tree, such as shown in Figure 10.19 on page 480, some nodes move higher in the tree and some lower. In a left rotation, the parent node moves down and its right child moves up one level. A double rotation, as shown in Figure 10.20 on page 481, is made up of two single rotations, and one node moves up two levels, while all the others move up or down by at most one level. By beginning with the just-accessed target node and working up the path to the root, we could do single rotations at each step, thereby lifting the target node all the way to the root. This method would achieve the goal of making the target node into the root, but, it turns out, the performance of the tree amortized over many accesses may not be good.

Instead, the key idea of splaying is to move the target node *two* levels up the tree at each step. First some simple terminology: Consider the path going from the root *down* to the accessed node. Each time we move left going down this path, *zig and zag* we say that we ***zig***, and each time we move right we say that we ***zag***. A move of two steps left (going down) is then called ***zig-zig***, two steps right ***zag-zag***, left then right ***zig-zag***, and right then left ***zag-zig***. These four cases are the only possibilities in moving two steps down the path. If the length of the path is odd, however, there will be one more step needed at its end, either a ***zig*** (left) move, or a ***zag*** (right) move.

The rotations done in splaying for each of zig-zig, zig-zag, and zig moves are shown in Figure 10.25. The other three cases, zag-zag, zag-zig, and zag are mirror images of these.

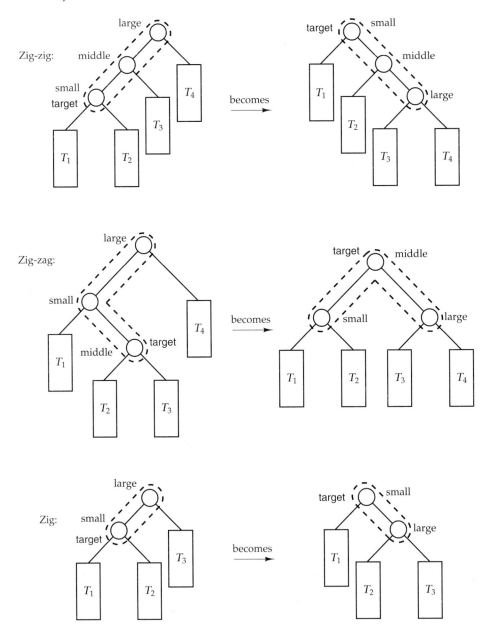

Figure 10.25. Splay rotations

The zig-zag case in Figure 10.25 is identical to that of an AVL double rotation, as shown in Figure 10.20 on page 481, and the zig case is identical to a single rotation (Figure 10.19 on page 480). The zig-zig case, however, is *not* the same as would be obtained by lifting the target node twice with single rotations, as shown in Figure 10.26.

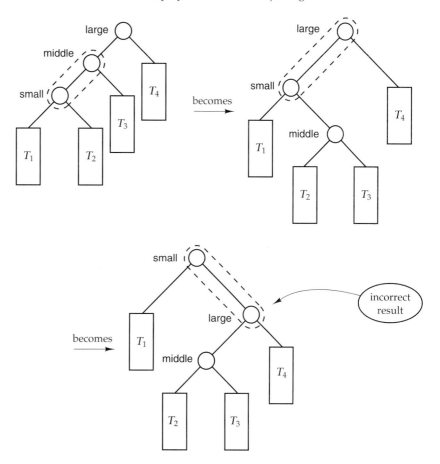

Figure 10.26. Zig-zig incorrectly replaced by single rotations

move two levels   To avoid the error shown in Figure 10.26, always think of lifting the target *two* levels at a time (except when only a single zig or zag step remains at the end). Also, note that it is *only* the nodes on the path from the target to the root whose relative positions are changed, and that only in the ways shown by colored dashed curves in Figure 10.25. None of the subtrees off the path (shown as T_1, T_2, T_3, and T_4 in Figure 10.25) changes its shape at all, and these subtrees are attached to the path in the only places they can possibly go to maintain the search-tree ordering of all the keys.

Let us fix these ideas in mind by working through an example, as shown in Figure 10.27.

example   We start with the top left tree and splay at *c*. The path from the root to *c* goes through *h, f, b, e, d, c*. From *e* to *d* to *c* is zig-zig (left-left, as shown by the dashed oval), so we perform a zig-zig rotation on this part of the tree, obtaining the second tree in Figure 10.27. Note that the remainder of the tree has not changed shape, and the modified subtree is hung in the same position it originally occupied.

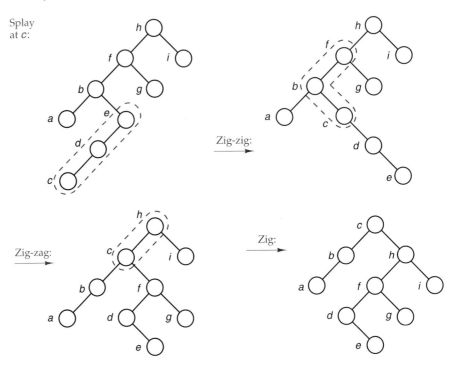

Figure 10.27. Example of splaying

For the next step, the path from *f* to *b* to *c* (shown inside the dashed curve in the second tree) is now a zig-zag move, and the resulting zig-zag rotation yields the third tree. Here the subtree *d, e* (off the path) does not change its shape but moves to a new position, as shown for T_3 in Figure 10.25.

In this third tree, *c* is only one step from the root, on the left, so a zig rotation yields the final tree of Figure 10.27. Here, the subtree rooted at *f* does not change shape but does change position.

bottom-up splaying   In this example, we have performed ***bottom-up*** splaying, beginning at the target node and moving up the path to the root two steps at a time. In working through examples by hand, this is the natural method, since, after searching from the top down, one would expect to turn around and splay from the bottom back up to the top of the tree. Hence, being done at the end of the process if necessary, a single zig or zag move occurs at the top of the tree. Bottom-up splaying is essentially a two-pass method, first searching down the tree and then splaying the target up to the root. In fact, if the target is not found but is then inserted, bottom-up splaying might even be programmed with three passes, one to search, one to insert, and one to splay.

top-down splaying   In writing a computer algorithm, however, it turns out to be easier and more efficient to splay from the top down *while* we are searching for the target node. When we find the target, it is immediately moved to the root of the tree, or, if the search is unsuccessful, a new root is created that holds the target. In top-down splaying, a single zig or zag move occurs at the bottom of the splaying process.

Hence, if you run the splaying function we shall develop on the example trees, you will obtain the same results as doing bottom-up splaying by hand when the target is moved an even number of levels, but the results will be different when it moves an odd number of levels.

10.5.3 Algorithm Development

We shall develop only one splaying function that can be used both for retrieval and for insertion. Given a target key, the function will search through the tree for the key, splaying as it goes. If it finds the key, then it retrieves it; if not, then the function inserts it as a new node. In either case, the node with the target key ends up as the root of the tree.

We shall implement splay trees as a derived class of the **class** Search_tree so that, in addition to the special **splay** method, all of the usual Search_tree methods can be applied to splay trees. The class specification follows:

```
template <class Record>
class Splay_tree: public Search_tree<Record> {
public:
    Error_code splay(const Record &target);
private:                          //   Add auxiliary function prototypes here.
};
```

A splay tree does *not* keep track of heights and does *not* use any balance factors like an AVL tree.

1. Three-Way Tree Partition

Top-down splaying uses the same moves (zig-zig, zig-zag, and the rest) illustrated in Figure 10.25, but, while splaying proceeds, the root must be left empty so that, at the end, the target node can be moved or inserted directly into the root. Hence, while splaying proceeds, the tree temporarily falls apart into separate subtrees, which are reconnected after the target is made the root. We shall use three subtrees, as follows:

three-way tree split

➡ The *central subtree* contains nodes within which the target will lie if it is present.

➡ The *smaller-key subtree* contains nodes with keys strictly less than the target; in fact, every key in the smaller-key subtree is less than every key in the central subtree.

➡ The *larger-key subtree* contains nodes with keys strictly greater than the target; in fact, every key in the larger-key subtree is greater than every key in the central subtree.

three-way invariant

These conditions will remain true throughout the splaying process, so we shall call them the ***three-way invariant***.

Initially, the central subtree is the whole tree, and the smaller-key and larger-key subtrees are empty, so the three-way invariant is initially correct. As the search proceeds, nodes are stripped off the central subtree and joined to one of the other two subtrees. When the search ends, the root of the central subtree will be the target node if it is present, and the central subtree will be empty if the target was not found. In either case, all the components will finally be joined together with the target as the root. See Figure 10.28.

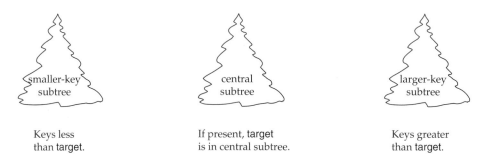

Keys less than target.	If present, target is in central subtree.	Keys greater than target.

Figure 10.28. Three-way tree split in splaying

2. Basic Action: link_right

At each stage of the search, we compare the target to the key in the root of the central subtree. Suppose the target is smaller. Then the search will move to the left, and we can take the root and its right subtree and adjoin them to the larger-key tree, reducing the central subtree to the former left subtree of the root. We call this process link_right, since it links nodes on the right into the larger-key subtree. Its action is shown in Figure 10.29.

zig compared to link_right

Note the similarity of link_right to a zig move: In both cases the left child node moves up to replace its parent node, which moves down into the right subtree. In fact, link_right is exactly a zig move except that the link from the former left child down to the former parent is deleted; instead, the parent (with its right subtree) moves into the larger-key subtree.

moving the parent

Where in the larger-key subtree should this parent (formerly the root of the central subtree) be attached? The three-way invariant tells us that every key in the central subtree comes before every key in the larger-key subtree; hence this parent (with its right subtree) must be attached on the left of the leftmost node (first in ordering of keys) in the larger-key subtree. This is shown in Figure 10.29. Note especially that, after link_right is performed, the three-way invariant continues to be true.

3. Programming the Splay Operations

The operation link_right accomplishes a zig transformation, and its symmetric analogue link_left will perform a zag transformation, but most of the time splaying requires a movement of two levels at a time. Surprisingly, all the remaining splay operations can be performed using only link_right, link_left, and ordinary (single) left and right rotations.

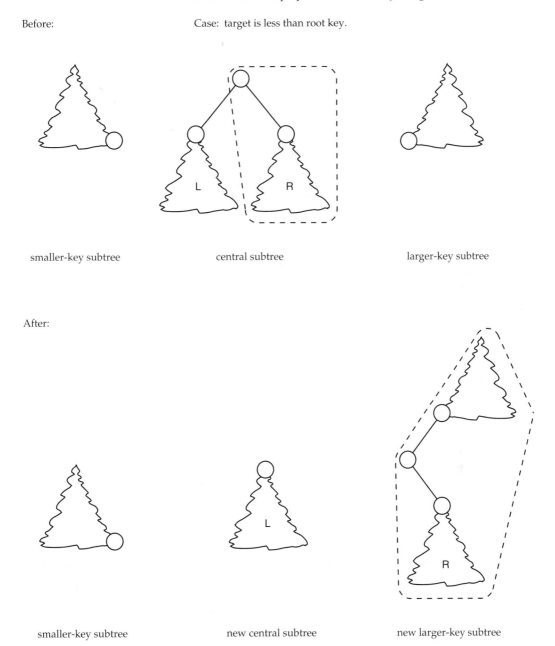

Figure 10.29. Action of link_right: a zig move

First consider the zig-zig case, as illustrated in Figure 10.30. In this case, the target key is not only less than that in the central subtree's root (called **large**) but also its left child (called **middle**), so the root, its left child, and their right subtrees should all be moved into the larger-key subtree. To do so, we first right-rotate the central tree around its root and then perform link_right.

Case: target is less than left child of root.

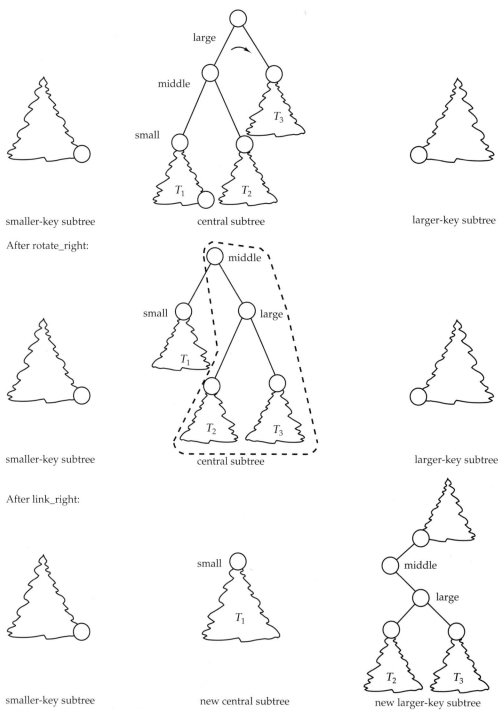

Figure 10.30. Zig-zig performed as rotate_right; link_right

Note that the change of relative positions in Figure 10.30 is the same as a zig-zig move: The chain moving leftward from large to middle to small becomes a chain moving rightward; small moves up the tree, and although a right link from small to middle is missing, the chain continues with a right link to large. Note also that, in the final arrangement, the three-way invariant continues to hold.

In the zig-zag case, illustrated in Figure 10.31, the target key comes somewhere between the root key (large) and its left child (small). Hence large and its right subtree can be moved into the larger-key subtree, and small and its left subtree can be moved into the smaller-key subtree. These steps are accomplished by first doing link_right and then link_left. Note again that, after the process is complete, the three-way invariant continues to hold.

4. Programming Conventions

The algorithm we develop uses five pointer variables to keep track of required positions in the three subtrees. The first four of these are as follows:

variables

➡ current gives the root of the central subtree of nodes not yet searched.

➡ child refers to either the left or right child of current, as required.

➡ last_small gives the largest (that is, the rightmost) node in the smaller-key subtree, which is the place where additional nodes must be attached.

➡ first_large gives the smallest (that is, the leftmost) node in the larger-key subtree, which is the place where additional nodes must be attached.

problem: empty subtrees

As we now turn to coding our functions, beginning with link_right, we immediately discover two problems we must solve. First is the problem of empty subtrees. Since the larger-key subtree is initially empty, it would be reasonable to initialize first_large to be NULL. We would then need to check for this case every time we execute link_right, or else we would attempt to follow a NULL pointer. Second, we

problem: lost roots

must have some way to find the roots of the smaller- and larger-key subtrees so that, after splaying is finished, we can link them back together as one tree. So far, we have not set up pointers to these roots, and for the splaying itself, we do not need them.

One way to solve these problems is to introduce conditional statements into our functions to check for various special cases. Instead, let us introduce a new programming device that is of considerable usefulness in many other applications, and one that will spare us both the need to check for NULL pointers and (as we shall see later) the need to keep track of the roots of the subtrees.

dummy node

This programming device is to use an additional node, called a ***dummy node***, which will contain no key or other data and which will simply be substituted for empty trees when convenient; that is, used when a NULL link might otherwise be dereferenced. Hence our fifth and last pointer variable:

Case: **target** is between root and its left child.

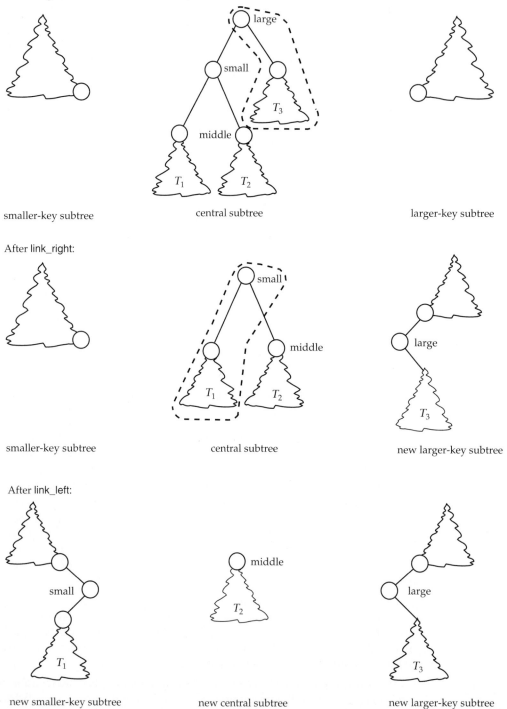

smaller-key subtree   central subtree   larger-key subtree

After link_right:

smaller-key subtree   central subtree   new larger-key subtree

After link_left:

new smaller-key subtree   new central subtree   new larger-key subtree

Figure 10.31. Zig-zag performed as link_right; link_left

➡ dummy points to a dummy node that is created at the beginning of the splaying function and is deleted at its end.

To indicate that the smaller- and larger-key subtrees are initially empty, we shall initialize both last_small and first_large to dummy. In this way, last_small and first_large will always refer to an actual Binary_node and therefore link_right and link_left will not attempt to dereference NULL pointers.

5. Subsidiary Functions

With all these decisions, coding link_right and link_left is straightforward:

```
template <class Record>
void Splay_tree<Record>::link_right(Binary_node<Record> * &current,
                                    Binary_node<Record> * &first_large)
```
/* **Pre:** *The pointer* first_large *points to an actual* Binary_node *(in particular, it is not* NULL*). The three-way invariant holds.*
 Post: *The node referenced by* current *(with its right subtree) is linked to the left of the node referenced by* first_large. *The pointer* first_large *is reset to* current. *The three-way invariant continues to hold.* */
```
{
   first_large->left = current;
   first_large = current;
   current = current->left;
}
```

```
template <class Record>
void Splay_tree<Record>::link_left(Binary_node<Record> * &current,
                                   Binary_node<Record> * &last_small)
```
/* **Pre:** *The pointer* last_small *points to an actual* Binary_node *(in particular, it is not* NULL*). The three-way invariant holds.*
 Post: *The node referenced by* current *(with its left subtree) is linked to the right of the node referenced by* last_small. *The pointer* last_small *is reset to* current. *The three-way invariant continues to hold.* */
```
{
   last_small->right = current;
   last_small = current;
   current = current->right;
}
```

The rotation functions are also easy to code; they do not use the dummy node, and they do not cause any change in the three-way partition.

```
template <class Record>
void Splay_tree<Record>::rotate_right(Binary_node<Record> * &current)
```
/* **Pre:** current *points to the root node of a subtree of a* Binary_tree. *This subtree has a nonempty left subtree.*
 Post: current *is reset to point to its former left child, and the former* current *node is the right child of the new* current *node.* */

```
  {
    Binary_node<Record> *left_tree = current->left;
    current->left = left_tree->right;
    left_tree->right = current;
    current = left_tree;
  }
```

```
template <class Record>
void Splay_tree<Record>::rotate_left(Binary_node<Record> * &current)
```
/* **Pre:**   current *points to the root node of a subtree of a* Binary_tree. *This subtree has a nonempty right subtree.*

   Post: current *is reset to point to its former right child, and the former* current *node is the left child of the new* current *node.* */
```
  {
    Binary_node<Record> *right_tree = current->right;
    current->right = right_tree->left;
    right_tree->left = current;
    current = right_tree;
  }
```

6. Finishing the Task

termination   When the search finishes, the root of the central subtree points at the target node or is NULL. If the target is found, it must become the root of the whole tree, but, before that, its left and right subtrees are now known to belong in the smaller-key and larger-key subtrees, respectively, so they should be moved there. If the search instead terminates unsuccessfully, with current == NULL, then a new root containing target must be created.

reassembly of the tree   Finally, the left and right subtrees of the new root should now be the smaller-key and larger-key subtrees. Now we must return to the second problem that we have not yet solved: How do we find the roots of these subtrees, since we have kept pointers only to their rightmost and leftmost nodes, respectively?

To answer this question, let us remember what happened at the beginning of the search. Initially, both pointers last_small and first_large were set to refer to the dummy node. When a node (and subtree) are attached to the larger-key subtree, they are attached on its left, by changing first_large->left. Since first_large *solution:* is initially dummy, we can now, at the end of the search, find the first node inserted *no lost roots* into the larger-key subtree, and thus its root, simply as dummy->left. Similarly, dummy->right points to the root of the smaller-key subtree. Hence the dummy node provides us with pointers to the roots of the smaller- and larger-key subtrees that would otherwise be lost. But note that the pointers are stored in positions reversed from what one might expect.

These steps are illustrated in Figure 10.32.

After splaying:

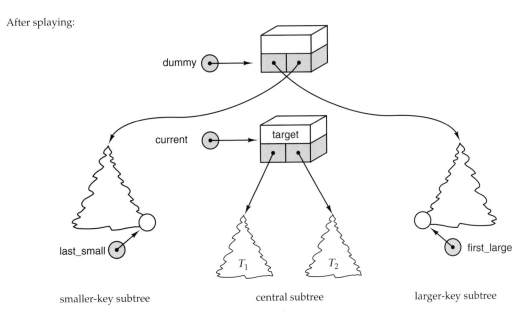

smaller-key subtree   central subtree   larger-key subtree

Reconnect into one tree:

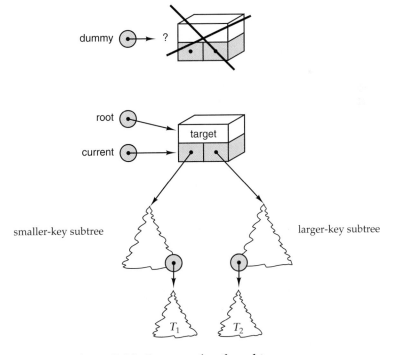

smaller-key subtree   larger-key subtree

Figure 10.32. Reconnecting the subtrees

7. Splaying: The Final Method

With all the preliminary work through which we have gone, we can finally write the function that actually retrieves and inserts a node in a binary search tree, simultaneously splaying the tree to make this target node into the root of the tree.

```
template <class Record>
Error_code Splay_tree<Record>::splay(const Record &target)
/* Post: If a node of the splay tree has a key matching that of target, it has been
         moved by splay operations to be the root of the tree, and a code of en-
         try_found is returned. Otherwise, a new node containing a copy of target
         is inserted as the root of the tree, and a code of entry_inserted is re-
         turned. */
{
  Binary_node<Record> *dummy = new Binary_node<Record>;
  Binary_node<Record> *current = root,
                      *child,
                      *last_small = dummy,
                      *first_large = dummy;
//   Search for target while splaying the tree.
  while (current != NULL && current->data != target)
    if (target < current->data) {
      child = current->left;
      if (child == NULL || target == child->data)  //   zig move
        link_right(current, first_large);
      else if (target < child->data) {  //   zig-zig move
        rotate_right(current);
        link_right(current, first_large);
      }
      else {                           //   zig-zag move
        link_right(current, first_large);
        link_left(current, last_small);
      }
    }
    else {                             //   case: target > current->data
      child = current->right;
      if (child == NULL || target == child->data)
        link_left(current, last_small);   //   zag move
      else if (target > child->data) {  //   zag-zag move
        rotate_left(current);
        link_left(current, last_small);
      }
      else {                           //   zag-zig move
        link_left(current, last_small);
        link_right(current, first_large);
      }
    }
```

```
//   Move root to the current node, which is created if necessary.
   Error_code result;
   if (current ==  NULL) {        //   Search unsuccessful: make a new root.
      current = new Binary_node<Record>(target);
      result = entry_inserted;
      last_small->right = first_large->left = NULL;
   }
   else {                         //   successful search
      result = entry_found;
      last_small->right = current->left;   //   Move remaining central nodes.
      first_large->left = current->right;
   }
   root = current;                //   Define the new root.
   root->right = dummy->left;   //   root of larger-key subtree
   root->left = dummy->right;   //   root of smaller-key subtree
   delete dummy;
   return result;
}
```

conclusion All things considered, this is really quite a subtle and sophisticated algorithm in its pointer manipulations and economical use of resources.

10.5.4 Amortized Algorithm Analysis: Introduction

We now wish to determine the behavior of splaying over long sequences of operations, but before doing so, let us introduce the amortized analysis of algorithms with simpler examples.

1. Introduction

In the past, we have considered two kinds of algorithm analysis, *worst-case* analysis and *average-case* analysis. In both of these, we have taken a single event or single situation and attempted to determine how much work an algorithm does to process it. Amortized analysis differs from both these kinds of analysis in that it considers *definition* a long *sequence* of events rather than a single event in isolation. Amortized analysis then gives a *worst-case* estimate of the cost of a long sequence of events.

It is quite possible that one event in a sequence affects the cost of later events. One task may be difficult and expensive to perform, but it may leave a data structure in a state where the tasks that follow become much easier. Consider, for example, a stack where any number of entries may be pushed on at once, and any number may be popped off at once. If there are n entries in the stack, then the worst-case cost of a multiple pop operation is obviously n, since all the entries might be popped off at once. If, however, almost all the entries are popped off (in one expensive pop operation), then a subsequent pop operation cannot be expensive, since few entries remain. Let us allow a pop of 0 entries at a cost of 0. Then, if we start with n entries in the stack and do a series of n multiple pops, the amortized worst-case *multiple pops*   cost of each pop is only 1, even though the worst-case cost is n, the reason being that the n multiple pops together can only remove the n entries from the stack, so their total cost cannot exceed n.

amortization   In the world of finance, *amortization* means to spread a large expense over a period of time, such as using a mortgage to spread the cost of a house (with interest) over many monthly payments. Accountants amortize a large capital expenditure over the income-producing activities for which it is used. Insurance actuaries amortize high-risk cases over the general population.

2. Average versus Amortized Analysis

independent vs. related events   Amortized analysis is not the same as average-case analysis, since the former considers a sequence of *related* situations and the latter all possible *independent* situations. For sorting methods, we did average-case analysis over all possible cases. It makes no sense to speak of sorting the same list twice in a row, and therefore amortized analysis does not usually apply to sorting.

sorting   We can, however, contrive an example where it does. Consider a list that is first sorted; then, after some use of the list, a new entry is inserted into a random position of the list. After further use, the list is then sorted again. Later, another entry is inserted at random, and so on. What sorting method should we use? If we rely on average-case analysis, we might choose quicksort. If we prefer worst-case analysis, then we might choose mergesort or heapsort with guaranteed performance of $O(n \log n)$. Amortized analysis, however, will lead us to insertion sort: Once the list is sorted and a new entry inserted at random, insertion sort will move it to its proper place with $O(n)$ performance. Since the list is nearly sorted, quicksort (with the best average-case performance) may provide the worst actual performance, since some choices of pivot may force it to nearly its worst case.

3. Tree Traversal

As another example, consider the inorder traversal of a binary tree, where we measure the cost of visiting one vertex as the number of branches traversed to reach that vertex from the last one visited. Figure 10.33 shows three binary trees, with the inorder traversal shown as a colored path, with the cost of visiting each vertex also shown in color.

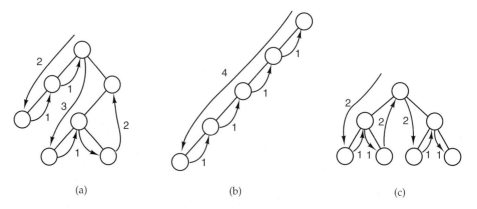

(a)   (b)   (c)

Figure 10.33. Cost of inorder traversal

The best-case cost of visiting a vertex is 1, when we go from a vertex to one of its children or to its parent. The worst-case cost, for a tree with n vertices, is $n - 1$, as shown by the tree that is one long chain to the left, where it takes $n - 1$ branches to reach the first (leftmost) vertex. [See part (b) of Figure 10.33.] In this chain, however, all the remaining vertices are reached in only 1 step each, as the traversal moves from each vertex to its parent. In a completely balanced binary tree of size n, some vertices require as many as $\lg n$ steps, others only 1. [See part (c) of Figure 10.33.]

If, however, we amortize the cost over a traversal of the entire binary tree, then the cost of going from each vertex to the next is less than 2. To see this, note first that every binary tree with n vertices has precisely $n - 1$ branches, since every vertex except the root has just one branch coming down into it. A complete traversal of the tree goes over every branch twice, once going down and once up. (Here we have included going up the path to the root after the last, rightmost vertex has been visited.) Hence the total number of steps in a full traversal is $2(n - 1)$, and the amortized number of steps from one vertex to the next is $2(n - 1)/n < 2$.

4. Credit Balance: Making Costs Level

Suppose you are working with your household budget. If you are employed, then (you hope) your income is usually fairly stable from month to month. Your expenses, however, may not be. Some months large amounts are due for insurance, or tuition, or a major purchase. Other months have no extraordinary expenses. To keep your bank account solvent, you then need to save enough during the months with low expenses so that you can pay all the large bills as they come due. At the beginning of the month with large bills, you have a large bank balance. After paying the bills, your bank balance is much smaller, but you are just as well off, because you now owe less money.

We wish to apply this idea to algorithm analysis. To do so, we invent a function, which we call a *credit balance*, that behaves like the bank balance of a well-budgeted family. The credit function will be chosen in such a way that it will be large when the next operation is expensive, and smaller when the next operation can be done quickly. We then think of the credit function as helping to bear some of the cost of expensive operations, and, for inexpensive operations, we set aside more than the actual cost, using the excess to build up the credit function for future use.

credit function

To make this idea more precise, suppose that we have a sequence of m operations on a data structure, and let t_i be the *actual* cost of operation i for $1 \le i \le m$. Let the values of our credit function be $c_0, c_1, \ldots, c_m$, where c_0 is the credit balance before the first operation and c_i is the credit balance after operation i, for $1 \le i \le m$. Then we make the fundamental definition:

Definition   The *amortized cost* a_i of each operation is defined to be

$$a_i = t_i + c_i - c_{i-1}$$

for $i = 1, 2, \ldots, m$, where t_i and c_i are as just defined.

This equation says that the amortized cost is the actual cost plus the amount that our credit balance has changed while doing the operation.

Remember that our credit balance is just an accounting tool: We are free to invent any function we wish, but some are much better than others. Our goal is to help with budgeting; therefore, our goal is:

goal   Choose the credit-balance function c_i so as to make the amortized costs a_i as nearly equal as possible, no matter how the actual costs t_i may vary.

We now wish to use the amortized cost to help us calculate the total actual cost of the sequence of m operations. The fundamental definition rearranges as $t_i = a_i + c_{i-1} - c_i$, and the total actual cost is then

$$\sum_{i=1}^{m} t_i = \sum_{i=1}^{m}(a_i + c_{i-1} - c_i) = \left(\sum_{i=1}^{m} a_i\right) + c_0 - c_m.$$

Except for the first and last values, all the credit balances cancel each other out and therefore do not enter the final calculation. For future reference, we restate this fact as a lemma:

Lemma 10.5   *The total actual cost and total amortized cost of a sequence of m operations on a data structure are related by*

$$\sum_{i=1}^{m} t_i = \left(\sum_{i=1}^{m} a_i\right) + c_0 - c_m.$$

Our goal is to choose the credit-balance function in such a way that the a_i are nearly equal; it will then be easy to calculate the right hand side of this equation, and therefore the total actual cost of the sequence of m operations as well.

telescoping sum   A sum like this one, where the terms have alternate plus and minus signs, so that they cancel when added, is called a **telescoping sum**, since it may remind you of a toy (or portable) telescope made up of several short tubes that slide inside each other but may be extended to make up one long telescope tube.

5. Incrementing Binary Integers

TimeOut   Let us tie down these ideas by studying one more simple example, and then it will be time to apply these ideas to prove a fundamental and surprising theorem about splay trees.

example   The example we consider is an algorithm that continually increments a binary (base 2) integer by 1. We start at the right side; while the current bit is 1, we change it to 0 and move left, stopping when we reach the far left or hit a 0 bit, which we change to 1 and stop. The cost of performing this algorithm is the number of bits

step i	integer	t_i	c_i	a_i
	0 0 0 0		0	
1	0 0 0 1	1	1	2
2	0 0 1 0	2	1	2
3	0 0 1 1	1	2	2
4	0 1 0 0	3	1	2
5	0 1 0 1	1	2	2
6	0 1 1 0	2	2	2
7	0 1 1 1	1	3	2
8	1 0 0 0	4	1	2
9	1 0 0 1	1	2	2
10	1 0 1 0	2	2	2
11	1 0 1 1	1	3	2
12	1 1 0 0	3	2	2
13	1 1 0 1	1	3	2
14	1 1 1 0	2	3	2
15	1 1 1 1	1	4	2
16	0 0 0 0	4	0	0

Figure 10.34. Cost and amortized cost of incrementing binary integers

(binary digits) that are changed. The results of applying this algorithm 16 times to a four digit integer are shown in the first three columns of Figure 10.34.

For the credit balance in this example, we take the total number of 1's in the binary integer. Clearly, the number of digits that must be changed is exactly one more than the number of 1's in the rightmost part of the integer, so it is reasonable that the more 1's there are, the more digits must be changed. With this choice, we can calculate the amortized cost of each step, using the fundamental formula. The result is shown in the last column of Figure 10.34 and turns out to be 2 for every step except the last, which is 0. Hence we conclude that we can increment a four-digit binary integer with an amortized cost of two digit changes, even though the actual cost varies from one to four.

10.5.5 Amortized Analysis of Splaying

After all this preliminary introduction, we can now use the techniques of amortized algorithm analysis to determine how much work our splay-tree algorithm does over a long sequence of retrievals and insertions.

measure of actual complexity   As the measure of the actual complexity, we shall take the depth within the tree that the target node has before splaying, which is, of course, the number of positions that the node will move up in the tree. All the actions of the algorithm—key comparisons and rotations—go in lock step with this depth. The number of iterations of the main loop that the function makes, for example, is about half this depth.

notation   First, let us introduce some simple notation. We let T be a binary search tree on which we are performing a splay insertion or retrieval. We let T_i denote the tree T as it has been transformed after step i of the splaying process, with $T_0 = T$. If x is any node in T_i, then we denote by $T_i(x)$ the subtree of T_i with root x, and we denote by $|T_i(x)|$ the number of nodes in this subtree.

We assume that we are splaying at a node x, and we consider a bottom-up splay, so x begins somewhere in the tree T, but, after m splaying steps, ends up as the root of T.

definition of   For each step i of the splaying process and each vertex x in T, we define the
rank function   **rank** at step i of x to be

$$r_i(x) = \lg |T_i(x)|.$$

This rank function behaves something like an idealized height: It depends on the size of the subtree with root x, not on its height, but it indicates what the height of the subtree would be if it were completely balanced.

If x is a leaf, then $|T_i(x)| = 1$, so $r_i(x) = 0$. Nodes close to the fringe of the tree have small ranks; the root has the largest rank in the tree.

 The amount of work that the algorithm must do to insert or retrieve in a subtree is clearly related to the height of the subtree, and so, we hope, to the rank of the subtree's root. We would like to define the credit balance in such a way that large and tall trees would have a large credit balance and short or small trees a smaller balance, since the amount of work in splaying increases with the height of the tree. We shall use the rank function to achieve this. In fact, we shall portion out the credit balance of the tree among all its vertices by always requiring the following to hold:

The Credit Invariant

the credit invariant   *For every node x of T and after every step i of splaying,*
node x has credit equal to its rank $r_i(x)$.

---

total credit balance   The total **credit balance** for the tree is then defined simply as the sum of the individual credits for all the nodes in the tree,

$$c_i = \sum_{x \in T_i} r_i(x).$$

If the tree is empty or contains only one node, then its credit balance is 0. As the tree grows, its credit balance increases, and this balance should reflect the work needed to build the tree. The investment of credit in the tree is done in two ways:

➡ We invest the actual work done in the operation. We have already decided to count this as one unit for each level that the target node rises during the splaying process. Hence each splaying step counts as two units, except for a zig or a zag step, which count as one unit.

➡ Since the shape of the tree changes during splaying, we must either add or remove credit invested in the tree so as to maintain the credit invariant at all times. (As we discussed in the last section, this is essentially an accounting device to even out the costs of different steps.)

amortized complexity

This investment is summarized by the equation defining the amortized complexity a_i of step i,

$$a_i = t_i + c_i - c_{i-1},$$

where t_i is the actual work and $c_i - c_{i-1}$ gives the change in the credit balance.

main goal

Our principal goal now is, by using the given definitions and the way splaying works, to determine bounds on a_i that, in turn, will allow us to find the cost of the whole splaying process, amortized over a sequence of retrievals and insertions.

First, we need a preliminary mathematical observation.

Lemma 10.6

If α, β, and γ are positive real numbers with $\alpha + \beta \leq \gamma$, then

$$\lg \alpha + \lg \beta \leq 2 \lg \gamma - 2.$$

Proof
We have $\left(\sqrt{\alpha} - \sqrt{\beta}\right)^2 \geq 0$, since the square of any real number is nonnegative. This expands and simplifies to

$$\sqrt{\alpha\beta} \leq \frac{\alpha + \beta}{2}.$$

arithmetic-geometric
mean inequality
end of proof

(This inequality is called the *arithmetic-geometric mean inequality*.) Since $\alpha + \beta \leq \gamma$, we obtain $\sqrt{\alpha\beta} \leq \gamma/2$. Squaring both sides and taking (base 2) logarithms gives the result in the lemma. ∎

We next analyze the various kinds of splaying steps separately.

Lemma 10.7

If the ith splaying step is a zig-zig or zag-zag step at node x, then its amortized complexity a_i satisfies

$$a_i < 3(r_i(x) - r_{i-1}(x)).$$

Proof
This case is illustrated as follows:

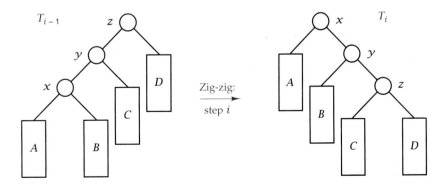

Zig-zig: step i

The actual complexity t_i of a zig-zig or a zag-zag step is 2 units, and only the sizes of the subtrees rooted at x, y, and z change in this step. Therefore, all terms in the summation defining c_i cancel against those for c_{i-1} except those indicated in the following equation:

$$
\begin{aligned}
a_i &= t_i + c_i - c_{i-1} \\
&= 2 + r_i(x) + r_i(y) + r_i(z) - r_{i-1}(x) - r_{i-1}(y) - r_{i-1}(z) \\
&= 2 + r_i(y) + r_i(z) - r_{i-1}(x) - r_{i-1}(y)
\end{aligned}
$$

We obtain the last line by taking the logarithm of $|T_i(x)| = |T_{i-1}(z)|$, which is the observation that the subtree rooted at z before the splaying step has the same size as that rooted at x after the step.

Lemma 10.6 can now be applied to cancel the 2 in this equation (the actual complexity). Let $\alpha = |T_{i-1}(x)|$, $\beta = |T_i(z)|$, and $y = |T_i(x)|$. From the diagram for this case, we see that $T_{i-1}(x)$ contains components x, A, and B; $T_i(z)$ contains components z, C, and D; and $T_i(x)$ contains all these components (and y besides). Hence $\alpha + \beta < y$, so Lemma 10.6 implies that $r_{i-1}(x) + r_i(z) \le 2r_i(x) - 2$, or $2r_i(x) - r_{i-1}(x) - r_i(z) - 2 \ge 0$. Adding this nonnegative quantity to the right side of the last equation for a_i, we obtain

$$
a_i \le 2r_i(x) - 2r_{i-1}(x) + r_i(y) - r_{i-1}(y).
$$

Before step i, y is the parent of x, so $|T_{i-1}(y)| > |T_{i-1}(x)|$. After step i, x is the parent of y, so $|T_i(x)| > |T_i(y)|$. Taking logarithms, we have $r_{i-1}(y) > r_{i-1}(x)$ and $r_i(x) > r_i(y)$. Hence we finally obtain

$$
a_i < 3r_i(x) - 3r_{i-1}(x),
$$

end of proof   which is the assertion in Lemma 10.7 that we wished to prove. ∎

Lemma 10.8   *If the ith splaying step is a zig-zag or zag-zig step at node x, then its amortized complexity a_i satisfies*

$$
a_i < 2(r_i(x) - r_{i-1}(x)).
$$

Lemma 10.9   *If the ith splaying step is a zig or a zag step at node x, then its amortized complexity a_i satisfies*

$$
a_i < 1 + (r_i(x) - r_{i-1}(x)).
$$

The proof of Lemma 10.8 is similar to that of Lemma 10.7 (even though the result is stronger), and the proof of Lemma 10.9 is straightforward; both of these are left as exercises.

Finally, we need to find the total amortized cost of a retrieval or insertion. To do so, we must add the costs of all the splay steps done during the retrieval or insertion. If there are m such steps, then at most one (the last) can be a zig or zag step to which Lemma 10.9 applies, and the others all satisfy the bounds in Lemmas 10.7 and 10.8, of which the coefficient of 3 in Lemma 10.7 provides the weaker bound. Hence we obtain that the total amortized cost is

$$\sum_{i=1}^{m} a_i = \sum_{i=1}^{m-1} a_i + a_m$$

$$\leq \sum_{i=1}^{m-1} \left(3r_i(x) - 3r_{i-1}(x)\right) + \left(1 + 3r_m(x) - 3r_{m-1}(x)\right)$$

$$= 1 + 3r_m(x) - 3r_0(x)$$

$$\leq 1 + 3r_m(x)$$

$$= 1 + 3\lg n.$$

telescoping sum   In this derivation, we have used the fact that the sum telescopes, so that only the first rank $r_0(x)$ and the final rank $r_m(x)$ remain. Since $r_0(x) \geq 0$, its omission only increases the right side, and since at the end of the splaying process x is the root of the tree, we have $r_m(x) = \lg n$, where n is the number of nodes in the tree.

With this, we have now completed the proof of the principal result of this section:

Theorem 10.10   *The amortized cost of an insertion or retrieval with splaying in a binary search tree with n nodes does not exceed*

$$1 + 3\lg n$$

upward moves of the target node in the tree.

Finally, we can relate this amortized cost to the actual cost of each of a long sequence of splay insertions or retrievals. To do so, we apply Lemma 10.5, noting that the summations now are over a sequence of retrievals or insertions, not over the steps of a single retrieval or insertion. We see that the total actual cost of a sequence of m splay accesses differs from the total amortized cost only by $c_0 - c_m$, where c_0 and c_m are the credit balances of the initial and final trees, respectively. If the tree never has more than n nodes, then the credit of any individual node is always somewhere between 0 and $\lg n$. Therefore, the initial and final credit balances of the tree are both between 0 and $n \lg n$, so we need not add more than $n \lg n$ to the cost in Theorem 10.10 to obtain:

Corollary 10.11   *The total complexity of a sequence of m insertions or retrievals with splaying in a binary search tree that never has more than n nodes does not exceed*

$$m(1 + 3\lg n) + n \lg n$$

upward moves of a target node in the tree.

In this result, each splaying step counts as two upward moves, except for zig or zag steps, which count as one move each.

The fact that insertions and retrievals in a splay tree, over a long sequence, are *guaranteed* to take only $O(\log n)$ time is quite remarkable, given that, at any time, it is quite possible for a splay tree to degenerate into a highly unbalanced shape.

Exercises
10.5

E1. Consider the following binary search tree:

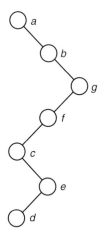

Splay this tree at each of the following keys in turn:

$$d \quad b \quad g \quad f \quad a \quad d \quad b \quad d$$

Each part builds on the previous; that is, use the final tree of each solution as the starting tree for the next part. [*Check*: The tree should be completely balanced after the last part, as well as after one previous part.]

E2. The *depth* of a node in a binary tree is the number of branches from the root to the node. (Thus the root has depth 0, its children depth 1, and so on.) Define the *credit balance* of a tree during preorder traversal to be the depth of the node being visited. Define the (actual) cost of visiting a vertex to be the number of branches traversed (either going down or up) from the previously visited node. For each of the following binary trees, make a table showing the nodes visited, the actual cost, the credit balance, and the amortized cost for a *preorder* traversal.

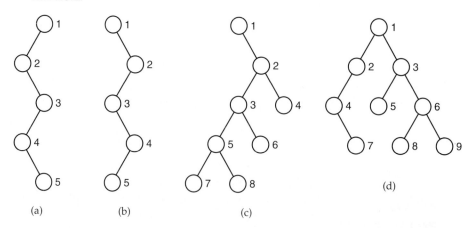

E3. Define a *rank* function $r(x)$ for the nodes of any binary tree as follows:

If x is the root, then $r(x)= 0$.

If x is the left child of a node y, then $r(x)= r(y)-1$.

If x is the right child of a node y, then $r(x)= r(y)+1$.

Define the *credit balance* of a tree during a traversal to be the rank of the node being visited. Define the (actual) cost of visiting a vertex to be the number of branches traversed (either going down or up) from the previously visited node. For each of the binary trees shown in Exercise E2, make a table showing the nodes visited, the actual cost, the credit balance, and the amortized cost for an *inorder* traversal.

E4. In analogy with Exercise E3, devise a rank function for binary trees that, under the same conditions as in Exercise E3, will make the amortized costs of a *postorder* traversal almost all the same. Illustrate your rank function by making a table for each of the binary trees shown in Exercise E2, showing the nodes visited, the actual cost, the credit balance, and the amortized cost for a *postorder* traversal.

E5. Generalize the amortized analysis given in the text for incrementing four-digit binary integers to n-digit binary integers.

E6. Prove Lemma 10.8. The method is similar to the proof of Lemma 10.7.

E7. Prove Lemma 10.9. This proof does not require Lemma 10.6 or any intricate calculations.

Programming Projects 10.5

P1. Substitute the splay tree class into the menu-driven demonstration program for binary search trees in Section 10.2, Project P2 (page 460), thereby obtaining a demonstration program for splay trees.

information retrieval

P2. Substitute the function for splay retrieval and insertion into the information-retrieval project of Project P5 of Section 10.2 (page 461). Compare the performance of splay trees with ordinary binary search trees for various combinations of input text files.

POINTERS AND PITFALLS

1. Consider binary search trees as an alternative to ordered lists (indeed, as a way of implementing the abstract data type *list*). At the cost of an extra pointer member in each node, binary search trees allow random access (with $O(\log n)$ key comparisons) to all nodes while maintaining the flexibility of linked lists for insertions, removals, and rearrangement.

2. Consider binary search trees as an alternative to tables (indeed, as a way of implementing the abstract data type *table*). At the cost of access time that is $O(\log n)$ instead of $O(1)$, binary search trees allow traversal of the data structure in the order specified by the keys while maintaining the advantage of random access provided by tables.

3. In choosing your data structures, always carefully consider what operations will be required. Binary trees are especially appropriate when random access, traversal in a predetermined order, and flexibility in making insertions and removals are all required.

4. While choosing data structures and algorithms, remain alert to the possibility of highly unbalanced binary search trees. If the incoming data are likely to be in random order, then an ordinary binary search tree should prove entirely adequate. If the data may come in a sorted or nearly sorted order, then the algorithms should take appropriate action. If there is only a slight possibility of serious imbalance, it might be ignored. If, in a large project, there is greater likelihood of serious imbalance, then there may still be appropriate places in the software where the trees can be checked for balance and rebuilt if necessary. For applications in which it is essential to maintain logarithmic access time at all times, AVL trees provide nearly perfect balance at a slight cost in computer time and space, but with considerable programming cost. If it is necessary for the tree to adapt dynamically to changes in the frequency of the data, then a splay tree may be the best choice.

5. Binary trees are defined recursively; algorithms for manipulating binary trees are usually best written recursively. In programming with binary trees, be aware of the problems generally associated with recursive algorithms. Be sure that your algorithm terminates under any condition and that it correctly treats the trivial case of an empty tree.

6. Although binary trees are usually implemented as linked structures, remain aware of the possibility of other implementations. In programming with linked binary trees, keep in mind the pitfalls attendant on all programming with linked lists.

REVIEW QUESTIONS

10.1 1. Define the term *binary tree*.

2. What is the difference between a binary tree and an ordinary tree in which each vertex has at most two branches?

3. Give the order of visiting the vertices of each of the following binary trees under (a) preorder, (b) inorder, and (c) postorder traversal.

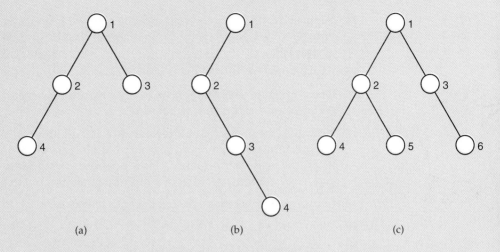

(a)   (b)   (c)

4. Draw the expression trees for each of the following expressions, and show the result of traversing the tree in **(a)** preorder, **(b)** inorder, and **(c)** postorder.

   (a) $a - b$.

   (b) $n/m!$.

   (c) $\log m!$.

   (d) $(\log x) + (\log y)$.

   (e) $x \times y \leq x + y$.

   (f) (a > b) || (b >= a)

10.2 5. Define the term *binary search tree*.

6. If a binary search tree with n nodes is well balanced, what is the approximate number of comparisons of keys needed to find a target? What is the number if the tree degenerates to a chain?

7. In twenty words or less, explain how treesort works.

8. What is the relationship between treesort and quicksort?

9. What causes removal from a search tree to be more difficult than insertion into a search tree?

10.3 10. When is the algorithm for building a binary search tree developed in Section 10.3 useful, and why is it preferable to simply using the function for inserting an item into a search tree for each item in the input?

11. How much slower, on average, is searching a random binary search tree than is searching a completely balanced binary search tree?

10.4 12. What is the purpose of AVL trees?

13. What condition defines an AVL tree among all binary search trees?

14. Suppose that A is a base class and B is a derived class, and that we declare: A *pA; B *pB; Can pA reference an object of **class** B? Can pB reference an object of **class** A?

15. Explain how the virtual methods of a class differ from other class methods.

16. Draw a picture explaining how balance is restored when an insertion into an AVL tree puts a node out of balance.

17. How does the worst-case performance of an AVL tree compare with the worst-case performance of a random binary search tree? How does it compare with its average-case performance? How does the average-case performance of an AVL tree compare with that of a random binary search tree?

10.5 18. In twenty words or less, describe what *splaying* does.

19. What is the purpose of splaying?

20. What is *amortized* algorithm analysis?

21. What is a *credit-balance function*, and how is it used?

22. In the big-*O* notation, what is the cost of splaying amortized over a sequence of retrievals and insertions? Why is this surprising?

REFERENCES FOR FURTHER STUDY

One of the most comprehensive source of information on binary trees is the series of books by KNUTH. The properties of binary trees, other classes of trees, traversal, path length, and history, altogether occupy pages 305–405 of Volume 1. Volume 3, pages 422–480, discusses binary search trees, AVL trees, and related topics. The proof of Theorem 10.2 is from Volume 3, page 427.

A mathematical analysis of the behavior of AVL trees appears in

E. M. REINGOLD, J. NIEVERGELT, and N. DEO, *Combinatorial Algorithms: Theory and Practice*, Prentice Hall, Englewood Cliffs, N. J., 1977.

The following book presents many interesting empirical studies and other analyses of various data structures, including binary trees:

ROBERT SEDGEWICK and PHILIPPE FLAJOLET, *An Introduction to the Analysis of Algorithms*, Addison-Wesley, Reading, Mass., 1996.

The original reference for AVL trees is

G. M. ADEL'SON-VEL'SKIĬ and E. M. LANDIS, *Dokl. Akad. Nauk SSSR* 146 (1962), 263–266; English translation: *Soviet Math. (Dokl.)* 3 (1962), 1259–1263.

Several algorithms for constructing a balanced binary search tree are discussed in

HSI CHANG and S. S. IYENGAR, "Efficient algorithms to globally balance a binary search tree," *Communications of the ACM* 27 (1984), 695–702.

The notions of splay trees and amortized algorithm analysis, together with the derivation of the algorithm we present, are due to:

D. D. SLEATOR and R. E. TARJAN, "Self-adjusting binary search trees," *Journal of the ACM* 32 (1985), 652–686.

Good sources for more advanced presentations of topics related to this chapter are:

HARRY R. LEWIS and LARRY DENENBERG, *Data Structures & Their Algorithms*, Harper-Collins, New York, 1991, 509 pages.

DERICK WOOD, *Data Structures, Algorithms, and Performance*, Addison-Wesley, Reading, Mass., 1993, 594 pages.

Another interesting method of adjusting the shape of a binary search tree, called *weighted path length* trees and based on the frequencies with which the nodes are accessed, appears in the following paper, easy to read and with a survey of related results:

G. ARGO, "Weighting without waiting: the weighted path length tree," *Computer Journal* 34 (1991), 444–449.

Multiway Trees

11

T HIS CHAPTER continues the study of trees as data structures, now concentrating on trees with possibly more than two branches at each node. We begin by establishing a connection with binary trees. Next, we study a class of trees called tries, which share some properties with table lookup. Then we investigate B-trees, which prove invaluable for problems of external information retrieval. Each of these sections is independent of the others. Finally, we apply the idea of B-trees to obtain another class of binary search trees, called red-black trees.

11.1 ORCHARDS, TREES, AND BINARY TREES

Binary trees, as we have seen, are a powerful and elegant form of data structure. Even so, the restriction to no more than two children at each node is severe, and there are many possible applications for trees as data structures where the number of children of a node can be arbitrary. This section elucidates a pleasant and helpful surprise: Binary trees provide a convenient way to represent what first appears to be a far broader class of trees.

11.1.1 On the Classification of Species

mathematical definition

Since we have already sighted several kinds of trees in the applications we have studied, we should, before exploring further, put our gear in order by settling the definitions. In mathematics, the term *tree* has a quite broad meaning: It is any set of points (called vertices) and any set of pairs of distinct vertices (called edges or branches) such that (1) there is a sequence of edges (a path) from any vertex to any other, and (2) there are no circuits, that is, no paths starting from a vertex and returning to the same vertex.

free tree

In computer applications we usually do not need to study trees in such generality, and when we do, for emphasis we call them *free trees*. Our trees are almost always tied down by having one particular vertex singled out as the *root*, and for emphasis we call such a tree a *rooted tree*.

rooted tree

A rooted tree can be drawn in our usual way by picking it up by its root and shaking it so that all the branches and vertices hang downward, with the leaves at the bottom. Even so, rooted trees still do not have all the structure that we usually use. In a rooted tree there is still no way to tell left from right, or, when one vertex has several children, to tell which is first, second, and so on. If for no other reason, the restraint of sequential execution of instructions (not to mention sequential organization of storage) usually imposes an order on the children of each vertex. Hence we define an *ordered tree* to be a rooted tree in which the children of each vertex are assigned an order.

ordered tree

Note that ordered trees for which no vertex has more than two children are still not the same class as binary trees. If a vertex in a binary tree has only one child, then it could be either on the left side or on the right side, and the two resulting binary trees are different, but both would be the same as ordered trees.

2-tree

As a final remark related to the definitions, let us note that the 2-trees that we studied as part of algorithm analysis are rooted trees (but not necessarily ordered trees) with the property that every vertex has either 0 or 2 children. Thus 2-trees do not coincide with any of the other classes we have introduced.

Figure 11.1 shows what happens for the various kinds of trees with a small number of vertices. Note that each class of trees after the first can be obtained by taking the trees from the previous class and distinguishing those that differ under the new criterion. Compare the list of five ordered trees with four vertices with the list of fourteen binary trees with four vertices constructed in Exercise E1 of Section 10.1 (page 441). You will find that, again, the binary trees can be obtained from the appropriate ordered trees by distinguishing a left branch from a right branch.

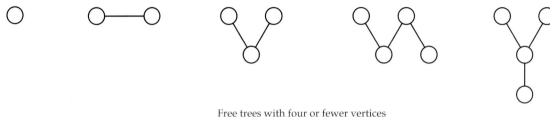

Free trees with four or fewer vertices
(Arrangement of vertices is irrelevant.)

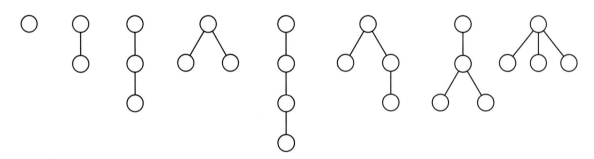

Rooted trees with four or fewer vertices
(Root is at the top of tree.)

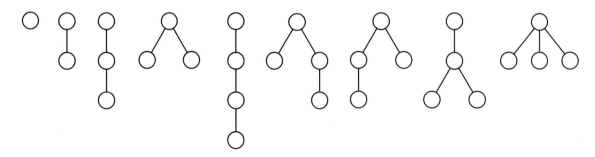

Ordered trees with four or fewer vertices

Figure 11.1. Various kinds of trees

11.1.2 Ordered Trees

1. Computer Implementation

If we wish to use an ordered tree as a data structure, the obvious way to implement it in computer memory would be to extend the standard way to implement a binary tree, keeping as many link members in each node as there may be subtrees, in place of the two links needed for binary trees. Thus in a tree where some nodes have *multiple links* as many as ten subtrees, we would keep ten link members in each node. But this will result in a great many of the link members being NULL. In fact, we can easily determine exactly how many. If the tree has n nodes and each node has k link members, then there are $n \times k$ links altogether. There is exactly one link that points to each of the $n - 1$ nodes other than the root, so the proportion of NULL links must be

$$\frac{(n \times k) - (n - 1)}{n \times k} > 1 - \frac{1}{k}.$$

wasted space   Hence if a vertex might have ten subtrees, then more than ninety percent of the links will be NULL. Clearly this method of representing ordered trees is very wasteful of space. The reason is that, for each node, we are maintaining a contiguous list of links to all its children, and these contiguous lists reserve much unused space. We now investigate a way that replaces these contiguous lists with linked lists and leads to an elegant connection with binary trees.

2. Linked Implementation

To keep the children of each node in a linked list, we shall need two kinds of links. First comes the header for a family of children; this will be a link from a parent

first_child *link*   node to its leftmost child, which we may call first_child. Second, each node except the root will appear in one of these lists, and hence requires a link to the next node

next_sibling *link*   on the list, that is, to the next child of the parent. We may call this second link next_sibling. This implementation is illustrated in Figure 11.2.

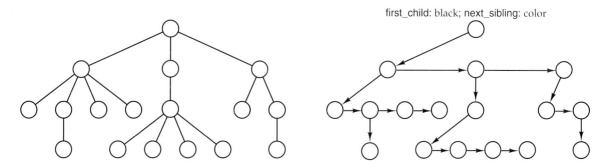

Figure 11.2. Linked implementation of an ordered tree

3. The Natural Correspondence

For each node of the ordered tree we have defined two links (that will be NULL if not otherwise defined), first_child and next_sibling. By using these two links we now have the structure of a binary tree; that is, the linked implementation of an ordered tree is a linked binary tree. If we wish, we can even form a better picture of a binary tree by taking the linked representation of the ordered tree and rotating it a few degrees clockwise, so that downward (first_child) links point leftward and the horizontal (next_sibling) links point downward and to the right. For the tree in Figure 11.2, we hence obtain the binary tree shown in Figure 11.3.

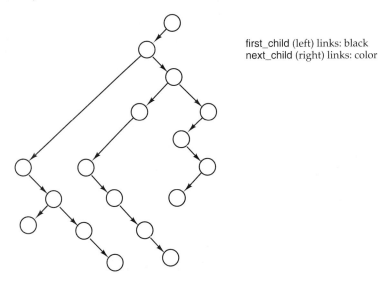

first_child (left) links: black
next_child (right) links: color

Figure 11.3. Rotated form of linked implementation

4. Inverse Correspondence

Suppose that we reverse the steps of the foregoing process, beginning with a binary tree and trying to recover an ordered tree. The first observation that we must make is that not every binary tree is obtained from a rooted tree by the foregoing process: Since the next_sibling link of the root is always NULL, the root of the corresponding binary tree will always have an empty right subtree. To study the inverse correspondence more carefully, we must consider another class of data structures.

11.1.3 Forests and Orchards

In our work so far with binary trees we have profited from using recursion, and for other classes of trees we shall continue to do so. Employing recursion means reducing a problem to a smaller one. Hence we should see what happens if we take a rooted tree or an ordered tree and strip off the root. What is then left is (if not empty) a set of rooted trees or an ordered set of ordered trees, respectively.

forest   The standard term for an arbitrary set of trees is *forest*, but when we use this term, we generally assume that the trees are rooted. The phrase *ordered forest* is sometimes used for an ordered set of ordered trees, but we shall adopt the equally *orchard*   descriptive (and more colorful) term ***orchard*** for this class.

Note that not only can we obtain a forest or an orchard by removing the root from a rooted tree or an ordered tree, respectively, but we can build a rooted or an ordered tree by starting with a forest or an orchard, attaching a new vertex at the top, and adding branches from the new vertex (which will be the root) to the roots of all trees in the forest or the orchard. These actions are illustrated in Figure 11.4.

recursive definitions   We shall use this process to give a new, recursive definition of ordered trees and orchards, one that yields a formal proof of the connection with binary trees. First, let us consider how to start. Recall that it is possible that a binary tree be empty; that is, it may have no vertices. It is also possible that a forest or an orchard be

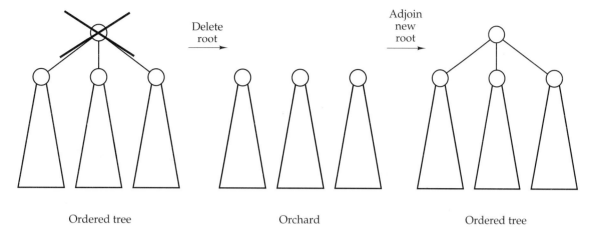

Ordered tree   Orchard   Ordered tree

Figure 11.4. Deleting and adjoining a root

empty; that is, that it contain no trees. It is, however, not possible that a rooted or an ordered tree be empty, since it is guaranteed to contain a root, at the minimum. If we wish to start building trees and forests, we can note that the tree with only one vertex is obtained by attaching a new root to an empty forest. Once we have this tree, we can make a forest consisting of as many one-vertex trees as we wish. Then we can attach a new root to build all rooted trees of height 1. In this way we can continue to construct all the rooted trees in turn in accordance with the following mutually recursive definitions.

Definition

A *rooted tree* consists of a single vertex v, called the *root* of the tree, together with a forest F, whose trees are called the *subtrees* of the root.

A *forest* F is a (possibly empty) set of rooted trees.

A similar construction works for ordered trees and orchards.

Definition

An *ordered tree* T consists of a single vertex v, called the *root* of the tree, together with an orchard O, whose trees are called the *subtrees* of the root v. We may denote the ordered tree with the ordered pair

$$T = \{v, O\}.$$

An *orchard* O is either the empty set $\varnothing$, or consists of an ordered tree T, called the *first tree* of the orchard, together with another orchard O' (which contains the remaining trees of the orchard). We may denote the orchard with the ordered pair

$$O = (T, O').$$

Notice how the ordering of trees is implicit in the definition of orchard. A nonempty orchard contains a first tree, and the remaining trees form another orchard, which again has a first tree that is the second tree of the original orchard. Continuing to

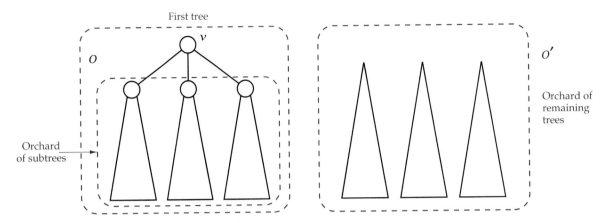

Figure 11.5. Recursive construction of ordered trees and orchards

examine the remaining orchard yields the third tree, and so on, until the remaining orchard is the empty one. See Figure 11.5.

11.1.4 The Formal Correspondence

We can now obtain the principal result of this section.

Theorem 11.1 *Let S be any finite set of vertices. There is a one-to-one correspondence f from the set of orchards whose set of vertices is S to the set of binary trees whose set of vertices is S.*

Proof Let us use the notation introduced in the definitions to prove the theorem. First, we need a similar notation for binary trees: A binary tree B is either the empty set $\varnothing$ or consists of a root vertex v with two binary trees B_1 and B_2. We may thus denote a nonempty binary tree with the ordered triple

$$B = [v, B_1, B_2].$$

We shall prove the theorem by mathematical induction on the number of vertices in S. The first case to consider is the empty orchard $\varnothing$, which will correspond to the empty binary tree:

$$f(\varnothing) = \varnothing.$$

If the orchard O is not empty, then it is denoted by the ordered pair

$$O = (T, O_2)$$

where T is an ordered tree and O_2 another orchard. The ordered tree T is denoted as the pair

$$T = \{v, O_1\}$$

where v is a vertex and O_1 is another orchard. We substitute this expression for T in the first expression, obtaining

$$O = (\{v, O_1\}, O_2).$$

By the induction hypothesis, f provides a one-to-one correspondence from orchards with fewer vertices than in S to binary trees, and O_1 and O_2 are smaller than O, so the binary trees $f(O_1)$ and $f(O_2)$ are determined by the induction hypothesis. We define the correspondence f from the orchard to a binary tree by

$$f(\{v, O_1\}, O_2) = [v, f(O_1), f(O_2)].$$

It is now obvious that the function f is a one-to-one correspondence between orchards and binary trees with the same vertices. For any way to fill in the symbols v, O_1, and O_2 on the left side, there is exactly one way to fill in the same symbols *end of proof* on the right, and vice versa. ■

11.1.5 Rotations

We can also use this notational form of the correspondence to help us form the picture of the transformation from orchard to binary tree. In the binary tree $[v, f(O_1), f(O_2)]$ the left link from v goes to the root of the binary tree $f(O_1)$, which in fact was the first child of v in the ordered tree $\{v, O_1\}$. The right link from v goes to the vertex that was formerly the root of the next ordered tree to the right. That is, "left link" in the binary tree corresponds to "first child" in an ordered tree, and "right link" corresponds to "next sibling." In geometrical terms, the transformation reduces to the following rules:

1. Draw the orchard so that the first child of each vertex is immediately below the vertex, rather than centering the children below the vertex.
2. Draw a vertical link from each vertex to its first child, and draw a horizontal link from each vertex to its next sibling.
3. Remove the remaining original links.
4. Rotate the diagram 45 degrees clockwise, so that the vertical links appear as left links and the horizontal links as right links.

This process is illustrated in Figure 11.6.

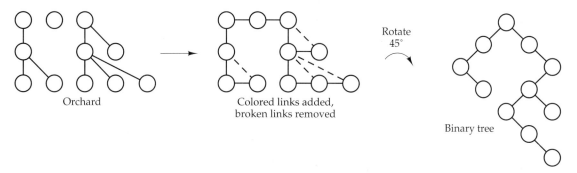

Figure 11.6. **Conversion from orchard to binary tree**

11.1.6 Summary

We have seen three ways to describe the correspondence between orchards and binary trees:

Highlights

➥ first_child and next_sibling links,

➥ rotations of diagrams,

➥ formal notational equivalence.

Most people find the second way, rotation of diagrams, the easiest to remember and to picture. It is the first way, setting up links to give the correspondence, that is usually needed in actually writing computer programs. The third way, the formal correspondence, finally, is the one that proves most useful in constructing proofs of various properties of binary trees and orchards.

Exercises 11.1

E1. Convert each of the following orchards into a binary tree.

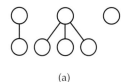

(a)

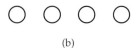

(b)

(c)

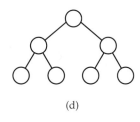

(d)

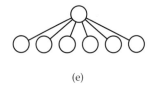

(e)

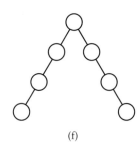

(f)

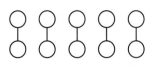

(g)

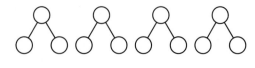

(h)

E2. Convert each of the following binary trees into an orchard.

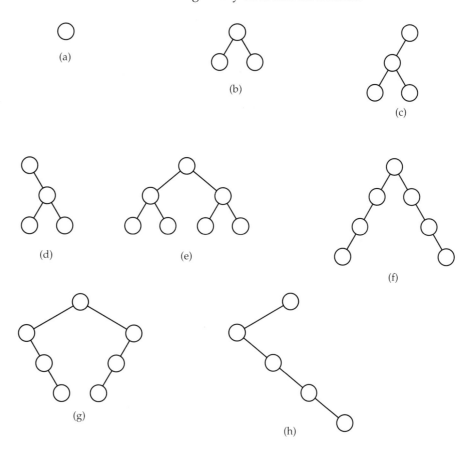

(a)

(b)

(c)

(d)

(e)

(f)

(g)

(h)

E3. Draw all the **(a)** free trees, **(b)** rooted trees, and **(c)** ordered trees with five vertices.

E4. We can define the *preorder traversal* of an orchard as follows: If the orchard is empty, do nothing. Otherwise, first visit the root of the first tree, then traverse the orchard of subtrees of the first tree in preorder, and then traverse the orchard of remaining trees in preorder. Prove that preorder traversal of an orchard and preorder traversal of the corresponding binary tree will visit the vertices in the same order.

E5. We can define the *inorder traversal* of an orchard as follows: If the orchard is empty, do nothing. Otherwise, first traverse the orchard of subtrees of the first tree's root in inorder, then visit the root of the first tree, and then traverse the orchard of remaining subtrees in inorder. Prove that inorder traversal of an orchard and inorder traversal of the corresponding binary tree will visit the vertices in the same order.

E6. Describe a way of traversing an orchard that will visit the vertices in the same order as postorder traversal of the corresponding binary tree. Prove that your traversal method visits the vertices in the correct order.

11.2 LEXICOGRAPHIC SEARCH TREES: TRIES ▬▬▬▬▬

multiway branching

Several times in previous chapters we have contrasted searching a list with looking up an entry in a table. We can apply the idea of table lookup to information retrieval from a tree by using a key or part of a key to make a *multiway branch*.

Instead of searching by comparison of entire keys, we can consider a key as a sequence of characters (letters or digits, for example), and use these characters to determine a multiway branch at each step. If our keys are alphabetic names, then we make a 26-way branch according to the first letter of the name, followed by another branch according to the second letter, and so on. This multiway branching is the idea of a thumb index in a dictionary. A thumb index, however, is generally used only to find the words with a given initial letter; some other search method is then used to continue. In a computer we can proceed two or three levels by multiway branching, but then the tree will become too large, and we shall need to resort to some other device to continue.

11.2.1 Tries

One method is to prune from the tree all the branches that do not lead to any key. In English, for example, there are no words that begin with the letters 'bb,' 'bc,' 'bf,' 'bg,' . . . , but there are words beginning with 'ba,' 'bd,' or 'be.' Hence all the branches and nodes for nonexistent words can be removed from the tree. The resulting tree is called a *trie*. (This term originated as letters extracted from the word *retrieval*, but it is usually pronounced like the word "try.")

A trie of order m can be defined formally as being either empty or consisting of an ordered sequence of exactly m tries of order m.

11.2.2 Searching for a Key

A trie describing the English words (as listed in the *Oxford English Dictionary*) made up only from the letters *a, b,* and *c* is shown in Figure 11.7. Along with the branches to the next level of the trie, each node contains a pointer to a record of information about the key, if any, that has been found when the node is reached. The search for a particular key begins at the root. The first letter of the key is used as an index to determine which branch to take. An empty branch means that the key being sought is not in the tree. Otherwise, we use the second letter of the key to determine the branch at the next level, and so continue. When we reach the end of the word, the information pointer directs us to the desired information. We shall use a NULL information pointer to show that the string is not a word in the trie. Note, therefore, that the word *a* is a prefix of the word *aba*, which is a prefix of the word *abaca*. On the other hand, the string *abac* is not an English word, and therefore its node has a NULL information pointer.

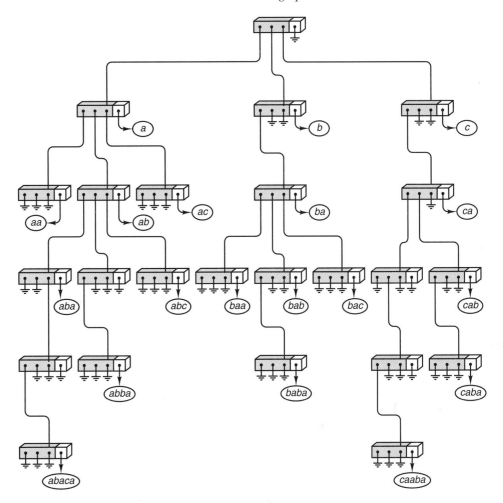

Figure 11.7. Trie of words constructed from *a*, *b*, *c*

11.2.3 C++ Algorithm

We shall translate the search process just described into a method for searching for records that have character arrays as their keys. We shall therefore assume that the classes **Record** and **Key** have the implementation described in Section 9.5, where we used similar keys for a radix sort: Every **Record** has a **Key** that is an alphanumeric string. We shall only make use of a single **Record** method, **char** key_letter(**int** position), that returns the character in the given **position** of the key (or returns a blank, if the key has length less than **position**). As in Section 9.5, an auxiliary function **int** alphabetic_order(**char** symbol) returns the alphabetic position of the character **symbol**. According to our earlier convention, this function will return a value of 27 for nonblank, nonalphabetic characters, and a value of 0 for blank characters. In a linked implementation, a trie contains a pointer to its root.

```
class Trie {
public:                          //   Add method prototypes here.

private:                         //   data members
   Trie_node *root;
};
```

Each node of the trie needs to store a pointer to a **Record** and an array of pointers to its branches. The branches correspond to the 28 results that can be returned by the function **position**. We thus arrive at the following specifications:

```
const int num_chars = 28;

struct Trie_node {
//   data members
   Record *data;
   Trie_node *branch[num_chars];
//   constructors
   Trie_node();
};
```

The constructor for a **Trie_node** simply sets all pointer members in the node to NULL.

11.2.4 Searching a Trie

The searching procedure becomes the following **Trie** method.

```
Error_code Trie :: trie_search(const Key &target, Record &x) const
/* Post:  If the search is successful, a code of success is returned, and the output pa-
          rameter x is set as a copy of the Trie's record that holds target. Otherwise,
          a code of not_present is returned.
   Uses:  Methods of class Key. */
{
   int position = 0;
   char next_char;
   Trie_node *location = root;
   while (location != NULL && (next_char = target.key_letter(position)) != ' ') {
                  //   Terminate search for a NULL location or a blank in the target.
      location = location->branch[alphabetic_order(next_char)];
                            //   Move down the appropriate branch of the trie.
      position++;
                  //   Move to the next character of the target.
   }
   if (location != NULL && location->data != NULL) {
      x = *(location->data);
      return success;
   }
   else
      return not_present;
}
```

The termination condition for the **while** loop is constructed to avoid either going beyond a NULL trie node or passing the end of a Key. At the conclusion of the loop, location (if not NULL) points to the node in the trie corresponding to the target.

11.2.5 Insertion into a Trie

Adding a new key to a trie is quite similar to searching for the key: We must trace our way down the trie to the appropriate point and set the **data** pointer to the information record for the new key. If, on the way, we hit a NULL branch in the trie, we must not terminate the search, but instead we must create new nodes and put them into the trie so as to complete the path corresponding to the new key. We thereby obtain the following method.

```
Error_code Trie :: insert(const Record &new_entry)
/* Post: If the Key of new_entry is already in the Trie, a code of duplicate_error is re-
          turned. Otherwise, a code of success is returned and the Record new_entry
          is inserted into the Trie.
   Uses: Methods of classes Record and Trie_node. */
{
    Error_code result = success;
    if (root == NULL) root = new Trie_node;  //   Create a new empty Trie.
    int position = 0;              //   indexes letters of new_entry
    char next_char;
    Trie_node *location = root;  //   moves through the Trie
    while (location != NULL &&
            (next_char = new_entry.key_letter(position)) != ' ') {
        int next_position = alphabetic_order(next_char);
        if (location->branch[next_position] == NULL)
            location->branch[next_position] = new Trie_node;
        location = location->branch[next_position];
        position++;
    }
    //   At this point, we have tested for all nonblank characters of new_entry.
    if (location->data != NULL) result = duplicate_error;
    else location->data = new Record(new_entry);
    return result;
}
```

11.2.6 Deletion from a Trie

The same general plan used for searching and insertion also works for deletion from a trie. We trace down the path corresponding to the key being deleted, and when we reach the appropriate node, we set the corresponding **data** member to NULL. If now, however, this node has all its members NULL (all branches and the **data** member), then we should delete this node. To do so, we can set up a stack of pointers to the nodes on the path from the root to the last node reached. Alternatively, we can use recursion in the deletion algorithm and avoid the need for an explicit stack. In either case, we shall leave the programming as an exercise.

11.2.7 Assessment of Tries

comparison with binary search

The number of steps required to search a trie (or insert into it) is proportional to the number of characters making up a key, not to a logarithm of the number of keys as in other tree-based searches. If this number of characters is small relative to the (base 2) logarithm of the number of keys, then a trie may prove superior to a binary tree. If, for example, the keys consist of all possible sequences of five letters, then the trie can locate any of $n = 26^5 = 11{,}881{,}376$ keys in 5 iterations, whereas the best that binary search can do is $\lg n \approx 23.5$ key comparisons.

In many applications, however, the number of characters in a key is larger, and the set of keys that actually occur is sparse in the set of all possible keys. In these applications, the number of iterations required to search a trie may very well exceed the number of key comparisons needed for a binary search.

dictionary
thumb index

The best solution, finally, may be to combine the methods. A trie can be used for the first few characters of the key, and then another method can be employed for the remainder of the key. If we return to the example of the thumb index in a dictionary, we see that, in fact, we use a multiway branch to locate the first letter of the word, but we then use some other search method to locate the desired word among those with the same first letter.

Exercises 11.2

E1. Draw the tries constructed from each of the following sets of keys.

   (a) All three-digit integers containing only 1, 2, 3 (in decimal representation).
   (b) All three-letter sequences built from a, b, c, d where the first letter is a.
   (c) All four-digit binary integers (built from 0 and 1).
   (d) The words

   > a   ear   re   rare   area   are   ere   era   rarer   rear   err

   built from the letters *a, e, r*.
   (e) The words

   > gig   i   inn   gin   in   inning   gigging   ginning

   built from the letters *g, i, n*.
   (f) The words

   > pal   lap   a   papa   al   papal   all   ball   lab

   built from the letters *a, b, l, p*.

E2. Write a method that will traverse a trie and print out all its words in alphabetical order.

E3. Write a method that will traverse a trie and print out all its words, with the order determined first by the length of the word, with shorter words first, and, second, by alphabetical order for words of the same length.

E4. Write a method that will delete a word from a trie.

Programming Project 11.2

P1. Construct a menu-driven demonstration program for tries. The keys should be words constructed from the 26 lowercase letters, up to 8 characters long. The only information that should be kept in a record (apart from the key) is a serial number indicating when the word was inserted.

11.3 EXTERNAL SEARCHING: B-TREES

In our work throughout this book we have assumed that all our data structures are kept in high-speed memory; that is, we have considered only *internal* information retrieval. For many applications, this assumption is reasonable, but for many other important applications, it is not. Let us now turn briefly to the problem of *external* information retrieval, where we wish to locate and retrieve records stored in a file.

11.3.1 Access Time

The time required to access and retrieve a word from high-speed memory is a few microseconds at most. The time required to locate a particular record on a disk is measured in milliseconds, and for floppy disks can exceed a second. Hence the time required for a single access is thousands of times greater for external retrieval than for internal retrieval. On the other hand, when a record is located on a disk, the normal practice is not to read only one word, but to read in a large *page* or *block*

block of storage of information at once. Typical sizes for blocks range from 256 to 1024 characters or words.

 Our goal in external searching must be to minimize the number of disk accesses, since each access takes so long compared to internal computation. With each access, however, we obtain a block that may have room for several records. Using these records we may be able to make a multiway decision concerning which block to access next. Hence multiway trees are especially appropriate for external searching.

11.3.2 Multiway Search Trees

Binary search trees generalize directly to multiway search trees in which, for some integer m called the *order* of the tree, each node has at most m children. If $k \leq m$ is the number of children, then the node contains exactly $k - 1$ keys, which partition all the keys in the subtrees into k subsets. If some of these subsets are empty, then the corresponding children in the tree are empty. Figure 11.8 shows a 5-way search tree (between 1 and 4 entries in each node) in which some of the children of some nodes are empty.

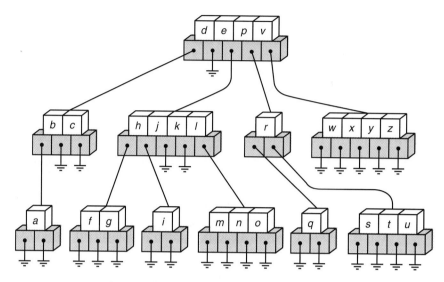

Figure 11.8. A 5-way search tree (not a B-tree)

11.3.3 Balanced Multiway Trees

Our goal is to devise a multiway search tree that will minimize file accesses; hence we wish to make the height of the tree as small as possible. We can accomplish this by insisting, first, that no empty subtrees appear above the leaves (so that the division of keys into subsets is as efficient as possible); second, that all leaves be on the same level (so that searches will all be guaranteed to terminate with about the same number of accesses); and, third, that every node (except the leaves) have at least some minimal number of children. We shall require that each node (except the leaves) have at least half as many children as the maximum possible. These conditions lead to the following formal definition:

Definition   A *B-tree of order* m is an m-way tree in which

1. All leaves are on the same level.
2. All internal nodes except the root have at most m nonempty children, and at least $\lceil m/2 \rceil$ nonempty children.
3. The number of keys in each internal node is one less than the number of its nonempty children, and these keys partition the keys in the children in the fashion of a search tree.
4. The root has at most m children, but may have as few as 2 if it is not a leaf, or none if the tree consists of the root alone.

The tree in Figure 11.8 is not a B-tree, since some nodes have empty children, some have too few children, and the leaves are not all on the same level. Figure 11.9 shows a B-tree of order 5 whose keys are the 26 letters of the alphabet.

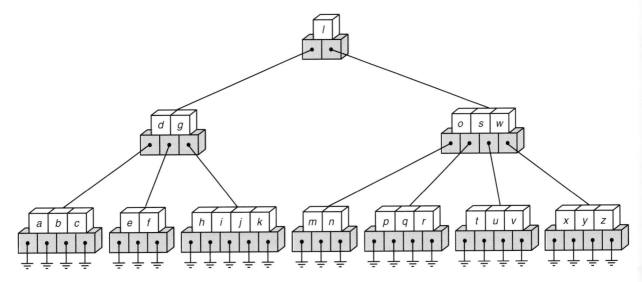

Figure 11.9. A B-tree of order 5

11.3.4 Insfrom into a B-Tree

method

The condition that all leaves be on the same level forces a characteristic behavior of B-trees: In contrast to binary search trees, B-trees are not allowed to grow at their leaves; instead, they are forced to grow at the root. The general method of insertion is as follows. First, a search is made to see if the new key is in the tree. This search (if the key is truly new) will terminate in failure at a leaf. The new key is then added to the leaf node. If the node was not previously full, then the insertion is finished.

When a key is added to a full node, then the node splits into two nodes, side by side on the same level, except that the median key is not put into either of the two new nodes; instead, it is sent up the tree to be inserted into the parent node. When a search is later made through the tree, therefore, a comparison with the median key will serve to direct the search into the proper subtree. When a key is added to a full root, then the root splits in two and the median key sent upward becomes a new root. This is the only time when the B-tree grows in height.

This process is greatly elucidated by studying an example such as the growth of the B-tree of order 5 shown in Figure 11.10. We shall insert the keys

$$a \quad g \quad f \quad b \quad k \quad d \quad h \quad m \quad j \quad e \quad s \quad i \quad r \quad x \quad c \quad l \quad n \quad t \quad u \quad p$$

into an initially empty tree, in the order given.

node splitting

The first four keys will be inserted into one node, as shown in the first diagram of Figure 11.10. They are sorted into the proper order as they are inserted. There is no room, however, for the fifth key, *k*, so its insertion causes the node to split into two, and the median key, *f*, moves up to enter a new node, which is a new root. Since the split nodes are now only half full, the next three keys can be inserted without difficulty. Note, however, that these simple insertions can require rearrangement of the keys within a node. The next insertion, *j*, again splits a node, and this time it is *j* itself that is the median key and therefore moves up to join *f* in the root.

1.

a, g, f, b:

2.

k:

3.

d, h, m:

4.

j:

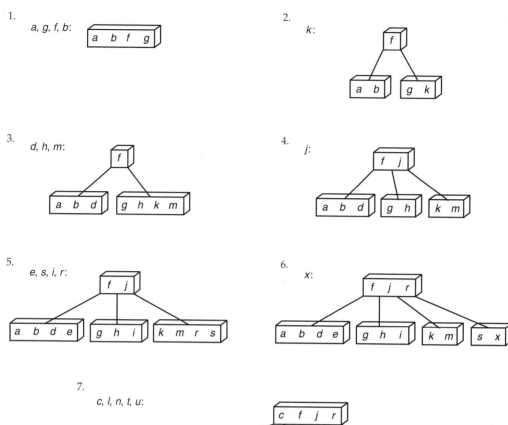

5.

e, s, i, r:

6.

x:

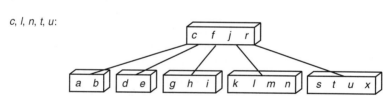

7.

c, l, n, t, u:

8.

p:

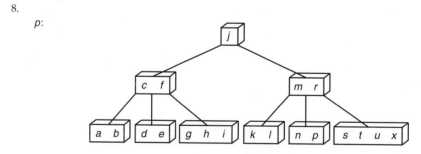

Figure 11.10. Growth of a B-tree

upward propagation   The next several insertions proceed similarly. The final insertion, that of *p*, is more interesting. This insertion first splits the node originally containing *k l m n*, sending the median key *m* upward into the node containing *c f j r*, which is, however, already full. Hence this node in turn splits, and a new root containing *j* is created.

improving balance   Two comments regarding the growth of B-trees are in order. First, when a node splits, it produces two nodes that are now only half full. Later insertions, therefore, can more likely be made without need to split nodes again. Hence one splitting prepares the way for several simple insertions. Second, it is always a median key that is sent upward, not necessarily the key being inserted. Hence repeated insertions tend to improve the balance of the tree, no matter in what order the keys happen to arrive.

11.3.5 C++ Algorithms: Searching and Insertion

To develop C++ algorithms for searching and insertion in a B-tree, let us begin with the declarations needed to set up a B-tree. For simplicity we shall construct our B-tree entirely in high-speed memory, using pointers to describe its structure. In *pointers and* most applications, these pointers would be replaced by the addresses of various *disk accesses* blocks or pages on a disk, and taking a pointer reference would become making a disk access.

1. Declarations

We leave clients free to choose what records they wish to store in a B-tree. Accordingly, our B-tree class, and the corresponding node class, will be templates *parameter: order* parameterized by the class **Record**. We shall also add a second template parameter, an integer representing the order of a B-tree. This allows a client to customize a B-tree object with a simple declaration such as: **B_tree<int, 5> sample_tree;** which declares **sample_tree** as a **B_tree** of order 5 that holds integer records. We arrive at the following class template specification:

```
template <class Record, int order>
class B_tree {
public:              //   Add public methods.
private:             //   data members
  B_node<Record, order> *root;
                     //   Add private auxiliary functions here.
};
```

contiguous lists   Within each node of a B-tree, we need a list of entries and a list of pointers to the children of the node. Since these lists are short, we shall, for simplicity, use contiguous arrays and a separate data member **count** for their representation.

```
template <class Record, int order>
struct B_node {
//   data members:
  int count;
  Record data[order − 1];
  B_node<Record, order> *branch[order];
//   constructor:
  B_node();
};
```

meanings of data *and* branch *indices*

The data member count gives the number of records in the B_node. If count is nonzero then the node has count + 1 children. branch[0] points to the subtree containing all records with keys less than that in data[0]; for each value of position between 1 and count − 1, inclusive, branch[position] points to the subtree with keys strictly between those of data[position − 1] and data[position]; and branch[count] points to the subtree with keys greater than that of data[count − 1].

The B_node constructor creates an empty node; emptiness is implemented by setting count to 0 in the newly created node.

2. Searching

As a simple first example we write a method to search through a B-tree for a record that matches the key of a target record. In our search method we shall assume, as usual, that records can be compared with the standard operators. As in a search through a binary tree, we begin by calling a recursive auxiliary function.

```
template <class Record, int order>
Error_code B_tree<Record, order> :: search_tree(Record &target)
/* Post: If there is an entry in the B-tree whose key matches that in target, the
         parameter target is replaced by the corresponding Record from the B-tree
         and a code of success is returned. Otherwise a code of not_present is
         returned.
   Uses: recursive_search_tree */
{
    return recursive_search_tree(root, target);
}
```

parameters

The input parameters for the auxiliary function recursive_search_tree are a pointer to the root of a subtree of the B-tree and a record holding the target key. The function returns an Error_code to report whether it matched the target with a B_tree entry: if it is successful it updates the value of its parameter target to match the record found in the B-tree.

searching a node

The general method of searching by working our way down through the tree is similar to a search through a binary search tree. In a multiway tree, however, we must examine each node more extensively to find which branch to take at the next step. This examination is done by another auxiliary B-tree function search_node that seeks a target among the records stored in a current node. The function search_node uses an output parameter position, which is the index of the target if found within the current node and otherwise is the index of the branch on which to continue the search.

```
template <class Record, int order>
Error_code B_tree<Record, order> :: recursive_search_tree(
            B_node<Record, order> *current, Record &target)
/* Pre:  current is either NULL or points to a subtree of the B_tree.
   Post: If the Key of target is not in the subtree, a code of not_present is re-
         turned. Otherwise, a code of success is returned and target is set to the
         corresponding Record of the subtree.
   Uses: recursive_search_tree recursively and search_node */
```

```
{
  Error_code result = not_present;
  int position;
  if (current != NULL) {
    result = search_node(current, target, position);
    if (result == not_present)
      result = recursive_search_tree(current->branch[position], target);
    else
      target = current->data[position];
  }
  return result;
}
```

tail recursion This function has been written recursively to exhibit the similarity of its structure to that of the insertion function to be developed shortly. The recursion is tail recursion, however, and can easily be replaced by iteration if desired.

3. Searching a Node

This function must determine whether the target is present in the current node, and, if not, find which of the count + 1 branches will contain the target key. We initialize the counter position to 0 and keep incrementing it until we either arrive at or pass beyond the target.

```
template <class Record, int order>
Error_code B_tree<Record, order> :: search_node(
    B_node<Record, order> *current, const Record &target, int &position)
/* Pre:   current points to a node of a B_tree.
   Post:  If the Key of target is found in *current, then a code of success is returned,
          the parameter position is set to the index of target, and the corresponding
          Record is copied to target. Otherwise, a code of not_present is returned,
          and position is set to the branch index on which to continue the search.
   Uses:  Methods of class Record. */
{
  position = 0;
  while (position < current->count && target > current->data[position])
    position++;                   //   Perform a sequential search through the keys.
  if (position < current->count && target == current->data[position])
    return success;
  else
    return not_present;
}
```

binary search For B-trees of large order, this function should be modified to use binary search instead of sequential search. In some applications, a significant amount of information is stored with each record of the B-tree, so that the order of the B-tree will be relatively small, and sequential search within a node is appropriate. In many applications, only keys are kept in the nodes, so the order is much larger, and binary search should be used to locate the position of a key within a node.

binary search tree   Yet another possibility is to use a linked binary search tree instead of a sequential array of entries for each node; this possibility will be investigated at length later in this chapter.

4. Insertion: The Main Function

Insertion into a B-tree can be most naturally formulated as a recursive function, since, after insertion in a subtree has been completed, a (median) record may remain that must be reinserted higher in the tree. Recursion allows us to keep track of the position within the tree and work our way back up the tree without need for an explicit auxiliary stack.

parameters   As usual, we shall require that the key being inserted is not already present in the tree. The insertion method then needs only one parameter: new_entry, the record being inserted. For the recursion, however, we need three additional output parameters. The first of these is current, the root of the current subtree under consideration. If *current needs to be split to accommodate new_entry, the recursive function will return a code of overflow (since there was no room for the key) and will determine a (median) record to be reinserted higher in the tree. When this happens, we shall adopt the convention that the old node *current contains the left half of the entries and a new node contains the right half of the entries. When such a split occurs, a second output parameter median gives the median record, and the third parameter right_branch gives a pointer to the new node, the right half of the former root *current of the subtree.

To keep all these parameters straight, we shall do the recursion in a function called push_down. This situation, when a nodes splits, is illustrated in Figure 11.11.

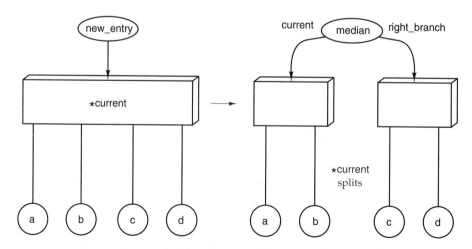

Figure 11.11. Action of push_down function when a node splits

The recursion is started by the **B_tree** method **insert**. If the outermost call to function **push_down** should return a code of **overflow**, then there is still one record, median, that remains to be (re-)inserted into the B-tree. A new root must then be created to hold this record, and the height of the entire B-tree will thereby increase. This is the only way that the B-tree grows in height.

The insertion method appears as follows:

template <**class** Record, **int** order>
Error_code B_tree<Record, order> :: insert(**const** Record &new_entry)
/* Post: *If the* Key *of* new_entry *is already in the* B_tree, *a code of* duplicate_error
    is returned. Otherwise, a code of success *is returned and the* Record
    new_entry *is inserted into the B-tree in such a way that the properties
    of a B-tree are preserved.*
  Uses: *Methods of* **struct** B_node *and the auxiliary function* push_down. */
{
  Record median;
  B_node<Record, order> *right_branch, *new_root;
  Error_code result = push_down(root, new_entry, median, right_branch);
  if (result == overflow) {   //   *The whole tree grows in height.*
                                //   *Make a brand new root for the whole B-tree.*
    new_root = **new** B_node<Record, order>;
    new_root->count = 1;
    new_root->data[0] = median;
    new_root->branch[0] = root;
    new_root->branch[1] = right_branch;
    root = new_root;
    result = success;
  }
  return result;
}

5. Recursive Insertion into a Subtree

Next we turn to the recursive function **push_down**, which uses a parameter **current** to point to the root of the subtree being searched. In a B-tree, a new record is first *stopping rule* inserted into a leaf. We shall thus use the condition **current == NULL** to terminate the recursion; that is, we shall continue to move down the tree searching for **new_entry** until we hit an empty subtree. Since the B-tree does not grow by adding new leaves, we do not then immediately insert **new_entry**, but instead we return a code of **overflow** (since an empty subtree cannot have a record inserted) and send the record back up (now called **median**) for later insertion.

When a recursive call returns a code of **overflow**, the record **median** has not been *reinserting a record* inserted, and we attempt to insert it in the current node. If there is room, then we are finished. Otherwise, the node *current splits into *current and *right_branch and a (possibly different) median record is sent up the tree. The function uses three auxiliary functions: **search_node** (same as for searching); **push_in** puts the median record into node *current provided that there is room; and **split** chops a full node *current into two nodes that will be siblings on the same level in the B-tree.

```
template <class Record, int order>
Error_code B_tree<Record, order>::push_down(
                B_node<Record, order> *current,
                const Record &new_entry,
                Record &median,
                B_node<Record, order> * &right_branch)
```

/* **Pre:** current *is either* NULL *or points to a node of a* B_tree.
   Post: *If an entry with a* Key *matching that of* new_entry *is in the subtree to which* current *points, a code of* duplicate_error *is returned. Otherwise,* new_entry *is inserted into the subtree: If this causes the height of the subtree to grow, a code of* overflow *is returned, and the* Record median *is extracted to be reinserted higher in the B-tree, together with the subtree* right_branch *on its right. If the height does not grow, a code of* success *is returned.*
   Uses: *Functions* push_down *(called recursively),* search_node, split_node, *and* push_in. */

```
{
  Error_code result;
  int position;
  if (current == NULL) {
              //    Since we cannot insert in an empty tree, the recursion terminates.
    median = new_entry;
    right_branch = NULL;
    result = overflow;
  }
  else {                         //    Search the current node.
    if (search_node(current, new_entry, position) == success)
      result = duplicate_error;
    else {
      Record extra_entry;
      B_node<Record, order> *extra_branch;
      result = push_down(current->branch[position], new_entry,
                    extra_entry, extra_branch);
      if (result == overflow) {
                  //    Record extra_entry now must be added to current
        if (current->count < order − 1) {
          result = success;
          push_in(current, extra_entry, extra_branch, position);
        }
        else split_node(   current, extra_entry, extra_branch, position,
                        right_branch, median);
        //    Record median and its right_branch will go up to a higher node.
      }
    }
  }
  return result;
}
```

6. Inserting a Key into a Node

The next auxiliary function, push_in, inserts the Record entry and its right-hand pointer right_branch into the node *current, provided there is room for the insertion. This situation is illustrated in Figure 11.12.

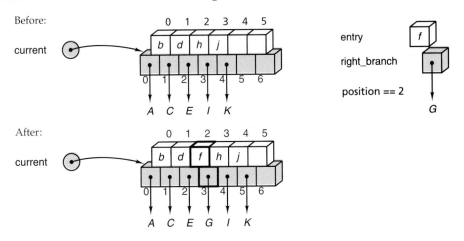

Figure 11.12. Action of push_in function

```
template <class Record, int order>
void B_tree<Record, order> :: push_in(B_node<Record, order> *current,
    const Record &entry, B_node<Record, order> *right_branch, int position)
/* Pre:   current points to a node of a B_tree. The node *current is not full and
            entry belongs in *current at index position.
    Post: entry has been inserted along with its right-hand branch right_branch into
            *current at index position. */
{
    for (int i = current->count; i > position; i--) {
                                // Shift all later data to the right.
        current->data[i] = current->data[i − 1];
        current->branch[i + 1] = current->branch[i];
    }
    current->data[position] = entry;
    current->branch[position + 1] = right_branch;
    current->count++;
}
```

7. Splitting a Full Node

The final auxiliary insertion function, split_node, must insert a record **extra_entry** with subtree pointer extra_branch into a full node *current, and split the right half *general outline* off as a new node *right_half. It must also remove the median record from its node and send it upward for reinsertion later.

It is, of course, not possible to insert record **extra_entry** directly into the full node: We must instead first determine whether **extra_entry** belongs in the left or right half, divide the node accordingly, and then insert **extra_entry** into the appropriate half. While all this work proceeds, we shall divide the node so that the Record median is the largest entry in the left half. This situation is illustrated in Figure 11.13.

```
template <class Record, int order>
void B_tree<Record, order> :: split_node(
   B_node<Record, order> *current,         //   node to be split
   const Record &extra_entry,       //   new entry to insert
   B_node<Record, order> *extra_branch,    //   subtree on right of extra_entry
   int position,                    //   index in node where extra_entry goes
   B_node<Record, order> * &right_half,    //   new node for right half of entries
   Record &median)                  //   median entry (in neither half)
/* Pre:   current points to a node of a B_tree.  The node *current is full, but if
            there were room, the record extra_entry with its right-hand pointer ex-
            tra_branch would belong in *current at position position, 0 ≤ position <
            order.
   Post:  The node *current with extra_entry and pointer extra_branch at position
            position are divided into nodes *current and *right_half separated by a
            Record median.
   Uses:  Methods of struct B_node, function push_in. */
{
   right_half = new B_node<Record, order>;
   int mid = order/2;               //   The entries from mid on will go to right_half.
   if (position <= mid) {           //   First case: extra_entry belongs in left half.
      for (int i = mid; i < order − 1; i++) {  //   Move entries to right_half.
         right_half->data[i − mid] = current->data[i];
         right_half->branch[i + 1 − mid] = current->branch[i + 1];
      }
      current->count = mid;
      right_half->count = order − 1 − mid;
      push_in(current, extra_entry, extra_branch, position);
   }
   else {                           //   Second case: extra_entry belongs in right half.
      mid++;                        //   Temporarily leave the median in left half.
      for (int i = mid; i < order − 1; i++) {  //   Move entries to right_half.
         right_half->data[i − mid] = current->data[i];
         right_half->branch[i + 1 − mid] = current->branch[i + 1];
      }
      current->count = mid;
      right_half->count = order − 1 − mid;
      push_in(right_half, extra_entry, extra_branch, position − mid);
   }
   median = current->data[current->count − 1];
                                    //   Remove median from left half.
   right_half->branch[0] = current->branch[current->count];
   current->count−−;
}
```

Case 1: position == 2; order == 5;
(extra_entry belongs in left half.)

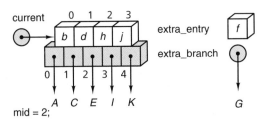

mid = 2;

Case 2: position == 3; order == 5;
(extra_entry belongs in right half.)

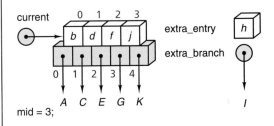

mid = 3;

Shift entries right:

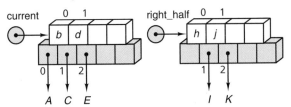

Shift entry right:

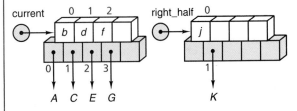

Insert extra_entry and extra_branch:

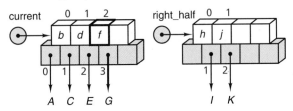

Insert extra_entry and extra_branch:

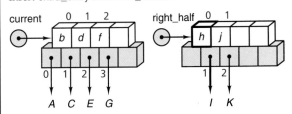

Remove median; move branch:

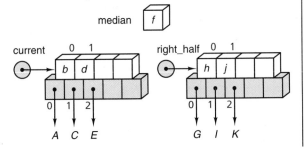

Remove median; move branch:

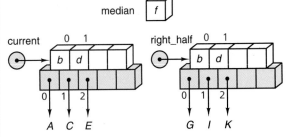

Figure 11.13. Action of split function

11.3.6 Deletion from a B-Tree

1. Method

During insertion, the new entry always goes first into a leaf. For deletion we shall also wish to remove an entry from a leaf. If the entry that is to be deleted is not in a leaf, then its immediate predecessor (or successor) under the natural order of keys is guaranteed to be in a leaf (prove it!). Hence we can promote the immediate predecessor (or successor) into the position occupied by the deleted entry, and delete the entry from the leaf.

moving entries

If the leaf contains more than the minimum number of entries, then one of them can be deleted with no further action. If the leaf contains the minimum number, then we first look at the two leaves (or, in the case of a node on the outside, one leaf) that are immediately adjacent to each other and are children of the same node. If one of these has more than the minimum number of entries, then one of them can be moved into the parent node, and the entry from the parent moved into the leaf where the deletion is occurring. If, finally, the adjacent leaf has only the minimum number of entries, then the two leaves and the median entry from the parent can all be combined as one new leaf, which will contain no more than the maximum number of entries allowed. If this step leaves the parent node with too few entries, then the process propagates upward. In the limiting case, the last entry is removed from the root, and then the height of the tree decreases.

2. Example

The process of deletion in our previous B-tree of order 5 is shown in Figure 11.14. The first deletion, *h*, is from a leaf with more than the minimum number of entries, and hence it causes no problem. The second deletion, *r*, is not from a leaf, and therefore the immediate successor of *r*, which is *s*, is promoted into the position of *r*, and then *s* is deleted from its leaf. The third deletion, *p*, leaves its node with too few entries. The key *s* from the parent node is therefore brought down and replaced by the key *t*.

combining nodes

Deletion of *d* has more extensive consequences. This deletion leaves the node with too few entries, and neither of its sibling nodes can spare an entry. The node is therefore combined with one of the siblings and with the median entry from the parent node, as shown by the dotted line in the first diagram and the combined node *a b c e* in the second diagram. This process, however, leaves the parent node with only the one key *f*. The top three nodes of the tree must therefore be combined, yielding the tree shown in the final diagram of Figure 11.14.

3. C++ Implementation

We can write a deletion algorithm with overall structure similar to that used for insertion. As usual, we shall employ recursion, with a separate method to start the recursion. Rather than attempting to pull an entry down from a parent node

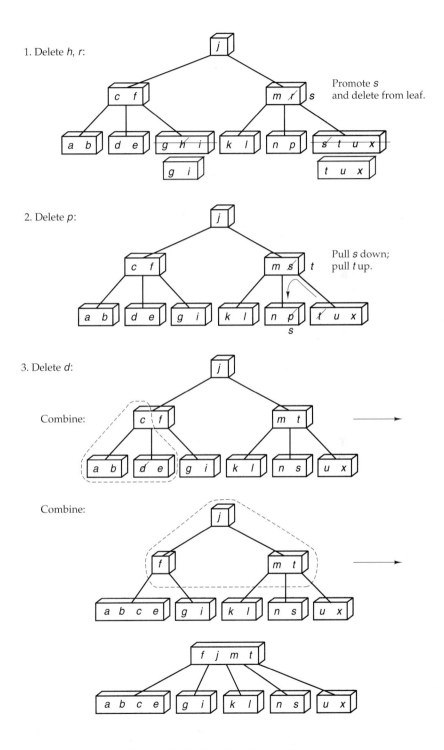

Figure 11.14. Deletion from a B-tree

postpone the work   during an inner recursive call, we shall allow the recursive function to return even though there are too few entries in its root node. The outer call will then detect this occurrence and move entries as required. When the last entry is removed from the root, then the empty node is deleted and the height of the B-tree shrinks.

The method implementation is:

```
template <class Record, int order>
Error_code B_tree<Record, order>::remove(const Record &target)
/* Post:  If a Record with Key matching that of target belongs to the B_tree, a code
          of success is returned and the corresponding node is removed from the
          B-tree. Otherwise, a code of not_present is returned.
   Uses: Function recursive_remove */
{
   Error_code result;
   result = recursive_remove(root, target);
   if (root != NULL && root->count == 0) {  //   root is now empty.
      B_node<Record, order> *old_root = root;
      root = root->branch[0];
      delete old_root;
   }
   return result;
}
```

4. Recursive Deletion

Most of the work is done in the recursive function recursive_remove. It first searches the current node for the target. If target is found and the current node is not a leaf, then the immediate successor of target is located and is placed in the current node; then the successor is deleted. Deletion from a leaf is straightforward, and otherwise the process continues by recursion. When a recursive call returns, the function checks to see if enough entries remain in the appropriate node, and, if not, it moves entries as required. Auxiliary functions are used in several of these steps.

```
template <class Record, int order>
Error_code B_tree<Record, order>::recursive_remove(
   B_node<Record, order> *current, const Record &target)
/* Pre:   current is either NULL or points to the root node of a subtree of a B_tree.
   Post: If a Record with Key matching that of target belongs to the subtree, a
          code of success is returned and the corresponding node is removed from
          the subtree so that the properties of a B-tree are maintained. Otherwise,
          a code of not_present is returned.
   Uses: Functions search_node, copy_in_predecessor, recursive_remove (recursive-
          ly), remove_data, and restore. */
```

```
{
   Error_code result;
   int position;
   if (current ==  NULL) result = not_present;
   else {
      if (search_node(current, target, position) ==  success) {
                                 //    The target is in the current node.
         result = success;
         if (current->branch[position] != NULL) { //   not at a leaf node
            copy_in_predecessor(current, position);
            recursive_remove(current->branch[position],
                             current->data[position]);
         }
         else remove_data(current, position);   //   Remove from a leaf node.
      }
      else result = recursive_remove(current->branch[position], target);
      if (current->branch[position] != NULL)
         if (current->branch[position]->count < (order − 1)/2)
            restore(current, position);
   }
   return result;
}
```

5. Auxiliary Functions

We now can conclude the process of B-tree deletion by writing several of the auxiliary functions required for various purposes. The function remove_data straightforwardly deletes an entry and the branch to its right from a node of a B-tree. This function is invoked only in the case when the entry is to be removed from a leaf of the tree.

```
template <class Record, int order>
void B_tree<Record, order>::remove_data(B_node<Record, order> *current,
                                        int position)
/* Pre:   current points to a leaf node in a B-tree with an entry at position.
   Post: This entry is removed from *current. */
{
   for (int i = position; i < current->count − 1; i++)
      current->data[i] = current->data[i + 1];
   current->count−−;
}
```

The function copy_in_predecessor is invoked when an entry must be deleted from a node that is not a leaf. In this case, the immediate predecessor (in order of keys) is found by first taking the branch to the left of the entry and then taking rightmost branches until a leaf is reached. The rightmost entry in this leaf then replaces the entry to be deleted.

template <**class** Record, **int** order>
void B_tree < Record, order > :: copy_in_predecessor(
                          B_node<Record, order> *current, **int** position)
/* **Pre:**   current *points to a non-leaf node in a B-tree with an entry at* position.
    Post: *This entry is replaced by its immediate predecessor under order of keys.* */
{
    B_node<Record, order> *leaf = current->branch[position];
                                // *First go left from the current entry.*
    while (leaf->branch[leaf->count] != NULL)
        leaf = leaf->branch[leaf->count]; // *Move as far rightward as possible.*
    current->data[position] = leaf->data[leaf->count − 1];
}

Finally, we must show how to restore root->branch[position] to the required minimum number of entries if a recursive call has reduced its count below this minimum. The function we write is somewhat biased to the left; that is, it looks first to
the sibling on the left to take an entry and uses the right sibling only when there
are no entries to spare in the left one. The steps that are needed are illustrated in
Figure 11.15.

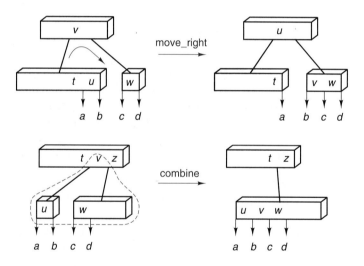

Figure 11.15. Restoration of the minimum number of entries

template <**class** Record, **int** order>
void B_tree<Record, order> :: restore(B_node<Record, order> *current,
                              int position)
/* **Pre:**   current *points to a non-leaf node in a B-tree; the node to which*
            current->branch[position] *points has one too few entries.*
    Post: *An entry is taken from elsewhere to restore the minimum number of en-*
            tries in the node to which current->branch[position] *points.*
    Uses: move_left, move_right, combine. */

```
  {
    if (position == current->count) //  case: rightmost branch
      if (current->branch[position − 1]->count > (order − 1)/2)
        move_right(current, position − 1);
      else
        combine(current, position);
    else if (position == 0)      //  case: leftmost branch
      if (current->branch[1]->count > (order − 1)/2)
        move_left(current, 1);
      else
        combine(current, 1);
    else                          //  remaining cases: intermediate branches
      if (current->branch[position − 1]->count > (order − 1)/2)
        move_right(current, position − 1);
      else if (current->branch[position + 1]->count > (order − 1)/2)
        move_left(current, position + 1);
      else
        combine(current, position);
  }
```

The actions of the remaining three functions move_left, move_right, and combine are clear from Figure 11.15.

```
template <class Record, int order>
void B_tree<Record, order> :: move_left(B_node<Record, order> *current,
                                                     int position)
/* Pre:   current points to a node in a B-tree with more than the minimum num-
          ber of entries in branch position and one too few entries in branch posi-
          tion − 1.
   Post:  The leftmost entry from branch position has moved into current, which
          has sent an entry into the branch position − 1. */
{
  B_node<Record, order> *left_branch = current->branch[position − 1],
                        *right_branch = current->branch[position];
  left_branch->data[left_branch->count] = current->data[position − 1];
                              //  Take entry from the parent.
  left_branch->branch[++left_branch->count] = right_branch->branch[0];
  current->data[position − 1] = right_branch->data[0];
                              //  Add the right-hand entry to the parent.
  right_branch->count−−;
  for (int i = 0; i < right_branch->count; i++) {
                              //  Move right-hand entries to fill the hole.
    right_branch->data[i] = right_branch->data[i + 1];
    right_branch->branch[i] = right_branch->branch[i + 1];
  }
  right_branch->branch[right_branch->count] =
    right_branch->branch[right_branch->count + 1];
}
```

```
template <class Record, int order>
void B_tree<Record, order> :: move_right(B_node<Record, order> *current,
                                          int position)
```
/* **Pre:** current *points to a node in a B-tree with more than the minimum num-*
           ber of entries in branch position *and one too few entries in branch* posi-
           tion + 1.
   Post: *The rightmost entry from branch* position *has moved into* current, *which*
           has sent an entry into the branch position + 1. */
```
{  B_node<Record, order> *right_branch = current->branch[position + 1],
                          *left_branch = current->branch[position];
   right_branch->branch[right_branch->count + 1] =
       right_branch->branch[right_branch->count];
   for (int i = right_branch->count ; i > 0; i--) {   //   Make room for new entry.
       right_branch->data[i] = right_branch->data[i - 1];
       right_branch->branch[i] = right_branch->branch[i - 1];
   }
   right_branch->count++;
   right_branch->data[0] = current->data[position];
                           //    Take entry from parent.
   right_branch->branch[0] = left_branch->branch[left_branch->count--];
   current->data[position] = left_branch->data[left_branch->count];
}
```

```
template <class Record, int order>
void B_tree<Record, order> :: combine(B_node<Record, order> *current,
                                       int position)
```
/* **Pre:** current *points to a node in a B-tree with entries in the branches* position
           and position − 1, *with too few to move entries.*
   Post: *The nodes at branches* position − 1 *and* position *have been combined*
           into one node, which also includes the entry formerly in current *at index*
           position − 1. */
```
{  int i;
   B_node<Record, order> *left_branch = current->branch[position - 1],
                          *right_branch = current->branch[position];
   left_branch->data[left_branch->count] = current->data[position - 1];
   left_branch->branch[++left_branch->count] = right_branch->branch[0];
   for (i = 0; i < right_branch->count; i++) {
       left_branch->data[left_branch->count] = right_branch->data[i];
       left_branch->branch[++left_branch->count] =
                               right_branch->branch[i + 1];
   }
   current->count--;
   for (i = position - 1; i < current->count; i++) {
       current->data[i] = current->data[i + 1];
       current->branch[i + 1] = current->branch[i + 2];
   }
   delete right_branch;
}
```

Exercises 11.3

E1. Insert the six remaining letters of the alphabet in the order

$$z, \quad v, \quad o, \quad q, \quad w, \quad y$$

into the final B-tree of Figure 11.10 (page 538).

E2. Insert the following entries, in the order stated, into an initially empty B-tree of order **(a)** 3, **(b)** 4, **(c)** 7:

$$a \quad g \quad f \quad b \quad k \quad d \quad h \quad m \quad j \quad e \quad s \quad i \quad r \quad x \quad c \quad l \quad n \quad t \quad u \quad p$$

E3. What is the smallest number of entries that, when inserted in an appropriate order, will force a B-tree of order 5 to have height 3 (that is, 3 levels)?

E4. Draw all the B-trees of order 5 (between 2 and 4 keys per node) that can be constructed from the keys 1, 2, 3, 4, 5, 6, 7, and 8.

E5. If a key in a B-tree is not in a leaf, prove that both its immediate predecessor and immediate successor (under the natural order) are in leaves.

E6. Suppose that disk hardware allows us to choose the size of a disk record any way we wish, but that the time it takes to read a record from the disk is $a + bd$, where a and b are constants and d is the order of the B-tree. (One node in the B-tree is stored as one record on the disk.) Let n be the number of entries in the B-tree. Assume for simplicity that all the nodes in the B-tree are full (each node contains $d - 1$ entries).

disk accesses

  (a) Explain why the time needed to do a typical B-tree operation (searching or insertion, for example) is approximately $(a + bd)\log_d n$.
  (b) Show that the time needed is minimized when the value of d satisfies $d(\ln d - 1) = a/b$. (Note that the answer does not depend on the number n of entries in the B-tree.) [*Hint:* For fixed a, b, and n, the time is a function of d: $f(d) = (a + bd)\log_d n$. Note that $\log_d n = (\ln n)/(\ln d)$. To find the minimum, calculate the derivative $f'(d)$ and set it to 0.]
  (c) Suppose a is 20 milliseconds and b is 0.1 millisecond. (The records are very short.) Find the value of d (approximately) that minimizes the time.
  (d) Suppose a is 20 milliseconds and b is 10 milliseconds. (The records are longer.) Find the value of d (approximately) that minimizes the time.

E7. Write a method that will traverse a linked B-tree, visiting all its entries in order of keys (smaller keys first).

traversal

E8. Define *preorder* traversal of a B-tree recursively to mean visiting all the entries in the root node first, then traversing all the subtrees, from left to right, in preorder. Write a method that will traverse a B-tree in preorder.

E9. Define *postorder* traversal of a B-tree recursively to mean first traversing all the subtrees of the root, from left to right, in postorder, then visiting all the entries in the root. Write a method that will traverse a B-tree in postorder.

E10. Remove the tail recursion from the function recursive_search_tree and integrate it into a nonrecursive version of search_tree.

E11. Rewrite the function search_node to use binary search.

E12. A ***B*-tree*** is a B-tree in which every node, except possibly the root, is at least two-thirds full, rather than half full. Insertion into a B*-tree moves entries between sibling nodes (as done during deletion) as needed, thereby delaying splitting a node until two sibling nodes are completely full. These two nodes can then be split into three, each of which will be at least two-thirds full.

B*-tree

(a) Specify the changes needed to the insertion algorithm so that it will maintain the properties of a B*-tree.

(b) Specify the changes needed to the deletion algorithm so that it will maintain the properties of a B*-tree.

(c) Discuss the relative advantages and disadvantages of B*-trees compared to ordinary B-trees.

Programming Projects 11.3

P1. Combine all the functions of this section into a menu-driven demonstration program for B-trees. If you have designed the demonstration program for binary search trees from Section 10.2, Project P2 (page 460) with sufficient care, you should be able to make a direct replacement of one package of operations by another.

P2. Substitute the functions for B-tree retrieval and insertion into the information-retrieval project of Project P5 of Section 10.2 (page 461). Compare the performance of B-trees with binary search trees for various combinations of input text files and various orders of B-trees.

11.4 RED-BLACK TREES

11.4.1 Introduction

B-tree nodes

In the last section, we used a contiguous list to store the entries within a single node of a B-tree. Doing so was appropriate because the number of entries in one node is usually relatively small and because we were emulating methods that might be used in external files on a disk, where dynamic memory may not be available, and records may be stored contiguously on the disk.

binary tree representation

In general, however, we may use any ordered structure we wish for storing the entries in each B-tree node. Small binary search trees turn out to be an excellent choice. We need only be careful to distinguish between the links within a single B-tree node and the links from one B-tree node to another. Let us therefore draw the links within one B-tree node as curly colored lines and the links between B-tree nodes as straight black lines. Figure 11.16 shows a B-tree of order 4 constructed this way.

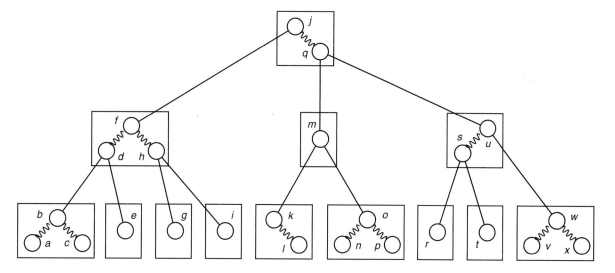

Figure 11.16. A B-tree of order 4 as a binary search tree

11.4.2 Definition and Analysis

This construction is especially useful for a B-tree of order 4 (like Figure 11.16), where each node of the tree contains one, two, or three entries. A node with one key is the same in the B-tree and the binary search tree; a node with three entries transforms as:

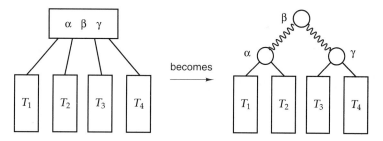

A node with two entries has two possible representations:

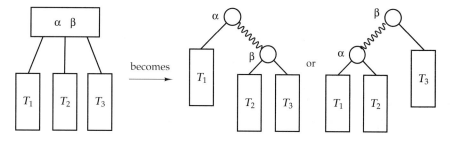

If we wished, we could always use only one of these two, but there is no reason to do so, and we shall find that our algorithms naturally produce both possible forms, so let us allow either form to represent a B-tree node with two entries.

first definition

Hence we obtain the fundamental definition of this section: A *red-black tree* is a binary search tree, with links colored red or black, obtained from a B-tree of order 4 in the way just described. After we have converted a B-tree into a red-black tree, we can use it like any other binary search tree. In particular, searching and traversal of a red-black tree are exactly the same as for an ordinary binary search tree; we simply ignore the color of the links. Insertion and deletion, however, require more care to maintain the underlying B-tree structure. Let us therefore translate the requirements for a B-tree into corresponding requirements for red-black trees.

colored nodes

First, however, let us adopt some more notation: We shall consider each *node* of a red-black tree as colored with the same color as the link immediately *above* it; hence we shall often speak of red nodes and black nodes instead of red links and black links. In this way, we need keep only one extra bit of information for each node to indicate its color.

root color

Since the root has no link above it, it does not obtain a color in this way. In order to simplify some algorithms, we adopt the convention that the root is colored black. Similarly, we shall consider that all the empty subtrees (corresponding to NULL links) are colored black.

black condition

The first condition defining a B-tree, that all its empty subtrees are on the same level, means that every simple path from the root to an empty subtree (NULL) goes through the same number of B-tree nodes. The corresponding red-black tree has one black node (and perhaps one or two red nodes) for each B-tree node. Hence we obtain the **black condition**:

> *Every simple path from the root to an empty subtree*
> *goes through the same number of black nodes.*

red condition

The assertion that a B-tree satisfies search-tree properties is automatically satisfied for a red-black tree, and, for order 4, the remaining parts of the definition amount to saying that each node contains one, two, or three entries. We need a condition on red-black trees that will guarantee that no more than three nodes are identified together (by red links) as one B-tree node, and that nodes with three entries are in the balanced form we are using. This guarantee comes from the **red condition**:

> *If a node is red, then its parent exists and is black.*

(Since we have required the root to be black, the parent of a red node always exists.)

We can summarize this discussion by presenting a formal definition that no longer refers to B-trees at all:

Definition

A *red-black tree* is a binary search tree in which each node has either the color *red* or *black* and that satisfies the following conditions:

black condition

1. Every simple path from the root to an empty subtree (a NULL link) goes through the same number of black nodes.

red condition

2. If a node is red, then its parent exists and is black.

From this definition it follows that no path from the root to an empty subtree can be more that twice as long as another, since, by the red condition, no more than half the nodes on such a path can be red, and, by the black condition, there are the same number of black nodes on each such path. Hence we obtain:

Theorem 11.2   *The height of a red-black tree containing n nodes is no more than $2 \lg n$.*

search performance   Hence the time for searching a red-black tree with n nodes is $O(\log n)$ in every case. We shall find that the time for insertion is also $O(\log n)$, but first we need to devise the associated algorithm.

Recall from Section 10.4, however, that an AVL tree, in its worst case, has height about $1.44 \lg n$ and, on average, has an even smaller height. Hence red-black trees do not achieve as good a balance as AVL trees. This does not mean, however, that red-black trees are necessarily slower than AVL trees, since AVL trees may require many more rotations to maintain balance than red-black trees require.

11.4.3 Red-Black Tree Specification

We could consider several options for the specification of a C++ class to represent red-black tree objects. We might go back to our original motivation and implement red-black trees as B-trees whose nodes store search trees rather than contiguous lists. This approach would force us to recode most of the methods and auxiliary functions of a B-tree, because the original versions relied heavily on the contiguous representation of node entries. We shall therefore investigate an alternative implementation, where we construct a red-black tree class that inherits the properties of our search-tree class of Section 10.2.

We must begin by incorporating colors into the nodes that will make up red-black trees:

```
enum Color {red, black};
template <class Record>
struct RB_node: public Binary_node<Record> {
   Color color;
   RB_node(const Record &new_entry) { color = red; data = new_entry;
                                       left = right = NULL; }

   RB_node()                       { color = red; left = right = NULL; }
   void set_color(Color c)         { color = c; }
   Color get_color() const         { return color; }
};
```

node constructors and methods   For convenience, we have included inline definitions for the constructors and other methods of a red-black node. We see that the **struct** RB_node is very similar to the earlier **struct** AVL_node that we used to store nodes of AVL-trees in Section 10.4: The only change is that we now maintain color information rather than balance information.

pointer access to methods   In order to invoke the node methods get_color and set_color via pointers, we need to add corresponding virtual functions to the base **struct** Binary_node. We added analogous virtual functions to access balance information in Section 10.4. The modified node specification takes the following form:

```
template <class Entry>
struct Binary_node {
  Entry data;
  Binary_node<Entry> *left;
  Binary_node<Entry> *right;
  virtual Color get_color() const { return red; }
  virtual void set_color(Color c)  { }
  Binary_node()                    { left = right = NULL; }
  Binary_node(const Entry &x)    { data = x; left = right = NULL; }
};
```

Just as in Section 10.4, once this modification is made, we can reuse all of our earlier methods and functions for manipulating binary search trees and their nodes. In particular, searching and traversal are identical for red-black trees and for binary search trees.

Our main objective is to create an updated insertion method for the class of red-black trees. The new method must insert new data into a red-black tree so that the red-black properties still hold after the insertion. We therefore require the following class specification:

```
template <class Record>
class RB_tree:  public Search_tree<Record> {
public:
  Error_code insert(const Record & new_entry);
private:                       //   Add prototypes for auxiliary functions here.
};
```

11.4.4 Insertion

overall outline

Let us begin with the standard recursive algorithm for insertion into a binary search tree. That is, we compare the new key of **target** with the key at the root (if the tree is nonempty) and then recursively insert the new entry into the left or right subtree of the root. This process terminates when we hit an empty subtree, whereupon we create a new node and attach it to the tree in place of the empty subtree.

new node

Should this new node be red or black? Were we to make it black, we would increase the number of black nodes on one path (and only one path), thereby violating the black condition. Hence the new node must be red. (Recall also that insertion of a new entry into a B-tree first goes into an existing node, a process that corresponds to attaching a new red node to a red-black tree.) If the parent of the new red node is black, then the insertion is finished, but if the parent is red, then we have introduced a violation of the red condition into the tree, since we have two adjacent red nodes on the path. The major work of the insertion algorithm is to remove such a violation of the red condition, and we shall find several different cases that we shall need to process separately.

postpone work

Our algorithm is considerably simplified, however, if we do not consider these cases immediately, but instead postpone the work as long as we can. Hence, when we make a node red, we do not immediately try to repair the tree, but instead

status variable   simply return from the recursive call with a status indicator set to indicate that the node just processed is red.

parent node: After this return, we are again processing the parent node. If it is black, then
red violation   the conditions for a red-black tree are satisfied and the process terminates. If it is red, then again we do not immediately attempt to repair the tree, but instead we set the status variable to indicate that we have two red nodes together, and then simply return from the recursive call. It turns out, in this case, to be helpful to use the status variable also to indicate if the two red nodes are related as left child or right child.

After returning from the second recursive call, we are processing the grandparent node. Here is where our convention that the root will always be black is helpful: Since the parent node is red, it cannot be the root, and hence the grandparent exists. This grandparent, moreover, is guaranteed to be black, since its child (the parent node) is red, and the only violation of the red condition is farther down the tree.

grandparent node: Finally, at the recursive level of the grandparent node, we can transform the
restoration   tree to restore the red-black conditions. We shall examine only the cases where the parent is the left child of the grandparent; those where it is the right child are symmetric. We need to distinguish two cases according to the color of the other (the right) child of the grandparent, that is, the "aunt" or "uncle" of the original node.

black aunt   First suppose this aunt node is black. This case also covers the possibility that the aunt node does not exist. (Recall that an empty subtree is considered black.) Then the red-black properties are restored by a single or double rotation to the right, as shown in the first two parts of Figure 11.17. You will need to verify that, in both these diagrams, the rotation (and associated color changes) removes the violation of the red condition and preserves the black condition by not changing the number of black nodes on any path down the tree.

Now suppose the aunt node is red, as shown in the last two parts of Figure 11.17.
red aunt   Here the transformation is simpler: No rotation occurs, but the colors are changed. The parent and aunt nodes become black, and the grandparent node becomes red. Again, you should verify that the number of black nodes on any path down the tree remains the same. Since the grandparent node has become red, however, it is quite possible that the red condition is still violated: The great-grandparent node may also be red. Hence the process may not terminate. We need to set the status indicator to show that we have a newly red node, and then we can continue to work out of the recursion. Any violation of the red condition, however, moves two levels up the tree, and, since the root is black, the process will eventually terminate. It is also possible that this process will change the root from black to red; hence, in the outermost call, we need to make sure that the root is changed back to black if necessary.

11.4.5 Insertion Method Implementation

Let us now take this procedure for insertion and translate it into C++. As usual, we shall do almost all the work within a recursive function, so the insertion method only does some setup and error checking. The most important part of this work is

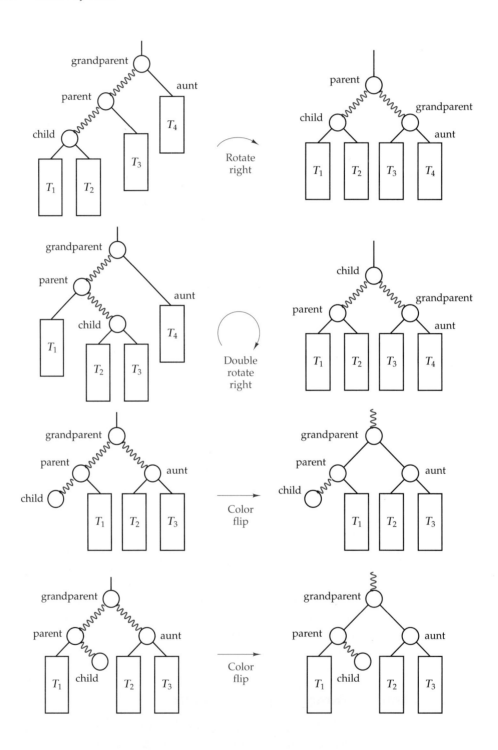

Figure 11.17. Restoring red-black conditions

to keep track of the status, indicating the outcome of the recursive insertion. For this status indicator, we set up a new enumerated type, as follows:

enum RB_code {okay, red_node, left_red, right_red, duplicate};

/* *These outcomes from a call to the recursive insertion function describe the following results:*

okay: *The color of the current root (of the subtree) has not changed; the tree now satisfies the conditions for a red-black tree.*

red_node: *The current root has changed from black to red; modification may or may not be needed to restore the red-black properties.*

right_red: *The current root and its right child are now both red; a color flip or rotation is needed.*

left_red: *The current root and its left child are now both red; a color flip or rotation is needed.*

duplicate: *The entry being inserted duplicates another entry; this is an error.*
      */

The only other task of the insertion method is to force the root to be colored black. Thus we have:

```
template <class Record>
Error_code RB_tree<Record>::insert(const Record &new_entry)
/* Post:  If the key of new_entry is already in the RB_tree, a code of duplicate_error
            is returned.  Otherwise, a code of success is returned and the Record
            new_entry is inserted into the tree in such a way that the properties of an
            RB-tree have been preserved.
    Uses: Methods of struct RB_node and recursive function rb_insert. */
{
  RB_code status = rb_insert(root, new_entry);
  switch (status) {          //   Convert private RB_code to public Error_code.
    case red_node:           //   Always split the root node to keep it black.
      root->set_color(black);  /* Doing so prevents two red nodes at the top of
                  the tree and a resulting attempt to rotate using a parent node that
                  does not exist. */
    case okay:
      return success;
    case duplicate:
      return duplicate_error;
    case right_red:
    case left_red:
      cout << "WARNING: Program error detected in RB_tree::insert" << endl;
      return internal_error;
  }
}
```

The recursive function rb_insert does the actual insertion, searching the tree in the usual way, proceeding until it hits the empty subtree where the actual insertion is placed by a call to the RB_node constructor. As the function then works its way out of the recursive calls, it uses either modify_left or modify_right to perform the rotations and color flips required by the conditions shown in Figure 11.17 and specified by the RB_code status.

```
template <class Record>
RB_code RB_tree<Record> :: rb_insert(Binary_node<Record> * &current,
                                     const Record &new_entry)
/* Pre:   current is either NULL or points to the first node of a subtree of an RB_tree
   Post:  If the key of new_entry is already in the subtree, a code of duplicate is
          returned.  Otherwise, the Record new_entry is inserted into the subtree
          pointed to by current.  The properties of a red-black tree have been re-
          stored, except possibly at the root current and one of its children, whose
          status is given by the output RB_code.
   Uses: Methods of class RB_node, rb_insert recursively, modify_left, and mod-
         ify_right. */
{
  RB_code status,
          child_status;
  if (current == NULL) {
    current = new RB_node<Record>(new_entry);
    status = red_node;
  }
  else if (new_entry == current->data)
    return duplicate;
  else if (new_entry < current->data) {
    child_status = rb_insert(current->left, new_entry);
    status = modify_left(current, child_status);
  }
  else {
    child_status = rb_insert(current->right, new_entry);
    status = modify_right(current, child_status);
  }
  return status;
}
```

The function modify_left updates the status variable and recognizes the situations shown in Figure 11.17 that require rotations or color flips. It is in this function that our decision to postpone the restoration of the red-black properties pays off. When modify_left is invoked, we know that the insertion was made in the left subtree of the current node; we know its color; and, by using the RB_code status variable, we know the condition of the subtree into which the insertion went. By using all this information, we can now determine exactly what actions, if any, are needed to restore the red-black properties.

```
template <class Record>
RB_code RB_tree<Record> :: modify_left(Binary_node<Record> * &current,
                                       RB_code &child_status)
```
/* **Pre:** *An insertion has been made in the left subtree of* *current *that has re-*
turned the value of child_status *for this subtree.*
   Post: *Any color change or rotation needed for the tree rooted at* current *has*
been made, and a status code is returned.
   Uses: *Methods of* **struct** RB_node, *with* rotate_right, double_rotate_right, *and*
flip_color. */
```
{
  RB_code status = okay;
  Binary_node<Record> *aunt = current->right;
  Color aunt_color = black;
  if (aunt != NULL) aunt_color = aunt->get_color();
  switch (child_status) {
  case okay:
    break;                        //    No action needed, as tree is already OK.
  case red_node:
    if (current->get_color() ==  red)
      status = left_red;
    else
      status = okay;              //    current is black, left is red, so OK.
    break;
  case left_red:
    if (aunt_color ==  black) status = rotate_right(current);
    else                      status = flip_color(current);
    break;
  case right_red:
    if (aunt_color ==  black) status = double_rotate_right(current);
    else                      status = flip_color(current);
    break;
  }
  return status;
}
```

The auxiliary function **modify_right** is similar, treating the mirror images of the situations shown in Figure 11.17. The actions of the rotation and color-flip functions are shown in Figure 11.17, and these may all safely be left as exercises. The rotation functions may be based on those for AVL trees, but for red-black trees it becomes important to set the colors and the status indicator correctly, as shown in Figure 11.17.

11.4.6 Removal of a Node

Just as removal of a node from a B-tree is considerably more complicated than insertion, removal from a red-black tree is much more complicated than insertion. Since insertion produces a new red node, which might violate the red condition, we needed to devote careful attention to restoring the red condition after an insertion. On the other hand, removal of a red node causes little difficulty, but removal of a black node can cause a violation of the black condition, and it requires consideration of many special cases in order to restore the black condition for the tree. There are so many special cases that we shall not even attempt to outline the steps that are needed. Consult the references at the end of this chapter for further information on removal algorithms.

Exercises 11.4

E1. Insert the keys *c, o, r, n, f, l, a, k, e, s* into an initially empty red-black tree.

E2. Insert the keys *a, b, c, d, e, f, g, h, i, j, k* into an initially empty red-black tree.

E3. Find a binary search tree whose nodes cannot be colored so as to make it a red-black tree.

E4. Find a red-black tree that is not an AVL tree.

E5. Prove that any AVL tree can have its nodes colored so as to make it a red-black tree. You may find it easier to prove the following stronger statement: An AVL tree of height h can have its nodes colored as a red-black tree with exactly $\lceil h/2 \rceil$ black nodes on each path to an empty subtree, and, if h is odd, then both children of the root are black.

Programming Projects 11.4

P1. Complete red-black insertion by writing the following missing functions:

    (a) modify_right   **(d)** rotate_right

    (b) flip_color   **(e)** double_rotate_left

    (c) rotate_left   **(f)** double_rotate_right

Be sure that, at the end of each function, the colors of affected nodes have been set properly, and the returned **RB_code** correctly indicates the current condition. By including extensive error testing for illegal situations, you can simplify the process of correcting your work.

P2. Substitute the function for red-black insertion into the menu-driven demonstration program for binary search trees from Section 10.2, Project P2 (page 460), thereby obtaining a demonstration program for red-black trees. You may leave removal not implemented.

P3. Substitute the function for red-black insertion into the information-retrieval project of Project P5 of Section 10.2 (page 461). Compare the performance of red-black trees with other search trees for various combinations of input text files.

POINTERS AND PITFALLS

1. Trees are flexible and powerful structures both for modeling problems and for organizing data. In using trees in problem solving and in algorithm design, first decide on the kind of tree needed (ordered, rooted, free, or binary) before considering implementation details.

2. Most trees can be described easily by using recursion; their associated algorithms are often best formulated recursively.

3. For problems of information retrieval, consider the size, number, and location of the records along with the type and structure of the entries while choosing the data structures to be used. For small records or small numbers of entries, high-speed internal memory will be used, and binary search trees will likely prove adequate. For information retrieval from disk files, methods employing multiway branching, such as tries, B-trees, and hash tables, will usually be superior. Tries are particularly well suited to applications where the keys are structured as a sequence of symbols and where the set of keys is relatively dense in the set of all possible keys. For other applications, methods that treat the key as a single unit will often prove superior. B-trees, together with various generalizations and extensions, can be usefully applied to many problems concerned with external information retrieval.

REVIEW QUESTIONS

11.1　**1.** Define the terms **(a)** *free tree*, **(b)** *rooted tree*, and **(c)** *ordered tree*.

2. Draw all the different **(a)** free trees, **(b)** rooted trees, and **(c)** ordered trees with three vertices.

3. Name three ways describing the correspondence between orchards and binary trees, and indicate the primary purpose for each of these ways.

11.2　**4.** What is a trie?

5. How may a trie with six levels and a five-way branch in each node differ from the rooted tree with six levels and five children for every node except the leaves? Will the trie or the tree likely have fewer nodes, and why?

6. Discuss the relative advantages in speed of retrieval of a trie and a binary search tree.

11.3　**7.** How does a multiway search tree differ from a trie?

8. What is a B-tree?

9. What happens when an attempt is made to insert a new entry into a full node of a B-tree?

10. Does a B-tree grow at its leaves or at its root? Why?

11. In deleting an entry from a B-tree, when is it necessary to combine nodes?

12. For what purposes are B-trees especially appropriate?

11.4　**13.** What is the relationship between red-black trees and B-trees?

14. State the black and the red conditions.

15. How is the height of a red-black tree related to its size?

REFERENCES FOR FURTHER STUDY

One of the most thorough available studies of trees is in the series of books by KNUTH. The correspondence from ordered trees to binary trees appears in Volume 1, pp. 332–347. Volume 3, pp. 471–505, discusses multiway trees, B-trees, and tries.
Tries were first studied in

EDWARD FREDKIN, "Trie memory," *Communications of the ACM* 3 (1960), 490–499.

The original reference for B-trees is

R. BAYER and E. McCREIGHT, "Organization and maintenance of large ordered indexes," *Acta Informatica* 1 (1972), 173–189.

An interesting survey of applications and variations of B-trees is

D. COMER, "The ubiquitous B-tree," *Computing Surveys* 11 (1979), 121–137.

For an alternative treatment of red-black trees, including a removal algorithm, see:

THOMAS H. CORMEN, CHARLES E. LEISERSON, and RONALD L. RIVEST, *Introduction to Algorithms*, M.I.T. Press, Cambridge, Mass., and McGraw-Hill, New York, 1990, 1028 pages.

This book gives comprehensive coverage of many different kinds of algorithms.
Another outline of a removal algorithm for red-black trees, with more extensive mathematical analysis, appears in

DERICK WOOD, *Data Structures, Algorithms, and Performance*, Addison-Wesley, Reading, Mass., 1993, pages 353–366.

Graphs

12

THIS CHAPTER introduces important mathematical structures called graphs that have applications in subjects as diverse as sociology, chemistry, geography, and electrical engineering. We shall study methods to represent graphs with the data structures available to us and shall construct several important algorithms for processing graphs. Finally, we look at the possibility of using graphs themselves as data structures.

12.1 MATHEMATICAL BACKGROUND

12.1.1 Definitions and Examples

A *graph* G consists of a set V, whose members are called the ***vertices*** of G, together with a set E of pairs of distinct vertices from V. These pairs are called the ***edges*** of G. If e = (v, w) is an edge with vertices v and w, then v and w are said to *lie on e*, and e is said to be ***incident*** with v and w. If the pairs are unordered, then

graphs and directed graphs
G is called an ***undirected graph***; if the pairs are ordered, then G is called a ***directed graph***. The term *directed graph* is often shortened to ***digraph***, and the unqualified term *graph* usually means *undirected graph*. The natural way to picture a graph is to represent vertices as points or circles and edges as line segments or arcs connecting the vertices. If the graph is directed, then the line segments or arcs have arrowheads

drawings
indicating the direction. Figure 12.1 shows several examples of graphs.

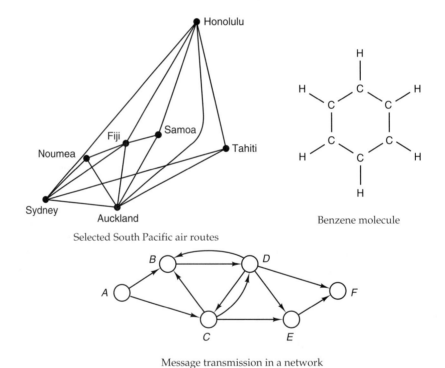

Selected South Pacific air routes

Benzene molecule

Message transmission in a network

Figure 12.1. Examples of graphs

The places in the first part of Figure 12.1 are the vertices of the graph, and the air routes connecting them are the edges. In the second part, the hydrogen and carbon atoms (denoted H and C) are the vertices, and the chemical bonds are the edges. The third part of Figure 12.1 shows a directed graph, where the nodes of the network (A, B, ..., F) are the vertices and the edges from one to another have the directions shown by the arrows.

applications Graphs find their importance as models for many kinds of processes or structures. Cities and the highways connecting them form a graph, as do the components on a circuit board with the connections among them. An organic chemical compound can be considered a graph with the atoms as the vertices and the bonds between them as edges. The people living in a city can be regarded as the vertices of a graph with the relationship *is acquainted with* describing the edges. People working in a corporation form a directed graph with the relation "supervises" describing the edges. The same people could also be considered as an undirected graph, with different edges describing the relationship "works with."

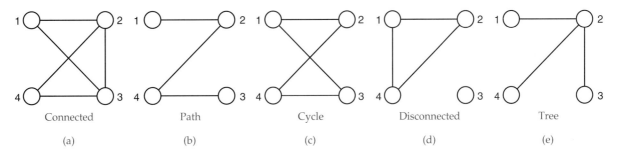

Connected	Path	Cycle	Disconnected	Tree
(a)	(b)	(c)	(d)	(e)

Figure 12.2. Various kinds of undirected graphs

12.1.2 Undirected Graphs

Several kinds of undirected graphs are shown in Figure 12.2. Two vertices in an undirected graph are called **adjacent** if there is an edge from one to the other. Hence, in the undirected graph of part (a), vertices 1 and 2 are adjacent, as are 3 and 4, but 1 and 4 are not adjacent. A **path** is a sequence of distinct vertices, each *paths, cycles,* adjacent to the next. Part (b) shows a path. A **cycle** is a path containing at least *connected* three vertices such that the last vertex on the path is adjacent to the first. Part (c) shows a cycle. A graph is called **connected** if there is a path from any vertex to any other vertex; parts (a), (b), and (c) show connected graphs, and part (d) shows a disconnected graph. If a graph is disconnected, we shall refer to a maximal subset of connected vertices as a **component**. For example, the disconnected graph in part (c) has two components: The first consists of vertices 1, 2, and 4, and the second has just the vertex 3. Part (e) of Figure 12.2 shows a connected graph with no cycles. You will notice that this graph is, in fact, a tree, and we take this property as the *free tree* definition: A **free tree** is defined as a connected undirected graph with no cycles.

12.1.3 Directed Graphs

For directed graphs, we can make similar definitions. We require all edges in a path or a cycle to have the same direction, so that following a path or a cycle means always moving in the direction indicated by the arrows. Such a path (cycle) is *directed paths and* called a **directed** path (cycle). A directed graph is called **strongly connected** if there *cycles* is a directed path from any vertex to any other vertex. If we suppress the direction of the edges and the resulting undirected graph is connected, we call the directed graph **weakly connected**. Figure 12.3 illustrates directed cycles, strongly connected directed graphs, and weakly connected directed graphs.

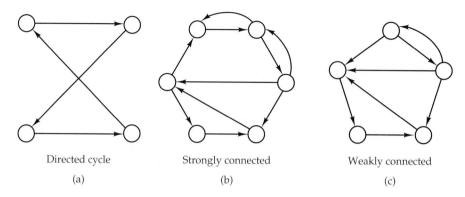

Figure 12.3. **Examples of directed graphs**

multiple edges

self-loops

The directed graphs in parts (b) and (c) of Figure 12.3 show pairs of vertices with directed edges going both ways between them. Since directed edges are ordered pairs and the ordered pairs (v, w) and (w, v) are distinct if $v \neq w$, such pairs of edges are permissible in directed graphs. Since the corresponding unordered pairs are not distinct, however, in an undirected graph there can be at most one edge connecting a pair of vertices. Similarly, since the vertices on an edge are required to be distinct, there can be no edge from a vertex to itself. We should remark, however, that (although we shall not do so) sometimes these requirements are relaxed to allow multiple edges connecting a pair of vertices and self-loops connecting a vertex to itself.

12.2 COMPUTER REPRESENTATION

If we are to write programs for solving problems concerning graphs, then we must first find ways to represent the mathematical structure of a graph as some kind of data structure. There are several methods in common use, which differ fundamentally in the choice of abstract data type used to represent graphs, and there are several variations depending on the implementation of the abstract data type. In other words, we begin with one mathematical system (a *graph*), then we study how it can be described in terms of abstract data types (*sets*, *tables*, and *lists* can all be used, as it turns out), and finally we choose implementations for the abstract data type that we select.

12.2.1 The Set Representation

Graphs are defined in terms of sets, and it is natural to look first to sets to determine their representation as data. First, we have a set of vertices, and, second, we have the edges as a set of pairs of vertices. Rather than attempting to represent this set of pairs directly, we divide it into pieces by considering the set of edges attached to each vertex separately. In other words, we can keep track of all the edges in the graph by keeping, for all vertices v in the graph, the set E_v of edges containing v, or, equivalently, the set A_v of all vertices adjacent to v. In fact, we can use this idea to produce a new, equivalent definition of a graph:

Definition   A *digraph* G consists of a set V, called the *vertices* of G, and, for all $v \in V$, a subset A_v of V, called the set of vertices *adjacent* to v.

From the subsets A_v we can reconstruct the edges as ordered pairs by the following rule: The pair (v, w) is an edge if and only if $w \in A_v$. It is easier, however, to work with sets of vertices than with pairs. This new definition, moreover, works for both directed and undirected graphs. The graph is undirected means that it satisfies the following symmetry property: $w \in A_v$ implies $v \in A_w$ for all v, $w \in V$. This property can be restated in less formal terms: It means that an undirected edge between v and w can be regarded as made up of two directed edges, one from v to w and the other from w to v.

1. Implementation of Sets

There are two general ways for us to implement sets of vertices in data structures and algorithms. One way is to represent the set as a *list* of its elements; this method we shall study presently. The other implementation, often called a *bit string*, keeps a Boolean value for each potential element of the set to indicate whether or not it is in the set. For simplicity, we shall consider that the potential elements of a set are indexed with the integers from 0 to max_set − 1, where max_set denotes the maximum number of elements that we shall allow. This latter strategy is easily implemented either with the standard template library class std :: bitset<max_set> or with our own class template that uses a template parameter to give the maximal number of potential members of a set.

sets as Boolean arrays

```
template <int max_set>
struct Set {
  bool is_element[max_set];
};
```

We can now fully specify a first representation of a graph:

first implementation: sets

```
template <int max_size>
class Digraph {
  int count;                      //   number of vertices, at most max_size
  Set<max_size> neighbors[max_size];
};
```

In this implementation, the vertices are identified with the integers from 0 to count − 1. If v is such an integer, the array entry neighbors[v] is the set of all vertices adjacent to the vertex v.

2. Adjacency Tables

sets as arrays

In the foregoing implementation, the structure Set is essentially implemented as an array of **bool** entries. Each entry indicates whether or not the corresponding vertex is a member of the set. If we substitute this array for a set of neighbors, we find that the array neighbors in the definition of **class** Graph can be changed to an array of arrays, that is, to a two-dimensional array, as follows:

second implementation: adjacency table

```
template <int max_size>
class Digraph {
   int count;                    //    number of vertices, at most max_size
   bool adjacency[max_size][max_size];
};
```

meaning

The adjacency table has a natural interpretation: adjacency[v][w] is true if and only if vertex v is adjacent to vertex w. If the graph is directed, we interpret adjacency[v][w] as indicating whether or not the edge from v to w is in the graph. If the graph is undirected, then the adjacency table must be symmetric; that is, adjacency[v][w] = adjacency[w][v] for all v and w. The representation of a graph by adjacency sets and by an adjacency table is illustrated in Figure 12.4.

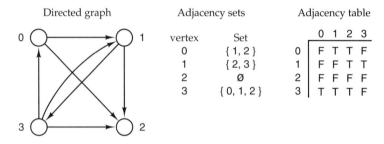

Directed graph   Adjacency sets

vertex	Set
0	{ 1, 2 }
1	{ 2, 3 }
2	∅
3	{ 0, 1, 2 }

Adjacency table

	0	1	2	3
0	F	T	T	F
1	F	F	T	T
2	F	F	F	F
3	T	T	T	F

Figure 12.4. Adjacency set and an adjacency table

12.2.2 Adjacency Lists

Another way to represent a set is as a *list* of its elements. For representing a graph, we shall then have both a list of vertices and, for each vertex, a list of adjacent vertices. We can consider implementations of graphs that use either contiguous lists or simply linked lists. For more advanced applications, however, it is often useful to employ more sophisticated implementations of lists as binary or multiway search trees or as heaps. Note that, by identifying vertices with their indices in the previous representations, we have *ipso facto* implemented the vertex set as a contiguous list, but now we should make a deliberate choice concerning the use of contiguous or linked lists.

1. List-based Implementation

We obtain list-based implementations by replacing our earlier sets of neighbors by lists. This implementation can use either contiguous or linked lists. The contiguous version is illustrated in part (b) of Figure 12.5, and the linked version is illustrated in part (c) of Figure 12.5.

third implementation: lists

```
typedef int Vertex;
template <int max_size>
class Digraph {
   int count;                    //    number of vertices, at most max_size
   List<Vertex> neighbors[max_size];
};
```

2. Linked Implementation

Greatest flexibility is obtained by using linked objects for both the vertices and the adjacency lists. This implementation is illustrated in part (a) of Figure 12.5 and results in a definition such as the following:

fourth implementation: linked vertices and edges

```
class Edge;                    //   forward declaration
class Vertex {
    Edge *first_edge;          //   start of the adjacency list
    Vertex *next_vertex;       //   next vertex on the linked list
};
class Edge {
    Vertex *end_point;         //   vertex to which the edge points
    Edge *next_edge;           //   next edge on the adjacency list
};
class Digraph {
    Vertex *first_vertex;      //   header for the list of vertices
};
```

12.2.3 Information Fields

Many applications of graphs require not only the adjacency information specified in the various representations but also further information specific to each vertex or each edge. In the linked representations, this information can be included as additional members within appropriate records, and, in the contiguous representations, it can be included by making array entries into records. An especially important *networks, weights* case is that of a ***network***, which is defined as a graph in which a numerical ***weight*** is attached to each edge. For many algorithms on networks, the best representation is an adjacency table, where the entries are the weights rather than Boolean values. We shall return to this topic later in the chapter.

12.3 GRAPH TRAVERSAL

12.3.1 Methods

In many problems, we wish to investigate all the vertices in a graph in some systematic order, just as with binary trees, where we developed several systematic traversal methods. In tree traversal, we had a root vertex with which we generally started; in graphs, we often do not have any one vertex singled out as special, and therefore the traversal may start at an arbitrary vertex. Although there are many possible orders for visiting the vertices of the graph, two methods are of particu-*depth-first* lar importance. ***Depth-first traversal*** of a graph is roughly analogous to preorder traversal of an ordered tree. Suppose that the traversal has just visited a vertex v, and let $w_1, w_2, \ldots, w_k$ be the vertices adjacent to v. Then we shall next visit w_1 and keep $w_2, \ldots, w_k$ waiting. After visiting w_1, we traverse all the vertices to which

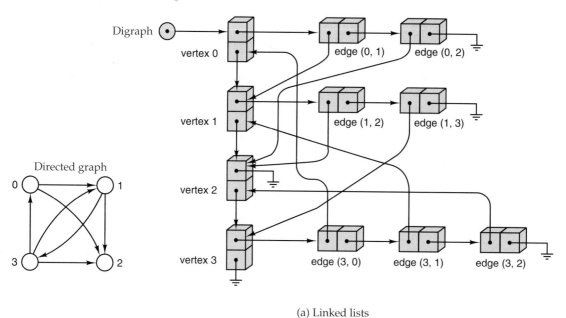

(a) Linked lists

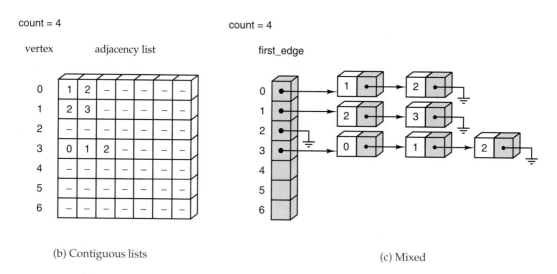

(b) Contiguous lists

(c) Mixed

Figure 12.5. Implementations of a graph with lists

breadth-first   it is adjacent before returning to traverse $w_2, \ldots, w_k$. **Breadth-first traversal** of a graph is roughly analogous to level-by-level traversal of an ordered tree. If the traversal has just visited a vertex v, then it next visits *all* the vertices adjacent to v, putting the vertices adjacent to these in a waiting list to be traversed after all vertices adjacent to v have been visited. Figure 12.6 shows the order of visiting the vertices of one graph under both depth-first and breadth-first traversals.

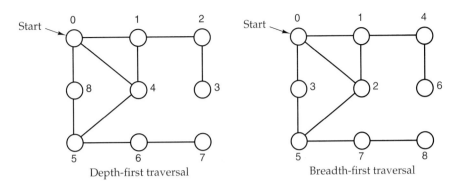

Figure 12.6. Graph traversal

12.3.2 Depth-First Algorithm

Depth-first traversal is naturally formulated as a recursive algorithm. Its action, when it reaches a vertex v, is:

```
visit(v);
for (each vertex w adjacent to v)
    traverse(w);
```

complications   In graph traversal, however, two difficulties arise that cannot appear for tree traversal. First, the graph may contain cycles, so our traversal algorithm may reach the same vertex a second time. To prevent infinite recursion, we therefore introduce a **bool** array visited. We set visited[v] to **true** immediately before visiting v, and check the value of visited[w] before processing w. Second, the graph may not be connected, so the traversal algorithm may fail to reach all vertices from a single starting point. Hence we enclose the action in a loop that runs through all vertices to make sure that we visit all components of the graph. With these refinements, we obtain the following outline of depth-first traversal. Further details depend on the choice of implementation of graphs and vertices, and we postpone them to application programs.

main function outline   **template <int** max_size>
void Digraph<max_size> :: depth_first(**void** (*visit)(Vertex &)) **const**
/* **Post:** *The function* *visit *has been performed at each vertex of the* Digraph *in depth-first order.*
    Uses: *Method* traverse *to produce the recursive depth-first order.* */
{ **bool** visited[max_size];
   Vertex v;
   for (all v in G) visited[v] = **false**;
   for (all v in G) **if** (!visited[v])
       traverse(v, visited, visit);
}

The recursion is performed in an auxiliary function **traverse**. Since **traverse** needs access to the internal structure of a graph, it should be a member function of the **class** Digraph. Moreover, since **traverse** is merely an auxiliary function, used in the construction of the method depth_first, it should be private to the **class** Digraph.

```
template <int max_size>
void Digraph<max_size>::traverse(Vertex &v, bool visited[ ],
                                           void (*visit)(Vertex &)) const
/* Pre:  v is a vertex of the Digraph.
   Post: The depth-first traversal, using function *visit, has been completed for v
         and for all vertices that can be reached from v.
   Uses: traverse recursively. */
{ Vertex w;
  visited[v] = true;
  (*visit)(v);
  for (all w adjacent to v)
    if (!visited[w])
      traverse(w, visited, visit);
}
```

12.3.3 Breadth-First Algorithm

Since using recursion and programming with stacks are essentially equivalent, we could formulate depth-first traversal with a **Stack**, pushing all unvisited vertices adjacent to the one being visited onto the **Stack** and popping the **Stack** to find the next vertex to visit. The algorithm for breadth-first traversal is quite similar to the resulting algorithm for depth-first traversal, except that a **Queue** is needed instead of a **Stack**. Its outline follows.

```
template <int max_size>
void Digraph<max_size>::breadth_first(void (*visit)(Vertex &)) const
/* Post: The function *visit has been performed at each vertex of the Digraph in
         breadth-first order.
   Uses: Methods of class Queue. */
{ Queue q;
  bool visited[max_size];
  Vertex v, w, x;
  for (all v in G) visited[v] = false;
  for (all v in G)
    if (!visited[v]) {
      q.append(v);
      while (!q.empty()){
        q.retrieve(w);
        if (!visited[w]) {
          visited[w] = true;
          (*visit)(w);
          for (all x adjacent to w)
            q.append(x);
        }
        q.serve();
      }
    }
}
```

12.4 TOPOLOGICAL SORTING

12.4.1 The Problem

topological order

If *G* is a directed graph with no directed cycles, then a ***topological order*** for *G* is a sequential listing of all the vertices in *G* such that, for all vertices $v, w \in G$, if there is an edge from *v* to *w*, then *v* precedes *w* in the sequential listing. Throughout this section, we shall consider only directed graphs that have no directed cycles. The term ***acyclic*** is often used to mean that a graph has no cycles.

applications

Such graphs arise in many problems. As a first application of topological order, consider the courses available at a university as the vertices of a directed graph, where there is an edge from one course to another if the first is a prerequisite for the second. A topological order is then a listing of all the courses such that all prerequisites for a course appear before it does. A second example is a glossary of technical terms that is ordered so that no term is used in a definition before it is itself defined. Similarly, the author of a textbook uses a topological order for the topics in the book. Two different topological orders of a directed graph are shown in Figure 12.7. As an example of algorithms for graph traversal, we shall develop functions that produce a topological ordering of the vertices of a directed graph that has no cycles. We shall develop two methods: first, using depth-first traversal, and, then, using breadth-first traversal. Both methods apply to an object of a **class** Digraph that uses the list-based implementation. Thus we shall assume

graph representation

the following class specification:

```
typedef int Vertex;

template <int graph_size>
class Digraph {
public:
   Digraph();
   void read();
   void write();
//   methods to do a topological sort
   void depth_sort(List<Vertex> &topological_order);
   void breadth_sort(List<Vertex> &topological_order);
private:
   int count;
   List <Vertex> neighbors[graph_size];
   void recursive_depth_sort(Vertex v, bool visited[ ],
                         List<Vertex> &topological_order);
};
```

The auxiliary member function recursive_depth_sort will be used by the method depth_sort. Both sorting methods should create a list giving a topological order of the vertices.

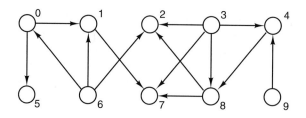

Directed graph with no directed cycles

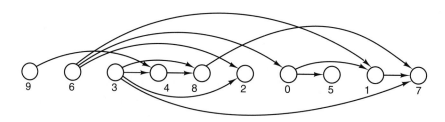

Depth-first ordering

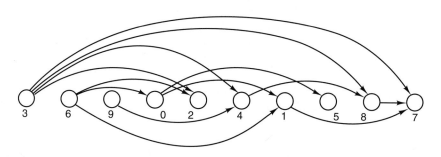

Breadth-first ordering

Figure 12.7. Topological orderings of a directed graph

12.4.2 Depth-First Algorithm

strategy

In a topological order, each vertex must appear before all the vertices that are its successors in the directed graph. For a depth-first topological ordering, we therefore start by finding a vertex that has no successors and place it last in the order. After we have, by recursion, placed all the successors of a vertex into the topological order, then we can place the vertex itself in a position before any of its successors. Since we first order the last vertices, we can repeatedly add vertices to the beginning of the List topological_order. The method is a direct implementation of the general depth first traversal procedure developed in the last section.

```
template <int graph_size>
void Digraph<graph_size> :: depth_sort(List<Vertex> &topological_order)
/* Post:  The vertices of the Digraph are placed into List topological_order with a
          depth-first traversal of those vertices that do not belong to a cycle.
   Uses:  Methods of class List, and function recursive_depth_sort to perform depth-
          first traversal. */
{
   bool visited[graph_size];
   Vertex v;
   for (v = 0; v < count; v++) visited[v] = false;
   topological_order.clear();
   for (v = 0; v < count; v++)
      if (!visited[v])           //   Add v and its successors into topological order.
         recursive_depth_sort(v, visited, topological_order);
}
```

The auxiliary function **recursive_depth_sort** that performs the recursion, based on
the outline for the general function **traverse**, first places all the successors of **v** into
their positions in the topological order and then places **v** into the order.

```
template <int graph_size>
void Digraph<graph_size> :: recursive_depth_sort(Vertex v, bool *visited,
                              List<Vertex> &topological_order)
/* Pre:   Vertex v of the Digraph does not belong to the partially completed List
          topological_order.
   Post:  All the successors of v and finally v itself are added to topological_order
          with a depth-first search.
   Uses:  Methods of class List and the function recursive_depth_sort. */
{
   visited[v] = true;
   int degree = neighbors[v].size();
   for (int i = 0; i < degree; i++) {
      Vertex w;                    //   A (neighboring) successor of v
      neighbors[v].retrieve(i, w);
      if (!visited[w])             //   Order the successors of w.
         recursive_depth_sort(w, visited, topological_order);
   }
   topological_order.insert(0, v);  //   Put v into topological_order.
}
```

performance

Since this algorithm visits each node of the graph exactly once and follows each
edge once, doing no searching, its running time is $O(n + e)$, where n is the number
of vertices and e is the number of edges in the graph.

12.4.3 Breadth-First Algorithm

method

In a breadth-first topological ordering of a directed graph with no cycles, we start
by finding the vertices that should be first in the topological order and then apply

the fact that every vertex must come before its successors in the topological order. The vertices that come first are those that are not successors of any other vertex. To find these, we set up an array predecessor_count whose entry at index v is the number of immediate predecessors of vertex v. The vertices that are not successors are those with no predecessors. We therefore initialize the breadth-first traversal by placing these vertices into a Queue of vertices to be visited. As each vertex is visited, it is removed from the Queue, assigned the next available position in the topological order (starting at the beginning of the order), and then removed from further consideration by reducing the predecessor count for each of its immediate successors by one. When one of these counts reaches zero, all predecessors of the corresponding vertex have been visited, and the vertex itself is then ready to be processed, so it is added to the Queue. We thereby obtain the following function:

```
template <int graph_size>
void Digraph<graph_size> :: breadth_sort(List<Vertex> &topological_order)
/* Post:  The vertices of the Digraph are arranged into the List topological_order
          which is found with a breadth-first traversal of those vertices that do not
          belong to a cycle.
   Uses: Methods of classes Queue and List. */
{
  topological_order.clear();
  Vertex v, w;
  int predecessor_count[graph_size];
  for (v = 0; v < count; v++) predecessor_count[v] = 0;
  for (v = 0; v < count; v++)
    for (int i = 0; i < neighbors[v].size(); i++) {
                              //    Loop over all edges v — w.
      neighbors[v].retrieve(i, w);
      predecessor_count[w] ++;
    }
  Queue ready_to_process;
  for (v = 0; v < count; v++)
    if (predecessor_count[v] == 0)
      ready_to_process.append(v);
  while (!ready_to_process.empty()) {
    ready_to_process.retrieve(v);
    topological_order.insert(topological_order.size(), v);
    for (int j = 0; j < neighbors[v].size(); j++) {  //    Traverse successors of v.
      neighbors[v].retrieve(j, w);
      predecessor_count[w] --;
      if (predecessor_count[w] == 0)
        ready_to_process.append(w);
    }
    ready_to_process.serve();
  }
}
```

This algorithm requires one of the packages for processing queues. The queue can be implemented in any of the ways described in Chapter 3 and Chapter 4. Since the entries in the Queue are to be vertices, we should add a specification: **typedef Vertex Queue_entry;** before the implementation of breadth_sort. As with depth-first traversal, the time required by the breadth-first function is $O(n + e)$, where n is the number of vertices and e is the number of edges in the directed graph.

performance

12.5 A GREEDY ALGORITHM: SHORTEST PATHS

12.5.1 The Problem

As another application of graphs, one requiring somewhat more sophisticated reasoning, we consider the following problem. We are given a directed graph G in which every edge has a nonnegative *weight* attached: In other words, G is a *directed network*. Our problem is to find a path from one vertex v to another w such that the sum of the weights on the path is as small as possible. We call such a *shortest path* path a **shortest path**, even though the weights may represent costs, time, or some quantity other than distance. We can think of G as a map of airline routes, for example, with each vertex representing a city and the weight on each edge the cost of flying from one city to the second. Our problem is then to find a routing from city v to city w such that the total cost is a minimum. Consider the directed graph shown in Figure 12.8. The shortest path from vertex 0 to vertex 1 goes via vertex 2 and has a total cost of 4, compared to the cost of 5 for the edge directly from 0 to 1 and the cost of 8 for the path via vertex 4.

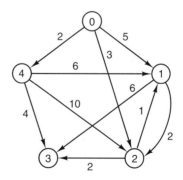

Figure 12.8. A directed graph with weights

It turns out that it is just as easy to solve the more general problem of starting at one vertex, called the **source**, and finding the shortest path to every other vertex, *source* instead of to just one destination vertex. In our implementation, the source vertex will be passed as a parameter. Our problem then consists of finding the shortest path from vertex **source** to every vertex in the graph. We require that the weights are all nonnegative.

12.5.2 Method

The algorithm operates by keeping a set S of those vertices whose shortest distance from source is known. Initially, source is the only vertex in S. At each step, we add to S a remaining vertex for which the shortest path from source has been found. The problem is to determine which vertex to add to S at each step. Let us think of the vertices already in S as having been labeled with some color, and think of the edges making up the shortest paths from source to these vertices as also colored.

distance table   We shall maintain a table **distance** that gives, for each vertex v, the distance from source to v along a path all of whose edges are colored, except possibly the last one. That is, if v is in S, then **distance[v]** gives the shortest distance to v and all edges along the corresponding path are colored. If v is not in S, then **distance[v]** gives the length of the path from source to some vertex w in S plus the weight of the edge from w to v, and all the edges of this path except the last one are colored. The table **distance** is initialized by setting **distance[v]** to the weight of the edge from source to v if it exists and to **infinity** if not.

greedy algorithm   To determine what vertex to add to S at each step, we apply the ***greedy*** criterion of choosing the vertex v with the smallest distance recorded in the table **distance**, such that v is not already in S. We must prove that, for this vertex v, the distance *verification*   recorded in **distance** really is the length of the shortest path from source to v. For suppose that there were a shorter path from source to v, such as shown in Figure 12.9. This path first leaves S to go to some vertex x, then goes on to v (possibly even reentering S along the way). But if this path is shorter than the colored path to v, then its initial segment from source to x is also shorter, so that the greedy criterion would have chosen x rather than v as the next vertex to add to S, since *end of proof*   we would have had **distance[x]** < **distance[v]**.

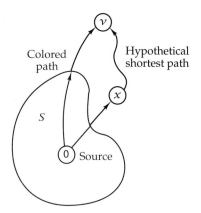

Figure 12.9. Finding a shortest path

When we add v to S, we think of v as now colored and also color the shortest path from source to v (every edge of which except the last was actually already colored). Next, we must update the entries of **distance** by checking, for each vertex w not in S, whether a path through v and then directly to w is shorter than the previously recorded distance to w. That is, we replace **distance[w]** by **distance[v]** *maintain the invariant*   plus the weight of the edge from v to w if the latter quantity is smaller.

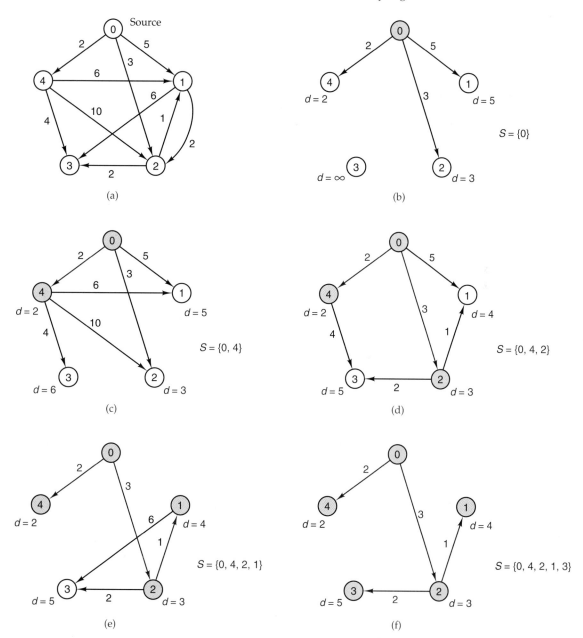

Figure 12.10. Example of shortest paths

12.5.3 Example

Before writing a formal function incorporating this method, let us work through the example shown in Figure 12.10. For the directed graph shown in part (a), the initial situation is shown in part (b): The set *S* (colored vertices) consists of **source**, vertex 0, alone, and the entries of the distance table **distance** are shown as numbers in color beside the other vertices. The distance to vertex 4 is shortest, so 4 is added to S in part (c), and the distance distance[3] is updated to the value 6. Since the distances to vertices 1 and 2 via vertex 4 are greater than those already recorded in T, their entries remain unchanged. The next closest vertex to source is vertex 2, and it is added in part (d), which also shows the effect of updating the distances to vertices 1 and 3, whose paths via vertex 2 are shorter than those previously recorded. The final two steps, shown in parts (e) and (f), add vertices 1 and 3 to S and yield the paths and distances shown in the final diagram.

12.5.4 Implementation

For the sake of writing a function to embody this algorithm for finding shortest distances, we must choose an implementation of the directed graph. Use of the adjacency-table implementation facilitates random access to all the vertices of the graph, as we need for this problem. Moreover, by storing the weights in the table, we can use the table to give weights as well as adjacencies. In the following Digraph specification, we add a template parameter to allow clients to specify the type of weights to be used. For example, a client using our **class** Digraph to model a network of airline routes might wish to use either integer or real weights for the cost of an airline route.

```
template <class Weight, int graph_size>
class Digraph {
public:
   //   Add a constructor and methods for Digraph input and output.
   void set_distances(Vertex source, Weight distance[ ]) const;
protected:
   int count;
   Weight adjacency[graph_size] [graph_size];
};
```

The data member count records the number of vertices in a particular Digraph. In applications, we would need to flesh out this class by adding methods for input and output, but since these will not be needed in the implementation of the method set_distances, which calculates shortest paths, we shall leave the additional methods as exercises.

We shall assume that the **class** Weight has comparison operators. Moreover, we shall expect clients to declare a largest possible Weight value called infinity. For example, client code working with integer weights could make use of the information in the ANSI C++ standard library <limits> and use a global definition:

$$\textbf{const } \text{Weight infinity} = \text{numeric\_limits}<\textbf{int}> :: \text{max}();$$

We shall place the value infinity in any position of the adjacency table for which the corresponding edge does not exist. The method set_distances that we now write will calculate the table of closest distances into its output parameter distance[ ].

shortest distance
procedure

```
template <class Weight, int graph_size>
void Digraph<Weight, graph_size>::set_distances(Vertex source,
                                    Weight distance[ ]) const
/* Post: The array distance gives the minimal path weight from vertex source to
         each vertex of the Digraph. */
{
   Vertex v, w;
   bool found[graph_size];    //   Vertices found in S
   for (v = 0; v < count; v++) {
      found[v] = false;
      distance[v] = adjacency[source][v];
   }
   found[source] = true;      //   Initialize with vertex source alone in the set S.
   distance[source] = 0;
   for (int i = 0; i < count; i++) {  //   Add one vertex v to S on each pass.
      Weight min = infinity;
      for (w = 0; w < count; w++) if (!found[w])
         if (distance[w] < min) {
            v = w;
            min = distance[w];
         }
      found[v] = true;
      for (w = 0; w < count; w++) if (!found[w])
         if (min + adjacency[v][w] < distance[w])
            distance[w] = min + adjacency[v][w];
   }
}
```

performance To estimate the running time of this function, we note that the main loop is executed $n - 1$ times, where n is the number of vertices, and within the main loop are two other loops, each executed $n - 1$ times, so these loops contribute a multiple of $(n - 1)^2$ operations. Statements done outside the loops contribute only $O(n)$, so the running time of the algorithm is $O(n^2)$.

12.6 MINIMAL SPANNING TREES

12.6.1 The Problem

The shortest-path algorithm of the last section applies without change to networks and graphs as well as to directed networks and digraphs. For example, in Figure 12.11 we illustrate the result of its application to find shortest paths (shown in color) from a source vertex, labeled 0, to the other vertices of a network.

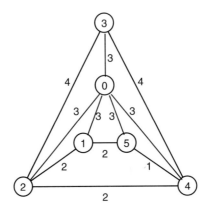

Figure 12.11. Finding shortest paths in a network

If the original network is based on a connected graph G, then the shortest paths from a particular source vertex link that source to all other vertices in G. Therefore, as we can see in Figure 12.11, if we combine the computed shortest paths together, we obtain a tree that links up all the vertices of G. In other words, we obtain a connected tree that is build up out of all the vertices and some of the edges of G. We shall refer to any such tree as a *spanning tree* of G. As in the previous section, we can think of a network on a graph G as a map of airline routes, with each vertex representing a city and the weight on each edge the cost of flying from one city to the second. A spanning tree of G represents a set of routes that will allow passengers to complete any conceivable trip between cities. Of course, passengers will frequently have to use several flights to complete journeys. However, this inconvenience for the passengers is offset by lower costs for the airline and cheaper tickets. In fact, spanning trees have been commonly adopted by airlines as hub-spoke route systems. If we imagine the network of Figure 12.11 as representing a hub-spoke system, then the source vertex corresponds to the hub airport, and the paths emerging from this vertex are the spoke routes. It is important for an airline running a hub-spoke system to minimize its expenses by choosing a system of routes whose costs have a minimal sum. For example, in Figure 12.12, where a pair of spanning trees of a network are illustrated with colored edges, an airline would prefer the second spanning tree, because the sum of its labels is smaller. To model an optimal hub-spoke system, we make the following definition:

Definition

minimal spanning tree

A *minimal spanning tree* of a connected network is a spanning tree such that the sum of the weights of its edges is as small as possible.

Although it is not difficult to compare the two spanning trees of Figure 12.12, it is much harder to see whether there are any other, cheaper spanning trees. Our problem is to devise a method that determines a minimal spanning tree of a connected network.

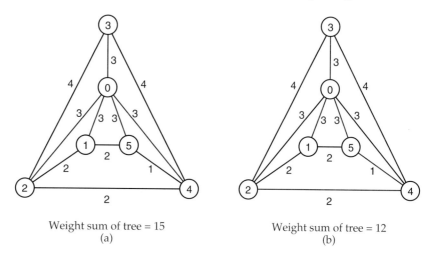

Weight sum of tree = 15
(a)

Weight sum of tree = 12
(b)

Figure 12.12. Two spanning trees in a network

12.6.2 Method

We already know an algorithm for finding a spanning tree of a connected graph, since the shortest path algorithm will do this. It turns out that we can make a small change to our shortest path algorithm to obtain a method, first implemented in 1957 by R. C. PRIM, that finds a minimal spanning tree.

We start out by choosing a starting vertex, that we call **source**, and, as we proceed through the method, we keep a set X of those vertices whose paths to the **source** in the minimal spanning tree that we are building have been found. We also need to keep track of the set Y of edges that link the vertices in X in the tree under construction. Thus, over the course of time, we can visualize the vertices in X and edges in Y as making up a small tree that grows to become our final spanning tree. Initially, **source** is the only vertex in X, and the edge set Y is empty. At each step, we add an additional vertex to X: This vertex is chosen so that an edge back to X has as small as possible a weight. This minimal edge back to X is added to Y.

It is quite tricky to prove that Prim's algorithm does give a minimal spanning tree, and we shall postpone this verification until the end of this section. However, we can understand the selection of the new vertex that we add to X and the new edge that we add to Y by noting that eventually we must incorporate an edge linking X to the other vertices of our network into the spanning tree that we are building. The edge chosen by Prim's criterion provides the cheapest way to accomplish this linking, and so according to the greedy criterion, we should use it. When we come to implement Prim's algorithm, we shall maintain a list of vertices that belong to X as the entries of a Boolean array **component**. It is convenient for us to store the edges in Y as the edges of a graph that will grow to give the output tree from our program.

neighbor table
distance table
We shall maintain an auxiliary table **neighbor** that gives, for each vertex v, the vertex of X whose edge to v has minimal cost. It is convenient to maintain a second table **distance** that records these minimal costs. If a vertex v is not joined by an edge to X we shall record its distance as the value infinity. The table **neighbor**

is initialized by setting neighbor[v] to source for all vertices v, and distance is initialized by setting distance[v] to the weight of the edge from source to v if it exists and to infinity if not.

To determine what vertex to add to X at each step, we choose the vertex v with the smallest value recorded in the table distance, such that v is not already in X. After this we must update our tables to reflect the change that we have made to X. We do this by checking, for each vertex w not in X, whether there is an edge linking v and w, and if so, whether this edge has a weight less than distance[w].

maintain the invariant   In case there is an edge (v, w) with this property, we reset neighbor[w] to v and distance[w] to the weight of the edge.

For example, let us work through the network shown in part (a) of Figure 12.13. The initial situation is shown in part (b): The set X (colored vertices) consists of source alone, and for each vertex w the vertex neighbor[w] is visualized by following any arrow emerging from w in the diagram. (The value of distance[w] is the weight of the corresponding edge.) The distance to vertex 1 is among the shortest, so 1 is added to X in part (c), and the entries in tables distance and neighbor are updated for vertices 2 and 5. The other entries in these tables remain unchanged. Among the next closest vertices to X is vertex 2, and it is added in part (d), which also shows the effect of updating the distance and neighbor tables. The final three steps are shown in parts (e), (f), and (g).

12.6.3 Implementation

To implement Prim's algorithm, we must begin by choosing a C++ **class** to represent a network. The similarity of the algorithm to the shortest path algorithm of the last section suggests that we should base a **class** Network on our earlier **class** Digraph.

```
template <class Weight, int graph_size>
class Network: public Digraph<Weight, graph_size> {
public:
   Network();
   void read();                    //   overridden method to enter a Network
   void make_empty(int size = 0);
   void add_edge(Vertex v, Vertex w, Weight x);
   void minimal_spanning(Vertex source,
                        Network<Weight, graph_size> &tree) const;
};
```

Here, we have overridden an input method, read, to make sure that the weight of any edge (v, w) matches that of the edge (w, v): In this way, we preserve our data structure from the potential corruption of undirected edges. The new method make_empty(int size) creates a Network with size vertices and no edges. The other new method, add_edge, adds an edge with a specified weight to a Network. Just as in the last section, we shall assume that the **class** Weight has comparison operators. Moreover, we shall expect clients to declare a largest possible Weight value called infinity. The method minimal_spanning that we now write will calculate a minimal spanning tree into its output parameter tree. Although the method can only compute a spanning tree when applied to a connected Network, it will always

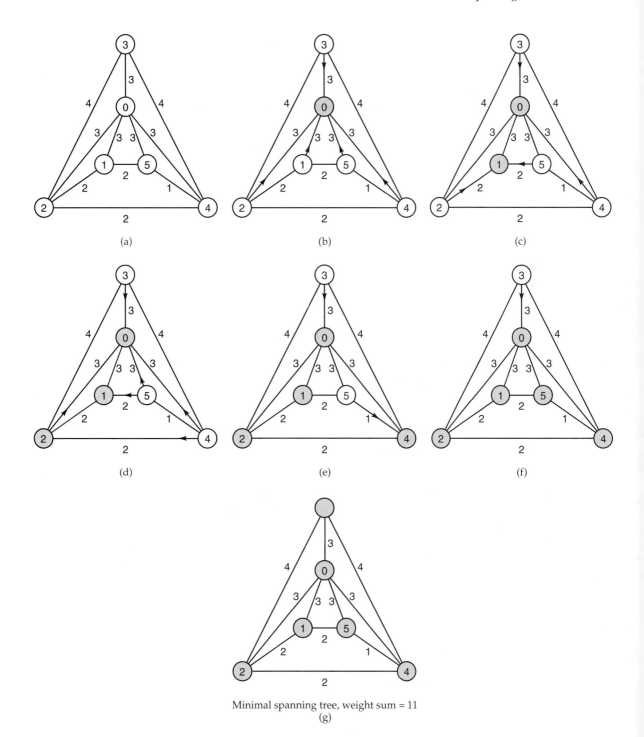

Minimal spanning tree, weight sum = 11
(g)

Figure 12.13. Example of Prim's algorithm

compute a spanning tree for the connected component determined by the vertex source in a **Network**.

```
template <class Weight, int graph_size>
void Network < Weight, graph_size > :: minimal_spanning(Vertex source,
                      Network<Weight, graph_size> &tree) const
/* Post: The Network tree contains a minimal spanning tree for the connected
         component of the original Network that contains vertex source. */
{
  tree.make_empty(count);
  bool component[graph_size];     //   Vertices in set X
  Weight distance[graph_size];    //   Distances of vertices adjacent to X
  Vertex neighbor[graph_size];    //   Nearest neighbor in set X
  Vertex w;
  for (w = 0; w < count; w++) {
    component[w] = false;
    distance[w] = adjacency[source][w];
    neighbor[w] = source;
  }
  component[source] = true;   //   source alone is in the set X.
  for (int i = 1; i < count; i++) {
    Vertex v;                 //   Add one vertex v to X on each pass.
    Weight min = infinity;
    for (w = 0; w < count; w++) if (!component[w])
      if (distance[w] < min) {
        v = w;
        min = distance[w];
      }
    if (min < infinity) {
      component[v] = true;
      tree.add_edge(v, neighbor[v], distance[v]);
      for (w = 0; w < count; w++) if (!component[w])
        if (adjacency[v][w] < distance[w]) {
          distance[w] = adjacency[v][w];
          neighbor[w] = v;
        }
    }
    else break;               //   finished a component in disconnected graph
  }
}
```

performance   To estimate the running time of this function, we note that the main loop is executed $n - 1$ times, where n is the number of vertices, and within the main loop are two other loops, each executed $n - 1$ times, so these loops contribute a multiple of $(n - 1)^2$ operations. Statements done outside the loops contribute only $O(n)$, so the running time of the algorithm is $O(n^2)$.

12.6.4 Verification of Prim's Algorithm

We must prove that, for a connected graph G, the spanning tree S that is produced by Prim's algorithm has a smaller edge-weight sum than any other spanning tree of G. Prim's algorithm determines a sequence of edges $s_1, s_2, \ldots, s_n$ that make up the tree S. Here, as shown in Figure 12.14, s_1 is the first edge added to the set Y in Prim's algorithm, s_2 is the second edge added to Y, and so on.

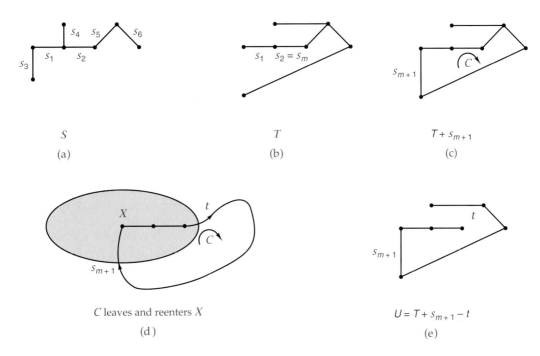

Figure 12.14. Optimality of the output tree of Prim's algorithm

induction: base case

final case

inductive step

In order to show that S is a minimal spanning tree, we prove instead that if m is an integer with $0 \le m \le n$, then there is a minimal spanning tree that contains the edges s_i with $i \le m$. We can work by induction on m to prove this result. The base case, where $m = 0$, is certainly true, since any minimal spanning tree does contain the requisite empty set of edges. Moreover, once we have completed the induction, the final case with $m = n$ shows that there is a minimal spanning tree that contains all the edges of S, and therefore agrees with S. (Note that adding any edge to a spanning tree creates a cycle, so any spanning tree that does contain all the edges of S must be S itself). In other words, once we have completed our induction, we will have shown that S is a minimal spanning tree.

We must therefore establish the inductive step, by showing that if $m < n$ and T is a minimal spanning tree that contains the edges s_i with $i \le m$, then there is a minimal spanning tree U with these edges and s_{m+1}. If s_{m+1} already belongs to T, we can simply set $U = T$, so we shall also suppose that s_{m+1} is not an edge of T. See part (b) of Figure 12.14.

Let us write X for the set of vertices of S belonging to the edges $s_1, s_2, \ldots, s_m$ and R for the set of remaining vertices of S. We recall that, in Prim's algorithm, the selected edge s_{m+1} links a vertex of X to R, and s_{m+1} is at least as cheap as any other edge between these sets. Consider the effect of adding s_{m+1} to T, as illustrated in part (c) of Figure 12.14. This addition must create a cycle C, since the connected network T certainly contains a multi-edge path linking the endpoints of s_{m+1}. The cycle C must contain an edge $t \neq s_{m+1}$ that links X to R, since as we move once around the closed path C we must enter the set X exactly as many times as we leave it. See part (d) of Figure 12.14. Prim's algorithm guarantees that the weight of s_{m+1} is less than or equal to the weight of t. Therefore, the new spanning tree U (see part (e) of Figure 12.14), obtained from T by deleting t and adding s_{m+1}, has a weight sum no greater than that of T. We deduce that U must also be a minimal spanning tree of G, but U contains the sequence of edges $s_1, s_2, \ldots, s_m, s_{m+1}$. This *end of proof* completes our induction.

12.7 GRAPHS AS DATA STRUCTURES

In this chapter, we have studied a few applications of graphs, but we have hardly begun to scratch the surface of the broad and deep subject of graph algorithms. In many of these algorithms, graphs appear, as they have in this chapter, as mathematical structures capturing the essential description of a problem rather than as computational tools for its solution. Note that in this chapter we have spoken of *mathematical* graphs as mathematical structures, and not as data structures, for we have used *structures and data* graphs to formulate mathematical problems, and, to write algorithms, we have *structures* then implemented the graphs within data structures like tables and lists. Graphs, however, can certainly be regarded as data structures themselves, data structures that embody relationships among the data more complicated than those describing a list or a tree. Because of their generality and flexibility, graphs are powerful data *flexibility and power* structures that prove valuable in more advanced applications such as the design of data base management systems. Such powerful tools are meant to be used, of course, whenever necessary, but they must always be used with care so that their power is not turned to confusion. Perhaps the best safeguard in the use of powerful tools is to insist on regularity; that is, to use the powerful tools only in carefully defined and well-understood ways. Because of the generality of graphs, it is not *irregularity* always easy to impose this discipline on their use. In this world, nonetheless, irregularities will always creep in, no matter how hard we try to avoid them. It is the bane of the systems analyst and programmer to accommodate these irregularities while trying to maintain the integrity of the underlying system design. Irregularity even occurs in the very systems that we use as models for the data structures we devise, models such as the family trees whose terminology we have always used. An excellent illustration of what can happen is the following classic story, quoted by N. WIRTH[1] from a Zurich newspaper of July 1922.

> I married a widow who had a grown-up daughter. My father, who visited us quite often, fell in love with my step-daughter and married her. Hence, my father became

---

[1] *Algorithms + Data Structures = Programs*, Prentice Hall, Englewood Cliffs, N. J., 1976, page 170.

OUCH!

my son-in-law, and my step-daughter became my mother. Some months later, my wife gave birth to a son, who became the brother-in-law of my father as well as my uncle. The wife of my father, that is my step-daughter, also had a son. Thereby, I got a brother and at the same time a grandson. My wife is my grandmother, since she is my mother's mother. Hence, I am my wife's husband and at the same time her step-grandson; in other words, I am my own grandfather.

Exercises 12.7

E1. **(a)** Find all the cycles in each of the following graphs. **(b)** Which of these graphs are connected? **(c)** Which of these graphs are free trees?

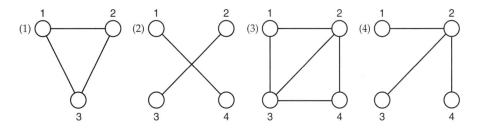

E2. For each of the graphs shown in Exercise E1, give the implementation of the graph as **(a)** an adjacency table, **(b)** a linked vertex list with linked adjacency lists, **(c)** a contiguous vertex list of contiguous adjacency lists.

E3. A graph is *regular* if every vertex has the same valence (that is, if it is adjacent to the same number of other vertices). For a regular graph, a good implementation is to keep the vertices in a linked list and the adjacency lists contiguous. The length of all the adjacency lists is called the *degree* of the graph. Write a C++ class specification for this implementation of regular graphs.

E4. The topological sorting functions as presented in the text are deficient in error checking. Modify the **(a)** depth-first and **(b)** breadth-first functions so that they will detect any (directed) cycles in the graph and indicate what vertices cannot be placed in any topological order because they lie on a cycle.

E5. How can we determine a maximal spanning tree in a network?

E6. Kruskal's algorithm to compute a minimal spanning tree in a network works by considering all edges in increasing order of weight. We select edges for a spanning tree, by adding edges to an initially empty set. An edge is selected if together with the previously selected edges it creates no cycle. Prove that the edges chosen by Kruskal's algorithm do form a minimal spanning tree of a connected network.

E7. Dijkstra's algorithm to compute a minimal spanning tree in a network works by considering all edges in any convenient order. As in Kruskal's algorithm, we select edges for a spanning tree, by adding edges to an initially empty set. However, each edge is now selected as it is considered, but if it creates a cycle together with the previously selected edges, the most expensive edge in this cycle is deselected. Prove that the edges chosen by Dijkstra's algorithm also form a minimal spanning tree of a connected network.

Programming Projects 12.7

P1. Write Digraph methods called read that will read from the terminal the number of vertices in an undirected graph and lists of adjacent vertices. Be sure to include error checking. The graph is to be implemented with

   (a) an adjacency table;
   (b) a linked vertex list with linked adjacency lists;
   (c) a contiguous vertex list of linked adjacency lists.

P2. Write Digraph methods called write that will write pertinent information specifying a graph to the terminal. The graph is to be implemented with

   (a) an adjacency table;
   (b) a linked vertex list with linked adjacency lists;
   (c) a contiguous vertex list of linked adjacency lists.

P3. Use the methods read and write to implement and test the topological sorting functions developed in this section for

   (a) depth-first order and
   (b) breadth-first order.

P4. Write Digraph methods called read and write that will perform input and output for the implementation of Section 12.5. Make sure that the method write( ) also applies to the derived **class** Network of Section 12.6.

P5. Implement and test the method for determining shortest distances in directed graphs with weights.

P6. Implement and test the methods of Prim, Kruskal, and Dijkstra for determining minimal spanning trees of a connected network.

POINTERS AND PITFALLS

1. Graphs provide an excellent way to describe the essential features of many applications, thereby facilitating specification of the underlying problems and formulation of algorithms for their solution. Graphs sometimes appear as data structures but more often as mathematical abstractions useful for problem solving.

2. Graphs may be implemented in many ways by the use of different kinds of data structures. Postpone implementation decisions until the applications of graphs in the problem-solving and algorithm-development phases are well understood.

3. Many applications require graph traversal. Let the application determine the traversal method: depth first, breadth first, or some other order. Depth-first traversal is naturally recursive (or can use a stack). Breadth-first traversal normally uses a queue.

4. Greedy algorithms represent only a sample of the many paradigms useful in developing graph algorithms. For further methods and examples, consult the references.

REVIEW QUESTIONS

12.1   **1.** In the sense of this chapter, what is a *graph*? What are *edges* and *vertices*?

         2. What is the difference between an *undirected* and a *directed* graph?

         3. Define the terms *adjacent*, *path*, *cycle*, and *connected*.

         4. What does it mean for a directed graph to be strongly connected? Weakly connected?

12.2   **5.** Describe three ways to implement graphs in computer memory.

12.3   **6.** Explain the difference between *depth-first* and *breadth-first* traversal of a graph.

         7. What data structures are needed to keep track of the waiting vertices during **(a)** depth-first and **(b)** breadth-first traversal?

12.4   **8.** For what kind of graphs is *topological sorting* defined?

         9. What is a *topological order* for such a graph?

12.5   **10.** Why is the algorithm for finding shortest distances called *greedy*?

12.6   **11.** Explain how Prim's algorithm for minimal spanning trees differs from Kruskal's algorithm.

REFERENCES FOR FURTHER STUDY

The study of graphs and algorithms for their processing is a large subject and one that involves both mathematics and computing science. Three books, each of which contains many interesting algorithms, are

> R. E. TARJAN, *Data Structures and Network Algorithms*, Society for Industrial and Applied Mathematics, Philadelphia, 1983, 131 pages.

> SHIMON EVEN, *Graph Algorithms*, Computer Science Press, Rockville, Md., 1979, 249 pages.

> E. M. REINGOLD, J. NIEVERGELT, N. DEO, *Combinatorial Algorithms: Theory and Practice*, Prentice-Hall, Englewood Cliffs, N. J., 1977, 433 pages.

The original reference for the greedy algorithm determining the shortest paths in a graph is

> E. W. DIJKSTRA, "A note on two problems in connexion with graphs," *Numerische Mathematik* 1 (1959), 269–271.

Prim's algorithm for minimal spanning trees is reported in

> R. C. PRIM, "Shortest connection networks and some generalizations," *Bell System Technical Journal* 36 (1957), 1389–1401.

Kruskal's algorithm is described in

> J. B. KRUSKAL, "On the shortest spanning tree of a graph and the traveling salesman problem," *Proceedings of the American Mathematical Society* 7 (1956), 48–50.

The original reference for Dijkstra's algorithm for minimal spanning trees is

> E. W. DIJKSTRA, "Some theorems on spanning subtrees of a graph," *Indagationes Mathematicæ* 28 (1960), 196–199.

Case Study: The Polish Notation

13

T HIS CHAPTER studies the Polish notation for arithmetic or logical expressions, first in terms of problem solving, and then as applied to a program that interactively accepts an expression, compiles it, and evaluates it. This chapter illustrates uses of recursion, stacks, tables, and trees, as well as their interplay in problem solving and algorithm design.

13.1 THE PROBLEM

One of the most important accomplishments of the early designers of computer languages was allowing a programmer to write arithmetic expressions in something close to their usual mathematical form. It was a real triumph to design a compiler that understood expressions such as

$$(x + y) * \exp(x - z) - 4.0$$
$$a * b + c/d - c * (x + y)$$
$$!(p \,\&\&\, q) \,||\, (x <= 7.0)$$

etymology: FORTRAN   and produced machine-language output. In fact, the name FORTRAN stands for

FORMULA TRANSLATOR

in recognition of this very accomplishment. It often takes only one simple idea that, when fully understood, will provide the key to an elegant solution of a difficult problem, in this case the translation of expressions into sequences of machine-language instructions.

The triumph of the method to be developed in this chapter is that, in contrast to the first approach a person might take, it is not necessary to make repeated scans through the expression to decipher it, and, after a preliminary translation, neither parentheses nor priorities of operators need be taken into account, so that evaluation of the expression can be achieved with great efficiency.

13.1.1 The Quadratic Formula

Before we discuss this idea, let us briefly imagine the problems an early compiler designer might have faced when confronted with a fairly complicated expression. Even the quadratic formula produces problems:

$$x = (-b + (b \uparrow 2 - (4 \times a) \times c) \uparrow \tfrac{1}{2})/(2 \times a)$$

notation   Here, and throughout this chapter, we denote exponentiation by '↑.' Of course, this operator does not exist in C++, but in this chapter we shall design our own system of expressions, and we are free to set our own conventions in any way we wish. When we take square roots, with $\uparrow \tfrac{1}{2}$, we limit our attention to only the non-negative root.

Which operations must be done before others? What are the effects of parentheses? When can they be omitted? As you answer these questions for this example, you will probably look back and forth through the expression several times.

In considering how to translate such expressions, the compiler designers soon settled on the conventions that are familiar now: Operations are ordinarily done left to right, subject to the priorities assigned to operators, with exponentiation highest, then multiplication and division, then addition and subtraction. This order can be altered by parentheses. For the quadratic formula the order of operations is

$$x \; = \; (-b + (b \uparrow 2 - (4 \times a) \times c) \uparrow \tfrac{1}{2}) \; / \; (2 \times a)$$

$$\begin{array}{ccccccccccc}
\uparrow & \uparrow & \uparrow & \uparrow & \uparrow & & \uparrow & & \uparrow & \uparrow & \uparrow & \uparrow \\
10 & 1 & 7 & 2 & 5 & & 3 & & 4 & 6 & 9 & 8
\end{array}$$

Note that assignment = really is an operator that takes the value of its right operand and assigns it to the left operand. The priority of = will be the lowest of any operator, since it cannot be done until the expression is fully evaluated.

1. Unary Operators and Priorities

With one exception, all the operators in the quadratic equation are **binary**, that is, they have two operands. The one exception is the leading minus sign in $-b$. This is a **unary** operator, and unary operators provide a slight complication in determining priorities. Normally we interpret -2^2 as -4, which means that negation is done after exponentiation, but we interpret 2^{-2} as $\frac{1}{4}$ and not as -4, so that here negation is done first. It is reasonable to assign unary operators the same priority as exponentiation and, in order to preserve the usual algebraic conventions, to evaluate operators of this priority from right to left. Doing this, moreover, also gives the ordinary interpretation of $2 \uparrow 3 \uparrow 2$ as

$$2^{(3^2)} \; = \; 512 \qquad \text{and not as} \qquad (2^3)^2 = 64.$$

There are unary operators other than negation. These include such operations as taking the factorial of x, denoted $x!$, the derivative of a function f, denoted f', as well as all functions of a single variable, such as the trigonometric, exponential, and logarithmic functions. In C++, there is also the Boolean operator !, which negates a Boolean variable. To avoid confusion with the factorial operator, we shall use 'not' to denote Boolean negation in the system of expressions that we design in this chapter.

Several binary operators also have Boolean results: the operators && and || as well as the comparison operators == , ! =, <, >, ≤, and ≥. These comparisons are normally done after the arithmetic operators, but before && , || , and assignment.

priority list   We thus obtain the following list of priorities to reflect our usual customs in evaluating operators:

Operators	Priority
↑, all unary operators	6
× / %	5
+ − (binary)	4
== ! = < > ≤ ≥	3
not	2
&& ||	1
=	0

C++ priorities for operators

Note that the priorities shown in this table are not the same as those used in C++. For example, under the syntax rules of C++, the operator ! has the same priority as the unary operators. This means that parentheses must often be used in C++ expressions, even though, by assigning 'not' a lower priority, the expression reads unambiguously to a person. For example, the expression

$$\text{not x} < 10$$

will be interpreted with C++ conventions as meaning

$$(!x) < 10,$$

which is always true.

13.2 THE IDEA

13.2.1 Expression Trees

Drawing a picture is often an excellent way to gain insight into a problem. For our current problem, the appropriate picture is the *expression tree*, as first introduced in Section 10.1.2. Recall that an expression tree is a binary tree in which the leaves are the simple operands and the interior vertices are the operators. If an operator is binary, then it has two nonempty subtrees that are its left and right operands (either simple operands or subexpressions). If an operator is unary, then only one of its subtrees is nonempty, the one on the left or right according to whether the operator is written on the right or left of its operand. You should review Figure 10.3 for several simple expression trees, as well as Figure 10.4 for the expression tree of the quadratic formula.

Let us determine how to evaluate an expression tree such as, for example, the one shown in part (a) of Figure 13.1. It is clear that we must begin with one of the leaves, since it is only the simple operands for which we know the values when starting. To be consistent, let us start with the leftmost leaf, whose value is 2.9. Since, in our example, the operator immediately above this leaf is unary negation, we can apply it immediately and replace both the operator and its operand by the result, −2.9. This step results in the diamond-shaped node in part (b) of the diagram.

The parent of the diamond-shaped node in part (b) is a binary operator, and its second operand has not yet been evaluated. We cannot, therefore, apply this operator yet, but must instead consider the next two leaves, as shown by the colored path. After moving past these two leaves, the path moves to their parent operator, which can now be evaluated, and the result is placed in the second diamond-shaped node, as shown in part (c).

At this stage, both operands of the addition are available, so we can perform it, obtaining the simplified tree in part (d). And so we continue, until the tree has been

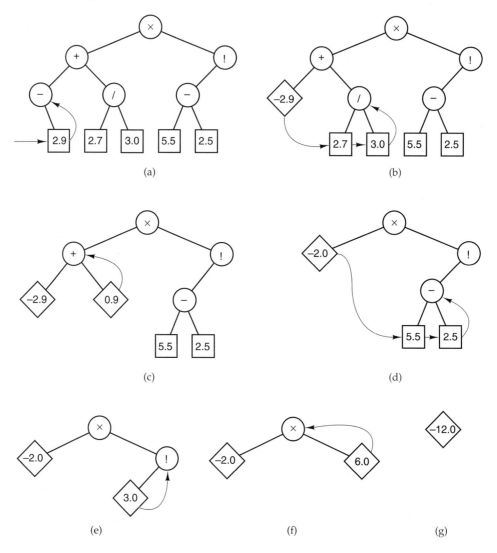

Figure 13.1. Evaluation of an expression tree

reduced to a single node, which is the final result. In summary, we have processed the nodes of the tree in the order

$$2.9 \quad - \quad 2.7 \quad 3.0 \quad / \quad + \quad 5.5 \quad 2.5 \quad - \quad ! \quad \times$$

postorder traversal   The general observation is that we should process the subtree rooted at any given operator in the order:

> *Evaluate the left subtree; evaluate the right subtree; perform the operator.*

(If the operator is unary, then one of these steps is vacuous.) This order is precisely a *postorder* traversal of the expression tree. We have already observed in Section

10.1.2 that the postorder traversal of an expression tree yields the postfix form of the expression, in which each operator is written after its operands, instead of between them.

This simple idea is the key to efficient calculation of expressions by computer.

As a matter of fact, our customary way to write arithmetic or logical expressions with the operator between its operands is slightly illogical. The instruction

Take the number 12 and multiply by . . . .

is incomplete until the second factor is given. In the meantime it is necessary to remember both a number and an operation. From the viewpoint of establishing uniform rules, it makes more sense either to write

Take the numbers 12 and 3; then multiply.

or to write

Do a multiplication. The numbers are 12 and 3.

13.2.2 Polish Notation

This method of writing all operators either before their operands or after them is called **Polish notation**, in honor of its discoverer, the Polish mathematician JAN ŁUKASIEWICZ. When the operators are written before their operands, it is called the **prefix form**. When the operators come after their operands, it is called the **postfix form**, or, sometimes, **reverse Polish form** or **suffix form**. Finally, in this context, it is customary to use the coined phrase **infix form** to denote the usual custom of writing binary operators between their operands.

The expression $a \times b$ becomes $\times\, a\, b$ in prefix form and $a\, b\, \times$ in postfix form. In the expression $a + b \times c$, the multiplication is done first, so we convert it first, obtaining first $a + (b\, c\, \times)$ and then $a\, b\, c\, \times\, +$ in postfix form. The prefix form of this expression is $+\, a \times b\, c$. Note that prefix and postfix forms are not related by taking mirror images or other such simple transformation. Note also that all parentheses have been omitted in the Polish forms. We shall justify this omission later.

As a more complicated example, we can write down the prefix and postfix forms of the quadratic formula, starting from its expression tree, as shown in Figure 10.4.

preorder traversal   First, let us traverse the tree in preorder. The operator in the root is the assignment '=,' after which we move to the left subtree, which consists only of the operand x. The right subtree begins with the division '/' and then moves leftward to '+' and to the unary negation '−.'

We now have an ambiguity that will haunt us later if we do not correct it. The first '−' (minus) in the expression is unary negation, and the second is binary subtraction. In Polish form it is not obvious which is which. When we go to evaluate the prefix string we will not know whether to take one operand for '−' or two, and the results will be quite different. To avoid this ambiguity we shall, in this *special symbol* ~   chapter, often reserve '−' to denote binary subtraction and use a special symbol '~' for unary negation. (This notation is certainly not standard. There are other ways to resolve the problem.)

The preorder traversal of Figure 10.4 up to this point has yielded

$$= \quad x \quad / \quad + \quad \sim \quad b$$

and the next step is to traverse the right subtree of the operator '+.' The result is the sequence

$$\uparrow \quad - \quad \uparrow \quad b \quad 2 \quad \times \quad \times \quad 4 \quad a \quad c \quad \tfrac{1}{2}$$

Finally, we traverse the right subtree of the division '/,' obtaining

$$\times \quad 2 \quad a.$$

Hence the complete prefix form for the quadratic formula is

$$= \quad x \quad / \quad + \quad \sim \quad b \quad \uparrow \quad - \quad \uparrow \quad b \quad 2 \quad \times \quad \times \quad 4 \quad a \quad c \quad \tfrac{1}{2} \quad \times \quad 2 \quad a.$$

You should verify yourself that the postfix form is

$$x \quad b \quad \sim \quad b \quad 2 \quad \uparrow \quad 4 \quad a \quad \times \quad c \quad \times \quad - \quad \tfrac{1}{2} \quad \uparrow \quad + \quad 2 \quad a \quad \times \quad / \quad = .$$

**Exercises
13.2**

(a) Draw the expression tree for each of the following expressions. Using the tree, convert the expression into **(b)** prefix and **(c)** postfix form. Use the table of priorities developed in this section, not those in C++.

E1. $a + b < c$

E2. $a < b + c$

E3. $a - b < c - d \; || \; e < f$

E4. $n! \, / \, (k! \times (n - k)!)$ (formula for binomial coefficients)

E5. $s = (n/2) \times (2 \times a + (n - 1) \times d)$ (This is the sum of the first n terms of an arithmetic progression.)

E6. $g = a \times (1 - r^n)/(1 - r)$ (sum of first n terms of a geometric progression)

E7. $a \; == \; 1 \; || \; b \times c \; == \; 2 \; || \; (a > 1 \; \&\& \; \text{not} \; b < 3)$

13.3 EVALUATION OF POLISH EXPRESSIONS

We first introduced the postfix form as a natural order of traversing an expression tree in order to evaluate the corresponding expression. Later in this section we shall formulate an algorithm for evaluating an expression directly from the postfix form, but first (since it is even simpler) we consider the prefix form.

13.3.1 Evaluation of an Expression in Prefix Form

Preorder traversal of a binary tree works from the top down. The root is visited first, and the remainder of the traversal is then divided into two parts. The natural way to organize the process is as a recursive, divide-and-conquer algorithm. The same situation holds for an expression in prefix form. The first symbol (if there is more than one) is an operator (the one that will actually be done last), and the remainder of the expression comprises the operand(s) of this operator (one for a unary operator, two for a binary operator). Our function for evaluating the prefix form should hence begin with this first symbol. If it is a unary operator, then the function should invoke itself recursively to determine the value of the operand. If the first symbol is a binary operator, then it should make two recursive calls for its two operands. The recursion terminates in the remaining case: When the first symbol is a simple operand, it is its own prefix form and the function should only return its value. Of course, if there is no first symbol, we must generate an Error_code.

The following outline thus summarizes the evaluation of an expression in prefix form:

Error_code Expression :: evaluate_prefix(Value &result)
/* *Outline of a method to perform prefix evaluation of an* Expression. *The details depend on further decisions about the implementation of expressions and values.* */

outline
```
{
    if (the Expression is empty) return fail;
    else {
        remove the first symbol from the Expression, and
            store the value of the symbol as t;
        if (t is a unary operation) {
            Value the_argument;
            if (evaluate_prefix(the_argument) == fail) return fail;
            else result = the value of operation t applied to the_argument;
        }
        else if (t is a binary operation) {
            Value first_argument, second_argument;
            if (evaluate_prefix(first_argument) == fail) return fail;
            if (evaluate_prefix(second_argument) == fail) return fail;
            result = the value of operation t
                    applied to first_argument and second_argument;
        }
        else                    //  t is a numerical operand.
            result = the value of t;
    }
    return success;
}
```

13.3.2 C++ Conventions

To tie down the details in this outline, let us establish some conventions and rewrite the algorithm in C++. Expressions will be represented by a fleshed-out version of the following class:

```
class Expression {
public:
   Error_code evaluate_prefix(Value &result);
   Error_code get_token(Token &result);
   //   Add other methods.
private:
   //   Add data members to store an expression.
};
```

The operators and operands in our expression may well have names that are more than one character long; hence we do not scan the expression one character at a time. Instead we define a *token* to be a single operator or operand from the expression. In our programs, we shall represent tokens as objects of a **struct** Token.

To emphasize that evaluation methods scan through an expression only once, we shall employ another method

$$\text{Token Expression :: get\_token( );}$$

that will move through an expression removing and returning one token at a time. We shall need to know whether the token is an operand, a unary operator, or a binary operator, so we assume the existence of a Token method kind() that will return one of the values of the following enumerated type:

```
enum Token_type {
   operand, unaryop, binaryop  //   Add any other legitimate token types.
};
```

For simplicity we shall assume that all the operands and the results of evaluating the operators are of the same type, which for now we leave unspecified and call Value. In many applications, this type would be one of **int**, **double**, or **bool**.

Finally, we must assume the existence of three auxiliary functions that return a result of type Value. The first two,

```
Value do_unary(const Token &operation, const Value &the_argument);
Value do_binary(const Token &operation,
                const Value &first_argument, const Value &second_argument);
```

actually perform the given operation on their operand(s). They need to recognize the symbols used for the operation and the arguments and invoke the necessary machine-language instructions. Similarly,

Value get_value(**const** Token &operand);

returns the actual value of a numerical operand, and might need, for example, to convert a constant from decimal to binary form or look up the value of a variable. The actual form of these functions will depend very much on the application. We cannot settle all these questions here, but want only to concentrate on designing one important part of a compiler or expression evaluator.

13.3.3 C++ Function for Prefix Evaluation

With these preliminaries we can now specify more details in our outline, translating it into a C++ method to evaluate prefix expressions.

```
Error_code Expression :: evaluate_prefix(Value &result)
/* Post: If the Expression does not begin with a legal prefix expression, a code of
         fail is returned. Otherwise a code of success is returned, and the Expression
         is evaluated, giving the Value result. The initial tokens that are evaluated
         are removed from the Expression. */
{
  Token t;
  Value the_argument, first_argument, second_argument;
  if (get_token(t) ==  fail) return fail;
  switch (t.kind()) {
  case unaryop:
    if (evaluate_prefix(the_argument) ==  fail) return fail;
    else result = do_unary(t, the_argument);
    break;
  case binaryop:
    if (evaluate_prefix(first_argument) ==  fail) return fail;
    if (evaluate_prefix(second_argument) ==  fail) return fail;
    else result = do_binary(t, first_argument, second_argument);
    break;
  case operand:
    result = get_value(t);
    break;
  }
  return success;
}
```

13.3.4 Evaluation of Postfix Expressions

It is almost inevitable that the prefix form should naturally call for a recursive function for its evaluation, since the prefix form is really a "top-down" formulation of the algebraic expression: The outer, overall actions are specified first, then later in the expression the component parts are spelled out. On the other hand, in the *comparison with prefix evaluation* postfix form the operands appear first, and the whole expression is slowly built up from its simple operands and the inner operators in a "bottom-up" fashion. Therefore, iterative programs using stacks appear more natural for the postfix form. (It is, of course, possible to write either recursive or nonrecursive programs for either form. We are here discussing only the motivation, or what first appears more natural.)

To evaluate an expression in postfix form, it is necessary to remember the operands until their operator is eventually found some time later. The natural way *stacks* to remember them is to put them on a stack. Then when the first operator to be applied is encountered, it will find its operands on the top of the stack. If it puts its result back on the stack, then its result will be in the right place to be an operand for a later operator. When the evaluation is complete, the final result will be the only value on the stack. In this way, we obtain a function to evaluate a postfix expression.

At this time we should note a significant difference between postfix and prefix expressions. There was no need, in the prefix function, to check explicitly that the end of the expression had been reached, since the entire expression automatically constituted the operand(s) for the first operator. Reading a postfix expression from left to right, however, we can encounter sub-expressions that are, by themselves, legitimate postfix expressions. For example, if we stop reading

$$b \quad 2 \quad \uparrow \quad 4 \quad a \quad \times \quad c \quad \times \quad -$$

after the '↑,' we find that it is a legal postfix expression. To remedy this problem we shall assume that a special token such as ';' marks the end of a postfix expression. Of course, this new token does not belong to any of the previous categories allowed by Token_type. Therefore, we shall augment the enumerated Token_type to include a new value **end_expression**. The other C++ classes and auxiliary functions are the same as for the prefix evaluation method.

```
typedef Value Stack_entry;     //   Set the type of entry to use in stacks.
Error_code Expression :: evaluate_postfix(Value &result)
/* Post: The tokens in Expression up to the first end_expression symbol are re-
         moved. If these tokens do not represent a legal postfix expression, a code
         of fail is returned. Otherwise a code of success is returned, and the re-
         moved sequence of tokens is evaluated to give Value result. */
{
   Token t;                    //   Current operator or operand
   Stack operands;             //   Holds values until operators are seen
   Value the_argument, first_argument, second_argument;
```

```
do {
  if (get_token(t) == fail) return fail;  //   No end_expression token
  switch (t.kind()) {
  case unaryop:
    if (operands.empty()) return fail;
    operands.top(the_argument);
    operands.pop();
    operands.push(do_unary(t, the_argument));
    break;
  case binaryop:
    if (operands.empty()) return fail;
    operands.top(second_argument);
    operands.pop();
    if (operands.empty()) return fail;
    operands.top(first_argument);
    operands.pop();
    operands.push(do_binary(t, first_argument, second_argument));
    break;
  case operand:
    operands.push(get_value(t));
    break;
  case end_expression:
    break;
  }
} while (t.kind() != end_expression);
if (operands.empty()) return fail;
operands.top(result);
operands.pop();
if (!operands.empty()) return fail;  //   surplus operands detected
return success;
}
```

13.3.5 Proof of the Program: Counting Stack Entries

So far we have given only an informal motivation for the preceding program, and
it may not be clear that it will produce the correct result in every case. Fortunately
it is not difficult to give a formal justification of the program and, at the same time,
to discover a useful criterion as to whether an expression is properly written in
postfix form or not.

The method we shall use is to keep track of the number of entries in the stack.
When each operand is obtained, it is immediately pushed onto the stack. A unary
operator first pops, then pushes the stack, and thus makes no change in the number
of entries. A binary operator pops the stack twice and pushes it once, giving a net
decrease of one entry in the stack. More formally, we have the following:

running-sum condition

> *For a sequence E of operands, unary operators, and binary operators, form a running sum by starting with 0 at the left end of E and counting +1 for each operand, 0 for each unary operator, and −1 for each binary operator. E satisfies the **running-sum condition** provided that this running sum never falls below 1 and is exactly 1 at the right-hand end of E.*

The sequence of running sums for the postfix form of an expression is illustrated in Figure 13.2.

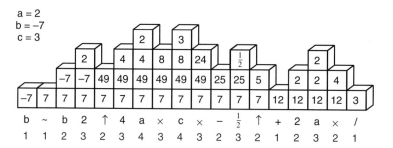

Figure 13.2. Stack frames and running sums, quadratic formula

We shall prove the next two theorems at the same time.

Theorem 13.1

> *If E is a properly formed expression in postfix form, then E must satisfy the running sum condition.*

Theorem 13.2

> *A properly formed expression in postfix form will be correctly evaluated by the method* evaluate_postfix.

Proof We shall prove the theorems together by using mathematical induction on the length of the expression E being evaluated.

induction proof
The starting point for the induction is the case that E is a single operand alone, with length 1. This operand contributes +1, and the running-sum condition is satisfied. The method, when applied to a simple operand alone, gets its value, pushes it on the stack (which was previously empty) and at the end pops it as the final value of the method, thereby evaluating it correctly.

induction hypothesis
For the induction hypothesis we now assume that E is a properly formed postfix expression of length more than 1, that the program correctly evaluates all postfix expressions of length less than that of E, and that all such shorter expressions satisfy the running-sum condition. Since the length of E is more than 1, E is constructed at its last step either as F op, where op is a unary operator and F a postfix expression, or as F G op, where op is a binary operator and F and G are postfix expressions.

In either case the lengths of F and G are less than that of E, so by induction hypothesis both of them satisfy the running-sum condition, and the method would evaluate either of them separately and would obtain the correct result.

unary operator   First, take the case when *op* is a unary operator. Since *F* satisfies the running-sum condition, the sum at its end is exactly +1. As a unary operator, *op* contributes 0 to the sum, so the full expression *E* satisfies the running-sum condition. When the method reaches the end of *F*, similarly, it will, by induction hypothesis, have evaluated *F* correctly and left its value as the unique stack entry. The unary operator *op* is then finally applied to this value, which is popped as the final result.

binary operator   Finally, take the case when *op* is binary, so *E* has the form *F G op* when *F* and *G* are postfix expressions. When the method reaches the last token of *F*, then the value of *F* will be the unique entry on the stack. Similarly, the running sum will be 1. At the next token the program starts to evaluate *G*. By the induction hypothesis the evaluation of *G* will also be correct and its running sum alone never falls below 1, and ends at exactly 1. Since the running sum at the end of *F* is 1, the combined running sum never falls below 2, and ends at exactly 2 at the end of *G*. Thus the evaluation of *G* will proceed and never disturb the single entry on the bottom of the stack, which is the result of *F*. When the evaluation reaches the final binary operator *op*, the running sum is correctly reduced from 2 to 1, and the operator finds precisely its two operands on the stack, where after evaluation it leaves its *end of proof*   unique result. This completes the proof of Theorems 13.1 and 13.2. ∎

Theorem 13.1 allows us to verify that a sequence of tokens is in fact a properly formed postfix expression by keeping a running count of the number of entries on the stack. This error checking is especially useful because its converse is also true:

Theorem 13.3   *If E is any sequence of operands and operators that satisfies the running-sum condition, then E is a properly formed expression in postfix form.*

Proof   We shall again use mathematical induction to prove Theorem 13.3. The starting point is an expression containing only one token. Since the running sum (same as final sum) for a sequence of length 1 will be 1, this one token must be a simple operand. One simple operand alone is indeed a syntactically correct expression.

induction proof   Now for the inductive step, suppose that the theorem has been verified for all expressions strictly shorter than *E*, and *E* has length greater than 1. If the last token of *E* were an operand, then it would contribute +1 to the sum, and since the final *case: operand*   sum is 1, the running sum would have been 0 one step before the end, contrary to the assumption that the running-sum condition is satisfied. Thus the final token of *E* must be an operator.

case: unary operator   If the operator is unary, then it can be omitted and the remaining sequence still satisfies the condition on running sums. Therefore, by induction hypothesis, it is a syntactically correct expression, and all of *E* then also is.

case: binary operator   Finally suppose that the last token is a binary operator *op*. To show that *E* is syntactically correct, we must find where in the sequence the first operand of *op* ends and the second one starts, by using the running sum. Since the operator *op* contributes −1 to the sum, it was 2 one step before the end. This 2 means that there were two items on the stack, the first and second operands of *op*. As we step backward through the sequence *E*, eventually we will reach a place where there is only one entry on the stack (running sum 1), and this one entry will be the first operand of *op*. Thus the place to break the sequence is at the last position before the end where the running sum is exactly 1. Such a position must exist, since at the far left end of E (if not before) we will find a running sum of 1. When we break E at its last 1, then it takes the form $F\ G\ op$. The subsequence F satisfies the condition on running sums, and ends with a sum of 1, so by induction hypothesis it is a correctly formed postfix expression. Since the running sums during G of $F\ G$ op never again fall to 1, and end at 2 just before op, we may subtract 1 from each of them and conclude that the running sums for G alone satisfy the condition. Thus by induction hypothesis G is also a correctly formed postfix expression. Thus both F and G are correct expressions and can be combined by the binary operator op

end of proof   into a correct expression E. Thus the proof of the theorem is complete.   ∎

We can take the proof one more step, to show that the last position where a sum of 1 occurs is the *only* place where the sequence E can be split into syntactically correct subsequences F and G. For suppose it was split elsewhere. If at the end of F the running sum is not 1, then F is not a syntactically correct expression. If the running sum is 1 at the end of F, but reaches 1 again during the G part of $F\ G\ op$, then the sums for G alone would reach 0 at that point, so G is not correct. We have now shown that there is only one way to recover the two operands of a binary operator. Clearly there is only one way to recover the single operand for a unary operator. Hence we can recover the infix form of an expression from its postfix form, together with the order in which the operations are done, which we can denote by bracketing the result of every operation in the infix form with another pair of parentheses.

We have therefore proved the following:

Theorem 13.4   *An expression in postfix form that satisfies the running-sum condition corresponds to exactly one fully bracketed expression in infix form. Hence no parentheses are needed to achieve the unique representation of an expression in postfix form.*

Similar theorems hold for the prefix form; their proofs are left as exercises. The preceding theorems provide both a theoretical justification of the use of Polish notation and a convenient way to check an expression for correct syntax.

13.3.6 Recursive Evaluation of Postfix Expressions

Most people find that the recursive function for evaluating prefix expressions is easier to understand than the stack-based, nonrecursive function for evaluating postfix expressions. In this (optional) section we show how the stack can be eliminated in favor of recursion for postfix evaluation.

First, however, let us see why the natural approach leads to a recursive function for prefix evaluation but not for postfix. We can describe both prefix and postfix expressions by the syntax diagrams of Figure 13.3. In both cases there are three possibilities: The expression consists of only a single operand, or the outermost operator is unary, or it is binary.

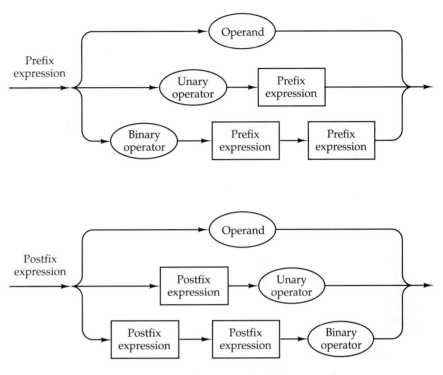

Figure 13.3. Syntax diagrams of Polish expressions

prefix evaluation   In tracing through the diagram for prefix form, the first token we encounter in the expression determines which of the three branches we take, and there are then no further choices to make (except within recursive calls, which need not be considered just now). Hence the structure of the recursive function for prefix evaluation closely resembles the syntax diagram.

postfix evaluation   With the postfix diagram, however, there is no way to tell from the first token (which will always be an operand) which of the three branches to take. It is only when the last token is encountered that the branch is determined. This fact does, however, lead to one easy recursive solution: Read the expression from right to left, reverse all the arrows on the syntax diagram, and use the essentially the same function as for prefix evaluation! (Of course, in the new function we have to reverse the order of arguments of operators such as − and /.)

   If we wish, however, to read the expression in the usual way from left to right, then we must work harder. Let us consider separately each of the three kinds of tokens in a postfix form. We have already observed that the first token in the expression must be an operand; this follows directly from the fact that the running sum after the first token is (at least) 1. Since unary operators do not change the running sum, unary operators can be inserted anywhere after the initial operand. It is the third case, binary operators, whose study leads to the solution.

running sum   Consider the sequence of running sums and the place(s) in the sequence where the sum drops from 2 to 1. Since binary operators contribute −1 to the sum, such places must exist if the postfix expression contains any binary operators, and they must correspond to the places in the expression where the two operands of the binary operator constitute the whole expression to the left. Such situations are illustrated in the stack frames of Figure 13.2. The entry on the bottom of the stack is the first operand; a sequence of positions where the height is at least 2, starting and ending at exactly 2, make up the calculation of the second operand. Taken in isolation, this sequence is itself a properly formed postfix expression. A drop in height from 2 to 1 marks one of the binary operators in which we are interested.

After the binary operator, more unary operators may appear, and then the process may repeat itself (if the running sums again increase) with more sequences that are self-contained postfix expressions followed by binary and unary operators. In summary, we have shown that postfix expressions are described by the syntax diagram of Figure 13.4, which translates easily into the recursive function that follows. The C++ conventions are the same as in the previous functions.

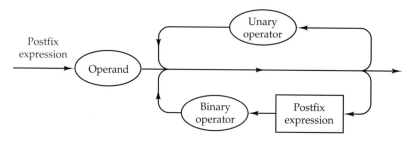

Figure 13.4. Alternative syntax diagram, postfix expression

left recursion   The situation appearing in the postfix diagram of Figure 13.3 is called **left recursion**, and the steps we have taken in the transition to the diagram in Figure 13.4 are typical of those needed to remove left recursion.

First is a function that initiates the recursion.

Error_code Expression :: evaluate_postfix(Value &result)
/* **Post:** *The tokens in* Expression *up to the first* end_expression *symbol are removed. If these tokens do not represent a legal postfix expression, a code of* fail *is returned. Otherwise a code of* success *is returned, and the removed sequence of tokens is evaluated to give* Value result. */

```
{
  Token first_token, final_token;
  Error_code outcome;
  if (get_token(first_token) ==  fail || first_token.kind() != operand)
    outcome = fail;
  else {
    outcome = recursive_evaluate(first_token, result, final_token);
    if (outcome ==  success && final_token.kind() != end_expression)
      outcome = fail;
  }
  return outcome;
}
```

The actual recursion uses the value of the first token separately from the remainder of the expression.

```
Error_code Expression :: recursive_evaluate(const Token &first_token,
                                            Value &result, Token &final_token)
/* Pre:  Token first_token is an operand.
   Post: If the first_token can be combined with initial tokens of the Expression
         to yield a legal postfix expression followed by either an end_expression
         symbol or a binary operator, a code of success is returned, the legal postfix
         subexpresssion is evaluated, recorded in result, and the terminating Token
         is recorded as final_token. Otherwise a code of fail is returned. The initial
         tokens of Expression are removed.
   Uses: Methods of classes Token and Expression, including recursive_evaluate
         and functions do_unary, do_binary, and get_value. */
{
  Value first_segment = get_value(first_token),
        next_segment;
  Error_code outcome;
  Token current_token;
  Token_type current_type;
  do {
    outcome = get_token(current_token);
    if (outcome != fail) {
      switch (current_type = current_token.kind()) {
      case binaryop:         //   Binary operations terminate subexpressions.
      case end_expression:   //   Treat subexpression terminators together.
        result = first_segment;
        final_token = current_token;
        break;
      case unaryop:
        first_segment = do_unary(current_token, first_segment);
        break;
      case operand:
        outcome = recursive_evaluate(current_token,
                                     next_segment, final_token);
        if (outcome == success && final_token.kind() != binaryop)
          outcome = fail;
        else
          first_segment = do_binary(final_token, first_segment,
                                    next_segment);
        break;
      }
    }
  } while (outcome == success && current_type != end_expression &&
                                 current_type != binaryop);
  return outcome;
}
```

Exercises 13.3

E1. Trace the action on each of the following expressions by the function evaluate_postfix in **(a)** nonrecursive and **(b)** recursive versions. For the recursive function, draw the tree of recursive calls, indicating at each node which tokens are being processed. For the nonrecursive function, draw a sequence of stack frames showing which tokens are processed at each stage.

(a) a b $+$ c $\times$

(b) a b c $+$ $\times$

(c) a $!$ b $!$ $/$ c d $-$ a $!$ $-$ $\times$

(d) a b $<$ $!$ c d $\times$ $<$ e $||$

E2. Trace the action of the function evaluate_prefix on each of the following expressions by drawing a tree of recursive calls showing which tokens are processed at each stage.

(a) $/$ $+$ x y $!$ n

(b) $/$ $+$ $!$ x y n

(c) $\&\&$ $<$ x y $||$ $!$ $=$ $+$ x y z $>$ x 0

E3. Which of the following are syntactically correct postfix expressions? Show the error in each incorrect expression. Translate each correct expression into infix form, using parentheses as necessary to avoid ambiguities.

(a) a b c $+$ $\times$ a $/$ c b $+$ d $/$ $-$

(b) a b $+$ c a $\times$ b c $/$ d $-$

(c) a b $+$ c a $\times$ $-$ c $\times$ $+$ b c $-$

(d) a $\sim$ b $\times$

(e) a $\times$ b $\sim$

(f) a b $\times$ $\sim$

(g) a b $\sim$ $\times$

E4. Translate each of the following expressions from prefix form into postfix form.

(a) $/$ $+$ x y $!$ n

(b) $/$ $+$ $!$ x y n

(c) $\&\&$ $<$ x y $||$ $!$ $=$ $+$ x y z $>$ x 0

E5. Translate each of the following expressions from postfix form into prefix form.

(a) a b $+$ c $\times$

(b) a b c $+$ $\times$

(c) a $!$ b $!$ $/$ c d $-$ a $!$ $-$ $\times$

(d) a b $<$ $!$ c d $\times$ $<$ e $||$

E6. Formulate and prove theorems analogous to Theorems **(a)** 13.1, **(b)** 13.3, and **(c)** 13.4 for the prefix form of expressions.

13.4 TRANSLATION FROM INFIX FORM TO POLISH FORM

Few programmers habitually write algebraic or logical expressions in Polish form, even though doing so might be more consistent and logical than the customary infix form. To make convenient use of the algorithms we have developed for evaluating Polish expressions, we must therefore develop an efficient method to translate arbitrary expressions from infix form into Polish notation.

As a first simplification, we shall consider only an algorithm for translating infix expressions into postfix form. Second, we shall not consider unary operators that are placed to the right of their operands. Such operators would cause no conceptual difficulty in the development of the algorithm, but they make the resulting function appear a little more complicated.

One method that we might consider for developing our algorithm would be, first, to build the expression tree from the infix form, and then to traverse the tree to obtain the postfix form. It turns out, however, that building the tree from the infix form is actually more complicated than constructing the postfix form directly.

Since, in postfix form, all operators come after their operands, the task of translation from infix to postfix form amounts to moving operators so that they come after their operands instead of before or between them. In other words,

delaying operators

> *Delay each operator until its right-hand operand has been translated. Pass each simple operand through to the output without delay.*

This action is illustrated in Figure 13.5.

Infix form:

$$x + y \qquad \sim x \qquad x + y \times z$$

Postfix form:

$$x \; y \; + \qquad x \sim \qquad x \; y \; z \; \times \; +$$

Infix form:

$$x = (\sim b + (b \uparrow 2 - 4 \times a \times c) \uparrow \tfrac{1}{2}) \, / \, (2 \times a)$$

Postfix form:

$$x \; b \sim b \; 2 \uparrow 4 \; a \times c \times - \tfrac{1}{2} \uparrow + 2 \; a \times / =$$

Figure 13.5. **Delaying operators in postfix form**

The major problem we must resolve is to find what token will terminate the right-hand operand of a given operator and thereby mark the place at which that operator should be placed. To do this, we must take both parentheses and priorities of operators into account.

The first problem is easy. If a left parenthesis is in the operand, then everything up to and including the matching right parenthesis must also be in the operand. For the second problem, that of taking account of the priorities of operators, we shall consider binary operators separately from operators of priority 6—namely, unary operators and exponentiation. The reason for this is that operators of priority 6 are evaluated from right to left, whereas binary operators of lower priority are evaluated from left to right.

finding the end of the right operand

Let op_1 be a binary operator of a priority evaluated from left to right, and let op_2 be the first nonbracketed operator to the right of op_1. If the priority of op_2 is less than or equal to that of op_1, then op_2 will not be part of the right operand of op_1, and its appearance will terminate the right operand of op_1. If the priority of op_2 is greater than that of op_1, then op_2 is part of the right operand of op_1, and we can continue through the expression until we find an operator of priority less than or equal to that of op_1; this operator will then terminate the right operand of op_1.

right-to-left evaluation

Next, suppose that op_1 has priority 6 (it is unary or exponentiation), and recall that operators of this priority are to be evaluated from right to left. If the first operand op_2 to the right of op_1 has equal priority, it therefore will be part of the right operand of op_1, and the right operand is terminated only by an operator of strictly smaller priority.

There are two more ways in which the right-hand operand of a given operator can terminate: The expression can end, or the given operator may itself be within a bracketed subexpression, in which case its right operand will end when an unmatched right parenthesis ')' is encountered. In summary, we have the following rules:

> If *op* is an operator in an infix expression, then its right-hand operand contains all tokens on its right until one of the following is encountered:
>
> 1. *the end of the expression;*
>
> 2. *an unmatched right parenthesis ')';*
>
> 3. *an operator of priority less than or equal to that of op, and not within a bracketed sub-expression, if op has priority less than 6; or*
>
> 4. *an operator of priority strictly less than that of op, and not within a bracketed subexpression, if op has priority 6.*

stack of operators

From these rules, we can see that the appropriate way to remember the operators being delayed is to keep them on a stack. If operator op_2 comes on the right of operator op_1 but has higher priority, then op_2 will be output before op_1 is. Thus the operators are output in the order last in, first out.

The key to writing an algorithm for the translation is to make a slight change in our point of view by asking, as each token appears in the input, which of the operators previously delayed (that is, on the stack) now have their right operands terminated because of the new token, so that it is time to move them into the output. The preceding conditions then become the following:

popping the stack

1. *At the end of the expression, all operators are output.*
2. *A right parenthesis causes all operators found since the corresponding left parenthesis to be output.*
3. *An operator of priority not 6 causes all other operators of greater or equal priority to be output.*
4. *An operator of priority 6 causes no operators to be output.*

To implement the second rule, we shall put each left parenthesis on the stack when it is encountered. Then, when the matching right parenthesis appears and the operators have been popped from the stack, the pair can both be discarded.

We can now incorporate these rules into a function. To do so, we shall use the same auxiliary types and functions as in the last section, except that now the method Token_type Token :: kind( ) can return two additional results:

leftparen   rightparen

that denote, respectively, left and right parentheses. The stack will now contain tokens (operators) rather than values.

In addition to the method Expression :: get_token( ) that obtains the next token from the input (infix expression), we use another method

void Expression :: put_token(**const** Token &t)

that puts the given token onto the end of a (postfix) expression. Thus these two methods might read and write with files or might only refer to lists already set up, depending on the desired application.

Finally, we shall use a new function

priority(**const** Token &operation)

that will return the priority of any Token that represents an operator.

With these conventions we can write a method that translates an expression from infix to postfix form. In this implementation, we have avoided the problem of checking whether the original expression is legal. Thus, we are forced to add this assumption as a precondition for the method.

```
Expression Expression :: infix_to_postfix( )
/* Pre:  The Expression stores a valid infix expression.
   Post: A postfix expression that translates the infix expression is returned. */
```

```
{
  Expression answer;
  Token current, prior;
  Stack delayed_operations;
  while (get_token(current) != fail) {
    switch (current.kind()) {
    case operand:
      answer.put_token(current);
      break;
    case leftparen:
      delayed_operations.push(current);
      break;
    case rightparen:
      delayed_operations.top(prior);
      while (prior.kind() != leftparen) {
        answer.put_token(prior);
        delayed_operations.pop();
        delayed_operations.top(prior);
      }
      delayed_operations.pop();
      break;
    case unaryop:
    case binaryop:               //   Treat all operators together.
      bool end_right = false; //   End of right operand reached?
      do {
        if (delayed_operations.empty()) end_right = true;
        else {
          delayed_operations.top(prior);
          if (prior.kind() == leftparen) end_right = true;
          else if (prior.priority() < current.priority()) end_right = true;
          else if (current.priority() == 6) end_right = true;
          else answer.put_token(prior);
          if (!end_right) delayed_operations.pop();
        }
      } while (!end_right);
      delayed_operations.push(current);
      break;
    }
  }
  while (!delayed_operations.empty()) {
    delayed_operations.top(prior);
    answer.put_token(prior);
    delayed_operations.pop();
  }
  answer.put_token(";");
  return answer;
}
```

example Figure 13.6 shows the steps performed to translate the quadratic formula

$$x = (\sim b + (b^2 - 4 \times a \times c)^{\frac{1}{2}})/(2 \times a)$$

into postfix form, as an illustration of this algorithm. (Recall that we are using '$\sim$' to denote unary negation.)

Input Token	Contents of Stack (rightmost token is on top)	Output Token(s)
x		x
$=$	$=$	
(	$=$ (	
$\sim$	$=$ ($\sim$	
b	$=$ ($\sim$	b
+	$=$ (+	$\sim$
(	$=$ (+ (	
b	$=$ (+ (	b
↑	$=$ (+ (↑	
2	$=$ (+ (↑	2
−	$=$ (+ (−	↑
4	$=$ (+ (−	4
×	$=$ (+ (− ×	
a	$=$ (+ (− ×	a
×	$=$ (+ (− ×	×
c	$=$ (+ (− ×	c
)	$=$ (+	× −
↑	$=$ (+ ↑	
$\frac{1}{2}$	$=$ (+ ↑	$\frac{1}{2}$
)	$=$	↑ +
/	$=$ /	
(	$=$ / (	
2	$=$ / (	2
×	$=$ / (×	
a	$=$ / (×	a
)	$=$ /	×
end of expression		/ =

Figure 13.6. Translation of the quadratic formula into postfix form

This completes the discussion of translation into postfix form. There will clearly be similarities in describing the translation into prefix form, but some difficulties arise because of the seemingly irrelevant fact that, in European languages, we read from left to right. If we were to translate an expression into prefix form working from left to right, then not only would the operators need to be rearranged but operands would need to be delayed until after their operators were output. But the relative order of operands is not changed in the translation, so the appropriate data structure to keep the operands would not be a stack (it would in fact be a queue). Since stacks would not do the job, neither would recursive programs with no explicit auxiliary storage, since these two kinds of programs can do equivalent tasks. Thus a left-to-right translation into prefix form would need a different approach. The trick is to translate into prefix form by working from right to left through the expression, using methods quite similar to the left-to-right postfix translation that we have developed. The details are left as an exercise.

Exercises 13.4

E1. Devise a method to translate an expression from prefix form into postfix form. Use the C++ conventions of this chapter.

E2. Write a method to translate an expression from postfix form into prefix form. Use the C++ conventions of this chapter.

E3. A *fully bracketed* expression is one of the following forms:

   i. a simple operand;

   ii. (*op E*) where *op* is a unary operator and *E* is a fully bracketed expression;

   iii. (*E op F*) where *op* is a binary operator and *E* and *F* are fully bracketed expressions.

Hence, in a fully bracketed expression, the results of every operation are enclosed in parentheses. Examples of fully bracketed expressions are $((a+b)-c)$, $(-a)$, $(a+b)$, $(a+(b+c))$. Write methods that will translate expressions from (a) prefix and (b) postfix form into fully bracketed form.

E4. Rewrite the method infix_to_postfix as a recursive function that uses no stack or other array.

Programming Project 13.4

P1. Construct a menu-driven demonstration program for Polish expressions. The input to the program should be an expression in any of infix, prefix, or postfix form. The program should then, at the user's request, translate the expression into any of fully bracketed infix, prefix, or postfix, and print the result. The operands should be single letters or digits only. The operators allowed are:

    binary: +   −   *   /   %   ∧   :   <   >   & | =

    left unary: #   ~

    right unary: !   ′   ″

Use the priorities given in the table on page 600, not those of C++. In addition, the program should allow parentheses '(' and ')' in infix expressions only. The meanings of some of the special symbols used in this project are:

&	Boolean **and** (same as **&&** in C++)	|	Boolean **or** (same as || in C++)
:	Assign (same as **=** in C++)	%	Modulus (binary operator)
∧	Exponentiation (same as ↑)	!	Factorial (on right)
'	Derivative (on right)	"	Second derivative (on right)
~	Unary negation	#	Boolean **not** (same as ! in C++)

13.5 AN INTERACTIVE EXPRESSION EVALUATOR

There are many applications for a program that can evaluate a function that is typed in interactively while the program is running. One such application is a program that will draw the graph of a mathematical function. Suppose that you are writing such a program to be used to help first-year calculus students graph functions. Most of these students will not know how to write or compile programs, so you wish to include in your program some way that the user can put in an expression for a function such as

$$x * \log(x) - x \wedge 1.25$$

while the program is running, which the program can then graph for appropriate values of x.

goal   The goal of this section is to describe such a program. We pay particular attention to two subprograms that help solve this problem. The first subprogram will take as input an expression involving constants, variable(s), arithmetic operators, and standard functions, with bracketing allowed, as typed in from the terminal. It will then translate the expression into postfix form and keep it in a list of tokens. The second subprogram will evaluate this postfix expression for values of the variable(s) given as its calling parameter(s) and return the answer, which can then be graphed.

purpose   We undertake this project for several reasons. It shows how to take the ideas already developed for working with Polish notation and build these ideas into a complete, concrete, and functioning program. In this way, the project illustrates a problem-solving approach to program design, in which we begin with solutions to the key questions and complete the structure with auxiliary functions as needed.

robustness   Finally, since this project is intended for use by people with little computer experience, it provides opportunity to test *robustness*; that is, the ability of the program to withstand unexpected or incorrect input without catastrophic failure.

13.5.1 Overall Structure

To allow the user flexibility in changing the graphing, let us make the program menu driven, so that the action of the main program has the following familiar form:

```
int main( )
/* Pre:   None
   Post:  Acts as a menu-driven graphing program.
   Uses:  Classes Expression and Plot, and functions introduction, get_command,
          and do_command. */
{
  introduction( );
  Expression infix;            //   Infix expression from user
  Expression postfix;          //   Postfix translation
  Plot graph;

  char ch;
  while ((ch = get_command( )) != 'q')
    do_command(ch, infix, postfix, graph);
}
```

In the main program, we use a pair of **Expression** objects to hold a user's infix expression and its postfix translation. We also make use of a class **Plot** to control all graphing activities. The division of work among various methods and functions is the task of **do_command**:

```
void do_command(char c, Expression &infix, Expression &postfix, Plot &graph)
/* Pre:   None
   Post:  Performs the user command represented by char c on the Expression infix,
          the Expression postfix, and the Plot graph.
   Uses:  Classes Token, Expression and Plot. */
{
  switch (c) {
  case 'r':                         //   Read an infix expression from the user.
    infix.clear( );
    infix.read( );
    if (infix.valid_infix( ) == success) postfix = infix.infix_to_postfix( );
    else cout << "Warning: Bad expression ignored. " << endl;
    break;
  case 'w':                         //   Write the current expression.
    infix.write( );
    postfix.write( );
    break;
  case 'g':                         //   Graph the current postfix expression.
    if (postfix.size( ) <= 0)
      cout << "Enter a valid expression before graphing!" << endl;
    else {
      graph.clear( );
      graph.find_points(postfix);
      graph.draw( );
    }
    break;
```

```
    case 'l':                    //   Set the graph limits.
        if (graph.set_limits( ) != success)
            cout << "Warning: Invalid limits" << endl;
        break;
    case 'p':                    //   Print the graph parameters.
        Token :: print_parameters( );
        break;
    case 'n':                    //   Set new graph parameters.
        Token :: set_parameters( );
        break;
    case 'h':                    //   Give help to user.
        help( );
        break;
    }
}
```

In response to the user command 'r', the program requests an expression and splits it apart into tokens. The method valid_infix( ) will determine whether the expression is syntactically correct. If so, it is converted into postfix form by the method infix_to_postfix( ) that we have already studied.

To graph an expression, in response to a user's command 'g', the postfix form is evaluated for many different values of the coordinate x, each value differing from the last by a small x_increment, and each result is plotted in turn as a single point on the screen.

The user can apply the command 'l' to select the domain of x values over which the graph will be plotted, the increment to use, and the range for showing the results of the expression evaluation. These values are kept within Plot graph and are reset with a method Plot :: set_limits( ).

expression parameters   In addition to the (independent) variable x used for plotting, an expression may contain further variables that we call *parameters* for the graph. For example, in the expression

$$a * \cos(x) + b * \sin(x),$$

a and b are parameters. The parameters will all retain fixed values while one graph is drawn, but these values can be changed, with the user command 'n', from one graph to the next without making any other change in the expression. The parameters will be stored as tokens, so we provide a static Token method set_parameters to reset values for all the parameters that appear in an expression.

Our program must also establish the definitions of the predefined tokens (such as the operators +, −, and *, amongst others, the operand x that will be used to represent a coordinate in the graphing, and perhaps some constants). However, before we can determine the details of these initializations, we must decide on data structures for tokens and expressions.

13.5.2 Representation of the Data: Class Specifications

Our first data-structure decisions concern how to store and retrieve the tokens used in Polish expressions. For each different token we must remember:

➡ Its name (as a **String**), so that we can recognize it in an input expression;

➡ Its kind, one of operand, unary operator, binary operator, and right unary operator (like factorial '!'), left parenthesis, or right parenthesis;

➡ For operators, a priority;

➡ For operands, a value.

It is reasonable to think of representing each token as a record containing this information. One small difficulty arises: The same token may appear several times in an expression. If it is an operand, then we must be certain that it is given the same value each time. If we put the records themselves into the expressions, then when a value is assigned to an operand we must be sure that it is updated in all the records corresponding to that operand.

lexicon

We can avoid having to keep chains of references to a given variable by associating an integer code with each token and placing this code in the expression, rather than the full record. We shall thus set up a *lexicon* for the tokens, which will include an array indexed by the integer codes; this array will hold the full records for the tokens. In this way, if k is the code for a variable, then every appearance of the variable in an expression will cause us to look in position k of the lexicon for the corresponding value, and we are automatically assured of getting the same value each time.

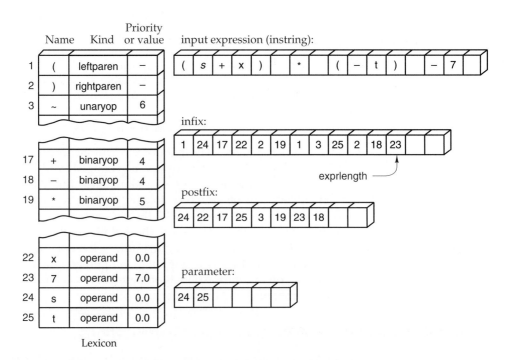

Figure 13.7. Data structures for tokens and expressions

We now introduce a structure to hold the token records that are stored as lexicon entries:

```
struct Token_record {
   String name;
   double value;
   int priority;
   Token_type kind;
};
```

In this structure, the member **name** that identifies a token is implemented with our **String** class of Section 6.3. Recall that **String** objects can be safely copied, passed across assignment operators, and compared by using the usual operators.

hash table

The lexicon must contain an array of **Token_record** objects; moreover, it must provide methods to locate a particular record, either from its integer code or from its name. We shall solve this information-retrieval problem by including a hash table called **index_code** as a member of the lexicon. In the hash table we shall store only codes and use these to look in the array of records to locate all the information about the token with a given name.

In a user's expression there will usually be no more than a few dozen tokens, and it is quite arguable that the best way to retrieve the code is by sequential search through the lexicon. Sequential search would be easy to program, would require no further data structures, and the cost in time over more sophisticated methods would be negligible.

symbol table

One of the objects of this project, however, is to illustrate larger applications, where the expense of sequential search may no longer be negligible. In a compiler, for example, there may be many hundreds of distinct symbols that must be recognized, and more sophisticated symbol tables must be used. A good choice is to use a hash table to make token names into integer codes.

We have now arrived at the following structure to represent the lexicon:

```
struct Lexicon {
   Lexicon();
   int hash(const String &x) const;
   void set_standard_tokens();   //   Set up the predefined tokens.
   int count;                    //   Number of records in the Lexicon
   int index_code[hash_size];    //   Declare the hash table.
   Token_record token_data[hash_size];
};
```

We can now return to the representation of tokens that we shall store in expressions. Every token should contain an integer code, representing the index of its **Token_record** in the array **token_data** of the Lexicon. This means that every **Token** needs access to the Lexicon, so that it can retrieve its associated record. We would, however, like to protect the Lexicon and its records from other access, to ensure

static data member

their integrity. We can accomplish both goals by declaring the Lexicon as a static data member of the **Token** class. Recall that a static data member is created and stored just once, but it can be accessed as a member of any object of the class.

We can now formulate the following outline of the **class Token**:

```
class Token {
public:

//    Add methods here.
private:
  int code;
  static Lexicon symbol_table;
  static List<int> parameters;
};
```

List<**int**> Token :: parameters;   //   *Allocate storage for static* Token *members.*
Lexicon Token :: symbol_table;

parameters

This **class** outline includes a second static data member, **parameters**, which holds a list of integer codes for those tokens that represent parameters. As an input expression is decoded, the program may find constants and new variables (parameters), which it will then add to the lexicon. These will all be classed as operands, but recall that, in the case of parameters, the user will be asked to give values before an expression is evaluated. To be able to prompt the user for these values, it is necessary to keep a list of those token codes that correspond to parameters. Because we shall need to have access to the parameter list from **Token** objects, it is convenient to declare **parameters** as another **static** data member of the **Token** class.

storage allocation for
static members

The two static members do not occupy storage within any **Token** object; therefore, storage must be allocated for them outside the class specification. Accordingly, we follow the class specification with appropriate definitions to reserve storage for the members **parameters** and **symbol_table**. These definitions will be processed at run time, before the **main** function starts to operate. This will ensure that the **List** and **Lexicon** constructors have carried out any required initializations before we ever start to use the objects **parameters** and **symbol_table**. Of course, when we create the **Lexicon symbol_table** we might add operands to the **List parameters**. Therefore, we must make sure to declare the **List parameters** before we declare the **Lexicon symbol_table**; in this way we ensure that the list is properly initialized before we start adding to it.

Placing tokens containing integer codes rather than records into expressions has the advantage of saving some space, but space for tokens is unlikely to be a critical restraint for this project. The time required to evaluate the postfix expression at many different values of the argument x is more likely to prove expensive.

We shall continue to use our earlier implementations of expressions as lists of tokens so that we can make use of our earlier efficient methods for translation and evaluation of expressions.

```
class Expression {
public:
//    Add method prototypes.
private:
  List<Token> terms;
  int current_term;
//    Add auxiliary function prototypes.
};
```

All these data structures are illustrated in Figure 13.7, along with some of the data structures used in the principal functions. A number of constants, auxiliary type specifications, and type identifications are needed along with these structures. Specifically, we need to create the enumerated type Token_type, declare and initialize the **const int** hash_size, and define the type identifier Value as a synonym for **double**. We must also include our earlier implementations of the classes String, List, and Stack. The classes String and List have already appeared in our specifications of tokens and expressions. Just as in Section 13.4, we shall need to use a Stack in translating expressions from infix to postfix form. Finally, our program uses a **class** Plot and other auxiliary graphing structures, which we shall discuss and implement later. We now consider the class implementations that we need for our program.

13.5.3 Tokens

Token methods

For consistency with the functions developed earlier in this chapter, we shall equip our **class** Token with a method kind() that reports the kind of a Token. For convenience, we shall use similar Token methods, priority(), name(), and value(), that report other token information. Moreover, a method code_number() will return a token's code.

Token constructors

We shall frequently need to produce a new Token object from its identification String: In other words, we shall need to recast the String as a Token. We can conveniently implement this cast operation as a Token constructor that takes a String argument. We also need to supply a second Token constructor with no arguments, which will be invoked when we declare but do not initialize a token. Finally, we shall need Token methods to set and examine the values of tokens representing parameters, and a method to assign a value to the coordinate x: These methods merely access or modify **static** data members and so have a modifier of **static** themselves. We have now settled on the following class:

```
class Token {
public:
  Token() {}
  Token (const String &x);
  Token_type kind() const;
  int priority() const;
  double value() const;
  String name() const;
  int code_number() const;
  static void set_parameters();
  static void print_parameters();
  static void set_x(double x_val);
private:
  int code;
  static Lexicon symbol_table;
  static List<int> parameters;
};
```

1. Accessing Token information

The methods that provide information about a token simply look in the Lexicon. For example, the method kind( ) is implemented as follows:

```
Token_type Token :: kind() const
{
    return symbol_table.token_data[code].kind;
}
```

2. Token Constructors and Initialization

The default constructor with no parameters does not assign an initial data code to a Token and so it is implemented with an empty code body. The other constructor takes a String argument and must assign an appropriate Token code. The String is first run through the method Lexicon :: hash, this hashing incorporates collision resolution and returns a location in the array Lexicon :: index_code. The resulting entry index_code[location] is either a previously assigned code for the String or the special code −1 indicating that the String has not been seen. In either case, the constructor can determine a correct initializing code to use as data in the new token.

```
Token :: Token(const String &identifier)
/* Post:  A Token corresponding to String identifier is constructed. It shares its code
          with any other Token object with this identifier.
     Uses: The class Lexicon. */
{
    int location = symbol_table.hash(identifier);
    if (symbol_table.index_code[location] == −1) {  //   Create a new record.
        code = symbol_table.count++;
        symbol_table.index_code[location] = code;
        symbol_table.token_data[code] = attributes(identifier);
        if (is_parameter(symbol_table.token_data[code]))
            parameters.insert(0, code);
    }
    else code = symbol_table.index_code[location];  //   Code of an old record
}
```

function attributes   The auxiliary function attributes examines the name of a token and sets up an appropriate Token_record according to our conventions. For example, if the parameter String identifier is "*", the function attributes returns a record including the data values: kind = binaryop and priority = 5. The implementation of attributes consists only of a series of assignment statements, which we omit. We should note that the function attributes merely provides a static initialization for each token, whereas the lexicon gives us dynamically changing information about tokens. For example, attributes will always assign a default value of 0.0 to a parameter, but the lexicon will record whatever value the user last entered.

function
is_parameter   The other auxiliary function is_parameter determines whether a Token is a parameter by examining its identifier.

3. Parameter Values

function set_parameters

Before evaluating an expression, we shall need to establish values for the parameters, if any. The function Token :: set_parameters that carries out this task traverses the list of parameters, printing information about each entry and requesting updated information from the user.

```
void Token :: set_parameters()
/* Post: All parameter values are printed for the user, and any changes specified
         by the user are made to these values.
   Uses: Classes List, Token_record, and String, and function read_num. */
{
  int n = parameters.size();
  int index_code;
  double x;
  for (int i = 0;  i < n;  i++) {
    parameters.retrieve(i, index_code);
    Token_record &r = symbol_table.token_data[index_code];
    cout  << "Give a new value for parameter "  << (r.name).c_str()
          << " with value "  << r.value << endl;
    cout  << "Enter a value or a new line to keep the old value: " << flush;
    if (read_num(x) ==  success) r.value = x;
  }
}
```

13.5.4 The Lexicon

The constructor of a Lexicon must set up the member hash table index_code[ ] as empty and then apply an auxiliary method Lexicon :: set_standard_tokens to enter information about all the predefined tokens. Thus the constructor takes the form

```
Lexicon :: Lexicon()
/* Post: The Lexicon is initialized with the standard tokens.
   Uses: set_standard_tokens */
{
  count = 0;
  for (int i = 0;  i < hash_size;  i++)
    index_code[i] = −1;      //   code for an empty hash slot
  set_standard_tokens();
}
```

function set_standard_tokens

The complete list of predefined tokens to be entered by set_standard_tokens is shown in Figure 13.8. Note that we include operations that are not a standard part of a computer language (such as the base 2 logarithm lg) and constants such as e and π. The expressions in which we are interested in this section always have real numbers as their results. Hence we do not include any Boolean valued operations.

Token	Name	Kind	Priority/Value	
0	;	end_expression		
1	(	leftparen		
2	)	rightparen		
3	~	unaryop	6	*negation*
4	abs	unaryop	6	
5	sqr	unaryop	6	
6	sqrt	unaryop	6	
7	exp	unaryop	6	
8	ln	unaryop	6	*natural logarithm*
9	lg	unaryop	6	*base 2 logarithm*
10	sin	unaryop	6	
11	cos	unaryop	6	
12	arctan	unaryop	6	
13	round	unaryop	6	
14	trunc	unaryop	6	
15	!	right unary	6	*factorial*
16	%	right unary	6	*percentage*
17	+	binaryop	4	
18	−	binaryop	4	
19	∗	binaryop	5	
20	/	binaryop	5	
21	∧	binaryop	6	
22	x	operand	0.00000	
23	pi	operand	3.14159	
24	e	operand	2.71828	

Figure 13.8. Predefined tokens for expression evaluation

In the following implementation, of Lexicon :: set_standard_tokens, we initialize a **String** to contain a list of all standard tokens, separated by spaces. We apply a function

get_word(**const** String &s, **int** n, String &t);

word: definition that finds the nth word in the **String** s and writes it to the **String** t. Here a word is defined to be any sequence of characters that does not contain a blank. The token named by this word is automatically added to the lexicon by use of the **Token** constructor. Of course, the token constructor calls the function **attributes** to look up the initial data record for the new token.

```
void Lexicon :: set_standard_tokens( )
{
   int i = 0;
   String symbols = (String)
      "; ( ) ˜ abs sqr sqrt exp ln lg sin cos arctan round trunc ! % + − * / ˆ x pi e";
   String word;
   while (get_word(symbols, i++, word) != fail) {
      Token t = word;
   }
   token_data[23].value = 3.14159;
   token_data[24].value = 2.71828;
}
```

1. Hash Table Processing

We need to devise the hash function used for indexing. Recall that, while the array Lexicon :: token_data takes an index and returns a token name and information about the token, the hash table Lexicon :: index_code takes a token name and returns an index.

It is often the case that the performance of a hash function can be enhanced by taking into account the application for which it will be used. In our graphing program many of the tokens are single characters (some letters and some one-character operators). The hash function that we develop therefore gives special emphasis to this fact.

```
int Lexicon :: hash(const String &identifier) const
/* Post:  Returns the location in table Lexicon :: index_code that corresponds to the
          String identifier. If the hash table is full and does not contain a record for
          identifier, the exit function is called to terminate the program.
   Uses: The class String, the function exit. */
{
   int location;
   const char *convert = identifier.c_str( );
   char first = convert[0], second;   //   First two characters of identifier
   if (strlen(convert) >= 2) second = convert[1];
   else second = first;
   location = first % hash_size;
   int probes = 0;
   while (index_code[location] >= 0 &&
          identifier != token_data[index_code[location]].name) {
      if (++probes >= hash_size) {
         cout << "Fatal Error: Hash Table overflow. Increase table size\n";
         exit(1);
      }
      location += second;
      location %= hash_size;
   }
   return location;
}
```

In this function we have responded to a hash table overflow by calling the system function `exit` from `<cstdlib>` to terminate the whole program, after printing a diagnostic message. Our program does not include any way for a user to discard data from the lexicon, and therefore once overflow occurs, there are no useful recovery options available. If we wished to upgrade the program to allow for deletion from the lexicon, the most convenient way to respond to overflow in the hash function would be to throw an exception.[1]

13.5.5 Expressions: Token Lists

required methods

We have already decided to represent expressions (both infix and postfix) with lists of token codes. Hence we may utilize the standard list operations. Our expressions must admit the methods get_token, put_token, infix_to_postfix, evaluate_postfix and recursive_evaluate that we used and developed earlier in the chapter. In addition, we shall certainly need methods to read, write, clear, and count the number of tokens in an expression.

error checking

In order to deal effectively with user errors, it is necessary to add a method valid_infix() to check whether an infix expression is syntactically valid. Finally, because the method get_token moves progressively forward through an expression, we shall need a method rewind to move back to the beginning of an expression. This method will need to be called when a user wants to graph the same function twice, with different graph limits or parameters. Hence, the specification for **class** Expression takes the form:

```
class Expression {
public:
  Expression();
  Expression(const Expression &original);
  Error_code get_token(Token &next);
  void put_token(const Token &next);
  Expression infix_to_postfix();
  Error_code evaluate_postfix(Value &result);
  void read();
  void clear();
  void write();
  Error_code valid_infix();
  int size();
  void rewind();
private:
  List<Token> terms;
  int current_term;
  Error_code recursive_evaluate(const Token &first_token,
                                Value &result, Token &final_token);
};
```

---

[1] We have not used exceptions in this book, but they are explained in advanced C++ textbooks.

1. Manipulating the Token List

The method **get_token** retrieves tokens from an **Expression** as it proceeds. In order to move forward through the **Expression**, it increments the data member current_term.

Error_code Expression :: get_token(Token &next)
/* **Post:** *The* Token next *records the* current_term *of the* Expression, current_term *is incremented, and an error code of* success *is returned, or if there is no such term a code of* fail *is returned.*
   Uses: *Class* List. */
{
  if (terms.retrieve(current_term, next) != success) **return** fail;
  current_term++;
  return success;
}

Similarly, the method **put_token** needs only to insert a token at the end of the expression's list, and the method **rewind** resets current_term to 0.

2. Reading an Expression

The method **Expression :: read** is used to read an expression in ordinary (infix) form, split it apart into tokens, and place their codes into the **Expression**.

input format   We must now establish conventions regarding the input format. Let us assume that an input expression is typed as one line, so that when we reach the end of the line, we have also reached the end of the input string. Let us use the conventions of C++ concerning spaces: Blanks are ignored between tokens, but the occurrence of a blank terminates a token. If a token is a word, then it begins with a letter, which can be followed by letters or digits.

Thus to read an expression we read a line of text with the **String** function **read_in** that we developed in Section 6.3. We apply a function **add_spaces** that inserts spaces on either side of every operator and separator in the input **String**: This ensures that the tokens appear as words of the **String**. Therefore, we can split the text apart with the **String** function **get_word**. We can finish by casting the individual words into tokens with our **Token** constructor. With this strategy, we obtain the following function:

void Expression :: read( )
/* **Post:** *A line of text, entered by the user, is split up into tokens and stored in the* Expression.
   Uses: *Classes* String, Token, *and* List. */

```
    {
      String input, word;
      int term_count = 0;
      int x;
      input = read_in(cin, x);
      add_spaces(input);           //   Tokens are now words of input.
      bool leading = true;
      for (int i = 0; get_word(input, i, word) != fail; i++) {  //   Process next token
        if (leading)
          if (word == "+") continue;                  //   unary +
          else if (word == "-") word = "~";           //   unary -
        Token current = word;
                                   //   Cast word to Token.
        terms.insert(term_count++, current);
        Token_type type = current.kind();
        if (type == leftparen || type == unaryop || type == binaryop)
          leading = true;
        else
          leading = false;
      }
    }
```

The method **read** contains a section of code that needs further explanation. This concerns the two symbols '+' and '−,' which can be either unary or binary operators. We introduce the Boolean variable **leading** to tell us which case occurs.

leading position   The value of **leading** detects whether an operator has a left argument. We shall show that if **leading** is true, then the current token can have no left argument and therefore cannot legally be a binary operator. In this way, our method is able to distinguish between unary and binary versions of the operators + and −. We shall take no action for a unary '+,' since it has no effect, and we replace a unary '−' by our private notation '~.' Note, however, that this change is local to our program. The user is not required—or even allowed—to use the symbol '~' for unary negation.

3. Leading and Non-Leading Positions

To motivate the inclusion of the variable **leading**, let us first consider a special case. Suppose that an expression is made up only from simple operands and binary operators, with no parentheses or unary operators. Then the only syntactically correct expressions are of the form

$$operand \quad binaryop \quad operand \quad binaryop \quad \ldots \quad operand$$

leading positions   where the first and last tokens are operands, and the two kinds of tokens alternate. It is illegal for two operands to be adjacent or for two binary operators to be adjacent. In the leading position there must be an operand, as there must be after each operator, so we can consider these positions also as "leading," since the preceding operator must lead to an operand.

Now suppose that unary operators are to be inserted into the preceding expression. Any number of left unary operators can be placed before any operand, but it is illegal to place a left unary operator immediately before a binary operator. That is, unary operators that go on the left can appear exactly where operands are allowed, in leading positions but only there. On the other hand, the appearance of a left unary operator leaves the position still as a "leading" position, since an operand must still appear before a binary operator becomes legal.

	Previous token *any one of:*	*Legal tokens* *any one of:*
Leading position:		
	start of expression binary operator unary operator left parenthesis	operand unary operator left parenthesis
Nonleading position:		
	operand right unary operator right parenthesis	binary operator right unary operator right parenthesis end of expression

Figure 13.9. Tokens legal in leading and nonleading positions

Right unary operators, similarly, can be placed in any non-leading position (that is, after operands or other right-unary operators), and the appearance of a right unary operator leaves the position as non-leading, since a binary operator must appear before another operand becomes legal.

Let us now, finally, also allow parentheses in the expression. A bracketed sub-expression is treated as an operand and, therefore, can appear exactly where operands are legal. Hence left parentheses can appear exactly in leading positions and leave the position as leading, and right parentheses can appear only in nonleading positions and leave the position as nonleading.

All the possibilities are summarized in Figure 13.9.

4. Error Checking for Correct Syntax

error checking It is in reading the input string that the greatest amount of error checking is needed to make sure that the syntax of the input expression is correct, and to make our program as robust as possible. This error checking will be done in a subsidiary method valid_infix, which checks for proper kinds of tokens in leading and non-leading positions. The following function also checks that parentheses are properly balanced:

```
Error_code Expression :: valid_infix( )
/* Post: A code of success or fail is returned according to whether the Expression
         is a valid or invalid infix sequence.
   Uses: Class Token. */
{
  Token current;
  bool leading = true;
  int paren_count = 0;
  while (get_token(current) != fail) {
    Token_type type = current.kind( );
    if (type ==  rightparen || type ==  binaryop || type ==  rightunaryop) {
      if (leading) return fail;
    }
    else if (!leading) return fail;
    if (type ==  leftparen) paren_count++;
    else if (type ==  rightparen) {
      paren_count--;
      if (paren_count < 0) return fail;
    }
    if (type ==  binaryop || type ==  unaryop || type ==  leftparen)
      leading = true;
    else leading = false;
  }
  if (leading) return fail;         //   An expected final operand is missing.
  if (paren_count > 0) return fail;  //   Right parentheses are missing.
  rewind( );
  return success;
}
```

5. Translation into Postfix Form

At the conclusion of the method **read( )**, the input expression has been converted into an infix sequence of tokens, in the form needed by function **infix_to_postfix** as derived in Section 13.4. In fact, we now arrive at the key step of our algorithm and can apply the previous work with just the minor change needed to allow for right unary operators.

When the method **infix_to_postfix** has finished, the output expression is a sequence of tokens in postfix form, and it can be evaluated efficiently in the next stage. This efficiency, in fact, is important so that a graph can be drawn without undue delay, even though it requires evaluation of the expression for a great many different values.

6. Postfix Evaluation

To evaluate a postfix expression, we again use a method developed in the first part of this chapter. Either the recursive or the nonrecursive version of the method evaluate_postfix can be used, again with no significant change. Of course, evaluate_postfix requires subsidiary functions get_value, do_unary, and do_binary, to which we next turn.

13.5.6 Auxiliary Evaluation Functions

In evaluating postfix expressions, we need auxiliary functions to evaluate operands and apply tokens that represent operators.

1. Evaluation of Operands

The function get_value need only call Token::value():

```
Value get_value(const Token &current)
/* Pre:   Token current is an operand.
   Post:  The Value of current is returned.
   Uses:  Methods of class Token. */
{
   return current.value();
}
```

2. Operators

Since we have integer codes for all the tokens, the application of operators can be done within a simple but long **switch** statement. We leave the one for unary operators as an exercise. For binary operators, we have the following function:

```
Value do_binary(const Token &operation,
                const Value &first_argument, const Value &second_argument)
/* Pre:   Token operation is a binary operator.
   Post:  The Value of operation applied to the pair of Value parameters is returned.
   Uses:  Methods of class Token. */
{
   switch (operation.code_number()) {
   case 17:
      return first_argument + second_argument;
   case 18:
      return first_argument – second_argument;
   case 19:
      return first_argument * second_argument;
   case 20:
      return first_argument/second_argument;
   case 21:
      return exp(first_argument, second_argument);
   }
}
```

exponentiation The exponentiation function, **exp(double)**, is supplied by one of the standard libraries <math.h> and <cmath>.

13.5.7 Graphing the Expression: The Class Plot

Now we come, finally, to the purpose of the entire program, graphing the expression on the computer screen. Graphics libraries in C++ are entirely system dependent, so what works on one machine may not necessarily work on another. We therefore begin with a system-independent approach that uses ordinary characters to draw crude graphs. The resulting **class** Plot can easily be replaced by more sophisticated implementations that make use of system graphics capabilities. Later, we shall illustrate an implementation of such an augmented **class** Plot that is appropriate for use with the Borland C++[2] compiler.

1. The Class Plot

The data members in a Plot object are used to store the graph limits and the data points to be plotted. The limits can simply be stored as floating-point data members x_low, x_high, y_low, and y_high. Another floating-point data member, x_increment, sets the gap between the x coordinates of successive data points.

When we come to draw a graph, we shall need to sort the points being plotted. We shall therefore store these points in a Sortable_list. Hence, the **class** Plot is specified as follows:

```
class Plot {
public:
  Plot();
  Error_code set_limits();
  void find_points(Expression &postfix);
  void draw();
  void clear();
  int get_print_row(double y_value);
  int get_print_col(double x_value);
private:
  Sortable_list<Point> points;   //  records of points to be plotted
  double x_low, x_high;          //  x limits
  double y_low, y_high;          //  y limits
  double x_increment;            //  increment for plotting
  int max_row, max_col;          //  screen size
};
```

The method find_points creates the Sortable_list of points to plot from its parameter Expression postfix.

The other significant class method, **draw**, plots a graph, from the point data stored in the Sortable_list, onto the user's screen.

The **class** Plot also has a constructor, a method to **clear** stored data, and methods to locate the row and column of the user's screen that will be used in plotting a particular point. We shall consider the output screen to be rectangular, with a size determined by the Plot data members max_row and max_col. We specify these

---

[2] Borland C++ is a trademark of Borland International, Inc.

data members in the Plot constructor. We would, for example, give them the values 19 and 79 to obtain a 20 × 80 text screen, or perhaps 780 and 1024 for a graphics screen. A position on the screen is specified by giving its integer row and column coordinates, from the ranges $0 \le$ row $\le$ max_row and $0 \le$ col $\le$ max_col. The method get_print_row uses the y-coordinate of a point of our graph to calculate a corresponding row of the screen.

int Plot :: get_print_row(**double** y_value)
/* **Post:** *Returns the row of the screen at which a point with* y-coordinate y_value *should be plotted, or returns* −1 *if the point would fall off the edge of the screen.* */
```
{
  double interp_y =
    ((double) max_row) * (y_high − y_value)/(y_high − y_low) + 0.5;
  int answer = (int) interp_y;
  if (answer < 0 || answer > max_row) answer = − 1;
  return answer;
}
```

The function returns a value of −1 to signify an input coordinate from outside the limits of the graph.

2. Points

The Sortable_list in a Plot stores objects of the **class** Point. Since these objects represent data points to be plotted, each Point must include two integer data members, row and col, that determine a location on the user's screen. These data members completely determine the ordering of points. We can therefore simply view a Point as its own sorting key. In our program, this decision is implemented with the definition

typedef Point Key;

To ensure compatibility with our earlier sorting methods, each Point must have overloaded comparison operators. The Point structure that we now define also includes two constructors. The constructors create either a Point with no useable data, or a Point storing the given row and col parameter values.

```
struct Point {
  int row;
  int col;
  Point();
  Point(int a, int b);
  bool operator == (const Point &p);
  bool operator != (const Point &p);
  bool operator >= (const Point &p);
  bool operator <= (const Point &p);
  bool operator >  (const Point &p);
  bool operator <  (const Point &p);
};
```

Eventually, when we plot data to the screen, we will first have to plot those data points that belong at the top of the screen and then plot lower points. Similarly, if two data points occupy the same row of the screen, we will plot the leftward one first. Let us therefore design **Point** comparison operators so that points that must be plotted earlier are considered smaller than points that must be plotted later. In this way, we can simply sort the points, to arrange them in the order that they must be plotted to the user's screen. For example, the **Point::operator** < has the following implementation:

```
bool Point::operator < (const Point &p)
{
   return (row < p.row) || (col < p.col && row ==  p.row);
}
```

3. Creating the Point Data

The method **Plot::find_points** produces the list of points to be plotted. It must repeatedly evaluate its postscript expression parameter and insert the resulting point into the **Sortable_list Plot::points**.

```
void Plot::find_points(Expression &postfix)
/* Post:  The Expression postfix is evaluated for values of x that range from x_low
          to x_high in steps of x_increment. For each evaluation we add a Point to
          the Sortable_list points.
   Uses:  Classes Token, Expression, Point, and List. */
{
   double x_val = x_low;
   double y_val;
   while (x_val <= x_high) {
      Token::set_x(x_val);
      postfix.evaluate_postfix(y_val);
      postfix.rewind();
      Point p(get_print_row(y_val), get_print_col(x_val));
      points.insert(0, p);
      x_val += x_increment;
   }
}
```

4. Drawing the Graph

As soon as we have generated a **Sortable_list** of points, we are ready to draw a graph. We simply sort the points, in our implementation with a mergesort, and then traverse through the sorted list, placing a symbol at each indicated screen location. Our care in first sorting the list of points to be plotted ensures that they are already arranged from top to bottom and, at any given height, from left to right in the output graph.

```
void Plot :: draw( )
/* Post:  All screen locations represented in points have been marked with the char-
          acter '#' to produce a picture of the stored graph.
    Uses: Classes Point and Sortable_list and its method merge_sort. */
{
    points.merge_sort( );
    int at_row = 0, at_col = 0;   //   cursor coordinates on screen
    for (int i = 0;  i < points.size( );  i++) {
        Point q;
        points.retrieve(i, q);
        if (q.row < 0 || q.col < 0) continue;   //    off the scale of the graph
        if (q.row < at_row || (q.row ==  at_row && q.col < at_col)) continue;
        if (q.row > at_row) {                    //    Move cursor down the screen.
            at_col = 0;
            while (q.row > at_row) {
                cout << endl;
                at_row++;
            }
        }
        if (q.col > at_col)                      //    Advance cursor horizontally.
            while (q.col > at_col) {
                cout << " ";
                at_col++;
            }
        cout << "#";
        at_col++;
    }
    while (at_row++ <= max_row) cout << endl;
}
```

13.5.8 A Graphics-Enhanced Plot Class

Although there is no graphics support in the standard library of C++, such support is often provided by particular systems. For example, the Borland C++ compiler includes a library of graphics routines in the header file `<graphics.h>`. This library includes functions to initialize the screen for graphics, to detect the number of pixels on the screen, to mark individual pixels, and to restore the screen.

We can incorporate these routines into our **class Plot** by changing the implementations of just four methods that have some interaction with the output screen. These methods are the constructor and the operations draw, find_points, and get_print_col.

In a very minor modification to the constructor, we should remove the predefined limits on max_row and max_col since these are now to be calculated by library functions. A similarly minor modification is required in the method get_print_col to reflect the numbering of pixel rows upwards from the bottom of the screen rather than downwards from the top of the screen.

In the method find_points, we begin by using Borland graphics functions to initialize the screen and record its dimensions. The output data points are then listed just as in our earlier implementation.

```
void Plot :: find_points(Expression &postfix)
/* Post:  The Expression postfix is evaluated for values of x that range from x_low
          to x_high in steps of x_increment. For each evaluation we add a Point of
          the corresponding data point to the Sortable_list points.
   Uses: Classes Token, Expression, Point, and List and the library <graphics.h>. */
{
    int graphicdriver = DETECT, graphicmode;
    initgraph( &graphicdriver,  &graphicmode, "");   //   screen detection and
    graphresult( );                                  //   initialization
    max_col = getmaxx( );                            //   with graphics.h library
    max_row = getmaxy( );
    double x_val = x_low;
    double y_val;
    while (x_val <= x_high) {
        Token :: set_x(x_val);
        postfix.evaluate_postfix(y_val);
        postfix.rewind( );
        Point p(get_print_row(y_val), get_print_col(x_val));
        points.insert(0, p);
        x_val += x_increment;
    }
}
```

Finally, the method **draw** has no need to sort the points, since pixels can be plotted in any order. The method simply lists points and marks corresponding pixels.

```
void Plot :: draw( )
/* Post:  All pixels represented in points have been marked to produce a picture of
          the stored graph.
   Uses: Classes Point and Sortable_list and the library <graphics.h> */
{
    for (int i = 0;  i < points.size( );  i++) {
        Point q;
        points.retrieve(i, q);
        if (q.row < 0 || q.col < 0) continue;   //   off the scale of the graph
        if (q.row > max_row || q.col > max_col) continue;
        putpixel(q.col, q.row, 3);               //   graphics.h library function
    }
    cout "Enter a character to clear screen and continue: " << flush;
    char wait_for;
    cin >> wait_for;
    restorecrtmode( );                           //   graphics.h library function
}
```

At this point, we have surveyed the entire project. There remain several functions and methods that do not appear in the text, but these are all sufficiently straight-forward that they can be left as exercises.

Exercises 13.5

E1. State precisely what changes in the program are needed to add the base 10 logarithm function log( ) as an additional unary operator.

E2. Naïve users of this program might (if graphing a function involving money) write a dollar sign '$' within the expression. What will the present program do if this happens? What changes are needed so that the program will ignore a '$'?

E3. C++ programmers might accidentally type a semicolon ';' at the end of the expression. What changes are needed so that a semicolon will be ignored at the end of the expression but will be an error elsewhere?

E4. Explain what changes are needed to allow the program to accept either square brackets [...] or curly brackets {...} as well as round brackets (...). The nesting must be done with the same kind of brackets; that is, an expression of the form (... [...)...] is illegal, but forms like [... (...)... {...}...] are permissible.

Programming Project 13.5

P1. Provide the missing functions and methods and implement the graphing program on your computer.

REFERENCES FOR FURTHER STUDY

The Polish notation is so natural and useful that one might expect its dis-covery to be hundreds of years ago. It may be surprising to note that it is a discovery of this century: JAN ŁUKASIEWICZ, *Elementy Logiki Matematyczny*, Warsaw, 1929; English translation: *Elements of Mathematical Logic*, Pergamon Press, 1963.

The development of iterative algorithms to form and evaluate Polish expressions (usually postfix form) can be found in several data structures books, as well as more advanced books on compiler theory. The iterative algorithm for translat-ing an expression from infix to postfix form appears to be due independently to E. W. DIJKSTRA and to C. L. HAMBLIN and appears in

E. W. DIJKSTRA, "Making a translator for ALGOL 60," *Automatic Programming Infor-mation* number 7 (May 1961); reprinted in *Annual Revue of Automatic Programming* 3 (1963), 347–356.

C. L. HAMBLIN, "Translation to and from Polish notation," *Computer Journal* 5 (1962), 210–213.

The recursive algorithm for evaluation of postfix expressions is derived, albeit from a rather different point of view, and for binary operators only, in

EDWARD M. REINGOLD, "A comment on the evaluation of Polish postfix expressions," *Computer Journal* 24 (1981), 288.

Mathematical Methods

A

THE FIRST PART of this appendix supplies several mathematical results used in algorithm analysis. The final two sections of the appendix, Fibonacci numbers and Catalan numbers, are optional topics intended for the mathematically inclined reader.

A.1 SUMS OF POWERS OF INTEGERS

The following two formulas are useful in counting the steps executed by an algorithm.

Theorem A.1

$$1 + 2 + \cdots + n = \frac{n(n + 1)}{2}.$$

$$1^2 + 2^2 + \cdots + n^2 = \frac{n(n + 1)(2n + 1)}{6}.$$

Proof The first identity has a simple and elegant proof. We let S equal the sum on the left side, write it down twice (once in each direction), and add vertically:

$$
\begin{array}{ccccccccc}
1 & + & 2 & + & 3 & + & \cdots & + & n-1 & + & n & = & S \\
n & + & n-1 & + & n-2 & + & \cdots & + & 2 & + & 1 & = & S \\
\hline
n+1 & + & n+1 & + & n+1 & + & \cdots & + & n+1 & + & n+1 & = & 2S
\end{array}
$$

end of proof   There are n columns on the left; hence $n(n+1) = 2S$ and the formula follows. ∎

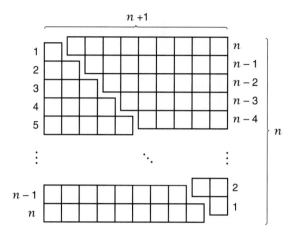

Figure A.1. Geometrical proof for sum of integers

The first identity also has the proof without words shown in Figure A.1.

proof by induction   We shall use the method of ***mathematical induction*** to prove the second identity. This method requires that we start by establishing an initial case, called the ***induction base***, which for our formula is the case $n = 1$. In this case the formula becomes

$$1^2 = \frac{1(1+1)(2+1)}{6},$$

which is true, so the induction base is established. Next, using the formula for the case $n - 1$, we must establish it for case n. For case $n - 1$ we thus shall assume

$$1^2 + 2^2 + \cdots + (n-1)^2 = \frac{(n-1)n(2(n-1)+1)}{6}$$

It follows that

$$
\begin{aligned}
1^2 + 2^2 + \cdots + (n-1)^2 + n^2 &= \frac{(n-1)n(2(n-1)+1)}{6} + n^2 \\
&= \frac{2n^3 - 3n^2 + n + 6n^2}{6} \\
&= \frac{n(n+1)(2n+1)}{6},
\end{aligned}
$$

which is the desired result, and the proof by induction is complete.

A convenient shorthand for a sum of the sort appearing in these identities is to use the capital Greek letter sigma

summation notation

$$\sum$$

in front of the typical summand, with the initial value of the index controlling the summation written below the sign, and the final value above. Thus the preceding identities can be written

$$\sum_{k=1}^{n} k = \frac{n(n+1)}{2}$$

and

$$\sum_{k=1}^{n} k^2 = \frac{n(n+1)(2n+1)}{6}.$$

Two other formulas are also useful, particularly in working with trees.

Theorem A.2

$$1 + 2 + 4 + \cdots + 2^{m-1} = 2^m - 1.$$

$$1 \times 1 + 2 \times 2 + 3 \times 4 + \cdots + m \times 2^{m-1} = (m-1) \times 2^m + 1.$$

In summation notation these equations are

$$\sum_{k=0}^{m-1} 2^k = 2^m - 1.$$

$$\sum_{k=1}^{m} k \times 2^{k-1} = (m-1) \times 2^m + 1.$$

Proof   The first formula will be proved in a more general form. We start with the following identity, which, for any value of $x \neq 1$, can be verified simply by multiplying both sides by $x - 1$:

$$\frac{x^m - 1}{x - 1} = 1 + x + x^2 + \cdots + x^{m-1}$$

for any $x \neq 1$. With $x = 2$ this expression becomes the first formula.

To establish the second formula we take the same expression in the case of $m + 1$ instead of m :

$$\frac{x^{m+1} - 1}{x - 1} = 1 + x + x^2 + \cdots + x^m$$

for any $x \neq 1$, and differentiate with respect to x:

$$\frac{(x-1)(m+1)x^m - (x^{m+1} - 1)}{(x-1)^2} = 1 + 2x + 3x^2 + \cdots + mx^{m-1}$$

end of proof   for any $x \neq 1$. Setting $x = 2$ now gives the second formula.   ■

Suppose that $|x| < 1$ in the preceding formulas. As m becomes large, it follows that x^m becomes small, that is

$$\lim_{m \to \infty} x^m = 0.$$

Taking the limit as $m \to \infty$ in the preceding equations gives

Theorem A.3   *If $|x| < 1$ then*

infinite series

$$\sum_{k=0}^{\infty} x^k = \frac{1}{1-x}.$$

$$\sum_{k=1}^{\infty} kx^{k-1} = \frac{1}{(1-x)^2}.$$

A.2 LOGARITHMS

The primary reason for using logarithms is to turn multiplication and division into addition and subtraction, and exponentiation into multiplication. Before the advent of pocket calculators, logarithms were an indispensable tool for hand calculation: Witness the large tables of logarithms and the once ubiquitous slide rule. Even though we now have other methods for numerical calculation, the fundamental properties of logarithms give them importance that extends far beyond their use as computational tools.

The behavior of many phenomena, first of all, reflects an intrinsically logarithmic structure; that is, by using logarithms we find important relationships that are not otherwise obvious. Measuring the loudness of sound, for example, is logarithmic: if one sound is 10 dB (decibels) louder than another, then the actual acoustic energy is 10 times as much. If the sound level in one room is 40 dB and it is 60 dB in another, then the human perception may be that the second room is half again as noisy as the first, but there is actually 100 times more sound energy in the second room. This phenomenon is why a single violin soloist can be heard above a full orchestra (when playing a different line), and yet the orchestra requires so many violins to maintain a proper balance of sound.

Earthquake intensity is also measured logarithmically: An increase of 1 on the RICHTER scale represents a ten-fold increase in energy released.

large numbers   Logarithms, secondly, provide a convenient way to handle very large numbers. The scientific notation, where a number is written as a small real number (often in the range from 1 to 10) times a power of 10, is really based on logarithms, since the power of 10 is essentially the logarithm of the number. Scientists who need to use very large numbers (like astronomers, nuclear physicists, and geologists) frequently speak of orders of magnitude and thereby concentrate on the logarithm of the number.

A logarithmic graph, thirdly, is a very useful device for displaying the properties of a function over a much broader range than a linear graph. With a logarithmic

physical measurements

graph, we can arrange to display detailed information on the function for small values of the argument and at the same time give an overall view for much larger values. Logarithmic graphs are especially appropriate when we wish to show percentage changes in a function.

A.2.1 Definition of Logarithms

base   Logarithms are defined in terms of a real number $a > 1$, which is called the **base** of the logarithms. (It is also possible to define logarithms with base a in the range $0 < a < 1$, but doing so would introduce needless complications into our discussion.) For any number $x > 0$, we define $\log_a x = y$, where y is the real number such that $a^y = x$. The logarithm of a negative number, and the logarithm of 0, are not defined.

A.2.2 Simple Properties

From the definition and from the properties of exponents we obtain

$$\log_a 1 = 0,$$
$$\log_a a = 1,$$
$$\log_a x < 0 \quad \text{for all } x \text{ such that } 0 < x < 1.$$
$$0 < \log_a x < 1 \quad \text{for all } x \text{ such that } 1 < x < a.$$
$$\log_a x > 1 \quad \text{for all } x \text{ such that } a < x.$$

The logarithm function has a graph like the one in Figure A.2.

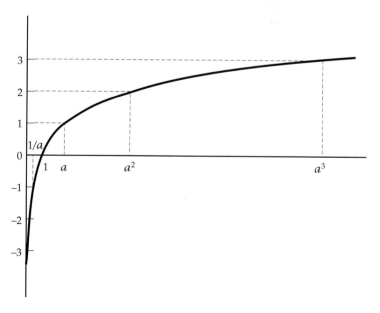

Figure A.2. Graph of the logarithm function

identities   We also obtain the identities

$$\log_a(xy) = (\log_a x) + (\log_a y)$$
$$\log_a(x/y) = (\log_a x) - (\log_a y)$$
$$\log_a x^z = z \log_a x$$
$$\log_a a^z = z$$
$$a^{\log_a x} = x$$

that hold for any positive real numbers x and y and for any real number z.

From the graph in Figure A.2 you will observe that the logarithm grows more and more slowly as x increases. The graphs of positive powers of x less than 1, such as the square root of x or the cube root of x, also grow progressively more slowly, but never become as flat as the graph of the logarithm. In fact,

> As x grows large, $\log x$ grows more slowly than x^c, for any $c > 0$.

A.2.3 Choice of Base

Any real number $a > 1$ can be chosen as the base of logarithms, but certain special choices appear much more frequently than others. For computation and for graphing, the base $a = 10$ is often used, and logarithms with base 10 are called **common**
common logarithm   **logarithms**. In studying computer algorithms, however, base 10 appears infrequently, and we do not often use common logarithms. Instead, logarithms with base 2 appear the most frequently, and we therefore reserve the special symbol

$$\lg x$$

to denote a logarithm with base 2.

A.2.4 Natural Logarithms

In studying mathematical properties of logarithms, and in many problems where logarithms appear as part of the answer, the number that appears as the base is

$$e = 2.718281828459\ldots.$$

natural logarithm   Logarithms with base e are called **natural logarithms**. In this book we always denote the natural logarithm of x by

$$\ln x.$$

In many mathematics books, however, other bases than e are rarely used, in which case the unqualified symbol $\log x$ usually denotes a natural logarithm. Figure A.3 shows the graph of logarithms with respect to the three bases 2, e, and 10.

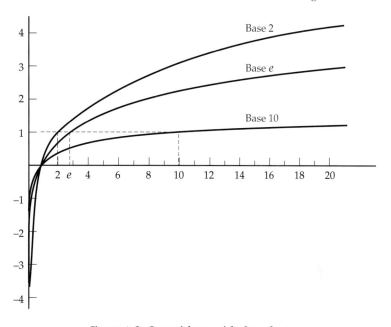

Figure A.3. Logarithms with three bases

The properties of logarithms that make e the natural choice for the base are thoroughly developed as part of the calculus, but we can mention two of these properties without proof. First, the graph of $\ln x$ has the property that its slope at each point x is $1/x$; that is, the derivative of $\ln x$ is $1/x$ for all real numbers $x > 0$. Second, the natural logarithm satisfies the infinite series

$$\ln(x + 1) = x - \frac{x^2}{2} + \frac{x^3}{3} - \frac{x^4}{4} + \cdots$$

exponential function

for $-1 < x < 1$, but this series requires many terms to give a good approximation and therefore, is not useful directly for computation. It is much better to consider instead the exponential function that "undoes" the logarithm and that satisfies the series

$$e^x = 1 + x + \frac{x^2}{2!} + \frac{x^3}{3!} + \cdots$$

for all real numbers x. This exponential function e^x also has the important property that it is its own derivative.

A.2.5 Notation

The notation just used for logarithms with different bases will be our standard. We thus summarize:

> ### Conventions
> *Unless stated otherwise, all logarithms will be taken with base 2.*
> *The symbol* lg *denotes a logarithm with base 2,*
> *and the symbol* ln *denotes a natural logarithm.*
> *If the base for logarithms is not specified or makes no difference,*
> *then the symbol* log *will be used.*

A.2.6 Change of Base

Logarithms with respect to one base are closely related to logarithms with respect to any other base. To find this relation, we start with the following relation that is essentially the definition

$$x = a^{\log_a x}$$

for any $x > 0$. Then

$$\log_b x = \log_b a^{\log_a x} = (\log_a x)(\log_b a).$$

The factor $\log_b a$ does not depend on x, but only on the two bases. Therefore:

> *To convert logarithms from one base to another, multiply by a constant factor, the logarithm of the first base with respect to the second.*

conversion factors   The most useful numbers for us in this connection are

$$\lg e \approx 1.442695041,$$
$$\ln 2 \approx 0.693147181,$$
$$\ln 10 \approx 2.302585093,$$
$$\lg 1000 \approx 10.0$$

The last value is a consequence of the important approximation $2^{10} = 1024 \approx 10^3 = 1000$.

A.2.7 Logarithmic Graphs

In a logarithmic scale the numbers are arranged as on a slide rule, with larger numbers closer together than smaller numbers. In this way, equal distances along the scale represent equal *ratios* rather than the equal *differences* represented on an ordinary linear scale. A logarithmic scale should be used when percentage change is important to measure, or when perception is logarithmic. Human perception of time, for example, sometimes seems to be nearly linear in the short term—what happened two days ago is twice as distant as what happened yesterday—but often seems more nearly logarithmic in the long term: We draw less distinction between one million years ago and two million years ago than we do between ten years ago and one hundred years ago.

log-log graphs   Graphs in which both the vertical and horizontal scales are logarithmic are called ***log-log graphs***. In addition to phenomena where the perception is naturally logarithmic in both scales, log-log graphs are useful to display the behavior of a function over a very wide range. For small values, the graph records a detailed view of the function, and for large values a broad view of the function appears on the same graph. For searching and sorting algorithms, we wish to compare methods both for small problems and large problems; hence log-log graphs are appropriate. (See Figure A.4.)

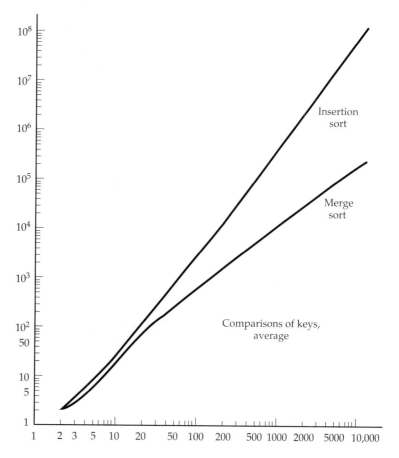

Figure A.4. Log-log graph, comparisons, insertion and merge sorts

One observation is worth noting: Any power of x graphs as a straight line with a log-log scale. To prove this, we start with an arbitrary power function $y = x^n$ and take logarithms on both sides, obtaining

$$\log y = n \log x.$$

A log-log graph in x and y becomes a linear graph in $u = \log x$ and $v = \log y$, and the equation becomes $v = nu$ in terms of u and v, which indeed graphs as a straight line.

A.2.8 Harmonic Numbers

As a final application of logarithms, we obtain an approximation to a sum that appears frequently in the analysis of algorithms, especially that of sorting methods. The nth *harmonic number* is defined to be the sum

$$H_n = 1 + \frac{1}{2} + \frac{1}{3} + \cdots + \frac{1}{n}$$

of the reciprocals of the integers from 1 to n.

To evaluate H_n, we consider the function $1/x$, and the relationship shown in Figure A.5. The area under the step function is clearly H_n, since the width of each step is 1, and the height of step k is $1/k$, for each integer k from 1 to n. This area is approximated by the area under the curve $1/x$ from $\frac{1}{2}$ to $n + \frac{1}{2}$. The area under the curve is

$$\int_{\frac{1}{2}}^{n+\frac{1}{2}} \frac{1}{x} dx = \ln(n + \tfrac{1}{2}) - \ln \tfrac{1}{2} \approx \ln n + 0.7.$$

When n is large, the fractional term 0.7 is insignificant, and we obtain $\ln n$ as a good approximation to H_n.

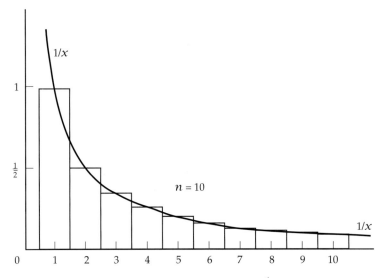

Figure A.5. Approximation of $\int_{\frac{1}{2}}^{n+\frac{1}{2}} \frac{1}{x} dx$

By refining this method of approximation by an integral, it is possible to obtain a very much closer approximation to H_n, if such is desired. Specifically,

Theorem A.4   *The harmonic number* H_n, $n \geq 1$, *satisfies*

$$H_n = \ln n + y + \frac{1}{2n} - \frac{1}{12n^2} + \frac{1}{120n^4} - \epsilon,$$

where $0 < \epsilon < 1/(252n^6)$, *and* $y \approx 0.577215665$ *is known as* **Euler's constant.**

A.3 PERMUTATIONS, COMBINATIONS, FACTORIALS

A.3.1 Permutations

A *permutation* of objects is an ordering or arrangement of the objects in a row. If we begin with n different objects, then we can choose any of the n objects to be the first one in the arrangement. There are then $n - 1$ choices for the second object, and since these choices can be combined in all possible ways, the number of choices multiplies. Hence the first two objects may be chosen in $n(n - 1)$ ways. There remain $n - 2$ objects, any one of which may be chosen as the third in the arrangement. Continuing in this way, we see that the number of permutations of n distinct objects is

count of permutations
$$n! = n \times (n - 1) \times (n - 2) \times \ldots \times 2 \times 1.$$

Objects to permute:	a b c d					
Choose a *first:*	a b c d	a b d c	a c b d	a c d b	a d b c	a d c b
Choose b *first:*	b a c d	b a d c	b c a d	b c d a	b d a c	b d c a
Choose c *first:*	c a b d	c a d b	c b a d	c b d a	c d a b	c d b a
Choose d *first:*	d a b c	d a c b	d b a c	d b c a	d c a b	d c b a

Figure A.6. Constructing permutations

Note that we have assumed that the objects are all distinct, that is, that we can tell each object from every other one. It is often easier to count configurations of distinct objects than when some are indistinguishable. The latter problem can sometimes be solved by temporarily labeling the objects so they are all distinct, then counting the configurations, and finally dividing by the number of ways in which the labeling could have been done. The special case in the next section is especially important.

A.3.2 Combinations

A *combination* of n objects taken k at a time is a choice of k objects out of the n, without regard for the order of selection. The number of such combinations is denoted either by

$$C(n, k) \quad \text{or by} \quad \binom{n}{k}.$$

We can calculate $C(n, k)$ by starting with the $n!$ permutations of n objects and form a combination simply by selecting the first k objects in the permutation. The order, however, in which these k objects appear is ignored in determining a combination, so we must divide by the number $k!$ of ways to order the k objects chosen. The order of the $n - k$ objects not chosen is also ignored, so we must also divide by $(n - k)!$. Hence:

count of combinations

$$C(n, k) = \frac{n!}{k!(n - k)!}$$

Objects from which to choose:		a b c d e f		
a b c	a c d	a d f	b c f	c d e
a b d	a c e	a e f	b d e	c d f
a b e	a c f	b c d	b d f	c e f
a b f	a d e	b c e	b e f	d e f

Figure A.7. Combinations of 6 objects, taken 3 at a time

binomial coefficients

The number of combinations $C(n, k)$ is called a **binomial coefficient**, since it appears as the coefficient of $x^k y^{n-k}$ in the expansion of $(x + y)^n$. There are hundreds of different relationships and identities about various sums and products of binomial coefficients. The most important of these can be found in textbooks on elementary algebra and on combinatorics.

A.3.3 Factorials

We frequently use permutations and combinations in analyzing algorithms, and for these applications we must estimate the size of $n!$ for various values of n. An excellent approximation to $n!$ was obtained by JAMES STIRLING in the eighteenth century:

Theorem A.5

$$n! \approx \sqrt{2\pi n} \left(\frac{n}{e}\right)^n \left[1 + \frac{1}{12n} + O\left(\frac{1}{n^2}\right)\right].$$

Stirling's approximation

We usually use this approximation in logarithmic form instead:

Corollary A.6

$$\ln n! \approx (n + \tfrac{1}{2})\ln n - n + \tfrac{1}{2}\ln(2\pi) + \frac{1}{12n} + O\left(\frac{1}{n^2}\right).$$

Note that, as n increases, the approximation to the logarithm becomes more and more accurate; that is, the difference approaches 0. The difference between the approximation directly to the factorial and $n!$ itself will not necessarily become small (that is, the difference need not go to 0), but the percentage error becomes arbitrarily small (the ratio goes to 1). KNUTH (Volume 1, page 111) gives refinements of Stirling's approximation that are even closer.

Proof The complete proof of Stirling's approximation requires techniques from advanced calculus that would take us too far afield here. We can, however, use a bit of elementary calculus to illustrate the first step of the approximation. First, we take the natural logarithm of a factorial, noting that the logarithm of a product is the sum of the logarithms:

$$
\begin{aligned}
\ln n! &= \ln(n \times (n-1) \times \cdots \times 1) \\
&= \ln n + \ln(n-1) + \cdots + \ln 1 \\
&= \sum_{x=1}^{n} \ln x.
\end{aligned}
$$

Next, we approximate the sum by an integral, as shown in Figure A.8.

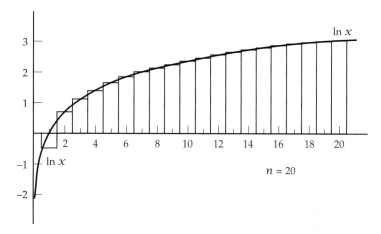

Figure A.8. Approximation of $\ln n!$ **by** $\int_{\frac{1}{2}}^{n+\frac{1}{2}} \ln x \, dx$

It is clear from the diagram that the area under the step function, which is exactly $\ln n!$, is approximately the same as the area under the curve, which is

$$
\begin{aligned}
\int_{\frac{1}{2}}^{n+\frac{1}{2}} \ln x \, dx &= (x \ln x - x) \Big|_{\frac{1}{2}}^{n+\frac{1}{2}} \\
&= (n + \tfrac{1}{2}) \ln(n + \tfrac{1}{2}) - n + \tfrac{1}{2} \ln 2.
\end{aligned}
$$

For large values of n, the difference between $\ln n$ and $\ln(n + \tfrac{1}{2})$ is insignificant, and hence this approximation differs from Stirling's only by the constant difference between $\tfrac{1}{2} \ln 2$ (about 0.35) and $\tfrac{1}{2} \ln(2\pi)$ (about 0.919).   ■

end of proof

A.4 FIBONACCI NUMBERS

The Fibonacci numbers originated as an exercise in arithmetic proposed by LEONARDO FIBONACCI in 1202:

rabbits   *How many pairs of rabbits can be produced from a single pair in a year? We start with a single newly born pair; it takes one month for a pair to mature, after which they produce a new pair each month, and the rabbits never die.*

In month 1, we have only one pair. In month 2, we still have only one pair, but they are now mature. In month 3, they have reproduced, so we now have two pairs. And so it goes. The number F_n of pairs of rabbits that we have in month n satisfies

recurrence relation $$F_0 = 0, \quad F_1 = 1, \quad \text{and} \quad F_n = F_{n-1} + F_{n-2} \quad \text{for} \quad n \geq 2.$$

This same sequence of numbers, called the **Fibonacci sequence**, appears in many other problems. In Section 10.4, for example, F_n appears as the minimum number of nodes in an AVL tree of height n. Our object in this section is to find a formula for F_n.

generating function   We shall use the method of **generating functions**, which is important for many other applications. The generating function is a formal infinite series in a symbol x, with the Fibonacci numbers as coefficients:

$$F(x) = F_0 + F_1 x + F_2 x^2 + \cdots + F_n x^n + \cdots .$$

We do not worry about whether this series converges, or what the value of x might be, since we are not going to set x to any particular value. Instead, we shall only perform formal algebraic manipulations on the generating function.

Next, we multiply by powers of x:

$$\begin{aligned}
F(x) &= F_0 + F_1 x + F_2 x^2 + \cdots + F_n \quad x^n + \cdots \\
x F(x) &= \qquad\quad F_0 x + F_1 x^2 + \cdots + F_{n-1} x^n + \cdots \\
x^2 F(x) &= \qquad\qquad\qquad F_0 x^2 + \cdots + F_{n-2} x^n + \cdots
\end{aligned}$$

and subtract the second two equations from the first:

$$(1 - x - x^2) F(x) = F_0 + (F_1 - F_0)x = x,$$

since $F_0 = 0, F_1 = 1$, and $F_n = F_{n-1} + F_{n-2}$ for all $n \geq 2$. We therefore obtain

$$F(x) = \frac{x}{1 - x - x^2}.$$

The roots of $1 - x - x^2$ are $\frac{1}{2}(-1 \pm \sqrt{5})$. By the method of partial fractions we can thus rearrange the formula for $F(x)$ as

closed form $$F(x) = \frac{1}{\sqrt{5}} \left(\frac{1}{1 - \phi x} - \frac{1}{1 - \psi x} \right)$$

where

$$\phi = \tfrac{1}{2}(1 + \sqrt{5}) \text{ and } \psi = 1 - \phi = \tfrac{1}{2}(1 - \sqrt{5}).$$

[Check this equation for $F(x)$ by putting the two fractions on the right over a common denominator.]

The next step is to expand the fractions on the right side by dividing their denominators into 1:

$$F(x) = \frac{1}{\sqrt{5}}(1 + \phi x + \phi^2 x^2 + \cdots - 1 - \psi x - \psi^2 x^2 - \cdots).$$

The final step is to recall that the coefficients of $F(x)$ are the Fibonacci numbers, and therefore to equate the coefficients of each power of x on both sides of this equation. We thus obtain

solution

$$F_n = \frac{1}{\sqrt{5}}(\phi^n - \psi^n).$$

Approximate values for ϕ and ψ are

$$\phi \approx 1.618034 \quad \text{and} \quad \psi \approx -0.618034.$$

This surprisingly simple answer to the values of the Fibonacci numbers is interesting in several ways. It is, first, not even immediately obvious why the right side should always be an integer. Second, ψ is a negative number of sufficiently small absolute value that we always have $F_n = \phi^n/\sqrt{5}$ rounded to the nearest *golden mean* integer. Third, the number ϕ is itself interesting. It has been studied since the times of the ancient Greeks—it is often called the **golden mean**—and the ratio of ϕ to 1 is said to give the most pleasing shape of a rectangle. The Parthenon and many other ancient Greek buildings have sides with this ratio.

A.5 CATALAN NUMBERS

The purpose of this section is to count the binary trees with n vertices. We shall accomplish this result via a slightly circuitous route, discovering along the way several other problems that have the same answer. The resulting numbers, called the **Catalan numbers**, are of considerable interest in that they appear in the answers to many apparently unrelated problems.

A.5.1 The Main Result

Definition   For $n \geq 0$, the nth **Catalan number** is defined to be

$$Cat(n) = \frac{C(2n, n)}{n + 1} = \frac{(2n)!}{(n + 1)!n!}.$$

Theorem A.7   *The number of distinct binary trees with n vertices, $n \geq 0$, is the nth Catalan number* *Cat(n).*

A.5.2 The Proof by One-to-One Correspondences

1. Orchards

Let us first recall the one-to-one correspondence from Theorem 11.1 (page 526) between the binary trees with n vertices and the orchards with n vertices. Hence to count binary trees, we may just as well count orchards.

2. Well-Formed Sequences of Parentheses

Second, let us consider the set of all well-formed sequences of n left parentheses '(' and n right parentheses ').' A sequence is *well formed* means that, when scanned from left to right, the number of right parentheses encountered never exceeds the number of left parentheses. Thus '((( )))' and '( ) ( ) ( )' are well formed, but '( )) (( )' is not, nor is '(( ),' since the total numbers of left and right parentheses in the expression must be equal.

Lemma A.8   *There is a one-to-one correspondence between the orchards with n vertices and the well-formed sequences of n left parentheses and n right parentheses, $n \geq 0$.*

bracketed form   To define this correspondence, we first recall that an orchard is either empty or is an ordered sequence of ordered trees. We define the **bracketed form** of an orchard to be the sequence of bracketed forms of its trees, written one after the next in the same order as the trees in the orchard. The bracketed form of the empty orchard is empty. We recall also that an ordered tree is defined to consist of its root vertex, together with an orchard of subtrees. We thus define the **bracketed form** of an ordered tree to consist of a left parenthesis '(' followed by the (name of the) root, followed by the bracketed form of the orchard of subtrees, and finally a right parenthesis ').'

The bracketed forms of several ordered trees and orchards appear in Figure A.9. It should be clear that the mutually recursive definitions we have given produce a unique bracketed form for any orchard and that the resulting sequence of parentheses is well formed. If, on the other hand, we begin with a well-formed sequence of parentheses, then the outermost pair(s) of parentheses correspond to the tree(s) of an orchard, and within such a pair of parentheses is the description of the corresponding tree in terms of its root and its orchard of subtrees. In this way, we have now obtained a one-to-one correspondence between the orchards with n vertices and the well-formed sequences of n left and n right parentheses.

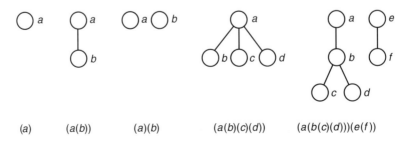

| (a) | (a(b)) | (a)(b) | (a(b)(c)(d)) | (a(b(c)(d)))(e(f)) |

Figure A.9. Bracketed form of orchards

In counting orchards we are not concerned with the labels attached to the vertices, and hence we shall omit the labels and, with the correspondence we have outlined, we shall now count well-formed sequences of n left and n right parentheses with nothing else inside the parentheses.

3. Stack Permutations

Let us note that, by replacing each left parenthesis by $+1$ and each right parenthesis by -1, the well-formed sequences of parentheses correspond to sequences of $+1$ and -1 such that the partial sums from the left are always nonnegative, and the total sum is 0. If we think of each $+1$ as pushing an item onto a stack, and -1 as popping the stack, then the partial sums count the items on the stack at a given time. From this it can be shown that the number of stack permutations of n objects (see Exercise E4 of Section 2.1, on page 56) is yet another problem for which the Catalan numbers provide the answer. Even more, if we start with an orchard and perform a complete traversal (walking around each branch and vertex in the orchard as though it were a decorative wall), counting $+1$ each time we go down a branch and -1 each time we go up a branch (with $+1 - 1$ for each leaf), then we thereby essentially obtain the correspondence with well-formed sequences over again.

4. Arbitrary Sequences of Parentheses

Our final step is to count well-formed sequences of parentheses, but to do this we shall instead count the sequences that are *not* well formed and subtract from the number of all possible sequences. We need a final one-to-one correspondence:

Lemma A.9   *The sequences of n left and n right parentheses that are not well formed correspond exactly to all sequences of $n - 1$ left parentheses and $n + 1$ right parentheses (in all possible orders).*

To prove this correspondence, let us start with a sequence of n left and n right parentheses that is not well formed. Let k be the first position in which the sequence goes wrong, so the entry at position k is a right parenthesis, and there is one more right parenthesis than left up through this position. Hence strictly to the right of position k there is one fewer right parenthesis than left. Strictly to the right of position k, then, let us replace all left parentheses by right and all right parentheses by left. The resulting sequence will have $n - 1$ left parentheses and $n + 1$ right parentheses altogether.

Conversely, let us start with a sequence of $n - 1$ left parentheses and $n + 1$ right parentheses, and let k be the first position where the number of right parentheses exceeds the number of left (such a position must exist, since there are more right than left parentheses altogether). Again let us exchange left for right and right for left parentheses in the remainder of the sequence (positions after k). We thereby obtain a sequence of n left and n right parentheses that is not well formed, and we have constructed the one-to-one correspondence as desired.

5. End of the Proof

With all these preliminary correspondences, our counting problem reduces to simple combinations. The number of sequences of $n-1$ left and $n+1$ right parentheses is the number of ways to choose the $n-1$ positions occupied by left parentheses from the $2n$ positions in the sequence; that is, the number is $C(2n, n-1)$. By Lemma A.9, this number is also the number of sequences of n left and n right parentheses that are not well formed. The number of all sequences of n left and n right parentheses is similarly $C(2n, n)$, so the number of well-formed sequences is

$$C(2n, n) - C(2n, n-1)$$

which is precisely the nth Catalan number.

Because of all the one-to-one correspondences, we also have:

Corollary A.10   *The number of well-formed sequences of n left and n right parentheses, the number of permutations of n objects obtainable by a stack, the number of orchards with n vertices, and the number of binary trees with n vertices are all equal to the nth Catalan number $Cat(n)$.*

A.5.3 History

Surprisingly, it was not for any of the preceding questions that Catalan numbers were first discovered, but rather for questions in geometry. Specifically, $\text{Cat}(n)$ provides the number of ways to divide a convex polygon with $n + 2$ sides into triangles by drawing $n - 1$ nonintersecting diagonals. (See Figure A.10.) This problem seems to have been proposed by L. EULER and solved by J. A. V. SEGNER in 1759. It was then solved again by E. CATALAN in 1838. Sometimes, therefore, the resulting numbers are called the *Segner numbers*, but more often they are called *Catalan numbers*.

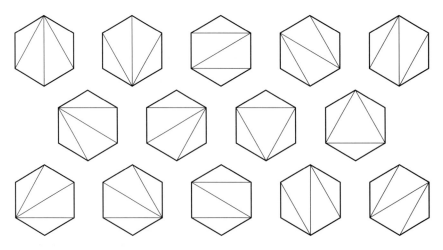

Figure A.10. Triangulations of a hexagon by diagonals

n	$Cat(n)$	n	$Cat(n)$
0	1	10	16,796
1	1	11	58,786
2	2	12	208,012
3	5	13	742,900
4	14	14	2,674,440
5	42	15	9,694,845
6	132	16	35,357,670
7	429	17	129,644,790
8	1,430	18	477,638,700
9	4,862	19	1,767,263,190

Figure A.11. The first 20 Catalan numbers

A.5.4 Numerical Results

We conclude this section with some indications of the sizes of Catalan numbers. The first 20 values are given in Figure A.11.

For larger values of n, we can obtain an estimate on the size of the Catalan numbers by using Stirling's approximation. When it is applied to each of the three factorials, and the result is simplified, we obtain

$$Cat(n) \approx \frac{4^n}{(n+1)\sqrt{\pi n}}.$$

When compared with the exact values in Figure A.11, this estimate gives a good idea of the accuracy of Stirling's approximation. When $n = 10$, for example, the estimated value for the Catalan number is 17,007, compared to the exact value of 16,796.

REFERENCES FOR FURTHER STUDY

More extensive discussions of proof by induction, the summation notation, sums of powers of integers, and logarithms appear in many algebra textbooks. These books will also provide examples and exercises on these topics. An excellent discussion of the importance of logarithms and of the subtle art of approximate calculation is N. DAVID MERMIN, "Logarithms!," *American Mathematical Monthly* 87 (1980), 1–7.

logarithms

Several interesting examples of estimating large numbers and thinking of them logarithmically are discussed in

DOUGLAS R. HOFSTADTER, "Metamagical themas," *Scientific American* 246, no. 5 (May 1982), 20–34.

harmonic numbers   Several surprising and amusing applications of harmonic numbers are given in the nontechnical article

RALPH BOAS, "Snowfalls and elephants, pop bottles and π," *Two-Year College Mathematics Journal* 11 (1980), 82–89.

The detailed estimates for both harmonic numbers and factorials (Stirling's approximation) are quoted from KNUTH, Volume 1, pp. 108–111, where detailed proofs may be found. KNUTH, Volume 1, is also an excellent source for further information regarding permutations, combinations, and related topics.

The original reference for Stirling's approximation is

factorials   JAMES STIRLING, *Methodus Differentialis* (1730), p. 137.

combinatorics   The branch of mathematics concerned with the enumeration of various sets or classes of objects is called ***combinatorics***. This science of counting can be introduced on a very simple level or studied with great sophistication. Two elementary textbooks containing many further developments of the ideas introduced here are

GERALD BERMAN and K. D. FRYER, *Introduction to Combinatorics*, Academic Press, 1972.

ALAN TUCKER, *Applied Combinatorics*, John Wiley, New York, 1980.

Fibonacci numbers   The derivation of the Fibonacci numbers will appear in almost any book on combinatorics, as well as in KNUTH, Volume 1, pp. 78–86, who includes some interesting history as well as many related exercises. The appearance of Fibonacci numbers in nature is illustrated in

PETER STEVENS, *Patterns in Nature*, Little, Brown, Boston, 1974.

Many hundreds of other properties of Fibonacci numbers have been and continue to be found; these are often published in the research journal *Fibonacci Quarterly*.

Catalan numbers   A derivation of the Catalan numbers (applied to triangulations of convex polygons) appears in the first of the cited books on combinatorics (BERMAN and FRYER, pp. 230–232). KNUTH, Volume 1, pp. 385–406, enumerates several classes of trees, including the Catalan numbers applied to binary trees. A list of 46 references providing both history and applications of the Catalan numbers appears in

W. G. BROWN, "Historical note on a recurrent combinatorial problem," *American Mathematical Monthly* 72 (1965), 973–977.

The following article expounds many other applications of Catalan numbers:

MARTIN GARDNER, "Mathematical games" (regular column), *Scientific American* 234, no. 6 (June, 1976), 120–125.

The original references for the derivation of the Catalan numbers are:

J. A. V. SEGNER, "Enumeratio modorum, quibus figuræ planæ rectilineæ per diagonales dividuntur in triangula," *Novi Commentarii Academiæ Scientiarum Imperialis Petropolitanæ* 7 (1758–1759), 203–209.

E. CATALAN, "Solution nouvelle de cette question: un polygone étant donné, de combien de manieres peut-on le partager en triangles au moyen de diagonales?," *Journal de Mathématiques Pures et Appliquées* 4 (1839), 91–94.

Random Numbers

B

RANDOM NUMBERS are a valuable tool for making computer programs display many outcomes. This appendix briefly treats the generation of random numbers, distinguishing several different kinds. These are then implemented as methods of a C++ **class** Random.

B.1 INTRODUCTION

Variety is the spice of life. Computers, on the other hand, tend to be entirely predictable and hence rather dull. Random numbers provide a way to inject unpredictability into computer programs and therefore, sometimes, to make them better imitate external events. When used as part of computer games, graphics displays, or simulations, random numbers can add a great deal of interest, and, when the program is run repeatedly, it may show a range of behavior not unlike that of the natural system it is imitating.

*system
random-number
generator*

The header files `<cstdlib>` and `<stdlib.h>` provide random number generation routines in C++ systems. These routines can be used in place of the ones developed here. But system random-number generators are sometimes not very good, so it is worthwhile to see how better ones can be constructed.

In any case, we should regard the random-number generator and all the subprograms in this section as a *package* for producing random numbers. Once we have developed the package, we should be able to use it in our simulation program or any other application we wish, but we should not need to look inside it to see how it functions. Hence all the details in this section (which are rather mathematical) should be considered part of the implementation with which we need not be concerned when we use random numbers in an application.

We shall implement these goals by designing a **class** Random whose methods generate and return random numbers of various kinds.

B.2 STRATEGY

seed for pseudorandom numbers

The idea we shall use to generate random numbers is to start with one number and apply a series of arithmetic operations that will produce another number with no obvious connection to the first. Hence the numbers we produce are not truly random at all, as each one depends in a definite way on its predecessor, and we should more properly speak of *pseudorandom* numbers. The number we use (and simultaneously change) is called the *seed*.

If the seed begins with the same value each time the program is run, then the whole sequence of pseudorandom numbers will be exactly the same, and we can reproduce any experimental results that we obtain. However, in case a client wishes

unreproducible behavior

to use random numbers that are not just unpredictable, but are also unreproducible, we shall include an option to initialize the seed according to the exact time measured in seconds. Since this time will most likely be different each time the program is run, this initialization should lead to different behavior every time the client program is run. Such unreproducible behavior is appropriate for implementing computer games, for example.

parameter: pseudo

We shall implement the two possible initialization operations by creating a constructor for the **class Random** that uses a parameter **bool** pseudo. When pseudo has the value **true**, we shall generate random numbers starting from a predefined seed, whereas when pseudo is **false** we shall generate unreproducible random numbers. In this way, the desired initialization is performed automatically each time the client program starts, and the client need make no special effort to initialize the seed.

seed private

The seed is used and changed by the random-number generator, but it should not be used by or, if possible, even accessible to the application program. That is, the user of the random-number package ought not necessarily be aware of the existence of a seed variable. Hence the seed should not be a parameter for the random-number generator. Nor is it reasonable that it should be declared as a global variable in the user's program, much less initialized by the user.

We shall therefore declare the seed as a **private** data member of the **class** Random. In this way, the seed will be accessible to all the methods and auxiliary functions in the class, but it cannot be accessed at all from outside the class.

We have now settled on the following outline of the **class Random**:

```
class Random {
public:
   Random(bool pseudo = true);
//   Declare random-number generation methods here.
private:
   int reseed();            //   Re-randomize the seed.
   int seed,
      multiplier, add_on;   //   constants for use in arithmetic operations
};
```

B.3 PROGRAM DEVELOPMENT

The heart of our **class** Random is the auxiliary function **reseed** that updates the seed. It is called upon to provide the randomized behavior of all of the other methods. The function operates as follows:

```
int Random :: reseed( )
/* Post: The seed is replaced by a psuedorandom successor. */
{
    seed = seed * multiplier + add_on;
    return seed;
}
```

In this function we perform a multiplication and an addition and then throw away the most significant part of the result, keeping only the less significant but more random digits.

The constants multiplier and add_on can be stored as data members in a Random object. They should not be chosen at random, but should be carefully chosen to make sure that the results pass various tests for randomness. For example, the values assigned by the following Random object constructor seem to work fairly well on 16-bit computers, but other choices should be made for other machines.

```
Random :: Random(bool pseudo)
/* Post: The values of seed, add_on, and multiplier are initialized.  The seed is
         initialized randomly only if pseudo ==  false. */
{
    if (pseudo) seed = 1;
    else seed = time(NULL) % max_int;
    multiplier = 2743;
    add_on = 5923;
}
```

The function time( ) that we use to generate an unpredictable seed comes from the header file `time.h`; it measures the number of seconds of elapsed time since the start of the year 1970.

1. Real Values

We shall not allow client code to use the function **reseed** directly; instead we convert its results into one of three forms more directly useful.

uniform distribution
The first of these imitates the random-number generators of most computer systems by returning as its result a real number uniformly distributed between 0 and 1. By **uniformly distributed** we mean that, if we take two intervals of the same length within the range of the method, then it is equally likely that the result will be in one interval as in the other. Since the range of our method is from 0 to 1, this definition means that the probability that the result is in any subinterval must equal the length of that subinterval.

One more restriction is usually placed on the range of the result: 0 may appear as a result but 1 may not. In mathematical terms, the range is the *half-open* interval $[0, 1)$.

Here is the resulting method of the **class** Random. It simply converts the result from **reseed** into the desired range. To carry out the conversion, we must first set the value of max_int to record the largest integer value that can be stored, this is obtained from one of the header files <limits>, <climits>, or <limits.h>.

```
double Random :: random_real()
/* Post: A random real number between 0 and 1 is returned. */
{
   double max = max_int + 1.0;
   double temp = reseed();
   if (temp < 0) temp = temp + max;
   return temp/max;
}
```

2. Integer Values

The second common form for random numbers is integers. We cannot, however, speak meaningfully about random integers since the number of integers is infinite but the number representable on a computer is finite. Hence the probability that a truly random integer is one of those representable on a computer is 0. We instead consider only the integers in a range between two integers low and high, inclusive. To calculate such an integer we start with a random real number in $[0, 1)$, multiply it by high − low + 1 since that is the number of integers in the desired range, truncate the result to an integer, and add low to put the result into the desired range of integers. Again, we implement this operation as a method of the **class** Random.

```
int Random :: random_integer(int low, int high)
/* Post: A random integer between low and high (inclusive) is returned. */
{
   if (low > high) return random_integer(high, low);
   else return ((int) ((high − low + 1) * random_real())) + low;
}
```

3. Poisson Values

expected value

example

A third, more sophisticated, form of random numbers is needed for the airport simulation of Section 3.5. This is called a *Poisson distribution* of random integers. We start with a positive real number called the ***expected value*** ν of the random numbers. If a sequence of nonnegative integers satisfies a ***Poisson distribution*** with expected value ν, then, over long subsequences, the mean (average) value of the integers in the sequence approaches ν.

If, for example, we start with an expected value of 1.5, then we might have a sequence reading $1, 0, 2, 2, 1, 1, 3, 0, 1, 2, 0, 0, 2, 1, 3, 4, 2, 3, 1, 1, \ldots$. If you calculate the average value for subsequences of this sequence, you will find that sometimes the average is less than 1.5 and sometimes it is more, but slowly it becomes more likely to be close to 1.5.

The following function generates pseudorandom integers according to a Poisson distribution. The derivation of this method and the proof that it works correctly require techniques from calculus and advanced mathematical statistics that are far outside the scope of this book, but that does not mean that we cannot apply the theory to calculate the numbers that we want. The result is a third method of the **class** Random:

```
int Random :: poisson(double mean)
/* Post:  A random integer, reflecting a Poisson distribution with parameter mean,
          is returned. */
{
   double limit = exp(−mean);
   double product = random_real();
   int count = 0;
   while (product > limit) {
      count++;
      product *= random_real();
   }
   return count;
}
```

Here, the function **exp(double** x) is the exponential function, and its implementation comes from one of the libraries <math.h> or <cmath>.

Programming Projects B.3

P1. Write a driver program that will test the three random number functions developed in this appendix. For each function, calculate the average value it returns over a sequence of calls (the number of calls specified by the user). For random_real, the average should be about 0.5; for random_integer(low, high) the average should be about (low + high)/2, where low and high are given by the user; for poisson(expected_value), the average should be approximately the expected value specified by the user.

P2. One test for uniform distribution of random integers is to see if all possibilities occur about equally often. Set up an array of integer counters, obtain from the user the number of positions to use and the number of trials to make, and then repeatedly generate a random integer in the specified range and increment the appropriate cell of the array. At the end, the values stored in all cells should be about the same.

P3. Generalize the test in the previous project to use a rectangular array and two random integers to determine which cell to increment.

scissors-paper-rock

P4. In a certain children's game, each of two players simultaneously puts out a hand held in a fashion to denote one of scissors, paper, or rock. The rules are that scissors beats paper (since scissors cut paper), paper beats rock (since paper covers rock), and rock beats scissors (since rock breaks scissors). Write a program to simulate playing this game with a person who types in S, P, or R at each turn.

P5. In the game of Hamurabi you are the emperor of a small kingdom. You begin

Hamurabi

with 100 people, 100 bushels of grain, and 100 acres of land. You must make decisions to allocate these resources for each year. You may give the people as much grain to eat as you wish, you may plant as much as you wish, or you may buy or sell land for grain. The price of land (in bushels of grain per acre) is determined randomly (between 6 and 13). Rats will consume a random percentage of your grain, and there are other events that may occur at random during the year. These are:

➥ Plague

➥ Bumper Crop

➥ Population Explosion

➥ Flooding

➥ Crop Blight

➥ Neighboring Country Bankrupt! Land Selling for Two Bushels per Acre

➥ Seller's Market

At the end of each year, if too many (again this is random) people have starved for lack of grain, they will revolt and dethrone you. Write a program that will determine the random events and keep track of your kingdom as you make the decisions for each year.

P6. After leaving a pub, a drunk tries to walk home, as shown in Figure B.1. The

random walk

streets between the pub and the home form a rectangular grid. Each time the drunk reaches a corner, he decides at random what direction to walk next. He never, however, wanders outside the grid.

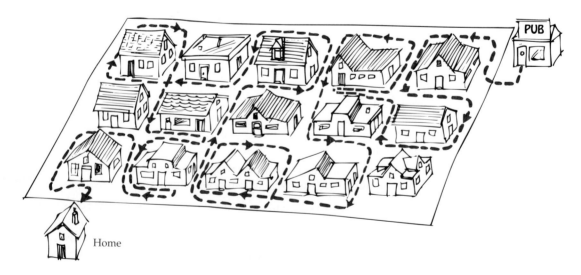

Figure B.1. A random walk

(a) Write a program to simulate this random walk. The number of rows and columns in the grid should be variable. Your program should calculate, over many random walks on the same grid, how long it takes the drunk to get home on average. Investigate how this number depends on the shape and size of the grid.

(b) To improve his chances, the drunk moves closer to the pub—to a room on the upper left corner of the grid. Modify the simulation to see how much faster he can now get home.

(c) Modify the original simulation so that, if the drunk happens to arrive back at the pub, then he goes in and the walk ends. Find out (depending on the size and shape of the grid) what percentage of the time the drunk makes it home successfully.

(d) Modify the original simulation so as to give the drunk some memory to help him, as follows. Each time he arrives at a corner, if he has been there before on the current walk, he remembers what streets he has already taken and tries a new one. If he has already tried all the streets from the corner, he decides at random which to take now. How much more quickly does he get home?

P7. Write a program that creates files of integers in forms suitable for testing and comparing the various searching, sorting, and information retrieval programs. A suitable approach to testing and comparing these programs is to use the program to create a small suite of files of varying size and various kinds of ordering, and then use the CPU timing unit to compare various programs operating on the same data file.

generation of searching and sorting data

The program should generate files of any size up to 15,000 positive integers, arranged in any of several ways. These include:

(a) Random order, allowing duplicate keys
(b) Random order with no duplicates
(c) Increasing order, with duplicates allowed
(d) Increasing order with no duplicates
(e) Decreasing order, with duplicates allowed
(f) Decreasing order with no duplicates
(g) Nearly, but not quite ordered, with duplicates allowed
(h) Nearly, but not quite ordered, with no duplicates

The nearly ordered files can be altered by entering user-specified data. The program should use pseudorandom numbers to generate the files that are not ordered.

REFERENCES FOR FURTHER STUDY

KNUTH, volume 2, pages 1–177, provides one of the most comprehensive treatments of pseudorandom number generators, testing methods, and related topics.

Packages and Utility Functions

C

T HIS APPENDIX describes the classes, definitions, and functions in the utility package that we have used throughout the book. The appendix also lists the contents of the other packages developed and used in various parts of this book. It concludes with a package for timing the execution of programs.

C.1 PACKAGES AND C++ TRANSLATION UNITS

purpose for packages

data structures

A large C++ program is normally broken up into several different files. The way that the program is partitioned into files is important, since it helps a human reader understand the logically separate parts of a large project. It can even help the compiler maintain this logical structure. Moreover, as we have seen, key building blocks of a program can be used over and over again in other programs. In this way, by dividing up a program wisely, we can facilitate code reuse by creating a *package* that can be plugged into other projects. For example, throughout this book we have been able to call on the package of **Stack** methods developed in Section 2.2 whenever it was convenient.

Usually, but not always, a package consists of a set of closely related tasks. In this book, for example, we use one package for calculating and keeping track of CPU times used in a program and another package (developed in Appendix B) for calculating pseudorandom numbers. Our utility package collects several frequently-used functions, even though they are not related to each other at all.

Packages are particularly appropriate holders for data structures. Hence, for example, a client that requires a **Stack** structure need only call on a **Stack** package to have the data structure. Of course, the client needs to know about the methods provided by the package, but as we have seen the client need not, and indeed should not, be concerned with the implementation details of the package.

interface and implementation

In general, a package should provide an *interface* containing details that clients need to know and an *implementation* that can be hidden from clients. Section 2.2.2, for example, specifies the operations for a stack but says nothing about implementation. The interface section of any stack package will contain exactly the same specifications. The implementation section will then contain full details for each of the stack methods specified in the interface.

change of implementation

Since the interface section stays exactly the same, a program that uses the stack package need not know which implementation is used. In fact, if the implementations are programmed properly, it should be impossible for the program to tell which implementation is in the package (except, perhaps, by measuring the speed with which various operations can be done).

files for packages

Although we often think in terms of building up a program out of reusable packages, when we come to implement the program we must work with the units that a C++ compiler accepts, that is, with files. When we consider the work done by the compiler and the subsequent action of a linker, we shall see that, in implementations, each package is generally broken up into a pair of files. These files correspond rather naturally to the concepts that we have already singled out as the interface and the implementation of the package.

declaration or header file

➡ The first file consists of declarations of the elements of the package, including name and type information for the classes, functions, objects, and templates in the package. This is called the *declaration file* or the *header file* for the package. The declaration file normally has the extension .h. This declaration information for a function is called a *function prototype*.

definition or code file

➡ The second file gives complete definitions of all the elements of the package, including their implementation code. This is called the *definition file* or the *code file* for the package. This file normally has the extension .c (or, on some systems, one of .C, .cpp, .cxx, or .cc).

The compiler can only process a single program file at any time. The file might use #include directives to read in other files or other directives to select what parts of the code to compile. In such cases, these directives are followed before any compilation takes place. The code resulting from following all the #include and other directives is known as a *translation unit*. The compiler operates on the translation unit and turns it into an *object file*. It is important that the compiler have access to declarations for all of the elements in the translation unit. In particular, we must #include the .h files corresponding to any packages that we call upon in the translation unit.

translation unit
object file

linking

The different object files that make up a program are linked together into executable code by a linker. The linker must make sure that a complete definition appears for every element of a program, and that among all of the different translation units, there is just one such definition. This means that a .c file should be included in just one translation unit of a program. We normally guarantee this by compiling the .c file itself, and we *never* include a .c file into another program file.

information hiding   In addition to aiding in the compilation and linking of large projects, the division of our packages into separate .h and .c files effectively enforces the principles of information hiding. The .h file provides a package interface and the .c file gives the implementation.

C.2 PACKAGES IN THE TEXT

Most of the packages developed in this book are for the various data structures that are studied. These are developed (quite often as exercises and projects) in the various sections of the book as the data structures are introduced. Here is a list of most of the packages that we have developed, with references to sections of the book. For the packages that represent our principal data structures, we list the methods and then give references to sections of the book that provide implementations. The last two packages, to supply general purpose utility code and program timing methods, have been used throughout the book but are discussed later in this appendix.

Stack package:
 Stack();
 bool empty() **const;**
 Error_code pop();
 Error_code top(Stack_entry &item) **const;**
 Error_code push(**const** Stack_entry &item);

Contiguous stack	*Section 2.2*
Linked stack	*Section 4.2*

Queue package:
 Queue();
 bool empty() **const;**
 Error_code serve();
 Error_code append(**const** Queue_entry &item);
 Error_code retrieve(Queue_entry &item) **const;**

Contiguous queue	*Section 3.2*
Linked queue	*Section 4.4*

List package:
 List();
 int size() **const;**
 bool full() **const;**
 bool empty() **const;**
 void clear();
 void traverse(**void** (*visit)(List_entry &));
 Error_code retrieve(**int** position, List_entry &x) **const;**
 Error_code replace(**int** position, **const** List_entry &x);
 Error_code remove(**int** position, List_entry &x);

Error_code insert(**int** position, **const** List_entry &x);

Tree packages:

Binary_tree( );
bool empty( ) **const;**
void preorder(**void** (*visit)(Entry &));
void inorder(**void** (*visit)(Entry &));
void postorder(**void** (*visit)(Entry &));
int size( ) **const;**
void clear( );
int height( ) **const;**
void insert(**const** Entry &);

Error_code remove(**const** Record &);
Error_code tree_search(Record &) **const;**

B-Tree package:

B_tree( );
Error_code search_tree(Record &target);
Error_code insert(**const** Record &new_node);
Error_code remove(**const** Record &target);
void print( );

C.3 THE UTILITY PACKAGE

Some program statements, while not logically related to each other, are used so frequently that they should be collected as a utility package and made available to all programs. Almost all programs developed in this book therefore include the clause

#include "utility.h";

which allows the program to access the contents of this utility package.

system dependencies

One purpose of the utility package is to include system libraries for commonly used tasks such as input and output. The names of the library files differ according to whether we use an ANSI version of C++ or an older version. By collecting these system-dependent features together in a single package, we make sure that our other programs do not depend on the precise version of C++ on our system. This practice thereby greatly improves the portability of our programs; that is, the ease with which we may compile them on different systems with different compilers.

An ANSI version of the interface file `utility.h` follows:

using namespace std;

```
#include <iostream>      //   standard iostream operations
#include <limits>        //   numeric limits
#include <cmath>         //   mathematical functions
#include <cstdlib>       //   C-string functions
#include <cstddef>       //   C library language support
#include <fstream>       //   file input and output
#include <cctype>        //   character classification
#include <ctime>         //   date and time functions
bool user_says_yes();
```

```
enum Error_code { success, fail, range_error, underflow, overflow, fatal,
                  not_present, duplicate_error, entry_inserted, entry_found,
                  internal_error };
```

standard library

In ANSI C++, the standard library is contained in the **namespace** std; . For this reason, in order that we can use the standard library without appealing to the scope resolution operator, we place the ANSI C++ instruction

using namespace std;

at the start of our utility package.

The next part of the package consists of instructions to include various system libraries. The comments that we have appended to the #include directives describe the purposes of the included files. Finally, we declare the function user_says_yes and the Error_code type that we use in many of our programs.

older versions of C++

A version of the utility interface file for a much older implementation of C++ might need to include a simulation of the Boolean type as well as slightly different standard header files. For example, the following interface might be appropriate on some systems with older C++ compilers:

```
#include <iostream.h>      //   standard iostream operations
#include <limits.h>        //   numeric limits
#include <math.h>          //   mathematical functions
#include <stdlib.h>        //   C-string functions
#include <stddef.h>        //   C library language support
#include <fstream.h>       //   file input and output
#include <ctype.h>         //   character classification
#include <time.h>          //   date and time functions
typedef int bool;
const bool false = 0;
const bool true = 1;
bool user_says_yes();

enum Error_code { success, fail, range_error, underflow, overflow, fatal,
                  not_present, duplicate_error, entry_inserted, entry_found,
                  internal_error };
```

user_says_yes   The only code that needs to be in the implementation file for the utility package is the definition of the function **user_says_yes()**, since this is the only utility function not found in a standard library. The following implementation is suitable for all C++ compilers:

```
bool user_says_yes()
{
   int c;
   bool initial_response = true;
   do {                           //   Loop until an appropriate input is received.
      if (initial_response)
         cout << " (y,n)? " << flush;
      else
         cout << "Respond with either y or n: " << flush;
      do {                        //   Ignore white space.
         c = cin.get();
      } while (c == '\n' || c == ' ' || c == '\t');
      initial_response = false;
   } while (c != 'y' && c != 'Y' && c != 'n' && c != 'N');
   return (c == 'y' || c == 'Y');
}
```

C.4 TIMING METHODS

When comparing different algorithms and data structures, it is often useful to keep track of how much computer time one program, or one phase of a program, uses in comparison with another. We therefore develop a package that implements a **class** Timer for this purpose. A constructor Timer starts the timer going, and in case

Timer :: reset
elapsed_time

we wish to reset the timer later, we shall supply a method **reset()**. The method **elapsed_time** returns the CPU time used since the start of the **Timer** object or the last call to **reset**, whichever is later. Hence **elapsed_time** is rather similar to the lap time shown on a stopwatch.

C++ systems provide a header file called <ctime> or <time.h> that contains a function **clock()** to tell the time as a value of type clock_t. By dividing a time interval by the number CLK_TCK of clock ticks in a second, we can compute elapsed times.

The file `timer.h` contains the following declaration of the **Timer class**.

```
class Timer{
public:
    Timer();
    double elapsed_time();
    void reset();
private:
    clock_t start_time;
};
```

The methods are coded as follows in the file `timer.c`.

```
Timer :: Timer()
{
    start_time = clock();
}

double Timer :: elapsed_time()
{
    clock_t end_time = clock();
    return ((double) (end_time − start_time))/((double) CLK_TCK);
}

void Timer :: reset()
{
    start_time = clock();
}
```

Programming Precepts, Pointers, and Pitfalls

D

THIS APPENDIX collects all the programming precepts, pointers, and pitfalls that appear in all the chapters of the text. These are arranged according to subject, beginning with a general survey of the data structures and algorithms studied in the book, then general criteria for designing data structures and algorithms, recursion, and then, finally, the construction, testing, and maintenance of computer programs.

D.1 CHOICE OF DATA STRUCTURES AND ALGORITHMS

D.1.1 Stacks

1. Stacks are among the simplest kind of data structures; use stacks when possible.

2. In any problem that requires a reversal of data, consider using a stack to store the data.

D.1.2 Lists

3. Don't confuse contiguous lists with arrays.

4. When working with general lists, first decide exactly what operations are needed, then choose the implementation that enables those operations to be done most easily.

linked and contiguous
5. In choosing between linked and contiguous implementations of lists, consider the necessary operations on the lists. Linked lists are more flexible in regard to insertions, deletions, and rearrangement; contiguous lists allow random access.

6. Contiguous lists usually require less computer memory, computer time, and programming effort when the items in the list are small and the algorithms are simple. When the list holds large data entries, linked lists usually save space, time, and often programming effort.

7. Dynamic memory and pointers allow a program to adapt automatically to a wide range of application sizes and provide flexibility in space allocation among different data structures. Static memory (arrays and indices) is sometimes more efficient for applications whose size can be completely specified in advance.

D.1.3 Searching Methods

8. Sequential search is slow but robust. Use it for short lists or if there is any doubt that the keys in the list are properly ordered.

9. Be extremely careful if you must reprogram binary search. Verify that your algorithm is correct and test it on all the extreme cases.

D.1.4 Sorting Methods

10. Many computer systems have a general-purpose sorting utility. If you can access this utility and it proves adequate for your application, then use it rather than writing a sorting program from scratch.

11. In choosing a sorting method, take into account the ways in which the keys will usually be arranged before sorting, the size of the application, the amount of time available for programming, the need to save computer time and space, the way in which the data structures are implemented, the cost of moving data, and the cost of comparing keys.

12. Mergesort, quicksort, and heapsort are powerful sorting methods, more difficult to program than the simpler methods, but much more efficient when applied to large lists. Consider the application carefully to determine whether the extra effort needed to implement one of these sophisticated algorithms will be justified.

13. Heapsort is like an insurance policy: It is usually slower than quicksort, but it guarantees that sorting will be completed in $O(n \log n)$ comparisons of keys, as quicksort cannot always do.

priority queues 14. Priority queues are important for many applications, and heaps provide an excellent implementation of priority queues.

D.1.5 Tables

15. Use the logical structure of the data to decide what kind of table to use: an ordinary array, a table of some special shape, a system of inverted tables, or a hash table. Choose the simplest structure that allows the required operations and that meets the space requirements of the problem. Don't write complicated functions to save space that will then remain unused.

index function, access array   16. Let the structure of the data help you decide whether an index function or an access array is better for accessing a table of data. Use the features built into your programming language whenever possible.

hash table   17. In using a hash table, let the nature of the data and the required operations help you decide between chaining and open addressing. Chaining is generally preferable if deletions are required, if the records are relatively large, or if overflow might be a problem. Open addressing is usually preferable when the individual records are small and there is no danger of overflowing the hash table.

18. Hash functions usually need to be custom-designed for the kind of keys used for accessing the hash table. In designing a hash function, keep the computations as simple and as few as possible while maintaining a relatively even spread of the keys over the hash table. There is no obligation to use every part of the key in the calculation. For important applications, experiment by computer with several variations of your hash function, and look for rapid calculation and even distribution of the keys.

D.1.6 Binary Trees

19. Consider binary search trees as an alternative to ordered lists (indeed, as a way of implementing the abstract data type *list*). At the cost of an extra pointer member in each node, binary search trees allow random access (with $O(\log n)$ key comparisons) to all nodes while maintaining the flexibility of linked lists for insertions, removals, and rearrangement.

20. Consider binary search trees as an alternative to tables (indeed, as a way of implementing the abstract data type *table*). At the cost of access time that is $O(\log n)$ instead of $O(1)$, binary search trees allow traversal of the data structure in the order specified by the keys while maintaining the advantage of random access provided by tables.

21. In choosing your data structures, always carefully consider what operations will be required. Binary trees are especially appropriate when random access, traversal in a predetermined order, and flexibility in making insertions and removals are all required.

unbalanced search tree   22. While choosing data structures and algorithms, remain alert to the possibility of highly unbalanced binary search trees. If the incoming data are likely to be in random order, then an ordinary binary search tree should prove entirely adequate. If the data may come in a sorted or nearly sorted order, then the algorithms should take appropriate action. If there is only a slight possibility of serious imbalance, it might be ignored. If, in a large project, there is greater likelihood of serious imbalance, then there may still be appropriate places in the software where the trees can be checked for balance and rebuilt if necessary. For applications in which it is essential to maintain logarithmic access time at all times, AVL trees provide nearly perfect balance at a slight cost in computer time and space, but with considerable programming cost. If it is necessary for the tree to adapt dynamically to changes in the frequency of the data, then a splay tree may be the best choice.

recursive structure   23. Binary trees are defined recursively; algorithms for manipulating binary trees are usually best written recursively. In programming with binary trees, be aware of the problems generally associated with recursive algorithms. Be sure that your algorithm terminates under any condition and that it correctly treats the trivial case of an empty tree.

24. Although binary trees are usually implemented as linked structures, remain aware of the possibility of other implementations. In programming with linked binary trees, keep in mind the pitfalls attendant on all programming with linked lists.

D.1.7 General Trees

25. Trees are flexible and powerful structures both for modeling problems and for organizing data. In using trees in problem solving and in algorithm design, first decide on the kind of tree needed (ordered, rooted, free, or binary) before considering implementation details.

26. Most trees can be described easily by using recursion; their associated algorithms are often best formulated recursively.

choice of tree structure   27. For problems of information retrieval, consider the size, number, and location of the records along with the type and structure of the entries while choosing the data structures to be used. For small records or small numbers of entries, high-speed internal memory will be used, and binary search trees will likely prove adequate. For information retrieval from disk files, methods employing multiway branching, such as tries, B-trees, and hash tables, will usually be superior. Tries are particularly well suited to applications where the keys are structured as a sequence of symbols and where the set of keys is relatively dense in the set of all possible keys. For other applications, methods that treat the key as a single unit will often prove superior. B-trees, together with various generalizations and extensions, can be usefully applied to many problems concerned with external information retrieval.

D.1.8 Graphs

28. Graphs provide an excellent way to describe the essential features of many applications, thereby facilitating specification of the underlying problems and formulation of algorithms for their solution. Graphs sometimes appear as data structures but more often as mathematical abstractions useful for problem solving.

29. Graphs may be implemented in many ways by the use of different kinds of data structures. Postpone implementation decisions until the applications of graphs in the problem-solving and algorithm-development phases are well understood.

graph traversal   30. Many applications require graph traversal. Let the application determine the traversal method: depth first, breadth first, or some other order. Depth-first traversal is naturally recursive (or can use a stack). Breadth-first traversal normally uses a queue.

31. Greedy algorithms represent only a sample of the many paradigms useful in developing graph algorithms. For further methods and examples, consult the references.

D.2 RECURSION

32. Recursion should be used freely in the initial design of algorithms. It is especially appropriate where the main step toward solution consists of reducing a problem to one or more smaller cases.

design from examples 33. Study several simple examples to see whether recursion should be used and how it will work.

34. Attempt to formulate a method that will work more generally. Ask, "How can this problem be divided into parts?" or "How will the key step in the middle be done?"

35. Ask whether the remainder of the problem can be done in the same or a similar way, and modify your method if necessary so that it will be sufficiently general.

36. Find a stopping rule that will indicate that the problem or a suitable part of it is done.

divide and conquer 37. Divide-and-conquer is one of the most widely applicable and most powerful methods for designing algorithms. When faced with a programming problem, see if its solution can be obtained by first solving the problem for two (or more) problems of the same general form but of a smaller size. If so, you may be able to formulate an algorithm that uses the divide-and-conquer method and program it using recursion.

38. Be very careful that your algorithm always terminates and handles trivial cases correctly.

analysis: 39. The key tool for the analysis of recursive algorithms is the recursion tree. Draw
recursion tree   the recursion tree for one or two simple examples appropriate to your problem.

40. The recursion tree should be studied to see whether the recursion is needlessly repeating work, or if the tree represents an efficient division of the work into pieces.

41. A recursive function can accomplish exactly the same tasks as an iterative function using a stack. Consider carefully whether recursion or iteration with a stack will lead to a clearer program and give more insight into the problem.

tail recursion 42. Tail recursion may be removed if space considerations are important.

43. Recursion can always be translated into iteration, but the general rules will often produce a result that greatly obscures the structure of the program. Such obscurity should be tolerated only when the programming language makes it unavoidable, and even then it should be well documented.

44. Study your problem to see if it fits one of the standard paradigms for recursive algorithms, such as divide and conquer, backtracking, or tree-structured algorithms.

45. Let the use of recursion fit the structure of the problem. When the conditions of the problem are thoroughly understood, the structure of the required algorithm will be easier to see.

D.3 DESIGN OF DATA STRUCTURES

46. Let your data structure your program. Refine your algorithms and data structures at the same time.

47. Once your data are fully structured, your algorithms should almost write themselves.

48. Use data structures to clarify the logic of your programs.

lists and tables

49. Before considering detailed structures, decide what operations on the data will be required, and use this information to decide whether the data belong in a *list* or a *table*. Traversal of the data structure or access to all the data in a prespecified order generally implies choosing a list. Access to any entry in time $O(1)$ generally implies choosing a table.

information hiding, encapsulation

50. Practice information hiding and encapsulation in implementing data structures: Use functions to access your data structures, and keep these in classes separate from your application program.

top-down design

51. Use top-down design for your data structures, just as you do for your algorithms. First determine the logical structure of the data, then slowly specify more detail, and delay implementation decisions as long as possible.

52. Postpone decisions on the details of implementing your data structures as long as you can.

53. Avoid tricky ways of storing your data; tricks usually will not generalize to new situations.

54. Before choosing implementations, be sure that all the data structures and their associated operations are fully specified on the abstract level.

55. Practice information hiding: Separate the application of data structures from their implementation.

56. Before choosing implementations, be sure that all the data structures and their associated operations are fully specified on the abstract level.

implementation

57. In choosing between implementations, consider the necessary operations on the data structure.

derived class

58. If every object of **class** A has all the properties of an object of **class** B, implement **class** A as a derived class of B.

59. Consider the requirements of derived classes when declaring the members of a base class.

is-a and has-a relationships

60. Implement is-a relationships between classes by using public inheritance.

61. Implement has-a relationships between classes by layering.

inheritance

62. Use private inheritance to model an "is implemented with" relationship between classes.

extreme cases

63. Always verify that your algorithm works correctly for an empty structure and for a structure with only one node.

D.4 ALGORITHM DESIGN AND ANALYSIS ━━━━━━━━━━

pre- and postconditions
64. Include precise preconditions and postconditions with every program, function, and method that you write.

65. Don't lose sight of the forest for its trees.

problem specification
66. Be sure you understand your problem completely. If you must change its terms, explain exactly what you have done.

user interface
67. Design the user interface with the greatest care possible. A program's success depends greatly on its attractiveness and ease of use.

simplicity
68. Keep your algorithms as simple as you can. When in doubt, choose the simple way.

69. Sometimes postponing problems simplifies their solution.

70. Keep your logic simple.

71. Keep your functions short; rarely should any function be more than a page long.

72. Choose your data structures as you design your algorithms, and avoid making premature decisions.

73. Avoid sophistication for sophistication's sake. If a simple method is adequate for your application, use it.

74. Don't reinvent the wheel. If a ready-made class template or function is adequate for your application, consider using it.

algorithm verification
75. Be sure your algorithm is correct before starting to code.

76. Verify the intricate parts of your algorithm.

77. In case of difficulty, formulate statements that will be correct both before and after each iteration of a loop, and verify that they hold.

78. Be sure you understand your problem before you decide how to solve it.

79. Be sure you understand the algorithmic method before you start to program.

80. In case of difficulty, divide a problem into pieces and think of each part separately.

Poisson distribution
81. Use Poisson random variables to model random event occurrences.

extreme cases
82. Always be careful of the extreme cases. Be sure that your algorithm terminates gracefully when it reaches the end of its task.

83. In designing algorithms be very careful of the extreme cases, such as empty lists, lists with only one item, or full lists (in the contiguous case).

algorithm analysis
84. Drawing trees is an excellent way both to trace the action of an algorithm and to analyze its behavior.

85. Rely on the big-O analysis of algorithms for large applications but not for small applications.

hash-table analysis
86. Recall from the analysis of hashing that some collisions will almost inevitably occur, so don't worry about the existence of collisions if the keys are spread nearly uniformly through the table.

87. For open addressing, clustering is unlikely to be a problem until the hash table is more than half full. If the table can be made several times larger than the space required for the records, then linear probing should be adequate; otherwise more sophisticated collision resolution may be required. On the other hand, if the table is many times larger than needed, then initialization of all the unused space may require excessive time.

D.5 PROGRAMMING

88. Never code until the specifications are precise and complete.

89. Act in haste and repent at leisure. Program in haste and debug forever.

names   90. Always name your classes, variables and functions with the greatest care, and explain them thoroughly.

91. The nouns that arise in describing a problem suggest useful classes for its solution; the verbs suggest useful functions.

documentation   92. Include careful documentation (as presented in Section 1.3.2) with each function as you write it.

93. Be careful to write down precise preconditions and postconditions for every function.

94. Keep your documentation concise but descriptive.

95. The reading time for programs is much more than the writing time. Make reading easy to do.

classes and functions   96. Use classes to model the fundamental concepts of the program.

97. Each function should do only one task, but do it well.

98. Each class or function should hide something.

99. The public methods for a data structure should be implemented without preconditions. The data members should be kept private.

global variables   100. Keep your connections simple. Avoid global variables whenever possible.

101. Never cause side effects if you can avoid it. If you must use global variables as input, document them thoroughly.

modular input and output   102. Keep your input and output as separate functions, so they can be changed easily and can be custom tailored to your computing system.

error checking   103. Include error checking at the beginning of functions to check that the preconditions actually hold.

104. Every time a function is used, ask yourself why you know that its preconditions will be satisfied.

105. Be sure to initialize your data structures.

106. In designing algorithms, always be careful about the extreme cases and handle them gracefully. Trace through your algorithm to determine what happens in extreme cases, particularly when a data structure is empty or full.

107. Do as thorough error checking as possible. Be sure that every condition that a function requires is stated in its preconditions, and, even so, defend your function from as many violations of its preconditions as conveniently possible.

108. Be sure that all your variables are properly initialized.

109. Double check the termination conditions for your loops, and make sure that progress toward termination always occurs.

D.6 PROGRAMMING WITH POINTER OBJECTS

choosing linked or 110. In choosing between linked and contiguous implementations, consider the
contiguous necessary operations on the data structure. Linked structures are more flexible in regard to insertions, deletions, and rearrangement; contiguous structures are sometimes faster.

111. Contiguous structures usually require less computer memory, computer time, and programming effort when the items in the structure are small and the algorithms are simple. When the structure holds large records, linked structures usually save space, time, and often programming effort.

112. Dynamic memory and pointers allow a program to adapt automatically to a wide range of application sizes and provide flexibility in space allocation among different data structures. Automatic memory is sometimes more efficient for applications whose size can be completely specified in advance.

pointer references 113. Uninitialized or random pointer objects should always be reset to NULL. After deletion, a pointer object should be reset to NULL.

114. Before reassigning a pointer, make sure that the object that it references will not become garbage.

safeguards 115. Linked data structures should be implemented with destructors, copy constructors, and overloaded assignment operators.

designing linked 116. Draw "before" and "after" diagrams of the appropriate part of a linked struc-
structures ture, showing the relevant pointers and the way in which they should be changed. If they might help, also draw diagrams showing intermediate stages of the process.

117. To determine in what order values should be placed in the pointer fields to carry out the various changes, it is usually better first to assign the values to previously undefined pointers, then to those with value NULL, and finally to the remaining pointers. After one pointer variable has been copied to another, the first is free to be reassigned to its new location.

undefined links 118. Be sure that no links are left undefined at the conclusion of a method of a linked structure, either as links in new nodes that have never been assigned or links in old nodes that have become dangling, that is, that point to nodes that no longer are used. Such links should either be reassigned to nodes still in use or set to the value NULL.

multiple dereferencing   119. Avoid the use of constructions such as (p->next)->next, even though they are syntactically correct. A single object should involve only a single pointer dereferencing. Constructions with repeated dereferencing usually indicate that the algorithms can be improved by rethinking what pointer variables should be declared in the algorithm, introducing new ones if necessary.

D.7 DEBUGGING AND TESTING

120. The quality of test data is more important than its quantity.

121. Program testing can be used to show the presence of bugs, but never their absence.

122. Use stubs and drivers, black-box and glass-box testing to simplify debugging.

123. Use plenty of scaffolding to help localize errors.

124. In programming with arrays, be wary of index values that are off by 1. Always use extreme-value testing to check programs that use arrays.

125. Keep your programs well formatted as you write them—it will make debugging much easier.

126. Keep your documentation consistent with your code, and when reading a program make sure that you debug the code and not just the comments.

127. Explain your program to somebody else: Doing so will help you understand it better yourself.

128. After a client uses a class method, it should decide whether to check the resulting error status. Classes should be designed to allow clients to decide how to respond to errors.

D.8 MAINTENANCE

129. For a large and important program, more than half the work comes in the maintenance phase, after it has been completely debugged, tested, and put into use.

optimization   130. Do not optimize your code unless it is necessary to do so. Do not start to optimize code until it is complete and correct.

131. Most programs spend 90 percent of their time doing 10 percent of their instructions. Find this 10 percent, and concentrate your efforts for efficiency there.

132. To improve your program, review the logic. Don't optimize code based on a poor algorithm.

133. Never optimize a program until it is correct and working.

134. Don't optimize code unless it is absolutely necessary.

135. Don't optimize your code until it works perfectly, and then only optimize it if improvement in efficiency is definitely required. First try a simple implementation of your data structures. Change to a more sophisticated implementation only if the simple one proves too inefficient.

prototypes 136. Always plan to build a prototype and throw it away. You'll do so whether you plan to or not.

137. Starting afresh is often easier than patching an old program.

Index